THE NEW TOPICAL TEXTBOOK will help you in your daily Bible study by making available, at your fingertips, thousands of topically arranged Scripture passages for easy reference. Also included is the Outline of the Fundamental Doctrines of the Bible, which contains hundreds of Scripture references covering such doctrines as the Trinity, sin and redemption.

Also included is R.A. Torrey's famous Methods of Bible Study, which is perfect for the beginner as well as the most seasoned Bible scholar.

THE
NEW TOPICAL TEXTBOOK

For Bible Students

BARBOUR BOOKS
Westwood, New Jersey

ISBN 1-55748-079-6

Published by: **BARBOUR AND COMPANY, INC.**
164 Mill Street
Westwood, New Jersey 07675

(In Canada, THE CHRISTIAN LIBRARY,
960 The Gateway, Burlington, Ontario L7L 5K7

EVANGELICAL CHRISTIAN PUBLISHERS ASSOCIATION ecpa MEMBER

Printed in the United States of America

METHODS OF BIBLE STUDY

By Rev. R. A. Torrey

First of all make up your mind that you will put some time *every day* into the study of the Word of God. That is an easy resolution to make, and not a very difficult one to keep; if the one who makes it is in earnest. It is one of the most fruitful resolutions that any Christian ever made. The forming of that resolution and the holding faithfully to it, has been the turning point in many a life. Many a life that has been barren and unsatisfactory has become rich and useful through the introduction into it of regular, persevering, daily study of the Bible. This study may not be very interesting at first, the results may not be very encouraging; but, if one will keep pegging away, it will soon begin to count as nothing else has ever counted in the development of character, and in the enrichment of the whole life. Nothing short of absolute physical inability should be allowed to interfere with this daily study.

It is impossible to make a rule that will apply to every one as to the amount of time that should be given each day to the study of the Word. I know many busy people, including not a few laboring men and women, who give an hour a day to Bible study, but if one cannot give more than fifteen minutes a great deal can be accomplished. Wherever it is possible the time set apart for the work should be in the daylight hours. The very best time is in the early morning hours. If possible lock yourself in with God alone.

2. Make up your mind to *study* the Bible. It is astounding how much heedless reading of the Bible is done. Men seem to think that there is some magic power in the book, and that, if they will but open its pages and skim over its words, they will get good out of it. The Bible is good only because of the truth that is in it, and to see this truth demands close attention. A verse must oftentimes be read and re-read and read again before the wondrous message of love and power that God has put into it begins to appear. Words must be turned over and

over in the mind before their full force and beauty takes possession of us. One must look a long time at the great masterpieces of art to appreciate their beauty and understand their meaning, and so one must look a long time at the great verses of the Bible to appreciate their beauty and understand their meaning. When you read a verse in the Bible ask yourself: What does this verse mean? Then ask: What does it mean for me? When that is answered ask yourself again: Is that all it means? and don't leave it until you are quite sure that is all it means for the present. You may come back at some future time and find it means yet a great deal more. If there are any important words in the verse weigh them, look up other passages where they are used, and try to get their full significance. God pronounces that man blessed who "meditates" on the Word of God "day and night." Ps. 1:2, 3. An indolent skimming over of a few verses or many chapters in the Bible is not meditation, and there is not much blessing in it. Jeremiah said: "Thy words were found and I did eat them." (Jer. 15:16.) Nothing is more important in eating than chewing. If one doesn't properly chew his food, he is quite as likely to get dyspepsia as nourishment. Don't let any one chew your spiritual food for you. Insist on doing it for yourself. Any one can be a student who makes up his mind to. It is hard at first but it soon becomes easy. I have seen very dull minds become keen by holding them right down to the grindstone.

3. *Study the Bible topically.* Take up the various subjects treated of in the Bible, one by one, and go through the Bible and find what it has to say on these subjects. It may be important to know what the great men have to say on important subjects; it is far more important to know what God has to say on these subjects. It is important also to know all that God has to say. A great many people know a part of what God has to say — and usually a very small part — and so their ideas are very imperfect and one-sided. If they only knew all God had to say on the subject, it would be far better for them and for their friends. The only way to know all God has to say on any subject is to go through the Bible on that subject. To do this is not necessary to read every verse in the Bible from Genesis to Revelation. It would be slow work, if we had to do that on every subject we took up. This would be necessary were it not for Textbooks and Concordances. But in these we have the results of the hard work of many minds. Here we have the

various passages that bear on any subject brought together and classified for use, so that now we can do in a few hours what would otherwise take months or years. The topical method of Bible study is the simplest, most fascinating and yields the largest immediate results. It is not the only method of Bible study, and the one who pursues it exclusively will miss much of the blessing God has for him in Bible study. But it is a very interesting and fruitful method of study. It is Mr. Moody's favorite method. It fills one's mind very full on any subject studied. Mr. Moody once gave several days to the study of "Grace." When he had finished he was so full of the subject that he rushed out on the street and going up to the first man he met he said: "Do you know anything about Grace?" "Grace who," the man asked. "The Grace of God that bringeth salvation." And then Mr. Moody poured out upon that man the rich treasures he had dug out of the Word of God. That is the way to master any subject and to get full of it. Go through the Bible and see what it has to say on this subject. This is easily done. Take your Textbook and turn to the subject. Suppose the subject you desire to study is "Prayer." On pages 198-200 will be found a long list of the various passages of Scripture that bear on this subject. Look them up one after another and study them carefully and see just what their teaching is. When you have gone through them you will know far more about prayer than you ever knew before, and far more than you could learn by reading any books that men have written about prayer, profitable as many of these books are. Sometimes it will be necessary to look up other subjects that are closely related to the one in hand. For example, you wish to study what the teaching of God's Word is regarding the atonement. In this case you will not only look under the head "Atonement" on page 23, but also under the head "Blood" on page 30, and under the head "Death of Christ," on page 60. To do this work a concordance is not necessary but it is often very helpful. For example, if you are studying the subject "Prayer" you can look up from the concordance the passages that contain the words "pray," "prayer," "cry," "ask," "call," "supplication," "intercession," etc. But the Textbook will give most of the passages on any subject regardless of what the words used in the passage may be. Other passages will be found in the section on Bible Doctrines under their proper headings.

There are four important suggestions to make regarding Topical Study of the Bible.

First: *Be systematic.* Do not take up subjects for study at random. Have a carefully prepared list of the subjects you wish to know about, and need to know about, and take them up one by one, in order. If you do not do this, the probability is that you will have a few pet topics and will be studying these over and over until you get to be a crank about them, and possibly a nuisance. You will know much about these subjects, but about many other subjects equally important you will know nothing. You will be a one-sided Christian.

Second: *Be thorough.* When you take up a subject do not be content to study a few passages on this subject, but find just as far as possible every passage in the Bible on this subject. If you find the Textbook incomplete make additions of your own to it.

Third: *Be exact.* Find the exact meaning of every passage given in the Textbook on any subject. The way to do this is simple. In the first place note the exact words used. In the next place get the exact meaning of the words used. This is done by finding how the word is used in the Bible. The Bible usage of the word is not always the common use of to-day. For example, the Bible use of the words "sanctification" and "justification" is not the same as the common use. Then notice what goes before and what comes after the verse. This will oftentimes settle the meaning of a verse when it appears doubtful. Finally see if there are any parallel passages. The meaning of many of the most diffucult passages in the Bible is made perfectly plain by some other passage that throws light upon them. Then parallel passages are given in the margin of a good reference Bible and still more fully in "The Treasury of Scripture Knowledge," a volume worthy of a place in the library of every Bible student.

Fourth: Arrange the results of your topical study in an orderly way and write them down. One should constantly use pen and paper in Bible study. When one has gone through the Textbook on any subject, he will have a large amount of material, but he will want to get it into usable shape. The various passages given on any topic in the Textbook are classified, but the classification is not always the one best adapted to our individual use. Take for example the subject "Prayer." The classification of texts in the Textbook is very suggestive, but a better one for some purposes would be: 1st. Who Can Pray so that God Will Hear? 2nd. To Whom to Pray. 3d. For Whom to Pray. 4th. When to Pray. 5th. Where to Pray. 6th. For What to Pray. 7th. How to Pray. 8th. Hindrances to Prayer. 9th. The results of Prayer. The passages given in the Textbook would come under these heads. It is well to make a trial division of the subject before taking up the individual passages given and to arrange such passage as we take it up under the appropriate head. We may have to add to the divisions with which we began as we find new passages. The best classification of passages for any individual is the one he makes for himself, although he will get helpful suggestions from others.

These are some subjects that every Christian should study and study as soon as possible. We give a list of these:

Sin.

The Atonement (or the Blood of Christ).

Justification.

The New Birth.

Adoption.

Sanctification.

Holiness.

Assurance.

The Flesh.

Cleansing.

Faith.

Repentance.

Prayer.

Thanksgiving.

Praise.

Worship.

Love: To God, to Jesus, to Christians, to all men.

The Future Destiny of Believers.

The Future Destiny of the Wicked. (Found under "Punishment of the Wicked," page 213; and "Death of the Wicked," page 61.)

The Character of Christ.

The Resurrection of Christ.

The Ascension of Christ.

The Second Coming of Christ: The fact, the manner, the purpose, the results, the time.

The Reign of Christ.

The Holy Spirit. Who and What He is; His Work.

God. His Attributes and Work.

Grace.

Messianic Prophecies (under head, "Prophecies Respecting Christ. page 207).

The Church.

The Jews.

Joy.

The Judgment.

Life.

Peace.

Perfection.

Persecution.

4. *Study the Bible by chapters.* This method of Bible study is not beyond any person of average intelligence who has fifteen minutes or more a day to put into Bible study. It will take, however, more than one day to the study of a chapter if only fifteen minutes a day are set apart for the work.

First: Select the chapters you wish to study. It is well to take a whole book and study the chapters in their order. The Acts of the Apostles (or the Gospel of John) is a good book to begin with. In time one may take up every chapter in the Bible, but it would not be wise to begin with Genesis.

Second: Read the chapter for to-day's study five times. It is well to read it aloud at least once. The writer sees many things when he read the Bible aloud that he does not see when he reads silently. Each new reading will bring out some new point.

Third: Divide the chapters into their natural divisions and find headings for them that describe in the most striking way their contents. For example, suppose the chapter studied is 1 Jno. 5. You might divide in this way: 1st Division, verses 1-3. The Believer's Noble Parentage. 2nd Division, verses 4, 5. The Believer's Glorious Victory. 3rd Division, verses 6-10. The Believer's Sure Ground of Faith. 4th Division, verses 11, 12. The Believer's Priceless Possession. 5th Division, verse 13. The Believer's Blessed Assurance. 6th Division, verses 14, 15. The Believer's Unquestioning Confidence. 7th Division, verses

16, 17. The Believer's Great Power and Responsibility. 8th Division, verses 18, 19. The Believer's Perfect Security. 9th Division, verse 20. The Believer's Precious Knowledge. 10th Division, verse 21. The Believer's Constant Duty. In many cases the natural divisions will be longer than in this chapter.

Fourth: Note the important differences between the Authorized Version and the Revised and write them in the margin of your Bible.

Fifth: Write down the leading facts of the chaper in their peoper order.

Sixth: Make a note of the persons mentioned in the chaper and of any light thrown upon their character. For example, your chapter is Acts 16. The persons mentioned are Timothy, Timothy's mother, Timothy's father, the brethren at Lystra and Iconium, Paul, the Jews of Lystra and Iconium, the apostles and elders at Jerusalem, a man of Macedonia, Luke, some women of Philippi, Lydia, the household of Lydia, a certain damsel possessed with a spirit of divination, the masters of this damsel, Silas, the praetors of Philippi, the Philippian mob, the jailor of Philippi, the prisoners in the Philippian jail, the household of the jailor, the lictors of Philippi, the brethren in Philippi. What light does the chaper throw upon the character of each?

Seventh: Note the principal lessons of the chapter. It would be well to classify these. *e.g.,* lessons about God, Christ, the Holy Spirit, etc., etc.

Eighth: The Central Truth of the chapter.

Ninth: The key verse of the chapter if there is one.

Tenth: The best verse in the chapter. Opinions will differ widely here. But the question is, which is the best verse to you at this present reading? Mark it and memorize it.

Eleventh: Note the verses that are usable as texts for sermons or talks or Bible readings. If you have time make an analysis of the thought of these verses and write it in the margin, or on the opposite leaf if you have an interleaved Bible.

Twelfth: Name the chapter. For example, Acts 1 might be called The Ascension Chapter; Acts 2, The Day of Pentecost Chapter; Acts 3, The Lame Man's Chapter; etc. Give your own names to the chapters. Give the name that sets forth the most important and characteristic feature of the chapter.

Thirteenth: Note subjects for further study. For example, you are studying Acts 1. Subjects suggested for further study are, The Baptism with the Holy Ghost (See Topical Textbook, page 26); The Ascension (page 20); The Second Coming of Christ (page 240).

Fourteenth: Words and phrases for further study. For example you are studying Jno. 3. You should look up such words and expressions as, "Eternal life," "Born again," "Water," "Believer," "The Kingdom of God."

Fifteenth: Write down what new truth you have learned from the chapter. If you have learned none, you had better go over it again.

Sixteenth: What truth already known has come to you with new power?

Seventeenth: What definite thing have you resolved to do as a result of studying this chapter? A permanent record should be kept of the results of the study of each chapter. It is well to have an interleaved Bible and keep the most important results in this.

5. *Study the Bible as the Word of God.* The Bible is the Word of God, and we get the most good out of any book by studying it as what it really is. It is often said that we should study the Bible just as we study any other book. That principle contains a truth, but it also contains a great error. The Bible it is true is a book as other books are books, the same laws of grammatical and literary construction and interpretation hold here as hold in other books. But the Bible is an entirely unique book. It is what no other book is — The Word of God. This can be easily proven to any candid man. The Bible ought then to be studied as no other book is. It should be studied as the Word of God. (1 Thes. 2: 13.) This involves five things.

First: A great eagerness and more careful and candid study to find out just what it teaches than is bestowed upon any other book or upon all other books. We must know the mind of God; here it is revealed.

Second: A prompt and unquestioning acceptance of and submission to its teachings when definitely ascertained, even when these teachings appear to us unreasonable or impossible. If this book is the Word of God how foolish to submit its teachings to the criticism of our finite reason. The little boy who discredits his wise father's statements because to his infant mind they appear unreasonable, is not a philosopher but a fool. When we are once satisfied that the Bible is the Word of God, its clear teachings must be the end of all controversy and discussion.

Third: Absolute reliance upon all its promises in all their length and breadth and depth and height. The one who studies the Bible as the Word of God will say of every promise no matter how vast and beyond belief it appears, "God who cannot lie has promised this, so I will claim it for myself." Mark the promises you thus claim. Look each day for some new promise from your infinite Father. He has put "His riches in glory" at your disposal. (Phil. 4: 19.)

Fourth: Obedience — prompt, exact, unquestioning, joyous obedience — to every command that it is evident from the context applies to you. Be on the lookout for new orders from the King. Blessing lies in the direction of obedience to them. God's commands are but signboards that mark the road to present success and blessedness and to eternal glory.

Fifth: Studying the Bible as the Word of God, involves studying it as His own voice speaking directly to you. When you open the Bible to study it realize that you have come into the very presence of God and that now He is going to speak to you. Every hour thus spent in Bible study will be an hour's walk and talk with God.

6. *Study the Bible prayerfully.* The author of the book is willing to act as interpreter of it. He does so when we ask Him to. The one who prays with earnestness and faith, the Psalmist's prayer, "Open thou mine eyes that I may behold wondrous things out of Thy law," will get his eyes opened to see beauties and wonders in the Word that he never dreamed of before. Be very definite about this. Each time you open the Bible to study it for a few minutes or many, ask God to give you the open and discerning eye, and expect Him to do it. Every time you come to a difficulty lay it before God and ask an explanation and expect it. How often we think as we puzzle over hard passages, "Oh if I only had so and so here to explain this." God is always present. Take it to Him.

7. *Look for "the things concerning Christ" "in all the Scriptures."* Christ is everywhere in the Bible (Luke 24: 27) be on the lookout for Him and mark His presence when you find it.

8. *Improve spare moments in Bible study.* In almost every man's life many minutes each day are lost; while waiting for meals or trains,

while riding on the cars, etc. Carry a pocket Bible or Testament with you and save these golden minutes by putting them to the very best use listening to the voice of God. The Topical Textbook can be easily carried in the pocket as a help in the work.

9. *Store away the Scripture in your mind and heart.* It will keep you from sin (Ps. 119: 11. R. V.), from false doctrine (Acts 20:29, 30, 32. 2 Tim. 3: 13-15), it will fill your heart with joy (Jer. 15: 16), and peace (Ps. 85: 8), it will give you victory over the Evil One (1 Jno. 2: 14), it will give you power in prayer (Jno. 15: 7), it will make you wiser than the aged and your enemies (Ps. 119: 100, 98, 130.) it will make you "complete, furnished completely unto every good work." (2 Tim. 3: 16, 17, R. V.) Try it. Do not memorize at random but memorize Scripture in a connected way. Memorize texts bearing on various subjects in proper order. Memorize by chapter and verse that you may know where to put your finger upon the text if any one disputes it.

THE NEW TOPICAL TEXTBOOK
For Bible Students

Access to God.

Is of God. Psa. 65: 4.
Is by Christ. Jno. 10: 7, 9. Jno. 14: 6. Rom. 5: 2. Eph. 2: 13. Eph. 3: 12. Heb. 7: 19, 25. Heb. 10: 19. 1 Pet. 3: 18.
Is by the Holy Ghost. Eph. 2: 18.
Obtained through faith. Acts 14: 27. Rom. 5: 2. Eph. 3: 12. Heb. 11: 6.
Follows upon reconciliation to God. Col. 1: 21, 22.
In prayer. Deu. 4: 7. Mat. 6: 6. 1 Pet. 1: 17. (See Prayer.)
In His temple. Psa. 15: 1. Psa. 27: 4. Psa. 43: 3. Psa. 65: 4.
To obtain mercy and grace. Heb. 4: 16.
A privilege of saints. Deu. 4: 7. Psa. 15th. Psa. 23: 6. Psa. 24: 3, 4.
Saints have, with confidence. Eph. 3: 12. Heb. 4: 16. Heb. 10: 19, 22.
Vouchsafed to repenting sinners. Hos. 14: 2. Joel 2: 12. (See Repentance.)
Saints earnestly seek. Psa. 27: 4. Psa. 42: 1, 2. Psa. 43: 3. Psa. 84: 1, 2.
The wicked commanded to seek. Isa. 55: 6. Jas. 4: 8.
Urge others to seek. Isa. 2: 3. Jer. 31: 6.
Promises connected with. Psa. 145: 18. Isa. 55: 3. Mat. 6: 6. Jas. 4: 8.
Blessedness of. Psa. 16: 11. Psa. 65: 4. Psa. 73: 28.
Typified. Lev. 16: 12—15, with Heb. 10: 19—22.
Exemplified. *Moses*, Exo. 24: 2. Exo. 34: 4—7.

Adoption.

Explained. 2 Cor. 6: 18.
Is according to promise. Rom. 9: 8. Gal. 3: 29.
Is by faith. Gal. 3: 7, 26.
Is of God's grace. Eze. 16: 3—6. Rom. 4: 16, 17. Eph. 1: 5, 6, 11.
Is through Christ. Jno. 1: 12. Gal. 4: 4, 5. Eph. 1: 5. Heb. 2: 10, 13.
Saints predestinated unto. Rom. 8: 29. Eph. 1: 5, 11.
Of Gentiles, predicted. Hos. 2: 23. Rom. 9: 24—26. Eph. 3: 6.
The Adopted are gathered together in one by Christ. Jno. 11: 52.
New birth connected with. Jno. 1: 12, 13.
The Holy Spirit is a Witness of. Rom. 8: 16.
Being led by the Spirit is an evidence of. Rom. 8: 14.
Saints receive the Spirit of. Rom. 8: 15. Gal. 4: 6.
A privilege of saints. Jno. 1: 12. 1 Jno. 3: 1.
Saints become brethren of Christ by. Jno. 20: 17. Heb. 2: 11, 12.
Saints wait for the final consummation of. Rom. 8: 19, 23. 1 Jno. 3: 2.
Subjects saints to the fatherly discipline of God. Deu. 8: 5. 2 Sam. 7: 14. Pro. 3: 11, 12, Heb. 12: 5—11.
God is long-suffering and merciful towards the partakers of. Jer. 31: 1, 9, 20.
Should lead to holiness. 2 Cor. 6: 17, 18, with 2 Cor. 7: 1. Phi. 2: 15. 1 Jno. 3: 2, 3.
SHOULD PRODUCE
- Likeness to God. Mat. 5: 44, 45, 48. Eph. 5: 1.
- Child-like confidence in God. Mat. 6: 25—34.
- A desire for God's glory. Mat. 5: 16.
- A spirit of prayer. Mat. 7: 7—11.
- A love of peace. Mat. 5: 9.
- A forgiving spirit. Mat. 6: 14.
- A merciful spirit. Luke 6: 35, 36.
- An avoidance of ostentation. Mat. 6: 1—4, 6, 18.

Safety of those who receive. Pro. 14: 26.

Confers a new name. Num. 6: 27. Isa. 62: 2. Acts 15: 17. (See Titles of of Saints.)
Entitles to an inheritance. Mat. 13: 43. Rom. 8: 17. Gal. 3: 29. Gal. 4: 7. Eph. 3: 6.
Is to be pleaded in prayer. Isa. 63: 16. Mat. 6: 9.
Illustrated. *Joseph's sons*, Gen. 48: 5, 14, 16, 22. *Moses*, Exo. 2: 10. *Esther*, Est. 2: 7.
Typified. *Israel*, Exo. 4: 22. Hos. 11: 1. Rom. 9: 4.
Exemplified. *Solomon*, 1 Chr. 28: 6.

Affections, The.

Should be supremely set upon God. Deu. 6: 5. Mar. 12: 30.
SHOULD BE SET
Upon the commandments of God. Psa. 19: 8—10. Psa. 119: 20, 97, 103, 167.
Upon the house and worship of God. 1 Chr. 29: 3. Psa. 26: 8. Psa. 27: 4. Psa. 84: 1, 2.
Upon the people of God. Psa. 16: 3. Rom. 12: 10. 2 Cor. 7: 13—15. 1 The. 2: 8.
Upon heavenly things. Col. 3: 1, 2.
Should be zealously engaged for God. Psa. 69: 9. Psa. 119: 139. Gal. 4:18.
Christ claims the first place in. Mat. 10: 37. Luke 14: 26.
Enkindled by communion with Christ. Luke 24: 32.
Blessedness of making God the object of. Psa. 91: 14.
Should not grow cold. Psa. 106: 12, 13. Mat. 24: 12. Gal. 4: 15. Rev. 2: 4.
Of saints, supremely set on God. Psa. 42: 1. Psa. 73: 25. Psa. 119: 10.
Of the wicked, not sincerely set on God. Isa. 58: 1, 2. Eze. 33: 31, 32. Luke 8: 13.
Carnal affections should be mortified. Rom. 8:13. Rom. 13: 14. 1 Cor 9: 27. Col. 3: 5. 1 The. 4: 5.
Carnal affections crucified in saints. Rom. 6: 6. Gal. 5: 24.
False teachers seek to captivate. Gal. 1: 10. Gal. 4: 17. 2 Tim. 3: 6. 2 Pet. 2: 3, 18. Rev. 2: 14, 20.
Of the wicked, are unnatural and perverted. Rom. 1 : 31. 2 Tim. 3: 3. 2 Pet. 2: 10.

Afflicted, Duty toward the.

To pray for them. Acts 12: 5. Phi. 1: 16, 19. Jas. 5: 14—16.
To sympathize with them. Rom. 12: 15. Gal. 6: 2.
To pity them. Job 6: 14.
To bear them in mind. Heb. 13: 3.
To visit them. Jas. 1: 27.
To comfort them. Job 16: 5. Job 29: 25. 2 Cor. 1: 4. 1 The. 4: 18.
To relieve them. Job. 31: 19, 20. Isa. 58: 10. Phi. 4: 14. 1 Tim. 5: 10.
To protect them. Psa. 82: 3. Pro. 22: 22. Pro. 31: 5.

Afflicted Saints.

God is with. Psa. 46: 5, 7. Isa. 43: 2.
God is a refuge and strength to. Psa. 27: 5, 6. Isa. 25: 4. Jer. 16: 19. Nah. 1: 7.
God comforts. Isa. 49: 13. Jer. 31: 13. Mat. 5: 4. 2 Cor. 1: 4, 5. 2 Cor. 7: 6.
God preserves. Psa. 34: 20.
God delivers. Psa. 34: 4, 19. Pro. 12: 13. Jer. 39: 17, 18.
Christ is with. Jno. 14: 18.
Christ supports. 2 Tim. 4: 17. Heb. 2: 18.
Christ comforts. Isa. 61: 2. Mat. 11: 28—30. Luke 7: 13. Jno. 14: 1. Jno. 16: 33.
Christ preserves. Isa. 63: 9. Luke 21: 18.
Christ delivers. Rev. 3: 10.
Should praise God. Psa. 13: 5, 6. Psa. 56: 8—10. Psa. 57: 6, 7. Psa. 71: 20—23.
Should imitate Christ. Heb. 12: 1—3. 1 Pet. 2: 21—23.
Should imitate the prophets. Jas. 5: 10.
Should be patient. Luke 21: 19. Rom. 12: 12. 2 The. 1: 4. Jas. 1: 4. 1 Pet. 2: 20.
Should be resigned. 1 Sam. 3: 18. 2 Kin. 20: 19. Job 1: 21. Psa. 39: 9.
Should not despise chastening. Job 5: 17. Pro. 3: 11. Heb. 12: 5.
Should acknowledge the justice of their chastisements. Neh. 9: 33. Job 2: 10. Isa. 64: 5—7. Lam. 3: 39. Mic. 7: 9.
Should avoid sin. Job 34: 31, 32. Jno. 5: 14. 1 Pet. 2: 12.
Should trust in the goodness of God. Job 13: 15. Psa. 71: 20. 2 Cor. 1: 9.
Should turn and devote themselves to God. Psa. 116: 7—9. Jer. 50: 3, 4. Hos. 6: 1.
Should keep the pious resolutions made during affliction. Psa. 66: 13—15.
Should be frequent in prayer. Psa. 50: 15. Psa. 55: 16, 17. (See Affliction, Prayer under.)
Should take encouragement from former mercies. Psa. 27: 9. 2 Cor. 1: 10.
Examples of afflicted saints. *Joseph*, Gen. 39: 20—23. Psa. 105: 17—19. *Moses*, Heb. 11: 25. *Eli*, 1 Sam. 3: 18. *Nehemiah*, Neh. 1: 4. *Job*, Job 1: 20—22. *David*, 2 Sam. 12: 15—23.

Paul, Acts 20: 22—24. Acts 21: 13.
Apostles, 1 Cor. 4: 13. 2 Cor. 6: 4—10.

Affliction, Consolation under.

God is the Author and Giver of. Psa. 23: 4. Rom. 15: 5. 2 Cor. 1: 3. 2 Cor. 7: 6. Col. 1: 11. 2 The. 2: 16, 17.
Christ is the Author and Giver of. Isa. 61: 2. Jno. 14: 18. 2 Cor. 1: 5.
The Holy Ghost is the Author and Giver of. Jno. 14: 16, 17. Jno. 15: 26. Jno. 16: 7. Acts 9: 31.
Promised. Isa. 51: 3, 12. Isa. 66: 13. Eze. 14: 22, 23. Hos. 2: 14. Zec. 1: 17.
Through the Holy Scriptures. Psa. 119: 50, 76. Rom. 15: 4.
By ministers of the gospel. Isa. 40: 1, 2. 1 Cor. 14: 3. 2 Cor. 1: 4, 6.
Is abundant. Psa. 71: 21. Isa. 66: 11.
Is strong. Heb. 6: 18.
Is everlasting. 2 The. 2: 16.
Is a cause of praise. Isa. 12: 1. Isa. 49: 13.
Pray for. Psa. 119: 82.
Saints should administer to each other. 1 The. 4: 18. 1 The. 5: 11, 14.
Is sought in vain from the world. Psa. 69: 20. Ecc. 4: 1. Lam. 1: 2.
To those who mourn for sin. Psa. 51: 17. Isa. 1: 18. Isa. 40: 1, 2. Isa. 61: 1. Mic. 7: 18, 19. Luke 4: 18.
To the troubled in mind. Psa. 42: 5. Psa. 94: 19. Jno. 14: 1, 27. Jno. 16: 20, 22.
To those deserted by friends. Psa. 27: 10. Psa. 41: 9—12. Jno. 14: 18. Jno. 15: 18, 19.
To the persecuted. Deu. 33: 27.
To the poor. Psa. 10: 14. Psa. 34: 6, 9, 10.
To the sick. Psa. 41: 3.
To the tempted. Rom. 16: 20. 1 Cor. 10: 13. 2 Cor. 12: 9. Jas. 1: 12. Jas. 4: 7. 2 Pet. 2: 9. Rev. 2: 10.
In prospect of death. Job. 19: 25, 26. Psa. 23: 4. Jno. 14: 2. 2 Cor. 5: 1. 1 The. 4: 14. Heb. 4: 9. Rev. 7: 14—17. Rev. 14: 13.
Under the infirmities of age. Psa. 71: 9, 18.

Affliction, Prayer under.

Exhortation to Jas. 5: 13.
That God would consider our trouble. 2 Kin. 19: 16. Neh. 9: 32. Psa. 9: 13. Lam. 5. 1.
For the presence and support of God. Psa. 10: 1. Psa. 102: 2.
That the Holy Spirit may not be withdrawn. Psa. 51: 11.
For divine comfort. Psa. 4: 6. Psa 119: 76.
For mitigation of troubles. Psa. 39: 12, 13.
For deliverance. Psa. 25: 17, 22. Psa. 39: 10. Isa. 64: 9—12. Jer. 17: 14.
For pardon and deliverance from sin. Psa. 39: 8. Psa. 51: 1. Psa. 79: 8.
That we may be turned to God. Psa. 80: 7. Psa. 85: 4—6. Jer. 31: 18.
For divine teaching and direction. Job 34: 32. Psa. 27: 11. Psa. 143: 10.
For increase of faith. Mar. 9: 24.
For mercy. Psa. 6: 2. Hab. 3: 2.
For restoration to joy. Psa. 51: 8, 12. Psa. 69: 29. Psa. 90: 14, 15.
For protection and preservation from enemies. 2 Kin. 19: 19. 2 Chr. 20: 12. Psa. 17: 8, 9.
That we may know the causes of our trouble. Job 6: 24. Job 10: 2. Job. 13: 23, 24.
That we may be taught the uncertainty of life. Psa. 39: 4.
That we may be quickened. Psa. 143; 11.

Afflictions.

God appoints. 2 Kin. 6: 33. Job 5: 6, 17. Psa. 66: 11. Amos 3: 6. Mic. 6: 9.
God dispenses, as He will. Job 11: 10. Isa. 10: 15. Isa. 45, 7.
God regulates the measure of. Psa. 80: 5. Isa. 9: 1. Jer. 46: 28.
God determines the continuance of. Gen. 15: 13, 14. Num. 14: 33. Isa. 10: 25. Jer. 29: 10.
God does not willingly send. Lam. 3: 33.
Man is born to. Job 5: 6, 7. Job 14: 1.
Saints appointed to. 1 The. 3: 3.
Consequent upon the fall. Gen. 3: 16—19.
Sin produces. Job 4: 8. Job 20: 11. Pro. 1: 31.
Sin visited with. 2 Sam. 12: 14. Psa. 89: 30—32. Isa. 57: 17. Acts 13: 10, 11.
Often severe. Job 16: 7—16. Psa. 42: 7. Psa. 66: 12. Jon. 2: 3. Rev. 7: 14.
Always less than we deserve. Ezr. 9: 13. Psa. 103: 10.
Frequently terminate in good. Gen. 50: 20. Exo. 1: 11, 12. Deu. 8: 15, 16. Jer. 24: 5, 6, Eze. 20: 37.
Tempered with mercy. Psa. 78: 38, 39. Psa. 106: 43—46. Isa. 30: 18—21. Lam. 3: 32. Mic. 7: 7—9. Nah. 1: 12.
Saints are to expect. Jno. 16: 33. Acts 14: 22.
Of saints, are comparatively light. Acts 20: 23, 24. Rom. 8: 18. 2 Cor. 4: 17.
Of saints, are but temporary. Psa. 30: 5. Psa. 103: 9. Isa. 54: 7, 8. Jno. 16: 20. 1 Pet. 1: 6. 1 Pet. 5: 10.
Saints have joy under. Job 5: 17. Jas. 5: 11.

Of saints, end in joy and blessedness. Psa. 126: 5, 6. Isa. 61: 2, 3. Mat. 5: 4. 1 Pet. 4: 13, 14.
Often arise from the profession of the gospel. Mat. 24: 9. Jno. 15: 21. 2 Tim. 3: 11, 12.
Exhibit the love and faithfulness of God. Deu. 8: 5. Psa. 119: 75. Pro. 3: 12. 1 Cor. 11: 32. Heb. 12: 6, 7. Rev. 3: 19.

Afflictions Made Beneficial.

In promoting the glory of God. Jno. 9: 1—3. Jno 11: 3, 4. Jno. 21: 18, 19.
In exhibiting the power and faithfulness of God. Psa. 34: 19, 20. 2 Cor. 4:8—11.
In teaching us thewill of God. Psa. 119: 71. Isa 26: 9. Mic. 6: 9.
In turning us to God. Deu. 4: 30, 31. Neh. 1: 8, 9. Psa. 78: 34. Isa. 10: 20, 21. Hos. 2: 6, 7.
In keeping us from again departing from God. Job 34: 31, 32. Isa. 10: 20. Eze. 14: 10, 11.
In leading us to seek God in prayer. Jud. 4: 3. Jer. 31: 18. Lam. 2: 17—19. Hos. 5: 14, 15. Jon. 2: 1.
In convincing us of sin. Job 36: 8, 9. Psa. 119: 67. Luke 15: 16—18.
In leading us to confession of sin. Num. 21: 7. Psa. 32: 5. Psa. 51: 3, 5.
In testing and exhibiting our sincerity. Job 23: 10. Psa. 66: 10. Pro. 17: 3.
In trying our faith and obedience. Gen. 22: 1, 2, with Heb. 11: 17. Exo. 15: 23—25. Deu. 8: 2, 16. 1 Pet. 1: 7. Rev. 2: 10.
In humbling us. Deu. 8: 3, 16. 2 Chr. 7: 13, 14. Lam. 3: 19, 20. 2 Cor. 12: 7.
In purifying us. Ecc. 7: 2, 3. Isa. 1: 25, 26. Isa. 48: 10. Jer. 9: 6, 7. Zec. 13: 9. Mal. 3: 2, 3.
In exercising our patience. Psa. 40: 1. Rom. 5: 3. Jas. 1: 3. 1 Pet. 2: 20.
In rendering us fruitful in good works. Jno. 15: 2. Heb. 12: 10, 11.
In furthering the gospel. Acts 8: 3, 4. Acts 11: 19—21. Phi. 1: 12. 2 Tim. 2: 9, 10. 2 Tim. 4: 16, 17.
Exemplified. *Joseph's brethren*, Gen. 42: 21. *Joseph*, Gen. 45: 5, 7, 8. *Israel*, Deu. 8: 3, 5. *Josiah*, 2 Kin. 22: 19. *Hezekiah*, 2 Chr. 32: 25, 26. *Manasseh*, 2 Chr. 33: 12. *Jonah*, Jon 2: 7. *Prodigal son*, Luke 15: 21.

Afflictions of the Wicked, The.

God is glorified in. Exo. 14: 4. Eze. 38: 22, 23.
God holds in derision. Psa. 37: 13. Pro. 1: 26, 27.
Are multiplied. Deu. 31: 17. Job 20: 12—18. Psa. 32: 10.
Are continual. Job 15: 20. Ecc. 2: 23. Isa. 32: 10.
Are often sudden. Psa. 73: 19. Pro. 6: 15. Isa. 30: 13. Rev. 18: 10.
Are often judicially sent. Job 21: 17. Psa. 107: 17. Jer. 30: 15.
Are for examples to others. Psa. 64: 7—9. Zep. 3: 6, 7. 1 Cor. 10: 5—11. 2 Pet. 2: 6.
Are ineffectual of themselves, for their conversion. Exo. 9: 30. Isa. 9: 13. Jer. 2: 30. Hag. 2: 17.
Their persecution of saints, a cause of. Deu. 30: 7. Psa. 55: 19. Zec. 2: 9. 2 The. 1: 6.
Impenitence is a cause of. Pro. 1: 30, 31. Eze. 24: 13. Amos 4: 6—12. Zec. 7: 11, 12. Rev. 2: 21, 22.
Sometimes humble them. 1 Kin. 21: 27.
Frequently harden. Neh. 9: 28, 29. Jer. 5: 3.
Produce slavish fear. Job 15: 24. Psa. 73: 19. Jer. 49: 3, 5.
Saints should not be alarmed at. Pro. 3: 25, 26.
Exemplified. *Pharaoh and the Egyptians*, Exo. 9: 14, 15. Exo. 14: 24, 25. *Ahaziah*, 2 Kin. 1: 1—4. *Gehazi*, 2 Kin. 5: 27. *Jehoram*, 2 Chr. 21: 12—19. *Uzziah*, 2 Chr. 26: 19—21. *Ahaz, &c.*, 2 Chr. 28: 5—8, 22.

Agriculture or Husbandry.

The cultivation of the earth. Gen. 3: 23.
The occupation of man before the fall. Gen. 2: 15.
Rendered laborious by the curse on the earth. Gen. 3: 17—19.
Man doomed to labor in, after the fall. Gen. 3: 23.
Contributes to the support of all. Ecc. 5: 9.
The providence of God to be acknowledged in the produce of. Jer. 5: 24. Hos. 2: 8.
REQUIRES
- Wisdom. Isa. 28: 26.
- Diligence. Pro. 27: 23—27. Ecc. 11: 6.
- Toil. 2 Tim. 2: 6.
- Patience in waiting. Jas. 5: 7.

Diligence in, abundantly recompensed. Pro. 12: 11. Pro. 13: 23. Pro. 28: 19. Heb. 6: 7.
PERSONS ENGAGED IN, CALLED
- Tillers of the ground. Gen. 4: 2.
- Husbandmen. 2 Chr. 26: 10.
- Laborers. Mat. 9: 37. Mat. 20: 1.

Peace favorable to. Isa. 2: 4. Jer. 31: 24.
War destructive to. Jer. 50: 16. Jer. 51: 23.

Patriarchs engaged in. Gen. 4: 2. Gen. 9: 20.
The labor of, supposed to be lessened by Noah. Gen. 5: 29, with Gen. 9: 20.
The Jews loved and followed. Jud. 6: 11. 1 Kin. 19: 19. 2 Chr. 26: 10.
Soil of Canaan suited to. Gen. 13: 10. Deu. 8: 7—9.
Climate of Canaan favorable to Deu. 11: 10, 11.

WAS PROMOTED AMONGST THE JEWS, BY
- Allotments to each family. Num. 36: 7—9.
- The right of redemption. Lev. 25: 23—28.
- Separation from other nations. Exo. 33: 16.
- The prohibition against usury. Exo. 22: 25.
- The promises of God's blessing on. Lev. 26: 4. Deu. 7: 13. Deu. 11: 14, 15.

ENACTMENTS TO PROTECT;
- Not to covet the fields of another. Deu. 5: 21.
- Not to move landmarks. Deu. 19: 14. Pro. 22: 28.
- Not to cut down crops of another. Deu. 23: 25.
- Against the trespass of cattle. Exo. 22: 5.
- Against injuring the produce of. Exo. 22: 6.

Often performed by hirelings. 1 Chr. 27: 26. 2 Chr. 26: 10. Mat. 20: 8. Luke 17: 7.
Not to be engaged in during the Sabbatical year. Exo. 23: 10, 11.
Produce of, given as rent for land. Mat. 21: 33, 34.
Produce of, often blasted because of sin. Isa. 5: 10. Isa. 7: 23. Jer. 12: 13. Joel 1: 10, 11.
Grief occasioned by the failure of the fruits of. Joel 1: 11. Amos 5: 16, 17.
Produce of, exported. 1 Kin. 5: 11. Eze. 27: 17.

OPERATIONS IN;
- Hedging. Isa. 5: 2, 5. Hos. 2: 6.
- Plowing. Job 1: 14.
- Digging. Isa. 5: 6. Luke 13: 8. Luke 16: 3.
- Manuring. Isa. 25: 10. Luke 14: 34, 35.
- Harrowing. Job 39: 10. Isa. 28: 24.
- Gathering out the stones. Isa. 5: 2.
- Sowing. Ecc. 11: 4. Isa. 32: 20. Mat. 13: 3.
- Planting. Pro. 31: 16. Isa. 44: 14. Jer. 31: 5.
- Watering. Deu. 11: 10. 1 Cor. 3: 6—8.
- Weeding. Mat. 13: 28.
- Grafting. Rom. 11: 17—19, 24.
- Pruning. Lev. 25: 3. Isa. 5: 6. Jno. 15: 2.
- Mowing. Psa. 129: 7. Amos 7: 1.
- Reaping. Isa. 17: 5.
- Binding. Gen 37: 7. Mat. 13: 30.
- Gleaning. Lev. 19: 9. Ruth 2: 3.
- Stacking. Exo. 22: 6.
- Threshing. Deu. 25: 4. Jud. 6: 11.
- Winnowing. Ruth 3: 2. Mat. 3: 12.
- Storing in barns. Mat. 6: 26. Mat. 13: 30.

BEASTS USED IN;
- The ox. Deu. 25: 4.
- The ass. Deu. 22: 10.
- The horse. Isa. 28: 28.

IMPLEMENTS OF;
- The plow. 1 Sam. 13: 20.
- The harrow. 2 Sam. 12: 31.
- The mattock. 1 Sam. 13: 20. Isa. 7: 25.
- The sickle. Deu. 16: 9. Deu. 23: 25.
- The pruning-hook. Isa. 18: 5. Joel 3: 10.
- The fork. 1 Sam. 13: 21.
- The ax. 1 Sam. 13: 20.
- The teethed threshing instrument. Isa. 41: 15.
- The flail, &c. Isa. 28: 27.
- The cart. 1 Sam. 6: 7. Isa. 28: 27, 28.
- The shovel. Isa. 30: 24.
- The sieve. Amos 9: 9.
- The fan. Isa. 30: 24. Mat. 3: 12.

ILLUSTRATIVE OF THE
- Culture of the Church. 1 Cor. 3: 9.
- Culture of the heart. Jer. 4: 3. Hos. 10: 12.

Alliance and Society with the Enemies of God.

Forbidden. Exo. 23: 32. Exo. 34: 12. Deu. 7: 2, 3. Deu. 13: 6, 8. Jos. 23: 6, 7. Jud. 2: 2. Ezr. 9: 12. Pro. 1: 10, 15. 2 Cor. 6: 14—17. Eph. 5: 11.
Lead to idolatry. Exo. 34: 15, 16. Num. 25: 1—8. Deu. 7: 4. Jud. 3: 5—7. Rev. 2: 20.
Have led to murder and human sacrifice. Psa. 106: 37, 38.
Provoke the anger of God. Deu. 7: 4. Deu. 31: 16, 17. 2 Chr. 19: 2. Ezr. 9: 13, 14. Psa. 106: 29, 40. Isa. 2: 6.
Provoke God to leave men to reap the fruits of them. Jos. 23: 12, 13. Jud. 2: 1—3.
Are ensnaring. Exo. 23: 33. Num. 25: 18. Deu. 12: 30. Deu. 13: 6. Psa. 106: 36.
Are enslaving. 2 Pet. 2: 18, 19.
Are defiling. Ezr. 9: 1, 2.
Are degrading. Isa. 1: 23.
Are ruinous to spiritual interests. Pro. 29. 24. Heb. 12: 14, 15. 2 Pet. 3: 17.
Are ruinous to moral character. 1 Cor. 15: 33.

Are a proof of folly. Pro. 12:11.
Children who enter into, bring shame upon their parents. Pro. 28:7.
Evil consequences of. Pro. 28:19. Jer. 51:7.
The wicked are prone to. Psa. 50:18. Jer. 2:25.
The wicked tempt saints to. Neh. 6:2—4.
Sin of, to be confessed, deeply repented of, and forsaken. Ezr. 10th Chap.
Involve saints in their guiltiness. 2 Jno. 9—11. Rev. 18:4.
Involve saints in their punishment. Num. 16:26. Jer. 51:6. Rev. 18:4.
Unbecoming in those called saints. 2 Chr. 19:2. 2 Cor. 6:14—16. Phi. 2:15.
Exhortations to shun all inducements to. Pro. 1:10—15. Pro. 4:14, 15. 2 Pet. 3:17.
Exhortations to hate and avoid. Pro. 14:7. Rom. 16:17. 1 Cor. 5:9—11. Eph. 5:6, 7. 1 Tim. 6:5. 2 Tim. 3:5.
A call to come out from. Num. 16:26. Ezr. 10:11. Jer. 51:6, 45. 2 Cor. 6:17. 2 The. 3:6. Rev. 18:4.
Means of preservation from. Pro. 2:10—20. Pro. 19:27.
Blessedness of avoiding. Psa. 1:1.
Blessedness of forsaking. Ezr. 9:12. Pro. 9:6. 2 Cor. 6:17, 18.
Saints grieve to meet with, in their intercourse with the world. Psa. 57:4. Psa. 120:5, 6. 2 Pet. 2:7, 8.
Saints grieve to witness in their brethren. Gen. 26:35. Ezr. 9:3. Ezr. 10:6.
Saints hate and avoid. Psa. 26:4, 5. Psa. 31:6. Psa. 101:7. Rev. 2:2.
Saints deprecate. Gen. 49:6. Psa. 6:8. Psa. 15:4. Psa. 101:4, 7. Psa. 119:115. Psa. 139:19.
Saints are separate from. Exo. 33:16. Ezr. 6:21.
Saints should be circumspect when undesignedly thrown into. Mat. 10:16. Col. 4:5. 1 Pet. 2:12.
Pious parents prohibit, to their children. Gen. 28:1.
Persons in authority should denounce. Ezr. 10:9—11. Neh. 13:23—27.
Punishment of. Num. 33:56. Deu. 7:4. Jos. 23:13. Jud. 2:3. Jud. 3:5—8. Ezr. 9:7, 14. Psa. 106:41, 42. Rev. 2:16, 22, 23.
Exemplified. *Solomon*, 1 Kin. 11:1—8. *Rehoboam*, 1 Kin. 12:8, 9. *Jehoshaphat.* 2 Chr. 18:3. 2 Chr. 19:2. 2 Chr. 20:35—38. *Jehoram*, 2 Chr. 21:6. *Ahaziah*, 2 Chr. 22:3—5. *Israelites*, Ezr. 9:1, 2. *Israel*, Eze. 44:7. *Judas Iscariot*, Mat. 26:14—16.
Examples of avoiding. *Man of God*, 1 Kin. 13:7—10. *Nehemiah, &c.*-Neh. 6:2—4. Neh. 10:29—31. *David*, Psa. 101:4—7. Psa. 119:115, *Jeremiah*, Jer. 15:17. *Joseph of Arimathea*, Luke 23:51. *Church of Ephesus.* Rev. 2:6.
Examples of forsaking. *Israelites*, Num. 16:27. Ezr. 6:21, 22. Ezr. 10:3, 4, 16, 17. *Sons of the Priests*, Ezr. 10:18, 19.
Examples of the judgments of God against. *Korah, &c.*, Num 16:32. *Ahaziah*, 2 Chr. 22:7, 8. *Judas Iscariot*, Acts 1:18.

Altars.

Designed for sacrifice. Exo. 20:24.
To be made of earth, or unhewn stone. Exo. 20:24, 25. Deu. 27:5, 6.
Of brick, hateful to God. Isa. 65:3.
Natural rocks sometimes used as. Jud. 6:19—21. Jud. 13:19, 20.
Were not to have steps up to them. Exo. 20:26.
For idolatrous worship, often erected on roofs of houses. 2 Kin. 23:12. Jer. 19:13. Jer. 32:29.
Idolaters planted groves near. Jud. 6:30. 1 Kin. 16:32, 33. 2 Kin. 21:3.
The Jews not to plant groves near. Deu. 16:21.
For idolatrous worship, to be destroyed. Exo. 34:13. Deu. 7:5.
Probable origin of inscriptions on. Deu. 27:8.
MENTIONED IN SCRIPTURE;
Of Noah. Gen. 8:20.
Of Abraham. Gen. 12:7, 8. Gen. 13:18. Gen. 22:9.
Of Isaac. Gen. 26:25.
Of Jacob. Gen. 33:20. Gen. 35:1, 3, 7.
Of Moses. Exo. 17:15. Exo. 24:4.
Of Balaam. Num. 23:1, 14, 29.
Of Joshua. Jos. 8:30, 31.
Of the temple of Solomon. 2 Chr. 4:1, 19.
Of the second temple. Ezr. 3:2, 3.
Of Reubenites, &c. East of Jordan. Jos. 22:10.
Of Gideon. Jud. 6:26, 27.
Of the people of Israel. Jud. 21:4.
Of Samuel. 1 Sam. 7:17.
Of David. 2 Sam. 24:21, 25.
Of Jeroboam at Bethel. 1 Kin. 12:33.
Of Ahaz. 2 Kin. 16:10—12.
Of the Athenians. Acts 17:23.
For burnt-offering. Exo. 27:1—8.
For incense. Exo. 30:1—6.
Protection afforded by. 1 Kin. 1:50, 51.
Afforded no protection to murderers, Exo. 21:14. 1 Kin. 2:18—34.

Altar of Burnt-offering, The.

Dimensions, &c. of. Exo. 27: 1. Exo. 38: 1.
Horns on the corners of. Exo. 27: 2. Exo. 38: 2.
Covered with brass. Exo. 27: 2.
All its vessels of brass. Exo. 27: 3. Exo. 38: 3.
A net-work grate of brass placed in. Exo. 27: 4, 5. Exo. 38: 4.
Furnished with rings and staves. Exo. 27: 6, 7. Exo. 38: 5—7.
Made after a divine pattern. Exo. 27: 8.
CALLED
  The brazen altar. Exo. 39: 39. 1 Kin. 8: 64.
  The altar of God. Psa. 43: 4.
  The altar of the Lord. Mal. 2: 13.
Placed in the court before the door of the tabernacle. Exo. 40: 6, 29.
Sanctified by God. Exo. 29: 44.
Anointed and sanctified with holy oil. Exo. 40: 10. Lev. 8: 10, 11.
Cleansed and purified with blood. Exo. 29: 36, 37.
Was most holy. Exo. 40: 10.
Sanctified whatever touched it. Exo. 29: 37.
All sacrifices to be offered on. Exo. 29: 38—42. Isa. 56: 7.
All gifts to be presented at. Mat. 5: 23, 24.
Nothing polluted or defective to be offered on. Lev. 22: 22. Mal. 1: 7, 8.
Offering at the dedication of. Num. 7 ch.
THE FIRE UPON,
  Came from before the Lord. Lev. 9: 24.
  Was continually burning. Lev. 6: 13.
  Consumed the sacrifices. Lev. 1: 8, 9.
Sacrifices bound to the horns of. Psa. 118: 27.
The blood of sacrifices put on the horns and poured at the foot of. Exo. 29: 12. Lev. 4: 7, 18, 25. Lev. 8: 15.
THE PRIESTS
  Alone to serve. Num. 18: 3, 7.
  Derived support from. 1 Cor. 9: 13.
Ahaz removed and profaned. 2 Kin. 16: 10—16.
The Jews condemned for swearing lightly by. Mat. 23: 18, 19.
A type of Christ. Heb. 13: 10.

Altar of Incense.

Dimensions, &c. of. Exo. 30: 1, 2. Exo. 37: 25.
Covered with gold. Exo. 30: 3. Exo. 37: 26.
Top of, surrounded with a crown of gold. Exo. 30: 3. Exo. 37: 26.
Had four rings of gold under the crown for the staves. Exo. 30: 4. Exo. 37: 27.
Staves of, covered with gold. Exo. 30: 5.
Called the golden altar. Exo 39: 38.
Placed before the vail in the outer sanctuary. Exo. 30: 6. Exo. 40: 5, 26.
Said to be before the Lord. Lev. 4: 7. 1 Kin. 9: 25.
Anointed with holy oil. Exo. 30: 26, 27.
The priest burned incense on, every morning and evening. Exo. 30: 7, 8.
No strange incense nor any sacrifice to be offered on. Exo. 30: 9.
Atonement made for, by the high priest once every year. Exo. 30: 10. Lev. 16: 18, 19.
The blood of all sin offerings put on the horns of. Lev. 4: 7, 18.
PUNISHMENT FOR;
  Offering strange fire on. Lev. 10. 1, 2.
  Unauthorized offering on. 2 Chr. 26: 16—19.
Covered by the priests before removal from the sanctuary. Num. 4: 11.
A type of Christ. Rev. 8: 3. Rev. 9: 3.

Amalekites, The.

Descent of. Gen. 36: 12, 16.
CHARACTER OF;
  Wicked. 1 Sam. 15: 18.
  Oppressive. Jud. 10: 12.
  Warlike and cruel. 1 Sam. 15: 33.
Governed by Kings. 1 Sam. 15: 20, 32.
A powerful and influential nation. Num. 24: 7.
Possessed cities. 1 Sam. 15: 5.
COUNTRY OF,
  In the south of Canaan. Num. 13: 29. 1 Sam. 27: 8.
  Extended from Havilah to Shur. 1 Sam. 15: 7.
  Was the scene of ancient warfare. Gen. 14: 7.
Part of the Kenites dwelt amongst. 1 Sam. 15: 6.
Were the first to oppose Israel. Exo. 17: 8.
Discomfited at Rephidim, through the intercession of Moses. Exo. 17: 9—13.
Doomed to utter destruction for opposing Israel. Exo. 17: 14, 16. Deu. 25: 19.
Their utter destruction foretold. Num. 24: 20.
Presumption of Israel punished by. Num. 14: 45.
United with Eglon against Israel. Jud. 3: 13,

Part of their possessions taken by Ephraim. Jud. 5: 14, with Jud. 12: 15.
With Midian, oppressed Israel. Jud. 6: 3—5.
Overcome by Gideon. Jud. 6: 33, 34. Jud. 7: 21, 22.
Saul
Overcame, and delivered Israel. 1 Sam. 14: 48.
Commissioned to destroy. 1 Sam. 15: 1—3.
Massacred. 1 Sam. 15: 4—8.
Condemned for not utterly destroying. 1 Sam. 15: 9—26. 1 Sam. 28: 18.
Agag, king of, slain by Samuel. 1 Sam. 5: 32, 33.
Invaded by David. 1 Sam. 27: 8, 9.
Pillaged and burned Ziklag. 1 Sam. 30: 1, 2.
Pursued and slain by David. 1 Sam. 30: 10—20.
Spoil taken from, consecrated. 2 Sam. 8: 11, 12.
Confederated against Israel. Psa. 83: 7.
Remnant of, completely destroyed during the reign of Hezekiah. 1 Chr. 4: 41—43.

Ambition.

God condemns. Gen. 11: 7. Isa. 5: 8.
Christ condemns. Matt. 18: 1, 3, 4. Matt. 20: 25, 26. Mat. 23: 11, 12.
Saints avoid. Psa. 131: 1, 2.
Vanity of. Job 20: 5—9. Job 24: 24. Psa. 49: 11—20.
Leads to strife and contention. Jas. 4: 1, 2.
Punishment of. Pro. 17: 19. Isa. 14: 12—15. Eze. 31: 10, 11. Obad. 3, 4.
Connected with
Pride. Hab. 2: 5.
Covetousness. Hab. 2: 8, 9.
Cruelty. Hab. 2: 12.
Exemplified. *Adam and Eve*, Gen. 3: 5, 6. *Builders of Babel*, Gen. 11: 4. *Miriam and Aaron*. Num. 12: 2. *Korah, &c.*, Num. 16: 3. *Absalom*, 2 Sam. 15: 4. 2 Sam. 18: 18. *Adonijah*, 1 Kin. 1: 5. *Sennacherib*, 2 Kin. 19: 23. *Shebna*, Isa. 22, 16. *Sons of Zebedee*, Mat. 20: 21. *Antichrist*, 2 The. 2: 4. *Diotrephes*, 3 Jno. 9.

Ammonites, The.

Descent of. Gen. 19: 38.
Called the
Children of Lot. Deu. 2: 19.
Children of Ammon. Jer. 25: 21.
Governed by hereditary kings. 2 Sam. 10: 1.
Country of,
Belonged to the Zamzummims. Deu. 2: 20, 21.
Bordered on the Amorites. Num. 21: 24.
Was fertile. Jer. 49: 4.
Well fortified. Num. 21: 24.
Half of, given to the Gadites. Jos. 13: 25.
Character of,
Cruel and covetous. Amos 1: 13.
Proud and reproachful. Zep. 2: 10.
Vindictive. Eze. 25: 3, 6.
Fond of ornaments. 2 Chr. 20: 25.
Idolatrous. Jud. 10: 6. 1 Kin. 11: 7, 33. 2 Kin. 23: 13.
Superstitious. Jer. 27: 3, with 9 v.
Chief cities of,
Rabbah. 2 Sam. 12: 26, 27. Jer. 49: 3.
Ai. Jer. 49: 3.
Jewish laws respecting
Perpetual exclusion from the congregation. Deu. 23: 3. Neh. 13: 1.
No covenant to be made with. Deu. 23: 6.
Not to be distressed. Deu. 2: 19. 2 Chr. 20: 10.
Assisted Eglon against Israel. Jud. 3: 12, 13.
With the Philistines oppressed Israel for eighteen years. Jud. 10: 6—9.
Jephthah raised up to deliver Israel from. Jud. 10: 15—18. Jud. 11 4—33.
Proposed a disgraceful treaty to Jabesh-gilead. 1 Sam. 11: 1—3.
Saul's victories over. 1 Sam. 11: 11. 1 Sam. 14: 47.
Ill-treated David's embassadors. 2 Sam. 10: 1—4.
Hired the Syrians against David. 2 Sam. 10: 6.
Victories of Joab over. 2 Sam. 10: 7—14. 2 Sam. 12: 26—29.
The royal treasure of, taken. 2 Sam. 12: 30.
Of Rabbah reduced to hard bondage. 2 Sam. 12: 31.
Spoil of, consecrated to God. 2 Sam. 8: 11, 12.
One of David's mighty men was of. 2 Sam. 23: 37.
Solomon intermarried with, and introduced idols of into Israel. 1 Kin. 11: 1—5.
Confederated against Jehoshaphat. 2 Chr. 20: 1. Psa. 83: 7.
Miraculous defeat of. 2 Chr. 20: 5—24.
Submitted to Uzziah. 2 Chr. 26: 8.
Defeated by Jotham. 2 Chr. 27: 5.
Seized upon the possessions of Gad. Jer. 49: 1.
Aided the Chaldeans against Judah. 2 Kin. 24: 2.
Vexed the Jews after captivity. Neh. 4: 3, 7, 8.

The Jews reprobated for intermarrying with. Ezr. 9: 1—3. Neh. 13 23—28.

PREDICTIONS RESPECTING

Subjection to Babylon. Jer. 25: 9—21. Jer. 27: 3, 6.

Destruction for hatred to Israel. Eze. 25: 2—10. Zep 2: 8, 9.

Punishment for oppressive cruelty. Jer. 49: 1—5. Amos 1: 13—15.

Restoration. Jer. 49: 6.

Subjection to the Jews. Isa. 11: 14.

Amorites, The.

Descent of. Gen. 10: 15, 16. 1 Chr. 1: 13, 14.

One of the seven nations of Canaan. Gen. 15: 21. Exo. 3: 8, 17.

Governed by many independent kings. Jos. 5: 1. Jos. 9: 10.

Kings of, great and powerful. Psa. 136: 18, 20.

Originally inhabited a mountain district in the south. Num. 13: 29. Deu. 1: 7, 20. Jud. 1: 36.

Acquired an extensive territory from Moab east of Jordan. Num. 21: 26, 30.

Had many and strong cities. Num. 32: 17, 33.

Of gigantic strength and stature. Amos 2: 9.

CHARACTER OF;

Profane and wicked. Gen. 15: 16.

Idolatrous. Jos. 24: 15.

Defeated by Chedorlaomer, &c. Gen. 14: 7.

Joined Abram against the kings. Gen. 14: 13, 24.

Jacob took a portion from. Gen. 48: 22.

Forbearance of God towards. Gen. 15: 16.

Doomed to utter destruction. Deu. 20: 17 18.

Refused a passage to Israel. Num. 21: 21—23. Deu. 2: 30.

Deprived of their eastern territory by Israel. Num. 21: 24—35.

Land of, given to Reubenites, &c. Jos. 13: 15—31.

Western kings of, confederated against Israel. Jos. 10: 1—5.

Miraculous overthrow of. Jos. 10: 11—14.

Kings of, degraded and slain. Jos. 10: 24—27.

The Gibeonites a tribe of, deceived Israel into a league. 2 Sam. 21: 2, with Jos. 9: 3—16.

The Israelites unable to expel, but exacted tribute from. Jud. 1: 34, 35.

Had peace with Israel in the days of Samuel. 1 Sam. 7: 14.

Brought into bondage by Solomon. 1 Kin. 9: 20, 21.

Ahab followed the abominations of. 1 Kin. 21: 26.

Manasseh exceeded abominations of. 2 Kin. 21: 11.

The Jews after the captivity condemned for intermarrying with. Ezr 9: 1, 2.

Descent from, illustrative of man's natural state. Eze. 16: 3.

Amusements and Pleasures, worldly.

Belong to the works of the flesh. Gal. 5: 19, 21.

Are transitory. Job. 21: 12, 13. Heb. 11: 25.

Are all vanity. Ecc. 2: 11.

Choke the word of God in the heart. Luke 8: 14.

Formed a part of idolatrous worship. Exo. 32: 4, 6, 19, with 1 Cor. 10: 7. Jud. 16: 23—25.

LEAD TO

Rejection of God. Job 21: 14, 15.

Poverty. Pro. 21: 17.

Disregard of the judgments and works of God. Isa. 5: 12. Amos 6: 1—6.

Terminate in sorrow. Pro. 14: 13.

Are likely to lead to greater evil Job 1: 5. Mat. 14: 6—8.

The wicked seek for happiness in. Ecc. 2: 1, 8.

INDULGENCE IN

A proof of folly. Ecc. 7: 4.

A characteristic of the wicked. Isa. 47: 8. Eph. 4: 17, 19. 2 Tim. 3: 4. Tit. 3: 3. 1 Pet. 4: 3.

A proof of spiritual death. 1 Tim. 5: 6.

An abuse of riches. Jas. 5: 1, 5.

Wisdom of abstaining from. Ecc. 7: 2, 3.

Shunned by the primitive saints. 1 Pet. 4: 3.

Abstinence from, seems strange to the wicked. 1 Pet. 4: 4.

Denounced by God. Isa. 5: 11, 12.

Punishment of. Ecc. 11: 9. 2 Pet. 2: 13.

Renunciation of, Exemplified. *Moses*, Heb. 11: 25.

Anakim, The.

Descent of. Num. 13: 22. Jos. 15: 13.

WERE CALLED

The sons of Anak. Num. 13: 33.

The sons of the Anakim. Deu. 1: 28.

The children of the Anakims. Deu. 9: 2.

Divided into three tribes. Jos. 15: 14.

Inhabited the mountains of Judah. Jos. 11: 21.

Hebron, chief city of. Jos. 14: 15, with Jos. 21: 11.
Of gigantic strength and stature. Deu. 2: 10, 11, 21.
Israel terrified by. Num. 14: 1, with Num. 13: 33.
Hebron a possession of, given to Caleb for his faithfulness. Jos. 14: 6—14.
Driven from Hebron by Caleb. Jos. 15: 13, 14.
Driven from Kirjath-sepher or Debir, by Othniel. Jos. 15: 15—17. Jud. 1: 12, 13.
Almost annihilated. Jos. 11: 21, 22.

Angels.

Created by God and Christ. Neh. 9. 6. Col. 1: 16.
Worship God and Christ. Neh. 9: 6. Phi. 2: 9—11. Heb. 1: 6.
Are ministering Spirits. 1 Kin. 19: 5. Psa. 68: 17. Psa. 104: 4. Luke 16: 22. Acts 12: 7—11. Acts 27: 23. Heb. 1· 7, 14.
Communicate the will of God and Christ. Dan. 8: 16, 17. Dan. 9: 21—23. Dan. 10: 11. Dan. 12: 6, 7. Mat. 2: 13, 20. Luke 1: 19, 28. Acts 5: 20. Acts 8: 26. Acts 10: 5. Acts 27: 23. Rev. 1: 1.
Obey the will of God. Psa. 103: 20. Mat. 6: 10.
Execute the purposes of God. Num. 22: 22. Psa. 103: 21. Mat. 13: 39—42. Mat. 28: 2. Jno. 5: 4. Rev. 5: 2.
Execute the judgments of God. 2 Sam. 24: 16. 2 Kin. 19: 35. Psa. 35: 5, 6. Acts 12: 23. Rev. 16: 1.
Celebrate the praises of God. Job 38: 7. Psa. 148: 2. Isa. 6: 3. Luke 2: 13, 14. Rev. 5: 11, 12. Rev. 7: 11, 12.
The law given by the ministration of. Psa. 68: 17. Acts 7: 53. Heb. 2: 2.
ANNOUNCED:
The conception of Christ. Mat. 1: 20, 21. Luke 1: 31.
The birth of Christ. Luke 2: 10—12.
The resurrection of Christ. Mat. 28: 5—7. Luke 24: 23.
The ascension and second coming of Christ. Acts 1: 11.
The conception of John the Baptist. Luke 1: 13, 36.
Minister to Christ. Mat. 4: 11. Luke 22: 43. Jno. 1: 51.
Are subject to Christ. Eph. 1: 21. Col. 1: 16. Col. 2: 10. 1 Pet 3: 22.
Shall execute the purposes of Christ. Mat. 13: 41. Mat. 24: 31.
Shall attend Christ at his second coming. Mat. 16: 27. Mat. 25: 31. Mar. 8: 38. 2 The. 1: 7.
Know and delight in the gospel of Christ. Eph. 3: 9, 10. 1 Tim. 3: 16. 1 Pet. 1: 12.
Ministration of, obtained by prayer. Mat. 26: 53. Acts 12: 5, 7.
Rejoice over every repentant sinner. Luke 15: 7, 10.
Have charge over the children of God. Psa. 34: 7. Psa. 91: 11, 12. Dan. 6. 22. Mat. 18: 10.
Are of different orders. Isa. 6: 2. 1 The. 4: 16. 1 Pet. 3: 22. Jude 9. Rev. 12: 7.
Not to be worshipped. Col. 2: 18. Rev. 19: 10. Rev. 22: 9.
Are examples of meekness. 2 Pet. 2: 11. Jude 9.
Are wise. 2 Sam. 14: 20.
Are mighty. Psa. 103: 20.
Are holy. Mat. 25: 31.
Are elect. 1 Tim. 5: 21.
Are innumerable. Job 25: 3. Heb. 12: 22.

Anger.

Forbidden. Ecc. 7: 9. Mat. 5: 22. Rom. 12: 19.
A work of the flesh. Gal. 5: 20.
A characteristic of fools. Pro. 12: 16. Pro. 14: 29. Pro. 27: 3. Ecc. 7: 9.
CONNECTED WITH
Pride. Pro. 21: 24.
Cruelty. Gen. 49: 7. Pro. 27: 3, 4.
Clamor and evil-speaking. Eph. 4: 31.
Malice and blasphemy. Col. 3: 8.
Strife and contention. Pro. 21: 19. Pro. 29: 22. Pro 30: 33.
Brings its own punishment. Job. 5: 2. Pro. 19: 19. Pro. 25: 28.
Grievous words stir up. Jud. 12: 4. 2 Sam. 19: 43. Pro. 15: 1.
Should not betray us into sin. Psa. 37: 8. Eph. 4: 26.
In prayer be free from. 1 Tim. 2: 8.
May be averted by wisdom. Pro. 29: 8.
Meekness pacifies. Pro. 15: 1. Ecc. 10: 4.
Children should not be provoked to. Eph. 6: 4. Col. 3: 21.
Be slow to. Pro. 15: 18. Pro. 16: 32. Pro. 19: 11. Tit. 1: 7. Jas. 1: 19.
Avoid those given to. Gen. 49: 6. Pro. 22: 24.
Justifiable, Exemplified. *Our Lord*, Mar. 3: 5. *Jacob*, Gen. 31: 36. *Moses*, Exo. 11: 8. Exo. 32: 19. Lev. 10: 16. Num. 16: 15. *Nehemiah*, Neh. 5: 6. Neh. 13: 17, 25.
Sinful, Exemplified. *Cain*, Gen. 4: 5, 6. *Esau*, Gen. 27: 45. *Simeon and Levi*, Gen. 49: 5—7. *Moses*, Num. 20: 10, 11. *Balaam*, Num. 22: 27. *Saul*, 1 Sam. 20: 30. *Ahab*, 1 Kin. 21: 4. *Naaman*, 2 Kin. 5: 11. *Asa*, 2 Chr. 16: 10. *Uzziah*, 2 Chr. 26: 19. *Haman*, Est. 3: 5. *Nebuchadnezzar*,

Dan. 3: 13. *Jonah*, Jon. 4: 4. *Herod*, Mat. 2: 16. *Jews*, Luke, 4: 28. *High Priest*, *&c.* Acts 5: 17. Acts 7: 54.

Anger of God, The.

Averted by Christ. Luke 2: 11, 14. Rom. 5: 9. 2 Cor. 5: 18, 19. Eph. 2: 14, 17. Col. 1: 20. 1 The. 1: 10.
Is averted from them that believe. Jno. 3: 14—18. Rom. 3: 25. Rom. 5: 1.
Is averted upon confession of sin and repentance. Job 33: 27, 28. Psa. 106: 43—45. Jer. 3: 12, 13. Jer. 18: 7, 8. Jer. 31: 18—20. Joel 2: 12—14. Luke 15: 18—20.
Is slow. Psa. 103: 8. Isa. 48: 9. Jon. 4: 2. Nah. 1: 3.
Is righteous. Psa. 58: 10, 11. Lam. 1: 18. Rom. 2: 6, 8. Rom. 3: 5, 6. Rev. 16: 6, 7.
The justice of, not to be questioned. Rom. 9: 18, 20, 22.
Manifested in terrors. Exo. 14: 24. Psa. 76: 6—8. Jer. 10: 10. Lam. 2: 20—22.
Manifested in judgments and afflictions. Job 21: 17. Psa. 78: 49—51. Psa. 90: 7. Isa. 9: 19. Jer. 7: 20. Eze. 7: 19. Heb. 3: 17.
Cannot be resisted. Job 9: 13. Job 14: 13. Psa. 76: 7. Nah. 1: 6.
Aggravated by continual provocation. Num. 32: 14.
Specially reserved for the day of wrath. Zep. 1: 14—18. Mat. 25: 41. Rom. 2: 5, 8. 2 The. 1: 8. Rev. 6: 17. Rev. 11: 18. Rev. 19: 15.

AGAINST

- The wicked. Psa. 7: 11. Psa. 21: 8, 9. Isa. 3: 8. Isa. 13: 9. Nah. 1: 2, 3. Rom. 1: 18. Rom. 2: 8. Eph. 5: 6. Col. 3: 6.
- Those who forsake him. Ezr. 8: 22. Isa. 1: 4.
- Unbelief. Psa. 78: 21, 22. Heb. 3: 18, 19. Jno. 3: 36.
- Impenitence. Psa. 7: 12. Pro. 1: 30, 31. Isa. 9: 13, 14. Rom. 2: 5.
- Apostacy. Heb. 10: 26, 27.
- Idolatry. Deu. 29: 20, 27, 28. Deu. 32: 19, 20, 22. Jos. 23: 16. 2 Kin. 22: 17. Psa. 78: 58, 59. Jer. 44: 3.
- Sin, in saints. Psa. 89: 30—32. Psa. 90: 7—9. Psa. 99: 8. Psa. 102: 9, 10. Isa. 47: 6.

Extreme, against those who oppose the gospel. Psa. 2: 2, 3, 5. 1 The. 2: 16.
Folly of provoking. Jer. 7: 19. 1 Cor. 10: 22.
To be dreaded. Psa. 2: 12. Psa. 76: 7. Psa. 90: 11. Mat. 10: 28.
To be deprecated. Exo. 32: 11. Psa. 6: 1. Psa 38: 1. Psa. 74: 1, 2. Isa. 64: 9.
Removal of, should be prayed for. Psa. 39: 10. Psa. 79: 5. Psa. 80: 4. Dan. 9: 16. Hab. 3: 2.
Tempered with mercy to saints. Psa. 30: 5. Isa. 26: 20. Isa. 54: 8. Isa. 57: 15, 16. Jer. 30: 11. Mic. 7: 11.
To be born with submission. 2 Sam. 24: 17. Lam. 3: 39, 43. Mic. 7: 9.
Should lead to repentance. Isa. 42: 24, 25. Jer. 4: 8.
Exemplified against, *The old world*, Gen. 7: 21—23. *Builders of Babel*, Gen. 11: 8. *Cities of the plain*, Gen. 19: 24, 25. *Egyptians*, Exo. 7: 20. Exo. 8: 6, 16, 24. Exo. 9: 3, 9, 23. Exo. 10: 13, 22. Exo 12: 29. Exo. 14: 27. *Israelites*, Exo. 32: 35. Num. 11: 1, 33. Num. 14: 40—45. Num. 21: 6. Num. 25: 9. 2 Sam. 24 1, 15. *Enemies of Israel*, 1 Sam. 5: 6. 1 Sam. 7: 10. *Nadab*, *&c.* Lev. 10. 2. *The Spies*, Num. 14: 37. *Korah*, *&c.* Num 16: 31, 35. *Aaron and Miriam*, Num. 12: 9, 10. *Five Kings*, Jos. 10: 25. *Abimelech*, Jud. 9: 56. *Men of Beth-shemesh*, 1 Sam. 6: 19. *Saul*, 1 Sam. 31: 6. *Uzzah*, 2 Sam. 6: 7. *Saul's family*, 2 Sam. 21: 1. Sennacherib, 2 Kin. 19: 28, 35, 37.

Anointing.

With oil. Psa. 92: 10.
With ointment. Jno. 11: 2.

WAS USED FOR

- Decorating the person. Ruth 3: 3.
- Refreshing the body. 2 Chr. 28: 15.
- Purifying the body. Est. 2: 12. Isa. 57: 9.
- Curing the sick. Mar. 6: 13. Jas. 5: 14.
- Healing wounds. Isa. 1: 6, Luke 10: 34.
- Preparing weapons for war. Isa. 21: 5.
- Preparing the dead for burial. Mat. 26: 12. Mar. 16: 1, with Luke 23: 56.
- The Jews very fond of. Pro. 27: 9. Amos 6: 6.

WAS APPLIED TO

- The head. Psa. 23: 5. Ecc. 9: 8.
- The face. Psa. 104: 15.
- The feet. Luke 7: 38, 39. Jno. 12: 3.
- The eyes. Rev. 3: 18.

OINTMENT FOR,

- Richly perfumed. So. of Sol. 4: 10. Jno. 12: 3.
- Most expensive. 2 Kin. 20: 13. Amos 6: 6. Jno. 12: 3, 5.
- Prepared by the apothecary. Ecc. 10: 1.
- An article of commerce. Eze. 27: 17. Rev. 18: 13.

Neglected in times of affliction. 2 Sam. 12: 20. 2 Sam. 14: 2. Dan. 10; 3.

Neglect of, to guests, a mark of disrespect. Luke 7: 46.
A token of joy. Ecc. 9: 7, 8.
Deprivation of, threatened as a punishment. Deu. 28: 40. Mic. 6: 15.
Why recommended by Christ in times of fasting. Mat. 6: 17, 18.

Anointing of the Holy Ghost.

Is from God. 2 Cor. 1: 21.
THAT CHRIST SHOULD RECEIVE
Foretold. Psa. 45: 7. Isa. 61: 1. Dan. 9: 24.
Fulfilled. Luke 4: 18, 21. Acts 4: 27. Acts 10: 38. Heb. 1: 9.
God preserves those who receive. Psa. 18: 50. Psa. 20: 6. Psa. 89: 20—23.
Saints receive. Isa. 61: 3. 1 Jno. 2: 20.
Is abiding in saints. 1 Jno. 2: 27.
Guides into all truth. 1 Jno. 2: 27.
Typified. Exo. 40: 13—15. Lev. 8: 12. 1 Sam. 16: 13. 1 Kin. 19: 16.

Anointing, Sacred.

Antiquity of. Gen. 28: 18. Gen. 35: 14.
Consecrates to God's service. Exo. 30: 29.
PERSONS WHO RECEIVED;
Prophets. 1 Kin. 19: 16. Isa. 61: 1.
Priests. Exo. 40: 13—15.
Kings. Jud. 9: 8. 1 Sam. 9: 16. 1 Kin. 1: 34.
THINGS WHICH RECEIVED;
Tabernacle, &c. Exo. 30: 26, 27. Exo. 40: 9.
Brazen altar. Exo. 29: 36. Exo. 40: 10.
Brazen laver. Exo. 40: 11.
THOSE WHO PARTOOK OF,
Protected by God. 1 Chr. 16: 22. Psa. 105: 15.
Not to be injured or insulted. 1 Sam. 24: 6. 1 Sam. 26: 9. 2 Sam. 1: 14, 15. 2 Sam. 19: 21.
OIL OR OINTMENT FOR;
Divinely prescribed. Exo. 30: 23—25.
Compounded by the priests. 1 Chr. 9: 30.
An holy anointing oil for ever. Exo. 30: 25, 31.
Not to be imitated. Exo. 30: 32.
To be put on no stranger. Exo. 30: 33.
Jews condemned for imitating. Eze. 23: 41.
ILLUSTRATIVE OF THE ANOINTING
Of Christ with the Holy Ghost. Psa. 45: 7. Isa. 61: 1, with Luke 4: 18.
Of saints with the Holy Ghost. 1 Jno 2: 27.

Antichrist.

Denies the Father and the Son. 1 Jno. 2: 22.
Denies the incarnation of Christ. 1 Jno. 4: 3. 2 Jno. 7.
Spirit of, prevalent in the Apostolic times. 1 Jno. 2: 18.
Deceit, a characteristic of. 2 Jno. 7.

Apostates.

Described. Deu. 13: 13. Heb. 3: 12.
Persecution tends to make. Mat. 24: 9, 10. Luke 8: 13.
A worldly spirit tends to make. 2 Tim. 4: 10.
Never belonged to Christ. 1 Jno. 2: 19.
Saints do not become. Psa. 44: 18, 19. Heb 6: 9. Heb. 10: 39.
It is impossible to restore. Heb. 6: 4—6.
Guilt and punishment of. Zep. 1: 4—6. Heb. 10: 25—31, 39. 2 Pet. 2: 17, 20—22.
Cautions against becoming. Heb. 3: 12. 2 Pet. 3: 17.
Shall abound in the latter days. Mat. 24: 12. 2 The. 2: 3. 1 Tim. 4: 1—3.
Exemplified. *Amaziah*, 2 Chr. 25: 14, 27. *Professed disciples*, Jno. 6: 66. *Hymeneus and Alexander*, 1 Tim. 1: 19, 20.

Apostles, The.

Christ pre-eminently called "The Apostle." Heb. 3: 1.
Ordained by Christ. Mar. 3: 14. Jno. 15: 16.
Received their title from Christ. Luke 6: 13.
CALLED BY
God. 1 Cor. 1: 1. 1 Cor. 12: 28. Gal. 1: 1, 15, 16.
Christ. Mat. 10: 1. Mar. 3: 13. Acts 20: 24. Rom. 1: 5.
The Holy Ghost. Acts 13: 2, 4.
Were unlearned men. Acts 4: 13.
Selected from obscure stations. Mat. 4: 18.
Sent first to the house of Israel. Mat. 10: 5, 6. Luke 24: 47. Acts 13: 46.
Sent to preach the gospel to all nations. Mat. 28: 19, 20. Mar. 16: 15. 2 Tim. 1: 11.
Christ always present with. Mat. 28: 20.
Warned against a timid profession of Christ. Mat. 10: 27—33.
The Holy Ghost given to. Jno. 20: 22. Acts 2: 1—4. Acts 9: 17.
Guided by the Spirit into all truth. Jno. 14: 26. Jno. 15: 26. Jno. 16: 13.
Instructed by the Spirit to answer adversaries. Mat. 10: 19, 20. Luke 12: 11, 12.

Specially devoted to the office of the ministry. Acts 6: 4. Acts 20: 27.
Humility urged upon. Mat. 20: 26, 27. Mar. 9: 33—37. Luke 22: 24—30.
Self-denial urged upon. Mat. 10: 37—39.
Mutual love urged upon. Jno. 15: 17.
Equal authority given to each of. Mat. 16: 19, with Mat. 18: 18. 2 Cor. 11: 5.
Were not of the world. Jno. 15: 19. Jno 17: 16.
Were hated by the world. Mat. 10: 22. Mat. 24: 9. Jno. 15: 18.
Persecutions and sufferings of. Mat. 10: 16, 18. Luke 21: 16. Jno. 15: 20. Jno. 16: 2.
Saw Christ in the flesh. Luke 1: 2. Acts 1: 22. 1 Cor. 9: 1. 1 Jno. 1: 1.
Witnesses of the resurrection and ascension of Christ. Luke 24: 33—41, 51. Acts 1: 2—9. Acts 10: 40, 41. 1 Cor. 15: 8.
Empowered to work miracles. Mat. 10: 1, 8. Mar. 16: 20. Luke 9: 1. Acts 2: 43.

Ark of the Covenant, The.

Dimensions, &c. of. Exo. 25: 10. Exo. 37: 1.
Entirely covered with gold. Exo. 25: 11. Exo. 37: 2.
Surrounded with a crown of gold. Exo. 25: 11.
Furnished with rings and staves. Exo. 25: 12—15. Exo. 37: 3—5.
Tables of testimony alone placed in. Exo. 25: 16, 21. 1 Kin. 8: 9, 21. 2 Chr. 5: 10. Heb. 9: 4.
Mercy-seat laid upon. Exo. 25: 21. Exo. 26: 34.
Placed in the Holy of Holies. Exo. 26: 33. Exo. 40: 21. Heb. 9: 3, 4.
The pot of manna and Aaron's rod laid up before. Heb. 9: 4, with Exo. 16: 33, 34. Num. 17: 10.
A copy of the law laid in the side of Deu. 31: 26.
Anointed with sacred oil. Exo. 30: 26.
Covered with the vail by the priests before removal. Num. 4: 5, 6.
Was called, the
- Ark of God. 1 Sam. 3: 3.
- Ark of God's strength. 2 Chr. 6: 41. Psa. 132: 8.
- Ark of the covenant of the Lord. Num. 10: 33.
- Ark of the testimony. Exo. 30: 6. Num. 7: 89.

A symbol of the presence and glory of God. Num. 14: 43, 44. Jos. 7: 6. 1 Sam. 14: 18, 19. Psa 132: 8.
Esteemed the glory of Israel. 1 Sam. 4: 21, 22.
Was holy. 2 Chr. 35: 3.
Sanctified its resting-place. 2 Chr. 8: 11.
The Israelites inquired of the Lord before. Jos. 7: 6—9. Jud. 20: 27. 1 Chr. 13: 3.
Was carried
- By priests or Levites alone. Deu. 10: 8. Jos. 3: 14. 2 Sam. 15: 24. 1 Chr. 15: 2.
- Before the Israelites in their journeys. Num. 10: 33. Jos. 3: 6.
- Sometimes to the camp in war. 1 Sam. 4: 4, 5.

Profanation of, punished. Num. 4: 5, 15. 1 Sam. 6: 19. 1 Chr. 15: 13.
Protecting of, rewarded. 1 Chr. 13: 14.
Captured by the Philistines. 1 Sam. 4: 11.
Miracles connected with
- Jordan divided. Jos. 4: 7.
- Fall of the walls of Jericho. Jos. 6: 6—20.
- Fall of Dagon. 1 Sam 5: 1—4.
- Philistines plagued. 1 Sam. 5: 6—12.
- Manner of its restoration. 1 Sam. 6: 1—18.

At Kirjath-jearim twenty years. 1 Sam. 7: 1, 2.
Removed from Kirjath-jearim to the house of Obed-edom. 2 Sam 6: 1—11.
David made a tent for. 2 Sam. 6: 17. 1 Chr. 15: 1.
Brought into the city of David. 2 Sam. 6: 12—15. 1 Chr. 15: 25—28.
Brought by Solomon into the temple with great solemnity. 1 Kin. 8: 1—6. 2 Chr. 5: 2—9.
A type of Christ. Psa. 40: 8. Rev. 11: 19.

Armies.

Antiquity of. Gen. 14: 1—8.
Ancient, often numerous. Jos. 11: 4. 1 Sam. 13: 5.
Of different nations often confederated. Jos. 9: 2. Jos. 10: 5. Jud. 3: 13. 1 Kin. 20: 1.
Troops often hired for. 1 Chr. 19: 7. 2 Chr. 25: 6.
Were composed of
- Bowmen and slingers. 1 Chr. 12: 2. Jer. 4: 29.
- Spearmen or heavy troops. Psa. 68: 30. Acts 23: 23.
- Cavalry. Exo. 14: 9. 1 Kin. 20: 20.
- War-chariots. Jos. 17: 16. Jud. 4: 3.

Often consisted of the whole effective strength of nations. Num. 21: 23. 1 Sam. 29: 1.
Furnished with standards. So. of Sol. 6: 4. Isa. 10: 18. Jer. 4: 21.
Accompanied by beasts of burden and wagons for baggage. Jud. 7: 12. 2 Kin. 7: 7. Eze. 23: 24.

Generally in three divisions. Gen. 14:15. Job. 1:17.
WERE LED BY
- Kings in person. 2 Kin. 18:13. 2 Kin. 25:1.
- Experienced captains. 2 Kin. 18:17, 24.

CALLED THE
- Wings of a nation. Isa. 8:8. Jer. 48:40.
- Power of Kings. 2 Chr. 32:9.
- Hosts. Jos. 10:5. Jud. 8:10.
- Bands. 2 Kin. 24:2. 1 Chr. 7:4.

Began their campaigns in the spring. 2 Sam. 11:1.
Often went on foreign service. Jer. 5:15. Jer. 50:3.
MARCHED
- Often in open line. Hab. 1:6, 8.
- With order and precision. Isa. 5:27. Joel 2:7, 8.
- With rapidity. Jer. 48:40. Hab. 1:8.
- With noise and tumult. Isa. 17:12, 13. Joel 2:5.

EMPLOYED IN
- Fighting battles. 1 Sam. 17:2, 3. 1 Chr. 19:17.
- Besieging cities. Deu. 20:12. Isa. 29:3.
- Assaulting cities. Jos 7:3, 4. Jud. 9:45.

Often surprised their enemies. Jos. 8:2. 2 Chr. 13:13. Jer. 51:12.
Commenced their battles with a shout. 1 Sam. 17:20. 2 Chr. 13:15. Jer. 51:14.
Toil and fatigue often endured by. Eze. 29:18.
Divided the spoil. Exo. 15:9. Zec. 14:1.
Sent out foraging parties. 2 Kin. 5:2.
Exercised savage cruelties on the vanquished. Jer. 50:42. Lam. 5:11—13. Amos 1:13.
Frequently the instrument of God's vengeance. Isa. 10:5, 6. Isa. 13:5.
In latter ages received pay. Luke 3:14. 1 Cor. 9:7.
ENCAMPED
- In the open fields. 2 Sam. 11:11. 1 Chr. 11:15.
- Before cities. Jos. 10:5. 1 Sam. 11:1.

Fear occasioned by. Num. 22:3. Jer. 6:25.
Devastation occasioned by. Isa 37:18. Jer. 5:17.
OFTEN DESTROYED BY
- Their enemies. Exo. 17:13. Jos. 10:10, 20. Jud. 11:33. 2 Sam. 18:7. 1 Kin. 20:21.
- Themselves through divine interposition. Jud. 7:22. 1 Sam. 14:15, 16. 2 Chr. 20:23.
- Supernatural means. Jos. 10:11. 2 Kin. 19:35.

Brought their idols with them. 1 Chr. 14:12.
COMPARED TO
- Whirlwinds. Jer. 25:32.
- Waters of a river. Isa. 8:7.
- Caterpillars. Jer. 51:14, 27.
- Grasshoppers. Jud. 6:3—5. Jud. 7:12.
- Locusts. Isa. 33:4. Rev. 9:3, 7.
- Flies. Isa. 7:18, 19.
- Clouds. Eze. 38:9—16.
- Overflowing torrents. Isa. 28:2. Dan. 11:10, 26.

ILLUSTRATIVE OF
- Multitudes of angels. 1 Kin. 22:19. Psa. 148:2. Dan. 4:35. Mat. 26:53.
- The Church. Dan. 8:10—13. So. of Sol. 6:4, 10.
- Numerous and heavy afflictions. Job 19:12.

Armies of Israel, The.

First mention of. Exo. 7:4.
COLLECTED BY
- Sound of trumpets. Jud. 3:27. Jud. 6:34.
- Special messengers. Jud. 6:35. 2 Sam. 20:14.
- Extraordinary means. Jud. 19:29, with Jud. 20:1. 1 Sam. 11:7.

Enrolled by the chief scribe. 2 Kin. 25:19.
CALLED
- The host. Deu. 23:9. 1 Sam. 28:19.
- The armies of the living God. 1 Sam. 17:26.

Composed of infantry. Num. 11:21. Jud. 5:15.
Horsemen and chariots introduced into, after David's reign. 1 Kin. 1:5. 1 Kin. 4:26.
DIVIDED INTO
- Three divisions. Jud. 7:16. 1 Sam. 11:11.
- Van and rear. Jos. 6:9.
- Companies of thousands, &c. Num. 31:14. 2 Kin. 1:9, 11. 1 Chr. 13:1. 1 Chr. 27:1.

Commanded by the captain of the host. 2 Sam. 2:8. 2 Sam. 17:25. 2 Sam. 20:23.
Often led by the king in person. 1 Sam. 8:20. 1 Sam. 15:4, 5. 2 Sam. 12:29. 1 Kin. 22 ch.
INFERIOR OFFICERS OF, APPOINTED BY
- The shoterim or chief officers. Deu. 20:9.
- The king. 2 Sam. 18:1. 2 Chr. 25:5.
- The captain of the host. 2 Sam. 18:11. 2 Kin. 4:13.

Persons liable to serve in. Num 1:2, 3.
PERSONS EXEMPTED FROM SERVING IN:
- Who had builded a house. Deu. 20:5.

Who had planted a vineyard. Deu. 20: 6.
Who were lately betrothed. Deu. 20: 7.
Who were newly married. Deu. 24: 5.
Refusing to join, stigmatized. Jud. 5: 15—17.
Refusing to join, often punished. Jud. 21: 5, 8—11. 1 Sam. 11: 7.
The fearful allowed to leave. Deu. 20: 8. Jud. 7: 3.
Sometimes consisted of the whole nation. Jud. 20: 11. 1 Sam. 11: 7.
Strict discipline observed in. Jos. 7: 16—21. 1 Sam. 14: 24—44.
Educated in the art of war. Isa. 2: 4. Mic. 4: 3.
Often supplied with arms from public armories. 2 Chr. 11: 12. 2 Chr. 26: 14.
BEFORE GOING TO WAR
Were numbered and reviewed. 2 Sam. 18: 1, 2, 4. 1 Kin. 10: 15, 27.
Required to keep from iniquity. Deu. 23: 9.
Consulted the Lord. Jud. 1: 1. Jud. 20: 27, 28.
Encouraged by their commanders. 2 Chr. 20: 20.
Ark of God frequently brought with. Jos. 6: 6, 7. 1 Sam. 4: 4, 5. 2 Sam. 11: 11. 2 Sam. 15: 24.
Attended by priests with trumpets. Num 10: 9. Num. 31: 6. 2 Chr. 13: 13, 14.
Praises of God often sung before. 2 Chr. 20: 21, 22.
Often disposed to battle with Judgment, &c. 2 Sam. 10: 9.
Bravery and fidelity in, rewarded. Jos. 15: 16. 1 Sam. 17: 25. 1 Sam. 18: 17. 2 Sam. 18: 11. 1 Chr. 11: 6.
Men selected from, for difficult enterprises. Exo. 17: 9. Num. 31: 5, 6. Jos. 7: 4. Jos. 8: 3. Jud. 7: 5, 6. 2 Sam. 17: 1.
Directed in their movements by God. Jos. 8: 1, 2. Jud. 1: 2. 2 Sam. 5: 25. 1 Chr. 14: 16.
With the aid of God all-powerful. Lev. 26: 3, 7, 8. Deu 7: 24. Deu 32: 30. Jos. 1: 5.
Without God easily overcome. Lev. 26: 17. Num. 14: 42, 45.
MODE OF PROVISIONING:
Food brought by themselves. Jos. 1: 11.
Food sent by their families. 1 Sam. 17: 17.
Contribution levied. Jud. 8: 5. 1 Sam. 25: 4—8.
By presents. 2 Sam. 17: 27—29.
Congratulated on returning victorious. 1 Sam. 18: 6, 7, with Exo. 15: 1—21.
Purified on returning from war. Num. 31: 19—24.
Disbanded after war. 1 Sam. 13: 2. 1 Kin. 22: 36.
Part of, retained in times of peace by the kings. 1 Sam. 13: 1, 2. 1 Chr. 27: 1—15.

Arms, Military.

Made of iron, steel, or brass. Job 20: 24. 1 Sam. 17: 5, 6.
OFFENSIVE:
Sword. Jud. 20: 15. Eze. 32: 27.
Two-edged sword. Psa. 149: 6. Pro. 5: 4.
Dagger. Jud. 3: 16, 21, 22.
Dart or javelin. 1 Sam. 18: 10, 11. 2 Sam. 18: 14.
Spear or lance. 1 Sam. 26: 7. Jer. 50: 42.
Battle-axe. Eze. 26: 9. Jer. 51: 20.
Bow and arrows. Gen. 48: 22. 1 Kin. 22: 34.
Sling. 1 Sam. 17: 50. 2 Kin. 3: 25.
Handstaff. Mat. 26: 47.
Called weapons of war. 2 Sam. 1: 27.
Called instruments of war. 1 Chr. 12: 33, 37.
Called instruments of death. Psa. 7: 13,
DEFENSIVE:
Helmet. 1 Sam. 17: 5, 38. 2 Chr. 26: 14.
Coat of mail, breastplate, habergeon, or brigandine. 1 Sam. 17: 5, 38. Exo. 28: 32. Jer. 46: 4. Rev. 9: 9.
Girdle. 1 Sam. 18: 4. 2 Sam. 18: 11.
Target. 1 Sam. 17: 6.
Greaves. 1 Sam. 17: 6.
Shield. 1 Kin. 10: 16, 17. 1 Kin. 14: 26, 27.
Buckler. 1 Chr. 5: 18. Eze. 26: 8
Called harness. 1 Kin. 22: 34.
Called armor. Luke 11: 22.
FOR SIEGES:
Battering rams. 2 Sam. 20: 15. Eze. 4: 2.
Engines for casting stones, &c. 2 Chr. 26: 15.
Not worn in ordinary. 1 Sam. 21: 8.
Put on at the first alarm. Isa. 8: 9. Jer. 46: 3, 4.
Armories built for. 2 Kin. 20: 13. So. of Sol. 4: 4.
Great stores of, prepared. 2 Chr. 32: 5.
WERE PROVIDED
By individuals themselves. 1 Chr. 12: 33, 37.
From the public arsenals. 2 Chr. 11: 12. 2 Chr. 26: 14.
Often given as presents. 1 Kin. 10: 25.
BEFORE USING
Tried and proved. 1 Sam. 17: 39.
Burnished. Jer. 46: 4. Eze. 21: 9—11, 28.
Anointed. Isa. 21: 5.

Part of, borne by armor-bearers. Jud. 9:54. 1 Sam. 14:1. 1 Sam. 16:21.
Hung on the walls of cities. Eze. 27: 10, 11.
OF THE VANQUISHED,
Taken off them. 2 Sam. 2: 21. Luke 11: 22.
Sometimes kept as trophies. 1 Sam. 17: 54.
Sometimes burned. Eze. 39: 9, 10.
Of conquered nations taken away to prevent rebellion. Jud. 5: 8. 1 Sam. 13:19—22.
Inferior to wisdom. Ecc. 9:18.
ILLUSTRATIVE OF
Spiritual armor. Rom. 13:12. 2 Cor. 6:7. Eph. 6:11—14. 1 The. 5:8.
Spiritual weapons. 2 Cor. 10: 4. Eph. 6: 17.
Judgments of God. Isa. 13: 5. Jer. 50: 25.

Arrows.

Deadly and destructive weapons. Pro. 26: 18.
Called shafts. Isa. 49: 2.
Sharp. Psa. 120: 4. Isa. 5: 28.
Bright and polished. Isa. 49: 2. Jer. 51: 11.
Sometimes poisoned. Job 6: 4.
Carried in a quiver. Gen. 27: 3. Isa. 49: 2. Jer. 5: 16. Lam. 3: 13.
DISCHARGED
Frow a bow. Psa. 11: 2. Isa. 7: 24.
From engines. 2 Chr. 26: 15.
At a mark for amusement. 1 Sam. 20: 20—22.
At the beasts of the earth. Gen. 27: 3.
Against enemies. 2 Kin. 19: 32. Jer. 50: 14.
With great force. Num. 24: 8. 2 Kin. 9: 24.
Fleetness of, alluded to. Zec. 9: 14.
The ancients divined by. Eze. 21: 21.
ILLUSTRATIVE
Of Christ. Isa. 49: 2.
Of the word of Christ. Psa. 45: 5.
Of God's judgment. Deu. 32: 23—42. Psa. 7: 13. Psa. 21: 12. Psa. 64: 7. Eze. 5: 16.
Of severe afflictions. Job 6: 4. Psa. 38: 2.
Of bitter words. Psa. 64: 3.
Of slanderous tongues. Jer. 9: 8.
Of false witnesses. Pro. 25: 18.
Of devices of the wicked. Psa. 11: 2.
Of young children. Psa. 127: 4.
Of lightnings. Psa. 77: 17, 18. Hab. 3: 11.
(Broken), of destruction of power. Psa. 76: 3.
(Falling from the hand), of the paralyzing power. Eze. 39: 3.

Arts of the.

Apothecary or perfumer. Exo. 30: 25, 35.
Armorer. 1 Sam. 8: 12.
Baker. Gen. 40: 1. 1 Sam. 8: 13.
Brick-maker. Gen. 11: 3. Exo. 5: 7, 8, 18.
Brazier. Gen. 4: 22. 2 Tim. 4: 14.
Blacksmith. Gen. 4: 22. 1 Sam. 13: 19.
Carver. Exo. 31: 5. 1 Kin. 6: 18.
Carpenter. 2 Sam. 5: 11. Mar. 6: 3.
Calker. Eze. 27: 9, 27.
Confectioner. 1 Sam. 8: 13.
Dyer. Exo. 25: 5.
Embroiderer. Exo. 35: 35. Exo. 38: 23.
Embalmer. Gen. 50: 2, 3, 26.
Engraver. Exo. 28: 11. Isa. 49: 16. 2 Cor. 3: 7.
Founder. Jud. 17: 4. Jer. 10: 9.
Fuller. 2 Kin. 18: 17. Mar. 9: 3.
Gardener. Jer. 29: 5. Jno. 20: 15.
Goldsmith. Isa. 40: 19.
Husbandman. Gen. 4: 2. Gen. 9: 20.
Mariner, &c. Eze. 27: 8, 9.
Mason. 2 Sam. 5: 11. 2 Chr. 24: 12.
Musician. 1 Sam. 18: 6. 1 Chr. 15: 16.
Potter. Isa. 64: 8. Jer. 18: 3. Lam. 4: 2. Zec. 11: 13.
Refiner of metals. 1 Chr. 28: 18. Mal. 3: 2, 3.
Ropemaker. Jud. 16: 11.
Silversmith. Acts 19: 24.
Stone-cutter. Exo. 20: 25. 1 Chr. 22: 15.
Ship-builder. 1 Kin. 9: 26.
Smelter of metals. Job 28: 2.
Spinner. Exo. 35: 25. Pro. 31: 19.
Tailor. Exo. 28: 3.
Tanner. Acts 9: 43. Acts 10: 6.
Tent-maker. Gen. 4: 20. Acts 18: 3.
Weaver. Exo. 35: 35. Jno. 19: 23.
Wine-maker. Neh. 13: 15. Isa. 63: 3.
Writer. Jud. 5: 14.

Ascension of Christ, The.

Prophecies respecting. Psa. 24: 7. Psa. 68: 18, with Eph. 4: 7, 8.
Foretold by Himself. Jno. 6: 62. Jno. 7: 33. Jno. 14: 28. Jno. 16: 5. Jno. 20: 17.
Forty days after His resurrection. Acts 1: 3.
Described. Acts 1: 9.
From Mount Olivet. Luke 24: 50, with Mar. 11: 1. Acts 1: 12.
While blessing His disciples. Luke 24: 50.
When He had atoned for sin. Heb. 9: 12. Heb. 10: 12.
Was triumphant. Psa. 68: 18.
Was to supreme power and dignity. Luke 24: 26. Eph. 1: 20, 21. 1 Pet. 3: 22.
As the Forerunner of His people. Heb. 6: 20.

To intercede. Rom. 8: 34. Heb. 9: 24.
To send the Holy Ghost. Jno. 16: 7. Acts 2: 33.
To receive gifts for men. Psa. 68: 18, with Eph. 4: 8, 11.
To prepare a place for His people. Jno. 14: 2.
His second coming shall be in like manner as. Acts 1: 10, 11.
Typified. Lev. 16: 15, with Heb. 6: 20. Heb. 9: 7, 9, 12.

Asher, The Tribe of.

Descended from Jacob's eighth son. Gen. 30: 12, 13.
Predictions concerning. Gen. 49: 20. Deu. 33: 24, 25.
Strength of, on leaving Egypt. Num. 1: 40, 41.
PERSONS SELECTED FROM,
To number the people. Num. 1: 13.
To spy out the land. Num. 13: 13.
To divide the land. Num. 34: 27.
The center of the fourth division of Israel in its journeys. Num. 10: 25, 26.
Encamped next to, and under the standard of Dan, north of the tabernacle. Num. 2: 25, 27.
Offering of, at the dedication. Num. 7: 72—77.
Families of. Num. 26: 44—47.
Strength of, on entering Canaan. Num. 26: 47.
On Ebal, said amen to the curses of the law. Deu. 27: 13.
Bounds of their inheritance. Jos. 19: 24—31.
Bordered on the sea. Jos. 19: 29. Jud. 5: 17.
Did not fully drive out Canaanites. Jud. 1: 31, 32.
Reproved for not aiding against Sisera. Jud. 5: 17.
Assisted Gideon against the Midianites. Jud. 6: 35. Jud. 7: 23.
Some of, at coronation of David. 1 Chr. 12: 36.
Officers placed over, by Solomon. 1 Kin. 4: 16.
Aided in Hezekiah's reformation. 2 Chr. 30: 11.
Remarkable persons of. 1 Chr. 7: 30—40. Luke 2: 36.

Asp, or Adder.

Dangerous to travelers. Gen. 49: 17.
DESCRIBED AS
Venomous. Job 20: 14, 16.
Not to be charmed. Psa. 58: 5.
ILLUSTRATIVE
Of obstinate rejecters of God's Word. Psa. 58: 4, 5.
Of the enemies of God's people. Psa. 91: 13.
(Venom of), of the speech of the wicked. Psa. 140: 3. Rom. 3: 13.
(Venom of), of injurious effects of wine. Deu. 32: 33. Pro. 23: 32.
(Deprived of its venom), of the effects of conversion. Isa. 11: 8, 9.

Ass, The Domestic.

Unclean. Lev. 11: 2, 3, 26, with Exo. 13: 13.
DESCRIBED AS
Not devoid of instinct. Isa. 1: 3.
Strong. Gen. 49: 14.
Fond of ease. Gen. 49: 14, 15.
Often fed on vine-leaves. Gen. 49: 11.
Formed a part of patriarchal wealth. Gen. 12: 16. Gen. 30: 43. Job 1: 3. Job 42: 12.
WAS USED
In agriculture. Isa. 30: 6, 24.
For bearing burdens. Gen. 42: 26. 1 Sam. 25: 18.
For riding. Gen. 22: 3. Num. 22: 21.
In harness. Isa. 21: 7.
In war. 2 Kin. 7: 7, 10.
Governed by a bridle. Pro. 26. 3.
Urged on with a staff. Num. 22: 23, 27.
Women often rode on. Jos. 15: 18. 1 Sam. 25: 20.
Persons of rank rode on. Jud. 10: 3, 4. 2 Sam. 16: 2.
Judges of Israel rode on white. Jud. 5: 10.
Young, most valued for labor. Isa. 30: 6, 24.
Trusty persons appointed to take care of. Gen. 36: 24. 1 Sam. 9: 3. 1 Chr. 27: 30.
Often taken unlawfully by corrupt rulers. Num. 16: 15. 1 Sam. 8: 16. 1 Sam. 12: 3.
Latterly counted an ignoble creature. Jer. 22: 19.
LAWS RESPECTING;
Not to be coveted. Exo. 20: 17.
Fallen under a burden, to be assisted. Exo. 23: 5.
Astray, to be brought back to its owner. Exo. 23: 4. Deu. 22: 1.
Astray, to be taken care of till its owner appeared. Deu. 22: 2, 3.
Not to be yoked with an ox. Deu. 22: 10.
To enjoy the rest of the Sabbath Deu. 5: 14.
First-born of, if not redeemed, to have its neck broken. Exo. 13: 13. Exo. 34: 20.
Christ entered Jerusalem on. Zec. 9: 9. Jno. 12: 14.
MIRACLES CONNECTED WITH;
Mouth of Balaam's opened to speak. Num. 22: 28. 2 Pet. 2: 16.
A thousand men slain by Samson with a jaw-bone of. Jud. 15: 19.

Water brought from the jaw-bone of. Jud. 15: 19.
Not torn by a lion. 1 Kin. 13: 28.
Eaten during famine in Samaria. 2 Kin. 6; 25.

Ass, The Wild.

Inhabits wild and solitary places. Job 39: 6. Isa. 32: 14. Dan. 5: 21.
Ranges the mountains for food. Job 39: 8.
Brays when hungry. Job 6: 5.
Suffers in time of scarcity. Jer. 14: 6.
DESCRIBED AS
Fond of liberty. Job 39: 5.
Intractable. Job 11: 12.
Unsocial. Hos. 8: 9.
Despises his pursuers. Job 39: 7.
Supported by God. Psa. 104: 10, 11.
ILLUSTRATIVE OF
Intractableness of natural man. Job 11: 12.
The wicked in their pursuit of sin. Job 24: 5.
Israel in their love of idols. Jer. 2: 23, 24.
The Assyrian power. Hos. 8: 9.
The Ishmaelites. Gen. 16: 12. (*Hebrew.*)

Assurance.

Produced by faith. Eph. 3: 12. 2 Tim. 1: 12. Heb. 10: 22.
Made full by hope. Heb. 6: 11, 19.
Confirmed by love. 1 Jno. 3: 14, 19. 1 Jno. 4: 18.
Is the effect of righteousness. Isa. 32: 17.
Is abundant in the understanding of the gospel. Col. 2: 2. 1 The. 1: 5.
SAINTS PRIVILEGED TO HAVE, OF
Their election. Psa. 4: 3. 1 The. 1: 4.
Their redemption. Job 19: 25.
Their adoption. Rom. 8: 16. 1 Jno. 3: 2.
Their salvation. Isa. 12: 2.
Eternal life. 1 Jno. 5: 13.
The unalienable love of God. Rom. 8: 38, 39.
Union with God and Christ. 1 Cor. 6: 15. 2 Cor. 13: 5. Eph. 5: 30. 1 Jno. 2: 5. 1 Jno. 4: 13.
Peace with God by Christ. Rom. 5: 1.
Preservation. Psa. 3: 6, 8. Psa. 27: 3—5. Psa. 46: 1—3.
Answers to prayer. 1 Jno. 3: 22. 1 Jno. 5: 14, 15.
Continuance in grace. Phi. 1: 6.
Comfort in affliction. Psa. 73: 26. Luke 4: 18, 19. 2 Cor. 4: 8—10, 16—18.
Support in death. Psa. 23: 4.
A glorious resurrection. Job 19: 26. Psa. 17: 15. Phi. 3: 21. 1 Jno. 3: 2.
A kingdom. Heb. 12: 28. Rev. 5: 10.
A crown. 2 Tim. 4: 7, 8. Jas. 1: 12.
Give diligence to attain to. 2 Pet. 1: 10, 11.
Strive to maintain. Heb. 3: 14, 18.
Confident hope in God restores. Psa. 42: 11.
Exemplified. *David*, Psa. 23: 4. Psa. 73: 24—26. *Paul*, 2 Tim. 1: 12. 2 Tim. 4: 18.

Assyria.

Antiquity and origin of. Gen. 10: 8—11.
Situated beyond the Euphrates. Isa. 7: 20.
Watered by the river Tigris. Gen. 2: 14.
CALLED
The land of Nimrod. Mic. 5: 6.
Shinar. Gen. 11: 2. Gen. 14: 1.
Asshur. Hos. 14: 3.
Nineveh, chief city of. Gen. 10: 11. 2 Kin. 19: 36.
Governed by kings. 2 Kin. 15: 19, 29.
CELEBRATED FOR
Fertility. 2 Kin. 18: 32. Isa. 36: 17.
Extent of conquests. 2 Kin. 18: 33—35. 2 Kin. 19: 11—13. Isa. 10: 9—14.
Extensive commerce. Eze. 27: 23, 24.
Idolatry, the religion of. 2 Kin. 19: 37.
AS A POWER, WAS
Most formidable. Isa. 28: 2.
Intolerant and oppressive. Nah. 3: 19.
Cruel and destructive. Isa. 10: 7.
Selfish and reserved. Hos. 8: 9.
Unfaithful, &c. 2 Chr. 28: 20, 21.
Proud and haughty. 2 Kin. 19: 22—24. Isa. 10: 8.
An instrument of God's vengeance. Isa. 7: 18, 19. Isa. 10: 5, 6.
Chief men of, described. Eze. 23: 6, 12, 23.
Armies of, described. Isa. 5: 26-29.
PUL KING OF,
Invaded Israel. 2 Kin. 15: 19.
Bought off by Menahem. 2 Kin. 15: 19, 20.
TIGLATH PILEZER KING OF,
Ravaged Israel. 2 Kin. 15: 29.
Asked to aid Ahaz against Syria. 2 Kin. 16: 7, 8.
Took money from Ahaz, but strengthened him not. 2 Chr. 28: 20, 21.
Conquered Syria. 2 Kin. 16: 9.
SHALMANESER KING OF,
Reduced Israel to tribute. 2 Kin. 17: 3.
Was conspired against by Hoshea. 2 Kin. 17: 4.
Imprisoned Hoshea. 2 Kin. 17: 4.
Carried Israel captive. 2 Kin. 17: 5, 6.

Re-peopled Samaria from Assyria. 2 Kin. 17: 24.
SENNACHERIB KING OF,
Invaded Judah. 2 Kin. 18: 13.
Bought off by Hezekiah. 2 Kin. 18: 14—16.
Insulted and threatened Judah. 2 Kin. 18: 17—32. 2 Kin. 19: 10—13.
Blasphemed the Lord. 2 Kin. 18: 33—35.
Prayed against by Hezekiah. 2 Kin. 19: 14—19.
Reproved for pride and blasphemy. 2 Kin. 12: 20—34. Isa. 37: 21—29.
His army destroyed by God. 2 Kin. 19: 35.
Assassinated by his sons. 2 Kin. 19: 36.
Condemned for oppressing God's people. Isa. 52: 4.
Manasseh taken captive to. 2 Chr. 33: 11.
The re-peopling of Samaria from, completed by Asnapper. Ezr. 4: 10.
Idolatry of, brought into Samaria. 2 Kin. 17: 29.
Judah condemned for trusting to. Jer. 2: 18, 36.
Israel condemned for trusting to. Hos. 5: 13. Hos. 7: 11. Hos. 8: 9.
The Jews condemned for following the idolatries of. Eze. 16: 28. Eze. 23: 5, 7, &c.
The greatness, extent, duration, and fall of, illustrated. Eze. 31: 3—17.
PREDICTIONS RESPECTING;
Conquest of the Kenites by. Num. 24: 22.
Conquest of Syria by. Isa. 8: 4.
Conquest and captivity of Israel by. Isa. 8: 4. Hos. 9: 3. Hos. 10: 6. Hos. 11: 5.
Invasion of Judah by. Isa. 5: 26. Isa. 7: 17—20. Isa. 8: 8. Isa. 10: 5, 6, 12.
Restoration of Israel from. Isa. 27: 12, 13. Hos. 11: 11. Zec. 10: 10.
Destruction of. Isa. 10: 12—19. Isa. 14: 24, 25. Isa. 30: 31—33. Isa. 31: 8, 9. Zec. 10: 11.
Participation in the blessings of the gospel. Isa. 19: 23—25. Mic. 7: 12.

Atonement, The.

Explained. Rom. 5: 8—11. 2 Cor. 5: 18, 19. Gal. 1: 4. 1 Jno. 2: 2. 1 Jno. 4: 10.
Foreordained. Rom. 3: 25 (*Margin*). 1 Pet. 1: 11, 20. Rev. 13: 8.
Foretold. Isa. 53: 4—6, 8—12. Dan. 9: 24—27. Zec. 13: 1, 7. Jno. 11: 50, 51.
Effected by Christ alone. Jno. 1: 29, 36. Acts 4: 10, 12. 1 The. 1: 10. 1 Tim. 2: 5, 6. Heb. 2: 9. 1 Pet. 2: 24.
Was voluntary. Psa. 40: 6—8, with Heb. 10: 5—9. Jno. 10: 11, 15, 17, 18.
EXHIBITS THE
Grace and mercy of God. Rom. 8: 32. Eph. 2: 4, 5, 7. 1 Tim. 2: 4. Heb. 2: 9.
Love of God. Rom. 5: 8. 1 Jno. 4: 9, 10.
Love of Christ. Jno. 15: 13. Gal. 2: 20. Eph. 5: 2, 25. Rev. 1: 5.
Reconciles the justice and mercy of God. Isa. 45: 21. Rom. 3: 25, 26.
Necessity for. Isa. 59: 16. Luke 19: 10. Heb. 9: 22.
Made but once. Heb. 7: 27. Heb. 9: 24—28. Heb. 10: 10, 12, 14. 1 Pet. 3: 18.
Acceptable to God. Eph. 5: 2.
Reconciliation to God effected by. Rom. 5: 10. 2 Cor. 5: 18—20. Eph. 2: 13—16. Col. 1: 20—22. Heb. 2: 17. 1 Pet. 3: 18.
Access to God by. Heb. 10: 19, 20.
Remission of sins by. Jno. 1: 29. Rom. 3: 25. Eph. 1: 7. 1 Jno. 1: 7. Rev. 1: 5.
Justification by. Rom. 5: 9. 2 Cor. 5: 21.
Sanctification by. 2 Cor. 5: 15. Eph. 5: 26, 27. Tit. 2: 14. Heb. 10: 10. Heb. 13: 12.
Redemption by. Mat. 20: 28. Acts 20: 28. 1 Tim. 2: 6. Heb. 9: 12. Rev. 5: 9.
HAS DELIVERED SAINTS FROM THE
Power of sin. Rom. 8: 3. 1 Pet. 1: 18, 19.
Power of the World. Gal. 1: 4. Gal. 6: 14.
Power of the devil. Col. 2: 15. Heb. 2: 14, 15.
Saints glorify God for. 1 Cor. 6: 20. Gal. 2: 20. Phi. 1: 20, 21.
Saints rejoice in God for. Rom. 5: 11.
Saints praise God for. Rev. 5: 9—13.
Faith in, indespensable. Rom. 3: 25. Gal. 3: 13, 14.
Commemorated in the Lord's supper. Mat. 26: 26—28. 1 Cor. 11: 23—26.
Ministers should fully set forth. Acts 5: 29—31, 42. 1 Cor. 15: 3. 2 Cor. 5: 18—21.
Typified. Gen. 4: 4, with Heb. 11: 4. Gen. 22: 2, with Heb. 11: 17, 19. Exo. 12: 5, 11, 14, with 1 Cor. 5: 7. Exo. 24: 8, with Heb. 9: 20. Lev. 16: 30, 34, with Heb. 9: 7, 12, 28. Lev. 17: 11, with Heb. 9: 22.

Atonement, The Day of.

Tenth day of seventh month. Lev. 23: 26, 27.
A day of humiliation. Lev. 16: 29, 31. Lev. 23: 27.

Observed as a sabbath. Lev. 23: 28, 32.
Offerings to be made on. Lev. 16: 3, 5—15.
The high priest entered into the holy place on. Lev. 16: 2, 3. Heb. 9: 7.
ATONEMENT MADE ON,
For the holy place. Exo. 30: 10. Lev. 16: 15, 16.
For the high priest. Lev. 16: 11. Heb. 9: 7.
For the whole congregation. Lev. 16: 17, 24. Lev. 23: 28. Heb. 9: 7.
The sins of the people borne off by the scapegoat on. Lev. 16: 21.
Punishment for not observing. Lev. 23: 29, 30.
Year of Jubilee commenced on. Lev. 25: 9.
Typical. Heb. 9: 8, 24.

Atonement, under the Law.

Made by sacrifice. Lev. 1: 4, 5.
By priests alone. 1 Chr. 6: 49. 2 Chr. 29: 24.
NECESSARY FOR
Propitiating God. Exo. 32: 30. Lev. 23: 27, 28. 2 Sam. 21: 3.
Ransoming. Exo. 30: 15, 16. Job. 33: 24.
Purifying. Exo. 29: 36.
OFFERED FOR
The congregation. Num. 15: 25. 2 Chr. 29: 24.
The priests. Exo. 29: 31—33. Lev. 8: 34.
Persons sinning ignorantly. Lev. 4: 20, &c.
Persons sinning wilfully. Lev. 6: 7.
Persons swearing rashly. Lev. 5: 4, 6.
Persons witholding evidence. Lev. 5: 1, 6.
Persons unclean. Lev. 5: 2, 3, 6.
Women after childbirth. Lev. 12: 8.
The altar. Exo. 29: 36, 37. Lev. 16: 18, 19.
The holy place. Lev. 16: 16, 17.
The healed leper. Lev. 14: 18.
The leprous house healed. Lev. 14: 53.
Extraordinary cases of. Exo. 32: 30—34. Num. 16: 47. Num. 25: 10—13.
Typical of Christ's atonement. Rom. 5: 6—11.

Babylon.

Origin of. Gen. 10: 8, 10. (*marg.*)
Origin of the name. Gen. 11: 8, 9.
WAS CALLED
Land of the Chaldeans. Eze. 12: 13.
Land of Shinar. Dan. 1: 2. Zec. 5: 11.
Land of Merathaim. Jer. 50: 1, 21.
Desert of the sea. Isa. 21: 1, 9.
Sheshach. Jer. 25: 12, 26.
Lady of kingdoms. Isa. 47: 5.
Situated beyond the Euphrates. Gen. 11: 31, with Jos. 24: 2, 3.
Formerly a part of Mesopotamia. Acts 7: 2.
Founded by the Assyrians, and a part of their empire. 2 Kin. 17: 24, with Isa. 23: 13.
Watered by the rivers Euphrates and Tigris. Psa. 137: 1. Jer. 51: 13.
Composed of many nations. Dan. 3: 4: 29.
Governed by Kings. 2 Kin. 20: 12. Dan. 5: 1.
With Media and Persia divided by Darius into one hundred and twenty provinces. Dan. 6: 1.
Presidents placed over. Dan. 2: 48. Dan. 6; 1.
Babylon the chief province of. Dan. 3: 1.
BABYLON THE CAPITAL OF,
Its antiquity. Gen. 11: 4, 9.
Enlarged by Nebuchadnezzar. Dan. 4: 30.
Surrounded with a great wall and fortified. Jer. 51: 53, 58.
Called the golden city. Isa. 14: 4.
Called the glory of kingdoms. Isa. 13: 19.
Called beauty of Chaldees, &c. Isa. 13: 19.
Called the city of merchants. Eze. 17: 4.
Called Babylon the great. Dan. 4: 30.
REMARKABLE FOR
Antiquity. Jer. 5: 15.
Naval power. Isa. 43: 14.
Military power. Jer. 5: 16. Jer 50: 23.
National greatness. Isa. 13: 19. Jer. 51: 41.
Wealth. Jer. 50: 37. Jer. 51: 13.
Commerce. Eze. 17: 4.
Manufacture of garments. Jos. 7: 21.
Wisdom of senators. Isa. 47: 10. Jer. 50: 35.
INHABITANTS OF,
Idolatrous. Jer. 50: 38. Dan. 3: 18.
Addicted to magic. Isa. 47: 9, 12, 13. Dan. 2: 1, 2.
Profane and sacrilegious. Dan. 5: 1—3.
Wicked. Isa. 47: 10.
AS A POWER WAS
Arrogant. Isa. 14: 13, 14. Jer. 50: 29, 31, 32.
Secure and self-confident. Isa. 47: 7, 8.
Grand and stately. Isa. 47: 1, 5.
Covetous. Jer. 51: 13.
Oppressive. Isa. 14: 4.

Cruel and destructive. Isa. 14: 17. Isa. 47: 6. Jer. 51: 25. Hab. 1: 6, 7.
An instrument of God's vengeance on other nations. Jer. 51: 7. Isa. 47: 6.
Languages spoken in. Dan. 1: 4. Dan. 2: 4.
Armies of, described. Hab. 1: 7—9.
REPRESENTED BY
A great eagle. Eze. 17: 3.
A head of gold. Dan. 2: 32, 37, 38.
A lion with eagle's wings. Dan. 7: 4.
Ambassadors of, sent to Hezekiah. 2 Kin. 20: 12.
NEBUCHADNEZZAR KING OF,
Made Jehoiakim tributary. 2 Kin. 24: 1.
Besieged Jerusalem. 2 Kin. 24: 10, 11.
Took Jehoiachin, &c. captive to Babylon. 2 Kin. 24: 12, 14—16. 2 Chr. 36: 10.
Spoiled the temple. 2 Kin. 24: 13.
Made Zedekiah king. 2 Kin. 24: 17.
Rebelled against by Zedekiah. 2 Kin. 24: 20.
Besieged and took Jerusalem. 2 Kin. 25: 1—4.
Burned Jerusalem. &c. 2 Kin. 25: 9, 10.
Took Zedekiah, &c. captive to Babylon. 2 Kin. 25: 7, 11, 18—21. 2 Chr. 36: 20.
Spoiled and burned the temple. 2 Kin. 25: 9, 13—17. 2 Chr. 36: 18, 19.
Revolt of the Jews from, and their punishment illustrated. Eze. 17 ch.
The Jews exhorted to be subject to, and settle in. Jer. 27: 17. Jer. 29: 1—7.
Treatment of the Jews in. 2. Kin. 25: 27—30. Dan. 1: 3—7.
Grief of the Jews in. Psa. 137: 1—6.
Destroyed by the Medes. Dan. 5: 30, 31.
Restoration of the Jews from. 2 Chr. 36: 23. Ezr. 1 ch. Ezr. 2: 1—67.
The gospel preached in. 1 Pet. 5: 13.
A type of Antichrist. Rev. 16: 19. Rev. 17: 5.
PREDICTIONS RESPECTING;
Conquests by. Jer. 21: 3—10. Jer. 27: 2—6. Jer. 49: 28—33. Eze. 21: 19—32. Eze. 29: 18—20.
Captivity of the Jews by. Jer. 20: 4—6. Jer. 22: 20—26. Jer. 25: 9—11. Mic 4: 10.
Restoration of the Jews from. Isa. 14: 1—4. Isa. 44: 28. Isa. 48: 20. Jer. 29: 10. Jer. 50: 4, 8, 19.
Destruction of. Isa. 13 ch. Isa. 14: 4—22. Isa. 21: 1—10. Isa. 47 ch. Jer. 25: 12. Jer. 50 ch. Jer. 51 ch.
Perpetual desolation of. Isa. 13: 19—22. Isa. 14: 22, 23. Jer. 50: 13, 39. Jer. 51: 37.
Preaching of the gospel in. Psa 87: 4.

Backsliding.

Is turning from God. 1 Kin. 11: 9.
Is leaving the first love. Rev. 2: 4.
Is departing from the simplicity of the gospel. 2 Cor. 11: 3. Gal. 3: 1—3. Gal. 5: 4, 7.
God is displeased at. Psa. 78: 57, 59.
Warnings against. Psa. 85: 8. 1 Cor. 10: 12.
Guilt and consequences of. Num. 14: 43. Psa. 125: 5. Isa. 59: 2, 9—11. Jer. 5: 6. Jer. 8: 5, 13. Jer. 15: 6. Luke 9: 62.
Brings its own punishment. Pro. 14: 14. Jer. 2: 19.
A haughty spirit leads to. Pro. 16: 18.
Proneness to. Pro. 24: 16. Hos. 11: 7.
Liable to continue and increase. Jer. 8: 5. Jer. 14: 7.
Exhortations to return from. 2 Chr. 30: 6. Isa. 31: 6. Jer. 3: 12, 14, 22. Hos. 6: 1.
Pray to be restored from. Psa. 80: 3. Psa. 85: 4. Lam. 5: 21.
Punishment of tempting others to the sin of. Pro. 28: 10. Mat. 18: 6.
Not hopeless. Psa. 37: 24. Pro. 24: 16.
Endeavor to bring back those guilty of. Gal. 6: 1. Jas. 5: 19, 20.
Sin of, to be confessed. Isa. 59: 12—14. Jer. 3: 13, 14. Jer. 14: 7—9.
Pardon of, promised. 2 Chr. 7: 14. Jer. 3: 12. Jer. 31: 20. Jer. 36: 3.
Healing of, promised. Jer. 3: 22. Hos. 14: 4.
Afflictions sent to heal. Hos. 5: 15.
Blessedness of those who keep from. Pro. 28: 14. Isa. 26: 3, 4. Col. 1: 21—23.
Hateful to Saints. Psa. 101: 3.
Exemplified. *Israel*, Exo. 32: 8. Neh. 9: 26. Jer. 3: 11. Hos. 4: 16. *Saul*, 1 Sam. 15: 11. *Solomon*, 1 Kin. 11: 3, 4. *Peter*, Mat. 26: 70—74.

Baptism.

As administered by John. Mat. 3: 5—12. Jno. 3: 23. Acts 13: 24. Acts 19: 4.
Sanctioned, by Christ's submission to it. Mat. 3: 13—15. Luke 3: 21.
Adopted by Christ. Jno. 3: 22. Jno. 4: 1, 2.
Appointed an ordinance of the Christian church. Mat. 28: 19, 20. Mar. 16: 15, 16.
To be administered in the name of the Father, the Son, and the Holy Ghost. Mat. 28: 19.

Water, the outward and visible sign in. Acts 8: 36. Acts 10: 47.
Regeneration, the inward and spiritual grace of. Jno. 3: 3, 5, 6. Rom. 6: 3, 4, 11.
Remission of sins, signified by. Acts 2: 38. Acts 22: 16.
Unity of the Church effected by. 1 Cor. 12: 13. Gal. 3: 27, 28.
Confession of sin necessary to. Mat. 3: 6.
Repentance necessary to. Acts 2: 38.
Faith necessary to. Acts 8: 37. Acts 18: 8.
There is but one. Eph. 4: 5.
ADMINISTERED TO
Individuals. Acts 8: 38. Acts 9: 18.
Households. Acts 16: 15. 1 Cor. 1: 16.
Emblematic of the influences of the Holy Ghost. Mat. 3: 11. Tit. 3: 5.
Typified. 1 Cor. 10: 2. 1 Pet. 3: 20, 21.

Baptism with the Holy Ghost.

Foretold. Eze. 36: 25.
Is through Christ. Tit. 3: 6.
Christ administered. Mat. 3: 11. Jno. 1: 33.
Promised to saints. Acts 1: 5. Acts 2: 38, 39. Acts 11: 16.
All saints partake of. 1 Cor. 12: 13.
Necessity for. Jno. 3: 5. Acts 19: 2—6.
Renews and cleanses the soul. Tit. 3: 5. 1 Pet. 3: 20, 21.
The Word of God instrumental to. Acts 10: 44. Eph. 5: 26.
Typified. Acts 2: 1—4.

Bear, The,

Inhabits woods. 2 Kin. 2: 24.
DESCRIBED AS
Voracious. Dan. 7: 5.
Cunning. Lam. 3: 10.
Cruel. Amos 5: 19.
Often attacks men. 2 Kin. 2: 24. Amos 5: 19.
Attacks the flock in the presence of the shepherd. 1 Sam. 17: 34.
Particularly fierce when deprived of its young. 2 Sam. 17: 8. Pro. 17: 12.
Growls when annoyed. Isa. 59: 11.
Miraculously killed by David. 1 Sam. 17: 36, 37.
ILLUSTRATIVE OF
God in His judgments. Lam. 3: 10. Hos. 13: 8.
The natural man. Isa. 11: 7.
Wicked rulers. Pro. 28: 15.
The kingdom of the Medes. Dan. 7: 5.
The kingdom of Antichrist. Rev. 13: 2.

Beard, The.

The Jews never appeared without. 2 Sam. 10: 5.
Worn even by the priests. Psa. 133: 2
Laying hold of, a token of respect Sam. 20: 9.
Shaving of, a great offence. 2 Sam. 10: 4, 6. 7.
Plucking of, a sign of scorn. Isa. 50: 6.
Dribbling on, a sign of derangement. 1 Sam. 21: 13.
IN AFFLICTION,
Was neglected and untrimmed. 2 Sam. 19: 24.
Was clipped. Jer. 48: 37.
Was shorn. Jer. 41: 5.
Sometimes plucked out. Ezr. 9: 3.
Corners of, not to be marred for the dead. Lev. 19: 27. Lev. 21: 5.
Subject to leprosy. Lev. 13: 29, 30.
Of the healed leper to be shaved. Lev. 14: 9.
Shaving, illustrative of severe judgments. Isa. 7: 20. Isa. 15: 2. Eze. 5: 1.

Beasts.

Created by God. Gen. 1: 24, 25. Gen. 2: 19.
Creation of, exhibits God's power. Jer. 27: 5.
Made for the praise and glory of God. Psa. 148: 10.
Differ in flesh from birds and fishes. 1 Cor. 15: 39.
Herb of the field given to, for food. Gen. 1: 30.
Power over, given to man. Gen. 1: 26, 28. Psa. 8: 7.
Instinctively fear man. Gen. 9: 2.
Received their names from Adam. Gen. 2: 19, 20.
Given to man for food after the flood. Gen. 9: 3.
Not to be eaten alive or with blood. Gen. 9: 4. Deu. 12: 16, 23.
That died naturally or were torn, not to be eaten. Exo. 22: 31. Lev. 17: 15. Lev. 22: 8.
Supply clothing to man. Gen. 3: 21. Job 31: 20.
The property of God. Psa. 50: 10.
Subjects of God's care. Psa. 36: 6. Psa. 104: 10, 11.
DESCRIBED AS
Devoid of speech. 2 Pet. 2: 16.
Devoid of understanding. Psa. 32: 9. Psa. 73: 22.
Devoid of immortality. Psa. 49: 12—15.
Possessed of instinct. Isa. 1: 3.
Being four-footed. Acts 10: 12.
By nature wild, &c. Psa. 50: 11. Mar. 1: 13.

Capable of being tamed. Jas. 3: 7.
Many kinds of, noisome and destructive. Lev. 26: 6: Eze. 5: 17.
Many kinds of, domestic. Gen. 36: 6. Gen. 45: 17.
Lessons of wisdom to be learned from. Job 12: 7.

FOUND IN
Deserts. Isa. 13: 21.
Fields. Deu. 7: 22. Joel 2: 22.
Mountains. So. of Sol. 4: 8.
Forests. Isa. 56: 9. Mic. 5: 8.

HABITATIONS OF;
Dens and caves. Job 37: 8. Job 38: 40.
Under spreading trees. Dan. 4: 12.
Deserted cities. Isa. 13: 21, 22. Zep. 2: 15.

Liable to diseases. Exo. 9: 3.
Frequently suffered on account of the sins of men. Joel 1: 18, 20. Hag. 1: 11.
Often cut off for the sins of men. Gen. 6: 7, with Gen. 7: 23. Exo. 11: 5. Hos. 4: 3.
Early distinguished into clean and unclean. Gen. 7: 2.

CLEAN;
Ox. Exo. 21: 28, with Deu. 14: 4.
Wild ox. Deu. 14: 5.
Sheep. Deu. 7: 13, with Deu. 14: 4.
Goat. Deu. 14: 4.
Hart. Deu. 14: 5, with Job 39: 1.
Roebuck. Deu. 14: 5, with 2 Sam. 2: 18.
Wild goat. Deu. 14: 5.
Fallow deer. Deu. 14: 5.
Chamois. Deu. 14: 5.
Pygarg. Deu. 14: 5.
How distinguished. Lev. 11: 3. Deu. 14: 6
Used for food. Lev. 11: 2. Deu. 12: 15.
Used for sacrifice. Gen. 8: 20.
First-born of, not redeemed. Num. 18: 17.

UNCLEAN;
Camel. Gen. 24: 64, with Lev. 11: 4.
Dromedary. 1 Kin. 4: 28. Est. 8: 10.
Horse. Job 39: 19—25.
Ass. Gen. 22: 3. Mat. 21: 2.
Wild ass. Job 6: 5. Job 39: 5—8.
Mule. 2 Sam. 13: 29. 1 Kin. 10: 25.
Lion. Jud. 14: 5, 6.
Leopard. So. of Sol. 4: 8.
Bear. 2 Sam. 17: 8.
Wolf. Gen. 49: 27. Jno. 10: 12.
Unicorn. Num. 23: 22.
Behemoth. Job 40: 15.
Ape. 1 Kin. 10: 22.
Fox. Psa. 63: 10. So. of Sol. 2: 5.
Dog. Exo. 22: 31. Luke 16: 2.
Swine. Lev. 11: 7. Isa. 66: 17.
Hare. Lev. 11: 6. Deu. 14: 7.
Coney. Lev. 11: 5. Psa. 104: 18.
Mouse. Lev. 11: 29. Isa. 66: 17.
Mole. Lev. 11: 30. Isa. 2: 20.
Weasel. Lev. 11: 29.
Ferret. Lev. 11: 30.
Badger. Exo. 25: 5. Eze. 16: 10.
How distinguished. Lev. 11: 26.
Not eaten. Lev. 11: 4—8. Deu. 1: 7, 8.
Not offered in sacrifice. Lev. 27: 11.
First-born of, redeemed. Num. 18: 15.
Caused uncleanness when dead. Lev. 5: 2.

DOMESTIC,
To enjoy the sabbath. Exo. 20: 10. Deu. 5: 14.
To be taken care of. Lev. 25: 7. Deu. 25: 4.
Not to be cruelly used. Num. 22: 27—32. Pro. 12: 10.

No likeness of, to be worshipped. Deu. 4: 17.
Representations of, worshipped by the heathen. Rom. 1: 23.
History of, written by Solomon. 1 Kin. 4: 33.
Often used as instruments of punishment. Lev. 26: 22. Deu. 32: 24. Jer. 15: 3. Eze. 5: 17.
Man by nature no better than. Ecc. 3: 18, 19.

ILLUSTRATIVE OF
The wicked. Psa. 49: 20. Tit. 1: 12.
Ungodly professors. 2 Pet. 2: 12. Jude 10.
Persecutors. 1 Cor. 15: 32. 2 Tim. 4: 17.
Kingdoms. Dan. 7: 11, 17. Dan. 8: 4.
People of different nations. Dan. 4: 12, 21, 22.
Antichrist. Rev. 13: 2. Rev. 20: 4.

Beds.

Antiquity of. Gen. 47: 31. Exo. 8: 3.
Couches or divans used as. Job 7: 13. Psa. 6: 6.
A small pallet or mattress used as. 1 Sam. 19: 15.
Considered necessary. 2 Kin. 4: 10.

MADE OF
Iron. Deu. 3: 11.
Ivory. Amos 6: 4.
Gold and silver. Est. 1: 6.

Wood. So. of Sol. 3: 7—9. (*marg.*)
Supplied with pillows. 1 Sam. 19: 13. 1 Sam. 26: 7.
Covered with tapestry and linen. Pro. 7: 16.
Often perfumed. Pro. 7: 17. Eze. 23: 41.
Of the poor covered with their upper garment. Exo. 22: 26, 27. Deu. 24: 12, 13.

USED FOR
Sleeping on. Job 33: 15. Luke 11: 7.
Reclining on by day. 2 Sam. 4: 5. 2 Sam. 11: 2.

Reclining on at meals. 1 Sam. 28: 23—25. Amos 6: 4—6. Luke 7: 36—38. Jno. 13: 23.
Not used in affliction. 2 Sam. 12: 16. 2 Sam. 13: 31.
Persons sometimes took to, in grief. 1 Kin. 21: 4. Hos. 7: 14.
Saints meditate and praise God while on. Psa. 4: 4. Psa. 149: 5. So. of Sol. 3: 1.
The wicked devise mischief while on. Psa. 36: 4. Mic. 2: 1.
The slothful too fond of. Pro. 26: 14.
Of the poor often sold for debt. Pro. 22: 27.
Subject to ceremonial defilement. Lev. 15: 4.
Purification of. Mar. 7: 4. (*marg.*)
ILLUSTRATIVE
Of the grave. Isa. 57: 2.
(Made in darkness,) of extreme misery. Job 17: 13.
(Made in sickness,) of divine support and comfort. Psa. 41: 3.
(Made on high,) of carnal security. Isa. 57: 7.
(Too short,) of plans which afford no rest or peace. Isa. 28: 20.

Benjamin, Tribe of.

Descended from Jacob's twelfth son. Gen. 35: 18.
Predictions respecting. Gen. 49: 27. Deu. 33: 12.
PERSONS SELECTED FROM,
To number the people. Num. 1: 11.
To spy out the land. Num. 13: 9.
To divide the land. Num. 34: 21.
Strength of, on leaving Egypt. Num. 1: 36, 37.
Formed the rear of the third division of Israel in their journeys. Num. 10: 22, 24.
Encamped on west side of the tabernacle under the standard of Ephraim. Num. 2: 18, 22.
Offering of, at dedication. Num. 7: 60—65.
Families of. Num. 26: 38—40.
Strength of, entering Canaan. Num. 26: 41.
On Gerizim said amen to the blessings. Deu. 27: 12.
Cities and bounds of inheritance. Jos. 18: 11—28.
Celebrated as bowmen and slingers. 1 Chr. 12: 2.
Assisted against Sisera. Jud. 5: 14.
Oppressed by the Ammonites. Jud. 10: 9.
Almost annihilated for protecting the men of Gibeah. Jud. 20: 12—48.
Remnant of, provided with wives to preserve the tribe. Jud. 21: 1—23.
Furnished the first king to Israel. 1 Sam. 9: 1, 2, 15—17. 1 Sam. 10: 20, 21. 2 Sam. 2: 8—10.
Adhered for a time to the house of Saul against David. 2 Sam. 2: 9, 15, 25, 31.
Some of, assisted David. 1 Chr. 12: 1—7, 16.
Revolted from the house of Saul. 2 Sam. 3: 19.
Some of, at David's coronation. 1 Chr. 12: 29.
A thousand of, with Shimei came to meet David on his return to Jerusalem. 2 Sam. 19: 16, 17.
Very numerous in David's time. 1 Chr. 7: 6—12.
Captains appointed over. 1 Kin. 4: 18. 1 Chr. 27: 12.
Remained faithful to Judah. 1 Kin. 12: 21.
Furnished an army to Jehoshaphat. 2 Chr. 17: 17.
Numbers of, returned from the captivity and dwelt at Jerusalem. Ezr. 1: 5. Neh. 11: 4.
Celebrated persons of; *Ehud*, Jud. 3: 15. *Kish*, 1 Sam. 9: 1. *Saul*, 1 Sam. 9: 1. 1 Sam. 10: 1. *Abner*, 1 Sam. 14: 51. 1 Sam. 17: 55. *Elhanan*, 2 Sam. 21: 19. *Paul*, Phi. 3: 5,

Birds.

Created by God. Gen. 1: 20, 21. Gen. 2: 19.
Created for the glory of God. Psa. 148: 10.
Herb of the field given as food to. Gen. 1: 30.
Differ in flesh from beasts and fishes. 1 Cor. 15: 39.
Power over given to man. Gen. 1: 26. Psa. 8: 8.
Names given to, by Adam. Gen. 2: 19, 20.
Instinctively fear man. Gen. 9: 2.
Instinct of, inferior to man's reason. Job 35: 11.
Lessons of wisdom to be learned from. Job 12: 7.
Can all be tamed. Jas. 3: 7.
Given as food to man. Gen. 9: 2, 3.
The blood of, not to be eaten. Lev. 7: 26.
The property of God. Psa. 50: 11.
God provides for. Psa. 104: 10—12. Mat. 6: 26. Luke 12: 23, 24.
CALLED
Fowls of the air. Gen. 7: 3.
Fowls of heaven. Job 35: 11.
Feathered fowl. Eze. 39: 17.
Winged fowl. Deu. 4: 17.
Birds of the air. Mat. 8: 20.
Many kinds of, granivorous. Mat. 13: 4.
Many kinds of, carnivorous. Gen. 15: 11. Gen. 40: 19. Deu. 28: 26.

Furnished with claws. Dan. 4: 33.
Propagated by eggs. Deu. 22: 6. Jer. 17: 11.
Make, and dwell in nests. Mat. 8: 20.
Are hostile to strange kinds. Jer. 12: 9.
Have each their peculiar note or song. Psa. 104: 12. Ecc. 12: 4. So. of Sol. 2: 12.
Fly above the earth. Gen. 1: 20.
Rapid flight of, alluded to. Isa. 31: 5. Hos. 9: 11. H[illegible]
Many kinds of, migratory. [illegible]er. 8: 7.
Often remove from places suffering calamities. Jer. 4: 25. Jer. 9: 10.
Rest on trees. Dan. 4: 12. Mat. 13: 32.

INHABIT

- Mountains. Psa. 50: 11.
- Deserts. Psa. 102: 6.
- Marshes. Isa. 14: 23.
- Deserted cities. Isa. 34: 11, 14, 15.

MAKE THEIR NESTS

- In trees. Psa. 104: 17. Eze. 31: 6.
- On the ground. Deu. 22: 6.
- In clefts of rocks. Num. 24: 21. Jer. 48: 28.
- In deserted cities. Isa. 34: 15.
- Under the roofs of houses. Psa. 84: 3.

Early distinguished into clean and unclean. Gen. 8: 20.

CLEAN;

- Dove. Gen. 8: 8.
- Turtle. Lev. 14: 22. So. of Sol. 2: 12.
- Pigeon. Lev. 1: 14. Lev. 12: 6.
- Quail. Exo. 16: 12, 13. Num. 11: 31, 32.
- Sparrow. Lev. 14: 4. (*marg.*) Mat. 10: 29–31.
- Swallow. Psa. 84: 3. Isa. 38: 14.
- Cock and hen. Mat. 23: 37. Mat. 26: 34, 74.
- Partridge. 1 Sam. 26: 20. Jer. 17: 11.
- Crane. Isa. 38: 14. Jer. 8: 7.
- To be eaten. Deu. 14: 11, 20.
- Offered in sacrifice. Gen. 8: 20. Lev. 1: 14.

UNCLEAN;

- Eagle. Lev. 11: 13. Job 39: 27.
- Ossifrage. Lev. 11: 13.
- Osprey. Lev. 11: 13.
- Vulture. Lev. 11: 14. Job 28: 7. Isa. 34: 15.
- Glede. Deu. 14: 13.
- Kite. Lev. 11: 14.
- Raven. Lev. 11: 15. Job 38: 41.
- Owl. Lev. 11: 16. Job 30: 29.
- Night hawk. Lev. 11: 16.
- Cuckoo. Lev. 11: 16.
- Hawk. Lev. 11: 16. Job 39: 26.
- Little owl. Lev. 11: 17.
- Cormorant. Lev. 11: 17. Isa. 34: 11.
- Great owl. Lev. 11: 17.
- Swan. Lev. 11: 18.
- Pelican. Lev. 11: 18. Psa. 102: 6.
- Gier Eagle. Lev. 11: 18.
- Stork. Lev. 11: 19. Psa. 104: 17.
- Heron. Lev. 11: 19.
- Lapwing. Lev. 11: 19.
- Bat. Lev. 11: 19. Isa. 2: 20.
- Ostrich. Job 39: 13, 18.
- Bittern. Isa. 14: 23. Isa. 34: 11.
- Peacock. 1 Kin. 10: 22. Job 39: 13.
- Not to be eaten. Lev. 11: 13, 17. Deu. 14: 12.

Not to be eaten with their young. Deu. 22: 6, 7.
Taken in snares or nets. Pro. 1: 17.
Often suffered for man's sin. Gen. 6: 7. Jer. 12: 4. Eze. 38: 20. Hos. 4: 3.
Solomon wrote the history of. 1 Kin. 4: 33.
Confinement of, in cages alluded to. Jer. 5: 27.
No likeness of, to be made for worship. Deu. 4: 17.
Often worshipped by idolaters. Rom. 1: 23.

ILLUSTRATIVE

- Of cruel and rapacious kings. Isa. 46: 11.
- Of hostile nations. Jer. 12: 9.
- Of people of different countries. Eze. 31: 6. Mat. 13: 32.
- Of unsettled persons, &c. Pro: 27: 8. Isa. 16: 2.
- Of the devil and his spirits. Mat. 13: 4, with 19 v.
- (Snaring,) of death. Ecc. 9: 12.
- (Snaring,) of designs of the wicked. Psa. 124: 7. Pro. 1: 10–17. Pro. 7: 23.

Blasphemy.

Christ assailed with. Mat. 10: 25. Luke 22: 64, 65. 1 Pet. 4: 14.
Charged upon Christ. Mat. 9: 2, 3. Mat. 26: 64, 65. Jno. 10: 33, 36.
Charged upon saints. Acts 6: 11, 13.
Proceeds from the heart. Mat. 15: 19.
Forbidden. Exo. 20: 7. Col. 3: 8.
The wicked addicted to. Psa. 74: 18. Isa. 52: 5. 2 Tim. 3: 2. Rev. 16: 11, 21.
Idolatry counted as. Isa. 65: 7. Eze. 20: 27, 28.
Hypocrisy counted as. Rev. 2: 9.
Saints grieved to hear. Psa. 44: 15, 16. Psa. 74: 10, 18, 22.
Give no occasion for. 2 Sam. 12: 14. 1 Tim. 6: 1.
Against the Holy Ghost, unpardonable. Mat. 12: 31, 32.
Connected with folly and pride. 2 Kin. 19: 22. Psa. 74: 18.
Punishment of. Lev. 24: 16. Isa. 65: 7. Eze. 20: 27–33. Eze. 35: 11, 12.
Exemplified. *The Danite*, Lev. 24: 11. *Sennacherib*, 2 Kin. 19: 4, 10, 22. *The Jews*, Luke 22: 65. *Hymeneus*, 1 Tim. 1: 20.

Blessed, The.

Whom God chooses. Psa. 65: 4. Eph. 1: 3, 4.
Whom God calls. Isa. 51: 2. Rev. 19: 9.
Who know Christ. Mat. 16: 16, 17.
Who know the gospel. Psa. 89: 15.
Who are not offended at Christ. Mat. 11: 6.
Who believe. Luke 1: 45. Gal. 3: 9.
Whose sins are forgiven. Psa. 32: 1, 2. Rom. 4: 7.
To whom God imputes righteousness without works. Rom. 4: 6—9.
Whom God chastens. Job 5: 17. Psa. 94: 12.
Who suffer for Christ. Luke 6: 22.
Who have the Lord for their God. Psa. 144: 15.
Who trust in God. Psa. 2: 12. Psa. 34: 8. Psa. 40: 4. Psa. 84: 12. Jer. 17: 7.
Who fear God. Psa. 112: 1. Psa. 128: 1, 4.
Who hear and keep the word of God. Psa. 119: 2. Jas. 1: 25. Mat. 13: 16. Luke 11: 28. Rev. 1: 3. Rev. 22: 7.
Who delight in the commandments of God. Psa. 112: 1.
Who keep the commandments of God. Rev. 22: 14.
Who wait for the Lord. Isa. 30: 18.
Whose strength is in the Lord. Psa. 84: 5.
Who hunger and thirst after righteousness. Mat. 5: 6.
Who frequent the house of God. Psa. 65: 4. Psa. 84: 4.
Who avoid the wicked. Psa. 1: 1.
Who endure temptation. Jas. 1: 12.
Who watch against sin. Rev. 16: 15.
Who rebuke sinners. Pro. 24: 25.
Who watch for the Lord. Luke 12: 37.
Who die in the Lord. Rev. 14: 13.
Who have part in the first resurrection. Rev. 20: 6.
Who favor saints. Gen. 12: 3. Ruth 2: 10.
The undefiled. Psa. 119: 1.
The pure in heart. Mat. 5: 8.
The just. Psa. 106: 3. Pro. 10: 6.
The children of the just. Pro. 20: 7.
The righteous. Psa. 5: 12.
The generation of the upright. Psa. 112: 2.
The faithful. Pro. 28: 20.
The poor in spirit. Mat. 5: 3.
The meek. Mat. 5: 5.
The merciful. Mat. 5: 7.
The bountiful. Deu. 15: 10. Psa. 41: 1. Pro. 22: 9. Luke 14: 13, 14.
The peace-makers. Mat. 5: 9.
Holy mourners. Mat. 5: 4. Luke 6: 21.
Saints at the judgment-day. Mat. 25: 34.
Who shall eat bread in the kingdom of God. Luke 14: 15. Rev. 19: 9.

Blindness, Spiritual.

Explained. Jno. 1: 5. 1 Cor. 2: 14.
The effect of sin. Isa. 29: 10. Mat. 6: 23. Jno. 3: 19, 20.
Unbelief the effect of. Rom. 11: 8. 2 Cor. 4: 3, 4.
Uncharitableness, a proof of. 1 Jno. 2: 9, 11.
A work of the devil. 2 Cor. 4: 4.
Leads to all evil. Eph. 4: 17—19.
Is inconsistent with communion with God. 1 Jno. 1: 6, 7.
Of ministers, fatal to themselves and to the people. Mat. 15: 14.
The wicked are in. Psa. 82: 5. Jer. 5: 21.
The self-righteous are in. Mat. 23: 19, 26. Rev. 3: 17.
The wicked wilfully guilty of. Isa. 26: 11. Rom. 1: 19—21.
Judicially inflicted. Psa. 69: 23. Isa. 29: 10. Isa. 44: 18. Mat. 13: 13, 14. Jno. 12: 40.
Pray for the removal of. Psa. 13: 3. Psa. 119: 18.
Christ appointed to remove. Isa. 42: 7. Luke 4: 18. Jno. 8: 12. Jno. 9: 39. 2 Cor. 4: 6.
Christ's ministers are lights to remove. Mat. 5: 14. Acts 26: 18.
Saints are delivered from. Jno. 8: 12. Eph. 5: 8. Col. 1: 13. 1 The. 5: 4, 5. 1 Pet. 2: 9.
Removal of, illustrated. Jno. 9: 7, 11, 25. Acts 9: 18. Rev. 3: 18.
Exemplified. *Israel*, Rom. 11: 25. 2 Cor. 3: 15. *Scribes and Pharisees*, Mat. 23: 16, 24. *Church of Laodicea*, Rev. 3: 17.

Blood.

The life of animals. Gen. 9: 4. Lev. 17: 11, 14.
Fluid. Deu. 12: 16.
Red. 2 Kin. 3: 22. Joel 2: 31.
Of all men the same. Acts 17: 26.
EATING OF, FORBIDDEN TO
- Man after the flood. Gen. 9: 4.
- The Israelites under the law. Lev. 3: 17. Lev. 17: 10, 12.
- The early Christians. Acts 15: 20, 29.

The Jews often guilty of eating. 1 Sam. 14: 32, 33. Eze. 33: 25.
Of animals slain for food to be poured on the earth and covered. Lev. 17: 13. Deu. 12: 16, 24.
Birds of prey delight in. Job 39: 30.
Beasts of prey delight in. Num. 23. 24. Psa. 68: 23.
SHEDDING OF HUMAN,
- Forbidden. Gen. 9: 5.
- Hateful to God. Pro. 6: 16, 17.

Defiling to the land. Psa. 106: 38.
Defiling to the person. Isa. 59: 3.
Jews often guilty of. Jer. 22: 17. Eze. 22: 4.
Always punished. Gen. 9: 6.
Mode of clearing those accused of. Deu. 21: 1—9.
The price of, not to be consecrated. Mat. 27: 6.
OF LEGAL SACRIFICES
For atonement. Exo. 30: 10. Lev. 17: 11.
For purification. Heb. 9: 13, 19—22.
How disposed of. Exo. 29: 12. Lev. 4: 7.
Not offered with leaven. Exo. 23: 18. Exo. 34: 25.
Ineffectual to remove sin. Heb. 10: 4.
Idolaters made drink-offerings of. Psa. 16: 4.
Water turned into, as a sign. Exo. 4: 30, with ver. 9.
Waters of Egypt turned into, as a judgment. Exo. 7: 17—21.
ILLUSTRATIVE
(Washing the feet in,) of victories. Psa. 58: 10. Psa. 68: 23.
(Building with,) of oppression and cruelty. Hab. 2: 12.
(Preparing unto,) of ripening for destruction. Eze. 35: 6.
(On one's own head,) of guilt. Lev. 20: 9. 2 Sam. 1: 16. Eze. 18: 13.
(Given to drink,) of severe judgments. Eze. 16: 38. Rev. 16: 6.

Boldness, Holy.

Christ set an example of. Jno. 7: 26.
Is through faith in Christ. Eph. 3: 12. Heb. 10: 19.
A characteristic of saints. Pro. 28: 1.
PRODUCED BY
Trust in God. Isa. 50: 7.
The fear of God. Acts 4: 19. Acts 5: 29.
Faithfulness to God. 1 Tim. 3: 13.
Express your trust in God with. Heb. 13: 6.
Have, in prayer. Eph. 3: 12. Heb. 4: 16.
Saints shall have, in judgment. 1 Jno. 4: 17.
Exhortations to. Jos. 1: 7. 2 Chr. 19: 11. Jer. 1: 8. Eze. 3: 9.
Pray for. Acts 4: 29. Eph. 6: 19, 20.
MINISTERS SHOULD EXHIBIT, IN
Faithfulness to their people. 2 Cor. 7: 4. 2 Cor. 10: 1.
Preaching. Acts 4: 31. Phi. 1: 14.
Reproving sin. Isa. 58: 1. Mic. 3: 8.
The face of opposition. Acts 13: 46. 1 The. 2: 2.
Exemplified. *Abraham*, Gen. 18: 22—32. *Jacob*, Gen. 32: 24—29. *Moses*, Exo. 32: 31, 32. Exo. 33: 18. *Aaron*, Num. 16: 47, 48. *David*, 1 Sam. 17: 45. *Elijah*, 1 Kin. 18: 15, 18. *Nehemiah*, Neh. 6: 11. *Shadrac*, Dan. 3: 17, 18. *Daniel*, Dan. 6: 10. *Joseph of Arimathea*, Mar. 15: 43. *Peter and John*, Acts 4: 8—13. *Stephen*, Acts 7: 51. *Paul*, Acts 9: 27, 29. Acts 19: 8. *Barnabas*, Acts 14: 3. *Apollos*, Acts 18: 26.

Bondage, Spiritual.

Is to the devil. 1 Tim. 3: 7. 2 Tim. 2: 26.
Is to the fear of death. Heb. 2: 14, 15.
Is to sin. Jno. 8: 34. Acts 8: 23. Rom. 6: 16. Rom. 7: 23. Gal. 4: 3. 2 Pet. 2: 19.
Deliverance from, promised. Isa. 42: 6, 7.
Christ delivers from. Luke 4: 18, 21. Jno. 8: 36. Rom. 7: 24, 25. Eph. 4: 8.
The gospel, the instrument of deliverance from. Jno. 8: 32. Rom. 8: 2.
Saints are delivered from. Rom. 6: 18, 22.
Deliverance from, illustrated. Deu. 4: 20.
Typified. *Israel in Egypt*, Exo. 1: 13, 14.

Books.

Probable origin of. Job 19: 23, 24.
MADE OF
Papyrus or paper reed. Isa. 19: 7.
Parchment. 2 Tim. 4: 13.
Made in a roll. Isa. 34: 4. Jer. 36: 2. Eze. 2: 9.
Written with pen and ink. Jer. 36: 18. 3 Jno. 13.
Often written on both sides. Eze. 2: 10.
Often sealed. Isa. 29: 11. Dan. 12: 4. Rev. 5: 1.
Often dedicated to persons of distinction. Luke 1: 3. Acts 1: 1.
Were numerous and most expensive. Acts 19: 19.
The ancients fond of making. Ecc. 12: 12.
Divine communicatons recorded in. Exo. 17: 14. Isa. 30: 8. Jer. 36: 2. Rev. 1: 19.
Important events recorded in. Ezr. 4: 15. Ezr. 6: 1, 2. (*marg.*) Est. 2: 23.
Erasures in, alluded to. Exo. 32: 33. Num. 5: 23.
NOT EXTANT, BUT MENTIONED IN SCRIPTURE;
Wars of the Lord. Num. 21: 14.
Jasher. Jos. 10: 13. 2 Sam. 1: 18.
Samuel concerning the kingdom. 1 Sam. 10: 25.
Chronicles of David. 1 Chr. 27: 24.

Acts of Solomon. 1 Kin. 11: 41.
Natural history by Solomon. 1 Kin. 4: 32, 33.
History of the kings. 1 Chr. 9: 1.
Samuel the seer. 1 Chr. 29: 29.
Nathan. 1 Chr. 29: 29. 2 Chr. 9: 29.
Shemaiah. 2 Chr. 12: 15.
Gad the seer. 1 Chr. 29: 29.
Ahijah the Shilonite. 2 Chr. 9: 29.
Visions of Iddo. 2 Chr. 9: 29. 2 Chr. 12: 15.
Jehu the son of Hanani. 2 Chr. 20: 34.
Sayings of the seers. 2 Chr. 33: 19.

ILLUSTRATIVE OF
Memorials of God's providence. Psa. 56: 8. Psa. 139: 16.
Memorials of conversation and conduct of men. Dan. 7: 10. Mal. 3: 16. Rev. 20: 12.
The record of the church of Christ. Dan. 12: 1. Heb. 12: 23. Rev. 20: 12, 15. Rev. 22: 19.

Bottles.

First mention of, in Scripture. Gen. 21: 14.
Ancients often drank from. Hab. 2: 15.

USED FOR HOLDING
Water. Gen. 21: 14, 15, 19.
Milk. Jud. 4: 19.
Wine. 1 Sam. 1: 24. 1 Sam. 16: 20.

Some, made of earthenware. Jer. 19: 1.

MADE OF SKINS
Shrivelled and dried by smoke. Psa. 119: 83.
Marred by age and use. Jos. 9: 4, 13.
When old, unfit for holding new wine. Mat. 9: 17. Mar. 2: 22.
Sometimes probably of large dimensions. 1 Sam. 25: 18. 2 Sam. 16: 1.

ILLUSTRATIVE
Of the clouds. Job 38: 37.
Of God's remembrance. Psa. 56: 8.
Of sinners ripe for judgment. Jer. 13: 12—14.
(Dried up,) of the afflicted. Psa. 119: 83.
(Ready to burst,) of the impatient. Job 32: 19.
(Broken,) of severe judgments. Isa. 30: 14. (*marg.*) Jer. 19: 10. Jer. 48: 12.

Bow, The.

An instrument of war. Gen. 48: 22. Isa. 7: 24.
Sometimes used in hunting. Gen. 27: 3.
For shooting arrows. 1 Chr. 12: 2. (*see marg.*)
Called the battle bow. Zec. 9: 10. Zec. 10: 4.

THOSE WHO USED, CALLED
Bowmen. Jer. 4: 29.
Archers. 1 Sam. 31: 3. (*marg.*) Jer. 51: 3.

Usually of steel. 2 Sam. 22: 35. Job 20: 24.
Held in the left hand. Eze. 39: 3.
Drawn with full force. 2 Kin. 9: 24.
The Jews taught to use. 2 Sam. 1: 18.

USED EXPERTLY BY
Lydians. Jer. 46: 9.
Elamites. Jer. 49: 35.
Philistines. 1 Sam. 31: 2, 3.
Sons of Reuben, Gad, and Manasseh. 1 Chr. 5: 18.
Benjamites. 1 Chr. 12: 2. 2 Chr. 14: 8.

Given as a token of friendship. 1 Sam. 18: 4.
Often furnished by the state. 2 Chr. 26: 14.
Of the vanquished, broken and burned. Psa. 37: 15. Eze. 39: 9.

ILLUSTRATIVE
Of strength and power. Job 29: 20.
Of the tongue of the wicked. Psa. 11: 2. Jer. 9: 3.
(When deceitful,) of the hypocrite. Psa. 78: 57. Hos. 7: 16.
(When broken,) of the overthrow of power. 1 Sam. 2: 4. Jer. 49: 35. Hos. 1: 5. Hos. 2: 18.

Brass, or Copper.

Dug out of the mountains. Deu. 8: 9.
Purified by smelting. Job 28: 2.

CHARACTERIZED BY
Strength. Job 40: 18.
Hardness. Lev. 26: 19.
Yellow color. Ezr. 8: 27. (*marg.*)
Fusibility. Eze. 22: 18, 20.
Sonorousness. 1 Cor. 13: 1.

Takes a high polish. 2 Chr. 4: 16. (*marg.*) Eze. 1: 7.
Inferior in value to gold and silver. Isa. 60: 17. Dan. 2: 32, 39.
Antiquity of working in. Gen. 4: 22.
Extensive commerce in. Eze. 27: 13. Rev. 18: 12.
Working in, a trade. Gen. 4: 22. 1 Kin. 7: 14. 2 Chr. 24: 12. 2 Tim. 4: 14.
Canaan abounded in. Deu. 8: 9, with Deu. 33: 25. (*marg.*)

TAKEN IN WAR;
Often in great quantities. Jos. 22: 8. 2 Sam. 8: 8. 2 Kin. 25: 13—16.
Cleansed by fire. Num. 31: 21—23.
Generally consecrated to God. Jos. 6: 19, 24. 2 Sam. 8: 10, 11.

Offerings of, for the tabernacle. Exo. 38: 29.
Collected by David for the temple. 1 Chr. 22: 3, 14, 16. 1 Chr. 29: 2.

Offerings of, for the temple. 1 Chr. 29:6, 7.
Coined for money. Mat. 10:9. Mar. 12:41. (*marg.*)
MADE INTO
Mirrors. Exo. 38:8. (*marg.*)
Gates. Psa. 107:16. Isa. 45:2.
Bars for gates. 1 Kin. 4:13.
Fetters. Jud. 16:21. 2 Kin. 25:7.
Shields. 1 Kin. 14:27. 2 Chr. 12:10.
Helmets. 1 Sam. 17:5.
Greaves for the legs. 1 Sam. 17:6.
Household vessels. Mar. 7:4.
Sacred vessels. Exo. 27:3. 1 Kin. 7:45.
Altars. Exo. 27:2. Exo. 39:39.
Sockets for pillars. Exo. 38:10, 11, 17.
Lavers. Exo. 30:18. 1 Kin. 7:38.
Pillars. 1 Kin. 7:15, 16.
Idols. Dan. 5:4. Rev. 9:20.
Instruments of music. 1 Chr. 15:19.
Moses made the serpent of. Num. 21:9. 2 Kin. 18:4.
ILLUSTRATIVE OF
Obstinate sinners. Isa. 48:4. Jer. 6:28.
The decrees of God. Zec. 6:1.
The strength and firmness of Christ. Dan. 10:6. Rev. 1:15.
Strength given to saints. Jer. 15:20. Mic. 4:13.
Macedonian empire. Dan. 2:39.
Extreme drought. Deu. 28:23.
The earth made barren. Lev. 26:19.

Bread.

Given by God. Ruth 1:6. Mat. 6:11.
Yielded by the earth. Job 28:5. Isa. 55:10.
MADE OF
Wheat. Exo. 29:2. Psa. 81:16.
Barley. Jud. 7:13. Jno. 6:9.
Beans, millet, &c. Eze. 4:9.
Manna (in the wilderness). Num. 11:8.
Corn ground for making. Isa. 28:28.
Was kneaded. Gen. 18:6. Jer. 7:18. Hos. 7:4.
Troughs used for kneading. Exo. 12:34.
Usually leavened. Lev. 23:17. Mat. 13:33.
Sometimes unleavened. Exo: 12:18. 1 Cor. 5:8.
WAS FORMED INTO
Loaves. 1 Sam. 10:3, 4. Mat. 14:17.
Cakes. 2 Sam. 6:19. 1 Kin. 17:13.
Wafers. Exo. 16:31. Exo. 29:23.
WAS BAKED
On hearths. Gen. 18:6.
On coals of fire. Isa. 44:19. Jno. 21:9.
In ovens. Lev. 26:26. Hos. 7:4—7.
Making of, a trade. Gen. 40:2. Jer. 37:21.
Ordinary, called common bread. 1 Sam. 21:4.
Sacred, called hallowed bread. 1 Sam. 21:4, 6.
Nutritious and strengthening. Psa. 104:15.
When old, dry and mouldy. Jos. 9:5, 12.
Often put for the whole sustenance of man. Gen 3:19. Gen. 39:6. Mat. 6:11.
The principal food used by the ancients. Gen. 18:5. Gen. 21:14. Gen. 27:17. Jud. 19:5.
Broken for use. Lam. 4:4. Mat. 14:19.
Kept in baskets. Gen. 40:16. Exo. 29:32.
Publicly sold. Mat. 14:15, with Mat. 15:33.
In times of scarcity, sold by weight. Lev. 26:26. Eze. 4:16.
Scarceness of, sent as a punishment. Psa. 105:16. Isa. 3:1. Eze. 5:16.
Plenty of, promised to the obedient. Lev. 26:5.
Often given as a present. 1 Sam. 25:18. 2 Sam. 16:2. 1 Chr. 12:40.
Served round after funerals. Eze. 24:17—22.
With water, the food of prisons. 1 Kin. 22:27.
Crumb of, used to wipe the fingers, thrown under the table. Mat. 15:27. Luke 16:21.
First fruit of, offered to God. Num. 15:19, 20.
Offered with sacrifices. Exo. 29:2, 23. Num. 28:2.
Placed on table of shew bread. Exo. 25:30.
Multitudes miraculously fed by Christ with. Mat. 14:19—21. Mat. 15:34—37.
ILLUSTRATIVE
Of Christ. Jno. 6:33—35.
(When broken,) of the death of Christ. Mat. 26:26, with 1 Cor. 11:23, 24.
(Partaking of,) of communion of saints. Acts 2:46. 1 Cor. 10:17.
(Want of,) of extreme poverty. Pro. 12:9. Isa. 3:7.
(Seeking or begging,) of extreme poverty. 1 Sam. 2:36. Psa. 37:25. Lam. 1:11.
(Fulness of,) of abundance. Eze. 16:49.
(Eating without scarceness,) of plenty. Deu. 8:9.
(Of adversity,) of heavy affliction. Isa. 30:20.
(Of tears,) of sorrow. Psa. 80:5.
(Of deceit,) of unlawful gain. Pro. 20:17.
(Of wickedness,) of oppression. Pro. 4:17.
(Of idleness,) of sloth. Pro. 31:27.

Breastplate.

A part of defensive armor. 1 Kin. 22:34. (*marg.*)
A part of the high priest's dress. Exo. 28:4.
FOR SOLDIERS,
Made of iron. Rev. 9:9.
Bright and shining. Rev. 9:17.
FOR THE HIGH PRIEST,
Materials of. Exo. 28:15. Exo. 39:8.
Form and dimensions of. Exo. 28:16. Exo. 39:9.
Made from the offering of the people. Exo. 35:9.
Had names of the tribes engraved on precious stones. Exo. 28:17—21. Exo. 39:10, 14.
Inseparably united to the ephod. Exo. 28:22—28. Exo. 39:15—21.
The Urim and Thummim placed in. Exo. 28:30. Lev. 8:8.
Worn as a memorial. Exo. 28:29, with Isa. 49:16.
ILLUSTRATIVE OF THE
Righteous judgment of Christ. Isa. 59:17.
Defence of righteousness. Eph. 6:14.
Defence of faith and love. 1 The. 5:8.

Brooks.

Canaan abounded with. Deu. 8:7.
Often ran over pebbles. 1 Sam. 17:40. Job 22:24.
BORDERS OF, FAVORABLE TO
Grass. 1 Kin. 18:5.
Willows. Lev. 23:40. Job 40:22.
Reeds. Isa. 19:7.
Abounded with fish. Isa. 19:8.
Afforded protection to a country. Isa. 19:6.
MENTIONED IN SCRIPTURE;
Arnon. Num. 21:14, 15.
Besor. 1 Sam. 30:9.
Gaash. 2 Sam. 23:30. 1 Chr. 11:32.
Cherith. 1 Kin. 17:3, 5.
Eschol. Num. 13:23, 24.
Kidron. 2 Sam. 15:23. 1 Kin. 15:13. Jno. 18:1.
Kishon. 1 Kin. 18:40. Psa. 83:9.
Zered. Deu. 2:13.
Of the willows. Isa. 15:7.
ILLUSTRATIVE
Of wisdom. Pro. 18:4.
Of temporal abundance. Job. 20:17.
(Deceptive,) of false friends. Job. 6:15.
(Drinking of, by the way,) of help in distress. Psa. 110:7.

Burial.

Probable origin of. Gen. 4:9, 10.
Design of. Gen. 23:3, 4.
ATTENDED BY
Family of the dead. Gen. 50:5, 6, 8. Mat. 8:21.
Numbers of friends, &c. Gen. 50:7, 9. 2 Sam. 3:31. Luke 7:12.
Female friends. Mar. 15:47. Luke 7:13.
Hired mourners. Jer. 9:17, 18.
Great lamentation at. Gen, 50:10, 11. 2 Sam. 3:31, 32.
Orations sometimes made at. 2 Sam. 3:33, 34.
THE BODY WAS
Washed before. Acts 9:37.
Anointed for. Mat. 26:12.
Wound in linen for. Jno. 11:44. Jno. 19:40.
Preserved with spices. Jno. 19:39, 40.
Sometimes burned before. 1 Sam. 31:12.
Carried on a bier to. 2 Sam. 3:31. Luke 7:14.
Perfumes burned at. 2 Chr. 16:14. Jer. 34:5.
Antiquity of coffins for. Gen. 50:26.
Often took place immediately after death. Jno. 11:17, with 39 v. Acts 5:6, 10.
Of persons embalmed, deferred for seventy days. Gen. 50:3, 4.
Of persons hanged, always on the days of execution. Deu. 21:23. Jno. 19:31.
The right of all nations. Jud. 16:31. Jno. 19:38.
Of enemies, sometimes performed by the conquerors. 1 Kin. 11:15. Eze. 39:11—14.
Of the friendless, a kind act. 2 Sam. 2:5.
PLACES USED FOR;
Natural caves. Gen. 23:19. Jno. 11:38.
Caves hewn out of rocks. Isa. 22:16. Mat. 27:60.
Gardens. 2 Kin. 21:18, 26. Jno. 19:41.
Under trees. Gen. 35:8. 1 Sam. 31:13.
Tops of the hills. Jos. 24:33. 2 Kin. 23:16.
Houses of the deceased. 1 Sam. 25:1. 1 Kin. 2:34.
The city of David for the kings of Judah. 1 Kin. 2:10. 2 Chr. 21:20. 2 Chr. 24:16.
Antiquity of purchasing places for. Gen 23:7—16.
PLACES OF,
Frequently prepared and pointed out during life. Gen. 50:5. 2 Chr. 16:14. Mat. 27:60.
Members of a family interred in the same. Gen. 25:10. Gen. 49:31. 2 Sam. 2:32.
Held in high veneration. Neh. 2:3, 5.

Provided for the common people. Jer. 26: 23.
Provided for aliens and strangers. Mat. 27: 7.
Visited by sorrowing friends. Jno. 11: 31.
Pillars erected on. Gen. 35: 20.
Tombs erected over. Mat. 23: 27—29.
Sometimes had inscriptions. 2 Kin. 23: 17.
Sometimes not apparent. Luke 11: 44.
For criminals, marked by heaps. Jos. 7: 26.
Were ceremonially unclean. Num. 19: 16, 18.
Often desecrated by idolatry. Isa. 65: 3, 4.
The Jews anxious to be interred in their family places of. Gen. 47: 29—31. Gen. 49: 29, 30. Gen. 50: 25. 2 Sam. 19: 37.
Followed by a feast. 2 Sam. 3: 35. Jer. 16: 7, 8. Hos. 9: 4.
Privation of, considered a calamity. Ecc. 6: 3.
Privation of, threatened as a punishment. 2 Kin. 9: 10. Jer. 8: 2. Jer. 16: 4.
An ignominious, compared to the burial of an ass. Jer. 22: 19.
Illustrative of regeneration. Rom. 6: 4. Col. 2: 12.

Burnt Offering, The.

To be offered only to the Lord. Jud. 13: 16.
Specially acceptable. Gen. 8: 21. Lev. 1: 9, 13, 17.
The most ancient of all sacrifices. Gen. 4: 4, with Gen. 8: 20. Gen. 22: 2, 13. Job 1: 5.
Offered by the Jews before the law. Exo. 10: 25. Exo. 24: 5.
To be taken from
The flock or herd. Lev. 1: 2.
The fowls. Lev. 1: 14.
Was an atonement for sin. Lev. 9: 7.
Guilt transferred to, by imposition of hands. Lev. 1: 4. Num. 8: 12.
Required to be
Killed, if a beast, by the person who brought it. Lev. 1: 5, 11.
Killed, if a bird, by the priest. Lev. 1: 15.
For the people at large, killed and prepared by the Levites. Eze. 44: 11.
A male without blemish. Lev. 1: 3. Lev. 22: 19.
Voluntary. Lev. 1: 3. Lev. 22: 18, 19.
Presented at the door of the tabernacle. Lev. 1: 3. Deu. 12: 6, 11, 14.
Offered by priests only. Lev. 1: 9. Eze. 44: 15.
Offered in righteousness. Psa. 51: 19.
Entirely burned. Lev. 1: 8, 9, 12, 13. Lev. 6: 9.
Blood of, sprinkled round about upon the altar. Lev. 1: 5, 11.
If a bird, the blood was wrung out at the side of the altar. Lev. 1: 15.
Ashes of, collected at foot of the altar, and conveyed without the camp. Lev. 6: 11.
Skin of, given to the priests for clothing. Lev. 7: 8. *See* Gen. 3: 21.
Was offered
Every morning and evening. Exo. 29: 38—42.
Every sabbath day. Num. 28: 9, 10.
The first day of every month. Num. 28: 11.
The seven days of unleavened bread. Num. 28: 19, 24.
The atonement day. Lev 16: 3, 5. Num. 29: 8.
At consecration of Levites. Num. 8: 12.
At consecration of priests. Lev. 9: 2, 12—14.
At consecration of kings. 1 Chr. 29: 21—23.
At purification of women. Lev. 12: 6.
For Nazarites after defilement, or at expiration of their vow. Num. 6: 11, 14.
For the healed leper. Lev. 14: 13, 19, 20.
At dedication of sacred places. Num. 7: 15, &c. 1 Kin. 8: 64.
After great mercies. 1 Sam. 6: 14. 2 Sam. 24: 22, 25.
Before going to war. 1 Sam. 7: 9.
With sound of trumpets at feasts. Num. 10: 10.
The fat, &c. of all peace offerings laid on, and consumed with the daily. Lev. 3: 5. Lev. 6: 12.
Of the wicked, not accepted by God. Isa. 1: 10, 11. Jer. 6: 19, 20. Amos 5: 22.
Obedience better than. 1 Sam. 15: 22. Jer. 7: 21—23.
Knowledge of God better than. Hos. 6: 6.
Love of God better than. Mar. 12: 33.
Abraham tried by the command to offer Isaac as. Gen. 22 ch.
Incapable of removing sin, and reconciling to God. Psa. 40: 6. Psa. 50: 8. Heb. 10: 6.
The most costly, no adequate tribute to God. Isa. 40: 16, with Psa. 50: 9—13.
Guilt of unauthorized persons offering. 1 Sam. 13: 12, 13.
Guilt of offering, except in the place appointed. Lev. 17: 8, 9.
Of human victims execrated. Deu. 12: 31. 2 Kin. 3:27. Jer. 7: 31. Jer. 19: 5.

ILLUSTRATIVE OF
The offering of Christ. Eph. 5: 2. Heb. 10: 8—10.
Devotedness to God. Rom. 12: 1.

Busy-bodies.

Fools are. Pro. 20: 3.
The idle are. 2 The. 3: 11. 1 Tim. 5: 13.
Are mischievous tale-bearers. 1 Tim. 5: 13.
Bring mischief upon themselves. 2 Kin. 14: 10. Pro. 26: 17.
Christians must not be. 1 Pet. 4: 15.

Calf, The.

The young of the herd. Job. 21: 10. Jer. 31: 12.
Playfulness of, alluded to. Psa. 29: 6.
FED ON
Milk. 1 Sam. 6: 10.
Branches of trees, &c. Isa. 27: 10.
Fattened in stalls, &c. 1 Sam. 28: 24. Amos 6: 4.
Offered in sacrifice. Lev. 9: 2, 3. Heb. 9: 12, 19.
Of a year old best for sacrifice. Mic. 6: 6.
If first-born not redeemed. Num. 18: 17.
Eaten in the patriarchal age. Gen. 18: 7, 8.
When fattened considered a delicacy. 1 Sam. 28: 24, 25. Amos 6: 4. Luke 15: 23, 27.
ILLUSTRATIVE OF
Saints nourished by grace. Mal. 4: 2.
Sacrifices of praise. Hos. 14: 2. Heb. 13: 5.
Patient endurance. Eze. 1: 7. Rev. 4: 7.

Calf of Gold.

Made on account of the delay of Moses in the mount. Exo. 32: 1.
WAS MADE
Of the ornaments of the women, &c. Exo. 32: 2, 3.
To represent God. Exo. 32: 4, 5. with Psa. 106: 20.
After an Egyptian model. Acts 7: 39, 41.
To go before the congregation. Exo. 32: 1.
Molten in the fire. Exo. 32: 4 Psa. 106: 19.
Fashioned with a graven tool. Exo. 32: 4.
An altar built before. Exo. 32: 5.
Sacrifices offered to. Exo. 32: 6. Acts 7: 41.
Worshipped with profane revelry. Exo. 32: 6, 18, 19, 25. 1 Cor. 10: 7.
MAKING OF
A very great sin. Exo. 32: 21, 30, 31.
A forgetting of God. Psa. 106: 21.
A turning aside from the divine command. Exo. 32: 8. Deu. 9: 12, 16.
Excited wrath against Aaron. Deu. 9: 20.
Excited wrath against Israel. Exo. 32: 10. Deu. 9: 14, 19.
Caused Moses to break the tables of the testimony. Exo. 32: 19. Deu. 9: 17.
Israel punished for. Exo. 32: 26—29, 35.
Moses interceded for those who worshipped. Exo. 32: 11—14, 30—34. Deu. 9: 18—20.
Destroyed by Moses. Exo. 32: 20. Deu. 9: 21.
Punishment of those who worshipped a warning to others. 1 Cor. 10: 5—7.

Call of God, The.

By Christ. Isa. 55: 5. Rom. 1: 6.
By His Spirit. Rev. 22: 17.
By His works. Psa. 19: 2, 3. Rom. 1: 20.
By His ministers. Jer. 35: 15. 2 Cor. 5: 20.
By His gospel. 2 The. 2: 14.
Is from darkness. 1 Pet. 2: 9.
Addressed to all. Isa. 45: 22. Mat. 20: 16.
Most reject. Pro. 1: 24. Mat. 20: 16.
Effectual to saints. Psa. 110: 3. Acts 2: 47. Acts 13: 48. 1 Cor. 1: 24.
TO MAN IS
Of grace. Gal. 1: 15. 2 Tim. 1: 9.
According to the purpose of God. Rom. 8: 28. Rom. 9: 11, 23, 24.
High. Phi. 3: 14.
Holy. 1 Tim. 1: 9.
Heavenly. Heb. 3: 1.
To fellowship with Christ. 1 Cor. 1: 9.
To holiness. 1 The. 4: 7.
To liberty. Gal. 5: 13.
To peace. 1 Cor. 7: 15. Col. 3: 15.
To glory and virtue. 2 Pet. 1: 3.
To the eternal glory of Christ. 2 The. 2: 14. 1 Pet. 5: 10.
To eternal life. 1 Tim. 6: 12.
Partakers of, justified. Rom. 8: 30.
Walk worthy of. Eph. 4: 1.
Blessedness of receiving. Rev. 19: 9.
Praise God for. 1 Pet. 2: 9.
Illustrated. Pro. 9: 3, 4. Mat. 23: 3—9.
REJECTION OF, LEADS TO
Judicial blindness. Isa. 6: 9, with Acts 28: 24—27. Rom. 11: 8—10.
Delusion. Isa. 66: 4. 2 The. 2: 10, 11.

Withdrawal of the means of grace. Jer. 26: 4—6. Acts 13: 46. Acts 18: 6. Rev. 2: 5.
Temporal judgments. Isa. 28: 12. Jer. 6: 16, 19. Jer. 35: 17. Zec. 7: 12—14.
Rejection by God. Pro. 1: 24—32. Jer. 6: 19, 30.
Condemnation. Jno. 12: 48. Heb. 2: 1—3. Heb. 12: 25.
Destruction. Pro. 29: 1. Mat. 22: 3—7.

Calves of Jeroboam.

Made of gold. 1 Kin. 12: 28.
Made to prevent the Israelites going to Jerusalem. 1 Kin. 12: 26, 27.
CALLED THE
Golden calves. 2 Kin. 10: 29. 2 Chr. 13: 8.
Calves of Bethaven. Hos. 10: 5.
Calves of Samaria. Hos. 8: 5.
Placed in Dan and Bethel. 1 Kin. 12: 29.
Probably from an Egyptian model. 1 Kin. 11: 40.
Designed to represent God. 1 Kin. 12: 28.
Priests appointed for. 1 Kin. 12: 31. 2 Chr. 11: 15.
Sacrifices offered to. 1 Kin. 12: 32. 1 Kin. 13: 1.
Feasts appointed for. 1 Kin. 12: 32, 33.
Were kissed in adoration. Hos. 13: 2.
WORSHIP OF
Denounced by a prophet. 1 Kin. 13: 1—3.
Adopted by succeeding kings. 1 Kin. 15: 34. 1 Kin. 16: 26. 2 Kin. 10: 29, 31. 2 Kin. 14: 24.
Became the sin of Israel. 1 Kin. 12: 30. 2 Kin. 10: 31. 2 Chr. 13: 8.
God's people refused to worship. 1 Kin. 19: 18. 2 Chr. 11: 16.
Guilt of making. 1 Kin. 14: 9, 10.
Guilt of worshipping. 1 Kin. 14: 15, 16. 2 Kin. 17: 22, 23.
PREDICTIONS RESPECTING;
Captivity. Hos. 10: 6.
Destruction. Hos. 8: 6. Hos. 10: 8.
Punishment of the worshippers. Hos. 8: 13, 14.

Camel, The.

Unclean. Lev. 11: 4. Deu. 14: 7.
Found in deserted places. Eze. 25: 5.
CHARACTERIZED BY
The bunches on its back. Isa. 30: 6.
Its docility. Gen. 24: 11.
The dromedary a species of, remarkable for swiftness. Jer. 2: 23.
Abounded in the east. 1 Chr. 5: 21. Isa. 60: 6.
A part of patriarchal wealth. Gen. 12: 16. Gen. 30: 43. Job 1: 3.
Kept in numbers by kings. 1 Chr. 27: 30.
USED FOR
Riding. Gen. 24: 61.
Drawing chariots. Isa 21: 7.
Carrying burdens. Gen. 37: 25. 1 Kin. 10: 2. 2 Kin. 8: 9.
Conveying posts and messengers. Est. 8: 10.
War. Jud. 7: 12. 1 Sam. 30: 17.
Of the rich adorned with chains. Jud 8: 21, 26.
Furniture of, alluded to. Gen. 31: 34.
Subject to plagues. Exo. 9: 3. Zec. 14: 15.
Treated with great care. Gen. 24: 31, 32.
Esteemed a valuable booty. 1 Chr. 5: 20, 21. 2 Chr. 14: 15. Job 1: 17. Jer. 49: 29, 32.
Coarse cloth made from its hair. Mat. 3: 4.
Referred to in illustrations by Christ. Mat. 19: 24. Mat. 23: 24.

Canaanites, The.

Descended from Ham. Gen. 10: 6.
An accursed race. Gen. 9: 25, 26.
Different families of. Gen. 10: 15—18.
Comprised seven distinct nations. Deu. 7: 1.
Possessions of, how bounded. Gen. 10: 19.
Country of, fertile. Exo. 3: 17. Num. 13: 27.
DESCRIBED AS
Great and mighty. Num. 13: 28. Deu. 7: 1.
Idolatrous. Deu. 29: 17.
Superstitious. Deu. 18: 9—11.
Profane and wicked. Lev. 18: 27.
Extremely numerous. Deu. 7: 17.
Had many strong cities. Num. 13: 28. Deu. 1: 28.
Expelled for wickedness. Deu. 9: 4. Deu. 18: 12.
ABRAHAM
Called to dwell amongst. Gen. 12: 1—5.
Was promised the country of, for inheritance. Gen. 13: 14—17. Gen. 15: 18. Gen. 17: 8.
Had his faith tried by dwelling amongst. Gen. 12: 6. Gen. 13: 7.
Kind to the patriarchs. Gen. 14: 13. Gen. 23: 6.
ISRAEL COMMANDED
To make no league with. Deu. 7: 2. Jud. 2: 2.
Not to intermarry with. Deu. 7: 3. Jos. 23: 12.
Not to follow idols of. Exo. 23: 24. Deu. 7: 25.

Not to follow customs of. Lev. 18: 26, 27.
To destroy, without mercy. Deu. 7: 2, 24.
To destroy all vestiges of their idolatry. Exo 23: 24. Deu. 7: 5, 25.
Not to fear. Deu. 7: 17, 18. Deu. 31: 7.
Terrified at the approach of Israel. Exo. 15: 15, 16, with Jos. 2: 9—11, and Jos. 5: 1.
Partially subdued by Israel. Jos. 10 ch. and Jos. 11 ch. with Jud. 1 ch.
PART OF LEFT
To try Israel. Jud. 2: 21, 22. Jud. 3: 1—4.
To chastise Israel. Num. 33: 55. Jud. 2: 3. Jud. 4: 2.
Israel ensnared by. Jud. 2: 3, 19. Psa. 106: 36—38.
Some descendants of, in our Lord's time. Mat. 15: 22. Mar. 7: 26.

Candlestick.

A part of household furniture. 2 Kin. 4: 10.
USED FOR HOLDING
Candles or torches. Mat. 5: 15.
Lamps. Exo. 25: 31, 37. Zec. 4: 2.
FOR THE TABERNACLE
Form, &c. of. Exo. 25: 31—36. Exo. 37: 17—22.
Held seven golden lamps. Exo. 25: 37. Exo. 37: 23.
Had snuffers, &c. of gold. Exo. 25: 38. Exo. 37: 23.
Weighed a talent of gold. Exo. 25: 39.
After a divine pattern. Exo. 25: 40. Num. 8: 4.
Called the lamp of God. 1 Sam. 3: 3.
Called the pure candlestick. Lev. 24: 4.
Placed in the outer sanctuary over against the table. Exo. 40: 24. Heb. 9: 2.
Lighted with olive oil. Exo. 27: 20. Lev. 24: 2.
Lighted &c. by priests. Exo. 27: 21. Lev. 24: 3, 4.
Directions for removing. Num. 4: 9, 10.
ILLUSTRATIVE OF
Christ. Zec. 4: 2. Jno. 8: 12. Heb. 9: 2.
The church. Rev. 1: 13, 20.
Ministers. Mat. 5: 14—16.

Care, Overmuch.

About eartly things, forbidden. Mat. 6: 25. Luke 12: 22, 29. Jno. 6: 27.
God's providential goodness should keep us from. Mat. 6: 26, 28, 30. Luke 22: 35.
God's promises should keep us from. Heb. 13: 5.
Trust in God should free us from. Jer. 17: 7, 8. Dan. 3: 16.
Should be cast on God. Psa. 37: 5. Psa. 55: 22. Pro. 16: 3. 1 Pet. 5: 7.
An obstruction to the Gospel. Mat. 13: 22. Luke 8: 14. Luke 14: 18—20.
Be without. 1 Cor. 7: 32. Phi. 4: 6.
Unbecoming in saints. 2 Tim. 2: 4.
Inutility of. Mat. 6: 27. Luke 12: 25, 26.
Vanity of. Psa. 39: 6. Ecc. 4: 8.
Warning against. Luke 21: 34.
Sent as a punishment to the wicked. Eze. 4: 16. Eze. 12: 19.
Exemplified. *Martha*, Luke 10: 41. *Persons who offered to follow Christ*, Luke 9: 57, &c.

Caves.

Natural. Heb. 11: 38.
Artificial. Jud. 6: 2.
FOUND IN THE
Open fields. Gen. 23: 20.
Rocks. Isa. 2: 19.
WERE USED AS
Dwelling-places. Gen. 19: 30.
Places of concealment. 1 Sam. 13: 6. 1 Sam. 14: 11. 1 Kin. 18: 4. Heb. 11: 38.
Resting places. 1 Sam. 24: 3. 1 Kin. 19: 9.
Burial places. Gen. 23: 19. Jno. 11: 38.
Haunts of robbers. Jer. 7: 11. Mat. 21: 13.
Hiding places of wild beasts. Nah. 2: 12.
Often capacious. 1 Sam. 22: 1, 2. 1 Sam. 24: 3.
Afford no protection from the judgments of God. Isa. 2: 19. Eze. 33: 27. Rev. 6: 15.
MENTIONED IN SCRIPTURE;
Adullam. 1 Sam. 22: 1.
Engedi. 1 Sam. 23: 29, with 1 Sam. 24: 1, 3.
Machpelah. Gen. 23: 9.
Makkedah. Jos. 10: 16, 17.

Cedar, The.

Planted by God. Psa. 104: 16. Isa. 41: 19.
Made to glorify God. Psa. 148: 9.
Lebanon celebrated for. Jud. 9: 15. Psa. 92: 12.
Banks of rivers favorable to the growth of. Num. 24: 6.
Imported largely by Solomon. 1 Kin. 10: 27.
DESCRIBED AS
High. Isa. 37: 24. Eze. 17: 22. Amos 2: 9.
Spreading. Psa. 80: 10, 11.

Fragrant. So. of Sol. 4:11.
Graceful and beautiful. Psa. 80:10. Eze. 17:23.
Strong and durable. Isa. 9:10.
Considered the first of trees. 1 Kin. 4:33.
Extensive commerce in. 1 Kin. 5:10, 11. Ezr. 3:7.
USED IN
Building temples. 1 Kin. 5: 5, 6. 1 Kin. 6: 9, 10.
Building palaces. 2 Sam. 5:11. 1 Kin. 7:2, 3.
Making masts of ships. Eze. 27:5.
Making wardrobes. Eze. 27:24.
Making chariots. So. of Sol. 3:9.
Purifying the leper. Lev. 14 : 4—7, 49—52.
Preparing the water of separation. Num. 19:6.
Making idols. Isa. 44:14.
THE EAGLE ALLUDED TO AS
Making its nest in. Jer. 22:23.
Perching on the high branches of. Eze. 17:3.
Instrumental in propagating. Eze. 17:4, 5.
Destruction of, a punishment. Jer. 22: 7.
Destruction of, exhibits God's power. Psa. 29: 5.
ILLUSTRATIVE OF
Majesty, strength, and glory of Christ. So of Sol. 5:15. Eze. 17: 22, 23.
Beauty and glory of Israel. Num. 24: 6.
Saints in their rapid growth. Psa. 92: 12.
Powerful nations. Eze. 31: 3. Amos 2:9.
Arrogant rulers. Isa. 2: 13. Isa. 10: 33, 34.

Censers.

For burning incense. Lev. 10:1. 2 Chr. 26: 19.
MADE OF
Brass. Num. 16: 39.
Gold. 1 Kin. 7: 50.
One of gold in the most holy place. Heb. 9: 4.
Directions for removing. Num. 4: 14.
Often used in idolatrous worship. Eze. 8: 11.
Of Korah, &c. made into plates to cover the altar. Num. 16: 18, 39.
Typical of Christ's intercession. Rev. 8: 3, 5.

Character of Saints.

Attentive to Christ's voice. Jno. 10: 3, 4.
Blameless and harmless. Phi. 2: 15.
Bold. Pro. 28: 1. Rom. 13: 3.
Contrite. Isa. 57: 15. Isa. 66: 2.
Devout. Acts 8: 2. Acts 22: 12.
Faithful. Rev. 17: 14.
Fearing God. Mat. 3: 16. Acts 10: 2.
Following Christ. Jno. 10: 4, 27.
Godly. Psa. 4: 3. 2 Pet. 2: 9.
Guileless. Jno. 1: 47.
Holy. Deu. 7:6. Deu. 14:2. Col. 3:12.
Humble. Psa. 34: 2. 1 Pet. 5: 5.
Hungering after righteousness. Mat. 5: 6.
Just. Gen 6: 9. Hab. 2: 4. Luke 2: 25.
Led by the Spirit. Rom. 8: 14.
Liberal. Isa. 32: 8. 2 Cor. 9: 13.
Loving. Col. 1: 4. 1 The. 4: 9.
Lowly. Pro. 16: 19.
Meek. Isa. 29: 19. Mat. 5: 5.
Merciful. Psa. 37: 26. Mat. 5: 7.
New Creatures. 2 Cor. 5:17. Eph. 2:10.
Obedient. Rom. 16: 19. 1 Pet 1: 14.
Poor in spirit. Psa. 51: 17. Mat. 5: 3.
Prudent. Pro. 16: 21.
Pure in heart. Mat. 5: 8. 1 Jno. 3: 3.
Righteous. Isa. 60: 21. Luke 1: 6.
Sincere. 2 Cor. 1: 12. 2 Cor. 2: 17.
Steadfast. Acts 2: 42. Col. 2: 5.
Taught of God. Isa. 54: 13. 1 Jno. 2: 27.
True. 2 Cor. 6: 8.
Undefiled. Psa. 119: 1.
Upright. 1 Kin. 3: 6. Psa. 15: 2.
Watchful. Luke 12: 37.
Zealous of good works. Tit. 2: 14. Tit. 3: 8.

Character of the wicked.

Abominable. Rev. 21: 8.
Alienated from God. Eph. 4: 18. Col. 1: 21.
Blasphemous. Luke 22: 65. Rev. 16: 9.
Blinded. 2 Cor. 4: 4. Eph. 4: 18.
Boastful. Psa. 10: 3. Psa. 49: 6.
Conspiring against God's people. Neh. 4: 8. Neh. 6: 2. Psa. 38: 12.
Covetous. Mic. 2: 2. Rom. 1: 29.
Deceitful. Psa. 5: 6. Rom. 3: 13.
Delighting in the iniquity of others. Pro. 2: 14. Rom 1: 32.
Despising the works of the faithful. Neh. 2: 19. Neh. 4: 2. 2 Tim. 3: 3, 4.
Destructive. Isa. 59: 7.
Disobedient. Neh. 9: 26. Tit. 3:3. 1 Pet. 2: 7.
Enticing to evil. Pro. 1: 10—14. 2 Tim. 3: 6.
Envious. Neh. 2: 10. Tit. 3: 3.
Fearful. Pro. 28: 1. Rev. 21: 8.
Fierce. Pro. 16: 29. 2 Tim. 3: 3.
Foolish. Deu. 32: 6. Psa. 5: 5.
Forgetting God. Job 8: 13.
Fraudulent. Psa. 37: 21. Mic. 6: 11.
Froward. Pro. 21: 8. Isa. 57: 17.
Glorying in their shame. Phi. 3: 19.
Hard-hearted. Eze. 3: 7.
Hating the light. Job. 24: 13. Jno. 3: 20.

Heady and high-minded. 2 Tim. 3: 4.
Hostile to God. Rom. 8: 7. Col. 1: 21.
Hypocritical. Isa. 29: 13. 2 Tim. 3: 5.
Ignorant of God. Hos. 4: 1. 2 The 1: 8.
Impudent. Eze. 2: 4.
Incontinent. 2 Tim. 3: 3.
Infidel. Psa. 10: 4. Psa 14: 1.
Loathsome. Pro. 13: 5.
Lovers of pleasure more than of God. 2 Tim. 3: 4.
Lying. Psa. 58: 3. Psa. 62: 4. Isa. 59: 4.
Mischievous. Pro. 24: 8. Mic. 7: 3.
Murderous. Psa. 10: 8. Psa. 94: 6. Rom. 1: 29.
Prayerless. Job 21: 15. Psa. 53: 4.
Persecuting. Psa. 69: 26. Psa. 109: 16.
Perverse. Deu. 32: 5.
Proud. Psa. 59: 12. Oba. 3. 2 Tim. 3: 2.
Rejoicing in the affliction of saints. Psa. 35: 15.
Reprobate. 2 Cor. 13: 5. 2 Tim. 3: 8. Tit. 1: 16.
Selfish. 2 Tim. 3: 2.
Sensual. Phi. 3: 19. Jude 19.
Sold under sin. 1 Kin. 21: 20. 2 Kin. 17: 17.
Stiff-hearted. Eze. 2: 4.
Stiff-necked. Exo. 33: 5. Acts 7: 51.
Uncircumcised in heart. Jer. 9: 26. Acts 7: 51.
Unjust. Pro. 11: 7. Isa. 26: 10.
Unmerciful. Rom. 1: 31.
Ungodly. Pro. 16: 27.
Unholy. 2 Tim. 3: 2.
Unprofitable. Mat. 25: 30. Rom. 3: 12.
Unruly. Tit. 1: 10.
Unthankful. Luke 6: 35. 2 Tim. 3: 2.
Untoward. Acts 2: 40.
Unwise. Deu. 32: 6.

Chariots.

Carriages for traveling, &c. Gen. 46: 29.
Carriages used in war. 1 Kin. 20: 25.
Wheels of, described. 1 Kin. 7: 33.
Bound with traces. Mic. 1: 13.
DRAWN BY
 Horses. 2 Kin. 10: 2. So. of Sol. 1: 9.
 Asses and camels. Isa. 21: 7.
Value of in Solomon's time. 1 Kin. 10: 29.
Drivers generally employed for. 1 Kin. 22: 34. 2 Chr. 18: 33.
Sometimes driven by the owners. 2 Kin. 9: 16, 20.
Sometimes driven furiously. 2 Kin. 9: 20. Isa. 5: 28. Jer. 4: 13.
Bounding motion of, referred to. Nah. 3: 2.
Noise occasioned by, referred to. 2 Kin. 7: 6. Joel 2: 5. Nah. 3: 2. Rev. 9: 9.
Introduced into Israel by David. 2 Sam. 8: 4.
Multiplied by Solomon. 1 Kin. 10: 26.
Imported from Egypt. 1 Kin. 10: 28, 29.
FOR WAR,
 Armed with iron. Jos. 17: 16. Jud. 1: 19.
 Lighted by night with torches. Nah. 2: 3.
 Commanded by captains. Exo. 14. 7. 1 Kin. 16: 9.
 Advantageously manœuvred in a flat country. Jud. 1: 19. 1 Kin. 20: 23—25.
 Formed part of the line of battle. 1 Kin. 20: 25.
 Used in pursuing enemies. Exo. 14: 9. 2 Sam. 1: 6.
 Kept in chariot cities. 1 Kin. 9: 19. 1 Kin. 10: 26.
USED IN WAR BY THE
 Egyptians. Exo. 14: 7. 2 Kin. 18: 24
 Canaanites. Jos. 17: 16. Jud. 4: 3.
 Philistines. 1 Sam. 13: 5.
 Syrians. 2 Sam. 10: 18. 1 Kin. 20: 1.
 Assyrians. 2 Kin. 19: 23.
 Ethiopians. 2 Chr. 14: 9. 2 Chr. 16: 8.
 Babylonians. Eze. 23: 24. Eze. 26: 7
 Jews. 2 Kin. 8: 21. 2 Kin. 10: 2.
Kings rode in, to battle. 1 Kin. 22: 35.
Kings used, in common. 1 Kin. 12: 18. 1 Kin. 18: 44.
Persons of distinction used. Gen. 41: 43. 2 Kin. 5: 9, 21. Jer. 17: 25. Acts 8: 28.
Often attended by running footmen. 1 Sam. 8: 11. 2 Sam. 15: 1. 1 Kin. 1: 5.
Consecrated to the sun. 2 Kin. 23: 11.
THE JEWS CONDEMNED FOR
 Multiplying. Isa. 2: 7.
 Trusting to. Isa. 22: 18. Isa. 31: 1.
 Taken in war, often destroyed. Jos. 11: 6, 9. Jer. 51: 21. Mic. 5: 10. Nah. 2: 13.
ILLUSTRATIVE OF
 The clouds. Psa. 104: 3.
 The judgments of God. Isa. 66: 15
 Angels. 2 Kin. 6: 16, 17, with Psa 68: 17.
 Prophets. 2 Kin. 2: 12. 2 Kin. 13: 14
 Christ's love to His church. So of Sol. 6: 12.
Elijah taken to heaven in one of fire. 2 Kin. 2: 11.

Charity.

Explained. 1 Cor. 13: 4—7.
Enjoined. Col. 3: 14. (See Love to Man.)

Chastity.

Commanded. Exo. 20: 14. Pro. 31 3. Acts 15: 20. Rom. 13: 13. Col. 3: 5. 1 The. 4: 3.
Required in look. Job 31: 1. Mat. 5: 28.

Required in heart. Pro. 6: 25.
Required in speech. Eph. 5: 3.
Keep the body in. 1 Cor. 6: 13, 15—18.
Preserved by wisdom. Pro. 2: 10, 11, 16. Pro. 7: 1—5.
Saints are kept in. Ecc. 7: 26.
Advantages of. 1 Pet. 3: 1, 2.
Shun those devoid of. 1 Cor. 5: 11. 1 Pet. 4: 3.
The wicked are devoid of. Rom. 1: 29. Eph. 4: 19. 2 Pet. 2: 14. Jude 8.
Temptation to deviate from, dangerous. 2 Sam. 11: 2—4.
Consequences of associating with those devoid of. Pro. 5: 3—11. Pro. 7: 25—27. Pro. 22: 14.
Want of, excludes from heaven. Gal. 5: 19—21.
Drunkenness destructive to. Pro. 23: 31—33.
Breach of, punished. 1 Cor. 3: 16, 17. Eph. 5: 5, 6. Heb. 13: 4. Rev. 22: 15.
Motives for. 1 Cor. 6: 19. 1 The. 4: 7.
Exemplified. *Abimelech*, Gen. 20: 4, 5. Gen. 26: 10, 11. *Joseph*, Gen. 39: 7—10. *Ruth*, Ruth 3: 10, 11. *Boaz*, Ruth 3: 13.

Cherubim.

Form and appearance of. Eze. 1: 5—11, 13, 14.
Animated by the Spirit of God. Eze. 1: 12, 20.
Engaged in accomplishing the purposes of God. Eze. 1: 15, 21. Eze. 10: 9—11, 16, 17.
The glory of God exhibited upon. Eze. 1: 22, 26—28. Eze. 10: 4, 18, 20.
Sound of their wings was as the voice of God. Eze. 1: 24. Eze. 10: 5.
Placed at the entrance of Eden. Gen. 3: 24.
Of gold,
- Formed out of, and at each end of the mercy seat. Exo. 25: 18—20.
- Placed over the ark of the covenant. 1 Sam. 4: 4. 1 Kin. 8: 6, 7. 2 Chr. 5: 7, 8.
- God's presence manifested between. 2 Sam. 6: 2. 2 Kin. 19: 15. Psa. 80: 1. Psa. 99: 1.
- The oracles or answers of God delivered from between. Exo. 25: 22. Num. 7: 89.

Called the cherubim of glory. Heb. 9: 5.
Representations of, made on the
- Curtains of the tabernacle. Exo. 26: 1, 31.
- Vail of the tabernacle. Exo. 26: 31.
- Vail of the temple. 2 Chr. 3: 14.
- Doors of the temple. 1 Kin. 6: 32, 35.
- Walls of the temple. 2 Chr. 3: 7.
- Bases of brazen lavers. 1 Kin. 7: 29: 36.

Riding on, illustrative of majesty and power of God. 2 Sam. 22: 11. Psa. 18: 10.

Children.

Christ was an example to. Luke 2: 51. Jno. 19: 26, 27.
Are a gift from God. Gen. 33: 5. Psa. 127: 3.
Are capable of glorifying God. Psa. 8: 2. Psa. 148: 12, 13. Mat. 21: 15, 16.
Should be
- Brought to Christ. Mar. 10: 13—16.
- Brought early to the house of God. 1 Sam. 1: 24.
- Instructed in the ways of God. Deu. 31: 12, 13. Pro. 22: 6.
- Judiciously trained. Pro. 22: 15. Pro. 29: 17. Eph. 6: 4.

Should
- Obey God. Deu. 30: 2.
- Fear God. Pro. 24: 21.
- Remember God. Ecc. 12: 1.
- Attend to parental teaching. Pro. 1: 8, 9.
- Honor parents. Exo. 20: 12. Heb. 12: 9.
- Fear parents. Lev. 19: 3.
- Obey parents. Pro. 6: 20. Eph. 6: 1.
- Take care of parents. 1 Tim. 5: 4.
- Honor the aged. Lev. 19: 32. 1 Pet. 5: 5.
- Not imitate bad parents. Eze. 20: 18.

An heritage from the Lord. Psa. 113: 9. Psa. 127: 3.
Not to have,
- Considered an affliction. Gen. 15: 2, 3. Jer. 22: 30.
- A reproach in Israel. 1 Sam. 1: 6, 7. Luke 1: 25.

Anxiety of the Jews for. Gen. 30: 1. 1 Sam. 1: 5, 8.
Often prayed for. 1 Sam. 1: 10, 11. Luke 1: 13.
Often given in answer to prayer. Gen. 25: 21. 1 Sam. 1: 27. Luke 1: 13.
Treatment of, after birth, noticed. Eze. 16: 4.
Mostly nursed by the mothers. 1 Sam. 1: 22. 1 Kin. 3: 21. Psa. 22: 9. So. of Sol. 8: 1.
Weaning of, a time of joy and feasting. Gen. 21: 8. 1 Sam. 1: 24.
Circumcised on the eighth day. Phi. 3: 5.
Named at circumcision. Luke 1: 59. Luke 2: 21.
Were named
- After relatives. Luke 1: 59, 61.
- From remarkable events. Gen. 21: 3, 6, with Gen. 18: 13. Exo. 2: 10. Exo. 18: 3, 4.
- From circumstances connected with their birth. Gen. 25: 25, 26. Gen. 35: 18. 1 Chr. 4: 9.

Often by God. Isa. 8: 3. Hos. 1: 4, 6, 9.
Often numerous. 2 Kin. 10: 1. 1 Chr. 4: 27.
Numerous, considered an especial blessing. Psa. 115: 14. Psa. 127: 4, 5.
Sometimes born when parents were old. Gen 15: 3, 6. Gen. 17: 17. Luke 1: 18.
MALE,
If first born, belonged to God and were redeemed. Exo. 13: 12, 13, 15.
Birth of, announced to the father by a messenger. Jer. 20: 15.
Under the care of tutors, till they came of age. 2 Kin. 10: 1. Gal. 4: 1. 2.
Usefully employed. 1 Sam. 9: 3. 1 Sam. 17: 15.
Inherited the possessions of their father. Deu. 21: 16, 17. Luke 12: 13, 14.
Received the blessing of their father before his death. Gen. 27: 1—4. Gen. 48: 15. Gen. 49 ch.
FEMALE,
Taken care of by nurses. Gen. 35: 8.
Usefully employed. Gen. 24: 13. Exo. 2: 16.
Inherited property in default of sons. Num. 27: 1-8. Jos. 17: 1—6.
Fondness and care of mothers for. Exo. 2: 2—10. 1 Sam. 2: 19. 1 Kin. 3: 27. Isa. 49: 15. 1 The. 2: 7, 8.
Of God's people, holy. Ezr. 9: 2. 1 Cor. 7: 14.
Of God's people, interested in the promises. Deu. 29: 29. Acts 2: 39
Prosperity of, greatly depended on obedience of parents. Deu. 4: 40. Deu. 12: 25, 28. Psa. 128: 1—3.
Frequently bore the curse of parents. Exo. 20: 5. Psa. 109: 9, 10.
WERE REQUIRED
To honor their parents. Exo. 20: 12.
To attend to instruction. Deu. 4: 9. Deu. 11: 19.
To submit to discipline. Pro. 29: 17. Heb. 12: 9.
To respect the aged. Lev. 19: 32.
Mode of giving public instruction to. Luke 2: 46. Acts 22: 3.
Power of parents over, during the patriarchal age. Gen. 9: 24, 25. Gen 21: 14. Gen. 38: 24.
Often wicked and rebellious. 2 Kin. 2: 23.
Rebellious, punished by the civil power. Exo. 21: 15—17. Deu. 21: 18—21.
Sometimes devoted their property to avoid supporting parents. Mat. 15: 5. Mar. 7: 11, 12.
Could demand their portion during their father's life. Luke 15: 12.
Amusements of, Zec. 8: 5. Mat. 11: 16, 17.
Casting out of weak, &c. alluded to. Eze. 16: 5.
Inhuman practice of offering to idols. 2 Kin. 17: 31. 2 Chr. 28: 3. 2 Chr. 33: 6.
ILLEGITIMATE,
Had no inheritance. Gen. 21: 10, 14. Gal. 4: 30.
Not cared for by the father. Heb. 12: 8.
Excluded from the congregation. Deu. 23: 2.
Sometimes sent away with gifts. Gen. 25: 6.
Despised by their brethren. Jud. 11: 2.
Destruction of, a punishment. Lev. 26: 22. Eze. 9: 6. Luke 19; 44.
Grief occasioned by loss of. Gen. 37: 35. Gen. 44: 27—29. 2 Sam. 13: 37. Jer. 6: 26. Jer. 31: 15.
Resignation manifested at loss of. Lev. 10: 19, 20. 2 Sam. 12: 18—23. Job 1: 19—21.

Children, Good.

The Lord is with. 1 Sam. 3:19.
Know the Scriptures. 2 Tim 3:15.
Observe the law of God. Prov. 28:7.
Their obedience to parents is well pleasing to God. Col. 3:20.
Partake of the promises of God. Acts 2:39.
Shall be blessed. Prov. 3:1—4. Eph. 6:2, 3.
Show love to parents. Gen. 46: 29.
Obey parents Gen. 28:7. Gen. 47:30.
Attend to parental teaching. Prov. 13:1.
Take care of parents. Gen. 45:9, 11. Gen. 47:12.
Make their parents' hearts glad. Pro. 10:1. Pro. 29:17.
Honor the aged. Job. 32:6, 7
Adduced as a motive for submission to God. Heb. 12:9.
Spirit of, a requisite for the kingdom of heaven. Mat. 18:3.
Illustrative of a teachable spirit. Mat. 18:4.
Exemplified. *Isaac*, Gen. 22 : 6—10. *Joseph*, Gen. 45:9. Gen. 46:29. *Jephthath's daughter*, Jud. 11:34, 36. *Samson*, Jud. 13: 24. *Samuel*, 1 Sam. 3:19. *Obadiah*, 1 Kin. 18: 12. *Josiah*, 2 Chr. 34 : 3. *Esther*, Est. 2 : 20. *Job*, Job 29:4. *David*. 1 Sam. 17:20. Psa. 71:5. *Daniel*, Dan. 1:6. *John the Baptist*, Luke 1:80. *Children in the Temple*, Mat. 21:15, 16. *Timothy*, 2 Tim. 3:15.

Children, Wicked.

Know not God. 1 Sam. 2:12.
Are void of understanding. Pro. 7:7.
Are proud. Isa. 3:5.

WITH REGARD TO PARENTS
Hearken not to them. 1 Sam. 2:25.
Despise them. Pro. 15:5, 20. Eze. 22:7.
Curse them. Pro. 30:11.
Bring reproach on them. Pro. 19:26.
Are a calamity to them. Pro. 19:13.
Are a grief to them. Pro. 17:25.
Despise their elders. Job 19:18.
PUNISHMENT OF, FOR
Setting light by parents. Deu. 27:16.
Disobeying parents. Deu. 21:21.
Mocking parents. Pro. 30:17.
Cursing parents. Exo. 21:15, with Mar. 7:10.
Smiting parents. Exo. 21:15.
Mocking a prophet. 2 Kin. 2:23, 24.
Gluttony and drunkenness. Deu. 21:20, 21.
Their guilt in robbing parents. Pro. 28:24.
Exemplified. *Esau*, Gen. 26: 34, 35. *Sons of Eli*, 1 Sam. 2:12, 17. *Sons of Samuel*, 1 Sam. 8:3. *Absalom*, 2 Sam, 15:10 *Adonijah*, 1 Kin. 1:5, 6. *Children at Bethel*, 2 Kin. 2:23. *Adrammelech and Sharezer*, 2 Kin. 19:37.

Christ, Character of.

Altogether lovely. So. of Sol. 5:16.
Holy. Luke 1:35. Acts 4:27. Rev. 3:7.
Righteous. Isa. 53:11. Heb. 1:9.
Good. Mat. 19:16.
Faithful. Isa. 11:5. 1 The. 5:24.
True. Jno. 1:14. Jno. 7:18. 1 Jno: 5:20.
Just. Zec. 9:9. Jno. 5:30. Acts 22:14.
Guileless. Isa. 53:9. 1 Pet. 2:22.
Sinless. Jno. 8:46. 2 Cor. 5:21.
Spotless. 1 Pet. 1:19.
Innocent. Mat. 27:4.
Harmless. Heb. 7:26.
Resisting temptation. Mat. 4:1—10.
Obedient to God the Father. Psa. 40:8. Jno. 4:34. Jno. 15:10.
Zealous. Luke 2:49. Jno. 2:17. Jno. 8:29.
Meek. Isa. 53:7. Zec. 9:9. Mat. 11:29.
Lowly in heart. Mat. 11:29.
Merciful. Heb. 2:17.
Patient. Isa. 53:7. Mat. 27:14.
Long-suffering. 1 Tim. 1:16.
Compassionate. Isa. 40:11. Luke 19:41.
Benevolent. Mat. 4:23, 24. Acts 10:38.
Loving. Jno. 13:1. Jno. 15:13.
Self-denying. Mat. 8:20. 2 Cor. 8:9.
Humble. Luke 22:27. Phi. 2:8.
Resigned. Luke 22:42.
Forgiving. Luke 23:34.
Subject to His parents. Luke 2:51.
Saints are conformed to. Rom. 8:29.

Christ is God.

As Jehovah. Isa. 40:3, with Mat. 3:3.
As Jehovah of glory. Psa. 24:7, 10, with 1 Cor. 2:8. Jas. 2:1.
As Jehovah, our RIGHTEOUSNESS. Jer. 23:5, 6, with 1 Cor. 1:30.
As Jehovah, above all. Psa. 97:9, with Jno. 3:31.
As Jehovah, the First and the Last. Isa. 44:6, with Rev. 1:17. Isa. 48: 12—16, with Rev. 22:13.
As Jehovah's Fellow and Equal. Zec. 13:7. Phi. 2:6.
As Jehovah of Hosts. Isa. 6:1—3, with Jno. 12:41, Isa. 8:13, 14, with 1 Pet. 2:8.
As Jehovah, the Shepherd. Isa. 40: 11. Heb. 13:20.
As Jehovah, for whose glory all things were created. Pro. 16:4, with Col 1:16.
As Jehovah, the Messenger of the covenant. Mal. 3:1, with Mark 1: 2, and Luke 2:27.
Invoked as Jehovah. Joel 2:32, with Acts 2:21, and 1 Cor. 1:2.
As the Eternal God and Creator. Psa. 102:24—27, with Heb. 1:8, 10—12.
As the mighty God. Isa. 9:6.
As the Great God and Saviour. Hos. 1:7, with Tit. 2:13.
As God over all. Psa. 45:6, 7. Rom. 9:5.
As the true God. Jer. 10:10, with 1 Jno. 5:20.
As God the Word. Jno. 1:1.
As God, the Judge. Ecc. 12:14, with 1 Cor. 4:5. 2 Cor. 5:10. 2 Tim. 4:1.
As Emmanuel. Isa. 7:14, with Mat. 1:23.
As King of kings and Lord of lords. Dan. 10:17, with Rev. 1:5. Rev. 17:14.
As the Holy One. 1 Sam. 2:2, with Acts 3:14.
As the Lord from heaven. 1 Cor. 15:47.
As Lord of the sabbath. Gen. 2:3, with Mat. 12:8.
As Lord of all. Acts 10:36. Rom. 10: 11—13.
As Son of God. Mat. 26:63—67.
As the Only-begotten Son of the Father. Jno. 1:14, 18. Jno 3:16, 18. 1 Jno. 4:9.
His blood is called the blood of God. Acts 20:28.
As one with the Father. Jno. 10:30, 38. Jno. 12:45. Jno. 14:7—10. Jno. 17:10.
As sending the Spirit, equally with the Father. Jno. 14:16, with Jno. 15:26.
As entitled to equal honor with the Father. Jno. 5:23.

As Owner of all things, equally with the Father. Jno. 16: 15.
As unrestricted by the law of the sabbath, equally with the Father. Jno. 5: 17.
As the Source of grace, equally with the Father. 1 The. 3: 11. 2 The. 2: 16, 17.
As unsearchable, equally with the Father. Pro. 30: 4. Mat. 11: 27.
As Creator of all things. Isa. 40: 28. Jno. 1: 3. Col. 1: 16. Heb. 1: 2.
As Supporter and Preserver of all things. Neh. 9: 6, with Col. 1: 17. Heb. 1: 3.
As possessed of the fulness of the Godhead. Col. 2: 9. Heb. 1: 3.
As raising the dead. Jno. 5: 21. Jno. 6: 40, 54.
As raising Himself from the dead. Jno. 2: 19, 21. Jno. 10: 18.
As Eternal. Isa. 9: 6. Mic. 5: 2 Jno. 1: 1. Col. 1: 17. Heb. 1: 8—10. Rev. 1: 8.
As Omnipresent. Mat. 18: 20. Mat. 28: 20. Jno. 3: 13.
As Omnipotent. Psa. 45: 3. Phi. 3: 21. Rev. 1: 8.
As Omniscient. Jno. 16: 30. Jno. 21: 17.
As discerning the thoughts of the heart. 1 Kin. 8: 39, with Luke 5: 22. Eze. 11: 5, with Jno. 2: 24, 25. Rev. 2: 23.
As unchangeable. Mal. 3: 6, with Heb. 1: 12. Heb. 13: 8.
As having power to forgive sins. Col. 3: 13, with Mar. 2: 7, 10.
As Giver of pastors to the Church. Jer. 3: 15, with Eph. 4: 11—13.
As Husband of the Church. Isa. 54: 5, with Eph. 5: 25—32. Isa 62: 5, with Rev. 21: 2, 9.
As the object of divine worship. Acts 7: 59. 2 Cor. 12: 8, 9. Heb. 1: 6. Rev. 5: 12.
As the object of faith. Psa. 2: 12, with 1 Pet. 2: 6. Jer. 17: 5, 7, with Jno. 14: 1.
As God, He redeems and purifies the Church unto Himself. Rev. 5: 9, with Tit. 2: 14.
As God, He presents the Church to Himself. Eph. 5: 27, with Jude 24, 25.
Saints live unto Him as God. Rom. 6: 11, and Gal. 2: 19, with 2 Cor. 5: 15.
Acknowledged by His Apostles. Jno. 20: 28.
Acknowledged by Old Testament saints. Gen. 17: 1, with Gen. 48: 15, 16. Gen. 32: 24—30, with Hos. 12: 3—5. Jude 6: 22—24. Jude 13: 21, 22. Job 19: 25—27.

Christ, the Head of the Church.

Predicted. Psa. 118: 22, with Mat. 21: 42.
Appointed by God. Eph. 1: 22.
Declared by Himself. Mat. 21: 42.
As His mystical body. Eph. 4: 12, 15, Eph. 5: 23.
Has the pre-eminence in all things. 1 Cor. 11: 3. Eph. 1: 22. Col. 1: 18.
Commissioned His Apostles. Mat. 10: 1, 7. Mat. 28: 19. Jno. 20: 21.
Instituted the sacraments. Mat. 28: 19. Luke 22: 19, 20.
Imparts gifts. Psa. 68: 18, with Eph. 4: 8.
Saints are complete in. Col. 2: 10.
Perverters of the truth do not hold. Col. 2: 18, 19.

Christ, the High Priest.

Appointed and called by God. Heb. 3: 1, 2. Heb. 5: 4, 5.
After the order of Melchizedek. Psa. 110: 4, with Heb. 5: 6. Heb. 6: 20. Heb. 7: 15, 17.
Superior to Aaron and the Levitical priests. Heb. 7: 11, 16, 22. Heb. 8: 1, 2, 6.
Consecrated with an oath. Heb. 7: 20, 21.
Has an unchangeable priesthood. Heb. 7: 23, 28.
Is of unblemished purity. Heb. 7: 26, 28.
Faithful. Heb. 3: 2.
Needed no sacrifice for Himself. Heb. 7: 27.
Offered Himself a sacrifice. Heb. 9: 14, 26.
His sacrifice superior to all others. Heb. 9: 13, 14, 23.
Offered sacrifice but once. Heb. 7: 27. Heb. 9: 25, 26.
Made reconciliation. Heb. 2: 17.
Obtained redemption for us. Heb. 9: 12.
Entered into heaven. Heb. 4: 14. Heb. 10: 12.
Sympathizes with those who are tempted. Heb. 2: 18. Heb. 4: 15.
Intercedes. Heb. 7: 25. Heb. 9: 24.
Blesses. Num. 6: 23—26, with Acts 3: 26.
On His throne. Zec. 6: 13.
Appointment of, and encouragement to steadfastness. Heb. 4: 14.
Typified. *Melchizedek*, Gen. 14: 18—20. *Aaron, &c.* Exo. 40: 12—15.

Christ, the King.

Foretold. Num. 24: 17. Psa. 2: 6. Psa. 45th. Isa. 9: 7. Jer. 23: 5. Mic. 5: 2.
Glorious. Psa. 24: 7—10. 1 Cor. 2: 8. Jas. 2: 1.
Supreme. Psa. 89: 27. Rev. 1: 5. Rev. 19: 16.
Sits in the throne of God. Rev. 3: 21.

Sits on the throne of David. Isa. 9: 7. Eze. 37: 24, 25. Luke 1: 32. Acts 2: 30
Is King of Zion. Psa. 2: 6. Isa. 52: 7. Zec. 9: 9. Mat. 21: 5. Jno. 12: 12—15.
Has a righteous kingdom. Psa. 45: 6, with Heb. 1: 8, 9. Isa. 32: 1. Jer. 23: 5.
Has an everlasting kingdom. Dan. 2: 44. Dan. 7: 14. Luke 1: 33.
Has an universal kingdom. Psa. 2: 8. Psa. 72: 8. Zec. 14: 9. Rev. 11: 15.
His kingdom not of this world. Jno. 18: 36.
Saints, the subjects of. Col. 1: 13. Rev. 15: 3.
Saints receive a kingdom from. Luke 22: 29, 30. Heb. 12: 28.
ACKNOWLEDGED BY
The wise men from the East. Mat. 2: 2.
Nathanael. Jno. 1: 49.
His followers. Luke 19: 38. Jno. 12: 13.
Declared by Himself. Mat. 25: 34. Jno. 18: 37.
Written on His cross Jno. 19: 19.
The Jews shall seek unto. Hos. 3: 5.
Saints shall behold. Isa. 33: 17. Rev. 22: 3, 4.
Kings shall do homage to. Psa. 72: 10. Isa. 49: 7.
Shall overcome all His enemies. Psa. 110: 1. Mar. 12: 36. 1 Cor. 15: 25. Rev. 17: 14.
Typified. *Melchizedek*, Gen. 14: 18. *David*, 1 Sam. 16: 1, 12, 13, with Luke 1: 32. *Solomon*, 1 Chr. 28: 6, 7.

Christ, the Mediator.

In virtue of His atonement. Eph. 2: 13—18. Heb. 9: 15. Heb. 12: 24.
The only One between God and man. 1 Tim. 2: 5.
Of the gospel covenant. Heb. 8: 6. Heb. 12: 24.
Typified. *Moses*, Deu. 5: 5. Gal. 3: 19. *Aaron*, Num. 16: 48.

Christ, the Prophet.

Foretold. Deu. 18: 15, 18. Isa. 52: 7. Nah. 1: 15.
Anointed with the Holy Ghost. Isa. 42: 1. Isa. 61: 1, with Luke 4: 18. Jno. 3: 34.
Alone knows and reveals God. Mat. 11: 27. Jno. 3: 2, 13, 34. Jno. 17: 6, 14, 26. Heb. 1: 1, 2.
Declared His doctrine to be that of the Father. Jno. 8: 26, 28. Jno. 12: 49, 50. Jno. 14: 10, 24. Jno. 15: 15. Jno. 17: 8, 16.
Preached the gospel, and worked miracles. Mat. 4: 23. Mat. 11: 5. Luke 4: 43.
Foretold things to come. Mat. 24: 3—35. Luke 19: 41, 44.
Faithful to His trust. Luke 4: 43. Jno. 17: 8. Heb. 3: 2. Rev. 1: 5. Rev. 3: 14.
Abounded in wisdom. Luke 2: 40, 47, 52. Col 2: 3.
Mighty in deed and word. Mat. 13: 54. Mar. 1: 27. Luke 4: 32. Jno. 7: 46.
Meek and unostentatious in His teaching. Isa. 42: 2. Mat. 12: 17—20.
God commands us to hear. Deu. 18: 15. Matt. 17: 25. Acts 3: 22. Acts 7: 37.
God will severely visit our neglect of. Deu. 18: 19. Acts 3: 23. Heb. 2: 3.
Typified. *Moses*, Deu. 18: 15.

Christ, the Shepherd.

Foretold. Gen. 49: 24. Isa. 40: 11. Eze. 34: 23. Eze. 37: 24.
The chief. 1 Pet. 5: 4.
The good. Jno. 10: 11, 14.
The great. Mic. 5: 4. Heb. 13: 20.
HIS SHEEP
He knows. Jno. 10: 14, 27.
He calls. Jno. 10: 3.
He gathers. Isa. 40: 11. Jno. 10: 16.
He guides. Psa. 23: 3. Jno. 10: 3, 4.
He feeds. Psa. 23: 1, 2. Jno. 10: 9.
He cherishes tenderly. Isa. 40: 11.
He protects and preserves. Jer. 31: 10. Eze. 34: 10. Zec. 9: 16. Jno. 10: 28.
He laid down His life for. Zec. 13: 7. Mat. 26: 31. Jno. 10: 11, 15. Acts 20: 28.
He gives eternal life to. Jno. 10: 28.
Typified. *David* 1 Sam. 16: 11.

Church, The.

Belongs to God. 1 Tim. 3: 15.
The body of Christ. Eph. 1: 23. Col. 1: 24.
Christ, the foundation-stone of. 1 Cor. 3: 11. Eph. 2: 20. 1 Pet. 2: 4, 6.
Christ, the head of. Eph. 1: 22. Eph. 5: 23.
Loved by Christ. So. of Sol. 7: 10. Eph. 5: 25.
Purchased by the blood of Christ. Acts 20: 28. Eph. 5: 25. Heb. 9: 12.
Sanctified and cleansed by Christ. 1 Cor. 6: 11. Eph. 5: 26, 27.
Subject to Christ. Rom. 7: 4. Eph. 5: 24.
The object of the grace of God. Isa. 27: 3. 2 Cor. 8: 1.

Displays the wisdom of God. Eph. 3:10.
Shews forth the praises of God. Isa. 60:6.
God defends. Psa. 89:18. Isa. 4:5. Isa. 49:25. Mat. 16:18.
God provides ministers for. Jer. 3:15. Eph. 4:11, 12.
Glory to be ascribed to God by. Eph. 3:21.
Elect. 1 Pet. 5:13.
Glorious. Psa. 45:13. Eph. 5:27.
Clothed in righteousness. Rev. 19:8.
Believers continually added to, by the Lord. Acts 2:47. Acts 5:14. Acts 11:24.
Unity of. Rom. 12:5. 1 Cor. 10:17. 1 Cor. 12:12. Gal. 3:28.
Saints baptized into, by one Spirit. 1 Cor. 12:13.
Ministers commanded to feed. Acts 20:28.
Is edified by the word. 1 Cor. 14:4, 13. Eph. 4:15, 16.
The wicked persecute. Acts 8:1—3. 1 The. 2:14, 15.
Not to be despised. 1 Cor. 11:22.
Defiling of, will be punished. 1 Cor. 3:17.
Extent of, predicted. Isa. 2:2. Eze. 17:22—24. Dan. 2:34, 35. Hab. 2:14.

Church of Israel.

Established by God. Deu. 4:5—14. Deu. 26:18, with Acts 7:35, 38.
Admission into, by circumcision. Gen. 17:10—14.
All Israelites members of. Rom. 9:4.
Was relatively holy. Exo. 31:13. Num. 16:3.
HAD
 An appointed place of worship. Deu. 12:5.
 Appointed ordinances. Exo. 18:20. Heb. 9:1, 10.
 Appointed feasts. Lev. 23:2. Isa. 1:14.
 An ordained ministry. Exo. 29:9. Deu. 10:8.
 The divine presence manifested in it. Exo. 29:45, 46. Lev. 26:11, 12. 1 Kin. 8:10, 11.
 A spiritual church within it. Rom. 9:6—8. Rom. 11:2—7.
In covenant with God. Deu. 4:13, 23. Acts 3:25.
The depository of holy writ. Rom. 3:2.
CALLED THE
 Congregation of Israel. Exo. 12:47. Lev. 4:13.
 Congregation of the Lord. Num. 27:17. Num. 31:16.
Privileges of. Rom. 9:4.
Proselytes admitted into. Num. 9:14. Num. 15:15, 29.
Supported by the people. Exo. 34:20. Deu. 16:17.
WORSHIP OF, CONSISTED IN
 Sacrifice. Exo. 10:25. Lev. 1:2. Heb. 10:1.
 Prayer. Exo. 24:1. Psa. 5:7. Psa. 95:6.
 Praise. 2 Chr. 5:13. 2 Chr. 30:21.
 Reading God's word. Exo. 24:7. Deu. 31:11.
 Preaching. Neh. 8:4, 7.
Attachment of the Jews to. Jno. 9:28, 29. Acts 6:11.
MEMBERS OF
 Required to know its statutes. Lev. 10:11.
 Required to keep its statutes. Deu. 16:12.
 Required to attend its worship. Exo. 23:17.
 Separated from, while unclean. Lev. 13:46. Lev. 15:31. Num. 5:2—4.
 Excommunicated for heavy offences. Num. 15:30, 31. Num. 19:20.
Persons excluded from. Exo. 12:48. Deu. 23:1—4. Eze. 44:7, 9.
A type of the church of Christ. Gal. 4:24—26. Heb. 12:23.

Circumcision.

Instituted by God. Gen. 17:9, 10.
Described. Gen. 17:11. Exo. 4:25.
Enforced by the law. Lev. 12:3, with Jno. 7:22.
CALLED THE
 Covenant of circumcision. Acts 7:8.
 Circumcision in the flesh. Eph. 2:11.
 Concision. Phi. 3:2.
A painful and bloody rite. Exo. 4:26. Jos. 5:8.
Promises to Abraham previous to. Rom. 4:9, 13.
A seal of the covenant. Gen. 17:11. Rom. 4:11.
Introductory Jewish sacrament. Gal. 5:3.
Outward sign of. Rom. 2:28.
Inward grace of. Rom. 2:29.
Necessary to enjoying the privileges of the Jewish Church. Exo. 11:48. Eze. 44:7.
WAS PERFORMED
 On males home-born and bought. Gen. 17:12, 13.
 On the eighth day. Gen. 17:12. Lev. 12:3.
 Even on the sabbath day. Jno. 7:22, 23.
 With knives of flint. Exo. 4:25. Jos. 5:3. (*marg.*)
 By the heads of families. Gen. 17:23. Exo. 4:25.

By persons in authority. Jos. 5:3.
In the presence of the family, &c. Luke 1:58—61.
Accompanied with naming the child. Gen. 21:3, 4. Luke 1:59. Luke 2:21.
First performed on Abraham and his family. Gen. 17: 24—27.
Not performed in the wilderness. Jos. 5:5.
Performed by Joshua at Gilgal. Jos. 5:2, 7.
Punishment for neglecting. Gen, 17: 14. Exo. 4: 24, 26.
Without faith, vain. Rom. 3: 30. Gal. 5: 6.
Without obedience, vain. Rom. 2: 25. 1 Cor. 7:19.
THE JEWS
Denominated by. Acts 10: 45. Gal. 2:9.
Held it unlawful to intermarry with those not of the. Gen. 34: 14. Jud. 14:3.
Held no intercourse with those not of the. Acts 10:28. Acts 11: 3. Gal. 2:12.
Despised as unclean those not of the. 1 Sam. 14:6. 1 Sam. 17: 26. Mat. 15:26, 27. Eph. 2:11.
Sometimes performed on slain enemies. 1 Sam. 18:25—27. 2 Sam. 3:14.
Abolished by the gospel. Eph. 2:11, 15. Col. 3:11.
Performed on Timothy as a matter of expediency because of the Jews, Acts 16: 3.
Necessity of, denied by Paul. Gal. 2:3—5.
Necessity of, asserted by false teachers. Acts 15: 24. Gal. 6: 12. Tit. 1:10.
Trusting to, a denial of Christ. Gal. 3:3, 4, with Gal. 5:3, 4.
Paul denounced for opposing. Acts 21:21.
Saints the true spiritual. Phi. 3: 3. Col. 2:11.
ILLUSTRATIVE OF
Readiness to hear and obey. Jer. 6:10.
Purity of heart. Deu. 10: 16. Deu. 30:6.
Purity of speech. Exo. 6:12.

Cities.

First mention of. Gen. 4:17.
Designed for habitations. Psa. 107: 7, 36.
Often built to perpetuate a name. Gen. 11: 4.
Often founded and enlarged by blood and rapine. Mic. 3:10. Hab. 2: 12.
BUILT
Of brick and slime. Gen. 11:3.
Of stone and wood. Psa. 102: 14. Eze. 26:12.
Of brick and mortar. Exo. 1:11, 14.
On solid foundations. Ezr. 6: 3. Rev. 21:14.
With compactness. Psa. 122: 3.
Often of a square form. Rev. 21:16.
Beside rivers. Psa. 46:4. Psa. 137:1.
On hills. Mat. 5: 14. Luke 4: 29. Rev. 17: 9.
In plains. Gen. 11: 2, 4. Gen. 13:12.
In desert places. 2 Chr. 8: 4. Psa. 107: 35, 36.
In pleasant situations. 2 Kin. 2: 19. Psa. 48: 2.
Arranged in streets and lanes. Num. 22:39. (*marg.*) Zec. 8:5. Luke 14:21.
Entered through gates. Gen. 34: 24. Neh. 13:19, 22.
Surrounded with walls. Deu. 1: 28. Deu. 3:5.
Often fortified by nature. Psa. 125: 2. Isa. 33: 16.
Often fortified by art. 2 Chr. 11: 5—10, 23. Psa. 48: 12, 13. Jer. 4: 5. Dan. 11:15.
Sometimes had suburbs. Num. 35: 2. Jos. 21:3.
WERE CALLED AFTER
The family of the founder. Gen. 4: 17. Jud. 18:29.
The proprietor of the land. 1 Kin. 16:24.
The country in which built. Dan. 4:29, 30.
Numerous. Jos. 15: 21. 1 Chr. 2: 22. Jer. 2:28.
Densely inhabited. Jon. 4:11. Nah. 3: 8.
Often great and goodly. Gen. 10: 12. Deu. 6:10. Dan. 4: 30. Jon. 3:3.
Often of great antiquity. Gen. 10: 11, 12.
Often insignificant. Gen. 19: 20. Ecc. 9:14.
DIFFERENT KINDS OF;
Royal. Num. 21: 26. Jos. 10: 2. 2 Sam. 12:26.
Fenced. Jos. 10:20. Isa. 36:1.
Treasure. Exo. 1: 11.
Commercial. Isa. 23:11. Eze. 27:3.
Chariot. 2 Chr. 1: 14. 2 Chr. 9: 25.
Store. 2 Chr. 8: 4, 6.
Levitical. Lev. 25: 32, 33. Num. 35: 7, 8.
Refuge. Num. 35: 6.
Inhabitants of, called citizens. Acts 21:39.
Prosperity of, increased by commerce. Gen. 49: 13, with Deu. 33: 18, 19. Eze. 28:5.
Artificial mode of supplying water to. 2 Kin. 18:17. 2 Kin. 20:20.
Infested by dogs. 1 Kin. 14: 11. Psa. 59:6, 14.
Under governors. 2 Chr. 33: 14. 2 Cor. 11:32.
Provided with judges. Deu. 16: 18. 2 Chr. 19:5.

Protected at night by watchmen. Psa 127:1 So. of Sol. 5: 7. Isa. 21: 11.
Furnished with stores. 2 Chr. 11:11, 12.
Garrisoned in war. 2 Chr. 17: 2, 19.
Often had citadels. Jud. 9: 51.
A great defence to a country. 2 Chr. 11: 5.
Afforded refuge in times of danger. Jer. 8: 14—16.
Often deserted on the approach of an enemy. 1 Sam. 31: 7. Jer, 4: 29.
WERE FREQUENTLY
Stormed. Jos. 8: 3—7. Jud. 9: 44.
Besieged. Deu. 28: 52. 2 Kin. 19: 24, 25.
Pillaged. Isa. 13: 16. Jer. 20: 5.
Wasted by pestilence. 1 Sam. 5: 11.
Wasted by famine. Jer. 52: 6. Amos 4: 6.
Depopulated. Isa. 17: 9. Eze. 26: 19.
Burned. Jud. 20: 38, 40. Isa. 1: 7.
Made heaps of ruins. Isa. 25: 2.
Razed and sown with salt. Jud. 9: 45.
Difficulty of taking, alluded to. Pro. 18: 19. Jer. 1: 18, 19.
Perishable nature of. Heb. 13: 14.
ILLUSTRATIVE OF
Saints. Mat. 5: 14.
Visible church. So. of Sol. 3: 2, 3. Rev. 11: 2.
Church triumphant. Rev. 21: 2. Rev. 22: 19.
Heavenly inheritance. Heb. 11: 16.
The apostacy. Rev. 16: 10. Rev. 17: 18.
Riches. Pro. 10: 15.

Cities of Refuge.

Design of. Exo. 21: 13. Num. 35: 11. Jos. 20: 3.
Names &c. of. Deu. 4: 41—43. Jos. 20: 7, 8.
REQUIRED TO BE
Easy of access. Deu. 19: 3. Isa. 62: 10.
Open to all manslayers. Jos. 20: 4.
Strangers might take advantage of. Num. 35: 15.
THOSE ADMITTED TO,
Were put on their trial. Num. 35: 12, 24.
Not protected outside of. Num. 35: 26: 27.
Obliged to remain in, until the high priest's death. Num. 35: 25, 28.
Afforded no asylum to murderers. Exo. 21: 14. Num. 35: 16—21.
ILLUSTRATIVE
Of Christ. Psa. 91: 2. Isa. 25: 4.
Of the hope of the gospel. Heb. 6: 18.
(The way to,) of Christ. Isa. 35: 8. Jno. 14: 6.

Clouds.

Formed from the sea. 1 Kin. 18: 44. Amos 9: 6.
Are the garment of the sea. Job 38: 9.
GOD
Established. Prov. 8: 28.
Balanced in the air. Job. 37: 16.
Disposed in order. Job 37: 15.
Brings over the earth. Gen. 9: 14.
Binds up. Job 26: 8.
Spreads out. Job 26: 9.
Scatters. Job 37: 11.
Power and wisdom of God exhibited in forming. Psa. 135: 6, 7. Psa. 147: 5, 8. Jer. 10: 13. Jer. 51: 16.
Power and wisdom of God exhibited in condensing. Job 36: 27, 28. Job 37: 10, 11. Pro. 3: 20.
Made for the glory of God. Psa. 148: 4.
CALLED THE
Clouds of heaven. Dan. 7: 13. Mat. 24: 30.
Windows of heaven. Gen. 7: 11. Isa. 24: 18.
Bottles of heaven. Job 38: 37.
Chambers of God. Psa. 104: 3, 13.
Waters above the firmament. Gen. 1: 7.
Dust of God's feet. Nah. 1: 3.
DIFFERENT KINDS OF, MENTIONED;
White. Rev. 14: 14.
Bright. Job 37: 11. Zec. 10: 1.
Thick. Job. 22: 14. Job 37: 11.
Black. 1 Kin. 18: 45.
Swift. Isa. 19: 1.
Great. Eze. 1: 4.
Small. 1 Kin. 18: 44.
Often cover the heavens. Psa. 147: 8.
Often obscure the sun, &c. Job. 36: 32. Eze. 32: 7.
Often dispersed by the wind. Hos. 13: 3.
USES OF;
To give rain. Jud. 5: 4. Psa. 104: 13, 14.
To supply dew. Pro. 3: 20. Isa. 18: 4.
To moderate heat. Isa. 25: 5.
From the west, bring rain. Luke 12: 54.
Though small, often bring much rain. 1 Kin. 18: 44, 45.
Thunder and lightning come from. Psa. 77: 17, 18.
The rainbow appears in. Gen. 9: 13, 14.
Frequently the instruments of God's judgments. Gen. 7: 11, 12. Job. 37: 13. Psa. 77: 17.
MAN
Ignorant of the spreading of. Job. 36: 29.

Ignorant of the disposing of. Job 37:15.
Ignorant of the balancing of. Job 37:16.
Cannot number. Job 38:37.
Cannot cause to rain. Job 38:34.
Cannot stay. Job 38:37.

ILLUSTRATIVE
Of multitudes of persons. Isa. 60:8. Heb. 12:1.
Of hostile armies. Jer. 4:13. Eze. 38:9, 16.
Of sins of men. Isa. 44:22.
Of judgments of God. Lam. 2:1. Eze. 30:3. Eze. 34:12. Joel 2:2.
Of unsearchableness of God. 2 Sam. 22:12. Psa. 97:2. Eze. 1:4.
(Riding upon,) of the power and greatness of God. Psa. 104:3. Isa. 19:1.
(Passing away,) of the goodness and prosperity of hypocrites. Hos. 6:4. Hos. 13:3.
(Without water,) of false teachers. Jude 12 v.
(Carried away by a tempest,) of false teachers. 2 Pet. 2:17.
(Without rain,) of the fraudulent. Pro. 25:14.
(A morning without,) of wise rulers. 2 Sam. 23:3, 4.
(When seasonable,) of the favor of good rulers. Pro. 16:15.

Cloud of Glory.

First manifestation of. Exo. 13:20, 21.

CALLED
The cloud. Exo. 34:5.
Pillar of cloud and pillar of fire. Exo. 13:22.
Cloudy pillar. Exo. 33:9, 10.
Cloud of the Lord. Num. 10:34.
The presence of God. Exo. 33:14, 15.

God's glory manifested in. Exo. 16:10. Exo. 40:35.
God came down in. Exo. 34:5. Num. 11:25.
God spoke from. Exo. 24:16. Psa. 99:7.

WAS DESIGNED TO
Regulate the movements of Israel. Exo. 40:36, 37. Num. 9:17—25.
Guide Israel. Exo. 13:21. Neh. 9:19.
Shew light to Israel. Psa. 78:14. Psa. 105:39.
Defend Israel. Exo. 14:19. Psa. 105:39.
Cover the tabernacle. Exo. 40:34. Num. 9:15.

Was dark to the enemies of Israel. Exo. 14:20.
Was the Shekinah over the mercy-seat. Lev. 16:2.
Continued during the journeyings of Israel. Exo. 13:22. Exo. 40:38.
Manifested in the temple of Solomon. 1 Kin. 8:10, 11. 2 Chr. 5:13. Eze. 10:4.

SPECIAL APPEARANCES OF;
At the murmuring for bread. Exo. 16:10.
At giving of the law. Exo. 19:9, 16. Exo. 24:16—18.
At sedition of Aaron and Miriam. Num. 12:5.
At the murmuring of Israel on report of the spies. Num. 14:10.
At the rebellion of Korah, &c. Num. 16:19.
At the murmuring of Israel on account of Korah's death. Num. 16:42.
At Christ's transfiguration. Mat. 17:5.
At Christ's ascension. Acts 1:9.

Our Lord shall make His second appearance in. Luke 21:27. Acts 1:11.

ILLUSTRATIVE OF
The glory of Christ. Rev. 10:1.
The protection of the church. Isa. 4:5.

Commandments, The Ten.

Spoken by God. Exo. 20:1. Deu. 5:4, 22.
Written by God. Exo. 32:16. Exo. 34:1, 28. Deu. 4:13. Deu. 10:4.
Enumerated. Exo. 20:3—17.
Summed up by Christ. Mat. 22:35—40.
Law of, is spiritual. Mat. 5:28. Rom. 7:14. (See Law of God.)

Commerce.

The barter of one commodity for another 1 Kin. 5:8, with 11 v.
The exchange of commodities for money. 1 Kin. 10:28, 29.

CALLED
Trade. Gen. 34:10. Mat. 25:16.
Traffic. Gen. 42:34. Eze. 17:4.
Buying and selling. Jas. 4:13.

ARTICLES OF, CALLED
Merchandise. Eze. 26:12. Mat. 22:5.
Wares. Jer. 10:17. Eze. 27:16. Jon. 1:5.

PERSONS ENGAGED IN, CALLED
Merchants. Gen. 37:28. Pro. 31:24.
Chapmen. 2 Chr. 9:14.
Traffickers. Isa. 23:8.
Sellers and buyers. Isa. 24:2.

Carried on in fairs, &c. Eze. 27:12, 19. Mat. 11:16.
Inland, by caravans. Job 6:19. Isa. 21:13.
Maritime, by ships. 2 Chr. 8:18. 2 Chr. 9:21.
Persons of distinction engaged in. Isa. 23:8.

Increased the wealth of nations and individuals. 2 Chr. 9:20—22. Pro. 31:14—18. Eze. 28:4, 5.

CARRIED ON BY
- Ishmaelites. Gen. 37:25.
- Egyptians. Gen. 42:2—34.
- Ethiopians. Isa. 45:14.
- Ninevites. Nah. 3:16.
- Syrians. Eze. 27:16, 18.
- People of Tarshish. Eze. 27:25.
- Tyrians. Eze. 28:5, 13, 16.
- Jews. Eze. 27:17.

OF THE JEWS
- Under strict laws. Lev. 19:36, 37. Lev. 25:14, 17.
- Commenced after their settlement in Canaan. Gen. 49:13, with Jud. 5:17.
- Greatly extended by Solomon. 1 Kin. 9:26, 27. 2 Chr. 9:21.
- Checked in Jehoshaphat's time. 1 Kin. 22:48, 49.

Success in, led to pride, &c. Eze. 28:2, 16—18.
Evil practices connected with. Pro. 20:14. Eze. 22:13. Hos. 12:7.
Denunciations connected with abuses of. Isa. 23:11. Eze. 7:12, 13. Eze. 27:32—36. Eze. 28:16—18.

ARTICLES OF;
- Blue cloth. Eze. 27:24.
- Brass. Eze. 27:13.
- Corn. 1 Kin. 5:11. Eze. 27:17.
- Cattle. Eze. 27:21.
- Chests of rich apparel. Eze. 27:24.
- Chariots. 1 Kin. 10:29.
- Clothes for chariots. Eze. 27:20.
- Embroidery. Eze. 27:16, 24.
- Gold. 2 Chr. 8:18.
- Honey. Eze. 27:17.
- Horses. 1 Kin. 10:29. Eze. 27:14.
- Ivory. 2 Chr. 9:21. Eze. 27:15.
- Iron and steel. Eze. 27:12, 19.
- Land. Gen. 23:13—16. Ruth 4:3.
- Lead. Eze. 27:12.
- Linen. 1 Kin. 10:28.
- Oil. 1 Kin. 5:11. Eze. 27:17.
- Perfumes. So. of Sol. 3:6.
- Precious stones. Eze. 27:16, 22. Eze. 28:13, 16.
- Purple. Eze. 27:16.
- Slaves. Gen. 37:28, 36. Deu. 24:7.
- Silver. 2 Chr. 9:21.
- Timber. 1 Kin. 5:6, 8.
- Tin. Eze. 27:12.
- White wool. Eze. 27:18.
- Wine. 2 Chr. 2:15. Eze. 27:18.

Illustrative of intercourse with the apostacy. Rev. 18:3—19.

Communion of Saints.

According to the prayer of Christ. Jno. 17:20, 21.

IS WITH
- God. 1 Jno. 1:3.
- Saints in heaven. Heb. 12:22—24.
- Each other. Gal. 2:9. 1 Jno. 1:3, 7.

God marks, with His approval. Mal. 3:16.
Christ is present in. Mat. 18:20.
In public and social worship. Psa. 34:3. Psa. 55:14. Acts 1:14. Heb. 10:25.
In the Lord's supper. 1 Cor. 10:17.
In holy conversation. Mal. 3:16.
In prayer for each other. 2 Cor. 1:11. Eph. 6:18.
In exhortation. Col. 3:16. Heb. 10:25.
In mutual comfort and edification. 1 The. 4:18. 1 The. 5:11.
In mutual sympathy and kindness. Rom. 12:15. Eph. 4:32.
Delight of. Psa. 16:3. Psa. 42:4. Psa. 133:1—3. Rom. 15:32.
Exhortation to. Eph. 4:1—3.
Opposed to communion with the wicked. 2 Cor. 6:14—17. Eph. 5:11.
Exemplified. *Jonathan*, 1 Sam. 23:16. *David*, Psa. 119:63. *Daniel*, Dan. 2:17, 18. *Apostles*, Acts 1:14. *The Primitive Church*, Acts 2:42. Acts 5:12. *Paul*, Acts 20:36—38.

Communion of the Lord's Supper.

Prefigured. Exo. 12:21—28. 1 Cor. 5:7, 8.
Instituted. Mat. 26:26. 1 Cor. 11:23.
Object of. Luke 22:19. 1 Cor. 11:24, 26.
Is the communion of the body and blood of Christ. 1 Cor. 10:16.
Both bread and wine are necessary to be received in. Mat. 26:27. 1 Cor. 11:26.
Self-examination commanded before partaking of. 1 Cor. 11:28, 31.
Newness of heart and life necessary to the worthy partaking of. 1 Cor. 5:7, 8.
Partakers of, should be wholly separate unto God. 1 Cor. 10:21.
Was continually partaken of, by the Primitive Church. Acts 2:42. Acts 20:7.

UNWORTHY PARTAKERS OF
- Are guilty of the body and blood of Christ. 1 Cor. 11:27.
- Discern not the Lord's body. 1 Cor. 11:29.
- Are visited with judgments. 1 Cor. 11:30.

Communion with God.

Is communion with the Father. 1 Jno. 1:3.
Is communion with the Son. 1 Cor. 1:9. 1 Jno. 1:3. Rev. 3:20.
Is communnion with the Holy Ghost. 1 Cor. 12:13. 2 Cor. 13:14. Phi. 2:1.
Reconciliation must precede. Amos 3:3.

Holiness essential to. 2 Cor. 6: 14—16.
Promised to the obedient. Jno. 14:23.
SAINTS
Desire. Psa. 42:1. Phi. 1:23.
Have, in meditation. Psa. 63:5, 6.
Have, in prayer. Phi. 4:6. Heb. 4:16.
Have, in the Lord's supper. 1 Cor. 10:16.
Should always enjoy. Psa. 16: 8. Jno. 14:16—18.
Exemplified. *Enoch*, Gen. 5: 24. *Noah*, Gen. 6:9. *Abraham*, Gen. 18: 33. *Jacob*, Gen. 32: 24—29. *Moses*, Exo. 33: 11—23.

Compassion and Sympathy.

Christ set an example of. Luke 19: 41, 42.
Exhortation to. Rom. 12:15. 1 Pet. 3:8.
EXERCISE TOWARDS
The afflicted. Job 6:14. Heb. 13:3.
The chastened. Isa. 22:4. Jer. 9:1.
Enemies. Psa. 35:13.
The poor. Pro. 19:17.
The weak. 2 Cor. 11: 29. Gal. 6: 2.
Saints. 1 Cor. 12: 25, 26.
Inseparable from love to God. 1 Jno. 3:17. Jno. 4:20.
MOTIVES TO
The compassion of God. Mat. 13: 27, 33.
The sense of our infirmities. Heb. 5: 2.
The wicked made to feel, for saints. Psa. 106:46.
Promise to those who show. Pro. 19:17. Mat. 10: 42.
Illustrated. Luke 10:33. Luke 15:20.
Exemplified. *Pharaoh's Daughter*, Exo. 2: 6. *Shobi*, *&c.* 2 Sam. 17: 27—29. *Elijah*, 1 Kin. 17: 18, 19. *Nehemiah*, Neh. 1:4. *Job's friends*, Job 2:11. *Job*, Job 30: 25. *David*, Psa. 35: 13, 14. *Jews*, Jno. 11: 19. *Paul*, 1 Cor. 9:22.

Compassion and Sympathy of Christ, The.

Necessary to His priestly office. Heb. 5: 2, with verse 7.
MANIFESTED FOR THE
Weary and heavy-laden. Mat. 11: 28—30.
Weak in faith. Isa. 40: 11. Isa. 42:3, with Mat. 12:20.
Tempted. Heb. 2:18.
Afflicted. Luke 7: 13. Jno. 11: 33, 35.
Diseased. Mat. 14:14. Mar. 1:41.
Poor. Mar. 8:2.
Perishing sinners. Mat. 9:36. Luke 19:41. Jno. 3:16.
An encouragement to prayer. Heb. 4:15.

Condemnation.

The sentence of God against sin. Mat. 25:41.
Universal, caused by the offence of Adam. Rom. 5: 12, 16, 18.
Inseparable consequence of sin. Pro. 12:2. Rom. 6: 23.
INCREASED BY
Impenitence. Mat. 11:20—24.
Unbelief. John. 3:18, 19.
Pride. 1 Tim. 3:6.
Oppression. Jas. 5:1—5.
Hypocrisy. Mat. 23:14.
Conscience testifies to the justice of. Job 9:20. Rom. 2:1. Tit. 3:11.
The law testifies to the justice of. Rom. 3:19.
According to men's deserts. Mat. 12. 37. 2 Cor. 11:15.
Saints are delivered from, by Christ. Jno. 3:18. Jno. 5:24. Rom. 8:1, 33, 34.
Of the wicked, an example. 2 Pet. 2: 6. Jude 7.
Chastisements are designed to rescue us from. Psa 94:12, 13. 1 Cor. 11: 32.
Apostates ordained unto. Jude 4.
Unbelievers remain under. Jno. 3: 18, 36.
The law is the ministration of. 2 Cor. 3:9.

Conduct, Christian.

Believing God. Mar. 11:22. Jno. 14: 11, 12.
Fearing God. Ecc. 12:13. 1 Pet. 2:17.
Loving God. Deu. 6:5. Mat. 22: 37.
Following God. Eph. 5:1. 1 Pet. 1: 15, 16.
Obeying God. Luke 1:6. 1 Jno. 5:3.
Rejoicing in God. Psa. 33:1. Hab. 3:18.
Believing in Christ. Jno. 6:29. 1 Jno. 3:23.
Loving Christ. Jno. 21: 15. 1 Pet. 1: 7, 8.
Following the example of Christ. Jno. 13:15. 1 Pet. 2:21—24.
Obeying Christ. Jno. 14:21. Jno. 15:14.
LIVING
To Christ. Rom. 14:8. 2 Cor. 5:15.
Unto righteousness. Mic. 6 : 8. Rom. 6:18. 1 Pet. 2:24.
Soberly, righteously, and godly. Tit. 2:12.
WALKING
Honestly. 1 The. 4:12.
Worthy of God. 1 The. 2:12.
Worthy of the Lord. Col. 1:10.

In the Spirit. Gal. 5:25.
After the Spirit. Rom. 8:1.
In newness of life. Rom. 6:4.
Worthy of our vocation. Eph. 4:1.
As children of light. Eph. 5:8.
Rejoicing in Christ. Phi. 3:1. Phi. 4:4.
Loving one another. Jno. 15:12. Rom. 12:10 1 Cor. 13. Eph. 5:2. Heb. 13:1.
Striving for the faith. Phi. 1:27. Jude 3.
Putting away all sin. 1 Cor. 5:7. Heb. 12:1.
Abstaining from all appearance of evil. 1 The. 5:22.
Perfecting holiness. Mat. 5:48. 2. Cor. 7:1. 2 Tim. 3:17.
Hating defilement. Jude 23.
Following after that which is good. Phi. 4:8. 1 The. 5:15. 1 Tim. 6:11.
Overcoming the world. 1 Jno. 5:4, 5.
Adorning the gospel. Mat. 5:16. Tit. 2:10.
Showing a good example. 1 Tim. 4:12. 1 Pet. 2:12. Tit. 2:7.
Abounding in the work of the Lord. 1 Cor. 15:58. 2 Cor. 8:7. 1 The. 4:1.
Shunning the wicked. Psa. 1:1. 2 The. 3:6.
Controlling the body. 1 Cor. 9:27. Col. 3:5.
Subduing the temper. Eph. 4:26. Jas. 1:19.
Submitting to injuries. Mat. 5:39—41. 1 Cor. 6:7.
Forgiving injuries. Mat. 6:14. Rom. 12:20.
Living peaceably with all. Rom. 12:18. Heb. 12:14.
Visiting the afflicted. Mat. 25:36. Jas 1:27.
Doing as we would be done by. Mat. 7:12. Luke 6:31.
Sympathizing with others. Gal. 6:2. 1 The. 5:14.
Honoring others. Psa. 15:4. Rom. 12:10.
Fulfilling domestic duties. Eph. 6:1—8. 1 Pet. 3:1—7.
Submitting to Authorities. Rom 13:1—7.
Being liberal to others. Acts 20:35. Rom. 12:13.
Being contented. Phi. 4:11. Heb. 13:5.
Blessedness of maintaining. Psa. 1:1—3. Psa. 19:9—11. Psa. 50:23. Mat. 5:3—12. Jno. 15:10. Jno. 7:17.

Confessing Christ.

Influences of the Holy Spirit necessary to. 1 Cor. 12:3. 1 Jno. 4:2.
A test of being saints. 1 Jno. 2:23. 1 Jno. 4:2, 3.
An evidence of union with God. 1 Jno. 4:15.
Necessary to salvation. Rom. 10:9, 10.
Ensures His confessing us. Mat. 10:32.
The fear of man prevents. Jno. 7:13. Jno. 12:42, 43.
Persecution should not prevent us from. Mar. 8:35. 2 Tim. 2:12.
Must be connected with faith. Rom 10:9.
Consequences of not. Mat. 10:33.
Exemplified. *Nathanael*, Jno. 1:49. *Peter*, Jno. 6:68, 69. Acts 2:22—36. *Man born blind*, Jno. 9:25, 33. *Martha*, Jno. 11:27. *Peter and John*, Acts 4:7—12. *Apostles*, Acts 5:29—32, 42, *Stephen*. Acts 7:52, 59. *Paul*, Acts 9:29. *Timothy*, 1 Tim. 6:12. *John*, Rev. 1:9. *Church in Pergamos*, Rev. 2:13. *Martyrs*, Rev. 20:4.

Confession of Sin.

God requires. Lev. 5:5. Hos. 5:15.
God regards. Job 33:27, 28. Dan. 9:20, &c.
Exhortation to. Jos. 7:19. Jer. 3:13. Jas. 5:16.
Promises to. Lev. 26:40—42. Pro. 28:13.
SHOULD BE ACCOMPANIED WITH
Submission to punishment. Lev. 26:41. Neh. 9:33. Ezra 9:13.
Prayer for forgiveness. 2 Sam. 24:10. Psa. 25:11. Psa. 51:1. Jer. 14:7—9, 20.
Self-abasement. Isa. 64:5, 6. Jer. 3:25.
Godly sorrow. Psa. 38:18. Lam. 1:20.
Forsaking sin. Pro. 28:13.
Restitution. Num. 5:6, 7.
Should be full and unreserved. Psa. 32:5. Psa. 51:3. Psa. 106:6.
Followed by pardon. Psa. 32:5. 1 Jno. 1:9.
Illustrated. Luke 15:21. Luke 18:13.
Exemplified. *Aaron*, Num. 12:11. *Israelites*, Num. 21:6, 7. 1 Sam. 7:6. 1 Sam. 12:19. *Saul*, 1 Sam. 15:24. *David*, 2 Sam. 24:10. *Ezra*. Ezr. 9:6. *Nehemiah*, Neh. 1:6, 7. *Levites*, Neh. 9:4, 33, 34. *Job*, Job 7:20. *Daniel*, Dan. 9:4. *Peter*, Luke 5:8. *Thief*, Luke 23:41.

Conscience.

Witnesses in man. Pro. 20:27. Rom. 2:15.
Accuses of sin. Gen. 42:21. 2 Sam. 24:10. Mat. 27:3. Acts 2:37.
We should have the approval of. Job 27:6. Acts 24:16. Rom. 9:1. Rom. 14:22.
The blood of Christ alone can purify. Heb. 9:14. Heb. 10:2—10, 22.

Keep the faith in purity of. 1 Tim. 1:19. 1 Tim. 3:9.
Of saints, pure and good. Heb. 13: 18. 1 Pet. 3:16, 21.
Submit to authority for. Rom. 13:5.
Suffer patiently for. 1 Pet. 2:19.
Testimony of, a source of joy. 2 Cor. 1:12. 1 Jno. 3:21.
Of others, not to be offended. Rom. 14:21. 1 Cor. 10:28—32.
Ministers should commend themselves to that of their people. 2 Cor. 4:2. 2 Cor. 5:11.
Of the wicked, seared. 1 Tim. 4:2.
Of the wicked, defiled. Tit. 1:15.
Without spiritual illumination, a false guide. Acts 23:1, with Acts 26:9.

Contempt.

Sin of. Job 31:13, 14. Pro. 14:21.
Folly of. Pro. 11:12.
A characteristic of the wicked. Pro. 18:3. Isa. 5:24. 2 Tim. 3:3.
FORBIDDEN TOWARDS
Parents. Pro. 23:22.
Christ's little ones. Mat. 18:10.
Weak brethren. Rom. 14:3.
Young ministers. 1 Cor. 16:11.
Believing masters. 1 Tim. 6:2.
The poor. Jas. 2:1—3.
Self-righteousness prompts to. Isa. 65:5. Luke 18:9, 11.
Pride and prosperity prompt to. Psa. 123:4.
Ministers should give no occasion for. 1 Tim. 4:12.
Of ministers, is a despising of God. Luke 10:16. 1 The. 4:8.
TOWARDS THE CHURCH
Often turned into respect. Isa. 60:14.
Often punished. Eze. 28:26.
Causes saints to cry unto God. Neh. 4:4. Psa. 123:3.
THE WICKED EXHIBIT TOWARDS
Christ. Psa. 22:6. Isa. 53:3. Mat. 27:29.
Saints. Psa. 119:141.
Authorities. 2 Pet. 2:10. Jude 8.
Parents. Pro. 15:5, 20.
The afflicted. Job 19:18.
The poor. Psa. 14:6. Ecc. 9:16.
Saints sometimes guilty of. Jas. 2:6.
Exemplified. *Hagar*, Gen. 16:4. *Children of Belial*, 1 Sam. 10:27. *Nabal*, 1 Sam. 25:10, 11. *Michal*, 2 Sam. 6:16. *Sanballat, &c.* Neh. 2:19. Neh. 4:2, 3. *False teachers*, 2 Cor. 10:10.

Contentment.

With godliness is great gain. Psa. 37:16. 1 Tim. 6:6.
SAINTS SHOULD EXHIBIT
In their respective callings. 1 Cor. 7:20.
With appointed wages. Luke 3:14.
With what things they have. Heb. 13:5.
With food and raiment. 1 Tim. 6:8.
God's promises should lead to. Heb. 13:5.
The wicked want. Isa. 5:8. Ecc. 5:10.
Exemplified. *Barzillai*, 2 Sam. 19:33—37. *Shunamite*, 2 Kin. 4:13. *David*, Psa. 16:6. *Agur*, Pro. 30:8, 9. *Paul*, Phi. 4:11, 12.

Conversion.

By God. 1 Kin. 18:37. Jno. 6:44. Acts 21:19.
By Christ. Acts 3:26. Rom. 15:18.
By the power of the Holy Ghost. Pro. 1:23.
Is of grace. Acts 11:21, with verse 23.
Follows repentance. Acts 3:19. Acts 26:20.
Is the result of faith. Acts 11:21.
THROUGH THE INSTRUMENTALITY OF
The scriptures. Psa. 19:7.
Ministers. Acts 26:18. 1 The. 1:9.
Self-examination. Psa. 119:59. Lam. 3:40.
Affliction. Psa. 78:34.
OF SINNERS, A CAUSE OF JOY.
To God. Eze. 18:23. Luke 15:32.
To saints. Acts 15:3. Gal. 1:23, 24.
Is necessary. Mat. 18:3.
Commanded. Job 36:10.
Exhortations to. Pro. 1:23. Isa. 31:6. Isa. 55:7. Jer. 3:7. Eze. 33:11.
Promises connected with. Neh. 1:9. Isa. 1:27. Jer. 3:14. Eze. 18:27.
Pray for. Psa. 80:7. Psa. 85:4. Jer. 31:18. Lam. 5:21.
Is accompanied by confession of sin, and prayer. 1 Kin. 8:35.
Danger of neglecting. Psa. 7:12. Jer. 44:5, 11. Eze. 3:19.
Duty of leading sinners to. Psa. 51:13.
Encouragement for leading sinners to. Dan. 12:3. Jas. 5:19, 20.
Of Gentiles, predicted. Isa. 2:2. Isa. 11:10. Isa. 60:5. Isa. 66:12.
Of Israel, predicted. Eze. 36:25—27.

Counsels and purposes of God, The.

Are great. Jer. 32:19.
Are wonderful. Isa. 28:29.
Are immutable. Psa. 33:11. Pro. 19:21. Jer. 4:28. Rom. 9:11. Heb. 6:17.
Are sovereign. Isa. 40:13, 14. Dan. 4:35.
Are eternal. Eph. 3:11.
Are faithfulness and truth. Isa. 25:1.

None can disannul. Isa. 14: 27.
Shall be performed. Isa. 14:24. Isa. 46: 11.
The sufferings and death of Christ were according to. Acts 2: 23. Acts 4: 28.
Saints called and saved according to. Rom. 8: 28. 2 Tim. 1: 9.
The union of all saints in Christ, is according to. Eph. 1: 9, 10.
The works of God according to. Eph. 1: 11.
Should be declared by ministers. Acts 20: 27.
Attend to. Jer. 49: 20. Jer. 50: 45.
Secret not to be searched into. Deu. 29: 29. Mat. 24: 36. Acts 1: 7.
THE WICKED
Understand not. Mic. 4: 12.
Despise. Isa. 5: 19.
Reject. Luke 7: 30.

Courts of Justice.

Have authority from God. Rom. 13: 1—5.
SUPERIOR COURT
Held first by Moses alone in the wilderness. Exo. 18: 13—20.
Consisted subsequently of priests and Levites. Deu. 17: 9, with Mal. 2: 7.
Presided over by the governor or the high priest. Deu. 17: 12. Jud. 4: 4, 5.
Held at the seat of government. Deu. 17: 8.
Decided on all appeals and difficult cases. Exo. 18: 26. Deu. 1: 17. Deu. 17: 8, 9.
Decisions of, conclusive. Deu. 17: 10, 11.
INFERIOR,
In all cities. Deu. 16: 18. 2 Chr. 19: 5—7.
Held at the gates. Gen. 34: 20. Deu. 16: 18. Deu. 21: 19. Job 5: 4.
Judges of, appointed by the governor. Exo. 18: 21, 25. Deu. 1: 9—15. 2 Sam. 15: 3.
All minor cases decided by. Exo. 18: 26. 2 Sam. 15: 4.
All transfers of property made before. Gen. 23: 17—20. Ruth 4: 1, 2.
Re-established by Jehoshaphat. 2 Chr. 19: 5—10.
Re-established by Ezra. Ezr. 7: 25.
SANHEDRIM OR COURT OF THE SEVENTY
Probably derived from the seventy elders appointed by Moses. Exo. 24: 9. Num. 11: 16, 17, 24—30.
Mentioned in the latter part of sacred history. Luke 22: 66. Jno. 11: 47. Acts 5: 27.
Consisted of chief priests, &c. Mat. 26: 57, 59.
Presided over by high priest. Mat. 26: 62—66.
Sat in high priest's palace. Mat. 26: 57, 58.
OF THE ROMANS IN JUDEA
Presided over by the governor or deputy. Mat. 27: 2, 11. Acts 18: 12.
Place of, called the hall of judgment. Jno. 18: 28, 33. Jno. 19: 9.
Never interfered in any dispute about minor matters or about religion. Acts 18: 14, 15.
Could alone award death. Jno. 18: 31.
Never examined their own citizens by torture. Acts 22: 25—29.
Appeals from, made to the emperor. Acts 25: 11. Acts 26: 32. Acts 28: 19.
Generally held in the morning. Jer. 21: 12. Mat. 27: 1. Luke 22: 66. Acts 5: 21.
Sometimes held in synagogues. Mat. 10: 17. Acts 22: 19. Acts 26: 11. Jas. 2: 2. (*Greek.*)
PROVIDED WITH
Judges. Deu. 16: 18.
Officers. Deu. 16: 18. Mat. 5: 25.
Tormentors or executioners. Mat. 18: 34.
JUDGES OF,
Called elders. Deu. 25: 7. 1 Sam. 16: 4.
Called magistrates. Luke 12: 58.
Rode often on white asses. Jud. 5: 10.
To judge righteously. Lev. 19: 15. Deu. 1: 16.
To judge without respect of persons. Exo. 23: 3, 6. Lev. 19: 15. Deu. 1: 17. Pro. 22: 22.
To investigate every case. Deu. 19: 18.
Not to take bribes. Exo. 23: 8. Deu. 16: 19.
To judge as for God. 2 Chr. 19: 6, 7, 9.
To decide according to law. Eze. 44: 24.
To promote peace. Zec. 8: 16.
Sat on the judgment-seat while hearing causes. Exo. 18: 13. Jud. 5: 10. Isa. 28: 6. Mat. 27: 19.
Examined the parties. Acts 24: 8.
Conferred together before giving judgment. Acts 5: 34—40. Acts 25: 12. Acts 26: 30, 31.
Pronounced the judgment of the court. Mat. 26: 65, 66. Luke 23: 24. Acts 5: 40.
Both the accusers and accused required to appear before. Deu. 25: 1. Acts 25: 16.
CAUSES IN, WERE OPENED BY
The complainant. 1 Kin. 3: 17—21. Acts 16: 19—21.

An advocate. Acts 24:1.

THE ACCUSED

Stood before the judge. Num. 35:12. Mat. 27:11.

Permitted to plead their own cause. 1 Kin. 3:22. Acts 24:10. Acts 26:1.

Might have advocates. Pro. 31:8, 9. Isa. 1:17.

Exhorted to confess. Jos. 7:19.

Examined on oath. Lev. 5:1. Mat. 26:63.

Sometimes examined by torture. Acts 22:24, 29.

Sometimes treated with insult. Mat. 26:67. Jno. 18:22, 23. Acts 23:2, 3.

The evidence of two or more witnesses required in. Deu. 17:6. Deu. 19:15. Jno. 8:17. 2 Cor. 13:1.

Witnesses sometimes laid their hands on the criminal's head before punishment. Lev. 24:14.

False witnesses in to receive the punishment of the accused. Deu. 19:19.

Corruption and bribery often practised in. Isa. 10:1. Amos 5:12. Amos 8:6.

THE JUDGMENT OF,

Not given till accused was heard. Jno. 7:51.

Recorded in writing. Isa. 10:1. (*marg.*)

Immediately executed. Deu. 25:2. Jos. 7:25. Mar. 15:15—20.

Witnesses first to execute. Deu. 17:7. Acts 7:58.

Allusions to. Job 5:4. Psa. 127:5. Mat. 5:22.

Illustrative of the last judgment. Mat. 19:28. Rom. 14:10. 1 Cor. 6:2.

Covenants.

Agreements between two parties. Gen. 26:28. Dan. 11:6.

DESIGNED FOR

Establishing friendship. 1 Sam. 18:3.

Procuring assistance in war. 1 Kin. 15:18, 19.

Mutual protection. Gen. 26:28, 29. Gen. 31:50—52.

Establishing peace. Jos. 9:15, 16.

Promoting commerce. 1 Kin. 5:6—11.

Selling land. Gen. 23:14—16.

CONDITIONS OF,

Clearly specified. 1 Sam. 11:1, 2.

Confirmed by oath. Gen. 21:23, 31. Gen. 26:31.

Witnessed. Gen. 23:17, 18. Ruth 4:9—11.

Written and sealed. Neh. 9:38. Neh. 10:1.

God often called to witness. Gen. 31:50, 53.

When confirmed, unalterable. Gal. 3:15.

Made by passing between the pieces of the divided sacrifices. Gen. 15:9—17. Jer. 34:18, 19.

Salt a sign of perpetuity in. Num. 18:19. 2 Chr. 13:5.

Ratified by joining hands. Pro. 11:21. Eze. 17:18.

Followed by a feast. Gen. 26:30. Gen. 31:54.

Presents given as tokens of. Gen. 21:27—30. 1 Sam. 18:3, 4.

Pillars raised in token of. Gen. 31:45, 46.

Names given to places where made. Gen. 21:31. Gen. 31:47—49.

THE JEWS

Forbidden to make, with the nations of Canaan. Exo. 23:32. Deu. 7:2.

Frequently made with other nations. 1 Kin. 5:12. 2 Kin. 17:4.

Condemned for making, with idolatrous nations. Isa. 30:2—5. Hos. 12:1.

Regarded, as sacred. Jos. 9:16—19. Psa. 15:4.

Violated by the wicked. Rom. 1:31. 2 Tim. 3:3.

ILLUSTRATIVE

Of the contract of marriage. Mal. 2:14.

Of God's promises to man. Gen. 9:9—11. Eph. 2:12.

Of the united determination of a people to serve God. 2 Kin, 11:17. 2 Chr. 15:12. Neh. 10:29.

Of good resolutions. Job 31:1.

(With death and hell,) of carnal security. Isa. 28:15, 18.

(With stones and beasts of the earth,) of peace and prosperity. Job 5:23. Hos. 2:18.

Covenant, The.

Christ, the substance of. Isa. 42:6. Isa. 49:8.

Christ, the Mediator of. Heb. 8:6. Heb. 9:15. Heb. 12:24.

Christ, the Messenger of. Mal. 3:1.

MADE WITH

Abraham. Gen. 15:7—18. Gen. 17:2—14. Luke 1:72—75. Acts 3:25. Gal. 3:16.

Isaac. Gen. 17:19, 21. Gen. 26:3, 4.

Jacob. Gen. 28:13, 14, with 1 Chr. 16:16, 17.

Israel. Exo. 6:4. Acts 3:25.

David. 2 Sam. 23:5. Psa. 89:3, 4.

Renewed under the gospel. Jer. 31:31—33. Rom. 11:27. Heb. 8:8—10, 13.

Fulfilled in Christ. Luke 1:68—79.

Confirmed in Christ. Gal. 3:17.
Ratified by the blood of Christ. Heb. 9:11—14, 16—23.
Is a covenant of peace. Isa. 54:9, 10. Eze. 34:25. Eze. 37:26.
Is unalterable. Psa. 89:34. Isa. 54:10. Isa. 59:21. Gal. 3:17.
Is everlasting. Psa. 111:9. Isa. 55:3. Isa. 61:8. Eze. 16:60—63. Heb. 13:20.
All saints interested in. Psa. 25:14. Psa. 89:29—37. Heb. 8:10.
The wicked have no interest in. Eph. 2:12.
Blessings connected with. Isa. 56:4—7. Heb. 8:10—12.
God is faithful to. Deu. 7:9. 1 Kin. 8:23. Neh. 1:5. Dan. 9:4.
God is ever mindful of. Psa. 105:8. Psa. 111:5. Luke 1:72.
Be mindful of. 1 Chr. 16:15.
Caution against forgetting. Deu. 4:23.
Plead, in prayer. Psa. 74:20. Jer. 14:21.
Punishment for despising. Heb. 10:29, 30.

Covetousness.

Comes from the heart. Mar. 7:22, 23.
Engrosses the heart. Eze. 33:31. 2 Pet. 2:14.
Is idolatry. Eph. 5:5. Col. 3:5.
Is the root of all evil. 1 Tim. 6:10.
Is never satisfied. Ecc. 5:10. Hab. 2:5.
Is vanity. Psa. 39:6. Ecc. 4:8.
IS INCONSISTENT
In saints. Eph. 5:3. Heb. 13:5.
Specially in ministers. 1 Tim. 3:3.
LEADS TO
Injustice and oppression. Pro. 28:20. Mic. 2:2.
Foolish and hurtful lusts. 1 Tim. 6:9.
Departure from the faith. 1 Tim. 6:10.
Lying. 2 Kin. 5:22—25.
Murder. Pro. 1:18, 19. Eze. 22:12.
Theft. Jos. 7:21.
Poverty. Pro. 28:22.
Misery. 1 Tim. 6:10.
Domestic affliction. Pro. 15:27.
Abhorred by God. Psa. 10:3.
Forbidden. Exo. 20:17.
A characteristic of the wicked. Rom. 1:29.
A characteristic of the slothful. Pro. 21:26.
Commended by the wicked alone. Psa. 10:3.
Hated by saints. Exo. 18:21. Acts 20:33.
To be mortified by saints. Col. 3:5.
Woe denounced against. Isa. 5:8. Hab. 2:9.
Punishment of. Job. 20:15. Isa. 57:17. Jer. 22:17—19. Mic. 2:2, 3.
Excludes from heaven. 1 Cor. 6:10. Eph. 5:5.
Beware of. Luke 12:15.
Avoid those guilty of. 1 Cor. 5:11.
Pray against. Psa. 119:36.
Reward of those who hate. Pro. 28:16.
Shall abound in the last days. 2 Tim. 3:2. 2 Pet. 2:1—3.
Exemplified. *Laban*, Gen. 31:41. *Achan*, Jos. 7:21. *Eli's sons*, 1 Sam. 2:12—14. *Samuel's sons*, 1 Sam. 8:3. *Saul*, 1 Sam. 15:9, 19. *Ahab*, 1 Kin. 21:2, &c. *Gehazi*, 2 Kin. 5:20—24. *Nobles of the Jews*, Neh. 5:7. Isa. 1:23. *Jewish People*, Isa. 56:11. Jer. 6:13. *Babylon*, Jer. 51:13. *Young man*, 19:22. *Judas*, Mat. 26:14, 15. Jno. 12:6. *Pharisees*, Luke 16:14. *Ananias, &c.* Acts 5:1—10. *Felix*, Acts 24:26. *Balaam*, 2 Pet. 2:15, with Jude 11.

Creation.

The formation of things which had no previous existence. Rom. 4:17, with Heb. 11:3.
EFFECTED
By God. Gen. 1:1. Gen. 2:4, 5. Pro. 26:10.
By Christ. Jno. 1:3, 10. Col. 1:16.
By the Holy Ghost. Job. 26:13. Psa. 104:30.
By the command of God. Psa. 33:9. Heb. 11:3.
In the beginning. Gen. 1:1. Mat. 24:21.
In six days. Exo. 20:11. Exo. 31:17.
According to God's purpose. Psa. 135:6.
For God's pleasure. Pro. 16:4. Rev. 4:11.
For Christ. Col. 1:16.
By faith we believe, to be God's work. Heb. 11:3.
ORDER OF;
First day, making light and dividing it from darkness. Gen. 1:3—5. 2 Cor. 4:6.
Second day, making the firmament or atmosphere, and separating the waters. Gen. 1:6—8.
Third day, separating the land from the water, and making it fruitful. Gen. 1:9—13.
Fourth day, placing the sun, moon, and stars to give light, &c. Gen. 1:14—19.
Fifth day, making birds, insects, and fishes. Gen. 1:20—23.
Sixth day, making beasts of the earth, and man. Gen. 1:24, 28.
God rested from, on the seventh day. Gen. 2:2, 3.

Approved of by God. Gen. 1:31.
A subject of joy to angels. Job 38: 7.
EXHIBITS
The deity of God. Rom. 1: 20.
The power of God. Isa. 40: 26, 28. Rom. 1: 20.
The glory and handiwork of God. Psa. 19: 1.
The wisdom of God. Psa. 104: 24. Psa. 136: 5.
The goodness of God. Psa. 33: 5.
God as the sole object of worship. Isa. 45: 16, with 18 v. Acts 17: 24, 27.
Glorifies God. Psa 145: 10. Psa. 148: 5.
God to be praised for. Neh. 9: 6. Psa. 136: 3–9.
Leads to confidence. Psa. 124: 8. Psa. 146: 5, 6.
Insignificance of man seen from. Psa. 8: 3, 4. Isa. 40: 12, 17.
Groaneth because of sin. Rom. 8: 22.
ILLUSTRATIVE OF
The new birth. 2 Cor. 5: 17. Eph. 2: 10.
Daily renewal of saints. Psa. 51: 40. Eph. 4: 24.
Renewal of the earth. Isa. 65: 17. 2 Pet. 3: 11, 13.

Creditors.

Defined. Philemon 18 v.
MIGHT DEMAND
Pledges. Deu. 24: 10, 11. Pro. 22: 27.
Security of others. Pro. 6: 1. Pro. 22: 26.
Mortgages on property. Neh. 5: 3.
Bills or promissory notes. Luke 16: 6, 7.
To return before sunset, garments taken in pledge. Exo. 22: 26, 27. Deu. 24: 12, 13. Eze. 18: 7, 12.
PROHIBITED FROM
Taking millstones in pledge. Deu. 24: 6.
Violently selecting pledges. Deu. 24: 10.
Exacting usury from brethren. Exo. 22: 25. Lev. 25: 36, 37.
Exacting debts from brethren during sabbatical year. Deu. 15: 2, 3.
Might take interest from strangers. Deu. 23: 20.
Sometimes entirely remitted debts. Neh. 5: 10–12. Mat. 18: 27. Luke 7: 42.
Often cruel in exacting debts. Neh. 5: 7–9. Job. 24: 3–9. Mat. 18: 28–30.
OFTEN EXACTED DEBTS
By selling the debtor or taking him for a servant. Mat. 18: 25, with Exo. 21: 2.
By selling the debtor's property. Mat. 18: 25.
By selling the debtor's family. 2 Kin. 4: 1. Job 24: 9. Mat. 18: 25.
By imprisonment. Mat. 5: 25, 26. Mat. 18: 34.
From the sureties. Pro. 11: 15. Pro. 22: 26, 27.
Were often defrauded. 1 Sam. 22: 2. Luke 16: 5–7.
ILLUSTRATIVE OF
God's claim upon men. Mat. 5: 25, 26, with Mat. 18: 23, 35. Luke 7: 41, 47.
The demands of the law. Gal. 5: 3.

Daily Sacrifice, The.

Ordained in mount Sinai. Num. 28: 6.
A lamb as a burnt offering morning and evening. Exo. 29: 38, 39. Num. 28: 3, 4.
Doubled on the sabbath. Num. 28: 9, 10.
REQUIRED TO BE
With a meat and drink offering. Exo. 29: 40, 41. Num. 28: 5–8.
Slowly and entirely consumed. Lev. 6: 9–12.
Perpetually observed. Exo. 29: 42. Num. 28: 3, 6.
Peculiarly acceptable. Num. 28: 8. Psa. 141: 2.
Secured God's presence and favor. Exo. 29: 43, 44.
Times of offering, were seasons of prayer. Ezr. 9: 5. Dan. 9: 20, 21, with Acts 3: 1.
Restored after the captivity. Ezr. 3: 3.
The abolition of, foretold. Dan. 9: 26, 27. Dan. 11: 31.
ILLUSTRATIVE OF
Christ. Jno. 1: 29, 36. 1 Pet. 1: 19.
Acceptable prayer. Psa. 141: 2.

Dan, The Tribe of.

Descended from Jacob's fifth son. Gen. 30: 6.
Predictions respecting. Gen. 49: 16 17. Deu. 33: 22.
PERSONS SELECTED FROM,
To number the people. Num. 1: 12.
To spy out the land. Num. 13: 12.
To divide the land. Num. 34: 22.
Strength of, on leaving Egypt. Num. 1: 38, 39.
Led the fourth and last division of Israel. Num. 2: 31. Num. 10: 25.
Encamped north of the tabernacle. Num. 2: 25.
Offering of, at dedication. Num. 7: 66–71.
Families of. Num. 26: 42.
Strength of, entering Canaan. Num. 26: 43.
On Ebal, said amen to the curses. Deu. 27: 13.

Bounds of its inheritance. Jos. 19: 40—46.
A commercial people. Jud. 5 : 17. Eze. 27 : 19.
Restricted to the hills by Amorites. Jud. 1 : 34.
A PART OF
Sent to seek new settlements. Jud. 18 : 1, 2.
Took Laish and called it Dan. Jos. 19 : 47. Jud. 18 : 8—13, 27—29.
Plundered Micah of his idols and his ephod. Jud. 18 : 17—21, 27.
Set up Micah's idols in Dan. Jud. 18 : 30, 31.
Reproved for not aiding against Sisera. Jud. 5 : 17.
Sampson was of. Jud. 13 : 2, 24, 25.
Some of, at coronation of David. 1 Chr. 12 : 35.
Ruler appointed over, by David. 1 Chr. 27 : 22.

Darkness.

Created by God. Psa. 104 : 20. Isa. 45 : 7.
Originally covered the earth. Gen. 1 : 2.
Separated from the light. Gen. 1 : 4.
Called night. Gen. 1 : 5.
Caused by setting of the sun. Gen. 15 : 17. Jno. 6 : 17.
Inexplicable nature of. Job 38 : 19, 20.
Exhibits God's power and greatness. Job 38 : 8, 9.
DEGREES OF, MENTIONED;
Great. Gen. 15 : 12.
That may be felt. Exo. 10 : 21.
Thick. Deu. 5 : 22. Joel 2 : 2.
Gross. Jer. 13 : 16.
Outer or extreme. Mat. 8 : 12.
EFFECTS OF;
Keeps us from seeing objects. Exo. 10 : 23.
Causes us to go astray. Jno. 12 : 35. 1 Jno. 2 : 11.
Causes us to stumble. Isa. 59 : 10.
Often put for night. Psa. 91 : 6.
Called the swaddling band of the sea. Job. 38 : 9.
Cannot hide us from God. Psa. 139 : 11, 12.
THE WICKED
The children of. 1 The. 5 : 5.
Live in. Psa. 107 : 10.
Walk in. Psa. 82 : 5.
Perpetrate their designs in. Job 24 : 16.
Are full of. Mat. 6 : 23.
MIRACULOUS,
On mount Sinai. Exo. 19 : 16, with Heb. 12 : 18.
Over the land of Egypt. Exo. 10 : 21, 22.
At the death of Christ. Mat. 27 : 45.
Before the destruction of Jerusalem. Mat. 24 : 29.
ILLUSTRATIVE OF
Greatness and unsearchableness of God. Exo. 20 : 21. 2 Sam. 22 : 10, 12. 1 Kin. 8 : 12. Psa. 97 : 2.
Abstruse and deep subjects. Job 28 : 3.
Secrecy. Isa. 45 : 19. Mat. 10 : 27.
Ignorance and error. Job 37 : 19. Isa. 60 : 2. Jno. 1 : 5. Jno. 3 : 19. Jno. 12 : 35. Acts 26 : 18.
Anything hateful. Job 3 : 4—9.
A course of sin. Pro. 2 : 13. Eph. 5 : 11.
Heavy afflictions. Job 23 : 17. Psa. 112 : 4. Ecc. 5 : 17. Isa. 5 : 30. Isa. 8 : 22. Isa. 59 : 9.
The power of Satan. Eph. 6 : 12. Col. 1 : 13.
The grave. 1 Sam. 2 : 9. Job 10 : 21, 22.
The punishment of devils and wicked men. Mat, 22 : 13. 2 Pet. 2 : 4, 17. Jude 6, 13 vs.

Day.

The light first called. Gen. 1 : 5.
Natural, from evening to evening. Gen. 1 : 5, &c. Lev. 23 : 32.
Artificial, the time of the sun's continuance above the horizon. Gen. 31 : 39, 40, Neh. 4 : 21, 22.
Prophetical, a year. Eze. 4 : 6. Dan. 12 : 12.
ARTIFICIAL, DIVIDED INTO
Break of. Gen. 32 : 24, 26. So. of Sol. 2 : 17.
Morning. Exo. 29 : 39. 2 Sam. 23 : 4.
Noon. Gen. 43 : 16. Psa. 55 : 17.
Decline of. Jud. 19 : 8, 9. Luke 9 : 12. Luke 24 : 29.
Evening. Gen. 8 : 11. Psa. 104 : 23. Jer. 6 : 4.
Sometimes divided into four parts. Neh. 9 : 3.
Latterly subdivided into twelve hours. Mat. 20 : 3, 5, 6. Jno. 11 : 9.
Time of, ascertained by the dial. 2 Kin. 20 : 11.
Succession of, secured by covenant. Gen. 8 : 22.
Made for the glory of God. Psa. 74 : 16.
Proclaims the glory of God. Psa. 19 : 2.
Under the control of God. Amos 5 : 8. Amos 8 : 9.
A TIME OF JUDGMENT CALLED A DAY OF
Anger. Lam. 2 : 21.
Wrath. Job. 20 : 28. Zep. 1 : 15, 18. Rom. 2 : 5.
Visitation. Mic. 7 : 4.
Destruction. Job 21 : 30.
Darkness. Joel 2 : 2. Zep. 1 : 15.
Trouble. Psa. 102 : 2.

Calamity Deu. 32: 35. Jer. 18: 17.
Adversity. Pro. 24: 10.
Vengeance. Pro. 6: 34. Isa. 61: 2.
Slaughter. Isa. 30: 25. Jer. 12: 3.
Evil. Jer. 17: 17. Amos 6: 3. Eph. 6: 13.
The Lord. Isa. 2: 12. Isa. 13: 6. Zep. 1: 14.

A TIME OF MERCY CALLED A DAY OF
Salvation. 2 Cor. 6: 2.
Redemption. Eph. 4: 30.
Visitation. Jer. 27: 22. 1 Pet. 2: 12.
God's power. Psa. 110: 3.

A TIME OF FESTIVITY CALLED A
Good day. Est. 8: 17. Est. 9: 19.
Day of good tidings. 2 Kin. 7: 9.
Day which the Lord has made. Psa. 118: 24.
Solemn day. Num. 10: 10. Hos. 9: 5.
Day of gladness. Num. 10: 10.

The time for labor. Psa 104: 23. Jno. 9: 4.
Wild beasts hide during. Psa. 104: 22.

ILLUSTRATIVE OF
Time of judgment. 1 Cor. 3: 13, with 1 Cor. 4: 3.
Spiritual light. 1 The. 5: 5, 8. 2 Pet. 1: 19.
The path of the just. Pro. 4: 18.

Dead, The.

They who have departed this life. Gen. 23: 2. Gen. 25: 8. Job 1: 19.

TERMS USED TO EXPRESS;
Corpses. 2 Kin. 19: 35. Nah. 3: 3.
Carcases. Num. 14: 29, 32, 33. 1 Kin. 13: 24.
Those who are not. Mat. 2: 18.
Deceased. Isa. 26: 14. Mat. 22: 25.

CHARACTERIZED BY
Being without the Spirit. Jas. 2: 26.
Being incapable of motion. Mat. 28: 4. Rev. 1: 17.
Ignorance of all human affairs. Ecc. 9: 5.
Absence of all human passions. Ecc. 9: 6.
Inability to glorify God. Psa. 115: 17.

Return not to this life. Job 7: 9, 10. Job 14: 10, 14.
Eyes of, closed by nearest of kin. Gen. 46: 4.
Were washed and laid out. Acts 9: 37.
Were wrapped in linen with spices. Jno. 19: 40.

MOURNING FOR, OFTEN
Very great. Gen. 37: 35. Jer. 31: 15. Mat. 2: 18. Jno. 11: 33.
Loud and clamorous. Jer. 16: 6. Mar. 5: 38.
By hired mourners. Jer. 9: 17, 18. Amos 5: 16.
With plaintive music. Jer. 48: 36. Mat. 9: 23.
Testified by change of apparel. 2 Sam. 14: 2.
Testified by tearing the hair. Jer. 16: 7.
Testified by covering the head. 2 Sam. 19: 4.
Testified by rending the garments. Gen. 37: 34. 2 Sam. 3: 31.
Lasted many days. Gen. 37: 34. Gen. 50: 3, 10.

Regard often shown to the memory of. Ruth 1: 8.
Too soon forgotten. Psa. 31: 12. Ecc. 9: 5.
Heathenish expressions of grief for, forbidden. Lev. 19: 28. Deu. 14: 1, 2.
All offerings to, forbidden. Deu. 26: 14.
Touching of, caused uncleanness. Num. 19: 11, 13, 16. Num. 9: 6, 7.
In a house rendered it unclean. Num. 19: 14, 15.
Even bones of, caused uncleanness. Num. 19: 16. *See* 2 Chr. 34: 5.
A priest not to mourn for, except when near of kin. Lev. 21: 1—3. Eze. 44: 25.
High priest in no case to mourn for. Lev. 21: 10, 11.
Nazarites not to touch or mourn for. Num. 6: 6, 7.
Those defiled by, removed from the camp. Num. 5: 2.
Uncleanness contracted from, removed by the water of separation. Num. 19: 12, 18.

IDOLATERS
Tore themselves for. Jer. 16: 7.
Offered sacrifices for. Psa. 106: 28.
Invoked and consulted. 1 Sam. 28: 7, 8.
Consecrated part of their crops to. Deu. 26: 14.

The Jews looked for a resurrection from. Isa. 26: 19. Acts 24: 15.
Instances of, restored to life before Christ. 1 Kin. 17: 22. 2 Kin. 4: 34—36. 2 Kin. 13: 21.
Instances of, restored by Christ. &c. Mat. 9: 25. Luke 7: 15. Jno. 11: 44. Acts 9: 40. Acts 20: 12.

ILLUSTRATIVE OF
Man's state by nature. 2 Cor. 5: 4. Eph. 2: 1, 5.
A state of deep affiiction, &c. Psa. 88: 5, 6. Psa. 143: 3. Isa. 59: 10.
Freedom from the power of sin. Rom. 6: 2, 8, 11. Col. 3: 3.
Freedom from the law. Rom. 7: 4.
Faith without works. 1 Tim. 5: 6. Jas. 2: 17, 26.
Diviners, &c. Isa. 8: 19.
Impotence. Gen. 20: 3. Rom. 4: 19.

Death, Eternal.

The necessary consequence of sin. Rom. 6: 16, 21. Rom. 8: 13. Jas. 1: 15.

The wages of sin. Rom. 6: 23.
The portion of the wicked. Mat. 25: 41, 46. Rom. 1: 32.
The way to, described. Psa. 9: 17. Mat. 7: 13.
Self-righteousness leads to. Pro. 14: 12.
God alone can inflict. Mat. 10: 28. Jas. 4: 12.
Is described as
- Banishment from God. 2 The. 1: 9.
- Society with the devil, &c. Mat. 25: 41.
- A lake of fire. Rev. 19: 20. Rev. 21: 8.
- The worm that dieth not. Mar. 9: 44.
- Outer darkness. Mat. 25: 30.
- A mist of darkness for ever. 2 Pet. 2: 17.
- Indignation, wrath, &c. Rom. 2: 8, 9.

Is called
- Destruction. Rom. 9: 22. 2 The. 1: 9.
- Perishing. 2 Pet. 2: 12.
- The wrath to come. 1 The. 1: 10.
- The second death. Rev. 2: 11.
- A resurrection to damnation. Jno. 5: 29.
- A resurrection to shame, &c. Dan. 12: 2.
- Damnation of hell. Mat. 23: 33.
- Everlasting punishment. Mat. 25: 46.

Shall be inflicted by Christ. Mat. 25: 31, 41. 2 The. 1: 7, 8.
Christ, the only way of escape from. Jno. 3: 16. Jno. 8: 51. Acts 4: 12.
Saints shall escape. Rev. 2: 11. Rev. 20: 6.
Strive to preserve others from. Jas. 5: 20.
Illustrated. Luke 16: 23—26.

Death, Natural.

By Adam. Gen. 3: 19. 1 Cor. 15: 21, 22.
Consequence of sin. Gen. 2: 17. Rom. 5: 12.
Lot of all. Ecc. 8: 8. Heb. 9: 27.
Ordered by God. Deu. 32: 39. Job 14: 5.
Puts an end to earthly projects. Ecc. 9: 10.
Strips of earthly possessions. Job 1: 21. 1 Tim. 6: 7.
Levels all ranks. Job 3: 17—19.
Conquered by Christ. Rom. 6: 9. Rev. 1: 18.
Abolished by Christ. 2 Tim. 1: 10.
Shall finally be destroyed by Christ. Hos. 13: 14. 1 Cor. 15: 26.
Christ delivers from the fear of. Heb. 2: 15.
Regard, as at hand. Job 14: 1, 2. Psa. 39: 4, 5. Psa. 90: 9. 1 Pet. 1: 24.
Prepare for. 2 Kin. 20: 1.
Pray to be prepared for. Psa. 39: 4, 13. Psa. 90: 12.
Consideration of, a motive to diligence. Ecc. 9: 10. Jno. 9: 4.
When averted for a season, is a motive to increased devotedness. Psa. 56: 12, 13. Psa. 118: 17. Isa. 38: 18, 20.
Enoch and Elijah were exempted from. Gen. 5: 24, with Heb. 11: 5. 2 Kin. 2: 11.
All shall be raised from. Acts 24: 15.
None subject to, in heaven. Luke 20: 36. Rev. 21: 4.
Illustrates the change produced in conversion. Rom. 6: 2. Col. 2: 20.
Is described as
- A sleep. Deu. 31: 16. Jno. 11: 11.
- The earthly house of this tabernacle being dissolved. 2 Cor. 5: 1.
- Putting off this tabernacle. 2 Pet. 1: 14.
- God requiring the soul. Luke 12: 20.
- Going the way whence there is no return. Job 16: 22.
- Gathering to our people. Gen. 49: 33.
- Going down into silence. Psa. 115: 17.
- Yielding up the ghost. Acts 5: 10.
- Returning to dust. Gen. 3: 19. Psa. 104: 29.
- Being cut down. Job 14: 2.
- Fleeing as a shadow. Job 14: 2.
- Departing. Phi. 1: 23.

Death of Christ, The.

Foretold. Isa. 53: 8. Dan. 9: 26. Zec. 13: 7.
Appointed by God. Isa. 53: 6, 10. Acts 2: 23.
Necessary for the redemption of man. Luke 24: 46. Acts 17: 3.
Acceptable, as a sacrifice to God. Mat. 20: 28. Eph. 5: 2. 1 The. 5: 10.
Was voluntary. Isa. 53: 12. Mat 26: 53. Jno. 10: 17, 18.
Was undeserved. Isa. 53: 9.
Mode of
- Foretold by Christ. Mat. 20: 18, 19. Jno. 12: 32, 33.
- Prefigured. Num. 21: 8, with Jno. 3: 14.
- Ignominious. Heb. 12: 2.
- Accursed. Gal. 3: 13.
- Exhibited His humility. Phi. 2: 8.
- A stumbling block to Jews. 1 Cor. 1: 23.
- Foolishness to Gentiles. 1 Cor. 1: 18, 23.

Demanded by the Jews. Mat. 27: 22, 23.
Inflicted by the Gentiles. Mat. 27: 26—35.

In the company of malefactors. Isa. 53: 12, with Mat. 27: 38.
Accompanied by preternatural signs. Mat. 27: 45, 51—53.
Emblematical of the death unto sin. Rom. 6: 3—8. Gal. 2: 20.
Commemorated in the sacrament of the Lord's Supper. Luke 22: 19, 20. 1 Cor. 11: 26—29.

Death of Saints, The.

A sleep in Christ. 1 Cor. 15: 18. 1 The. 4: 14.
Is blessed. Rev. 14: 13.
Is gain. Phi. 1: 21.
Is FULL OF
  Faith. Heb. 11: 13.
  Peace. Isa. 57: 2.
  Hope. Pro. 14: 32.
Sometimes desired. Luke 2: 29.
Waited for. Job 14: 14.
Met with resignation. Gen. 50: 24. Jos. 23: 14. 1 Kin. 2: 2.
Met without fear. 1 Cor. 15: 55.
Precious in God's sight. Psa. 116: 15.
God preserves them unto. Psa. 48: 14.
God is with them in. Psa. 23: 4.
Removes from coming evil. 2 Kin. 22: 20. Isa. 57: 1.
LEADS TO
  Rest. Job 3: 17. 2 The. 1: 7.
  Comfort. Luke 16: 25.
  Christ's presence. 2 Cor. 5: 8. Phi. 1: 23.
  A crown of life. 2 Tim. 4: 8. Rev. 2: 10.
  A joyful resurrection. Isa. 26: 19. Dan. 12: 2.
Disregarded by the wicked. Isa. 57: 1.
Survivors consoled for. 1 The. 4: 13—18.
The wicked wish theirs to resemble. Num. 23: 10.
Illustrated. Luke 16: 22.
Exemplified. *Abraham*, Gen. 25: 8. *Isaac*, Gen. 35: 29. *Jacob*, Gen. 49: 33. *Aaron*, Num. 20: 28. *Moses*, Deu. 34: 5. *Joshua*, Jos. 24: 29. *Elisha*, 2 Kin. 13: 14, 20. *One thief*, Luke 23: 43. *Dorcas*, Acts 9: 37.

Death of the Wicked, The.

Is in their sins. Eze. 3: 19. Jno. 8: 21.
Is without hope. Pro 11: 7.
Sometimes without fear. Jer. 34: 5, with 2 Chr. 36: 11—13.
Frequently sudden and unexpected. Job 21: 13, 23. Job 27: 21. Pro. 29: 1.
Frequently marked by terror. Job 18: 11—15. Job 27: 19—21. Psa. 73: 19.
Punishment follows. Isa. 14: 9. Acts 1: 25.
The remembrance of them perishes in. Job 18: 17. Psa. 34: 16. Pro. 10: 7.
God has no pleasure in. Eze. 18: 23, 32.
Like the death of beasts. Psa. 49: 14.
Illustrated. Luke 12: 20. Luke 16: 22, 23.
Exemplified. *Korah, &c.*, Num. 16: 32. *Absalom*, 2 Sam. 18: 9, 10. *Ahab*, 1 Kin. 22: 34. *Jezebel*, 2 Kin. 9: 33. *Athaliah*, 2 Chr. 23: 15. *Haman*, Est. 7: 10. *Belshazzar*, Dan. 5: 30. *Judas*, Mat. 27: 5, with Acts 1: 18. *Ananias, &c.*, Acts 5: 5, 9, 10. *Herod*, Acts 12: 23.

Death, Spiritual.

Alienation from God is. Eph. 4: 18.
Carnal-mindedness is. Rom. 8: 6.
Walking in trespasses and sins is. Eph. 2: 1. Col. 2: 13.
Spiritual ignorance is. Isa. 9: 2. Mat. 4: 16. Luke 1: 79. Eph. 4: 18.
Unbelief is. Jno. 3: 36. 1 Jno. 5: 12.
Living in pleasure is. 1 Tim. 5: 6.
Hypocrisy is. Rev. 3: 1, 2.
Is a consequence of the fall. Rom. 5: 15.
Is the state of all men by nature. Rom. 6: 13. Rom. 8: 6.
The fruits of, are dead works. Heb. 6: 1. Heb. 9: 14.
A call to arise from. Eph. 5: 14.
Deliverance from, is through Christ. Jno. 5: 24, 25. Eph. 2: 5. 1 Jno. 5: 12.
Saints are raised from. Rom. 6: 13.
Love of the brethren, a proof of being raised from. 1 Jno. 3: 14.
Illustrated. Eze. 37: 2, 3. Luke 15: 24.

Deceit.

Is falsehood. Psa. 119: 118.
The tongue, the instrument of. Rom. 3: 13.
Comes from the heart. Mar. 7: 22.
Characteristic of the heart. Jer. 17: 9.
God abhors. Psa. 5: 6.
Forbidden. Pro. 24: 28. 1 Pet. 3: 10.
Christ was perfectly free from. Isa. 53: 9, with 1 Pet. 2: 22.
SAINTS
  Free from. Psa. 24: 4. Zep. 3: 13. Rev. 14: 5.
  Purpose against. Job 27: 4.
  Avoid. Job 31: 5.
  Shun those addicted to. Psa. 101: 7.
  Pray for deliverance from those who use. Psa. 43: 1. Psa. 120: 2.
  Delivered from those who use. Psa. 72: 14.
  Should beware of those who teach. Eph. 5: 6. Col. 2: 8.

Should lay aside, in seeking truth. 1 Pet. 2: 1.
Ministers should lay aside. 2 Cor. 4: 2. 1 The. 2: 3.
THE WICKED
Are full of. Rom. 1: 29.
Devise. Psa. 35: 20. Psa. 38: 12. Pro. 12: 5.
Utter. Psa. 10: 7. Psa. 36: 3
Work. Pro. 11: 18.
Increase in. 2 Tim. 3: 13.
Use, to each other. Jer. 9: 5.
Use, to themselves. Jer. 37: 9. Oba. 3: 7.
Delight in. Pro. 20: 17.
FALSE TEACHERS
Are workers of. 2 Cor. 11: 13.
Preach. Jer. 14: 14. Jer. 23: 26.
Impose on others by. Rom. 16: 18. Eph. 4: 14.
Sport themselves with. 2 Pet. 2: 13.
Hypocrites devise. Job 15: 35.
Hypocrites practice. Hos. 11: 12.
False witnesses use. Pro. 12: 17. Pro. 14: 5.
A characteristic of Antichrist. 2 Jno. 7.
A characteristic of the Apostacy. 2 The. 2: 10.
EVIL OF
Keeps from knowledge of God. Jer. 9: 6.
Keeps from turning to God. Jer. 8: 5.
Leads to pride and oppression. Jer. 5: 27, 28.
Leads to lying. Pro. 14: 25.
Often accompanied by fraud and injustice. Psa. 10: 7. Psa. 43: 1.
Hatred often concealed by. Pro. 26: 24—28.
The folly of fools is. Pro. 14: 8.
The kisses of an enemy are. Pro. 27: 6.
Blessedness of being free from. Psa. 24: 4, 5. Psa. 32: 2.
Punishment of. Psa. 55: 23. Jer. 9: 7—9.
Exemplified. *The devil*, Gen. 3: 1, 4, 5, with Jno. 8: 44. *Rebecca and Jacob*, Gen. 27: 9, 19. *Laban*, Gen. 31: 7. *Joseph's brethren*, Gen. 37: 31, 32. *Pharaoh*, Exo. 8: 29. *David*, 1 Sam. 21: 13. *Job's friends*, Job 6: 15. *Doeg*. Psa. 52: 2, compared with the title. *Herod*, Mat. 2: 8. *Pharisees*, Mat. 22: 16. *Chief Priests*, Mar. 14: 1.

Decision.

Necessary to the service of God. Luke 9: 62.
Exhortations to. Jos. 24: 14, 15.
EXHIBITED IN
Seeking God with the heart. 2 Chr. 15: 12.
Keeping the commandments of God. Neh. 10: 29.
Being on the Lord's side. Exo. 32: 26.
Following God fully. Num. 14: 24. Num. 32: 12. Jos. 14: 8.
Serving God. Isa. 56: 6.
Loving God perfectly. Deu. 6: 5.
Blessedness of. Jos. 1: 7.
OPPOSED TO
A divided service. Mat. 6: 24.
Double-mindedness Jas. 1: 8.
Halting between two opinions. 1 Kin. 18: 21.
Turning to the right or left. Deu. 5: 32.
Not setting the heart aright. Psa. 78: 8, 37.
Exemplified. *Moses*, Exo. 32: 26. *Caleb*, Num. 13: 30. *Joshua*, Jos. 24: 15. *Ruth*, Ruth 1: 16. *Asa*, 2 Chr. 15: 8. *David*, Psa. 17: 3. *Peter*, Jno. 6: 68. *Paul*, Acts 21: 13. *Abraham*, Heb. 11: 8.

Dedication.

Consecration of a place of worship. 2 Chr. 2: 4.
Solemn confirmation of a covenant. Heb. 9: 18.
Devoting any thing to sacred uses. 1 Chr. 28: 12.
SUBJECTS OF;
Tabernacle. Num. 7 ch.
Temple of Solomon. 1 Kin. 8: 1—63. 2 Chr. 7: 5.
Second temple. Ezr. 6: 16, 17.
Persons. Exo. 22: 29. 1 Sam. 1: 11.
Property. Lev. 27: 28. Mat. 15: 5.
Spoils of war. 2 Sam. 8: 11. 1 Chr. 18: 11.
Tribute from foreigners. 2 Sam 8: 10, 11.
Walls of cities. Neh. 12: 27.
Houses when built. Deu. 20: 5. Psa. 30, *title*.
By idolaters in setting up idols. Dan. 3: 2, 3.
THINGS DEDICATED TO GOD:
Esteemed holy. Lev. 27: 28. 2 Kin. 12: 18.
Placed with the treasures of the Lord's house. 1 Kin. 7: 51. 2 Chr. 5: 1.
Special chambers prepared for. 2 Chr. 31: 11, 12.
Levites placed over. 1 Chr. 26: 20, 26. 2 Chr. 31: 12.
Applied to the repair and maintenance of the temple. 2 Kin. 12: 4, 5. 1 Chr. 26: 27.
For support of priests. Num. 18: 14. Eze. 44: 29.
Given to propitiate enemies. 2 Kin. 12: 17, 18.

Law respecting the release of. Lev. 27 ch.
Of property often perverted. Mar. 7: 9—13.
Illustrative of devotedness to God. Psa. 119: 38.

Defilement.

Forbidden to the Jews. Lev. 11: 44, 45.
THINGS LIABLE TO CEREMONIAL;
The person. Lev. 5: 3.
Garments. Lev. 13: 59.
Furniture, &c. Lev. 15: 9, 10. Num. 19: 14, 15.
Houses. Lev. 14: 44.
The land. Lev. 18: 25. Deu. 21: 23.
The sanctuary. Lev. 20: 3. Zep. 3: 4.
CEREMONIAL, CAUSED BY
Eating unclean things. Lev. 11: 8. Acts 10: 11, 14.
Eating things that died. Lev. 17: 15.
Touching a dead body or a bone. Num. 9: 6, 7. Num. 19: 11, 16.
Touching a grave. Num. 19: 16.
Touching a dead beast. Lev. 5: 2. Lev. 11: 24—28.
Being alone with a dead body. Num. 19: 14.
Mourning for the dead. Lev. 21: 1—3.
Having a leprosy. Lev. 13: 3, 11. Num. 5: 2, 3.
Having an issue, &c. Lev. 15: 2. Num. 5: 2.
Touching anything defiled by an issue, &c. Lev. 15: 5—11.
Going into a leprous house. Lev. 14: 46.
Sacrificing the red heifer. Num. 19: 7
Burning the red heifer. Num. 19: 8.
Gathering ashes of red heifer. Num. 19: 10.
Touching an unclean person. Num. 19: 22.
Child-bearing. Lev. 12: 2.
Causes of, improperly enlarged by tradition. Mar. 7: 2, with Mat. 15: 20.
MORAL, CAUSED BY
Following the sins of the heathen. Lev. 18: 24.
Seeking after wizards. Lev. 19: 31.
Giving children to Molech. Lev. 20: 3.
Making and serving idols. Eze. 20: 17, 18. Eze. 22: 3, 4. Eze. 23: 7.
Blood shedding. Isa. 59: 3.
Moral, punished. Lev. 18: 24, 25, 28, 29.
Those under, removed from the camp. Num. 5: 3, 4. Deu. 23: 14.
PRIESTS
To decide in all cases of. Lev. 10: 10. Lev. 13: 3.
Specially required to avoid. Lev. 21: 1—6, 11, 12.
Not to eat holy things while under. Lev. 22: 2, 4—6.
Punished for eating of the holy things while under. Lev. 22: 3.
Cleansed by legal ablutions. Num. 19: 18, 19. Heb. 9: 13.
Neglecting purification from, punished by cutting off. Num. 19: 13, 20.
Ceremonial, abolished under the gospel. Acts 10: 15. Rom. 14: 14. Col. 2: 20—22.
ILLUSTRATIVE
Of sin. Mat. 15: 11, 18. Jude 8 v.
Of unholy doctrines. 1 Cor. 3: 16, 17.

Delighting in God.

Commanded. Psa. 37: 4.
Reconciliation leads to. Job 22: 21, 26.
Observing the sabbath leads to. Isa. 58: 13, 14.
SAINTS' EXPERIENCE, IN
Communion with God. So. of Sol. 2: 3.
The law of God. Psa. 1: 2. Psa. 119: 24, 35.
The goodness of God. Neh. 9: 25.
The comforts of God. Psa. 94: 19.
HYPOCRITES
Pretend to. Isa. 58: 2.
In heart despise. Job 27: 10. Jer. 6: 10.
Promises to. Psa. 37: 4.
Blessedness of. Psa. 112: 1.

Deluge, The.

Sent as a punishment for the extreme wickedness of man. Gen. 6: 5—7, 11—13, 17.
CALLED THE
Flood. Gen. 9: 28.
Waters of Noah. Isa. 54: 9.
Noah forewarned of. Gen. 6: 13. Heb. 11: 7.
Long-suffering of God exhibited in deferring. Gen. 6: 3, with 1 Pet. 3: 20.
The wicked warned of. 1 Pet. 3: 19, 20. 2 Pet. 2: 5.
Noah, &c., saved from. Gen. 6: 18—22. Gen. 7: 13, 14.
Date of its commencement. Gen. 7: 11.
Came suddenly and unexpectedly. Mat. 24: 38, 39.
PRODUCED BY
Forty days' incessant rain. Gen. 7: 4, 12, 17.

Opening up of the fountains of the great deep. Gen. 7: 11.
Increased gradually. Gen. 7: 17, 18.
Extreme height of. Gen. 7: 19, 20.
Time of its increase and prevailing. Gen. 7: 24.
Causes of its abatement. Gen. 8: 1, 2.
Decrease of, gradual. Gen. 8: 3, 5.
Date of its complete removal. Gen. 8: 13.
Complete destruction effected by. Gen. 7: 23.
Face of the earth changed by. 2 Pet. 3: 5, 6.
Traditional notice of. Job 22: 15—17.
THAT IT SHALL NEVER AGAIN OCCUR
Promised. Gen. 8: 21, 22.
Confirmed by covenant. Gen. 9: 9—11.
The rainbow a token. Gen. 9: 12—17.
A pledge of God's faithfulness. Isa. 54: 9, 10.
ILLUSTRATIVE
Of the destruction of sinners. Psa. 32: 6. Isa. 28: 2, 18.
Of baptism. 1 Pet. 3: 20, 21.
(Unexpectedness of,) of suddenness of Christ's coming. Mat. 24: 36—39. Luke 17: 26, 27—30.

Denial of Christ.

In doctrine. Mar. 8: 38. 2 Tim. 1: 8.
In practice. Phi. 3: 18, 10. Tit. 1: 16.
A characteristic of false teachers. 2 Pet. 2: 1. Jude 4.
Is the spirit of Antichrist. 1 Jno. 2: 22, 23. 1 Jno. 4: 3.
Christ will deny those guilty of. Mat. 10: 33. 2 Tim. 2: 12.
Leads to destruction. 2 Pet. 2: 1. Jude 4, 15.
Exemplified. *Peter*, Mat. 26: 69—75. *The Jews*, Jno. 18: 40. Acts 3: 13, 14.

Desert, Journey of Israel through the.

Date of its commencement. Exo. 12: 41, 42.
Their number commencing. Exo. 12: 37.
Their healthy state commencing. Psa. 105: 37.
A mixed multitude accompanied them in. Exo. 12: 38. Num. 11: 4.
Commenced in haste. Exo. 12: 39.
Conducted with regularity. Exo. 13: 18.
Under Moses as leader. Exo. 3: 10—12, with Acts 7: 36, 38.
By a circuitous route. Exo. 13: 17, 18.
Order of marching during. Num. 10: 14—28.
Order of encamping during. Num. 2 ch.
Difficulty and danger of. Deu. 8: 15.
CONTINUED FORTY YEARS
As a punishment. Num. 14: 33, 34.
To prove and humble them, &c Deu. 8: 2.
To teach them to live on God's word. Deu. 8: 3.
Under God's guidance. Exo. 13: 21, 22. Exo. 15: 13. Neh. 9: 12. Psa. 78: 52. Isa. 63: 11—14.
Under God's protection. Exo. 14: 19, 20, with Psa. 105: 39. Exo. 23: 20, with Psa. 78: 53.
With miraculous provision. Exo. 16: 35. Deu. 8: 3.
Their clothing preserved during. Deu. 8: 4. Deu. 29: 5. Neh. 9: 21.
Worship of God celebrated during, Exo. 24: 5—8. Exo. 29: 38—42. Exo. 40: 24—29.
Justice administered during. Exo. 18: 13, 26.
Circumcision omitted during. Jos. 5: 5.
Caused universal terror and dismay. Exo. 15: 14—16. Num. 22: 3, 4.
Obstructed, &c. by the surrounding nations. Exo. 17: 8. Num. 20: 21.
Territory acquired during. Deu. 29: 7, 8.
Marked by constant murmurings and rebellions. Psa. 78: 40. Psa. 95: 10. Psa. 106: 7—39.
Constant goodness and mercy of God to them during. Psa. 106: 10, 43—46. Psa. 107: 6, 13.
Commenced from Rameses in Egypt. Exo. 12: 37.
TO SUCCOTH. Exo. 12: 37. Num. 33: 5.
TO ETHAM. Exo. 13: 20. Num. 33: 6.
BETWEEN BAALZEPHON AND PIHAHIROTH. Exo. 14: 2. Num. 33: 7.
Overtaken by Pharaoh. Exo. 14: 9.
Exhorted to look to God. Exo. 14: 13, 14.
The cloud removed to the rear. Exo. 14: 19, 20.
Red Sea divided. Exo. 14: 16, 21.
THROUGH THE RED SEA. Exo. 14: 22, 29.
Faith exhibited in passing. Heb. 11: 29.
Pharaoh and his host destroyed. Exo. 14: 23—28. Psa. 106: 11.
Israel's song of praise. Exo. 15: 1—21. Psa. 106: 12.
THROUGH THE WILDERNESS OF SHUR OR ETHAM. Exo. 15: 22. Num. 33: 8.
TO MARAH. Exo. 15: 23. Num. 33: 8.
Murmuring of the people on account of bitter water. Exo. 15: 24.
Water sweetened. Exo. 15: 25.
To ELIM. Exo. 15: 27. Num. 33: 9.
BY THE RED SEA. Num. 33: 10.
THROUGH THE WILDERNESS OF SIN.

Exo. 16:1. Num. 33:11.
Murmuring for bread. Exo. 16:2, 3.
Quails given for one night. Exo. 16:8, 12, 13.
Manna sent. Exo. 16:4, 8, 16—31.
To DOPHKAH. Num. 33:12.
To ALUSH. Num. 33:13.
To REPHIDIM. Exo. 17:1. Num. 33:14.
Murmuring for water. Exo. 17:2, 3.
Water brought from the rock. Exo. 17:5, 6.
Called Massah and Meribah. Exo. 17:7.
Amalek opposes Israel. Exo. 17:8.
Amalek overcome. Exo. 17:9—13.
To MOUNT SINAI. Exo. 19:1, 2. Num. 33:15.
Jethro's visit. Exo. 18:1—6.
Judges appointed. Exo. 18:14—26. Deu. 1:9—15.
Moral law given. Exo. 19:3. Exo. 20 ch.
Covenant made. Exo. 24:3—8.
Moral law written on tables. Exo. 31:18.
Order for making the tabernacle, &c. Exo. 24 ch. to Exo. 27 ch.
Tribe of Levi taken instead of the first-born. Num. 3:11—13.
Aaron and his sons selected for priesthood. Exo. 28 ch. Exo. 29 ch. Num. 3:1—3, 10.
Levites set apart. Num. 3:5—9.
Golden calf made. Exo. 32:1, 4.
Tables of testimony broken. Exo. 32:19.
People punished for idolatry. Exo. 32:25—29, 35.
God's glory shown to Moses. Exo. 33:18—23. Exo. 34:5—8.
The tables of testimony renewed. Exo. 34:1—4, 27—29. Deu. 10:1—5.
Tabernacle first set up. Exo. 40 ch.
Nadab and Abihu destroyed for offering strange fire. Lev. 10:1, 2. Num. 3, 4.
Passover first commemorated. Num. 9:1—5.
Second numbering of the people. Num. 1:1—46, with Exo. 38:25, 26.
To KIBROTH-HATTAAVAH. Num. 33:16.
Complaining punished by fire. Num. 11:1—3.
Called Taberah. Num. 11:3.
Murmuring of the mixed multitude and of Israel, for flesh. Num. 11:4—9.
Flesh promised. Num. 11: 10—15, 18—23.
Seventy elders appointed to assist Moses. Num. 11:16, 17, 24—30.
Quails sent for a month. Num 11:19, 20, 31, 32.
Their murmuring punished. Num. 11:33. Psa. 78:30, 31.
Why called Kibroth-hattaavah. Num. 11:34.
To HAZEROTH. Num. 11:35. Num. 33:17.
Aaron and Miriam envy Moses. Num. 12:1, 2.
Miriam punished by leprosy. Num. 12:10.
Delayed seven days for Miriam. Num. 12:14, 15.
To KADESH-BARNEA IN WILDERNESS OF RITHMAH OR PARAN. Deu. 1:19, and Num 32:8, with Num. 12:16, and Num. 33:18.
The people anxious to have the land of Canaan searched. Deu. 1:22.
Moses commanded to send spies. Num. 13:1, 2.
Persons selected as spies. Num. 13:3—16.
Spies sent. Jos. 14:7, with Num. 13:17—20.
Spies bring back evil report. Num. 13:26—33.
The people terrified and rebel. Num. 14:1—4.
Punishment for rebellion. Num. 14:26, 35. Num. 32:11—13. Deu. 1:35, 36, 40.
Guilty spies slain by plague. Num. 14:36, 37.
People smitten by Amalek for going up without the Lord. Num. 14:40—45. Deu. 1:41—44.
RETURNED BY THE WAY TO THE RED SEA. Num. 14:25. Deu. 1:40. Deu. 2:1.
Sabbath breaker stoned. Num. 15:32—26.
Rebellion of Korah. Num. 16:1—19.
Korah, &c. punished. Num. 16:30—35.
Plague sent. Num. 16:41—46.
Plague stayed. Num. 16:47—50.
God's choice of Aaron confirmed. Num. 17 ch.
To RIMMON-PAREZ. Num. 33:19.
To LIBNAH OR LABAN. Num. 33:20. Deu. 1:1.
To RISSAH. Num. 33:21.
To KEHELATHAH. Num. 33:22.
To MOUNT SHAPHER. Num. 33:23.
To HARADAH. Num. 33:24.
To MAKHELOTH. Num. 33:25.
To TAHATH. Num. 33:26.
To TARAH. Num. 33:27.
To MITHCAH. Num. 33:28.
To HASHMONAH. Num. 33:29.
To MOSEROTH OR MOSERA. Num. 33 30.
To BENE-JAAKAN. Num. 33:31.
To HORHAGIDGAD OR GUDGODAH. Num. 33:32. Deu. 10:7.
To JOTBATHAH OR LAND OF RIVERS. Num. 33:33. Deu. 10:7.
Several of these stations probably revisited. Deu. 10:6, 7, with Num. 33:30—32.

To Ebronah. Num. 33:34.
To Ezion-gaber. Num. 33:35.
To Kadesh in the wilderness of Zin. Num. 20:1. Num. 33:36. Jud. 11:16.
Miriam dies and is buried. Num. 20:1.
Second murmuring for water. Num. 20:2—6.
Moses striking the rock instead of speaking to it, disobeys God. Num. 20:7—11.
Moses and Aaron punished. Num. 20:12.
Called Meribah to commemorate the murmuring. Num. 20:13. Num. 27:14.
Orders given respecting Edom. Deu. 2:3—6.
The king of Edom refuses a passage. Num. 20:14—21. Jud. 11:17.
To Mount Hor. Num. 20:22. Num. 33:37.
Aaron dies. Num. 20:28, 29. Num. 33:38, 39.
Arad conquered. Num. 21:1—3. Num. 33:40.
Called Hormah. Num. 21:2, 3.
To Zalmonah. Num. 33:41.
Murmuring of the people. Num. 21:4, 5.
Fiery serpents sent. Num. 21:6.
Brazen serpent raised up. Num. 21:7—9.
To Punon. Num. 33:42.
To Oboth. Num. 21:10. Num. 33:43.
To Ije-abarim before Moab. Num. 21:11. Num. 33:44.
Orders given respecting Moab. Deu. 2:8, 9.
To Zared or Dibon-gad. Num. 21:12. Num. 33:45.
To Almon-Diblathaim. Num. 33:46.
Across the brook Zered. Deu. 2:13.
Time occupied in going from Kadesh-barnea to this station. Deu. 2:14.
Order to pass through Ar. Deu. 2:18.
Orders given respecting Ammon. Deu. 2:19.
Across the Arnon. Num. 21:13—15. Deu. 2:24.
To Beer or the Well. Num. 21:16.
To Mattanah. Num. 21:18.
To Nahaliel. Num. 21:19.
To Bamoth. Num. 21:19.
To the Mountains of Abarim. Num. 21:20. Num. 33:47.
The Amorites refuse a passage to Israel. Num. 21:21—23. Deu. 2:26—30.
Sihon conquered. Num. 21:23—32. Deu. 2:32—36.
Og conquered. Num. 21:33—35. Deu. 3:1—11.
Reubenites, &c. obtained the land taken from the Amorites. Num. 32 ch. Deu. 3:12—17.
Return to the plains of Moab. Num. 22:1. Num. 33:48, 49.
Balak sends for Balaam. Num. 22:5, 6, 15—17.
Balaam not permitted to curse Israel. Num. 22:9—41. Num. 23 ch. Num. 24 ch.
Israel seduced to idolatry, &c. by advice of Balaam. Num. 25:1—3. Rev. 2:14.
Israel punished. Num. 25:5, 9.
Third numbering. Num. 26:1—62.
All formerly numbered over twenty years old, except Caleb and Joshua, dead. Num. 26:63—65, with Num. 14:29.
The law of female inheritance settled. Num. 27:1—11, with Num. 36:1—9.
Appointment of Joshua. Num. 27:15—23.
Midianites destroyed and Balaam slain. Num. 31 ch. with Num. 25:17, 18.
The law rehearsed. Deu. 1:3.
The law written by Moses. Deu. 31:9.
Moses beholds Canaan. Deu. 34:1—4.
Moses dies and is buried. Deu. 34:5, 6.
Joshua ordered to cross Jordan. Jos. 1:2.
Two spies sent to Jerico. Jos. 2:1.
Across the river Jordan. Jos. 4:10.
Illustrative of the pilgrimage of the church. So. of Sol. 8:5. 1 Pet. 1:17.

Deserts.

Vast barren plains. Exo. 5:3. Jno. 6:13.
Uninhabited places. Mat. 14:15. Mar. 6:31.
Described as
Uninhabited and lonesome. Jer. 2:6.
Uncultivated. Num. 20:5. Jer. 2:2.
Desolate. Eze. 6:14.
Dry and without water. Exo. 17:1. Deu. 8:15.
Trackless. Isa. 43:19.
Great and terrible. Deu. 1:19.
Waste and howling. Deu. 32:10.
Infested with wild beasts. Isa. 13:21. Mar. 1:13.
Infested with serpents. Deu. 8:15.
Infested with robbers. Jer. 3:2. Lam. 4:19.
Danger of travelling in. Exo. 14:3. 2 Cor. 11:26.
Guides required in. Num. 10:31. Deu. 32:10.

PHENOMENA OF, ALLUDED TO;
- Mirage or deceptive appearance of water. Jer. 15: 18. (*marg.*)
- Simoon or deadly wind. 2 Kin. 19: 7. Jer. 4: 11.
- Tornadoes or whirlwinds. Isa. 21: 1.
- Clouds of sand and dust. Deu. 28: 24. Jer. 4: 12, 13.

MENTIONED IN SCRIPTURE;
- Arabian or great desert. Exo. 23: 31.
- Bethaven. Jos. 18: 12.
- Beersheba. Gen. 21: 14. 1 Kin. 19: 3, 4.
- Damascus. 1 Kin. 19: 15.
- Edom. 2 Kin. 3: 8.
- Engedi. 1 Sam. 24: 1.
- Gibeon. 2 Sam. 2: 24.
- Judea. Mat. 3: 1.
- Jeruel. 2 Chr. 20: 16.
- Kedemoth. Deu. 2: 26.
- Kadesh. Psa. 29: 8.
- Maon. 1 Sam. 23: 24, 25.
- Paran. Gen. 21: 21. Num. 10: 12.
- Shur. Gen. 16: 7. Exo. 15: 22.
- Sin. Exo. 16: 1.
- Sinai. Exo. 19: 1, 2. Num. 33: 16.
- Ziph. 1 Sam. 23: 14, 15.
- Zin. Num. 20: 1. Num. 27: 14.
- Of the Red Sea. Exo. 13: 18.
- Near Gaza. Acts 8: 26.

Heath often found in. Jer. 17: 6.
Parts of, afforded pasture. Gen. 36: 24. Exo. 3: 1.
Inhabited by wandering tribes. Gen. 21: 20, 21. Psa. 72: 9. Jer. 25: 24.
The persecuted fled to 1 Sam. 23: 14 Heb. 11: 38.
The disaffected fled to. 1 Sam. 22: 2. Acts 21: 38.

ILLUSTRATIVE OF
- Barrenness. Psa. 106: 9. Psa. 107: 33, 35.
- Those deprived of all blessings. Hos. 2: 3.
- The world. So. of Sol. 3: 6. So. of Sol. 8: 5.
- The Gentiles. Isa. 35: 1, 6. Isa. 41: 19.
- What affords no support. Jer. 2: 31.
- Desolation by armies. Jer. 12: 10—13. Jer. 50: 12.

Despair.

Produced in the wicked by divine judgments. Deu. 28: 34, 67. Rev. 9: 6. Rev. 16: 10.

LEADS TO
- Continuing in sin. Jer. 2: 25. Jer. 18: 12.
- Blasphemy. Isa. 8: 21. Rev. 16: 10, 11.

Shall seize upon the wicked at the appearing of Christ. Rev. 6: 16.
Saints sometimes tempted to. Job 7: 6. Lam. 3: 18.
Saints enabled to overcome. 2 Cor. 4: 8, 9.
Trust in God, a preservative against. Psa. 42: 5, 11.
Exemplified. *Cain*, Gen. 4: 13, 14. *Ahithophel*, 2 Sam. 17: 23. *Judas*, Mat. 27: 5.

Devil, The.

Sinned against God. 2 Pet. 2: 4. 1 Jno. 3: 8.
Cast out of heaven. Luke 10: 18.
Cast down to hell. 2 Pet. 2: 4. Jude 6.
The author of the fall. Gen. 3: 1, 6, 14, 24.
Tempted Christ. Mat. 4: 3—10.
Perverts the Scriptures. Mat. 4: 6, with Psa. 91: 11, 12.
Opposes God's work. Zec. 3: 1. 1 The. 2: 18.
Hinders the gospel. Mat. 13: 19. 2 Cor. 4: 4.
Works lying wonders. 2 The. 2: 9. Rev. 16: 14.
Assumes the form of an angel of light. 2 Cor. 11: 14.

THE WICKED
- Are the children of. Mat. 13: 38. Acts 13: 10. 1 Jno. 3: 10.
- Turn aside after. 1 Tim. 5: 15.
- Do the lusts of. Jno. 8: 44.
- Possessed by. Luke 22: 3. Acts 5: 3. Eph. 2: 2.
- Blinded by. 2 Cor. 4: 4.
- Deceived by. 1 Kin. 22: 21, 22. Rev. 20: 7, 8.
- Ensnared by. 1 Tim. 3: 7. 2 Tim. 2: 26
- Troubled by. 1 Sam. 16: 14.
- Punished, together with. Mat. 25: 41.

SAINTS
- Afflicted by, only as God permits. Job 1: 12. Job 2: 4—7.
- Tempted by. 1 Chr. 21: 1. 1 The. 3: 5.
- Sifted by. Luke 22: 31.
- Should resist. Jas. 4: 7. 1 Pet. 5: 9.
- Should be armed against. Eph. 6: 11—16.
- Should be watchful against. 2 Cor. 2: 11.
- Overcome. 1 Jno. 2: 13. Rev. 12: 10, 11.
- Shall finally triumph over. Rom. 16: 20.

TRIUMPH OVER, BY CHRIST
- Predicted. Gen. 3: 15.
- In resisting his temptations. Mat. 4: 11.
- In casting out the spirits of. Luke 11: 20. Luke 13: 32.
- In empowering His disciples to cast out. Mat. 10: 1. Mar. 16: 17.

In destroying the works of. 1 Jno. 3:8.
Completed by His death. Col. 2:15. Heb. 2. 14.
Illustrated. Luke 11:21, 22.

CHARACTER OF,
Presumptuous. Job 1:6. Mat. 4: 5, 6.
Proud. 1 Tim. 3:6.
Powerful. Eph. 2:2. Eph. 6:12.
Wicked. 1 Jno. 2:13.
Malignant. Job 1:9. Job 2:4.
Subtle. Gen. 3:1, with 2 Cor. 11:3.
Deceitful. 2 Cor. 11:14. Eph. 6:11.
Fierce and cruel. Luke 8:29. Luke 9:39, 42. 1 Pet. 5:8.
Cowardly. Jas. 4:7.

The Apostacy is of. 2 Thes. 2:9. Tim. 4:1.
Shall be condemned at the judgment. Jude 6. Rev. 20:10.
Everlasting fire is prepared for. Mat. 25:41.
Compared to, *A fowler*, Psa. 91:3. *Fowls*, Mat. 13:4. *A sower of tares*, Mat. 13:25, 28. *A wolf*, Jno. 10:12. *A roaring lion*, 1 Pet. 5:8. *A serpent*, Rev. 12:9. Rev. 20:2.

Devotedness to God.

A characteristic of saints. Job 23:12.
Christ, an example of. Jno. 4:34. Jno. 17:4.

GROUNDED UPON
The mercies of God. Rom. 12:1.
The goodness of God. 1 Sam. 12:24.
The call of God. 1 The. 2:12.
The death of Christ. 2 Cor. 5:15.
Our creation. Psa. 86:9.
Our preservation. Isa. 46:4.
Our redemption. 1 Cor. 6:19, 20.

SHOULD BE
With our spirit. 1 Cor. 6:20. 1 Pet. 4:6.
With our bodies. Rom. 12:1. 1 Cor. 6:20.
With our members. Rom. 6:12, 13. 1 Pet. 4:2.
With our substance. Exo. 22:29. Pro. 3:9.
Unreserved. Mat. 6:24. Luke 14:33.
Abounding. 1 The. 4:1.
Persevering. Luke 1:74, 75. Luke 9:62.
In life and death. Rom. 14:8. Phi. 1:20.

SHOULD BE EXIBITED IN
Loving God. Deu. 6:5. Luke 10:27.
Serving God. 1 Sam. 12:24. Rom. 12:11.
Walking worthy of God. 1 The. 2:12.
Doing all to God's glory. 1 Cor. 10:31.
Bearing the cross. Mar. 8:34.
Self-denial. Mar. 8:34.
Living to Christ. 2 Cor. 5:15.
Giving up all for Christ. Mat. 19:21, 28, 29.
Want of, condemned. Rev. 3:16.

Exemplified. *Joshua*, Jos. 24:15. *Peter*, *Andrew*, *James*, *John*, Mat. 4:20–22. *Joanna*, *&c*. Luke 8:3. *Paul*, Phi. 1:21. *Timothy*, Phi, 2:19–22. *Epaphroditus*, Phi. 2:30.

Diet of the Jews, The.

In patriarchial age. Gen. 18:7, 8. Gen. 27:4.
In Egypt. Exo. 16:3. Num. 11:5.
In the wilderness. Exo. 16:4–12.
Of the poor, frugal. Ruth 2:14. Pro. 15:17.
Of the rich. luxurious. Pro. 23:1–3. Lam. 4:5. Amos 6:4, 5. Luke 16:19.

ARTICLES USED FOR;
Milk. Gen. 49:12. Pro. 27:27.
Butter. Deu. 32:14. 2 Sam. 17:29.
Cheese. 1 Sam. 17:18. Job 10:10.
Bread. Gen. 18:5. 1 Sam. 17:17.
Parched corn. Ruth 2:14. 1 Sam. 17:17.
Flesh. 2 Sam. 6:19. Pro. 9:2.
Fish. Mat. 7:10. Luke 24:42.
Herbs. Pro. 15:17. Rom. 14:2. Heb. 6:7.
Fruit. 2 Sam. 16:2.
Dried fruit. 1 Sam. 25:18. 1 Sam. 30:12.
Honey. So. of Sol. 5:1. Isa. 7:15.
Oil. Deu. 12:17. Pro. 21:17. Eze. 16:13.
Vinegar. Num. 6:3. Ruth 2:14.
Wine. 2 Sam. 6:19. Jno. 2:3, 10.
Water. Gen. 21:14. Mat. 10:42.

Expressed by bread and water. 1 Kin. 13:9, 16.
Generally prepared by females. Gen. 27:9. 1 Sam. 8:13. Pro. 31:15.

WAS TAKEN
In the morning, sparingly. Jud. 19:5, with Ecc. 10:16, 17.
At noon. Gen. 43:16. Jno. 4:6, 8.
In the evening. Gen. 24:11, 33. Luke 24:29, 30.
Often sitting. Gen. 27:19. Gen. 43:33.
Often reclining. Amos 6:4. Jno. 13:23.
With the hand. Mat. 26:23, with Luke 22:21.

Thanks given before. Mar. 8:6. Acts 27:35.
Purification before. 2 Kin. 3:11. Mat. 15:2.
A hymn sung after. Mat. 26:30.
Men and women did not partake of, together. Gen. 18:8, 9. Est. 1:3, 9.
Articles of, often sent as presents. 1 Sam. 17:18. 1 Sam. 25:18, 27. 2 Sam. 16:1, 2.

Diligence.

Christ, an example. Mar. 1: 35. Luke 2: 49.
REQUIRED BY GOD IN
Seeking Him. 1 Chr. 22: 19. Heb. 11: 6.
Obeying Him. Deu. 6: 17. Deu. 11: 13.
Hearkening to Him. Isa. 55: 2.
Striving after perfection. Phi. 3: 13, 14.
Cultivating Christian graces. 2 Pet. 1: 5.
Keeping the soul. Deu. 4: 9.
Keeping the heart. Pro. 4: 23.
Labors of love. Heb. 6: 10—12.
Following every good work. 1 Tim. 5: 10.
Guarding against defilement. Heb. 12: 15.
Seeking to be found spotless. 2 Pet. 3: 14.
Making our calling, &c., sure. 2 Pet. 1: 10.
Self-examination. Psa. 77: 6.
Lawful business. Pro. 27: 23. Ecc. 9: 10.
Teaching religion. 2 Tim. 4: 2. Jude 3.
Instructing children. Deu. 6: 7. Deu. 11: 19.
Discharging official duties. Deu. 19: 18.
Saints should abound in. 2 Cor. 8: 7.
IN THE SERVICE OF GOD
Should be persevered in. Gal. 6: 9.
Is not in vain. 1 Cor. 15: 58.
Preserves from evil. Exo. 15: 26.
Leads to assured hope. Heb. 6: 11.
God rewards. Deu. 11: 14. Heb. 11: 6.
IN TEMPORAL MATTERS, LEADS TO
Favor. Pro. 11: 27.
Prosperity. Pro. 10: 4. Pro. 13: 4.
Honor. Pro. 12: 24. Pro. 22: 29.
Illustrated. Pro. 6: 6—8.
Exemplified. *Jacob*, Gen. 31: 40. *Ruth*, Ruth 2: 17. *Hezekiah*, 2 Chr. 31: 21. *Nehemiah, &c.* Neh. 4: 6. *Psalmist*, Psa. 119: 60. *Apostles*, Acts 5: 42. *Apollos*, Acts 18: 25. *Titus*, 2 Cor. 8: 22. *Paul*, 1 The. 2: 9. *Onesiphorus*, 2 Tim. 1: 17.

Discipline of the Church.

Ministers authorized to establish. Mat. 16: 19. Mat. 18: 18.
CONSISTS IN
Maintaining sound doctrine. 1 Tim. 1: 3. Tit. 1: 13.
Ordering its affairs. 1 Cor. 11: 34. Tit. 1: 5.
Rebuking offenders. 1 Tim. 5: 20. 2 Tim. 4: 2.
Removing obstinate offenders. 1 Cor. 5: 3—5, 13. 1 Tim. 1: 20.
Should be submitted to. Heb. 13: 17.
Is for edification. 2 Cor. 10: 8. 2 Cor. 13: 10.
Decency and order, the objects of. 1 Cor. 14: 40.
Exercise, in a spirit of charity. Cor. 2: 6—8.
Prohibits women preaching. 1 Cor. 14: 34. 1 Tim. 2: 12.

Diseases.

Often sent as punishment. Deu. 28: 21. Jno. 5: 14.
Often brought from other countries. Deu. 7: 15.
Often through Satan. 1 Sam. 16: 14—16. Job 2: 7.
Regarded as visitations. Job 2: 7—10. Psa. 38: 2, 7.
Intemperance a cause of. Hos. 7: 5.
Sins of youth a cause of. Job 20: 11.
Over-excitement a cause of. Dan. 8: 27.
Were many and divers. Mat. 4: 24.
MENTIONED IN SCRIPTURE;
Ague. Lev. 26: 16.
Abscess. 2 Kin. 20: 7.
Atrophy. Job 16: 8. Job 19: 20.
Blindness. Job 29: 15. Mat. 9: 27.
Boils and blains. Exo. 9: 10.
Consumption. Lev. 26: 16. Deu. 28: 22.
Demoniacal possession. Mat. 15: 22. Mar. 5: 15.
Deafness. Psa. 38: 13. Mar. 7: 32.
Debility. Psa. 102: 23. Eze. 7: 17.
Dropsy. Luke 14: 2.
Dumbness. Pro. 31: 8. Mat. 9: 32.
Dysentery. 2 Chr 21: 12—19. Acts 28: 8.
Emerods. Deu. 28: 27. 1 Sam. 5: 6, 12.
Fever. Deu. 28: 22. Mat 8: 14.
Impediment speech. Mar. 7: 32.
Itch. Deu. 28: 27.
Inflammation. Deu. 28: 22.
Issue of blood. Mat. 9: 20.
Lameness. 2 Sam. 4: 4. 2 Chr. 16: 12.
Leprosy. Lev. 13: 2. 2 Kin. 5: 1.
Loss of appetite. Job 33: 20. Psa. 107: 18.
Lunacy. Mat. 4: 24. Mat. 17: 15.
Melancholy. 1 Sam. 16: 14.
Palsy. Mat. 8: 6. Mat. 9: 2.
Plague. Num. 11: 33. 2 Sam. 24 15, 21, 25.
Scab. Deu. 28: 27.
Sunstroke. 2 Kin. 4: 18—20. Isa. 49: 10.
Ulcers. Isa. 1: 6. Luke 16: 20.
Worms. Acts 12: 23.
Children subject to. 2 Sam. 12: 15. 1 Kin. 17: 17.
FREQUENTLY
Loathsome. Psa. 38: 7. Psa. 41: 8.

Painful. 2 Chr. 21:15. Job 33:19.
Tedious. Deu. 28:59. Jno. 5:5. Luke 13:16.
Complicated. Deu. 28:60, 61. Acts 28:8.
Incurable. 2 Chr. 21:18. Jer. 14:19.
Physicians undertook the cure of. Jer. 8:22. Mat. 9:12. Luke 4:23.
Medicine used for curing. Pro. 17:22. Isa. 1:6.
Art of curing, defective. Job 13:4. Mar. 5:26.
God often entreated to cure. 2 Sam. 12:16. 2 Kin. 20:1-3. Psa. 6:2. Jas. 5:14.
Not looking to God in, condemned. 2 Chr. 16:12.
THOSE AFFLICTED WITH,
Anointed. Mar. 6:13. Jas. 5:14.
Often laid in the streets to receive advice from passers by. Mar. 6:56. Acts 5:15.
Often divinely supported. Psa. 41:3.
Often divinely cured. 2 Kin. 20:5. Jas. 5:15.
Illustrative of sin. Isa. 1:5.

Disobedience to God.

Provokes His anger. Psa. 78:10, 40. Isa. 3:8.
Forfeits His favor. 1 Sam. 13:14.
Forfeits His promised blessings. Jos. 5:6. 1 Sam. 2:30. Jer. 18:10.
Brings a curse. Deu. 11:28. Deu. 28:15, &c.
A characteristic of the wicked. Eph. 2:2. Tit. 1:16. Tit. 3:3.
The wicked persevere in. Jer. 22:21.
Heinousness of, illustrated. Jer. 35:14, &c.
Men prone to excuse. Gen. 3:12, 13.
Shall be punished. Isa. 42:24, 25. Heb. 2:2.
Acknowledge the punishment of, to be just. Neh. 9:32, 33. Dan. 9:10, 11, 14.
Warnings against. 1 Sam. 12:15. Jer. 12:17.
Bitter results of, illustrated. Jer. 9:13, 15.
Exemplified. *Adam and Eve*, Gen. 3:6, 11. *Pharaoh*, Exo. 5:2. *Nadab, &c.* Lev. 10:1. *Moses, &c.* Num. 20:8, 11, 24. *Saul*, 1 Sam. 28:18. *The prophet*, 1 Kin. 13:20—23. *Israel*, 2 Kin. 18:9—12. *Jonah*, Jon. 1:2, 3.

Divination.

An abominable practice. 1 Sam. 15:23. (*marg.*)
All who practised it, abominable. Deu. 18:12.
PRACTISED BY
Diviners. Deu. 18:14.
Enchanters. Deu. 18:10. Jer. 27:9.
Witches. Exo. 22:18. Deu. 18:10.
Charmers. Deu: 18:11.
Wizards. Deu. 18:11. 1 Sam. 28:3.
Consulters of familiar spirits. Deu. 18:11.
Magicians. Gen. 41:8. Dan. 4:7.
Astrologers. Isa. 47:13. Dan. 4:7.
Sorcerers. Jer. 27:9. Acts 13:6, 8.
Necromancers. Deu. 18:11.
Soothsayers. Isa. 2:6. Dan. 2:27.
False prophets. Jer. 14:14. Eze. 13:3, 6.
EFFECTED THROUGH
Enchantments. Exo. 7:11. Num. 24:1.
Sorcery. Isa. 47:12. Acts 8:11.
Observing times. 2 Kin. 21:6.
Observing heavenly bodies. Isa. 37:13. (*marg.*)
Raising the dead. I Sam. 28:11, 12.
Inspecting the inside of beasts. Eze. 21:21.
The flight of arrows. Eze. 21:21, 22.
Cups. Gen. 44:2, 5.
Rods. Hos. 4:12.
Dreams. Jer. 29:8. Zec. 10:2.
Connected with idolatry. 2 Chr. 33:5, 6.
Books of, numerous and expensive. Acts 19:19.
A lucrative employment. Num. 22:7. Acts 16:16.
THOSE WHO PRACTISED,
Regarded as wise men. Dan. 2:12, 27.
Regarded with awe. Acts 8:9, 11.
Consulted in difficulties. Dan. 2:2. Dan. 4:6, 7.
Used mysterious words and gestures. Isa. 8:19.
A system of fraud. Eze. 13:6, 7. Jer. 29:8.
Frustrated by God. Isa. 44:25.
Could not injure the Lord's people. Num. 23:23.
THE LAW
Forbade to the Israelites the practice of. Lev. 19:26. Deu. 18:10, 11.
Forbade seeking to. Lev. 19:31. Deu. 18:14.
Punished with death those who used. Exo. 22:18. Lev. 20:27.
Punished those who sought to. Lev. 20:6.
The Jews prone to. 2 Kin. 17:17. Isa. 2:6.

Divisions.

Forbidden in the church. 1 Cor. 1:10.
Condemned in the church. 1 Cor. 1:11—13. 1 Cor. 11:18.
Unbecoming in the church. 1 Cor. 12:24, 25.

ARE CONTRARY TO THE
Unity of Christ. 1 Cor. 1: 13. 1 Cor. 12: 13.
Desire of Christ. Jno. 17: 21—23.
Purpose of Christ. Jno. 10: 16.
Spirit of the primitive church. 1 Cor. 11: 16.
Are a proof of a carnal spirit. 1 Cor. 3: 3.
Avoid those who cause. Rom. 16: 17.
Evil of, illustrated. Mat. 12: 25.

Divorce.

Law of marriage against. Gen. 2: 24. Mat. 19: 6.
PERMITTED
By the Mosaic law. Deu. 24: 1.
On account of hardness of heart. Mat. 19: 8.
Often sought by the Jews. Mic. 2: 9. Mal. 2: 14.
Sought on slight grounds. Mat. 5: 31. Mat. 19: 3.
Not allowed to those who falsely accused their wives. Deu. 22: 18, 19.
WOMEN
Could obtain. Pro. 2: 17, with Mar. 10: 12.
Could marry after. Deu. 24: 2.
Responsible for vows after. Num. 30: 9.
Married after, could not return to first husband. Deu. 24: 3, 4. Jer. 3: 1.
Afflicted by. Isa. 54: 4, 6.
Priests not to marry women after. Lev. 21: 14.
Of servants, regulated by law. Exo. 21: 7, 11.
Of captives, regulated by law. Deu. 21: 13, 14.
Forced on those who had idolatrous wives. Ezr. 10: 2—17. Neh. 13: 23, 30.
Jews condemned for love of. Mal. 2: 14—16.
Forbidden by Christ except for adultery. Mat. 5: 32. Mat. 19: 9.
Prohibition of, offended the Jews. Mat. 19: 10.
Illustrative of God's casting off of the Jewish church. Isa. 50: 1. Jer. 3: 8.

Doctrines, False.

Destructive to faith. 2 Tim. 2: 18.
Hateful to God. Rev. 2: 14, 15.
Unprofitable and vain. Tit. 3: 9. Heb. 13: 9.
SHOULD BE AVOIDED BY
Ministers. 1 Tim. 1: 4. 1 Tim. 6: 20.
Saints. Eph. 4: 14. Col. 2: 8.
All men. Jer. 23: 16. Jer. 29: 8.
The wicked love. 2 Tim. 4: 3, 4.
The wicked given up to believe. 2 The. 2: 11.
TEACHERS OF
Not to be countenanced. 2 Jno. 10.
Should be avoided. Rom. 16: 17, 18.
Bring reproach on religion. 2 Pet. 2: 2.
Speak perverse things. Acts 20: 30.
Attract many. 2 Pet. 2: 2.
Deceive many. Mat. 24: 5.
Shall abound in the latter days. 1 Tim. 4: 1.
Pervert the gospel of Christ. Gal. 1: 6, 7.
Shall be exposed. 2 Tim. 3: 9.
TEACHERS OF, ARE DESCRIBED AS
Cruel. Acts 20: 29.
Deceitful. 2 Cor. 11: 13.
Covetous. Tit. 1: 11. 2 Pet. 2: 3.
Ungodly. Jude 4, 8.
Proud and ignorant. 1 Tim. 6: 3, 4.
Corrupt and reprobate. 2 Tim. 3: 8.
Try, by Scripture. Isa. 8: 20. 1 Jno. 4: 1.
Curse on those who teach. Gal. 1: 8, 9.
Punishment of those who teach. Mic. 3: 6, 7. 2 Pet. 2: 1, 3.

Doctrines of the Gospel, The.

Are from God. Jno. 7: 16. Acts 13: 12.
Are taught by Scripture. 2 Tim. 3: 16.
Are godly. 1 Tim. 6: 3. Tit. 1: 1.
Immorality condemned by. 1 Tim. 1: 9—11.
Lead to fellowship with the Father and with the Son. 1 Jno. 1: 3. 2 Jno. 9.
Lead to holiness. Rom. 6: 17—22. Tit. 2: 12.
Bring no reproach on. 1 Tim. 6: 1. Tit. 2: 5.
MINISTERS SHOULD
Be nourished up in. 1 Tim. 4: 6.
Attend to. 1 Tim. 4: 13, 16.
Hold, in sincerity. 2 Cor. 2: 17. Tit. 2: 7.
Hold steadfastly. 2 Tim. 1: 13. Tit. 1: 9.
Continue in. 1 Tim. 4: 16.
Speak things which become. Tit. 2: 1.
Saints obey, from the heart. Rom. 6: 17.
Saints abide in. Acts 2: 42.
A faithful walk adorns. Tit. 2: 10.
The obedience of saints leads to surer knowledge of. Jno. 7: 17.
THOSE WHO OPPOSE, ARE
Proud. 1 Tim. 6: 3, 4.
Ignorant. 1 Tim. 6: 4.
Doting about questions, &c. 1 Tim. 6: 4.
Not to be received. 2 Jno. 10.
To be avoided. Rom. 16: 17.
Not endured by the wicked. 2 Tim. 4: 3.

Dog, The.

Despised by the Jews. 2 Sam. 3: 8.
DESCRIBED AS
- Impatient of injury. Pro. 26: 17.
- Unclean. Luke 16: 21. 2 Pet. 2: 22.
- Carnivorous. 1 Kin. 14: 11. 2 Kin. 9: 35, 36.
- Fond of blood. 1 Kin. 21: 19. 1 Kin. 22: 38.
- Dangerous and destructive. Psa. 22: 16.

Infested cities by night. Psa. 59: 14, 15.
Nothing holy to be given to. Mat. 7: 6. Mat. 15: 26.
Things torn by beasts given to. Exo. 22: 31.
Sacrificing of, an abomination. Isa. 66: 3.
Price of, not to be consecrated. Deu. 23: 18.
WHEN DOMESTICATED,
- Employed in watching flocks. Job 30: 1.
- Fed with the crumbs, &c. Mat. 15: 27.

Manner of, in drinking alluded to. Jud. 7: 5.
ILLUSTRATIVE
- Of Gentiles. Mat. 15: 22, 26.
- Of covetous ministers. Isa. 56: 11.
- Of fools. Pro. 26: 11.
- Of apostates. 2 Pet. 2: 22.
- Of persecutors. Psa. 22: 16, 20.
- Of obstinate sinners. Mat. 7: 6. Rev. 22: 15.
- Of false teachers. Phi. 3: 2.
- (Dumb,) of unfaithful ministers. Isa. 56: 10.
- (Dead,) of the mean. 1 Sam 24: 14. 2 Sam. 9: 8.

Dove, The.

Clean and used as food. Deu. 14: 11.
Offered in sacrifice. Gen. 15: 9. Lev. 1: 14.
Impiously sold in the court of the temple. Mat. 21: 12. Jno. 2: 16.
CHARACTERIZED BY
- Simplicity. Mat. 10: 16.
- Comeliness of countenance. So. of Sol. 2: 14.
- Softness of eyes. So. of Sol. 1: 15.
- Sweetness of voice. So. of Sol. 2: 14.
- Richness of plumage. Psa. 68: 13.

Mournful tabering of, alluded to. Nah. 2: 7.
Dwells in rocks. So. of Sol. 2: 14, Jer. 48: 28.
Frequents streams and rivers. So. of Sol. 5: 12.
Sent from the ark by Noah. Gen. 8: 8, 10, 12.
Why considered the emblem of peace. Gen. 8: 11.
The harbinger of spring. So. of Sol. 2: 12.
ILLUSTRATIVE
- Of the Holy Ghost. Mat. 3: 16. Jno. 1: 32.
- Of the meekness of Christ. So. of Sol. 5: 12.
- Of the church. So. of Sol. 2: 14. So. of Sol. 5: 2.
- Of mourners. Isa. 38: 14. Isa. 59: 11.
- Of converts to the church. Isa. 60: 8.
- (In its flight,) of the return of Israel from captivity. Hos. 11: 11.

Dragon, The.

Often of a red color. Rev. 12: 3.
DESCRIBED AS
- Powerful. Rev. 12: 4.
- Poisonous. Deu. 32: 33.
- Of solitary habits. Job 30: 29.

Its mournful voice alluded to. Mic. 1: 8.
Its wailing alluded to. Mic. 1: 8.
Its snuffing up the air alluded to. Jer. 14: 6.
Its swallowing of its prey alluded to. Jer. 51: 34.
FOUND IN
- The wilderness. Mal. 1: 3.
- Deserted cities. Isa. 13: 22. Jer. 9: 11.
- Dry places. Isa. 34: 13. Isa. 43: 20.

A species of, in rivers. Psa. 74: 13. Isa. 27: 1.
ILLUSTRATIVE
- Of cruel and persecuting kings. Isa. 27: 1. Isa. 51: 9. Eze. 29: 3.
- Of enemies of the church. Psa. 91: 13.
- Of wicked men. Psa. 44: 19.
- Of the devil. Rev. 13: 2. Rev. 20: 2, 7.
- (Poison of,) of wine. Deu. 32: 33.

Dreams.

Visions in sleep. Job 33: 15. Dan. 2: 28.
Often but imaginary. Job 20: 8. Isa. 29: 8.
Excess of business frequently leads to. Ecc. 5: 3.
God's will often revealed in. Num. 12: 6. Job 33: 15.
FALSE PROPHETS
- Pretended to. Jer. 23: 25—28. Jer. 29: 8.
- Not to be regarded in. Deu. 13: 1—3. Jer. 27: 9.
- Condemned for pretending to. Jer. 23: 32.

Vanity of trusting to natural. Ecc. 5: 7.
THE ANCIENTS
- Put great faith in. Jud. 7: 15.

Often perplexed by. Gen. 40: 6. Gen. 41: 8. Job 7: 14. Dan. 2: 1. Dan. 4: 5.
Anxious to have, explained. Gen. 40: 8. Dan. 2: 3.
Consulting magicians on. Gen. 41: 8. Dan. 2: 2–4.
God the only interpreter of. Gen. 40: 8. Gen. 41: 16. Dan. 2: 27—30. Dan. 7: 16.
MENTIONED IN SCRIPTURE, OF
Abimelech. Gen. 20: 3—7.
Jacob. Gen. 28: 12. Gen. 31: 10.
Laban. Gen. 31: 24.
Joseph. Gen. 37: 5—9.
Pharaoh's butler and baker. Gen. 40: 5—19.
Pharaoh. Gen. 41: 1—7.
Midianite. Jud. 7: 13—15.
Solomon. 1 Kin. 3: 5—15.
Nebuchadnezzar. Dan. 2: 1, 31. Dan. 4: 5, 8.
Daniel. Dan. 7 ch.
Joseph. Mat. 1: 20, 21. Mat. 2: 13, 19, 20.
Wise men. Mat. 2: 11, 12.
Pilate's wife. Mat. 27: 19.
ILLUSTRATIVE OF
Prosperity of sinners. Job 20: 5—8. Psa. 73: 19, 20.
Impure imaginations. Jude 8 v.
Enemies of the church. Isa. 29: 7, 8.

Drink Offering.

Antiquity of. Gen. 35: 14.
Sacrifices accompanied by. Exo. 29: 40. Lev. 23: 13.
Quantity appointed to be used for each kind of sacrifice. Num. 15: 3—10.
For public sacrifices provided by the state. Ezr. 7: 17. Eze. 45: 17.
Not poured on the altar of incense. Exo. 30: 9.
Omission of, caused by bad vintage. Joel 1: 9, 13.
IDOLATROUS JEWS
Offered to the queen of heaven. Jer. 7: 18. Jer. 44: 17—19.
Reproved for offering, to idols. Isa. 57: 5, 6. Isa. 65: 11. Jer. 19: 13. Eze. 20: 28.
Idolaters often used blood for. Psa. 16: 4.
Vanity of offering, to idols. Deu. 32: 37, 38.
ILLUSTRATIVE OF THE
Offering of Christ. Isa. 53: 12.
Pouring out of the Spirit. Joel 2: 28.
Devotedness of ministers. Phi. 2: 17. (*Greek.*)

Drunkenness.

Forbidden. Eph. 5: 18.
Caution against. Luke 21: 34.
Is a work of the flesh. Gal. 5: 21.
Is debasing. Isa. 28: 8.
Is inflaming. Isa. 5: 11.
Overcharges the heart. Luke 21: 34.
Takes away the heart. Hos. 4: 11.
LEADS TO
Poverty. Pro. 21: 17. Pro. 23: 21.
Strife. Pro. 23: 29, 30.
Woe and sorrow. Pro. 23: 29, 30.
Error. Isa. 28: 7.
Contempt of God's works. Isa. 5: 12.
Scorning. Hos. 7: 5.
Rioting and wantonness. Rom. 13: 13.
The wicked addicted to. Dan. 5: 1—4.
False teachers often addicted to. Isa. 56: 12.
Folly of yielding to. Pro. 20: 1.
Avoid those given to. Pro. 23: 20. 1 Cor. 5: 11.
DENUNCIATIONS AGAINST
Those given to. Isa. 5: 11, 12. Isa. 28: 1—3.
Those who encourage. Hab. 2: 15.
Excludes from heaven. 1 Cor. 6: 10. Gal. 5: 21.
Punishment of. Deu. 21: 20, 21. Joel 1: 5, 6. Amos 6: 6, 7. Mat. 24: 49—51.
Exemplified. *Noah*, Gen. 9: 21. *Nabal*, 1 Sam. 25: 36. *Uriah*, 2 Sam. 11: 13. *Elah*, 1 Kin. 16: 9, 10. *Benhadad*, 1 Kin. 20: 16. *Belshazzar*, Dan. 5. 4. *Corinthians*, 1 Cor. 11: 21.

Eagle, The.

A bird of prey. Job 9: 26. Mat. 24: 28.
Unclean. Lev. 11: 13. Deu. 14: 12.
Different kinds of. Lev. 11: 13, 18. Eze. 17: 3.
Called the eagle of the heavens. Lam. 4: 19.
DESCRIBED AS
Longsighted. Job 39: 29.
Swift. 2 Sam. 1: 23.
Soaring to heaven. Pro. 23: 5.
Strength of its feathers alluded to. Dan. 4: 33.
Greatness of its wings alluded to. Eze. 17: 3, 7.
Peculiarity of its flight alluded to. Pro. 30: 19.
Delights in the lofty cedars. Eze. 17. 3, 4.
Dwells in the high rocks. Job 39: 27, 28.
Feeds her young with blood. Job 39: 29, 30.
ILLUSTRATIVE
Of wisdom and zeal of God's ministers. Eze. 1: 10. Rev. 4: 7.
Of great and powerful kings. Eze. 17: 3. Hos. 8: 1.

(Renewed strength and beauty of,) of the renewal of saints. Psa. 103: 5.
(Mode of teaching her young to fly,) of God's care of His church. Exo. 19: 4. Deu. 32: 11.
(Wings of,) of protection afforded to the church. Rev. 12: 14.
(Upward flight of,) of the saint's rapid progress toward heaven. Isa. 40: 31.
(Swiftness of,) of the melting away of riches. Pro. 23: 5.
(Swiftness of,) of the swiftness of hostile armies. Deu. 28: 49. Jer. 4: 13. Jer. 48: 40. Lam. 4: 19.
(Height and security of its dwelling,) of the fancied but fatal security of the wicked. Jer. 49: 16. Oba. 4 v.
(Increased baldness of, in the moulting season,) of calamities. Mic. 1: 16.
(Hasting to the prey,) of the swiftness of man's days. Job 9: 26.
Was the standard of the Roman armies. Mat. 24: 15, with 28 v.

Ear, The.

The organ of hearing. Job 13: 1. Job 29: 11.
Capable of trying and distinguishing words. Job 12: 11.
God
Made. Pro. 20: 12.
Planted. Psa. 94: 9.
Opens. Job 33: 16. Job 36: 10.
Judicially closes. Isa. 6: 10, with Mat. 13: 15.
Christ opens. Isa. 35: 5. Isa. 43: 8, 10.
Instruction received through. Isa. 30: 21.
That hears and receives the word of God, blessed. Exo. 15: 26. Mat. 13: 16.
Should
Seek knowledge. Pro. 18: 15.
Be bowed down to instructions. Pro. 5: 1.
Be inclined to wisdom. Pro. 2: 2.
Be given to the law of God. Isa. 1: 10.
Receive the word of God. Jer. 9: 20.
Hear and obey reproof. Pro. 15: 31. Pro. 25: 12.
Not satisfied with earthly things. Ecc. 1: 8.
Of the wicked
Uncircumcised. Jer. : 10. Acts 7: 51.
Itching. 2 Tim. 4: 3.
Not inclined to hear God. Jer. 7: 24. Jer. 35: 15.
Turned away from God's law. Pro. 28: 9.
Stopped against God's word. Psa. 58: 4. Zec. 7: 11.
Not to be stopped at cry of the poor. Pro. 21: 13.
Blood put on the right ear of
Priests at consecration. Exo. 29: 20. Lev. 8: 23.
The healed leper in cleansing him. Lev. 14: 14.
Often adorned with rings. Eze. 16: 12. Hos. 2: 13.
Of servants who refused to leave their masters, bored to the door. Exo. 21: 6. Deu. 15: 17.

Early Rising.

Christ set an example of. Mar. 1: 35. Luke 21: 38. Jno. 8: 2.
Requisite for
Devotion. Psa. 5: 3. Psa. 59: 16. Psa. 63: 1. Psa. 88: 13. Isa. 26: 9.
Executing God's commands. Gen. 22: 3.
Discharge of daily duties. Pro. 31: 15.
Neglect of, leads to poverty. Pro. 6: 9—11.
Practised by the wicked, for
Deceit. Pro. 27: 14.
Executing plans of evil. Mic. 2: 1.
Illustrates spiritual diligence. Rom. 13: 11, 12.
Exemplified. *Abraham*, Gen. 19: 27. *Isaac, &c.* Gen. 26: 31. *Jacob*, Gen. 28: 18. *Joshua, &c.* Jos. 3: 1. *Gideon*, Jud. 6: 38. *Samuel*, 1 Sam. 15: 12. *David*, 1 Sam. 17: 20. *Mary, &c.* Mar. 16: 2. *Apostles*, Acts 5: 21.

Earth, The.

The world in general. Gen. 1: 2.
The dry land as divided from waters. Gen. 1: 10.
God
Created. Gen. 1: 1. Neh. 9: 6.
Laid the foundation of. Job 38: 4. Psa. 102: 25.
Formed. Psa. 90: 2.
Spread abroad. Isa. 42: 5. Isa. 44: 24.
Suspended in space. Job 26: 7.
Supports. Psa. 75: 3.
Establishes. Psa. 78: 69. Psa. 119: 90.
Enlightens. Gen. 1: 14—16. Jer. 33: 25.
Waters. Psa. 65: 9. Psa. 147: 8.
Makes fruitful. Gen. 1: 11. Gen. 27: 28.
Inspects. Zec. 4: 10.
Governs supremely. Job 34: 13. Psa. 135: 6.
Reigns in. Exo. 8: 22. Psa. 97: 1.

Shall be exalted in. Psa. 46: 10.
Is the Lord's. Exo. 9: 29. 1 Cor. 10: 26.
Created to be inhabited. Isa. 45: 18.
First division of. Gen. 10: 25.
Ideas of the ancients respecting the form of. Job 11: 9. Job 38: 18. Pro. 25: 3.
Diversified by hills and mountains. Hab. 3: 6.
Full of minerals. Deu. 8: 9. Job 28: 1—5, 15—19.
DESCRIBED AS
God's footstool. Isa. 66: 1. Mat. 5: 35.
Full of God's goodness. Psa. 33: 5.
Full of God's riches. Psa. 104: 24.
Full of God's mercy. Psa. 119: 64.
Full of God's glory. Num. 14: 21. Isa. 6: 3.
Shining with God's glory. Eze. 43: 2.
Trembling before God. Psa. 68: 8. Jer. 10: 10.
Melting at God's voice. Psa. 46: 6.
Burning at God's presence. Nah. 1: 5.
MAN
Formed out of. Gen. 2: 7. Psa. 103: 14.
Given dominion over. Gen. 1: 26. Psa. 115: 16.
By nature is of. 1 Cor. 15: 47, 48.
By nature minds the things of. Phi. 3: 19.
Brought a curse on. Gen. 3: 17.
Shall return to. Gen 3: 19. Psa. 146: 4.
Subject to God's judgments. Psa. 46: 8. Isa. 11: 4.
Corrupted by sin. Gen. 6: 11, 12. Isa. 24: 5.
Made barren by sin. Deu. 28: 23. Psa. 107: 34.
Made to mourn and languish by sin. Isa. 24: 4. Jer. 4: 28. Jer. 12: 4. Hos. 4: 3.
Satan goes to and fro in. Job 1: 7. 1 Pet. 5: 8.
Shall be filled with the knowledge of God. Isa. 11: 9. Hab. 2: 14.
Once inundated. Gen. 7: 17—24.
Not to be again inundated. Gen. 9: 11. 2 Pet. 3: 6, 7.
To be dissolved by fire. 2 Pet. 3: 7, 10, 12.
To be renewed. Isa. 65: 17. 2 Pet. 3: 13.
Saints shall inherit. Psa. 25: 13. Mat. 5: 5.

Earthquakes.

Islands and mountainous districts liable to. Psa. 114: 4, 6. Rev. 6: 14. Rev. 16: 18, 20.
FREQUENTLY ACCOMPANIED BY
Volcanic eruptions. Psa. 104: 32. Nah. 1: 5.
Convulsion and receding of the sea. 2 Sam. 22: 8, 16. Psa. 18: 7, 15. Psa. 46: 3.
Opening of the earth. Num. 16: 31, 32.
Overturning of mountains. Psa. 46: 2. Zec. 14: 4.
Rending of rocks. Mat. 27: 51.
ARE VISIBLE TOKENS OF
God's power. Job 9: 6. Heb. 12: 26.
God's presence. Psa. 68: 7, 8. Psa. 114: 7.
God's anger. Psa. 18: 7. Psa. 60: 2. Isa. 13: 13.
Men always terrified by. Num. 16: 34. Zec. 14: 5. Mat. 27: 54. Rev. 11: 13.
MENTIONED IN SCRIPTURE;
At Mount Sinai. Exo. 19: 18.
In the wilderness. Num. 16: 31, 32.
In strongholds of Philistines. 1 Sam. 14: 15.
When Elijah fled from Jezebel. 1 Kin. 19: 11.
In Uzziah's reign. Amos 1: 1. Zec. 14: 5.
At our Lord's death. Mat. 27: 51.
At our Lord's resurrection. Mat. 28: 2.
At Philippi. Acts 16: 26.
Before destruction of Jerusalem, predicted. Mat. 24: 7. Luke 21: 11.
At Christ's second coming, predicted. Zec. 14: 4.
ILLUSTRATIVE OF
The judgments of God. Isa. 24: 19, 20. Isa. 29: 6. Jer. 4: 24. Rev. 8: 5.
The overthrow of kingdoms. Hag. 2: 6, 22. Rev. 6: 12, 13. Rev. 16: 18, 19.

Edification.

Described. Eph. 4: 12—16.
IS THE OBJECT OF
The ministerial office. Eph. 4: 11, 12.
Ministerial gifts. 1 Cor. 14: 3—5, 12.
Ministerial authority. 2 Cor. 10: 8. 2 Cor. 13: 10.
The Church's union in Christ. Eph. 4: 16.
The gospel, the instrument of. Acts 20: 32.
Love leads to. 1 Cor. 8: 1.
Exhortation to. Jude 20, 21.
Mutual, commanded. Rom. 14: 19. 1 The. 5: 11.
All to be done to. 2 Cor. 12: 19. Eph. 4: 29.
Use self-denial to promote, in others. 1 Cor. 10: 23, 33.
The peace of the Church favors. Acts 9: 31.
Foolish questions opposed to. 1 Tim. 1: 4.

Edomites, The.

Descended from Esau. Gen. 36:9.
Dwelt in Mount Seir. Gen. 32:3. Deu. 2:4, 5.
WERE CALLED
Children of Esau. Deu. 2:4.
Brethren of Israel. Num. 20:14.
Governed by dukes. Gen. 36:15—30, 40—43. Exo. 15:15.
Afterwards had kings. Gen. 36:31—39. Num 20:14.
Under a deputy or viceroy while subject to Judah. 1 Kin. 22:47.
CHARACTER OF;
Wise. Jer. 49:7.
Proud and self-confident. Jer. 49:16. Oba. 3 v.
Strong and cruel. Jer. 49:19.
Vindictive. Eze. 25:12.
Idolatrous. 2 Chr. 25:14, 20.
Superstitious. Jer. 27:3, with 9 v.
Carried on extensive commerce. Eze. 27:20.
COUNTRY OF,
Specially given to them. Deu. 2:5.
Fertile and rich. Gen. 27:39.
Mountainous and rocky. Jer. 49:16. Mal. 1:3.
Traversed by roads. Num. 20:17.
Well fortified. Psa. 60:9.
Called Mount Seir. Eze. 35:2.
Called Mount of Esau. Oba. 21 v.
Called Dumah. Isa. 21:11.
Called Idumea. Isa. 34:6. Mar. 3:8.
Called Edom. Isa. 63:1.
CITIES OF;
Dinhabah or Dedan. Gen. 36:32. Jer. 49:8.
Avith. Gen. 36:35.
Pau. Gen. 36:39.
Bozra. Jer. 49:22. Amos 1:12.
Teman. Jer. 49:7. Eze. 25:13.
Ezion-geber, a sea port. 1 Kin. 9:26.
Implacable enemies of Israel. Eze. 35:5.
Israel forbidden to hate. Deu. 23:7.
Israel forbidden to spoil. Deu. 2:4, 6. 2 Chr. 20:10.
Might be received into the congregation in third generation. Deu. 23:8.
Refused Israel a passage. Num. 20:21. Jud. 11:17.
Saul made war against. 1 Sam. 14:47.
David subdued, &c. 2 Sam. 8:14. 1 Chr. 18:11, 13.
Slaughter of, by Joab and Abishai. 1 Kin. 11:16. 1 Chr. 18:12.
Took refuge in Egypt. 1 Kin. 11:17—19.
Returned after David's death. 1 Kin. 11:21—22.
Were stirred up against Solomon. 1 Kin. 11:14.
Confederated with enemies of Israel against Jehoshaphat. 2 Chr. 20:10. Psa. 83:4—6.
Miraculous overthrow of. 2 Chr. 20:22.
Revolted from Joram, king of Judah. 2 Kin. 8:20—22. 2 Chr. 21:8—10.
Re-conquered by Amaziah. 2 Kin. 14:7, 10. 2 Chr. 25:11, 12.
The Jews ensnared by the idols of, and punished. 2 Chr. 25:14, 15, 20.
Rebelled against Ahaz. 2 Chr. 28:17.
Aided Babylon against Judah. Psa. 137:7. Oba. 11.
PREDICTIONS RESPECTING;
Subjection to Israel. Gen. 25:23 Gen. 27:29, 37.
Revolt from Israel. Gen. 27:40.
Israel's occupation of their country. Num. 24:18. Oba. 17—19 vs.
To share in the punishment of the nations. Jer. 9:26. Jer. 25:15—27. Eze. 32:29.
Punishment for persecuting Israel. Isa. 34:5—8. Isa. 63:1—4. Lam. 4:21. Eze. 25:13, 14. Amos 1:11, 12. Oba. 10, 15 vs.
Exterminating slaughter of. Oba. 18 v.
Utter desolation of their country. Isa. 34:9—17. Eze. 35:7—15.
The king of Babylon an instrument of their punishment. Jer. 27:3–6.
Israel an instrument of their punishment. Eze. 25:14. Oba. 18 v.
Their ruin to be an astonishment. Jer. 49:17, 21.
Their future subjection to the Jews. Isa. 11:14. Amos 9:12.
Remarkable persons of. *Doeg*, 1 Sam. 22:18. *Hadad*, 1 Kin. 11, 14, 19. *Eliphaz*, Job 2:11.

Egypt.

Peopled by Mizraim's posterity. Gen. 10:6, 13, 14.
Boundaries of. Eze. 29:10.
Dry climate of. Deu. 11:10, 11.
Watered by the Nile. Gen. 41:1—3. Exo. 1:22.
Inundations of, alluded to. Amos 8:8.
Subject to plague, &c. Deu. 7:15. Deu. 28:27, 60.
Sometimes visited by famine. Gen. 41:30.
CALLED
The land of Ham. Psa. 105:23. Psa. 106:22.
The South. Jer. 13:19. Dan. 11:14, 25.
Sihor. Isa. 23:3.
Rahab. Psa. 87:4. Psa. 89:10.
House of Bondmen. Exo. 13, 3, 14. Deu. 7:8.
CELEBRATED FOR
Fertility. Gen. 13:10. Gen. 45. 18.

Wealth. Heb. 11: 26.
Literature. 1 Kin. 4: 30. Acts 7: 22.
Fine horses. 1 Kin. 10: 28, 29.
Fine linen, &c. Pro. 7: 16. Isa. 19: 9.
Commerce. Gen. 41: 57. Eze. 27: 7.
Religion of, idolatrous. Exo. 12: 12. Num. 33: 4. Isa. 19: 1. Eze. 29: 7.
Idolatry of, followed by Israel. Exo. 32: 4, with Eze. 20: 8, 19.
Magic practised in. Exo. 7: 11, 12, 22. Exo. 8: 7.
Ruled by kings who assumed the name of Pharaoh. Gen. 12: 14, 15. Gen. 40: 1, 2. Exo. 1: 8, 22.
Under a governor. Gen. 41: 41—44.
Had princes and counsellors. Gen. 12: 15. Isa. 19: 11.

As a power was

Proud and arrogant. Eze. 29: 3. Eze. 30: 6.
Pompous. Eze. 32: 12.
Mighty. Isa. 30: 2, 3.
Ambitious of conquests. Jer. 46: 8.
Treacherous. Isa. 36: 6. Eze. 29: 6, 7.

Inhabitants of,

Superstitious. Isa. 19: 3.
Hospitable. Gen. 47: 5, 6. 1 Kin. 11: 18.
Often intermarried with strangers. Gen. 21: 21. 1 Kin. 3: 1. 1 Kin. 11: 19. 1 Chr. 2: 34, 35.
Abhorred shepherds. Gen. 46: 34.
Abhorred the sacrifice of oxen, &c. Exo. 8: 26.
Not to be abhorred by Israel. Deu. 23: 7.
Might be received into the congregation in third generation. Deu. 23: 8.
Mode of entertaining in. Gen. 43: 32—34.
Diet used in. Num. 11: 5.
Mode of enbalming in. Gen. 50: 3.
Often a refuge to strangers. Gen. 12: 10. Gen. 47: 4. 1 Kin. 11: 17, 40. 2 Kin. 25, 26. Mat. 2: 12, 13.

The armies of,

Described. Exo. 14: 7—9.
Destroyed in the Red Sea. Exo. 14: 23—28.
Captured and burned Gezer. 1 Kin. 9: 16.
Besieged and plundered Jerusalem in Rehoboam's time. 1 Kin. 14: 25, 26.
Invaded Assyria and killed Josiah who assisted it. 2 Kin. 23: 29.
Deposed Jehoahaz and made Judea tributary. 2 Kin. 23: 31–35.
Assistance of, sought by Judah against the Chaldees. Eze. 17: 15, with Jer. 37: 5, 7.

History of Israel in;

Their sojourn in it, foretold. Gen. 15: 13.
Joseph sold into. Gen. 37: 28. Gen. 39: 1.
Potiphar blessed for Joseph's sake. Gen. 39: 2—6.
Joseph unjustly cast into prison. Gen. 39: 7—20.
Joseph interprets the chief baker's and the chief butler's dreams. Gen. 40: 5—19.
Joseph interprets Pharaoh's dreams. Gen. 41: 14—32.
Joseph counsels Pharaoh. Gen. 41: 33—36.
Joseph made governor. Gen. 41: 41—44.
Joseph's successful provision against the years of famine. Gen. 41: 46—56.
Joseph's ten brethren arrive. Gen. 42: 1—6.
Joseph recognizes his brethren. Gen. 42: 7, 8.
Benjamin brought. Gen. 43: 15.
Joseph makes himself known to his brethren. Gen. 45: 1—8.
Joseph sends for his father. Gen. 45: 9—11.
Pharaoh invites Jacob into. Gen. 45: 16—20.
Jacob's journey Gen. 46: 5—7.
Jacob, &c., presented to Pharaoh. Gen. 47: 1—10.
Israel placed in the land of Goshen. Gen. 46: 34. Gen. 47: 11, 27.
Joseph enriches the king. Gen. 47: 13—26.
Jacob's death and burial. Gen. 49: 33. Gen. 50: 1—13.
Israel increase and are oppressed. Exo. 1: 1—14.
Male children destroyed. Exo. 1: 15—22.
Moses born and hid for three months. Exo. 2: 2.
Moses exposed on the Nile. Exo. 2: 3, 4.
Moses adopted and brought up by Pharaoh's daughter. Exo. 2: 5—10.
Moses slays an Egyptian. Exo. 2: 11, 12.
Moses flies to Midian. Exo. 2: 15.
Moses sent to Pharaoh. Exo. 3: 2—10.
Pharaoh increases their affliction. Exo. 5 ch.
Moses proves his divine mission by miracles. Exo. 4: 29—31. Exo. 7: 10.
Egypt is plagued for Pharaoh's obstinacy. Exo. 7: 14, to Exo. 10 ch.
The passover instituted. Exo. 12: 1—28.
Destruction of the first-born. Exo. 12: 29, 30.
Israel spoil the Egyptians. Exo. 12: 35, 36.
Israel driven out of. Exo. 12: 31—33.
Date of the Exodus. Exo. 12: 41. Heb. 11: 27.

Pharaoh pursues Israel and is miraculously destroyed. Exo. 14: 5—25.

PROPHECIES RESPECTING;
- Dismay of its inhabitants. Isa. 19: 1, 16, 17.
- Infatuation of its princes. Isa. 19: 3, 11—14.
- Failure of internal resources. Isa. 19: 5—10.
- Civil war and domestic strife. Isa. 19: 2.
- Armies destroyed by Babylon. Jer. 46: 2—12.
- Invasion by Babylon. Jer. 46: 13, 24. Eze. 32: 11.
- Destruction of its power. Eze. 30: 24, 25.
- Destruction of its cities. Eze. 30: 14—18.
- Destruction of its idols. Jer. 43: 12, 13. Jer. 46: 25. Eze. 30: 13.
- Spoil of, a reward to Babylon for services against Tyre. Eze. 29: 18—20.
- Captivity of its people. Isa. 20: 4. Jer. 46: 19, 24, 26. Eze. 30: 4.
- Utter desolation of, for forty years. Eze. 29: 8—12. Eze. 30: 12. Eze. 32: 15.
- Allies to share its misfortunes. Eze. 30: 4, 6.
- The Jews who practised its idolatry to share its punishments. Jer. 44. 7—28.
- Terror occasioned by its fall. Eze. 32: 9, 10.
- Ever to be a base kingdom. Eze. 29: 15.
- Christ to be called out of. Hos. 11: 1. Mat. 2: 15.
- Conversion of. Isa. 19: 18—20.
- To be numbered and blessed along with Israel. Isa. 19: 23—25.
- Prophetic illustration of its destruction. Jer. 43: 9, 10. Eze. 30: 21, 22. Eze. 32: 4—6.

Election.

Of Christ, as Messiah. Isa. 42: 1. 1 Pet. 2: 6.

Of good angles. 1 Tim. 5: 21.

Of Israel. Deu. 7: 6. Isa. 45: 4.

Of ministers. Luke 6: 13. Acts 9: 15.

Of churches. 1 Pet. 5: 13.

OF SAINTS, IS
- Of God. 1 The. 1: 4. Tit. 1: 1.
- By Christ. Jno. 13: 18. Jno. 15: 16.
- In Christ. Eph. 1: 4.
- Personal. Mat. 20: 16, with Jno. 6: 44. Acts 22: 14. 2 Jno. 1: 13.
- According to the purpose of God. Rom. 9: 11. Eph. 1: 11.
- According to the foreknowledge of God. Rom. 8: 29. 1 Pet. 1: 2.
- Eternal. Eph. 1: 4.
- Sovereign. Rom. 9: 15, 16. 1 Cor. 1: 27. Eph. 1: 11.
- Irrespective of merit. Rom. 9: 11.
- Of grace. Rom. 11: 5.
- Recorded in heaven. Luke 10: 20.
- For the glory of God. Eph. 1: 6.
- Through faith. 2 The. 2: 13.
- Through sanctification of the Spirit. 1 Pet. 1: 2.
- To adoption. Eph. 1: 5.
- To salvation. 2 The. 2: 13.
- To conformity with Christ. Rom. 8: 29.
- To good works. Eph. 2: 10.
- To spiritual warfare. 2 Tim. 2: 4.
- To eternal glory. Rom. 9: 23.

ENSURES TO SAINTS
- Effectual calling. Rom. 8: 30.
- Divine teaching. Jno. 17: 6.
- Belief in Christ. Acts 13: 48.
- Acceptance with God. Rom. 11: 7.
- Protection. Mar. 13: 20.
- Vindication of their wrongs. Luke 18: 7.
- Working of all things for good. Rom. 8: 28.
- Blessedness. Psa. 33: 12. Psa. 65: 4.
- The inheritance. Isa. 65: 9. 1 Pet. 1: 4, 5.

Should lead to cultivation of graces. Col. 3: 12.

Should be evidenced by diligence. 2 Pet. 1: 10.

Saints may have assurance of. 1 The. 1: 4.

Exemplified. *Isaac*, Gen. 21: 12. *Abram*, Neh. 9: 7. *Zerubbabel*, Hag. 2: 23. *Apostles*, Jno. 13: 18. Jno. 15: 19. *Jacob*, Rom. 9: 12, 13. *Rufus*, Rom. 16: 13. *Paul*, Gal. 1: 15.

Embalming.

Unknown to early patriarchs. Gen. 23: 4.

Learned by the Jews in Egypt. Gen. 50: 2, 26.

Time required for. Gen. 50: 3.

How performed by the Jews. 2 Chr. 16: 14. Luke 23: 56, with Jno. 19: 40.

Not always practised by the Jews. Jno. 11: 39.

An attempt to defeat God's purpose. Gen. 3: 19.

Emblems of the Holy Ghost, The.

WATER. Jno. 3: 5. Jno. 7: 38, 39.
- Cleansing. Eze. 16: 9. Eze 36: 25. Eph. 5: 26. Heb. 10: 22.
- Fertilizing. Psa. 1: 3. Isa. 27: 3, 6. Isa. 44: 3, 4. Isa. 58: 11.
- Refreshing. Psa. 46: 4. Isa. 41: 17, 18.
- Abundant. Jno. 7: 37, 38.

Freely given. Isa. 55: 1. Jno. 4: 14. Rev. 22: 17.
FIRE. Mat. 3: 11.
Purifying. Isa. 4: 4. Mal. 3: 2, 3.
Illuminating. Exo. 13: 21. Psa. 78: 14.
Searching. Zep. 1: 12, with 1 Cor. 2: 10.
WIND.
Independent. Jno. 3: 8. 1 Cor. 12: 11.
Powerful. 1 Kin. 19: 11, with Acts 2: 2.
Sensible in its effects. Jno. 3: 8.
Reviving. Eze. 37: 9, 10, 14.
OIL. Psa. 45: 7.
Healing. Luke 10: 34. Rev. 3: 18.
Comforting. Isa. 61: 3. Heb. 1: 9.
Illuminating. Mat. 25: 3, 4. 1 Jno. 2: 20, 27.
Consecrating. Exo. 29: 7. Exo. 30: 30. Isa. 61: 1.
RAIN AND DEW. Psa. 72: 6.
Fertilizing. Eze. 34: 26, 27 Hos. 6: 3. Hos. 10: 12. Hos. 14: 5.
Refreshing. Psa. 68: 9. Isa. 18: 4.
Abundant. Psa. 133: 3.
Imperceptible. 2 Sam. 17: 12, with Mar. 4: 26—28.
A DOVE. Mat. 3: 16.
Gentle. Mat. 10: 16, with Gal. 5: 22.
A VOICE. Isa. 6: 8.
Speaking. Mat. 10: 20.
Guiding. Isa. 30: 21, with Jno. 16: 13.
Warning. Heb. 3: 7—11.
A SEAL. Rev. 7: 2.
Securing. Eph. 1: 13, 14. Eph. 4: 30.
Authenticating. Jno. 6: 27. 2 Cor. 1: 22.
CLOVEN TONGUES. Acts 2: 3, 6—11.

Enemies.

Christ prayed for His. Luke 23: 34.
The lives of, to be spared. 1 Sam. 24: 10. 2 Sam. 16: 10, 11.
The goods of, to be taken care of. Exo. 23: 4, 5.
SHOULD BE
Loved. Mat. 5: 44.
Prayed for. Acts 7: 60.
Assisted. Pro. 25: 21, with Rom. 12: 20.
Overcome by kindness. 1 Sam. 26: 21.
Rejoice not at the misfortunes of. Job 31: 29.
Rejoice not at the failings of. Pro. 24: 17.
Desire not the death of. 1 Kin. 3: 11.
Curse them not. Job 31: 30.
Be affectionately concerned for. Psa. 35: 13.
The friendship of, deceitful. 2 Sam. 20: 9, 10. Pro. 26: 26. Pro. 27: 6. Mat. 26: 48, 49.
God defends against. Psa. 59: 9. Psa. 61: 3.
God delivers from. 1 Sam. 12: 11. Ezr. 8: 31. Psa. 18: 48.
Made to be at peace with saints. Pro. 16: 7.
Pray for deliverance from. 1 Sam. 12: 10. Psa. 17: 9. Psa. 59: 1. Psa. 64: 1.
Of saints, God will destroy. Psa. 60: 12.
Praise God for deliverance from. Psa. 136: 24.

Entertainments.

Often great. Gen. 21: 8. Dan. 5: 1. Luke 5: 29.
GIVEN ON OCCASIONS OF
Marriage. Mat. 22: 2.
Birth days. Mar. 6: 21.
Weaning children. Gen. 21. 8.
Taking leave of friends. 1 Kin. 19: 21.
Return of friends. 2 Sam. 12: 4. Luke 15: 23, &c.
Ratifying covenants. Gen. 26: 30. Gen 31: 54.
Sheep-shearing. 1 Sam. 25: 2, 36. 2 Sam. 13: 23.
Harvest home. Ruth 3: 2—7. Isa. 9: 3.
Vintage. Jud. 9: 27.
Coronation of Kings. 1 Kin. 1: 9, 18, 19. 1 Chr. 12: 39, 40. Hos. 7: 5.
Offering voluntary sacrifice. Gen. 31: 54. Deu. 12: 6, 7. 1 Sam. 1: 4, 5, 9.
Festivals. 1 Sam. 20: 5, 24—26.
National deliverance. Est. 8: 17. Est. 9: 17—19.
Preparations made for. Gen. 18: 6, 7. Pro. 9: 2. Mat. 22: 4. Luke 15: 23.
KINDS OF, MENTIONED IN SCRIPTURE;
Dinner. Gen. 43: 16. Mat. 22: 4. Luke 14: 12.
Supper. Luke 14: 12. Jno. 12: 2.
Banquet of wine. Est. 5: 6
Under the direction of a symposiarch or master of the feast. Jno. 2: 8, 9.
Served often by hired servants. Mat. 22: 13. Jno. 2: 5.
Served often by members of the family. Gen. 18: 8. Luke 10: 40. Jno. 12: 2.
INVITATIONS TO,
Often addressed to many. Luke 14: 16.
Often only to relatives and friends. 1 Kin. 1: 9. Luke 14: 12.
Often by the master in person. 2 Sam. 13: 24. Est. 5: 4. Zep. 1: 7. Luke 7: 36.

Repeated through servants when all things were ready. Pro. 9: 1—5. Luke 14: 17.
Should be sent to the poor, &c. Deu. 14: 29, with Luke 14: 13.

OFTEN GIVEN IN
The house. Luke 5: 29.
The air, beside fountains. 1 Kin. 1: 9.
The court of the house. Est. 1: 5, 6. Luke 7: 36: 37.
The upper room or guest chamber. Mar. 14: 14, 15.

GUESTS AT,
Saluted by the master. Luke 7: 45.
Usually anointed. Psa. 23: 5. Luke 7: 46.
Had their feet washed when they came a distance. Gen. 18: 4. Gen. 43: 24. Luke 7: 38, 44.
Arranged according to rank. Gen. 43: 33. 1 Sam. 9: 22. Luke 14: 10.
Often had separate dishes. Gen. 43: 34. 1 Sam. 1: 4.
Often ate from the same dish. Mat. 26: 23.

Forwardness to take chief seats at, condemned. Mat. 23: 6. Luke 14: 7, 8.
A choice portion reserved in, for principal guests. Gen. 43: 34. 1 Sam. 1: 5. 1 Sam. 9: 23, 24.
Custom of presenting the sop at, to one of the guests, alluded to. Jno. 13: 26.
Portions of, often sent to the absent. 2 Sam. 11: 8. Neh. 8: 10. Est. 9: 19.
Offence given by refusing to go to. Luke 14: 18, 24.
Anxiety to have many guests at, alluded to. Luke 14: 22, 23.
Men and women did not usually meet at. Est. 1: 8, 9. Mar. 6: 21, with Mat. 14: 11.
None admitted to, after the master had risen and shut the door. Luke 13: 24, 25.
Began with thanksgiving. 1 Sam. 9: 13. Mar. 8: 6.
Concluded with a hymn. Mar. 14: 26.
None asked to eat or to drink more than he liked at. Est. 1: 8.
Music and dancing often introduced at. Amos 6: 5. Mar. 6: 22. Luke 15: 25.
Often scenes of great intemperance. 1 Sam. 25: 36. Dan. 5: 3, 4. Hos. 7: 5.
Given by the guests in return. Job 1: 4. Luke 14: 12.

Envy.

Forbidden. Pro. 3: 31. Rom. 13: 13.
Produced by foolish disputations. 1 Tim. 6: 4.
Excited by good deeds of others. Ecc. 4: 4.
A work of the flesh. Gal. 5: 21. Jas. 4: 5.
Hurtful to the envious. Job 5: 2. Pro. 14: 30.
None can stand before. Pro. 27: 4.
A proof of carnal-mindedness. 1 Cor. 3: 1, 3.
Inconsistent with the gospel. Jas. 3: 14.
Hinders growth in grace. 1 Pet. 2: 1, 2.

THE WICKED
Are full of. Rom. 1: 29.
Live in. Tit. 3: 3.

Leads to every evil work. Jas. 3: 16.
Prosperity of the wicked should not excite. Psa. 37: 1, 35. Psa. 73: 3, 17—20.
Punishment of. Isa. 26: 11.
Exemplified. *Cain*, Gen. 4: 5. *Philistines*, Gen. 26: 14. *Laban's sons*, Gen. 31: 1. *Joseph's brethren*, Gen. 37: 11. *Joshua*, Num. 11: 28, 29. *Aaron, &c.* Num. 12: 2. *Korah, &c.* Num. 16: 3, with Psa. 106: 16. *Saul*, 1 Sam. 18: 8. *Sanballat, &c.* Neh. 2: 10. *Haman*, Est. 5: 13. *Edomites*, Eze. 35: 11. *Princes of Babylon*, Dan. 6: 3, 4. *Chief Priests*, Mar. 15: 10. *Jews*, Acts 13: 45. Acts 17: 5.

Ephod, The.

The emblem of the priestly office. Hos. 3: 4.

WORN BY
The high priest. 1 Sam. 2: 28. 1 Sam. 14: 3.
Ordinary priests. 1 Sam. 22: 18.
Persons engaged in the service of God. 1 Sam. 2: 18. 2 Sam. 6: 14.
Generally of linen. 1 Sam. 2: 18. 2 Sam. 6: 14.

FOR THE HIGH PRIEST,
Commanded to be made. Exo. 28: 4.
Made of offerings of the people. Exo. 25: 4, 7.
Made of gold, blue, purple, scarlet, &c. Exo. 28: 6. Exo. 29: 2, 3.
Shoulders of, joined by onyx stones engraved with names of the twelve tribes of Israel. Exo. 28: 7, 9—12. Exo. 39: 4, 6, 7.
Had a girdle of curious work. Exo. 28: 8.
Breastplate of judgment inseparably united to. Exo. 28: 25—28. Exo. 39: 20, 21.
Worn over the robe. Exo. 28: 31. Lev. 8: 7.
Fastened on with its own girdle. Lev. 8: 7.
Worn or held by him when consulted. 1 Sam. 23: 6, 9—12. 1 Sam. 30: 7, 8.

Used by idolatrous priests. Jud. 8: 27. Jud. 17: 5. Jud. 18: 14.
Israel deprived of, for sin. Hos. 3: 4.

Ephraim, Tribe of.

Descended from Joseph's second son adopted by Jacob. Gen. 41: 52. Gen. 48: 5.
Predictions respecting. Gen. 48: 20. Deu. 33: 13—17.
PERSONS SELECTED FROM,
To number the people. Num. 1: 10.
To spy out the land. Num. 13: 8.
To divide the land. Num. 34: 24.
Strength of, on leaving Egypt. Num. 1: 32, 33.
Led the third division of Israel. Num. 10: 22.
Encamped west of the tabernacle. Num. 2: 18.
Offering of, at the dedication. Num. 7: 48—53.
Families of, Num. 26: 35, 36.
Strength of, on entering Canaan. Num. 26: 37.
On Gerizim, said amen to blessings. Deu. 27: 12.
Bounds of its inheritance. Jos. 16: 5—9.
Could not drive out the Canaanites but made them tributary. Jos 16: 10. Jud. 1: 29.
ASSISTED
Manasseh in taking Bethel. Jud. 1: 22—25.
Deborah and Barak against Sisera. Jud. 5: 14.
Gideon against Midian. Jud. 7: 24, 25.
Remonstrated with Gideon for not calling them sooner against Midian. Jud. 8: 1—3.
Quarrelled with Jephtha for not seeking their aid against Ammon. Jud. 12: 1—4.
Defeated and many slain. Jud. 12: 5, 6.
Some of, at coronation of David. 1 Chr. 12: 30.
Officers appointed over, by David. 1 Chr. 27: 10, 20.
The leading tribe of the kingdom of Israel. Isa. 7: 2 17. Jer. 31: 9, 20.
Many of, joined Judah under Asa. 2 Chr. 15: 9.
Many of, joined in Hezekiah's passover and reformation. 2 Chr. 30: 18. 2 Chr. 31: 1.
The tabernacle continued a long time in Shiloh, a city of. Jos. 18: 1. Jos. 19: 51.
One of Jeroboam's calves set up in Bethel, a city of. 1 Kin. 12: 29.
Remarkable persons of. *Joshua*, Num. 13: 8. Jos. 1: 1. *Abdon*, Jud. 12: 13—15. *Zichri*, 2 Chr. 28: 7.

Euphrates, The.

A branch of the river of Eden. Gen. 2: 14.
CALLED
The river. Exo. 23: 31. Neh. 2: 7. Psa. 72: 8.
The great river. Gen. 15: 18. Deu. 1: 7.
The flood. Jos. 24: 2.
Waters of, considered wholesome. Jer. 2: 18.
Often overflowed its banks. Isa. 8: 7, 8.
Assyria bounded by. 2 Kin. 23: 29. Isa. 7: 20.
Babylon situated on. Jer. 51: 13, 36.
Extreme eastern boundary of the promised land. Gen. 15: 18. Deu. 1: 7. Deu. 11: 24.
Egyptian army destroyed at. Jer. 46: 2, 6, 10.
Frequented by the captive Jews. Psa. 137: 1.
Captivity of Judah represented by the marring of Jeremiah's girdle in. Jer. 13: 3—9.
Prophecies respecting Babylon thrown into, as a sign. Jer. 51: 63.
Shall be the scene of future judgments. Rev. 16: 12.

Evening, The.

The day originally began with. Gen. 1: 5, &c.
Divided into two, commencing at 3 o'clock, and sunset. Exo. 12: 6. (*marg.*) Num. 9: 3. (*marg.*)
CALLED
Even. Gen. 19: 1. Deu. 28: 67.
Eventide. Jos. 8: 29. Acts 4: 3.
Cool of the day. Gen. 3: 8.
Stretches out its shadows. Jer. 6: 4.
The outgoings of, praise God. Psa. 65: 8.
Man ceases from labor in. Ruth 2: 17. Psa. 104: 23.
Wild beasts come forth in. Psa. 59: 6, 14. Jer. 5: 6.
A SEASON FOR
Meditation. Gen 24: 63.
Prayer. Psa. 55: 17. Mat. 14: 15, 23.
Exercise. 2 Sam. 11: 2.
Taking food. Mar. 14: 17, 18. Luke 24: 29, 30.
Humiliation often continued until. Jos. 7: 6. Jud. 20: 23, 26. Jud. 21: 2. Ezr. 9: 4, 5.
Custom of sitting at the gates in. Gen. 19: 1.
All defiled persons unclean until. Lev. 11: 24—28. Lev. 15: 5—7. Lev. 17: 15. Num. 19: 19.
Part of the daily sacrifice offered in. Exo. 29: 41. Psa. 141: 2. Dan. 9: 21.
Paschal lamb killed in. Exo. 12: 6, 18.

The golden candlestick lighted in. Exo. 27: 21, with Exo. 30: 8.
The sky red in, a token of fair weather. Mat. 16: 2.

Example of Christ, The.

Is perfect. Heb. 7: 26.
CONFORMITY TO, REQUIRED IN
- Holiness. 1 Pet. 1: 15, 16, with Rom. 1: 6.
- Righteousness. 1 Jno. 2: 6.
- Purity. 1 Jno. 3: 3.
- Love. Jno. 13: 34. Eph. 5: 2. 1 Jno. 3: 16.
- Humility. Luke 22: 27. Phi. 2: 5, 7.
- Meekness. Mat. 11: 29.
- Obedience. Jno. 15: 10.
- Self-denial. Mat. 16: 24. Rom. 15: 3.
- Ministering to others. Mat. 20: 28. Jno. 13: 14, 15.
- Benevolence. Acts 20: 35. 2 Cor. 8: 7, 9.
- Forgiving injuries. Col. 3: 13.
- Overcoming the world. Jno. 16: 33, with 1 Jno. 5: 4.
- Being not of the world. Jno. 17: 16.
- Being guileless. 1 Pet. 2: 21, 22.
- Suffering wrongfully. 1 Pet. 2: 21—23.
- Suffering for righteousness. Heb. 12: 3, 4.

Saints predestinated to follow. Rom. 8: 29.
Conformity to, progressive. 2 Cor. 3: 18.

Excellency and Glory of Christ, The.

As God. Jno. 1: 1—5. Phi. 2: 6, 9, 10.
As the Son of God. Mat. 3: 17. Heb. 1: 6, 8.
As one with the Father. Jno. 10: 30, 38.
As the First-born. Col. 1: 15, 18.
As the First-begotten. Heb. 1: 6.
As Lord of lords, &c. Rev. 17: 14.
As the image of God. Col. 1: 15. Heb. 1: 3.
As Creator. Jno. 1: 3. Col. 1: 16. Heb. 1: 2.
As the Blessed of God. Psa. 45: 2.
As Mediator. 1 Tim. 2: 5. Heb. 8: 6.
As Prophet. Deu. 18: 15, 16, with Acts 3: 22.
As Priest. Psa. 110: 4. Heb. 4: 15.
As King. Isa. 6: 1—5, with Jno. 12: 41.
As Judge. Mat. 16: 27. Mat. 25: 31, 33.
As Shepherd. Isa. 40: 10, 11. Jno. 10: 11, 14.
As Head of the Church. Eph. 1: 22.
As the true Light. Luke 1: 78, 79. Jno. 1: 4, 9.
As the foundation of the Church. Isa. 28: 16.
As the way. Jno. 14: 6. Heb. 10: 19, 20.
As the truth. 1 Jno. 5: 20. Rev. 3: 7.
As the life. Jno. 11: 25. Col. 3: 4. 1 Jno. 5: 11.
As incarnate. Jno. 1: 14.
In His words. Luke 4: 22. Jno. 7: 46.
In His works. Mat. 13: 54. Jno. 2: 11.
In His sinless perfection. Heb. 7: 26—28.
In the fulness of His grace and truth. Psa. 45: 2, with Jno. 1: 14.
In His transfiguration. Mat. 17: 2, with 2 Pet. 1: 16—18.
In His exaltation. Acts 7: 55, 56. Eph. 1: 21.
In the calling of the Gentiles. Psa. 72: 17. Jno. 12: 21, 23.
In the restoration of the Jews. Psa. 102: 16.
In His triumph. Isa. 63: 1—3, with Rev. 19: 11, 16.
Followed His sufferings. 1 Pet. 1: 10, 11.
Followed His resurrection. 1 Pet. 1: 21.
Is unchangeable. Heb. 1: 10—12.
Is incomparable. So. of Sol. 5: 10. Phi. 2: 9.
Imparted to saints. Jno. 17: 22. 2 Cor. 3: 18.
Celebrated by the redeemed. Rev. 5: 8—14. Rev. 7: 9—12.
Revealed in the gospel. Isa. 40: 5.
Saints shall rejoice at the revelation of. 1 Pet. 4: 13.
Saints shall behold, in heaven. Jno 17: 24.

Excellency and Glory of the Church, The.

Derived from God. Isa. 28: 5.
Derived from Christ. Isa. 60: 1. Luke 2: 34.
Result from the favor of God. Isa. 43: 4.
God delights in. Psa. 45: 11. Isa. 62 3—5.
Saints delight in. Isa. 66: 11.
CONSIST IN ITS
- Being the seat of God's worship. Psa. 96: 6.
- Being the temple of God. 1 Cor. 3: 16, 17. Eph. 2: 21, 22.
- Being the body of Christ. Eph. 1: 22, 23.
- Being the bride of Christ. Psa. 45: 13, 14. Rev. 19: 7, 8. Rev. 21: 2.
- Being established. Psa. 48: 8. Isa. 33: 20.
- Eminent position. Psa. 48: 2. Isa. 2: 2.
- Graces of character. So. of Sol. 2: 14.
- Perfection of beauty. Psa. 50: 2.

Members being righteous. Isa. 60: 21. Rev. 19: 8.
Strength and defence. Psa. 48: 12, 13.
Sanctification. Eph. 5: 26, 27.
Augmented by increase of its members. Isa. 49: 18. Isa. 60: 4—14.
Are abundant. Isa. 66: 11.
Sin obscures. Lam. 2: 14, 15.

Eye, The.

The light of the body. Mat. 6: 22. Luke 11: 34.
GOD
Made. Pro. 20: 12.
Formed. Psa. 94: 9.
Opens. 2 Kin. 6: 17. Psa. 146: 8.
Enlightens. Ezr. 9: 8. Psa. 13: 3.
Frequently fair. 1 Sam. 16: 12 (*marg.*)
Sometimes tender. Gen. 29: 17.
Sometimes blemished. Lev. 21: 20.
PARTS OF, MENTIONED IN SCRIPTURE;
The apple or ball. Deu. 32: 10.
The lid. Job 16: 16.
The brow. Lev. 14: 9.
ACTIONS OF, MENTIONED IN SCRIPTURE.
Seeing. Job 7: 8. Job 28: 10.
Winking. Pro. 10: 10.
Weeping. Job 16: 20. Psa. 88: 9. Lam. 1: 16.
Directing. Num. 10: 31. Psa. 32: 8.
The light of, rejoices the heart. Pro. 15: 30.
Not satisfied with seeing. Prov. 27: 20. Ecc. 1: 8.
Not satisfied with riches. Ecc. 4: 8.
No evil thing to be set before. Psa. 101: 3.
A guard to be set on. Job 31: 1. Pro. 23: 31.
Made red by wine. Gen. 49: 12. Pro. 23: 29.
Grows dim by sorrow. Job 17: 7.
Grows dim by age. Gen. 27: 1. 1 Sam. 3: 2.
Consumed by grief. Psa. 6: 7. Psa. 31: 9.
Consumed by sickness. Lev. 26: 16.
THE JEWS
Wore their phylacteries between. Exo. 13: 16, with Mat. 23: 5.
Not to make baldness between. Deu. 14: 1.
Raised up, in prayer. Psa. 121: 1. Psa. 123: 1.
Cast, on the ground in humiliation. Luke 18: 13.
The Jewish women often painted. 2 Kin. 9: 30. (*marg.*) Jer. 4: 30. (*marg.*) Eze. 23: 40.
Often put out as a punishment. Jud. 16: 21. 1 Sam. 11: 2. 2 Kin. 25: 7.
Punishment for injuring. Exo. 21: 24, 26. Lev. 24: 20. Mat. 5: 38.
ILLUSTRATIVE
Of the mind. Mat. 6: 22, 23.
(Open,) of spiritual illumination. Psa. 119: 18, 37.
(Anointing with eyesalve,) of healing by the Spirit. Rev. 3: 18.

Faith.

Is the substance of things hoped for. Heb. 11: 1.
Is the evidence of things not seen. Heb. 11: 1.
Commanded. Mar. 11: 22. 1 Jno. 3: 23.
THE OBJECTS OF, ARE
God. Jno. 14: 1.
Christ. Jno. 6: 29. Acts 20: 21.
Writings of Moses. Jno. 5: 46. Acts 24: 14,
Writings of the prophets. 2 Chr. 20: 20. Acts 26: 27.
The gospel. Mar. 1: 15.
Promises of God. Rom. 4: 21. Heb. 11: 13.
IN CHRIST, IS
The gift of God. Rom. 12: 3. Eph. 2: 8. Eph. 6: 23. Phi. 1: 29.
The work of God. Acts 11: 21. 1 Cor. 2: 5.
Precious. 2 Pet. 1: 1.
Most holy. Jude 20.
Fruitful. 1 The. 1: 3.
Accompanied by repentance. Mar. 1: 15. Luke 24: 47.
Followed by conversion. Acts 11: 21.
Christ is the Author and Finisher of. Heb. 12: 2.
Is a gift of the Holy Ghost. 1 Cor. 12: 9.
The Scriptures designed to produce. Jno. 20: 31. 2 Tim. 3: 15.
Preaching designed to produce. Jno. 17: 20. Acts 8: 12. Rom. 10: 14, 15, 17. 1 Cor. 3: 5.
THROUGH IT IS
Remission of sins. Acts 10: 43. Rom. 3: 25.
Justification. Acts 13: 39. Rom. 3: 21, 22, 28, 30. Rom. 5: 1. Gal. 2: 16.
Salvation. Mar. 16: 16. Acts 16: 31.
Sanctification. Acts 15: 9. Acts 26: 18.
Spiritual light. Jno. 12: 36, 46.
Spiritual life. Jno. 20: 31. Gal. 2: 20.
Eternal life. Jno. 3: 15, 16. Jno. 6: 40, 47.
Rest in heaven. Heb. 4: 3.
Edification. 1 Tim. 1: 4. Jude 20.
Preservation. 1 Pet. 1: 5.
Adoption. Jno. 1: 12. Gal. 3: 26.
Access to God. Rom. 5: 2. Eph. 3: 12.
Inheritance of the promises. Gal. 3: 22. Heb. 6: 12.

The gift of the Holy Ghost. Acts 11:15—17. Gal. 3:14. Eph. 1:13.
Impossible to please God without. Heb. 11:6.
Justification is by, to be of grace. Rom. 4:16.
Essential to the profitable reception of the gospel. Heb. 4:2.
Necessary in the Christian warfare. 1 Tim. 1:18, 19. 1 Tim. 6:12.
The gospel effectual in those who have. 1 The. 2:13.
Excludes self-justification. Rom. 10:3, 4.
Excludes boasting. Rom. 3:27.
Works by love. Gal. 5:6. 1 Tim. 1:5. Phile. 5.
PRODUCES
  Hope. Rom. 5:2.
  Joy. Acts 16:34. 1 Pet. 1:8.
  Peace. Rom. 15:13.
  Confidence. Isa. 28:16, with 1 Pet. 2:6.
  Boldness in preaching. Psa. 116:10, with 2 Cor. 4:13.
Christ is precious to those having. 1 Pet. 2:7.
Christ dwells in the heart by. Eph. 3:17.
Necessary in prayer. Mat. 21:22. Jas. 1:6.
Those who are not Christ's have not. Jno. 10:26, 27.
An evidence of the new birth. 1 Jno. 5:1.
BY IT SAINTS
  Live. Gal. 2:20.
  Stand. Rom. 11:20. 2 Cor. 1:24.
  Walk. Rom. 4:12. 2 Cor. 5:7.
  Obtain a good report. Heb. 11:2.
  Overcome the world. 1 Jno. 5:4, 5.
  Resist the devil. 1 Pet. 5:9.
  Overcome the devil. Eph. 6:16.
  Are supported. Psa. 27:13. 1 Tim. 4:10.
Saints die in. Heb: 11:13.
SAINTS SHOULD
  Be sincere in. 1 Tim. 1:5. 2 Tim 1:5.
  Abound in. 2 Cor. 8:7.
  Continue in. Acts 14:22. Col. 1:23.
  Be strong in. Rom. 4:20—24.
  Stand fast in. 1 Cor. 16:13.
  Be grounded and settled in. Col. 1:23.
  Hold, with a good conscience. 1 Tim. 1:19.
  Pray for the increase of. Luke 17:5.
  Have full assurance of. 2 Tim. 1:12. Heb. 10:22.
True, evidenced by its fruits. Jas. 2:21—25.
Without fruits, is dead. Jas. 2:17, 20, 26.
Examine whether you be in. 2 Cor. 13:5.
All difficulties overcome by. Mat. 17:20. Mat. 21:21. Mar. 9:23.
All things should be done in. Rom. 14:22.
Whatsoever is not of, is sin. Rom. 14:23.
Often tried by affliction. 1 Pet. 1:6, 7.
Trial of, works patience. Jas. 1:3.
The wicked often profess. Acts 8:13, 21.
The wicked destitute of. Jno. 10:25. Jno. 12:37. Acts 19:9. 2 The. 3:2.
Protection of, illustrated. *A shield*, Eph, 6:16. *A breastplate*, 1 The. 5:8.
Exemplified. *Caleb*, Num. 13:0. *Job*, Job 19:25. *Shadrach, &c.* Dan. 3:17. *Daniel*, Dan. 6:10, 23. *Peter*, Mat. 16:16. *Woman who was a sinner*, Luke 7:50. *Nathanael*, Jno. 1:49. *Samaritans*, Jno. 4:39. *Martha*, Jno. 11:27. *The Disciples*, Jno. 16:30. *Thomas*, Jno. 20:28. *Stephen*, Acts 6:5. *Priests*, Acts 6:7. *Ethiopian*, Acts 8:37. *Barnabas*, Acts 11:24. *Sergius Paulus*, Acts 13:12. *Philippian jailor*, Acts 16:31, 34. *Romans*, Rom. 1:8. *Colossians*, Col. 1:4. *Thessalonians*, 1 The. 1:3. *Lois*, 2 Tim. 1:5. *Paul*, 2 Tim. 4:7. *Abel*, Heb. 11:4. *Enoch*, Heb. 11:5. *Noah*, Heb. 11:7. *Abraham*, Heb. 11:8, 17. *Isaac*, Heb. 11:20. *Jacob*, Heb. 11:21. *Joseph*, Heb: 11:22. *Moses*, Heb. 11:24, 27. *Rahab*, Heb. 11:31. *Gideon &c.* Heb. 11:32, 33, 39.

Faithfulness.

A characteristic of saints. Eph. 1:1. Col. 1:2. 1 Tim. 6:2. Rev. 17:14.
EXHIBITED IN
  The service of God. Mat. 24:45.
  Declaring the word of God. Jer. 23:28. 2 Cor. 2:17. 2 Cor. 4:2.
  The care of dedicated things. 2 Chr. 31:12.
  Helping the brethren. 3 Jno. 5.
  Bearing witness. Pro. 14:5.
  Reproving others. Pro. 27:6. Psa. 141:5.
  Situations of trust. 2 Kin. 12:15. Neh. 13:13. Acts 6:1—3.
  Doing work. 2 Chr. 34:12.
  Keeping secrets. Pro. 11:13.
  Conveying messages. Pro. 13:17. Pro. 25:13.
  All things. 1 Tim. 3:11.
  The smallest matters. Luke 16:10—12.
Should be unto death. Rev. 2:10.
ESPECIALLY REQUIRED IN
  Ministers. 1 Cor. 4:2. 2 Tim. 2:2.
  The wives of ministers. 1 Tim. 3:11.

The children of ministers. Tit. 1: 6.
Difficulty of finding Pro. 20: 6.
The wicked devoid of. Psa. 5: 9.
Associate with those who exhibit. Psa. 101: 6.
Blessedness of. 1 Sam. 26: 23. Pro. 28: 20.
Blessedness of, illustrated. Mat. 24: 45, 46. Mat. 25: 21, 23.
Exemplified. *Joseph*, Gen. 39: 22, 23. *Moses*, Num. 12: 7, with Heb. 3: 2, 5. *David*, 1 Sam. 22: 14. *Hananiah*, Neh. 7: 2. *Abraham*, Neh. 9: 8. Gal. 3: 9. *Daniel*, Dan. 6: 4. *Paul*, Acts 20: 20, 27. *Timothy*, 1 Cor. 4: 17. *Tychicus*, Eph. 6: 21. *Epaphras*, Col. 1: 7. *Onesimus*, Col. 4: 9. *Silvanus*, 1 Pet. 5: 12. *Antipas*, Rev. 2: 13.

Faithfulness of God, The.

Is part of His character. Isa. 49: 7. 1 Cor. 1: 9. 1 The 5: 24.
DECLARED TO BE
Great. Lam. 3: 23.
Established. Psa. 89: 2.
Incomparable. Psa. 89: 8.
Unfailing Psa. 89: 33. 2 Tim. 2: 13.
Infinite. Psa. 36: 5.
Everlasting. Psa 119: 90. Psa. 146: 6.
Should be pleaded in prayer. Psa. 143: 1.
Should be proclaimed. Psa. 40: 10. Psa. 89: 1.
MANIFESTED
In His counsels. Isa. 25: 1.
In afflicting His saints. Psa. 119: 75.
In fulfilling His promises. 1 Kin. 8: 20. Psa. 132: 11. Mic. 7: 20. Heb. 10: 23.
In keeping His covenant. Deu. 7: 9. Psa. 111: 5.
In His testimonies. Psa. 119: 138.
In executing His judgments. Jer. 23: 20. Jer. 51: 29.
In forgiving sins. 1 Jno. 1: 9.
To His saints. Psa 89: 24. 2 The. 3: 3.
Saints encouraged to depend on. 1 Pet. 4: 19.
Should be magnified. Psa. 89: 5. Psa. 92: 2.

Fall of Man, The.

By the disobedience of Adam. Gen. 3: 6, 11, 12, with Rom. 5: 12, 15, 19.
Through temptation of the devil. Gen. 3: 1—5. 2 Cor. 11: 3. 1 Tim. 2: 14.
MAN IN CONSEQUENCE OF;
Made in the image of Adam. Gen. 5: 3, with 1 Cor. 15: 48, 49.
Born in sin. Job. 15: 14. Job. 25: 4. Psa. 51: 5. Isa. 48: 8. Jno. 3: 6.
A child of wrath. Eph. 2: 3.
Evil in heart. Gen. 6: 5. Gen. 8: 21. Jer. 16: 12. Mat. 15: 19.
Blinded in heart. Eph. 4: 18.
Corrupt and perverse in his ways. Gen. 6: 12. Psa. 10: 5. Rom. 3: 12—16.
Depraved in mind. Rom. 8: 5—7. Eph. 4: 17. Col. 1: 21. Tit. 1: 15.
Without understanding. Psa. 14: 2, 3, with Rom. 3: 11. Rom. 1: 31.
Receives not the things of God. 1 Cor. 2: 14.
Comes short of God's glory. Rom. 3: 23.
Defiled in conscience. Tit. 1: 15. Heb. 10: 22.
Intractable. Job 11: 12.
Estranged from God. Gen. 3: 8. Psa. 58: 3. Eph. 4: 18. Col. 1: 21.
In bondage to sin. Rom. 6: 19. Rom. 7: 5, 23. Gal. 5: 17. Tit. 3: 3.
In bondage to the devil. 2 Tim. 2: 26. Heb. 2: 14, 15.
Constant in evil. Psa 10: 5. 2 Pet. 2: 14.
Conscious of guilt. Gen. 3: 7, 8, 10.
Unrighteous. Ecc. 7: 20. Rom. 3. 10.
Abominable. Job 15: 16. Psa. 14: 3.
Turned to his own way. Isa. 53: 6.
Loves darkness. Jno. 3: 19.
Corrupt, &c. in speech. Rom. 3: 13, 14.
Devoid of the fear of God. Rom. 3: 18.
Totally depraved. Gen 6: 5. Rom. 7: 18.
Dead in sin. Eph. 2: 1. Col. 2: 13.
All men partake of the effects of. 1 Kin. 8: 46. Gal. 3: 22. 1 Jno. 1: 8. 1 Jno. 5: 19.
PUNISHMENT CONSEQUENT UPON,
Banishment from Paradise. Gen. 3: 24.
Condemnation to labor and sorrow. Gen. 3: 16, 19. Job. 5: 6, 7.
Temporal death. Gen. 3: 19. Rom. 5: 12. 1 Cor. 15: 22.
Eternal death. Job 21: 30. Rom. 5: 18, 21. Rom. 6: 23.
Cannot be remedied by man. Pro. 20: 9. Jer. 2: 22. Jer. 13: 23.
Remedy for, provided by God. Gen. 3: 15. Jno. 3: 16.

Families.

Of saints blessed. Psa. 128: 3—6.
SHOULD
Be taught the Scriptures. Deu. 4: 9, 10.
Worship God together. 1 Cor. 16: 19.

Be duly regulated. Pro. 31: 27. 1 Tim. 3: 4, 5, 12.
Live in unity. Gen. 45: 24. Psa. 133: 1.
Live in mutual forbearance. Gen. 50: 17—21. Mat. 18: 21, 22.
Rejoice together before God. Deu. 14: 26.
Deceivers and liars should be removed from. Psa. 101: 7.
Warning against departing from God. Deu. 29: 18.
Punishment of irreligious. Jer. 10: 25.
Good—Exemplified. *Abraham*, Gen. 18: 19. *Jacob*, Gen. 35: 2. *Joshua*, Jos. 24: 15. *David*, 2 Sam. 6: 20. *Job*, Job 1: 5. *Lazarus of Bethany*, Jno. 11: 1—5. *Cornelius*, Acts 10: 2, 33. *Lydia*, Acts 16: 15. *Jailor of Philippi*, Acts 16: 31—34. *Crispus*, Acts 18: 8. *Lois*, 2 Tim. 1: 5.

Famine.

Sent by God. Psa. 105: 16.
Often on account of sin. Lev. 26: 21, 26. Lam. 4: 4—6.
One of God's four sore judgments. Eze. 14: 21.
CAUSED BY
God's blessing withheld. Hos. 2: 8, 9. Hag. 1: 6.
Want of seasonable rain. 1 Kin. 17: 1. Jer. 14: 1—4. Amos 4: 7.
Rotting of the seed in the ground. Joel 1: 17.
Swarms of insects. Deu. 28: 38, 42. Joel 1: 4.
Blasting and mildew. Amos 4: 9. Hag. 2: 17.
Devastation by enemies. Deu. 28: 33, 51.
Often long continued. Gen. 41: 27. 2 Kin. 8: 1, 2.
Often severe. Gen. 12: 10. 1 Kin. 18: 2. Jer. 52: 6.
EXPRESSED BY
Taking away the stay of bread, &c. Isa. 3: 1.
Cleanness of teeth. Amos 4: 6.
The arrows of famine. Eze. 5: 16.
Often accompanied by war. Jer. 14: 15. Jer. 29: 18.
Often followed by pestilence. Jer. 42: 17. Eze. 7: 15. Mat. 24: 7.
THINGS EATEN DURING;
Wild herbs. 2 Kin. 4: 39, 40.
Ass's flesh. 2 Kin. 6: 25.
Ordure. 2 Kin. 6: 25. Lam. 4: 5.
Human flesh. Lev. 26: 29. 2 Kin. 6: 28, 29.
Provisions sold by weight during. Eze. 4: 16.
Suffering of brute creation from. Jer. 14: 5, 6.
CAUSED
Burning and fever. Deu. 32: 24.
Blackness of the skin. Lam. 4: 8. Lam. 5: 10.
Grief and mourning. Joel 1: 11—13.
Faintness. Gen. 47: 13.
Wasting of the body. Lam. 4: 8. Eze. 4: 17.
Death. 2 Kin. 7: 4. Jer. 11: 22.
God provided for His people during. 1 Kin. 17: 4, 9. Job 5: 20. Psa. 33: 19. Psa. 37: 19.
INSTANCES OF, IN SCRIPTURE;
In the days of Abraham. Gen. 12: 10.
In the days of Isaac. Gen. 26: 1.
In the days of Joseph. Gen. 41: 53—56.
In the days of the Judges. Ruth 1: 1.
In the reign of David. 2 Sam. 21: 1
In the reign of Ahab. 1 Kin. 17: 1 1 Kin. 18: 5.
In the time of Elisha. 2 Kin. 4: 38.
During the siege of Samaria. 2 Kin. 6: 25.
Of seven years foretold by Elisha. 2 Kin. 8: 1.
In the time of Jeremiah. Jer. 14: 1.
During the siege of Jerusalem. 2 Kin. 25: 3.
After the captivity. Neh. 5: 3.
In the reign of Claudius Cæsar. Acts 11: 28.
Before destruction of Jerusalem. Mat. 24: 7.
The Jews in their restored state not to be afflicted by. Eze. 36: 29, 30.
ILLUSTRATIVE OF
A dearth of the means of grace. Amos 8: 11, 12.
Destruction of idols. Zep. 2: 11.

Fasting.

Spirit of, explained. Isa. 58: 6, 7.
Not to be made a subject of display. Mat. 6: 16—18.
Should be unto God. Zec. 7: 5. Mat. 6: 18.
For the chastening of the soul. Psa. 69: 10.
For the humbling of the soul. Psa. 35: 13.
OBSERVED ON OCCASIONS OF
Judgments of God. Joel 1: 14. Joel 2: 12.
Public calamities. 2 Sam. 1: 12.
Afflictions of the Church. Luke 5 33—35.
Afflictions of others. Psa. 35: 13. Dan. 6: 18.
Private afflictions. 2 Sam. 12: 16.
Approaching danger. Est. 4: 16.
Ordination of ministers. Acts 13: 3. Acts 14: 23.
ACCOMPANIED BY
Prayer. Ezr. 8: 23. Dan. 9: 3.
Confession of sin. 1 Sam, 7: 6. Neh. 9: 1, 2.
Mourning. Joel 2: 12.

Humiliation. Deu. 9: 18. Neh. 9: 1.
Promises connected with. Isa. 58: 8—12. Mat. 6: 18.
Of hypocrites
Described. Isa. 58: 4, 5.
Ostentatious. Mat. 6: 16.
Boasted of, before God. Luke 18: 12.
Rejected. Isa. 58: 3. Jer. 14: 12.
Extraordinary—Exemplified. *Our Lord*, Mat. 4: 2. *Moses*, Exo. 34: 28. Deu. 9: 9, 18. *Elijah*, 1 Kin. 19: 8.
National—Exemplified. *Israel*, Jud. 20: 26. Ezr. 8: 21. Est. 4: 3, 16. Jer. 36: 9. *Men of Jabesh-gilead*, 1 Sam. 31: 13. *Ninevites*, Jon. 3: 5—8.
Of Saints—Exemplified. *David*, 2 Sam. 12: 16. Psa. 109: 24. *Nehemiah*, Neh. 1: 4. *Esther*, Est. 4: 16. *Daniel*, Dan. 9: 3. *Disciples of John*, Mat. 9: 14. *Anna*, Luke 2: 37. *Cornelius*, Acts 10: 30. *Primitive Christians*, Acts 13: 2. *Apostles*, 2 Cor. 6: 5. *Paul*, 2 Cor. 11: 27.
Of the wicked—Exemplified. *Elders of Jezreel*, 1 Kin. 21: 12. *Ahab*, 1 Kin. 21: 27. *Pharisees*, Mar. 2: 18. Luke 18: 12.

Fatherless, The.

Find mercy in God. Hos. 14: 3.
God will
Be a father of. Psa. 68: 5.
Be a helper of. Psa. 10: 14.
Hear the cry of. Exo. 22: 23.
Execute the judgment of. Deu, 10: 18. Psa. 10: 18.
Punish those who oppress. Exo. 22: 24. Isa. 10: 1—3. Mal. 3: 5.
Punish those who judge not. Jer. 5: 28, 29.
Visit in affliction. Jas. 1: 27.
Let them share in our blessings. Deu. 14: 29.
Defend. Psa. 82: 3. Isa. 1: 17.
Wrong not, in judgment. Deu. 24: 17.
Defraud not. Pro. 23: 10.
Afflict not. Exo. 22: 22.
Oppress not. Zec. 7: 10.
Do no violence to. Jer. 22: 3.
Blessedness of taking care of. Deu. 14: 29. Job 29: 12, 13. Jer. 7: 6, 7.
The wicked
Rob. Isa. 10: 2.
Overwhelm. Job 6: 27.
Vex. Eze. 22: 7.
Oppress. Job 24: 3.
Murder. Psa. 94: 6.
Judge not for. Isa. 1: 23. Jer. 5: 28.
A curse on those who oppress. Deu. 27: 19.
Promises with respect to. Jer. 49: 11.
A type of Zion in affliction. Lam. 5: 3.
Exemplified. *Lot*, Gen. 11: 27, 28. *Daughter of Zelophehad*, Num. 27: 1—5. *Jotham*, Jud. 9: 16—21. *Mephibosheth*, 2 Sam. 9: 3. *Joash*, 2 Kin. 11: 1—12. *Esther*, Est. 2: 7.

Favor of God, The.

Christ the especial object of. Luke 2: 52.
Is the source of
Mercy. Isa. 60: 10.
Spiritual life. Psa. 30: 5.
Spiritual wisdom leads to. Pro. 8: 35.
Mercy and truth lead to. Pro. 3: 3, 4.
Saints
Obtain. Pro. 12: 2.
Encompassed by. Psa. 5: 12.
Strengthened by. Psa. 30: 7.
Victorious through. Psa. 44: 3.
Preserved through. Job 10: 12.
Exalted in. Psa. 89: 17.
Sometimes tempted to doubt. Psa. 77: 7.
Domestic blessings traced to. Pro. 18: 22.
Disappointment of enemies an assured evidence of. Psa. 41: 11.
Given in answer to prayer. Job 33: 26.
Pray for. Psa. 106: 4. Psa. 119: 58.
Plead, in prayer. Exo. 33: 13. Num. 11: 15.
To be acknowledged. Psa. 85: 1.
The wicked
Uninfluenced by. Isa. 26: 10.
Do not obtain. Isa. 27: 11. Jer. 16: 13.
Exemplified. *Naphtali*, Deu. 33: 23. *Samuel*, 1 Sam. 2: 26. *Job*, Job 10: 12. *The Virgin Mary*, Luke 1: 28, 30. *David*, Acts 7: 46.

Fear, Godly.

God is the object of. Isa. 8: 13.
God is the author of. Jer. 32: 39, 40.
Searching the Scriptures gives the understanding of. Pro. 2: 3—5.
Described as
Hatred of evil. Pro. 8: 13.
Wisdom. Job 28: 28. Psa. 111: 10.
A treasure to saints. Pro. 15: 16. Isa. 33: 6.
A fountain of life. Pro. 14: 27.
Sanctifying. Psa. 19: 9.
Filial and reverential. Heb. 12: 9, 28.
Commanded. Deu. 13: 4. Psa. 22: 23. Ecc. 12: 13. 1 Pet. 2: 17.
Motives to
The holiness of God. Rev. 15: 4.
The greatness of God. Deu. 10: 12, 17.
The goodness of God. 1 Sam. 12: 24.
The forgiveness of God. Psa. 130: 4.
Wondrous works of God. Jos. 4: 23. 24.
Judgments of God. Rev. 14: 7.
A characteristic of saints. Mal. 3: 16.
Should accompany the joy of saints. Psa. 2: 11.
Necessary to
The worship of God. Psa. 5: 7. Psa. 89: 7.

The service of God. Psa. 2:11. Heb. 12:28.
Avoiding of sin. Exo. 20:20.
Righteous government. 2 Sam. 23:3.
Impartial administration of justice. 2 Chr. 19:6—9.
Perfecting holiness. 2 Cor. 7:1.

THOSE WHO HAVE
Afford pleasure to God. Psa. 147:11.
Are pitied by God. Psa. 103:13.
Are accepted of God. Acts 10:35.
Receive mercy from God. Psa 103:11, 17. Luke 1:50.
Are blessed. Psa. 112:1. Psa. 115:13.
Confide in God. Psa. 115:11. Pro. 14:26.
Depart from evil. Pro. 16:6.
Converse together of holy things. Mal. 3:16.
Should not fear man. Isa. 8:12, 13. Mat. 10:28.
Desires of, fulfilled by God. Psa. 145:19.
Days of, prolonged. Pro. 10:27.

SHOULD BE
Prayed for. Psa. 86:11.
Exhibited in our callings. Col. 3:22.
Exhibited in giving a reason for our hope. 1 Pet. 3:15.
Constantly maintained. Deu. 14:23. Jos. 4:24. Pro. 23:17.
Taught to others. Psa. 34:11.

Advantages of. Pro. 15:16. Pro. 19:23. Ecc. 8:12, 13.
The wicked destitute of. Psa. 36:1. Pro. 1:29. Jer. 2:19. Rom. 3:18.
Exemplified. *Abraham*, Gen. 22:12. *Joseph*, Gen. 39:9. Gen. 42:18. *Obadiah*, 1 Kin. 18:12. *Nehemiah*, Neh. 5:15. *Job*, Job 1:1, 8. *Primitive Christians*, Acts 9:31. *Cornelius*, Acts 10:2 *Noah*, Heb. 11:7.

Fear, Unholy.

A characteristic of the wicked. Rev. 21:8.

IS DESCRIBED AS
A fear of idols. 2 Kin. 17:38.
A fear of man 1 Sam. 15:24. Jno. 9:22.
A fear of judgments Isa. 2:19. Luke 21:26. Rev. 6:16, 17.
A fear of future punishment. Heb. 10:27.
Overwhelming. Exo. 15:16. Job 15:21, 24.
Consuming. Psa. 73:19.

A guilty conscience leads to. Gen. 3:8, 10. Psa. 53:5. Pro. 28:1.
Seizes the wicked. Job 15:24. Job 18:11.
Surprises the hypocrite. Isa. 33:14, 18.
The wicked judicially filled with. Lev. 26:16, 17. Deu. 28:65—67. Jer. 49:5.
Shall be realized. Pro. 1:27. Pro. 10:24.
God mocks. Pro. 1:26.
Saints sometimes tempted to. Psa. 55:5.
Saints delivered from. Pro. 1:33. Isa. 14:3.
Trust in God, a preservative from. Psa. 27:1.
Exhortations against. Isa. 8:12. Jno. 14:27.
Exemplified. *Adam*, Gen. 3:10. *Cain*, Gen. 4:14. *Midianites*, Jud. 7:21, 22, *Philistines*, 1 Sam. 14:15. *Saul*, 1 Sam. 28:5, 20. *Adonijah's guests*, 1 Kin. 1:49. *Haman*, Est. 7:6. *Ahaz*, Isa. 7:2. *Belshazzar*, Dan. 5:6. *Pilate*, Jno. 19:8. *Felix*, Acts 24:25

Feast of Dedication, The.

To commemorate the cleansing of the temple after its defilement by Antiochus. Dan. 11:31.
Held in the winter month, Chisleu. Jno. 10:22.

Feast of Jubilee, The.

Held every fiftieth year. Lev. 25:8, 10.
Began upon the day of atonement. Lev. 25:9.

CALLED THE
Year of liberty. Eze. 46:17.
Year of the redeemed. Isa. 63:4.
Acceptable year. Isa. 61:2.

Was specially holy. Lev. 25:12.
Proclaimed by trumpets. Lev. 25:9. Psa. 89:15.

ENACTMENTS RESPECTING;
Cessation of all field labor. Lev. 25:11.
The fruits of the earth to be common property. Lev. 25:12.
Redemption of sold property. Lev. 25:23—27.
Restoration of all inheritances. Lev. 25:10, 13, 28. Lev. 27:24.
Release of Hebrew servants. Lev. 25:40, 41, 54.

Houses in walled cities not redeemed within a year, exempted from the benefit of. Lev. 25:30.
Sale of property calculated from. Lev. 25:15, 16.
Value of devoted property calculated from. Lev. 27:14—23.
Illustrative of the Gospel. Isa. 61:1, 2. Luke 4:18, 19,

Feast of the New Moon, The.

Held first day of the month. Num. 10:10.
Celebrated with blowing of trumpets. Num. 10:10. Psa. 81:3, 4.

Sacrifices at. Num. 28:11—15.
A SEASON FOR
Inquiring of God's messengers. 2 Kin. 4:23.
Worship in God's house. Isa. 66:23. Eze. 46:1.
Entertainments. 1 Sam. 20:5, 18.
Observed with great solemnity. 1 Chr. 23:31. 2 Chr. 2:4. 2 Chr. 8:13. 2 Chr. 31:3.
Restored after captivity. Ezr. 3:5. Neh. 10:33.
Mere outward observance of, hateful to God. Isa. 1:13, 14.
Disliked by the ungodly. Amos 8:5.
The Jews deprived of, for sin. Hos. 2:11.
Observance of, by Christians, condemned. Col. 2:16, with Gal. 4:10.

Feast of Pentecost, The.

Held fiftieth day after offering first sheaf of barley harvest. Lev. 23:15, 16. Deu. 16:9.
CALLED THE
Feast of harvest. Exo. 23:16.
Feast of weeks. Exo. 34:22. Deu. 16:10.
Day of the first fruits. Num. 28:26.
Day of Pentecost. Acts 2:1.
To be perpetually observed. Lev. 23:21.
All males to attend. Exo. 23:16, 17. Deu. 16:16.
A holy convocation. Lev. 23:21. Num. 28:26.
A time of holy rejoicing. Deu. 16:11, 12.
The first fruits of bread presented at. Lev. 23:17. Deu. 16:10.
Sacrifices at. Lev. 23:18, 19. Num. 28:27—31.
The law given from Mount Sinai upon. Exo. 19:1, 11, with Exo. 12:6, 12.
The Holy Ghost given to apostles at. Acts 2:1—3.
Observed by early church. Acts 20:16. 1 Cor. 16:8.

Feast of Purim, or Lots, The.

Instituted by Mordecai. Est. 9:20.
To commemorate the defeat of Haman's wicked design. Est. 3:7—15, with Est. 9:24—26.
Began fourteenth of twelfth month. Est. 9:17.
Lasted two days. Est. 9:21.
Mode of celebrating. Est. 9:17—19, 22.
The Jews bound themselves to keep. Est. 9:27, 28.
Confirmed by royal authority. Est. 9:29—32.

Feast of Sabbatical Year, The.

A sabbath for the land. Lev. 25:2.
Kept every seventh year. Exo. 23:11. Lev. 25:4.
Surplus of sixth year to provide for. Lev. 25:20—22.
ENACTMENTS RESPECTING;
Cessation of all field labor. Lev. 25:4, 5.
The fruits of the earth to be common property. Exo. 23:11. Lev. 25:6, 7.
Remission of debts. Deu. 15:1—3. Neh. 10:31.
Release of all Hebrew servants. Exo. 21:2. Deu. 15:12.
Public reading of the law at feast of tabernacles. Deu. 31:10—13.
No release to strangers during. Deu. 15:3.
Release of, not to hinder the exercise of benevolence. Deu. 15:9—11.
Jews threatened for neglecting. Lev. 26:34, 35, 43. Jer. 34:13—18.
The seventy years' captivity a punishment for neglecting. 2 Chr. 36:20, 21.
Restored after the captivity. Neh. 10:31.

Feast of Tabernacles, The.

Held after harvest and vintage. Deu. 16:13.
Began fifteenth of seventh month. Lev. 23:34, 39.
Lasted seven days. Lev. 23:34, 41. Deu. 16:13, 15.
Called the feast of ingathering. Exo. 34:22.
All males obliged to appear at. Exo. 23:16, 17.
First and last days of, holy convocations. Lev. 23:35, 39. Num. 29:12, 35.
Sacrifices during. Lev. 23:36, 37. Num. 29:13—39.
TO BE OBSERVED
With rejoicing. Deu. 16:14, 15.
Perpetually. Lev. 23:41.
The people dwelt in booths during. Lev. 23:42. Neh. 8:15, 16.
The law publicly read every seventh year at. Deu. 31:10—12. Neh. 8:18.
CUSTOMS OBSERVED AT;
Bearing branches of palms. Lev. 23:40. Rev. 7:9.
Drawing water from the pool of Siloam. Isa. 12:3. Jno. 7:2, 37—39.
Singing hosannas. Psa. 118:24—29. Mat. 21:8, 9.
To commemorate the sojourn of Israel in the desert. Lev. 23:43.

REMARKABLE CELEBRATIONS OF;
At the dedication of Solomon's temple. 1 Kin. 8: 2, 65.
After the captivity. Ezr. 3: 4. Neh. 8: 17.

Feast of the Passover, The.

Ordained by God. Exo. 12:1, 2.
Commenced the fourteenth of the first month at even. Exo. 12: 2, 6, 18. Lev. 23: 5. Num. 9: 3.
Lasted seven days. Exo. 12: 15. Lev. 23: 6.
CALLED THE
Passover. Num. 9: 5. Jno. 2: 23.
Jew's passover. Jno. 2: 13. Jno. 11: 55.
Lord's passover. Exo. 12: 11, 27.
Feast of unleavened bread. Mar. 14: 1. Luke 22: 1.
Days of unleavened bread. Acts 12: 3. Acts 20: 6.
All males to appear at. Exo. 23: 17. Deu. 16: 16.
Paschal lamb eaten first day of. Exo. 12: 6, 8.
Unleavened bread eaten at. Exo. 12: 15. Deu. 16: 3.
LEAVEN
Not to be in their houses during. Exo. 12: 19.
Not to be in any of their quarters. Exo. 13: 7. Deu. 16: 4.
Nothing with, to be eaten. Exo. 12: 20.
Punishment for eating. Exo. 12: 15, 19.
First and last days of, holy convocations. Exo. 12: 16. Num. 28: 18, 25.
Sacrifices during. Lev. 23: 8. Num. 28: 19—24.
The first sheaf of barley harvest offered the day after the Sabbath in. Lev. 23: 10—14.
TO COMMEMORATE THE
Passing over the first-born. Exo. 12: 12, 13.
Deliverance of Israel from bondage of Egypt. Exo. 12: 17, 42. Exo. 13: 9. Deu. 16: 3.
To be perpetually observed during the Mosaic dispensation. Exo. 12: 14. Exo. 13: 10.
Children to be taught the nature and design of. Exo. 12: 26, 27. Exo. 13: 8.
Purification necessary to the due observance of. 2 Chr. 30: 15—19. Jno. 11: 55.
Might be kept in second month by those who were unclean at the appointed time. Num. 9: 6—11. 2 Chr. 30: 2, 3, 15.
No uncircumcised person to keep. Exo. 12: 43, 45.
Strangers and servants when circumcised might keep. Exo. 12: 44, 48.
Neglect of, punished with death. Num. 9: 13.
Improper keeping of, punished. 2 Chr. 30: 18, 20.
REMARKABLE CELEBRATIONS OF:
On leaving Egypt. Exo. 12: 28, 50.
In the wilderness of Sinai. Num. 9: 3—5.
On entering the land of promise. Jos. 5: 10, 11.
In Hezekiah's reign. 2 Chr. 30: 1.
In Josiah's reign. 2 Kin. 23: 22, 23. 2 Chr. 35: 1, 18.
After the captivity. Ezr. 6: 19, 20.
Before the death of Christ. Luke 22: 15.
Moses kept through faith. Heb. 11: 28.
Christ always observed. Mat. 26: 17—20. Luke 22: 15. Jno. 2: 13, 23.
The people of Jerusalem lent their rooms to strangers for. Luke 22: 11, 12.
The Lord's Supper instituted at. Mat. 26: 26—28.
Custom of releasing a prisoner at. Mat. 27: 15. Luke 23: 16, 17.
The Sabbath in, a high day. Jno. 19: 31.
The day before the Sabbath in, called the preparation. Jno. 19: 14, 31.
Illustrative of redemption through Christ. 1 Cor. 5: 7, 8.

Feasts of Trumpets, The.

Held the first day of seventh month. Lev. 23: 24. Num. 29: 1.
A memorial of blowing of trumpets. Lev. 23: 24.
A holy convocation and rest. Lev. 23: 24, 25.
Sacrifices at. Num. 29: 2—6.

Feasts, The Anniversary.

Instituted by God. Exo. 23: 14.
Enumerated. Exo. 23: 15, 16.
CALLED
Appointed feasts. Isa. 1: 14.
Feasts of the Lord. Lev. 23: 4.
Solemn feasts. 2 Chr. 8: 13. Lam. 1: 4.
Solemn meetings. Isa. 1: 13.
Were eucharistic. Psa. 122: 4.
All males to attend. Exo. 23: 17. Exo. 34: 23.
Children commenced attending, when twelve years old. Luke 2: 42.
Females often attended. 1 Sam. 1: 3, 9. Luke 2: 41.
The Jews attended gladly. Psa. 122: 1, 2.
The Jews went up to, in large companies. Psa. 42: 4. Luke 2: 44.

The dangers and difficulties encountered in going up to, alluded to. Psa. 84: 6. 7.
The land divinely protected during. Exo 34: 24.
Offerings to be made at. Exo. 34: 20. Deu. 16: 16, 17.
WERE SEASONS OF
Joy and gladness. Psa. 42: 4. Isa. 30: 29.
Sacrificing. 1 Sam. 1: 3. 1 Kin. 9: 25. 2 Chr. 8: 13.
Entertainments. 1 Sam. 1: 4, 9.
The ten tribes seduced by Jeroboam from attending. 1 Kin. 12: 27.
The Jews dispersed in distant parts often attended. Acts 2: 5—11. Acts 8: 27.
Christ attended. Jno. 5: 1. Jno. 7: 10.
Rendered unavailing by the impiety of the Jews. Isa. 1: 13, 14. Amos 5: 21.
Illustrative of general assembly of the church. Heb. 12: 23.

Feet, The.

Necessary members of the body. 1 Cor. 12: 15, 21.
PARTS OF, MENTIONED IN SCRIPTURE;
Heel. Psa. 41: 9. Psa. 49: 5. Hos. 12: 3.
Sole. Deu. 11: 24. 1 Kin. 5: 3.
Toes. Exo. 29: 20. 2 Sam. 21: 20. Dan. 2: 41.
Often swift. 2 Sam. 2: 18. 2 Sam. 22: 34.
WERE LIABLE TO
Disease. 1 Kin. 15: 23.
Swelling from walking. Deu. 8: 4.
Injury from stones, &c. Psa. 91: 12.
Early use of shoes for. Exo. 12: 11.
Of women often adorned with tinkling ornaments. Isa. 3: 16, 18.
OF THE JEWS
Neglected in affliction. 2 Sam. 19: 24. Eze. 24: 17.
Bare in affliction. 2 Sam. 15: 30.
Washed frequently. 2 Sam. 11: 8. So. of Sol. 5: 3.
Stamped on the ground in extreme joy or grief. Eze. 6: 11. Eze. 25: 6.
Washing for others, a menial office. 1 Sam. 25: 41. Jno. 13: 5—14.
Of strangers and travellers washed. Gen. 18: 4. Gen. 19: 2. Gen. 24: 32. 1 Tim. 5: 10.
Neglect of washing, disrespectful to guest. Luke 7: 44.
Respect exhibited by falling at. 1 Sam. 25: 24. 2 Kin. 4: 37. Est. 8: 3. Mar. 5: 22. Acts 10: 25.
Reverence expressed by kissing. Luke 7: 38, 45.
Sleep expressed by covering. 1 Sam. 24: 3.
Subjection expressed by licking the dust of. Isa. 49: 23.
Condemnation expressed by shaking the dust from. Mat. 10: 14. Mar. 6: 11.
Subjugation of enemies expressed by placing on their necks. Jos. 10: 24. Psa. 110: 1.
Origin of uncovering in consecrated places. Exo. 3: 5. Jos. 5: 15.
Of enemies often maimed and cut off. Jud. 1: 6, 7. 2 Sam. 4: 12.
OF CRIMINALS
Bound with fetters. Psa. 105: 18.
Placed in stocks. Job 13: 27. Acts 16: 24.
Path of, to be pondered. Pro. 4: 26.
To be refrained from evil. Pro. 1: 15. Heb. 12: 13.
To be turned to God's testimonies. Psa. 119: 59.
To be directed by God's word. Psa. 119: 105.
To be guided by wisdom and discretion. Pro. 3: 21, 23, 26.
OF THE WICKED
Swift to mischief. Pro. 6: 18.
Swift to shed blood. Pro. 1: 16. Rom. 3: 15.
Ensnared. Job 18: 8. Psa. 9: 15.
OF SAINTS
At liberty. Psa. 18: 36. Psa. 31: 8.
Kept by God. 1 Sam. 2: 9. Psa. 116: 8.
Established by God. Psa. 66: 9. Psa. 121: 3.
Guided by Christ. Isa. 48: 17. Luke 1: 79.
ILLUSTRATIVE
(Set on a rock,) of stability. Psa. 40: 2.
(Set in a large place,) of liberty. Psa. 31: 8.
(Sliding,) of yielding to temptation. Job 12: 5. Psa. 17: 5. Psa. 38: 16. Psa. 94: 18.
(Treading under,) of complete destruction. Isa. 18: 7. Lam. 1: 15.
(Washed or dipped in oil,) of abundance. Deu. 33: 24. Job 29: 6.
(Dipped in blood,) of victory. Psa. 68: 23.

Fig-tree, The.

Produces a rich sweet fruit. Jud. 9: 11.
Not found in desert places. Num. 20: 5.
ABOUNDED IN
Egypt. Psa. 105: 33.
Canaan. Num. 13: 23. Deu. 8: 8.
Often grew wild. Amos 7: 14. (*marg.*)
Sometimes planted in vineyards. Luke 13: 6.
Propagated by the Jews. Amos 4: 9.
Required cultivation. Luke 13: 8.

Fruit of, formed after winter. So. of Sol. 2:11, 13.
Leaves of, put forth, a sign of the approach of summer. Mat. 24:32.
Reasonableness of expecting fruit upon, when full of leaves. Mar. 11:13.
FRUIT OF,
Eaten fresh from the tree. Mat. 21:18, 19.
Eaten dried in cakes. 1 Sam. 30:12.
Gathered and kept in baskets. Jer. 24:1.
First ripe esteemed. Jer. 24:2. Hos. 9:10.
Used in the miraculous healing of Hezekiah. 2 Kin. 20:7. Isa. 38:21.
Sold in the markets. Neh. 13:15.
Sent as presents. 1 Sam. 25:18. 1 Chr. 12:40.
A species of, produced vile and worthless fruit. Jer. 29:17.
Leaves of, used by Adam for covering. Gen. 3:7.
Afforded a thick shade. Jno. 1:48, 50.
Often unfruitful. Luke 13:7.
Failure of, a great calamity. Hab. 3:17.
THE JEWS PUNISHED BY
God's breaking down. Hos. 2:12.
Failure of fruit on. Jer. 8:13. Hag. 2:19.
Enemies devouring fruit of. Jer. 5:17
Barking and eating of, by locusts, &c. Joel 1:4, 7, 12. Amos 4:9.
ILLUSTRATIVE
(Barren,) of mere professors of religion. Mat. 21:19. Luke 13:6, 7.
(Sitting under one's own,) of prosperity and peace. 1 Kin. 4:25. Mic. 4:4.
FRUIT OF, ILLUSTRATIVE
Of good works. Mat. 7:16.
(Good,) of saints. Jer. 24:2, 3.
(Bad,) of wicked men. Jer: 24:2, 3—8.
(First ripe,) of the fathers of the Jewish church. Hos. 9:10.
(Untimely and dropping,) of the wicked ripe for judgment. Isa. 34:4. Nah. 3:12. Rev. 6:13.

Fire.

Can be increased in intensity. Dan. 3:19, 22.
Though small, kindles a great matter. Jas. 3:5.
THINGS CONNECTED WITH;
Burning coals. Pro. 26:21.
Flame. So. of Sol. 8:6. Isa. 66:15.
Sparks. Job 18:5. Isa. 1:31.
Ashes. 1 Kin. 13:3. 2 Pet. 2:6.
Smoke. Isa. 34:10. Joel 2:30.
Kept alive by fuel. Pro. 26:20. Isa. 9:5.
CHARACTERIZED AS
Bright. Eze. 1:13.
Spreading. Jas. 3:5.
Enlightening. Psa. 78:14. Psa. 105:39.
Heating. Mar. 14:54.
Melting. Psa. 68:2. Isa. 64:2.
Purifying. Num. 31:23. 1 Pet. 1:7. Rev. 3:18.
Drying. Job 15:30. Joel 1:20.
Consuming. Jud. 15:4, 5. Psa. 46:9. Isa. 10:16, 17.
Insatiable. Pro. 30:16.
SACRED,
Came from before the Lord. Lev. 9:24.
Always burning on the altar. Lev. 6:13.
All burnt offerings consumed by. Lev. 6:9, 12.
Incense burned with. Lev. 16:12. Num. 16:46.
Guilt of burning incense without. Lev. 10:1.
Restored to the temple. 2 Chr. 7:1—3.
Frequently employed as an instrument of divine vengeance. Psa. 97:3. Isa. 47:14. Isa. 66:16.
MIRACULOUS,
In the burning bush. Exo. 3:2.
Plagued the Egyptians. Exo. 9:23, 24.
Led the people of Israel in the desert. Exo. 13:22. Exo. 40:38.
On Mount Sinai at giving of law. Deu. 4:11, 36.
Destroyed Nadab and Abihu. Lev. 10:2.
Destroyed the people at Taberah. Num. 11:1.
Consumed the company of Korah. Num. 16:35.
Consumed the sacrifice of Gideon. Jud. 6:21.
Angel ascended in. Jud. 13:20.
Consumed the sacrifice of Elijah. 1 Kin. 18:38.
Destroyed the enemies of Elijah. 2 Kin. 1:10, 12.
Elijah taken up in a chariot of. 2 Kin. 2:11.
God appeared in. Exo. 3:2. Exo. 19:18.
Christ shall appear in. Dan. 7:10. 2 The. 1:8.
Punishment of the wicked shall be in. Mat. 13:42. Mat. 25:41.
IN HOUSES
Lighted in the winter. Jer. 36:22.
Lighted in spring mornings. Jno. 18:18.

Not to be lighted on the Sabbath. Exo. 35:3.
Made of charcoal. Jno. 18:18.
Made of wood. Acts 28:3.
Injury from, to be made good by the person who kindled it. Exo. 22:6.
ILLUSTRATIVE OF
God's protection. Num. 9:16. Zec. 2:5.
God's vengeance. Deu. 4:24. Heb. 12:29.
Christ as judge. Isa. 10:17. Mal. 3:2.
The Holy Spirit. Isa. 4:4. Acts 2:3.
The church destroying her enemies. Oba. 18 v.
The word of God. Jer. 5:14. Jer. 23:29.
Zeal of saints. Psa. 39:3. Psa. 119:139.
Zeal of angels. Psa. 104:4. Heb. 1:7.
God's enemies. Isa. 10:17. Oba. 18 v.
Lust. Pro. 6:27, 28.
Wickedness. Isa. 9:18.
The tongue. Pro. 16:27. Jas. 3:6.
The self-righteous. Isa. 65:5.
The hope of hypocrites. Isa. 50:11.
Persecution. Luke 12:49—53.
Affliction. Isa. 43:2.
Judgments. Jer. 48:45. Lam. 1:13. Eze. 39:6.

First-born, The.

Of man and beast dedicated to God. Exo. 13:2, 12. Exo. 22:29.
Dedicated to commemorate the sparing of the first-born of Israel. Exo. 13:15. Num. 3:13. Num. 8:17.
OF CLEAN BEASTS
Not to labor. Deu. 15:19.
Not shorn. Deu. 15:19.
Not taken from the dam for seven days. Exo. 22:30. Lev. 22:27.
Offered in sacrifice. Num. 18:17.
Could not be a free-will offering. Lev. 27:26.
Antiquity of offering. Gen. 4:4.
Flesh of, the priests' portion. Num. 18:18.
OF UNCLEAN BEASTS
To be redeemed. Num. 18:15.
Law of redemption for. Num. 18:16.
Of the ass to be redeemed with a lamb or its neck broken. Exo. 13:13. Exo. 34:20.
OF ISRAEL
Tribe of Levi taken for. Num. 3:12, 40—43. Num. 8:18.
To be redeemed. Exo. 34:20. Num. 18:15.
Price of redemption for. Num. 3:46, 47.
Price of, given to the priests. Num. 3:48—51.
Laws respecting, restored after the captivity. Neh. 10:36.
Laws respecting, observed at Christ's birth. Luke 2:22, 23.
The beginning of strength and excellency of power. Gen. 49:3. Deu. 21:17.
Precious and valuable. Mic. 6:7. Zec. 12:10.
Objects of special love. Gen. 25:28. Jer. 31:9, 20.
PRIVILEGES OF;
Precedence in the family. Gen. 48:13, 14.
Authority over the younger children. Gen. 27:29. 1 Sam. 20:29.
Special blessing by the father. Gen. 27:4, 35.
The father's title and power. 2 Chr. 21:3.
A double portion of inheritance. Deu. 21:17.
In case of death the next brother to raise up seed to. Deu. 25:5, 6. Mat. 22:24—28.
Not to be alienated by parents through caprice. Deu. 21:15, 16.
Could be forfeited by misconduct. Gen. 49:3, 4, 8. 1 Chr. 5:1.
Could be sold. Gen. 25:31, 33. Heb. 12:16, 17.
INSTANCES OF, SUPERSEDED;
Cain. Gen. 4:4, 5.
Japheth. Gen. 10:21.
Ishmael. Gen. 17:19—21.
Esau. Gen. 25:23. Rom. 9:12, 13.
Manasseh. Gen. 48:15—20.
Reuben, &c. 1 Chr. 5:1, 2.
Aaron. Exo. 7:1, 2, with Num. 12:2, 8.
David's brothers. 1 Sam. 16:6—12.
Adonijah. 1 Kin. 2:15, 22.
ILLUSTRATIVE OF
The dignity, &c. of Christ. Psa. 89:27. Rom. 8:29. Col. 1:18.
The dignity, &c. of the church. Heb. 12:23.

First-fruits, The.

To be brought to God's house. Exo. 34:26.
DIFFERENT KINDS OF;
Barley harvest. Lev. 23:10—14.
Wheat harvest. Exo. 23:16. Lev. 23:16, 17.
Wine and oil. Deu. 18:4.
Wool. Deu. 18:4.
Honey. 2 Chr. 31:5.
Fruit of new trees in fourth year. Lev. 19:23, 24.
All agricultural produce. Deu. 26:2.
To be the very best of their kind. Num. 18:12.

Holy to the Lord. Eze. 48: 14.
God honored by the offering of. Pro. 3: 9.
Offering of, consecrated the whole. Rom. 11: 16.
TO BE OFFERED
Without delay. Exo. 22: 29.
In a basket. Deu. 26: 2.
With thanksgiving. Deu. 26: 3—10.
Allotted to the priests. Num. 18: 12, 13. Lev. 23: 20. Deu. 18: 3—5.
Law of, restored after the captivity. Neh. 10: 35, 37. Neh. 13: 31.
ILLUSTRATIVE OF
Early Jewish church. Jer. 2: 3.
First converts in any place. Rom. 16: 5.
Church of Christ. Jas. 1: 18. Rev. 14: 4.
Resurrection of Christ. 1 Cor. 15: 20, 23.

Fishes.

Created by God. Gen. 1: 20, 21. Exo. 20: 11.
Made for God's glory. Job 12: 8, 9. Psa. 69: 34.
INHABIT
Seas. Num. 11: 22. Eze. 47: 10.
Rivers. Exo. 7: 18. Eze. 29: 5.
Ponds. So. of Sol. 7: 4. Isa. 19: 10.
Number and variety of. Psa. 104: 25.
Different in flesh from beasts, &c. 1 Cor. 15: 39.
Cannot live without water. Isa. 50: 2.
Man given dominion over. Gen. 1: 26, 28. Psa. 8: 8.
Man permitted to eat. Gen. 9: 2, 3.
USED AS FOOD
By the Egptians. Num. 11: 5.
By the Jews. Mat. 7: 10.
Mode of cooking alluded to. Luke 24: 42. Jno. 21: 9.
The Tyrians traded in. Neh. 13: 16.
Sold near the fish gate at Jerusalem. 2 Chr. 33: 14. Zep. 1: 10.
Distinction between clean, and unclean. Lev. 11: 9—12. Deu. 14: 9, 10.
MENTIONED IN SCRIPTURE;
Leviathan. Job 41: 1. Psa. 74: 14.
Whale. Gen. 1: 21. Mat. 12: 40.
Solomon wrote the history of. 1 Kin. 4: 33.
No likeness of, to be made for worship. Exo. 20: 4. Deu. 4: 18.
Catching of, a trade. Mat. 4: 18. Luke 5: 2.
TAKEN WITH
Nets. Luke 5: 4—6. Jno. 21: 6—8.
Hooks. Amos 4: 2. Mat. 17: 27.
Spears. Job 41: 7.
Often suffered for man's sin. Exo. 7: 21. Eze. 38: 20.
MIRACLES CONNECTED WITH;
Multiplying a few. Mat. 14: 17—21. Mat. 15: 34.
Immense draughts of. Luke 5: 6, 9. Jno. 21: 6, 11.
Procuring tribute money from. Mat. 17: 27.
Dressed on the shore. Jno. 21: 9.
ILLUSTRATIVE
Of the whole population of Egypt. Eze. 29: 45.
Of the visible church. Mat. 13: 48.
Of men ignorant of future events. Ecc. 9: 12.
Of those ensnared by the wicked. Hab. 1: 14.
(Good,) of saints. Mat. 13: 48, 49.
(Bad,) of mere professors. Mat. 13: 48, 49.

Flattery.

Saints should not use. Job 32: 21, 22.
Ministers should not use. 1 The. 2: 5.
THE WICKED USE, TO
Others. Psa. 5: 9. Psa. 12: 2.
Themselves. Psa. 36: 2.
HYPOCRITES USE, TO
God. Psa. 78: 36.
Those in authority. Dan. 11: 34.
False prophets and teachers use. Eze. 12: 24, with Rom. 16: 18.
Wisdom, a preservative against. Pro. 4: 5.
Worldly advantage obtained by. Dan. 11: 21, 22.
Seldom gains respect. Pro. 28: 23.
Avoid those given to. Pro. 20: 19.
Danger of. Pro. 7: 21—23. Pro. 29: 5.
Punishment of. Job 17: 5. Psa. 12: 3.
Exemplified. *Woman of Tekoah*, 2 Sam. 14: 17, 20. *Absalom*, 2 Sam. 15: 2—6. *False prophets*, 1 Kin. 22: 13. *Darius's courtiers*, Dan. 6: 7. *Pharisees, &c.* Mat. 12: 14. *Tyrians, &c.* Acts 12: 22.

Flowers.

Wild in fields. Psa. 103: 15.
Cultivated in gardens. So. of Sol. 6: 2, 3.
DESCRIBED AS
Beautiful. Mat. 6: 29.
Sweet. So. of Sol. 5: 13.
Evanescent. Psa. 103: 16. Isa. 40: 8.
Appear in spring. So. of Sol. 2: 12.
MENTIONED IN SCRIPTURE;
The lily. Hos. 14: 5. Mat. 6: 28.
The lily of the valley. So. of Sol. 2: 1.
The rose. Isa. 35: 1.
The rose of Sharon. So. of Sol. 2: 1.
Of the grass. 1 Pet. 1: 24.
Garlands of, used in worship of idols. Acts 14: 13.

REPRESENTATIONS OF, ON THE
Golden candlestick. Exo. 25: 31, 33. 2 Chr. 4: 21.
Sea of brass. 1 Kin. 7: 26. 2 Chr. 4: 5.
Wood work of the temple. 1 Kin. 6: 18, 29, 33, 35.
ILLUSTRATIVE OF
The graces of Christ. So. of Sol. 5: 13.
Shortness of man's life. Job 14: 2. Psa. 103: 15.
Kingdom of Israel. Isa. 28: 1.
Glory of man. 1 Pet. 1: 24.
Rich men. Jas. 1: 10, 11.

Fools.

All men are, without the knowledge of God. Tit. 3: 3.
Deny God. Psa. 14: 1. Psa. 53: 1.
Blaspheme God. Psa. 74: 18.
Reproach God. Psa. 74: 22.
Make a mock at sin. Pro. 14: 9.
Despise instruction. Pro. 1: 7. Pro. 15: 5.
Hate knowledge. Pro. 1: 22.
Delight not in understanding. Pro. 18: 2.
Sport themselves in mischief. Pro. 10: 23.
Walk in darkness. Ecc. 2: 14.
Hate to depart from evil. Pro. 13: 19.
Worship of, hateful to God. Ecc. 5: 1.
ARE
Corrupt and abominable. Psa. 14: 1.
Self-sufficient. Pro. 12: 15. Rom. 1: 22.
Self-confident. Pro. 14: 16.
Self-deceivers. Pro. 14: 8.
Mere professors of religion. Mat. 25: 2—12.
Full of words. Ecc. 10: 14.
Given to meddling. Pro. 20: 3.
Slanderers. Pro. 10: 18.
Liars. Pro. 10: 18.
Slothful. Ecc. 4: 5.
Angry. Ecc. 7: 9.
Contentious. Pro. 18: 6.
A grief to parents. Pro. 17: 25. Pro. 19: 13.
Come to shame. Pro. 3: 35.
Destroy themselves by their speech. Pro. 10: 8, 14. Ecc. 10: 12.
The company of, ruinous. Pro. 13: 20.
Lips of, a snare to the soul. Pro. 18: 7.
Cling to their folly. Pro. 26: 11. Pro. 27: 22.
Worship idols. Jer. 10: 8. Rom. 1: 22, 23.
Trust to their own hearts. Pro. 28: 26.
Depend upon their wealth. Luke 12: 20.
Hear the gospel and obey it not. Mat. 7: 26.
The mouth of, pours out folly. Pro. 15: 2.
Honor is unbecoming for. Pro. 26: 1, 8.
God has no pleasure in. Ecc. 5: 4.
Shall not stand in the presence of God. Psa. 5: 5.
Avoid them. Pro. 9: 6. Pro. 14: 7.
Exhorted to seek wisdom. Pro. 8: 5.
Punishment of. Psa. 107: 17. Pro. 19: 29. Pro. 26: 10.
Exemplified. *Rehoboam*, 1 Kin. 12: 8. *Israel*, Jer. 4: 22. *Pharisees*, Mat. 23: 17, 19.

Forests.

Tracts of land covered with trees. Isa. 44: 14.
Underwood often in. Isa. 9: 18.
Infested by wild beasts. Psa. 50: 10. Psa. 104: 20. Isa. 56: 9. Jer. 5: 6. Mic. 5: 8.
Abounded with wild honey. 1 Sam. 14: 25, 26.
Often afforded pasture. Mic. 7: 14.
MENTIONED IN SCRIPTURE;
Bashan, Isa. 2: 13. Eze. 27: 6. Zec. 11: 2.
Hareth. 1 Sam. 22: 5.
Ephraim. 2 Sam. 18: 6, 8.
Lebanon. 1 Kin. 7: 2. 1 Kin. 10: 17.
Carmel. 2 Kin. 19: 23. Isa. 37: 24.
Arabian. Isa. 21: 13.
The south. Eze. 20: 46, 47.
The king's. Neh. 2: 8.
Supplied timber for building. 1 Kin. 5: 6—8.
Were places of refuge. 1 Sam. 22: 5. 1 Sam. 23: 16.
Jotham built towers, &c. in. 2 Chr. 27: 4.
The power of God extends over. Psa. 29: 9.
Called on to rejoice at God's mercy, Isa. 44: 23.
Often destroyed by enemies. 2 Kin. 19: 23. Isa. 37: 24. Jer. 46: 23.
ILLUSTRATIVE
Of the unfruitful world. Isa. 32: 19.
(A fruitful field turned into,) of the Jews rejected by God. Isa. 29: 17. Isa. 32: 15.
(Destroyed by fire,) of destruction of the wicked. Isa. 9: 18. Isa. 10: 17, 18. Jer. 21: 14.

Forgetting God.

A characteristic of the wicked. Pro. 2: 17. Isa. 65: 11.
Backsliders are guilty of. Jer. 3: 21, 22.
IS FORGETTING HIS
Covenant. Deu. 4: 23. 2 Kin. 17: 38.
Works. Psa. 78: 7, 11. Psa. 106: 13.
Benefits. Psa. 103: 2. Psa. 106: 7.

Word. Heb. 12:5. Jas. 1:25.
Law. Psa. 119:153, 176. Hos. 4:6.
Past deliverance. Jud. 8:34. Psa. 78:42.
Power to deliver. Isa. 51:13–15.
Encouraged by false teachers. Jer. 23:27.
Prosperity often leads to. Deu. 8:12—14. Hos. 13:6.
Trials should not lead to. Psa. 44:17–20.
Resolve against. Psa. 119:16, 93.
Cautions against. Deu. 6:12. Deu. 8:11..
Exhortation to those guilty of. Psa. 50:22.
Punishment of. Job 8:12, 13. Psa. 9:17. Isa. 17:10, 11. Eze. 23:35. Hos. 8:14.

Forgiveness of Injuries.

Christ set an example of. Luke 23:34.
Commanded. Mar. 11:25. Rom. 12:19.
To be unlimited. Mat. 18:22. Luke 17:4.
A characteristic of saints. Psa. 7:4.
MOTIVES TO,
The mercy of God. Luke 6:36.
Our need of forgiveness. Mar. 11:25.
God's forgiveness of us. Eph. 4:32.
Christ's forgiveness of us. Col. 3:13.
A glory to saints. Pro. 19:11.
SHOULD BE ACCOMPANIED BY
Forbearance. Col. 3:13.
Kindness. Gen. 45:5—11 Rom. 12:20.
Blessing and prayer. Mat. 5:44.
Promises to. Mat. 6:14. Luke 6:37.
No forgiveness without. Mat. 6:15. Jas. 2:13.
Illustrated. Mat. 18:23—35.
Exemplified, *Joseph*, Gen. 50:20, 21. *David*, 1 Sam. 24:7. 2 Sam. 18:5. 2 Sam. 19:23. *Solomon*, 1 Kin. 1:53. *Stephen*, Acts 7:60. *Paul*, 2 Tim. 4:16.

Forsaking God.

Idolaters guilty of. 1 Sam. 8:8. 1 Kin. 11:33.
The wicked guilty of. Deu. 28:20.
Backsliders guilty of. Jer. 15:6.
IS FORSAKING
His house. 2 Chr. 29:6.
His covenant. Deu. 29:25. 1 Kin. 19:10. Jer. 22:9. Dan. 11:30.
His commandments. Ezr. 9:10.
The right way. 2 Pet. 2:15.
Trusting in man is. Jer. 17:5.
Leads men to follow their own devices. Jer. 2:13.
Prosperity tempts to. Deu. 31:20. Deu. 32:15.
Wickedness of. Jer. 2:13. Jer. 5:7.
Unreasonableness and ingratitude of. Jer. 2:5, 6.
Brings confusion. Jer. 17:13.
Followed by remorse. Eze. 6:9.
Brings down His wrath. Ezr. 8:22.
Provokes God to forsake men. Jud. 10:13. 2 Chr. 15:2. 2 Chr. 24:20, 24.
Resolve against. Jos. 24:16. Neh. 10:29—39.
Curse pronounced upon. Jer. 17:5.
Sin of, to be confessed. Ezr. 9:10.
Warnings against. Jos 24:20. 1 Chr. 28:9.
Punishment of. Deu. 28:20. 2 Kin. 22:16, 17 Isa. 1:28. Jer. 1:16. Jer. 5:19
Exemplified. *Children of Israel*, 1 Sam. 12:10. *Saul*, 1 Sam. 15:11. *Ahab*, 1 Kin. 18:18. *Amon*, 2 Kin. 21:22. *Kingdom of Judah*, 2 Chr. 12:1, 5. 2 Chr. 21:10. Isa. 1:4. Jer. 15:6. *Kingdom of Israel*, 2 Chr. 13:11, with 2 Kin. 17:7—18. *Many disciples*, Jno. 6:66. *Phygellus, &c.* 2 Tim. 1:15. *Balaam*, 2 Pet. 2:15.

Fortresses.

Places strong by nature. Num. 24:31.
Places fortified by art. Jer. 51:53.
The security of a nation. Isa. 33:16. Dan. 11:10.
PLACES USED AS;
Cities. Jud. 9:31. Neh. 4:2.
Strong-holds. Jud. 6:2. 2 Chr. 11:11.
Forts. 2 Sam. 5:9. Isa. 25:12.
Strong towers. 2 Chr. 26:9.
Afforded protection in danger. Jud. 6:2.
Defended against enemies. Nah. 2:1.
OFTEN
Entered by the enemy. Dan. 11:7.
Spoiled. Hos. 10:14.
Levelled. Isa. 25:12.
Deserted, &c. Isa. 34:13.
Destruction of, threatened. Isa. 17:3.
ILLUSTRATIVE OF
God's protection. Psa. 18:2. Jer. 16:19.
Christ, the defence of saints. Isa. 33:16.
Protection afforded to ministers. Jer. 6:27.

Foundation.

The lowest part of a building, and on which it rests. Luke 14:29. Acts 16:26.
FIGURATIVELY APPLIED TO
The heavens. 2 Sam 22:8.
The earth. Job 38:4. Psa. 104:5.
The world. Psa. 18:15. Mat. 13:35.
The mountains. Deu. 32:22.
The ocean. Psa. 104:8.
Kingdoms. Exo. 9:18.
LAID FOR
Cities. Jos. 6:26. 1 King 16:34.

Walls. Ezr. 4: 12. Rev. 21: 14.
Houses. Luke 6: 48.
Temples. 1 Kin. 6: 37. Ezr. 3: 10.
Towers. Luke 14: 28, 29.

DESCRIBED AS
Of stone. 1 Kin. 5: 17.
Deep laid. Luke 6: 48.
Strongly laid. Ezr. 6: 3.
Joined together by corner stones. Ezr. 4: 12, with 1 Pet. 2: 6, and Eph. 2: 20.

Security afforded by. Mat. 7: 25. Luke 6: 48.

ILLUSTRATIVE OF
Christ. Isa. 28: 16. 1 Cor. 3: 11.
Doctrines of the apostles, &c. Eph. 2: 20.
First principles of the gospel. Heb. 6: 1, 2.
Decrees and purposes of God. 2 Tim. 2: 19.
Magistrates. Psa. 82: 5.
The righteous. Pro. 10: 25.
Hope of saints. Psa. 87: 1.
Security of saints' inheritance. Heb. 11: 10.

Fountains and Springs.

Created by God. Psa. 74: 15. Psa. 104: 10.
God to be praised for. Rev. 14: 7.
Come from the great deep. Gen. 7: 11. Job 38: 16.
Found in hills and valleys. Deu. 8: 7. Psa. 104: 10.
Send forth each but one kind of water. Jas. 3: 11.

AFFORD
Drink to the beasts. Psa. 104: 11.
Refreshment to the birds. Psa. 104: 12.
Fruitfulness to the earth. 1 Kin. 18: 5. Joel 3: 18.

Frequented by travellers. Gen. 16: 7.
Abound in Canaan. Deu. 8: 7. 1 Kin. 18: 5.
Sometimes dried up. Isa. 58: 11.
Drying up of, a severe punishment. Psa. 107: 33, 34. Hos. 13: 15.

CONSTANTLY FLOWING
Especially esteemed. Isa. 58: 11.
Could not be ceremonially defiled. Lev. 11: 36.

Sometimes stopped or turned off to distress enemies. 2 Chr. 32: 3, 4.

MENTIONED IN SCRIPTURE;
In the way to Shur. Gen. 16: 7.
Of the waters of Nephtoah. Jos. 15: 9.
Of Jezreel. 1 Sam. 29: 1.
Of Pisgah. Deu. 4: 49.
Upper and nether springs. Jos. 15: 19. Jud. 1: 15.

ILLUSTRATIVE
Of God. Psa. 36: 9. Jer. 2: 13. Jer. 17: 13.
Of Christ. Zec. 13: 1.
Of the Holy Ghost. Jno. 7: 38, 39.
Of constant supplies of grace. Psa. 87: 7.
Of eternal life. Jno. 4: 14. Rev. 21: 6.
Of the means of grace. Isa. 41: 18. Joel 3: 18.
Of a good wife. Pro. 5: 18.
Of a numerous posterity. Deu. 33: 28.
Of spiritual wisdom. Pro. 16: 22. Pro. 18: 4.
Of the law of the wise. Pro. 13: 14.
Of godly fear. Pro. 14: 27.
(Sealed up,) of the church. So. of Sol. 4: 12.
(Not failing,) of the church. Isa. 58: 11.
(Always flowing,) of unceasing wickedness of the Jews. Jer. 6: 7.
(Corrupt,) of the natural heart. Jas. 3: 11, with Mat. 15: 18, 19.
(Troubled,) of saints led astray. Pro. 25: 26.

Fox, The.

Found in deserts. Eze. 13: 4.
Abounded in Palestine. Jud. 15: 4. Lam. 15: 18.

DESCRIBED AS
Active. Neh. 4: 3.
Crafty. Luke 13: 32.
Carnivorous. Psa. 63: 10.

Destructive to vines. So. of Sol. 2: 15.
Dwells in holes. Mat. 8: 20. Luke 9: 58.

ILLUSTRATIVE OF
False prophets. Eze. 13: 4.
Cunning and deceitful persons. Luke 13: 32.
Enemies of the church. So. of Sol. 2: 15.

Used by Samson for annoying the Philistines. Jud. 15: 4—6.

Fruits.

The produce of corn, &c. Deu. 22: 9. Psa. 107: 37.
The produce of trees. Gen. 1: 29. Ecc. 2: 5.

CALLED THE
Fruit of the ground. Gen. 4: 3. Jer. 7: 20.
Fruit of the earth. Isa. 4: 2.
Increase of the land. Psa. 85: 12.

Given by God. Acts 14: 17.
Preserved to us by God. Mal. 3: 11.

REQUIRE
A fruitful land. Psa. 107: 34.
Rain from heaven. Psa. 104: 13. Jas. 5: 18.
Influence of the sun and moon. Deu. 33: 14.

Produced in their due seasons. Mat. 21: 41.
First of, devoted to God. Deu. 26: 2.

DIVIDED INTO
- Hasty or precocious. Isa. 28: 4.
- Summer fruits. 2 Sam. 16: 1.
- New and old. So. of Sol. 7: 13.
- Goodly. Jer. 11: 16.
- Pleasant. So. of Sol. 4: 16.
- Precious. Deu. 33: 14.
- Evil or bad. Mat. 7: 17.

To be waited for with patience. Jas. 5: 7.
Often sent as presents. Gen. 43: 11.
OFTEN DESTROYED
- In God's anger. Jer. 7: 20.
- By blight. Joel 1: 12.
- By locusts, &c. Deu. 28: 38, 39. Joel 1: 4.
- By enemies. Eze. 25: 4.
- By drought. Hag. 1: 10.

ILLUSTRATIVE
- Of effects of repentance. Mat. 3: 8.
- Of works of the Spirit. Gal. 5: 22, 23. Eph. 5: 9.
- Of doctrines of Christ. So. of Sol. 2: 3.
- Of good works. Mat. 7: 17, 18. Phi. 4: 17.
- Of a holy conversation. Pro. 12: 14. Pro. 18: 20.
- Of praise. Heb. 13: 15.
- Of the example, &c. of the godly. Pro. 11: 30.
- Of effects of industry. Pro. 31: 16, 31.
- Of the reward of saints. Isa. 3: 10.
- Of the reward of the wicked. Jer. 17: 9, 10.
- Of converts to the church. Psa. 72: 16. Jno. 4: 36.
- (Bad,) of the conduct and conversation of evil men. Mat. 7: 17. Mat. 12: 33.

Gad, The Tribe of.

Descended from Jacob's seventh son. Gen. 30: 11.
Predictions respecting. Gen. 49: 19. Deu. 33: 20, 21.
PERSONS SELECTED FROM,
- To number the people. Num. 1: 14.
- To spy out the land. Num. 13: 15.

Strength of, on leaving Egypt. Num. 1: 24, 25.
The rear of second division of Israel in their journeys. Num. 10: 18—20.
Encamped south of the tabernacle under the standard of Reuben. Num. 2: 10, 14.
Offering of, at the dedication. Num. 7: 42—47.
Families of. Num. 26: 15—17.
Strength of, on entering Canaan. Num. 26: 18.
On Ebal, said amen to the curse. Deu. 27: 13.
Sought and obtained its inheritance east of Jordan. Num. 32: 1—33.
Bounds of its inheritance. Jos. 13: 24—28.
Cities built by. Num. 32: 34—36.
Assisted in conquest of Canaan. Jos. 4: 12, 13.
After the conquest, returned home. Jos. 22: 9.
Assisted in building the altar of witness, which excited the jealousy of Israel. Jos. 22: 10—29.
Many from other tribes sought refuge with, from the Philistines. 1 Sam. 13: 7.
Eleven of, swam the Jordan, and joined David in the hold. 1 Chr. 12: 8—15.
Some of, at coronation of David. 1 Chr. 12: 37, 38.
David appointed rulers over. 1 Chr. 26: 32.
Spoiled the Hagarites. 1 Chr. 5: 18—22.
Subdued by Hazael king of Syria. 2 Kin. 10: 33.
Taken captive to Assyria. 2 Kin. 15: 29, with 1 Chr. 5: 22, 26.
Land of, seized by the Moabites and Ammonites. Jer. 48: 18—24. Jer. 49: 1.

Galilee.

Separated from Judea by Samaria. Jno. 4: 3, 4.
Upper part of, called Galilee of the Gentiles. Isa. 9: 1. Mat. 4: 15.
Lake of Gennesaret, called the sea of. Mat. 15: 29. Luke 5: 1.
Kadesh the city of refuge for. Jos. 21: 32.
INHABITANTS OF,
- Called Galileans. Acts 2: 7.
- Used a peculiar dialect. Mat. 26: 73. Mar. 14: 70.
- Despised by the Jews. Jno. 7: 41, 52.
- Opposed the Roman taxation. Acts 5: 37.
- Cruelly treated by Pilate. Luke 13: 1.

Twenty cities of, given to Hiram. 1 Kin. 9: 11.
Conquered by the Syrians. 1 Kin. 15: 20.
Conquered by the Assyrians. 2 Kin. 15: 29.
Jurisdiction of, granted to Herod by the Romans. Luke 3: 1. Luke 23: 6, 7.
Supplied Tyre, &c. with provisions. Acts 12: 20.
CHRIST
- Brought up in. Mat. 2: 22. Luke 2: 39, 51.
- Despised as of. Mat. 26: 69, with Jno. 7: 52.
- Chose His apostles from. Mat. 4: 18, 21. Jno. 1: 43, 44. Acts 1: 11.

Preaching in, predicted. Isa. 9:1, 2. Mat. 4:14, 15.
Preached throughout. Mar. 1:39. Luke 4:44.
Commenced, and wrought many miracles in. Mat. 4:23, 24. Mat. 15:29—31.
Kindly received in. Jno. 4:45.
Followed by the people of. Mat. 4:25.
Ministered to by women of. Mat. 27:55. Mar. 15:41. Luke 8:3.
Sought refuge in. Jno. 4:1, 3.
Appeared in, to His disciples after His resurrection. Mat. 26:32. Mat. 28:7.

MODERN TOWNS OF;
Accho or Ptolemais. Jud. 1:31.
Tiberias. Jno. 6:23.
Nazareth. Mat. 2:22, 23. Luke 1:26.
Cana. Jno. 2:1. Jno. 21:2.
Capernaum. Mat. 4 13.
Chorazin. Mat. 11:21.
Bethsaida. Mar. 6:45. Jno. 1:44.
Nain. Luke 7:11.
Cesarea. Acts 9:30. Acts 10:24.
Cesarea Philippi. Mat. 16:13. Mar. 8:27.

Christian churches established in. Acts 9:31.

Gardens.

Often made by the banks of rivers. Num. 24:6.

KINDS OF, MENTIONED IN SCRIPTURE;
Herbs. Deu. 11:10. 1 Kin. 21:2.
Cucumbers. Isa. 1:8.
Fruit trees. Ecc. 2:5, 6.
Spices, &c. So. of Sol. 4:16. So. of Sol. 6:2.

Often enclosed. So. of Sol. 4:12.
Often refreshed by fountains. So. of Sol. 4:15.
Taken care of by gardeners. Jno. 20:15.
Lodges erected in. Isa. 1:8.

OFTEN USED FOR
Entertainments. So. of Sol. 5:1.
Retirement. Jno. 18:1.
Burial places. 2 Kin. 21:18, 26. Jno. 19:41.
Idolatrous worship. Isa 1:29. Isa. 65:3.

Blasting of, a punishment. Amos 4:9.
Jews ordered to plant, in Babylon. Jer. 29:5, 28.

OF EDEN
Planted by the Lord. Gen. 2:8.
Called the garden of the Lord. Gen. 13:10.
Called the garden of God. Eze. 28:13.
Had every tree good for food. Gen. 2:9.
Watered by a river. Gen. 2:10—14.
Man placed in, to dress and keep. Gen. 2:8, 15.
Man driven from, after the fall. Gen. 3:23, 24.
Fertility of Canaan like. Gen. 13:10. Joel 2:3.
The future state of the Jews shall be like. Isa. 51:3. Eze. 36:35.

ILLUSTRATIVE
Of the church. So. of Sol. 5:1. So. of Sol. 6:2, 11.
(Enclosed,) of the pleasantness, fruitfulness, and security of the church. So. of Sol. 4:12.
(Well watered,) of spiritual prosperity of the church. Isa. 58:11. Jer. 31:12.
(When dried up,) of the wicked. Isa. 1:30.

Garments.

Origin of. Gen. 3:7, 21.

CALLED
Raiment. Gen. 28:20. Deu. 8:4.
Clothes. Pro. 6:27. Eze. 16:39.
Clothing. Job 22:6. Job 31:19.
Vesture. Gen. 41:42. Rev. 19:16.

MATERIALS USED FOR,
Wool. Pro. 27:26. Eze. 34:3.
Silk. Pro. 31:22.
Linen. Lev. 6:10. Est. 8:15.
Camel's hair. Mat. 3:4.
Skins. Heb. 11:37.
Sackcloth. 2 Sam. 3:31. 2 Kin. 19:1.

Not to be made of mixed materials. Deu. 22:11.
Of the sexes, not to be interchanged. Deu. 22:5.

COLORS OF, MENTIONED;
White. Ecc. 9:8.
Blue. Eze. 23:6.
Purple. Eze. 7:27. Luke 16:19.
Scarlet. 2 Sam. 1:24. Dan. 5:7.
Different colors. Gen. 37:3. 2 Sam. 13:18.

Were often fringed and bordered. Num. 15:38. Deu. 22:12.
Scribes and Pharisees condemned for making broad the borders of. Mat. 23:5.
Worn long and flowing. Luke 20:46. Rev. 1:13.
Girt up during employment. Luke 17:8. Jno. 13:4.

MENTIONED IN SCRIPTURE;
Hyke or upper garment. Deu. 24:13. Mat. 21:8.
Burnoose or cloak. Luke 6:29. 2 Tim. 4:13.
Tunic or coat. Jno. 19:23. Jno. 21:7.
Girdle. 1 Sam. 18:4. Acts 21:11.
Bonnet or hat. Lev. 8:13. Dan. 3:21.
Shoe or sandal. Exo. 3:5. Mar. 6:9.

Vail. Gen. 24: 65.
Liable to plague and leprosy. Lev. 13: 47—59.
Cleansed by water from ceremonial uncleanness. Lev. 11: 32. Num. 31: 20.
OF THE RICH,
Of the finest materials. Mat. 11: 8.
Gay. Jas. 2: 2, 3.
Gorgeous. Luke 7: 25. Acts 12: 21.
Embroidered. Psa. 45: 14. Eze. 16: 18.
Perfumed. Psa. 45: 8. So. of Sol. 4: 11.
Multiplied and heaped up. Job 27: 16. Isa. 3: 22.
Often moth-eaten. Job 13: 28. Jas. 5: 2.
OF THE POOR,
Provided specially by God. Deu. 10: 18.
Vile. Jas. 2: 2.
Used as a covering by night. Deu. 24: 13.
Not to be retained in pledge. Deu. 24: 12, 13.
Grew old and wore out. Jos. 9: 5. Psa. 102: 26.
Of Israel preserved for forty years. Deu. 8: 4.
Were often changed. Gen. 35: 2. Gen. 41: 14.
Of those slain with a sword not used. Isa. 14: 19.
Given as a token of covenants. 1 Sam. 18: 4.
Given as presents. Gen. 45: 22. 2 Kin. 5: 22.
Often rent in affliction. 2 Sam. 15: 32. Ezr. 9: 3, 5.
ILLUSTRATIVE
(White,) of righteousness. Mat. 28: 3. Rev. 3: 18.
(Rolled in blood,) of victory. Isa. 9: 5.
(Washed in wine,) of abundance. Gen. 49: 11.

Gates.

Design of Isa. 62: 10.
MADE OF
Brass. Psa. 107: 16. Isa. 45: 2.
Iron. Acts 12: 10.
Often two-leaved. Isa. 45: 1.
Fastened with bars of iron. Psa. 107: 16. Isa. 45: 2.
MADE TO
Cities. 1 Kin. 17: 10.
Houses. Luke 16: 20. Acts 12: 14.
Temples. Acts 3: 2.
Palaces. Est. 5: 13,
Prisons. Acts 12: 10.
Camps. Exo. 32: 26.
Rivers. Nah. 2: 6.
OF CITIES
Chief places of concourse. Pro. 1: 21.
Courts of justice held at. Deu. 16: 18. 2 Sam. 15: 2. Pro. 22: 22, 23.
Land sold at. Gen. 23: 10, 16.
Land redeemed at. Ruth 4: 1.
Markets held at. 2 Kin. 7: 1, 18.
Proclamations made at. Pro. 1: 21. Jer. 17: 19.
Councils of state held at. 2 Chr. 18: 9. Jer. 39: 3.
Conferences held at. Gen. 34: 20. 2 Sam. 3: 27.
Public commendation given at. Pro. 31: 23, 31.
Public censure passed at. Job 5: 4. Isa. 29: 21.
Shut at night-fall. Jos. 2: 5. Neh. 13: 19.
Chief points of attack in war. Jud. 5: 8. Isa. 22: 7. Eze. 21: 15.
Battering rams used against. Eze. 21: 22.
Experienced officers placed over. 2 Kin. 7: 17.
Troops reviewed at, going to war. 2 Sam. 18: 4.
Often razed and burned. Neh. 1: 3. Lam. 2: 9.
Idolatrous rites performed at. Acts 14: 13.
Criminals punished at. Deu. 17: 5. Jer. 20: 2.
Custom of sitting at, in the evening, alluded to. Gen. 19: 1.
OF THE TEMPLE
Called gates of Zion. Lam. 1: 4.
Called gates of righteousness. Psa. 118: 19.
Called gates of the Lord. Psa. 118: 20.
Overlaid with gold. 2 Kin. 18: 16.
One specially beautiful. Acts 3: 2.
Levites the porters of. 2 Chr. 8: 14. 2 Chr. 23: 4.
Charge of, given by lot. 1 Chr. 26: 13—19.
The treasury placed at. 2 Chr. 24: 8. Mar. 12: 41.
The pious Israelites delighted to enter. Psa. 118: 19, 20. Psa. 100: 4.
Frequented by beggars. Acts 3: 2.
OF JERUSALEM,
High gate of Benjamin. Jer. 20: 2. Jer. 37: 13.
Fish gate. 2 Chr. 33: 14. Neh. 3: 3.
Sheep gate. Neh. 3: 1. Jno. 5: 2. (*marg.*)
Gate of Miphkad. Neh. 3: 31.
Gate of Ephraim. Neh. 12: 39.
Valley gate. 2 Chr. 26: 29. Neh. 2: 13.
Water gate. Neh. 3: 26. Neh. 8: 3.
Horse gate. 2 Chr. 23: 15. Neh. 3: 28.
Old gate. Neh. 3: 6. Neh. 12: 39.
Corner gate. 2 Chr. 26: 9.
Dung gate. Neh. 3: 14. Neh. 12: 31.
Gate of the fountain. Neh. 3: 15.

Carcase of sin-offering burned without. Lev. 4:12. Heb. 13:11—13.
Criminals generally punished without. Lev. 24:23. Jno. 19:17, with Heb. 13:12.
ILLUSTRATIVE
Of Christ. Jno. 10:9.
(Of heaven,) of access to God. Gen. 28:12—17.
(Of hell,) of Satan's power. Mat. 16:18.
(Of the grave,) of death. Isa. 38:10.
(Strait,) of the entrance to life. Mat. 7:14.
(Wide,) of the entrance to ruin. Mat. 7:13.

Genealogies.

The Jews reckoned by. 1 Chr. 9:1. 2 Chr. 31:19.
Public registers kept of. 2 Chr. 12:15. Neh. 7:5.
OF CHRIST
Given. Mat. 1:1—17. Luke 3:23—38.
Prove His descent from Judah. Heb. 7:14.
Priests who could not prove their own, excluded from the priesthood. Ezr. 2:62. Neh. 7:64.
Subject of, to be avoided. 1 Tim. 1:4. Tit. 3:9.
Illustrative of the record of saints in the book of life. Luke 10:20. Heb. 12:23. Rev. 3:5.

Gentiles.

Comprehend all nations except the Jews. Rom. 2:9. Rom. 3:9. Rom. 9:24.
CALLED
Heathen. Psa. 2:1. Gal. 3:8.
Nations. Psa. 9:20. Psa. 22:28. Isa. 9:1.
Uncircumcised. 1 Sam. 14:6. Isa. 52:1.
Uncircumcision. Rom. 2:26.
Greeks. Rom. 1:16. Rom. 10:12.
Strangers. Isa. 14:1. Isa. 60:10.
Ruled by God. 2 Chr. 20:6. Psa. 47:8.
Chastised by God. Psa. 9:5. Psa. 94:10.
Counsel of, brought to nought. Psa. 33:10.
CHARACTERIZED AS
Ignorant of God. Rom. 1:21. 1 The. 4:5.
Refusing to know God. Rom. 1:28.
Without the law. Rom. 2:14.
Idolatrous. Rom. 1:23, 25. 1 Cor. 12:2.
Superstitious. Deu. 18:14.
Depraved and wicked. Rom. 1:28—32. Eph. 4:19.
Blasphemous and reproachful. Neh. 5:9.
Constant to their false gods. Jer. 2:11.
Hated and despised the Jews. Est. 9:1, 5. Psa. 44:13, 14. Psa. 123:3.
Often ravaged and defiled the holy land and sanctuary. Psa. 79:1. Lam. 1:10
THE JEWS
Not to follow the ways of. Lev. 18 3. Jer. 10:2.
Not to intermarry with. Deu. 7:3.
Permitted to have, as servants. Lev. 25:44.
Despised, as if dogs. Mat. 15:26.
Never associated with. Acts 10:28. Acts 11:2, 3.
Often corrupted by. 2 Kin. 17:7, 8.
Dispersed amongst. Jno. 7:35.
Excluded from Israel's privileges Eph. 2:11, 12.
Not allowed to enter the temple. Acts 21:28, 29.
Outer court of temple for. Eph. 2:14. Rev. 11:2.
Given to Christ as His inheritance Psa. 2:8.
Christ given as a light to. Isa. 42:6. Luke 2:32.
Conversion of, predicted. Isa. 2:2. Isa. 11:10.
United with the Jews against Christ. Acts 4:27.
The gospel not to be preached to, till preached to the Jews. Mat. 10:5. Luke 24:47. Acts 13:46.
First special introduction of the gospel to. Acts 10:34—45. Acts 15:14.
First general introduction of the gospel to. Acts 13:48, 49, 52. Acts 15:12.
Paul the apostle of. Acts 9:15. Gal. 2:7, 8.
Jerusalem trodden down by, &c. Luke 21:24.
Israel rejected till the fulness of. Rom. 11:25.

Gibeonites.

Descended from the Hivites and Amorites. Jos. 9:3, 7, with 2 Sam 21:2.
A mighty and warlike people. Jos. 10:2.
Cities of. Jos. 9:17.
ISRAEL
Deceived by. Jos. 9:4—13.
Made a league with. Jos. 9:15.
Spared on account of their oath. Jos. 9:18, 19.
Appointed, hewers of wood, &c. Jos. 9:20—27.
Attacked by the kings of Canaan. Jos. 10:1—5.
Delivered by Israel. Jos. 10:6—10.
Saul sought to destroy. 2 Sam. 21:2.

Israel plagued for Saul's cruelty to. 2 Sam. 21:1.
Effected the destruction of the remnant of Saul's house. 2 Sam. 21:4—9.
The office of the Nethinim probably orginated in. 1 Chr. 9:2.
Part of, returned from the captivity. Neh. 7:25.

Gift of the Holy Ghost, The.

By the Father. Neh. 9:20. Luke 11:13.
By the Son. Jno. 20:22.
To Christ without measure. Jno. 3:34.
GIVEN
  According to promise. Acts 2:38, 39.
  Upon the exaltation of Christ. Psa. 68:18. Jno. 7:39.
  Through the intercession of Christ. Jno. 14:16.
  In answer to prayer. Luke 11:13. Eph. 1:16, 17.
  For instruction. Neh. 9:20.
  For comfort of saints. Jno. 14:16.
  To those who repent and believe. Acts 2:38.
  To those who obey God. Acts 5:32.
  To the Gentiles. Acts 10:44, 45. Acts 11:17. Acts 15:8.
Is abundant. Psa. 68:9. Jno. 7:38, 39.
Is permanent. Isa. 59:21. Hag. 2:5. 1 Pet. 4:14.
Is fructifying. Isa. 32:15.
Received through faith. Gal. 3:14.
An evidence of union with Christ. 1 Jno. 3:24. 1 Jno. 4:13.
An earnest of the inheritance of the saints. 2 Cor. 1:22. 2 Cor. 5:5. Eph. 1:14.
A pledge of the continued favor of God. Eze. 39:29.

Gifts of God, The.

All blessings are. Jas. 1:17. 2 Pet. 1:3.
Are dispensed according to His will. Ecc. 2:26. Dan. 2:21. Rom. 12:6. 1 Cor. 7:7.
Are free and abundant. Num. 14:8. Rom. 8:32.
SPIRITUAL,
  Christ the chief of. Isa. 42:6. Isa. 55:4. Jno. 3:16. Jno. 4:10. Jno. 6:32, 33.
  Are through Christ. Psa. 68:18, with Eph. 4:7, 8. Jno. 6:27.
  The Holy Ghost. Luke 11:13. Acts 8:20.
  Grace. Psa. 84:11. Jas. 4:6.
  Wisdom. Pro. 2:6. Jas. 1. 5.
  Repentance. Acts 11:18.
  Faith. Eph. 2:8. Phi. 1:29.
  Righteousness. Rom. 5:16, 17.
  Strength and power. Psa. 68:35.
  A new heart. Eze. 11:19.
  Peace. Psa. 29:11.
  Rest. Mat. 11:28. 2 The. 1:7.
  Glory. Psa. 84:11. Jno. 17:22.
  Eternal life. Rom. 6:23.
  Not repented of by Him. Rom. 11:29.
  To be used for mutual profit. 1 Pet. 4:10.
  Pray for. Mat. 7:7, 11. Jno. 16:23, 24.
Acknowledge. Psa. 4:7. Psa. 21:2.
TEMPORAL,
  Life. Isa. 42:5.
  Food and raiment. Mat. 6:25—33.
  Rain and fruitful seasons. Gen. 27:28. Lev. 26:4, 5. Isa. 30:23.
  Wisdom. 2 Chr. 1:12.
  Peace. Lev. 26:6. 1 Chr. 22:9.
  All good things Psa. 34:10. 1 Tim. 6:17.
  To be used and enjoyed. Ecc. 3:13. Ecc. 5:19, 20. 1 Tim. 4:4, 5.
  Should cause us to remember God. Deu. 8:18.
  All creatures partake of. Psa. 136:25. Psa. 145:15, 16.
  Pray for. Zec. 10:1. Mat. 6:11.
Illustrated. Mat. 25:15—30.

Girdles.

Worn upon the loins. 1 Kin 2:5. Jer. 13:1, 11.
Worn by priests about the breasts. Rev. 1:13.
MADE OF
  Fine linen. Eze. 16:10.
  Twined linen with blue, purple, &c. Exo. 39:29.
  Gold. Rev. 1:13. Rev. 15:6.
  Leather. 2 Kin. 1:8. Mat. 3:4.
  Sackcloth. Isa. 3:24. Lam. 2:10.
Made for sale by industrious women. Pro. 31:24.
USED FOR
  Strengthening the loins. Pro. 31:17. Isa. 22:21. Isa. 23:10. (*marg.*)
  Girding up the garments when walking. 1 Kin. 18:46. 2 Kin. 4:29.
  Girding up the garments when working. Luke 12:37. Luke 17:8. Jno. 13:4.
  Suspending the sword. 2 Sam. 20:8. Neh. 4:18.
  Suspending the inkhorn. Eze. 9:2. (*marg.*)
  Holding money. Mat. 10:9. Mar. 6:8. (*Greek.*)
  Taken off when at rest. Isa. 5:27, with Jno 13:4.
GIVEN AS
  A token of friendship. 1 Sam. 18:4.
  A reward of military service. 2 Sam. 18:11.
ILLUSTRATIVE OF
  Strength. Psa. 18:39. Isa. 22:21.
  Gladness. Psa. 30:11.
  Righteousness of Christ. Isa. 11:5.

Faithfulness of Christ. Isa. 11:5.
Truth. Eph. 6:14.

Glorifying God.

Commanded. 1 Chr. 16:28. Psa. 22:23. Isa. 42:12.
Due to Him. 1 Chr. 16:29.
FOR HIS
Holiness. Psa. 99:9. Rev. 15:4.
Mercy and truth. Psa. 115:1. Rom. 15:9.
Faithfulness and truth. Isa. 25:1.
Wondrous works. Mat. 15:31. Acts 4:21.
Judgments. Isa. 25:3. Eze. 28:22. Rev. 14:7.
Deliverance. Psa. 50:15.
Grace to others. Acts 11:18. 2 Cor. 9:13. Gal. 1:24.
Obligation of saints to. 1 Cor. 6:20.
Is acceptable through Christ. Phi. 1:11. 1 Pet. 4:11.
Christ, an example of. Jno. 17:4.
ACCOMPLISHED BY
Relying on His promises. Rom. 4:20.
Praising Him. Psa. 50:23.
Doing all to Him. 1 Cor. 10:31.
Dying for Him. Jno. 21:19.
Confessing Christ. Phi. 2:11.
Suffering for Christ. 1 Pet. 4:14:16.
Glorifying Christ. Acts 19:17. 2 The. 1:12.
Bringing forth fruits of righteousness. Jno. 15:8. Phi. 1:11.
Patience in affliction. Isa. 24:15.
Faithfulness. 1 Pet. 4:11.
Required in body and spirit. 1 Cor. 6:20.
Shall be universal. Psa. 86:9. Rev. 5:13.
SAINTS SHOULD
Resolve on. Psa. 69:30. Psa. 118:28.
Unite in. Psa. 34:3. Rom. 15:6.
Persevere in. Psa. 86:12.
All the blessings of God are designed to lead to. Isa. 60:21. Isa. 61:3.
The holy example of saints may lead others to. Mat. 5:16. 1 Pet. 2:12.
All, by nature, fail in. Rom. 3:23.
The wicked averse to. Dan. 5:23. Rom. 1:21.
Punishment for not. Dan. 5:23, 30. Mal. 2:2. Acts 12:23. Rom. 1:21.
Heavenly hosts engaged in. Rev. 4:11.
Exemplified. *David*, Psa. 57:5. *The Multitude*, Mat. 9:8. Mat. 15:31. *The Virgin Mary*, Luke 1:46. *Angels*, Luke 2:14. *Shepherds*, Luke 2:20. *Man sick of the Palsy*, Luke 5:25. *Woman with infirmity*, Luke 13:13. *Leper*, Luke 17:15. *Blind man*, Luke 18:43. *Centurion*, Luke 23:47. *The Church at Jerusalem*, Acts 11:18. *Gentiles at Antioch*, Acts 13:48. *Abraham*, Rom. 4:20. *Paul*, Rom. 11:36.

Glory.

God is, to His people. Psa. 3:3. Zec 2:5.
Christ is, to His people. Isa. 60:1 Luke 2:32.
The gospel ordained to be, to saints. 1 Cor. 2:7.
Of the gospel, exceeds that of the law. 2 Cor. 3:9, 10.
The joy of saints is full of. 1 Pet. 1:8
SPIRITUAL,
Is given by God. Psa. 84:11.
Is given by Christ. Jno. 17:22.
Is the work of the Holy Ghost. 2. Cor. 3:18.
ETERNAL,
Procured by the death of Christ. Heb. 2:10.
Accompanies salvation by Christ. 2 Tim. 2:10.
Inherited by saints. 1 Sam. 2:8. Psa. 73:24. Pro. 3:35. Col. 3:4. 1 Pet. 5:10.
Saints called to. 2 The. 2:14. 1 Pet. 5:10.
Saints afore prepared unto. Rom. 9:23.
Enhanced by present afflictions. 2 Cor. 4:17.
Present afflictions not worthy to be compared with. Rom. 8:18.
Of the Church shall be rich and abundant. Isa. 60:11—13.
The bodies of saints shall be raised in. 1 Cor. 15:43. Phi. 3:21.
Saints shall be, of their ministers. 1 The. 2:19, 20.
TEMPORAL,
Is given by God. Dan. 2:37.
Passeth away. 1 Pet. 1:24.
The devil tries to seduce by. Mat. 4:8.
Of hypocrites turned to shame. Hos. 4:7.
Seek not, from man. Mat. 6:2. 1 The. 2:6.
OF THE WICKED
Is in their shame. Phi. 3:19.
Ends in destruction. Isa. 5:14.

Glory of God, The.

Exhibited in Christ. Jno 1:14. 2 Cor. 4:6. Heb. 1:3.
EXHIBITED IN
His name. Deu. 28:58. Neh. 9:5.
His majesty. Job 37:22. Psa. 93:1. Psa. 104:1. Psa. 145:5, 12. Isa. 2:10.
His power. Exo. 15:1, 6. Rom. 6:4.
His works. Psa. 19:1. Psa. 111:3.
His holiness. Exo. 15:11.
DESCRIBED AS
Great. Psa. 138:5.
Eternal. Psa. 104:31.

Rich. Eph. 3:16.
Highly exalted. Psa. 8: 1. Psa. 113:4.
EXHIBITED TO
Moses. Exo. 34: 5—7, with Exo. 33: 18—23.
Stephen. Acts 7:55.
His Church. Deu. 5:24. Psa. 102:16.
Enlightens the Church. Isa. 60: 1, 2. Rev. 21:11, 23.
Saints desire to behold. Psa. 63: 2. Psa. 90:16.
God is jealous of. Isa. 42:8.
Reverence. Isa. 59:19.
Plead in prayer. Psa. 79:9.
Declare. 1 Chr. 16:24. Psa. 145: 5, 11.
Magnify. Psa. 57:5.
The earth is full of. Isa. 6:3.
The knowledge of, shall fill the earth. Hab. 2:14.

Gluttony.

Christ was falsely accused of. Mat. 11:19.
The wicked addicted to. Phi. 3: 19. Jude 12.
LEADS TO
Carnal security. Isa. 22:13, with 1 Cor. 15:32. Luke 12:19.
Poverty. Pro. 23:21.
Of princes, ruinous to their people. Ecc. 10:16, 17.
Is inconsistent in saints 1 Pet. 4: 3.
Caution against. Pro. 23:2, 3. Luke 21:34. Rom. 13:13, 14.
Pray against temptations to. Psa. 141:4.
Punishment of. Num. 11:33, 34, with Psa. 78:31. Deu. 21:21. Amos 6: 4, 7.
Danger of, illustrated. Luke 12:45, 46.
Exemplified. *Esau*, Gen. 25: 30—34, with Heb. 12:16, 17 *Israel*, Num. 11:4, with Psa. 78:18. *Sons of Eli*, 1 Sam. 2: 12—17. *Belshazzar*, Dan. 5:1.

Goat, The.

Clean and fit for food. Deu. 14:4, 5.
Offered in sacrifice. Gen. 15:9. Lev. 16:5, 7.
The male, best for sacrifice. Lev. 22: 19. Psa. 50:9.
First-born of, not redeemed. Num. 18:17.
Jews had large flocks of. Gen. 32: 14. 1 Sam. 25:2.
Most profitable to the owner. Pro. 27:26.
Milk of, used as food. Pro. 27:27.
THE YOUNG OF,
Called kids. Gen. 37:31.
Kept in small flocks. 1 Kin. 20:27.
Fed near the shepherds' tents. So. of Sol. 1:8.
Not to be seethed in milk of mother. Exo. 23:19.
Offered in sacrifice. Lev. 4: 23. Lev. 5:6.
Offered at the passover. Exo. 12:5. 2 Chr. 35:7.
Considered a delicacy. Gen. 27:9. Jud. 6:19.
Given as a present. Gen. 38:17. Jud. 15:1.
THE HAIR OF,
Offered for tabernacle. Exo. 25:4. Exo. 35:23.
Made into curtains, for covering the tabernacle. Exo. 35:26. Exo. 36:14—18.
Made into pillows. 1 Sam. 19:13.
Skin of, often used as clothing. Heb. 11:37.
Bashan celebrated for. Deu. 32:14.
The Arabians traded in. Eze. 27:21.
Flocks of, always led by a male. Jer. 50:8.
When wild dwelt in the hills and rocks. 1 Sam. 24: 2. Job 39:1. Psa. 104:18.
ILLUSTRATIVE
Of Macedonian empire. Dan. 8: 5, 21.
Of the wicked. Zec. 10: 3. Mat. 25:32, 33.
(Flock of,) of the church. So. of Sol. 4:1.

God.

Is a spirit. Jno. 4:24. 2 Cor. 3:17.
IS DECLARED TO BE
Light. Isa. 60:19. Jas. 1:17. 1 Jno. 1:5.
Love. 1 Jno. 4:8, 16.
Invisible. Job 23:8, 9. Jno. 1:18. Jno. 5:37. Col. 1:15. 1 Tim. 1:17.
Unsearchable. Job 11:7. Job 37:23. Psa. 145:3. Isa. 40:28. Rom. 11:33.
Incorruptible. Rom. 1:23.
Eternal. Deu. 33:27. Psa. 90:2. Rev. 4:8—10.
Immortal. 1 Tim. 1:17. 1 Tim. 6:16.
Omnipotent. Gen. 17:1. Exo. 6:3.
Omniscient. Psa. 139:1—6. Pro 5:21.
Omnipresent. Psa. 139: 7. Jer. 23:23.
Immutable. Psa. 102:26, 27. Jas. 1:17.
Only-wise. Rom. 16: 27. 1 Tim. 1:17.
Glorious. Exo. 15:11. Psa. 145:5.
Most High. Psa. 83:18. Acts 7:48.
Perfect. Mat. 5:48.
Holy. Psa. 99:9. Isa. 5:16.
Just. Deu. 32:4. Isa. 45:21.
True. Jer. 10:10. Jno. 17:3.
Upright. Psa. 25:8. Psa. 92:15.
Righteous. Ezr. 9:15. Psa. 145:17.
Good. Psa. 25:8. Psa. 119:68.
Great. 2 Chr. 2:5. Psa. 86:10.

Gracious. Exo. 34: 6. Psa. 116: 5.
Faithful. 1 Cor. 10: 13. 1 Pet. 4: 19.
Merciful. Exo. 34: 6, 7. Psa. 86: 5.
Long-suffering. Num. 14: 18. Mic. 7: 1.
Jealous. Jos. 24: 19. Nah. 1: 2.
Compassionate. 2 Kin. 13: 23.
A consuming fire. Heb. 12: 29.
None beside Him. Deu. 4: 35. Isa. 44: 6.
None before Him. Isa. 43: 10.
None like to Him. Exo. 9: 14. Deu. 33: 26. 2 Sam. 7: 22. Isa. 46: 5, 9. Jer. 10: 6.
None good but He. Mat. 19: 17.
Fills heaven and earth. 1 Kin. 8: 27. Jer. 23: 24.
Should be worshipped in spirit and in truth. Jno. 4: 24.

Gold.

Found in the earth. Job 28: 1, 6.
ABOUNDED IN
Havilah. Gen. 2: 11.
Ophir. 1 Kin. 9: 28. Psa. 45: 9.
Sheba. Psa. 72: 15. Isa. 60: 6.
Parvaim. 2 Chr. 3: 6.
Belongs to God. Joel 3: 5. Hag. 2: 8.
DESCRIBED AS
Yellow. Psa. 68: 13.
Malleable. Exo. 39: 3. 1 Kin. 10: 16, 17.
Fusible. Exo. 32: 3, 4. Pro. 17: 3.
Precious. Ezr. 8: 27. Isa. 13: 12.
Valuable. Job 28: 15, 16.
Most valuable when pure and fine. Job 28: 19. Psa. 19: 10. Psa. 21: 3. Pro. 3: 14.
Refined and tried by fire. Zec. 13: 9. 1 Pet. 1: 7.
Working in, a trade. Neh. 3: 8. Isa. 40: 19.
An article of commerce. Eze. 27: 22.
The patriarchs were rich in. Gen. 13: 2.
Imported by Solomon. 1 Kin. 9: 11, 28. 1 Kin. 10: 11.
Abundance of, in Solomon's reign. 2 Chr. 1: 15.
Offerings of, for tabernacle. Exo. 35: 22.
Offering of, for temple. 1 Chr. 22: 14. 1 Chr. 29: 4, 7.
Used as money. Mat. 10: 9. Acts 3: 6.
Priestly and royal garments adorned with. Exo. 28: 4—6. Psa. 45: 9, 13.
WAS USED FOR
Overlaying the tabernacle. Exo 36: 34, 38.
Overlaying the temple. 1 Kin. 6: 21, 22.
Overlaying cherubims in temple. 2 Chr. 3: 10.
Overlaying the ark, &c. Exo. 25: 11—13.
Overlaying floor of temple. 1 Kin. 6: 30.
Overlaying throne of Solomon. 1 Kin. 10: 18.
Mercy seat and cherubims. Exo. 25: 17, 18.
Sacred candlesticks. Exo. 25: 31. 2 Chr. 4: 7, 20.
Sacred utensils. Exo. 25: 29, 38. 2 Chr. 4: 19—22.
Crowns. 2 Sam. 12: 30. Psa. 21: 3.
Sceptres. Est. 4: 11.
Chains. Gen. 41: 42. Dan. 5: 29.
Rings. So. of Sol. 5: 14. Jas. 2: 2.
Earrings. Jud. 8: 24, 26.
Ornaments. Jer. 4: 30.
Shields. 2 Sam. 8: 7. 1 Kin. 10: 16, 17.
Vessels. 1 Kin. 10: 21. Est. 1: 7.
Idols. Exo. 20: 23. Psa. 115: 4. Dan. 5: 4.
Couches. Est. 1: 6.
Footstools. 2 Chr. 9: 18.
Estimated by weight. 1 Chr. 28: 14.
Given as presents. 1 Kin. 15: 19. Mat. 2: 11.
Exacted as tribute. 1 Kin. 20: 3, 5. 2 Kin. 23: 33, 35.
Taken in war, dedicated to God. Jos. 6: 19. 2 Sam. 8: 11. 1 Kin. 15: 15.
Kings of Israel not to multiply. Deu. 17: 17.
Jews condemned for multiplying. Isa. 2: 7.
Vanity of heaping up. Ecc. 2: 8, 11.
LIABLE TO
Grow dim. Lam. 4: 1.
Canker and rust. Jas. 5: 3.
ILLUSTRATIVE OF
Saints after affliction. Job 23: 10.
Tried faith. 1 Pet. 1: 7.
The doctrines of grace. Rev. 3: 18.
True converts. 1 Cor. 3: 12.
Babylonish empire. Dan. 2: 38.

Goodness of God, The.

Is part of His character. Psa. 25: 8. Nah. 1: 7. Mat. 19: 17.
DECLARED TO BE
Great. Neh. 9: 35. Zec. 9: 17.
Rich. Psa. 104: 24. Rom. 2: 4.
Abundant. Exo. 34: 6. Psa. 33: 5.
Satisfying. Psa. 65: 4. Jer. 31: 12, 14.
Enduring. Psa. 23: 6. Psa. 52: 1.
Universal. Psa. 145: 9. Mat. 5: 45.
MANIFESTED
To His Church. Psa. 31: 19. Lam. 3: 25.
In doing good. Psa. 119: 68. Psa. 145: 9.
In supplying temporal wants. Acts 14: 17.
In providing for the poor. Psa. 68: 10.
In forgiving sins. 2 Chr. 30: 18, Psa. 86: 5.
Leads to repentance. Rom. 2: 4.
Recognize, in His dealings. Ezr. 8: 18. Neh. 2: 18.

Pray for the manifestation of. 2 The. 1:11.
Despise not. Rom. 2:4.
Reverence. Jer. 33:9. Hos. 3:5.
Magnify. Psa. 107:8. Jer. 33:11.
Urge others to confide in. Psa. 34:8.
The wicked disregard. Neh. 9:35.

Gospel, The.

Is good tidings of great joy for all people. Luke 2:10, 11, 31, 32.
Foretold. Isa. 41:27. Isa. 52:7. Isa. 61:1—3. Mark 1:15.
Preached under the old testament. Heb. 4:2.
Exhibits the grace of God. Acts 14:3. Acts 20:32.
The knowledge of the glory of God is by. 2 Cor. 4:4, 6.
Life and immortality are brought to light by Jesus through. 2 Tim. 1:10.
Is the power of God unto salvation. Rom. 1:16. 1 Cor. 1:18. 1 The. 1:5.
Is glorious. 2 Cor. 4:4.
Is everlasting. 1 Pet. 1:25. Rev. 14:6.
Preached by Christ. Mat. 4:23. Mar. 1:14.
Ministers have a dispensation to preach. 1 Cor. 9:17.
Preached beforehand to Abraham. Gen. 22:18, with Gal. 3:8.
PREACHED TO
  The Jews first. Luke 24:47. Acts 13:46.
  The Gentiles. Mar. 13:10. Gal. 2:2, 9.
  The poor. Mat. 11:5. Luke 4:18.
  Every creature. Mar. 16:15. Col. 1:23.
Must be believed. Mar. 1:15. Heb. 4:2.
Brings peace. Luke 2:10, 14. Eph. 6:15.
Produces hope. Col. 1:23.
Saints have fellowship in. Phi. 1:5.
There is fulness of blessing in. Rom. 15:29.
THOSE WHO RECEIVE, SHOULD
  Adhere to the truth of. Gal. 1:6, 7. Gal. 2:14. 2 Tim. 1:13.
  Not be ashamed of. Rom. 1:16. 2 Tim. 1:8.
  Live in subjection to. 2 Cor. 9:13.
  Have their conversation becoming. Phi. 1:27.
  Earnestly contend for the faith of. Phi. 1:17, 27. Jude 3.
  Sacrifice friends and property for. Mat. 10:37.
  Sacrifice life itself for. Mar. 8:35.
Profession of, attended by afflictions. 2 Tim. 3:12.
Promises to sufferers for. Mar. 8:35. Mar. 10:30.
Be careful not to hinder. 1 Cor. 9:12.
Is hid to them that are lost. 2 Cor. 4:3.
Testifies to the final judgment. Rom. 2:16.
Let him who preaches another, be accursed. Gal. 1:8.
Awful consequences of not obeying. 2 The. 1:8, 9.
IS CALLED, THE
  Dispensation of the grace of God. Eph. 3:2.
  Gospel of peace. Eph. 6:15.
  Gospel of God. Rom. 1:1. 1 The. 2:8. 1 Pet. 4:17.
  Gospel of Christ. Rom. 1:9, 16. 2 Cor. 2:12. 1 The. 3:2.
  Gospel of the grace of God. Acts 20:24.
  Gospel of the kingdom. Mat. 24:14.
  Gospel of salvation. Eph. 1:13.
  Glorious gospel of Christ. 2 Cor. 4:4.
  Preaching of Jesus Christ. Rom. 16:25.
  Mystery of the gospel. Eph. 6:19.
  Word of God. 1 The. 2:13.
  Word of Christ. Col. 3:16.
  Word of grace. Acts 14:3. Acts 20:32.
  Word of salvation. Acts 13:26.
  Word of reconciliation. 2 Cor. 5:19.
  Word of truth. Eph. 1:13. Jas. 1:18.
  Word of faith. Rom. 10:8.
  Word of life. Phi. 2:16.
  Ministration of the Spirit. 2. Cor. 3:8.
  Doctrine according to godliness. 1 Tim. 6:3.
  Form of sound words. 2 Tim. 1:13.
Rejection of, by many, foretold. Isa. 53:1, with Rom. 10:15, 16.
Rejection of, by the Jews, a means of blessing to the Gentiles. Rom. 11:28.

Grace.

God is the God of all. 1 Pet. 5:10.
God is the Giver of. Psa. 84:11. Jas. 1:17.
God's throne, the throne of. Heb. 4:16.
The Holy Ghost is the Spirit of. Zec. 12:10. Heb. 10:29.
Was upon Christ. Luke 2:40. Jno. 3:34.
Christ spake with. Psa. 45:2, with Luke 4:22.
Christ was full of. Jno. 1:14.
Came by Christ. Jno. 1:17. Rom. 5:15,
Given by Christ. 1 Cor. 1:4.
Foretold by the prophets. 1 Pet. 1:10.
Riches of, exhibited in God's kindness through Christ. Eph. 2:7.
Glory of, exhibited in our acceptance in Christ. Eph. 1:6.
IS DESCRIBED AS
  Great. Acts 4:33.
  Sovereign. Rom. 5:21.

Rich. Eph. 1: 7. Eph. 2: 7.
Exceeding. 2 Cor. 9: 14.
Manifold. 1 Pet. 4: 10.
All-sufficient. 2 Cor. 12: 9.
All-abundant. Rom. 5: 15, 17, 20.
Glorious. Eph. 1: 6.
The gospel, a declaration of. Acts 20: 24, 32.
IS THE SOURCE OF
Election. Rom. 11: 5.
The call of God. Gal. 1: 15.
Justification. Rom. 3: 24. Tit. 3: 7.
Faith. Acts 18: 27.
Forgiveness of sins. Eph. 1: 7.
Salvation. Acts 15: 11. Eph. 2: 5, 8.
Consolation. 2 The. 2: 16.
Hope. 2 The. 2: 16.
Necessary to the service of God. Heb. 12: 28.
God's work completed in saints by. 2 The. 1: 11, 12.
The success and completion of the work of God to be attributed to. Zec. 4: 7.
Inheritance of the promises by. Rom. 4: 16.
Justification by, opposed to that by works. Rom. 4: 4, 5. Rom. 11: 6. Gal. 5: 4.
SAINTS
Are heirs of. 1 Pet. 3: 7.
Are under. Rom. 6: 14.
Receive, from Christ. Jno. 1: 16.
Are what they are by. 1 Cor. 15: 10. 2 Cor. 1: 12.
Abound in gifts of. Acts 4: 33. 2 Cor. 8: 1. 2 Cor. 9: 8, 14.
Should be established in. Heb. 13: 9.
Should be strong in. 2 Tim. 2: 1.
Should grow in. 2 Pet. 3: 18.
Should speak with. Eph. 4: 29. Col. 4: 6.
SPECIALLY GIVEN
To ministers. Rom. 12: 3, 6. Rom. 15: 15. 1 Cor. 3: 10. Gal. 2: 9. Eph. 3: 7.
To the humble. Pro. 3: 34, with Jas. 4: 6.
To those who walk uprightly. Psa. 84: 11.
Not to be received in vain. 2 Cor. 6: 1.
PRAY FOR,
For yourselves. Heb. 4: 16.
For others. 2 Cor. 13: 14. Eph. 6: 24.
Beware lest you fail of. Heb. 12: 15.
Manifestation of, in others, a cause of gladness. Acts 11: 23. 3 Jno. 3: 4.
Special manifestation of, at the second coming of Christ. 1 Pet. 1: 13.
Not to be abused. Rom. 3: 8. Rom. 6: 1, 15.
Antinomians abused. Jude 4.

Grass.

A green herb. Mar. 6: 39.
CALLED
Grass of the earth. Rev. 9: 4.
Grass of the field. Num. 22: 4.
Springs out of the earth. 2 Sam. 23: 4.
GOD
Originally created. Gen. 1: 11, 12.
The giver of. Deu. 11: 15.
Causes to grow. Psa. 104: 14. Psa. 147: 8.
Adorns and clothes. Mat. 6: 30.
Often grew on the tops of houses. Psa. 129: 6.
When young, soft and tender. Pro. 27: 25.
Refreshed by rain and dew. Deu. 32: 2. Pro. 19: 12.
Cattle fed upon. Job 6: 5. Jer. 50: 11.
Ovens often heated with. Mat. 6: 30.
DESTROYED BY
Locusts. Rev. 9: 4.
Hail and lightning. Rev. 8: 7.
Drought. 1 Kin. 17: 1, with 1 Kin. 18: 5.
Failure of, a great calamity. Isa. 15: 5, 6.
Sufferings of cattle from failure of, described. Jer. 14: 5, 6.
ILLUSTRATIVE
Of shortness and uncertainty of life. Psa. 90: 5, 6. Psa. 103: 15. Isa. 40: 6, 7. 1 Pet. 1: 24.
Of prosperity of the wicked. Psa. 92: 7.
(Refreshed by dew and showers,) of saints refreshed by grace. Psa. 72: 6. Mic. 5: 7.
(On tops of houses,) of the wicked. 2 Kin. 19: 26. Isa. 37: 27.

Groves.

Antiquity of. Gen. 21: 33.
Often on tops of hills. 1 Kin. 14: 23. Hos. 4: 13.
Often used as resting places. 1 Sam. 22: 6. (*marg.*)
Idols were worshipped in. Deu. 12: 2.
Not to be planted near God's altar. Deu. 16: 21.
Of Canaanites, to be destroyed. Exo. 34: 13. Deu. 7: 5. Deu. 12: 3.
FOR IDOL WORSHIP PLANTED
By Ahab. 1 Kin. 16: 33.
By Manasseh. 2 Kin. 21: 3.
By Israelites. 2 Kin. 17: 16.
Fondness of Israel for. Jer. 17: 2.
Punishment for making and serving. 1 Kin. 14: 15. Isa. 1: 28, 29. Mic. 5: 14.
DESTROYED BY
Gideon. Jud. 6: 25—28.
Hezekiah. 2 Kin. 18: 4.
Asa. 2 Chr. 14: 3.
Jehoshaphat. 2 Chr. 17: 6.
Josiah. 2 Kin. 23: 14. 2 Chr. 34: 3, 7.
God promised to wean Israel from. Isa. 17: 7, 8.

Hair, The.

The natural covering of the head. Psa. 68: 21.
Innumerable. Psa. 40: 12. Psa. 69: 4.
Growth of. Jud. 16: 22.
GOD
Numbers. Mat. 10: 30.
Takes care of. Dan. 3: 27. Luke 21: 18.
Black, particularly esteemed. So. of Sol. 5: 11.
WHITE OR GRAY,
A token of age. 1 Sam. 12: 2. Psa. 71: 18.
A token of weakness and decay. Hos. 7: 9.
An emblem of wisdom. Dan. 7: 9, with Job 12: 12.
With righteousness, a crown of glory. Pro. 16: 31.
To be reverenced. Lev. 19: 32.
Man cannot even change the color of. Mat. 5: 36.
OF WOMEN
Worn long for a covering. 1 Cor. 11: 15.
Plaited and broidered. 1 Tim. 2: 9. 1 Pet. 3: 3.
Well set and ornamented. Isa. 3: 24.
Neglected in grief. Luke 7: 38. Jno. 12: 3.
Sometimes worn long by men. 2 Sam. 14: 26.
Men condemned for wearing long. 1 Cor. 11: 14.
Often expensively anointed. Ecc. 9: 8.
OF NAZARITES
Not to be cut or shorn during their vow. Num. 6: 5. Jud. 16: 17, 19, 20.
Shorn after completion of vow. Num. 6: 18.
Of the healed leper to be shorn. Lev. 14: 9.
Color of, changed by leprosy. Lev. 13: 3, 10.
Cut off in affliction. Jer 7: 29.
Plucked out in extreme grief. Ezr. 9: 3.
Plucking out of, a reproach. Neh. 13: 25. Isa. 50: 6.
JUDGMENTS EXPRESSED BY
Sending baldness for. Isa. 3: 24. Jer. 47: 5.
Shaving. Isa. 7: 20.

Hands, The.

Necessary members of the body. 1 Cor. 12: 21.
PARTS OF, MENTIONED;
The palm. Isa. 49: 16. Mat. 26: 67.
The thumb. Exo. 29: 20. Lev. 14: 14, 17.
The fingers. 2 Sam. 21: 20. Dan. 5: 5.
God strengthens. Gen. 49: 24.
God makes impotent. Job 5: 12.
OPERATIONS OF, MENTIONED;
Feeling. Psa. 115: 7. 1 Jno. 1: 1.
Taking. Gen. 3: 22. Exo. 4: 4.
Holding. Jud. 7: 20. Rev. 10: 2.
Working. Pro. 31: 19. 1 The. 4: 11.
Writing. Isa. 44: 5. Gal. 6: 11.
Making signs. Isa. 13: 2. Acts 12: 17.
Striking. Mar. 14: 65. Jno. 19: 3.
DISTINGUISHED AS
The right. Acts 3: 7.
The left. Gen. 14: 15. Acts 21: 3.
Many alike expert with both. 1 Chr. 12: 2.
Many had more command of the left. Jud. 3: 15, 21. (*marg.*) Jud. 20: 16.
THE RIGHT HAND,
Place of honor. 1 Kin. 2: 19. Psa. 45: 9.
Place of power. Psa. 110: 1. Mar. 14: 62.
Signet worn on. Jer. 22: 24.
Given in token of friendship. Gal. 2: 9.
Used in embracing. 2 Sam. 20: 9. So. of Sol. 2: 6. So. of Sol. 8: 3.
Sworn by. Isa. 62: 8.
The accuser stood at, of the accused. Psa. 109: 6. Zec. 3: 1.
Of priests touched with blood of consecration-ram. Exo. 29: 20. Lev. 8: 23, 24.
Of healed leper touched with blood of his sacrifice. Lev. 14: 14, 17, 25.
Of healed leper touched with oil. Lev. 14: 28.
The Jews carried a staff in, when walking. Exo. 12: 11. 2 Kin. 4: 29.
The Jews eat with. Mat. 26: 23.
WERE WASHED
Before eating. Mat. 15: 2. Mar. 7: 3.
After touching an unclean person. Lev. 15: 11.
In token of innocency. Deu. 21: 6, 7. Mat. 27: 24.
Custom of domestics pouring water upon, alluded to. 2 Kin. 3: 11.
Servants directed by movements of. Psa. 123: 2.
Kissed in idolatrous worship. Job. 31: 27.
Treaties made by joining. 2 Kin. 10: 15. Pro. 11: 21.
Suretiship entered into by striking. Job 17: 3. Pro. 6: 1. Pro. 17: 18. Pro. 22: 26.
WERE LIFTED UP
In prayer. Psa. 141: 2. Lam. 3: 41.
In praise. Psa. 134: 2.
In taking an oath. Gen. 14: 22, Rev. 10: 5.

In blessing. Lev. 9: 22.
Often spread out in prayer. Psa. 68: 31. Isa. 1: 15.
Placed under the thigh of a person to whom an oath was made. Gen. 24: 2, 3. Gen. 47: 29, 31.
Clapped together in joy. 2 Kin. 11: 12. Psa. 47: 1.
Smitten together in extreme anger. Num. 24: 10. Eze. 21: 14, 17.
Stretched out in derision. Hos. 7: 5. Zep. 2: 15.
IMPOSITION OF, USED IN
Transferring guilt of sacrifices. Lev. 1: 4. Lev. 3: 2. Lev. 16: 21, 22.
Setting apart the Levites. Num. 8: 10.
Conferring civil power. Num. 27: 18. Deu. 34: 9.
Blessing. Gen. 48: 14. Mar. 10: 16.
Ordaining ministers. Acts 6: 6. 1 Tim. 4: 14.
Imparting the gifts of the Holy Ghost. Acts 8: 17. Acts 19: 6.
Imposition of, a first principle of the doctrine of Christ. Heb. 6: 1, 2.
SHOULD BE EMPLOYED
Industriously. Eph. 4: 28. 1 The. 4: 11.
In God's service. Neh. 2: 18. Zec. 8: 9, 13.
In acts of benevolence. Pro. 3: 27. Pro. 31: 20.
OF THE WICKED, DESCRIBED AS
Bloody. Isa. 1: 15. Isa. 59: 3.
Violent. Psa. 58: 2. Isa. 59: 6.
Mischievous. Psa. 26: 10. Mic. 7: 3.
Slothful. Pro. 6: 10. Pro. 21: 25.
Ensnaring to themselves. Psa. 9: 16.
The wicked recompensed for the work of. Psa. 28: 4. Pro. 12: 14. Isa. 3: 11.
Saints blessed in the work of. Deu. 2: 7. Deu. 30: 9. Job 1: 10. Psa. 90: 17.
CRIMINALS OFTEN
Bound by. Mat. 22: 13.
Deprived of. Deu. 25: 12. 2 Sam. 4: 12.
Mutilated in. Jud. 1: 6, 7.
Hung by. Lam. 5: 12.
ILLUSTRATIVE
Of power. 1 Kin. 18: 46. 2 Kin. 13: 5.
(Lifted up against another,) of rebellion. 2 Sam. 20: 21.
(Opened,) of liberality. Deu. 15: 8. Psa. 104: 28.
(Shut,) of illiberality. Deu. 15: 7.
RIGHT HAND, ILLUSTRATIVE
Of strength and power. Exo. 15: 6. Psa. 17: 7.
(Holding by,) of support. Psa. 73. 23. Isa. 41: 13.
(Standing at,) of protection. Psa. 16; 8, Psa. 109: 31. Psa. 110: 5.
(Full of bribes,) of corruption. Psa. 26: 10.
(Full of falsehood,) of deceitfulness. Psa. 144: 8, 11, *see* Isa. 44: 20.
(Withdrawn,) of support withheld. Psa. 74: 11.
(Cutting off,) of extreme self-denial. Mat. 5: 30.

Happiness of Saints in this Life.

Is in God. Psa. 73: 25, 26.
Only found in the ways of wisdom. Pro. 3: 17, 18.
Described by Christ in the beatitudes. Mat. 5: 3—12.
IS DERIVED FROM
Fear of God. Psa. 128: 1, 2. Pro. 28: 14.
Trust in God. Pro. 16: 20. Phi. 4: 6, 7.
The words of Christ. Jno. 17: 13.
Obedience to God. Psa. 40: 8. Jno. 13: 17.
Salvation. Deu. 33: 29. Isa. 12: 2, 3.
Hope in the Lord. Psa. 146: 5.
Hope of glory. Rom. 5: 2.
God being their Lord. Psa. 144: 15.
God being their help. Psa. 146: 5.
Praising God. Psa. 135: 3.
Their mutual love. Psa. 133: 1.
Divine chastening. Job 5: 17. Jas. 5: 11.
Suffering for Christ. 2 Cor. 12: 10. 1 Pet. 3: 14. 1 Pet. 4: 13, 14.
Having mercy on the poor. Pro. 14: 21.
Finding wisdom. Pro. 3: 13.
Is abundant and satisfying. Psa. 36: 8. Psa. 63: 5.

Happiness of the Wicked, The.

Is limited to this life. Psa. 17: 14. Luke 16: 25.
Is short. Job 20: 5.
Is uncertain. Luke 12: 20. Jas. 4: 13, 14.
Is vain. Ecc. 2: 1. Ecc. 7: 6.
IS DERIVED FROM
Their wealth. Job 21: 13. Psa. 52: 7.
Their power. Job 21: 7. Psa. 37: 35.
Their worldy prosperity. Psa. 17: 14. Psa. 73: 3, 4, 7.
Popular applause. Acts 12: 22.
Gluttony. Isa. 22: 13. Hab. 1: 16.
Drunkenness. Isa. 5: 11. Isa. 56: 12.
Vain pleasure. Job 21: 12. Isa. 5: 12.
Successful oppression. Hab. 1: 15. Jas. 5: 6.
Marred by jealousy. Est. 5: 13.
Often interrupted by judgments. Num. 11: 33. Job 15: 21. Psa. 73: 18—20. Jer. 25: 10, 11.
Leads to sorrow. Pro. 14: 13.
Leads to recklessness. Isa. 22: 13.

Sometimes a stumbling-block to saints. Psa. 73: 3, 16. Jer. 12: 1. Hab. 1: 13.
Saints often permitted to see the end of. Psa. 73: 17—20.
Envy not. Psa. 37: 1.
Woe against. Amos 6: 1. Luke 6: 25.
Illustrated. Psa. 37: 35, 36. Luke 12: 16—20. Luke 16: 19—25.
Exemplified. *Israel*, Num. 11: 33. *Haman*, Est. 5: 9—11. *Belshazzar*, Dan. 5: 1. *Herod*, Acts 12: 21—23.

Hart, The.

Clean and used as food. Deu. 12: 15. Deu. 14: 5.
Often hunted. Lam. 1: 6.
FEMALE OF,
Called the hind. So. of Sol. 2: 7.
Delights in freedom. Gen. 49: 21.
Kind and affectionate. Pro. 5: 19.
Brings forth at appointed time. Job 39: 1, 2.
Brings forth with difficulty. Job 39: 3.
Brings forth at the voice of God. Psa. 29: 9.
Forsakes her young in famine. Jer. 14: 5.
Young of, abundantly provided for. Job 39: 4.
ILLUSTRATIVE
Of Christ. So. of Sol. 2: 9, 17. So. of Sol. 8: 14.
Of converted sinners. Isa. 35: 6.
(Sure-footedness of,) of experienced saints. Psa. 18: 33. Hab. 3: 19.
(Panting for water,) of afflicted saints longing for God. Psa. 42: 1, 2.
(Without pasture,) of the persecuted. Lam. 1: 6.

Harvest, The.

Ingathering of fruits of the fields. Mar. 4: 29.
To continue without intermission. Gen. 8: 22.
CALLED THE
Appointed weeks of harvest. Jer. 5: 24.
Harvest time. 2 Sam. 23: 13. Jer. 50: 16.
Fields appeared white before. Jno. 4: 35.
Of barley at the passover. Lev. 23: 6, 10. Ruth 1: 22.
Of wheat at Pentecost. Exo. 34: 22. 1 Sam. 12: 17.
Men and women engaged in. Ruth 2: 8, 9.
PERSONS ENGAGED IN,
Reapers. Ruth 2: 4.
Binders. Gen. 37: 7. Psa. 129: 7.
Called harvest-men. Isa. 17: 5.
Called laborers. Mat. 9: 37.
Fed by the husbandman during. Ruth 2: 14.
Received wages. Jno. 4: 36.
Often defrauded of their wages. Jas. 5: 4.
Former and latter rain necessary to abundance of. Jer. 5: 24. Amos 4: 7.
Patience required in waiting for. Jas. 5: 7.
Not to be commenced until the first fruits had been offered to God. Lev. 23: 10, 14.
A time of great joy. Psa. 126: 6. Isa. 9: 3.
Omitted in the sabbatical year. Lev. 25: 5.
Omitted in year of jubilee. Lev. 25: 11, 12.
The Sabbath to be observed during. Exo. 34: 21.
Legal provision for the poor during. Lev. 19: 9, 10. Lev. 23: 22. Deu. 24: 19.
FAILURE OF,
Occasioned by drought. Amos 4: 7.
Occasioned by locusts. Joel 1: 4.
Sometimes continued for years. Gen. 45: 6.
A cause of great grief. Isa. 16: 9. Joel 1: 11.
A punishment for sin. Isa. 17: 10, 11.
Slothfulness during, ruinous. Pro. 10: 5.
Miraculous thunder, &c. in. 1 Sam. 12: 17, 18.
ILLUSTRATIVE
Of seasons of grace. Jer. 8: 20.
Of the end of the world. Mat. 13: 30, 39.
Of a time when many are ready to receive the gospel. Mat. 9: 37, 38. Jno. 4: 35.
Of a time of judgment. Jer. 51: 33. Hos. 6: 11.
Of ripeness for wrath. Joel 3: 13. Rev. 14: 15.
(Dew in,) of God's protection, &c. Isa. 18: 4.
(Cold in,) of a refreshing message. Pro. 25: 13.
(Rain in,) of honor given to fools. Pro. 26: 1.

Hatred.

Forbidden. Lev. 19: 17. Col. 3: 8.
Is murder. 1 Jno. 3: 15.
A work of the flesh. Gal. 5: 20.
Often cloaked by deceit. Pro. 10: 18. Pro. 26: 26.
Leads to deceit. Pro. 26: 24, 25.
Stirs up strife. Pro. 10: 12.
Embitters life. Pro. 15: 17.
INCONSISTENT WITH
The knowledge of God. 1 Jno. 2: 9, 11.
The love of God. 1 Jno. 4: 20.

Liars prone to. Pro. 26:28.
THE WICKED EXHIBIT,
Towards God. Rom. 1:30.
Towards saints. Psa. 25:19. Pro. 29:10.
Towards each other. Tit. 3:3.
Christ experienced. Psa. 35:19, with Jno. 7:7. Jno. 15:18, 24, 25.
SAINTS SHOULD
Expect. Mat. 10:22. Jno. 15:18, 19.
Not marvel at. 1 Jno. 3:13.
Return good for. Exo. 23:5. Mat. 5:44.
Not rejoice in the calamities of those who exhibit. Job 31:29, 30. Psa. 35:13, 14.
Give no cause for. Pro. 25:17.
Punishment of. Psa. 34:21. Psa. 44:7. Psa. 89:23. Amos 1:11.
WE SHOULD EXHIBIT AGAINST
False ways. Psa. 119:104, 128.
Lying. Psa. 119:163.
Evil. Psa. 97:10. Pro. 8:13.
Backsliding. Psa. 101:3.
Hatred and opposition to God. Psa. 139:21, 22.
Exemplified. *Cain*, Gen. 4:5, 8. *Esau*, Gen. 27:41. *Joseph's brethren*, Gen. 37:4. *Men of Gilead*, Jud. 11:7. *Saul*, 1 Sam. 18:8, 9. *Ahab*, 1 Kin. 22:8. *Haman*, Est. 3:5, 6. *Enemies of the Jews*, Est. 9:1, 5. Eze. 35:5, 6. *Chaldeans*, Dan. 3:12. *Enemies of Daniel*, Dan. 6:4—15. *Herodias*, Mat. 14:3, 8. *The Jews*, Acts 23:12, 14.

Hatred to Christ.

Is without cause. Psa. 69:4, with Jno. 15:25.
Is on account of His testimony against the world. Jno. 7:7.
INVOLVES
Hatred to His Father. Jno. 15:23, 24.
Hatred to His people. Jno. 15:18.
Punishment of. Psa. 2:2, 9. Psa. 21:8.
No escape for those who persevere in. 1 Cor. 15:25. Heb. 10:29—31.
Illustrated. Luke 19:12—14, 17.
Exemplified. *Chief Priests, &c.* Mat. 27:1, 2. Luke 22:5. *Jews*, Mat. 27:22, 23. *Scribes, &c.* Mar. 11:18. Luke 11:53, 54.

Head.

The uppermost and chief member of the body. Isa. 1:6. 2 Kin. 6:31.
All the other members necessary to. 1 Cor. 12:21.
The body supported and supplied by. Eph. 4:16.
Put for the whole person. Gen. 49:26. Pro. 10:6.
Put for the life. Dan. 1:10. 1 Sam. 28:2.
PARTS OF, MENTIONED;
The skull. 2 Kin. 9:35. Mat. 27:33.
The crown. Gen. 49:26. Isa. 3:17.
The forehead. 1 Sam. 17:49. Eze. 9:4.
The temples. Jud. 4:21, 22. So. of Sol. 4:3.
The face. Gen. 48:12. 2 Kin. 9:30.
The hair. Jud. 16:22. Psa. 40:12.
The scalp. Psa. 68:21.
Often anointed. Ecc. 9:8. Mat. 6:17.
BOWED DOWN
In worshipping God. Gen. 24:26. Exo. 4:31.
As a token of respect. Gen. 43:28.
IN GRIEF
Covered up. 2 Sam. 15:30. Est. 6:12.
Shorn. Job 1:20.
Sprinkled with dust. Jos. 7:6. Job 2:12.
The hands placed on. 2 Sam. 13:19. Jer. 2:37.
Priests forbidden to shave, &c. Lev. 21:5, 10.
Nazarites forbidden to shave. Num. 6:5.
Derision expressed by shaking, &c. 2 Kin. 19:21. Psa. 22:7. Psa. 109:25. Mat. 27:39.
The Jews censured for swearing by. Mat. 5:36.
When hoary with age to be respected. Lev. 19:32.
LIABLE TO
Leprosy. Lev. 13:42—44.
Scab. Isa. 3:17.
Internal disease. 2 Kin. 4:19. Isa. 1:5.
Baldness. Lev. 13:40, 41. Isa. 15:2.
Of the leper always uncovered. Lev. 13:45.
Of women generally covered in public. Gen. 24:65. 1 Cor. 11:5.
Of criminals often cut off. Mat. 14:10.
Of enemies slain in war, often cut off. Jud. 5:26. 1 Sam. 17:51, 57. 1 Sam. 31:9.
ILLUSTRATIVE
Of God. 1 Cor. 11:3.
Of Christ. 1 Cor. 11:3. Eph. 1:22. Col. 2:19.
Of rulers. 1 Sam. 15:17. Dan. 2:38.
Of chief men. Isa. 9:14, 15.
Of the chief city of a kingdom. Isa. 7:8.
(Covered,) of defense and protection. Psa. 140:7.
(Covered,) of subjection. 1 Cor. 11:5, 10.
(Made bald,) of heavy judgments. Isa. 3:24. Isa. 15:2. Isa. 22:12. Mic. 1:16.
(Lifted up,) of joy and confidence. Psa. 3:3. Luke 21:28.
(Lifted up,) of pride, &c. Psa. 83:2.

(Lifted up,) of exaltation. Gen. 40: 13. Psa. 27: 6.
(Anointed,) of joy and prosperity. Psa. 23: 5. Psa. 92: 10.

Heart, The.

Issues of life are out of. Pro. 4: 23.
GOD.
Tries. 1 Chr. 29: 17. Jer. 12: 3.
Knows. Psa. 44: 21. Jer. 20: 12.
Searches. 1 Chr. 28: 9. Jer. 17: 10.
Understands the thoughts of. 1 Chr. 28: 9. Psa. 139: 2.
Ponders. Pro. 21: 2. Pro. 24: 12.
Influences. 1 Sam. 10: 26. Ezr. 6: 22. Ezr. 7: 27. Pro. 21: 1. Jer. 20: 9.
Creates a new. Psa. 51: 10. Eze. 36: 26.
Prepares. 1 Chr. 29: 18. Pro. 16: 1.
Opens. Acts 16: 14.
Enlightens. 2 Cor. 4: 6. Eph. 1: 18.
Strengthens. Psa. 27: 14.
Establishes. Psa. 112: 8. 1 The. 3: 13.
SHOULD BE
Prepared unto God. 1 Sam. 7: 3.
Given to God. Pro. 23: 26.
Perfect with God. 1 Kin. 8: 61.
Applied unto wisdom. Psa. 90: 12. Pro. 2: 2.
Guided in the right way. Pro. 23: 19.
Purified. Jas. 4: 8.
Single. Eph. 6: 5. Col. 3: 22.
Tender. Eph. 4: 32.
Kept with diligence. Pro. 4: 23.
WE SHOULD
Believe with. Acts 8: 37. Rom. 10: 10.
Serve God with all. Deu. 11: 13.
Keep God's statutes with all. Deu. 26: 16.
Walk before God with all. 1 Kin. 2: 4.
Trust in God with all. Pro. 3: 5.
Love God with all. Mat. 22: 37.
Return to God with all. Deu. 30: 2.
Do the will of God from. Eph. 6: 6.
Sanctify God in. 1 Pet. 3: 15.
Love one another with a pure. 1 Pet. 1: 22.
No man can cleanse. Pro. 20: 9.
Faith, the means of purifying. Acts 15: 9.
Renewal of, promised under the gospel. Eze. 11: 19. Eze. 36: 26. Heb. 3: 10.
When broken and contrite, not despised by God. Psa. 51: 17.
The pure in, shall see God. Mat. 5: 8.
PRAY THAT IT MAY BE
Cleansed. Psa. 51: 10.
Inclined to God's testimonies. Psa. 119: 36.
United to fear God. Psa. 86: 11.
Directed into the love of God. 2 The. 3: 5.
Harden not, against God. Psa. 95: 8, with Heb. 4: 7.
Harden not against the poor. Deu. 15: 7.
Regard not iniquity in. Psa. 66: 18.
Take heed lest it be deceived. Deu. 11: 16.
Know the plague of. 1 Kin. 8: 38.
He that trusteth in, is a fool. Pro. 28: 26.

Heart, Character of the Renewed.

Prepared to seek God. 2 Chr. 19: 3. Ezr. 7: 10. Psa. 10: 17.
Fixed on God. Psa. 57: 7. Psa. 112: 7.
Joyful in God. 1 Sam. 2: 1. Zec. 10: 7.
Perfect with God. 1 Kin. 8: 61. Psa. 101: 2.
Upright. Psa. 97: 11. Psa. 125: 4.
Clean. Psa. 73: 1.
Pure. Psa. 24: 4. Mat. 5: 8.
Tender. 1 Sam. 24: 5. 2 Kin. 22: 19.
Single and sincere. Acts 2: 46. Heb. 10: 22.
Honest and good. Luke 8: 15.
Broken, contrite. Psa. 34: 18. Psa. 51: 17.
Obedient. Psa. 119: 112. Rom. 6: 17.
Filled with the law of God. Psa. 40: 8. Psa. 119: 11.
Awed by the word of God. Psa. 119: 161.
Filled with the fear of God. Jer. 32: 40.
Meditative. Psa. 4: 4. Psa. 77: 6.
Circumcised. Deu. 30: 6. Rom. 2: 29.
Void of fear. Psa. 27: 3.
Desirous of God. Psa. 84: 2.
Enlarged. Psa. 119: 32. 2 Cor. 6: 11.
Faithful to God. Neh. 9: 8.
Confident in God. Psa. 112: 7.
Sympathizing. Jer. 4: 19. Lam. 3: 51.
Prayerful. 1 Sam. 1: 13. Psa. 27: 8.
Inclined to obedience. Psa. 119: 112.
Wholly devoted to God. Psa. 9: 1. Psa. 119: 10, 69, 145.
Zealous. 2 Chr. 17: 6. Jer. 20: 9.
Wise. Pro. 10: 8. Pro. 14: 33. Pro. 23: 15.
A treasury of good. Mat. 12: 35.

Heart, Character of the Unrenewed.

Hateful to God. Pro. 6: 16, 18. Pro. 11: 20.
Full of evil. Ecc. 9: 3.
Full of evil imaginations. Gen. 6: 5. Gen. 8: 21. Pro. 6: 18.
Full of vain thoughts. Jer. 4: 14.
Fully set to do evil. Ecc. 8: 11.
Desperately wicked. Jer. 17: 9.
Far from God. Isa. 29: 13, with Mat. 15: 8.
Not perfect with God. 1 Kin. 15: 3. Acts 8: 21. Pro. 6: 18.

Not prepared to seek God. 2 Chr. 12: 14.
A treasury of evil. Mat. 12: 35. Mar. 7: 21.
Darkened. Rom. 1: 21.
Prone to error. Psa. 95: 10.
Prone to depart from God. Deu. 29: 18. Jer. 17: 5.
Impenitent. Rom. 2: 5.
Unbelieving. Heb. 3: 12.
Blind. Eph. 4: 18.
Uncircumcised. Lev. 26: 41. Acts 7: 51.
Of little worth. Pro. 10: 20.
Deceitful. Jer. 17: 9.
Deceived. Isa. 44: 20. Jas. 1: 26.
Divided. Hos. 10: 2.
Double. 1 Chr. 12: 33. Psa. 12: 2.
Hard. Eze. 3: 7. Mar. 10: 5. Rom. 2: 5.
Haughty. Pro. 18: 12. Jer. 48: 29.
Influenced by the devil. Jno. 13: 2.
Carnal. Rom. 8: 7.
Covetous. Jer. 22: 17. 2 Pet. 2: 14.
Despiteful. Eze. 25: 15.
Ensnaring. Ecc. 7: 26.
Foolish. Pro. 12: 23. Pro. 22: 15.
Froward. Psa. 101: 4. Pro. 6: 14. Pro. 17: 20.
Fretful against the Lord, Pro. 19: 3.
Idolatrous. Eze. 14: 3, 4.
Mad. Ecc. 9: 3.
Mischievous. Psa. 28: 3. Psa. 140: 2.
Proud. Psa. 101: 5. Jer. 49: 16.
Rebellious. Jer. 5: 23.
Perverse. Pro. 12: 8.
Stiff. Eze. 2: 4.
Stony. Eze. 11: 19. Eze. 36: 26.
Stout. Isa. 10: 12. Isa. 46: 12.
Elated by sensual indulgence. Hos. 13: 6.
Elated by prosperity. 2 Chr. 26: 16. Dan. 5: 20.
Studieth destruction. Pro. 24: 2.
Often judicially stupified. Isa, 6: 10. Acts 28: 26, 27.
Often judicially hardened. Exo. 4: 21. Jos. 11: 20.

Heathen, The.

Are without God and Christ. Eph. 2: 12.
DESCRIBED AS
- Ignorant. 1 Cor. 1: 21. Eph. 4: 18.
- Idolatrous. Psa. 135: 15. Rom. 1: 23, 25.
- Worshippers of the devil. 1 Cor. 10: 20.
- Cruel. Psa. 74: 20. Rom. 1: 31.
- Filthy. Ezr. 6: 21. Eph. 4: 19. Eph. 5: 12.
- Persecuting. Psa. 2: 1, 2. 2 Cor. 11: 26.
- Scoffing at saints. Psa. 79: 10.
- Strangers to the covenant of promise. Eph. 2: 12.
- Having no hope. Eph. 2: 12.

Degradation of. Lev. 25: 44.
HAVE
- Evidence of the power of God. Rom. 1: 19, 20. Acts 17: 27.
- Evidence of the goodness of God. Acts 14: 17.
- The testimony of conscience. Rom. 2: 14, 15.

Evil of imitating. 2 Kin. 16: 3. Eze. 11: 12.
Cautions against imitating. Jer. 10: 2. Mat. 6: 7.
Danger of intercourse with. Psa 106: 35.
Employed to chastise the Church Lev. 26: 33. Jer. 49: 14. Lam. 1: 3. Eze. 7: 24. Eze. 25: 7. Dan. 4: 27. Hab. 1: 5—9.
The Church shall be avenged of. Psa. 149: 7. Jer. 10: 25. Oba. 15.
GOD
- Rules over. 2 Chr. 20: 6. Psa. 47: 8.
- Brings to nought the counsels of. Psa. 33: 10.
- Will be exalted among. Psa. 46: 10. Psa. 102: 15.
- Punishes. Psa. 44: 2. Joel 3: 11—13. Mic. 5: 15. Hab. 3: 12. Zec. 14: 18.
- Will finally judge. Rom. 2: 12—16.

Given to Christ. Psa. 2: 8. Dan. 7: 14.
Salvation of, foretold. Gen. 12: 3, with Gal. 3: 8. Isa. 2: 2—4. Isa. 52: 10. Isa. 60: 1—8.
Salvation provided for. Acts 28: 28. Rom. 15: 9—12.
The glory of God to be declared amongst. 1 Chr. 16: 24. Psa. 96: 3.
The gospel to be preached to. Mat. 24: 14. Mat. 28: 19. Rom. 16: 26. Gal. 1: 16.
Necessity for preaching to. Rom. 10: 14.
The gospel received by. Acts 11: 1. Acts 13: 48. Acts 15: 3, 23.
Baptism to be administered to. Mat. 28: 19.
The Holy Ghost poured out upon Acts 10: 44, 45. Acts 15: 8.
Praise God for success of the gospel amongst. Psa. 98: 1—3. Acts 11: 18.
Pray for. Psa. 67: 2—5.
Aid missions to. 2 Cor. 11: 9. 3 Jno. 6, 7.
Conversion of, acceptable to God. Acts 10: 35. Rom. 15: 16.

Heaven.

Created by God. Gen. 1: 1. Rev. 10: 6.
Everlasting. Psa. 89: 29. 2 Cor. 5: 1.
Immeasurable. Jer. 31: 37.
High. Psa. 103: 11. Isa. 57: 15.
Holy. Deu. 26: 15. Psa. 20: 6. Isa. 57: 15.
God's dwelling-place. 1 Kin. 8: 30. Mat. 6: 9.

God's throne. Isa. 66: 1, with Acts 7: 49.
GOD
Is the Lord of. Dan. 5: 23. Mat. 11: 25.
Reigns in. Psa. 11: 4. Psa. 135: 6. Dan. 4: 35.
Fills. 1 Kin. 8: 27. Jer. 23: 24.
Answers His people from. 1 Chr. 21: 26. 2 Chr. 7: 14. Neh. 9: 27. Psa. 20: 6.
Sends His judgments from. Gen. 19: 24. 1 Sam. 2: 10. Dan. 4: 13, 14. Rom. 1: 18.
CHRIST
As Mediator, entered into. Acts 3: 21. Heb. 6: 20. Heb. 9: 12, 24.
Is all-powerful in. Mat. 28: 18. 1 Pet. 3: 22.
Angels are in. Mat. 18: 10. Mat. 24: 36.
Names of saints are written in. Luke 10: 20. Heb. 12: 23.
Saints rewarded in. Mat. 5: 12. 1 Pet. 1: 4.
Repentance occasions joy in. Luke 15: 7.
Lay up treasure in. Mat. 6: 20. Luke 12: 33.
Flesh and blood cannot inherit. 1 Cor. 15: 50.
Happiness of, described. Rev. 7: 16, 17.
IS CALLED
A garner. Mat. 3: 12.
The kingdom of Christ and of God. Eph. 5: 5.
The Father's house. Jno. 14: 2.
A heavenly country. Heb. 11: 16.
A rest. Heb. 4: 9.
Paradise. 2 Cor. 12: 2, 4.
The wicked excluded from. Gal. 5: 21. Eph. 5: 5. Rev. 22: 15.
Enoch and Elijah were translated into. Gen. 5: 24, with Heb. 11: 5. 2 Kin. 2: 11.

Heave-offering.

To be brought to God's house. Deu. 12: 6.
CONSISTED OF
First fruits of bread. Num. 15: 19—21.
Right shoulder of peace offerings. Lev. 7: 32.
Part of the meat offering of all peace offerings. Lev. 7: 14.
Shoulder of the priest's consecration-ram. Exo. 29: 27.
Tenth of all tithes. Num. 18: 26.
Part of all gifts. Num. 18: 29.
Part of spoil taken in war. Num. 31: 26—47.
To be the best of their kind. Num. 18: 29.
To be heaved up by the priest. Exo. 29: 27.
Sanctified the whole offering. Num. 18: 27, 30.
Given to the priests. Exo. 29: 28. Lev. 7: 34.
To be eaten in a clean place. Lev. 10: 12—15.

Hedges.

Antiquity of. 1 Chr. 4: 23.
Designed for protection. Isa. 5: 2.
Often made of thorns. Mic. 7: 4.
PLACED AROUND
Gardens. So. of Sol. 4: 12. Lam. 2: 6. (*marg.*)
Vineyards. Mat. 21: 33. Mar. 12: 1.
Difficulty of breaking through. Pro. 15: 19.
Danger of breaking through. Ecc. 10: 8.
Desolation caused by removing. Psa. 80: 12, 13.
Filled with grasshoppers. Nah. 3: 17.
Poor travellers sought rest under. Luke 14: 23.
Afforded protection in danger. Jer. 49: 3.
Making up gaps in, alluded to. Eze. 13: 5. Eze. 22: 30.
ILLUSTRATIVE
Of God's protection. Job 1: 10.
Of numerous afflictions. Job 3: 23. Job 19: 8.
Of heavy judgments. Lam. 3: 7. Hos. 2: 6.
Of holy ordinances, &c. Isa. 5: 2. Mat. 21: 33.
Of the way of the slothful. Pro. 15: 19.
(Broken down,) of the taking away of protection. Psa. 80: 12. Isa. 5: 5.

Heedfulness.

Commanded. Exo. 23: 13. Pro. 4: 25—27.
NECESSARY
In the care of the soul. Deu. 4: 9.
In the house and worship of God. Ecc. 5: 1.
In what we hear. Mar. 4: 24.
In how we hear. Luke 8: 18.
In keeping God's commandments. Jos. 22: 5.
In conduct. Eph. 5: 15.
In speech. Pro. 13: 3. Jas. 1: 19.
In worldly company. Psa. 39: 1. Col. 4: 5.
In giving judgment. 1 Chr. 19: 6, 7.
Against sin. Heb. 12: 15, 16.
Against unbelief. Heb. 3: 12.
Against idolatry. Deu. 4: 15, 16.
Against false Christs, and false prophets. Mat. 24: 4, 5, 23, 24.
Against false teachers. Phi. 3: 2. Col. 2: 8. 2 Pet. 3: 16, 17.
Against presumption. 1 Cor. 10: 12.
Promises to. 1 Kin. 2: 4. 1 Chr. 22: 13.

Hell.

1. THE PLACE OF DISEMBODIED SPIRITS, Acts 2: 31.
   Which Christ visited. Luke 23: 43. Acts 2: 31. 1 Pet. 3: 19.
   Contains, a place of rest, Abraham's bosom. Luke 16: 23.
   Paradise. Luke 23: 43.
   And a place of torment. Luke 16: 23.
2. THE PLACE OF FUTURE PUNISHMENT.
   Destruction from the presence of God. 2 The. 1: 9.

DESCRIBED AS
- Everlasting punishment. Mat. 25: 46.
- Everlasting fire. Mat. 25: 41.
- Everlasting burnings. Isa. 33: 14.
- A furnace of fire. Mat. 13: 42, 50.
- A lake of fire. Rev. 20: 15.
- Fire and brimstone. Rev. 14: 10.
- Unquenchable fire. Mat. 3: 12.
- Devouring fire. Isa. 33: 14.

Prepared for the devil, &c. Mat. 25: 41.
Devils are confined in, until the judgment-day. 2 Pet. 2: 4. Jude 6.
Punishment of, is eternal. Isa. 33: 14. Rev. 20: 10.
The wicked shall be turned into. Psa. 9: 17.
Human power cannot preserve from. Eze. 32: 27.
The body suffers in. Mat. 5: 29. Mat. 10: 28.
The soul suffers in. Mat. 10: 28.
The wise avoid. Pro. 15: 24.
Endeavor to keep others from. Pro. 23: 14. Jude 23.
The society of the wicked leads to. Pro. 5: 5. Pro. 9: 18.
The beast, false prophets, and the devil shall be cast into. Rev. 19: 20. Rev. 20: 10.
The powers of, cannot prevail against the Church. Mat. 16: 18.
Illustrated. Isa. 30: 33.

Herbs, &c.

Called the green herbs. 2 Kin. 19: 26.
GOD
- Created. Gen. 1: 11, 12. Gen. 2: 5.
- Causes, to grow. Job 38: 27. Psa. 104: 14.

Each kind of, contains its own seed. Gen. 1: 11, 12.
Given as food to man. Gen. 1: 28, 29. Gen. 9: 3.
FOUND IN
- The fields. Jer. 12: 4.
- The mountains. Pro. 27: 25.
- The marshes. Job 8: 11.
- The deserts. Job 24: 5. Jer. 17: 6.

Cultivated in gardens. Deu. 11: 10. 1 Kin. 21: 2.
Cultivated for food. Pro. 15: 17. Heb. 6: 7.
Require rain and dew. Deu. 32: 2. Job 38: 26, 27.
Mode of watering, alluded to. Deu. 11: 10.
MENTIONED IN SCRIPTURE;
- Aloe. So. of Sol. 4: 14.
- Anise. Mat. 23: 23.
- Barley. Exo. 9: 31. 2 Sam. 14: 30.
- Beans. 2 Sam. 17: 28.
- Bulrushes. Exo. 2: 3. Isa. 58: 5.
- Calamus. So. of Sol. 4: 14.
- Cummin. Isa. 28: 27. Mat. 23: 23.
- Cucumber. Num. 11: 5. Isa. 1: 8.
- Fitches. Isa. 28: 25, 27.
- Flag. Exo. 2: 3. Job 8: 11.
- Flax. Exo. 9: 31.
- Garlic. Num. 11: 5.
- Gourds. 2 Kin. 4: 39.
- Grass. Num. 22: 4.
- Heath. Jer. 17: 6. Jer. 48: 6.
- Hyssop. Exo. 12: 22. 1 Kin. 4: 33.
- Leeks. Num. 11: 5.
- Lentiles. Gen. 25: 34.
- Mandrakes. Gen. 30: 14. So. of Sol. 7: 13.
- Mallows. Job 30: 4.
- Millet. Eze. 4: 9.
- Melon. Num. 11: 5.
- Mint. Mat. 23: 23.
- Myrrh. So. of Sol. 4: 14.
- Onions. Num. 11: 5.
- Reeds. Job 40: 21. Isa. 19: 6.
- Rushes. Job 8: 11.
- Rye. Exo. 9: 32.
- Saffron. So. of Sol. 4: 14.
- Spikenard. So. of Sol. 4: 14.
- Tares or Darnel. Mat. 13: 30.
- Wheat. Exo. 9: 32. Jer. 12: 13.

Bitter, used at passover. Exo. 12: 8. Num. 9: 11.
Poisonous, not fit for man's use. 2 Kin. 4: 39, 40.
DESTROYED BY
- Hail and lightning. Exo. 9: 22—25.
- Locusts, &c. Exo. 10: 12, 15. Psa. 105: 34, 35.
- Drought. Isa. 42: 15.
- Titheable among the Jews. Luke 11: 42.

Were sometimes used instead of animal food by weak saints. Rom. 14: 2.
ILLUSTRATIVE
- Of the wicked. 2 Kin 19: 26. Psa. 37: 2.
- (Dew on,) of grace given to saints. Isa. 18: 4.

High Places.

Used for idolatrous worship. 1 Kin. 11: 7, 8.
God sometimes worshipped on. 1 Sam. 9: 12. 1 Kin. 3: 2, 4. 2 Chr. 33: 17.

MENTIONED IN SCRIPTURE;
Gibeon. 1 Kin. 3: 4.
Arnon. Num. 21: 28.
Baal. Num. 22: 41.
Tophet. Jer. 7: 31.
Bamah. Eze. 20: 29.
Aven. Hos. 10: 8.
Adorned with tapestry. Eze. 16: 16.
Surrounded with groves. 1 Kin. 14: 23.
BUILT BY
Solomon. 1 Kin. 11: 7.
Jeroboam. 1 Kin. 12: 31.
Jehoram. 2 Chr. 21: 11.
Ahaz. 2 Chr. 28: 25.
Manasseh. 2 Kin. 21: 3. 2 Chr. 33: 3.
People of Judah. 1 Kin. 14: 23.
People of Israel. 2 Kin. 17: 9.
Priests ordained for. 1 Kin. 12: 32. 1 Kin. 13: 33.
Sacrifices and incense offered to idols upon. 2 Kin. 12: 3. 2 Kin. 16: 4.
Enchantments used upon. Num. 23: 3. Num. 24: 1.
Of the Canaanites to be destroyed. Num. 33: 52.
THE JEWS
Built, in their cities. 2 Kin. 17: 9.
Built, in all their streets. Eze. 16: 24, 31.
Condemned for building. Eze. 16: 23—35.
Provoked God with. 1 Kin. 14: 22, 23. Psa. 78: 58.
Threatened with destruction of. Lev. 26: 30.
Punished for. 2 Kin. 17: 11, with 18 v.
DESTROYED BY
Asa, partially. 2 Chr. 14: 3, 5, with 2 Chr. 15: 17.
Jehoshaphat. 2 Chr. 17: 6.
Hezekiah. 2 Kin. 18: 4. 2 Chr. 31: 1.
Josiah. 2 Kin. 23: 8. 2 Chr. 34: 3.
NOT REMOVED BY
Jehoash. 2 Kin. 12: 3.
Amaziah. 2 Kin. 14: 4.
Azariah. 2 Kin. 15: 4.
Jotham. 2 Kin. 15: 35.

High Priest, The.

Specially called of God. Exo 28: 1, 2. Heb. 5: 4.
Consecrated to his office. Exo. 40: 13. Lev. 8: 12.
WAS CALLED
The priest. Exo. 29: 30. Neh. 7: 65.
God's high priest. Acts 23: 4.
Ruler of the people. Exo. 22: 28, with Acts 23: 5.
The office of, hereditary. Exo. 29: 29.
Next in rank to the king. Lam. 2: 6.
Often exercised chief civil power. 1 Sam. 4: 18.
DUTIES OF;
Offering gifts and sacrifices. Heb. 5: 1.
Lighting the sacred lamps. Exo. 30: 8. Num. 8: 3.
Making atonement in the most holy place once a year. Lev. 16 ch. Heb. 9: 7.
Bearing before the Lord the names of Israel for a memorial. Exo. 28: 12, 29.
Enquiring of God by Urim and Thummim. 1 Sam. 23: 9—12. 1 Sam. 30: 7, 8.
Consecrating the Levites. Num. 8 11—21.
Appointing priests to offices. 1 Sam 2: 36.
Taking charge of money collected in the sacred treasury. 2 Kin. 12: 10. 2 Kin. 22: 4.
Presiding in the superior court. Mat. 26: 3, 57—62. Acts 5: 21—28. Acts 23: 1—5.
Taking the census of the people. Num. 1: 3.
Blessing the people. Lev. 9: 22, 23.
Sometimes enabled to prophesy. Jno. 11: 49—52.
Assisted by a deputy. 2 Sam. 15: 24. Luke 3: 2.
THE DEPUTY OF,
Called the second priest. 2 Kin. 25: 18.
Had oversight of the tabernacle. Num. 4: 16.
Had oversight of the Levites. Num. 3: 32.
To marry a virgin of Aaron's family. Lev. 21: 13, 14.
Forbidden to mourn for any. Lev. 21: 10—12.
To be tender and compassionate. Heb. 5: 2.
Needed to sacrifice for himself. Heb. 5: 1—3.
SPECIAL GARMENTS OF;
Ephod with its curious girdle. Exo. 28: 6, 7.
Girdle. Exo. 28: 4, 39.
Broidered coat. Exo. 28: 4, 39.
Robe of the ephod. Exo. 28: 31—35.
Breastplate. Exo. 28: 15—29.
Linen mitre. Exo. 28: 4, 39.
Plate or crown of gold, &c. Exo. 28: 36—38.
Made by divine wisdom given to Bezaleel, &c. Exo. 28: 3. Exo. 36: 1. Exo. 39: 1.
Were for beauty and ornament. Exo. 28: 2.
Worn at his consecration. Lev. 8: 7, 9.
Worn seven days after consecration. Exo. 29: 30.
Descended to his successors. Exo. 29: 29.
Wore the ordinary priest's garments when making atonement in the holy place. Lev. 16: 4.
Office of, promised to the posterity of Phinehas for his zeal. Num. 25: 12, 13.

Family of Eli degraded from office of, for bad conduct. 1 Sam. 2: 27—36.
Sometimes deposed by the kings. 1 Kin. 2: 27.
Office of, made annual by the Romans. Jno. 11: 49—51, with Acts 4: 6.
TYPIFIED CHRIST IN
Being called of God. Heb. 5: 4, 5,
His title. Heb. 3: 1.
His appointment. Isa. 61: 1. Jno. 1: 32—34.
Making atonement. Lev. 16: 33. Heb. 2: 17.
Splendid dress. Exo. 28: 2, with Jno. 1: 14.
Being liable to temptation. Heb. 2: 18.
Compassion and sympathy for the weak and ignorant. Heb. 4: 15. Heb. 5: 1, 2.
Marrying a virgin. Lev. 21: 13, 14. 2 Cor. 11: 2.
Holiness of office. Lev. 21: 15, with Heb. 7: 26.
Performing by himself all the services on day of atonement. Lev. 16 ch. with Heb. 1: 3.
Bearing the names of Israel upon his heart. Exo. 28: 29, with So. of Sol. 8: 6.
Alone entering into most holy place. Heb. 9: 7, with 12, 24 vs. and Heb. 4: 14.
Interceding. Num. 16: 43—48. Heb. 7: 25.
Blessing. Lev. 9: 22, 23. Acts 3: 26.
INFERIOR TO CHRIST IN
Needing to make atonement for his own sins. Heb. 5: 2, 3. Heb. 7: 26—28. Heb. 9: 7.
Being of the order of Aaron. Heb. 6: 20. Heb. 7: 11—17. Heb. 8: 4, 5, with 1, 2, 6 vs.
Being made without an oath. Heb. 7: 20—22.
Not being able to continue. Heb. 7: 23, 24.
Offering oftentimes the same sacrifices. Heb. 9: 25, 26, 28. Heb. 10: 11, 12, 14.
Entering into holiest every year. Heb. 9: 7, 12, 25.

High-ways.

Roads for public use. Num. 20: 19. Deu. 2: 27.
Called the king's highway. Num. 20: 17.
Marked out by heaps of stones. Jer. 31: 21.
Generally broad. Jud. 20: 32, 45. Mat. 7: 13.
Generally straight. 1 Sam. 6: 12. Isa. 40: 3.
Made to all cities of refuge. Deu. 19: 2, 3.
Often made in deserts. Isa. 40: 3.
INFESTED WITH
Serpents. Gen. 49: 17.
Wild beasts. 1 Kin. 13: 24, with Isa. 35: 9.
Robbers. Jer. 3: 2. Luke 10: 30—33.
Beggars sat by sides of. Mat. 20: 30. Mar. 10: 46.
Often obstructed. Jer. 18: 15.
All obstructions removed from, before persons of distinction. Isa. 40: 3, 4, with Mat. 3: 3.
By-paths more secure in times of danger. Jud. 5: 6.
Desolation of, threatened as a punishment. Lev. 26: 22. Isa. 33: 8.
ILLUSTRATIVE
Of Christ. Jno. 14: 6.
Of the way of holiness. Isa. 35: 8.
Of facilities for the restoration of the Jews. Isa. 11: 16. Isa. 62: 10.
(Made in the deserts,) of facilities for the spread of the gospel. Isa. 40: 3. Isa. 43: 19.
(Narrow,) of the way to life. Mat. 7: 14.
(Broad,) of the way to destruction. Mat. 7: 13.

Hittites.

Descended from Canaan's son, Heth. Gen. 10: 15.
CALLED THE
Sons of Heth. Gen. 23: 3, 20.
Children of Heth. Gen. 23: 5.
One of the seven nations of Canaan. Deu. 7: 1.
Dwelt in Hebron. Gen. 23 : 2, 3, 19.
Governed by kings. 1 Kin. 10: 29. 2 Kin. 7: 6.
Land of, promised to Israel. Gen. 15: 20. Exo. 3: 8.
Israel commanded to destroy. Deu. 7: 1, 2, 24.
Part of their land given to Caleb. Jos. 14: 13.
Not entirely destroyed by Israel. Jud. 3: 5.
The remnant of, made tributary in the reign of Solomon. 1 Kin. 9: 20, 21.
Luz built in the country of. Jud. 1: 26.
INTERMARRIAGES WITH, BY
Esau. Gen. 36: 2.
Solomon. 1 Kin. 11: 1, 2.
Israel after conquest of Canaan. Jud. 3: 5, 6.
Israelites after the captivity. Ezr. 9: 1.
Descent from, illustrative of the degradation of the Jews. Eze. 16: 3.

Remarkable persons of. *Ephron*, Gen. 49: 30. *Abimelech*, 1 Sam. 26: 6. *Uriah*, 2 Sam. 11: 6, 21.

Hivites.

Descended from Canaan. Gen. 10: 15, 17.
Supposed to be the ancient Avim, or Avites. Deu. 2: 33. Jos. 13: 3.
One of the seven nations of Canaan. Deu. 7: 1.
Dwelt near Lebanon. Jud. 3: 3.
The Shechemites a people of. Gen. 34: 2.
The Gibeonites a people of. Jos. 9: 3, 7.
Esau intermarried with. Gen. 36: 2.
Land of, promised to Israel. Exo. 3: 8. Exo. 23: 23.
Israel commanded to destroy. Deu. 7: 1, 2, 24.
A part of, left to prove Israel. Jud. 3: 3.
Remnant of, made tributary in the reign of Solomon. 1 Kin. 9: 20, 21.

Holiness.

Commanded. Lev. 11: 45. Lev. 20: 7. Eph. 5: 8. Col. 3: 12. Rom. 12: 1.
CHRIST
- Desires, for His people. Jno. 17: 17.
- Effects, in His people. Eph. 5: 25—27.
- An example of. Heb. 7: 26. 1 Pet. 2: 21, 22.

The character of God, the standard of. Lev. 19: 2, with 1 Pet. 1: 15, 16. Eph. 5: 1.
The character of Christ, the standard of. Rom. 8: 29. 1 Jno. 2: 6. Phi. 2: 5.
The gospel the way of. Isa. 35: 8.
Necessary to God's worship. Psa. 24: 3, 4.
None shall see God without. Eph. 5: 5. Heb. 12: 14.
SAINTS
- Elected to. Rom. 8: 29. Eph. 1: 4.
- Called to. 1 The. 4: 7. 2 Tim. 1: 9.
- New created in. Eph. 4: 24.
- Possess. 1 Cor. 3: 17. Heb. 3: 1.
- Have their fruit unto. Rom. 6: 22.
- Should follow after. Heb. 12: 14.
- Should serve God in. Luke 1: 74, 75.
- Should yield their members as instruments of. Rom. 6: 13, 19.
- Should present their bodies to God in. Rom. 12: 1.
- Should have their conversation in. 1 Pet. 1: 15. 2 Pet. 3: 11.
- Should continue in. Luke 1: 75.
- Should seek perfection in. 2 Cor. 7: 1.
- Shall be presented to God in. Col. 1: 22. 1 The. 3: 13.
- Shall continue in, for ever. Rev. 22: 11.

Behavior of aged women should be as becomes. Tit. 2: 3.
Promise to women who continue in. 1 Tim. 2: 15.
Promised to the Church. Isa. 35: 8. Oba. 17. Zec. 14: 20, 21.
Becoming in the Church. Psa. 93: 5.
The Church is the beauty of. 1 Chr. 16: 29. Psa. 29: 2.
The word of God the means of producing. Jno. 17: 17. 2 Tim. 3: 16, 17.
IS THE RESULT OF
- The manifestation of God's grace. Tit. 2: 3, 11, 12.
- Subjection to God. Rom. 6: 22.
- God's keeping. Jno. 17: 15.
- Union with Christ. Jno. 15: 4, 5. Jno. 17: 9.

Required in prayer. 1 Tim. 2: 8.
MINISTERS SHOULD
- Possess. Tit. 1: 8.
- Avoid everything inconsistent with. Lev. 21: 6. Isa. 52: 11.
- Be examples of. 1 Tim. 4: 12.
- Exhort to. Heb. 12: 14. 1 Pet. 1: 14—16.

MOTIVES TO;
- The glory of God. Jno. 15: 8. Phi. 1: 11.
- The love of Christ. 2 Cor. 5: 14, 15.
- The mercies of God. Rom. 12: 1, 2.
- The dissolution of all things. 2 Pet. 3: 11.

Chastisements are intended to produce, in saints. Heb. 12: 10. Jas. 1: 2, 3.
Should lead to separation from the wicked. Num. 16: 21, 26. 2 Cor. 6: 17, 18.
The wicked are without. 1 Tim. 1: 9. 2 Tim. 3: 2.
Exemplified. *David*, Psa. 86: 2. *Israel*, Jer. 2: 3. *John the Baptist*, Mar. 6: 20. *Prophets*, Luke 1: 70. *Paul*, 1 The. 2: 10. *Wives of Patriarchs*, 1 Pet. 3: 5.

Holiness of God, The.

Is incomparable. Exo. 15: 11. 1 Sam. 2: 2.
EXHIBITED IN HIS
- Character. Psa. 22: 3. Jno. 17: 11.
- Name. Isa. 57: 15. Luke 1: 49.
- Words. Psa. 60: 6. Jer. 23: 9.
- Works. Psa. 145: 17.
- Kingdom. Psa. 47: 8. Mat. 13: 41. Rev. 21: 27. 1 Cor. 6: 9, 10.

IS PLEDGED FOR THE FULFILMENT OF
- His promises. Psa. 89: 35.
- His judgments. Amos 4: 2.

Saints are commanded to imitate. Lev. 11: 44, with 1 Pet. 1: 15, 16.
Saints should praise. Psa. 30: 4.

Should produce reverential fear. Rev. 15:4.
Requires holy service. Jos. 24:19. Psa. 93:5.
Heavenly hosts adore. Isa. 6:3. Rev. 4:8.
Should be magnified. 1 Chr. 16:10. Psa. 48:1. Psa. 99:3, 5. Rev. 15:4.

Holy Ghost, the Comforter, The.

Proceeds from the Father. Jno. 15:26.
GIVEN
By the Father. Jno. 14:16.
By Christ. Isa. 61:3.
Through Christ's intercession. Jno. 14:16.
Sent in the name of Christ. Jno. 14:26.
Sent by Christ from the Father. Jno. 15:26. Jno. 16:7.
AS SUCH HE
Communicates joy to saints. Rom. 14:17. Gal. 5:22. 1 The. 1:6.
Edifies the Church. Acts 9:31.
Testifies of Christ. Jno. 15:26.
Imparts the love of God. Rom. 5:3—5.
Imparts hope. Rom. 15:13. Gal. 5:5.
Teaches saints. Jno. 14:26.
Dwells with, and in saints. Jno. 14:17.
Abides for ever with saints. Jno. 14:16.
Is known by saints. Jno. 14:17.
The world cannot receive. Jno. 14:17.

Holy Ghost, The, is God.

As Jehovah. Exo. 17:7, with Heb. 3:7—9. Num. 12:6, with 2 Pet. 1:21.
As Jehovah of hosts. Isa. 6:3, 8—10, with Acts 28:25.
As Jehovah, Most High. Psa. 78:17, 21, with Acts 7:51.
Being invoked as Jehovah. Luke 2:26—29. Acts 4:23—25, with Acts 1:16, 20. 2 The. 3:5.
As called God. Acts 5:3, 4.
As joined with the Father and the Son in the baptismal formula. Mat. 28:19.
As eternal. Heb. 9:14.
As omnipresent. Psa. 139:7—13.
As omniscient. 1 Cor. 2:10.
As omnipotent. Luke 1:35. Rom. 15:19.
As the Spirit of glory and of God. 1 Pet. 4:14.
As Creator. Gen. 1:26, 27, with Job 33:4.
As equal to, and one with the Father. Mat. 28:19. 2 Cor. 13:14.
As Sovereign Disposer of all things. Dan. 4:35, with 1 Cor. 12:6, 11.
As Author of the new birth. Jno. 3:5, 6, with 1 Jno. 5:4.
As raising Christ from the dead. Acts 2:24, with 1 Pet. 3:18. Heb. 13:20, with Rom. 1:4.
As inspiring Scripture. 2 Tim. 3:16, with 2 Pet. 1:21.
As the source of wisdom. 1 Cor. 12:8. Isa. 11:2. Jno. 16:13. Jno. 14:26.
As the source of miraculous power. Mat. 12:28, with Luke 11:20. Acts 19:11, with Rom. 15:19.
As appointing and sending ministers. Acts 13:2, 4, with Mat. 9:38. Acts 20:28.
As directing where the gospel should be preached. Acts 16:6, 7, 10.
As dwelling in saints. Jno. 14:17, with 1 Cor. 14:25. 1 Cor. 3:16, with 1 Cor. 6:19.
As Comforter of the Church. Acts 9:31, with 2 Cor 1:3.
As sanctifying the Church. Eze. 37:28, with Rom. 15:16.
As the Witness. Heb. 10:15, with 1 Jno. 5:9.
As convincing of sin, of righteousness, and of judgment. Jno. 16:8—11.

Holy Ghost, The, Personality of.

He creates and gives life. Job 33:4.
He appoints and commissions ministers. Isa. 48:16. Acts 13:2. Acts 20:28.
He directs ministers where to preach. Acts 8:29. Acts 10:19, 20.
He directs ministers where not to preach. Acts 16:6, 7.
He instructs ministers what to preach. 1 Cor. 2:13.
He spoke in, and by, the Prophets. Acts 1:16. 1 Pet. 1:11, 12. 2 Pet. 1:21.
He strives with sinners. Gen. 6:3.
He reproves. Jno. 16:8.
He comforts. Acts 9:31.
He helps our infirmities. Rom. 8:26.
He teaches. Jno. 14:26. 1 Cor. 12:3.
He guides. Jno. 16:13.
He sanctifies. Rom. 15:16. 1 Cor. 6:11.
He testifies of Christ. Jno. 15:26.
He glorifies Christ. Jno. 16:14.
He has a power of His own. Rom. 15:13.
He searches all things. Rom. 11:33, 34, with 1 Cor. 2:10, 11.
He works according to His own will. 1 Cor. 12:11.
He dwells with saints. Jno. 14:17.
He can be grieved. Eph. 4:30.
He can be vexed. Isa. 63:10.
He can be resisted. Acts 7:51.
He can be tempted. Acts 5:9.

Holy Ghost, the teacher, The.

Promised. Pro. 1:23.
As the Spirit of wisdom. Isa. 11:2. Isa. 40:13, 14.
GIVEN
In answer to prayer. Eph. 1:16, 17.
To saints. Neh. 9:20. 1 Cor. 2:12, 13.
Necessity for. 1 Cor. 2:9, 10.
AS SUCH HE
Reveals the things of God. 1 Cor. 2:10, 13.
Reveals the things of Christ. Jno. 16:14.
Reveals the future. Luke 2:26. Acts 21:11.
Brings the words of Christ to remembrance. Jno. 14:26.
Directs in the way of godliness. Isa. 30:21. Eze. 36:27.
Teaches saints to answer persecutors. Mar. 13:11. Luke 12:12.
Enables ministers to teach. 1 Cor. 12:8.
Guides into all truth. Jno. 14:26. Jno. 16:13.
Directs the decisions of the Church. Acts 15:28.
Attend to the instruction of. Rev. 2:7, 11, 29.
The natural man will not receive the things of. 1 Cor. 2:14.

Holy Land.

Extremely fruitful. Exo. 3:8. Num. 13:27. Deu. 8:7—9. Deu. 11:10—12.
Abounded in minerals. Deu. 8:9. Deu. 33:25.
CALLED
The land. Lev. 26:42. Luke 4:25.
The Lord's land. Hos. 9:3.
Land of Canaan. Gen. 11:31. Lev. 14:34.
Land of Israel. 1 Sam. 13:19. Mat. 2:20, 21.
Land of Judah. Isa. 26:1.
Land of the Hebrews. Gen. 40:15.
Land of promise. Heb. 11:9.
Land of Immanuel. Isa. 8:8.
Pleasant land. Psa. 106:24. Dan. 8:9.
Good land. Num. 14:7. Deu. 3:25.
Glorious land. Dan. 11:16.
Palestina. Exo. 15:14. Isa. 14:29, 31.
Original inhabitants of. Gen. 10:15—20. Deu. 7:1.
Inhabitants of, expelled for wickedness. Gen. 15:16. Exo. 23:23. Lev. 18:25. Deu. 18:12.
PROMISED TO
Abraham. Gen. 12:7. Gen. 13:15. Gen. 17:8.
Isaac. Gen. 26:3.
Jacob. Gen. 28:13, 15. Gen. 35:12.
Given by covenant to Israel. Ex[...] 6:4.
EXTENT OF,
As promised. Gen. 15:18. Deu. 1[...] 7. Jos. 1:4.
As at first divided. Num. 34:1—1[...]
Under Solomon. 1 Kin. 4:21, 2[...] 2 Chr. 9:26.
Twelve men sent to spy. Num. 13 ch[...]
Conquered by Joshua. Jos. 6 ch. t[...] Jos. 12 ch.
Divided by lot. Num. 34:16—29, wit[...] Jos. 13:7—14.
Allotment of, specified. Jos. 14 ch[...] to Jos. 19 ch.
All inheritances in, inalienable. Lev[...] 25:10, 23.
A sabbath of rest appointed for[...] Lev. 25:2—5.
Obedience the condition of continuing in. Lev. 26:3, &c. Deu. 5:3[...] Deu. 11:16, 17, 22—25.
DIVIDED INTO
Twelve provinces by Solomon. [...] Kin. 4:7—19.
Two kingdoms in the time of Rehoboam. 1 Kin. 11:35, 36. 1 Kin[...] 12:19, 20.
Four provinces by the Romans[...] Luke 3:1.
Numerous population of, in Solomon's reign. 1 Kin. 3:8. 2 Chr[...] 1:9.
Extensive commerce of, in Solomon's reign. 1 Kin. 9:26—28. 1 Kin. 10[...] 22—29.
Prosperity of, in Solomon's reign. [...] Kin. 4:20.
Was the burial place of the patriarchs. Gen. 49:29—31. Gen. 50:13[...] 25. Jos. 24:32.
A type of the rest that remaineth for[...] saints. Heb. 4:1, 2, 9. 1 Pet. 1:4.

Holy of Holies.

Divided from the outward tabernacle by a vail. Exo. 26:31—33.
WAS CALLED THE
Sanctuary. Lev. 4:6. Psa. 20:2[...]
Holy sanctuary. Lev. 16:33.
Holy place. Exo. 28:29. Lev. 16[...] 2, 3.
Most holy place. Exo. 26:31—33[...]
Holiest of all. Heb. 9:3.
Oracle. 1 Kin. 6:5, 16, 20.
CONTAINED
Ark of testimony. Exo. 26:33. Exo[...] 40:3, 21.
Mercy-seat. Exo. 26:34.
Cherubim. Exo. 25:18—22. 1 Kin[...] 6:23—28.
Golden censer. Heb. 9:4.
Pot of manna. Exo. 16:33. Heb[...] 9:4.
Aaron's rod. Num. 17:10. Heb. 9:4.

A written copy of the divine law. Deu. 31:26. 2 Kin. 22:8.
God appeared in. Exo. 25:22. Lev. 16:2.
THE HIGH PRIEST
Not to enter, at all times. Lev. 16:2.
Alone to enter, once a year. Heb. 9:7.
Entered, in ordinary priest's dress. Lev. 16:4.
Entered, not without blood of atonement. Lev. 16:14, 15. Heb. 9:7.
Offered incense in. Lev. 16:12.
Made atonement for. Lev. 16:15, 16, 20, 33.
The priests allowed to enter, and prepare the holy things for removal. Num. 4:5.
Laid open to view at Christ's death. Mat. 27:51.
A type of heaven. Psa. 102:19. Heb. 9:12, 13, 24.
Saints have boldness to enter the true. Heb. 10:19.

Homicide.

Distinguished from murder. Exo. 21:13, 14. Num. 35:16—21, with 25 v.
JUSTIFIABLE, DESCRIBED AS
Killing persons condemned by law. Gen. 9:6. Exo. 35:2. Lev. 24:16.
Killing a thief in the night. Exo. 22:2.
Killing enemies in battle. Num. 31:7, 8.
Killing a manslayer by next of kin. Num. 35:27.
UNJUSTIFIABLE, DESCRIBED AS
Killing without enmity. Num. 35:22.
Killing without lying in wait. Exo. 21:13. Num. 35:22.
Killing by accident. Num. 35:23. Deu. 19:5.
The avenger of blood might slay those guilty of unjustifiable. Num. 35:19, 27.
Protection afforded in the cities of refuge to those guilty of unjustifiable. Num. 35:11, 15.
Confinement in the city of refuge the punishment for unjustifiable. Num. 35:25, 28.

Honey.

God the giver of. Psa. 81:16. Eze. 16:19.
Gathered and prepared by bees. Jud. 14:18.
FOUND IN
Rocks. Deu. 32:13. Psa. 81:16.
Woods. 1 Sam. 14:25, 26. Jer. 41:8.
Carcases of dead animal's. Jud. 14:8.
Sweetness of. Jud. 14:18.
In the comb sweetest and most valuable. Pro. 16:24. Pro. 24:13.
ABOUNDED IN
Egypt. Num. 16:13.
Assyria. 2 Kin. 18:32.
Canaan. Exo. 3:8. Lev. 20:24. Deu. 8:8.
Esteemed a wholesome food. Pro. 24:13.
Moderation needful in the use of. Pro. 25:16, 27.
Loathed by those who are full. Pro. 27:7.
WAS EATEN
Plain. 1 Sam. 14:25, 26, 29.
With the comb. So. of Sol. 5:1. Luke 24:42.
With milk. So. of Sol. 4:11.
With butter. Isa. 7:15, 22.
With locusts. Mat. 3:4. Mar. 1:6.
Mixed with flour. Exo. 16:31. Eze. 16:13.
Not to be offered with any sacrifice. Lev. 2:11.
First fruits of, offered to God. 2 Chr. 31:5.
Often sent as a present. Gen. 43:11. 1 Kin. 14:3.
Exported from Canaan. Eze. 27:17.
ILLUSTRATIVE OF
The word of God. Psa. 19:10. Psa. 119:103.
Wisdom. Pro. 24:13, 14.
Holy speech of saints. So. of Sol. 4:11.
Pleasant words. Pro 16:24.
Lips of a strange woman. Pro. 5:3.

Hope.

In God. Psa. 39:7. 1 Pet. 1:21.
In Christ. 1 Cor. 15:19. 1 Tim. 1:1.
In God's promises. Acts 26:6, 7. Tit. 1:2.
In the mercy of God. Psa. 33:18.
Is the work of the Holy Ghost. Rom. 15:13. Gal. 5:5.
OBTAINED THROUGH
Grace. 2 The. 2:16.
The word. Psa. 119:81.
Patience and comfort of the Scriptures. Rom. 15:4.
The gospel. Col. 1:5, 23.
Faith. Rom. 5:1, 2. Gal. 5:5.
The result of experience. Rom. 5:4.
A better hope brought in by Christ. Heb. 7:19.
DESCRIBED AS
Good. 2 The. 2:16.
Lively. 1 Pet. 1:3.
Sure and steadfast. Heb. 6:19.
Gladdening. Pro. 10:28.
Blessed. Tit. 2:13.
Makes not ashamed. Rom. 5:5,

Triumphs over difficulties. Rom. 4: 18.
Is an encouragement to boldness in preaching. 2 Cor. 3: 12.
SAINTS
Are called to. Eph. 4: 4.
Rejoice in. Rom. 5: 2. Rom. 12: 12.
Have all, the same. Eph. 4: 4.
Have, in death. Pro. 14: 32.
Should abound in. Rom. 15: 13.
Should look for the object of. Tit. 2: 13.
Should not be ashamed of. Psa. 119: 116.
Should hold fast. Heb. 3: 6.
Should not be moved from. Col. 1: 23.
Should continue in. Psa. 71: 14. 1 Pet. 1: 13.
Connected with faith and love. 1 Cor. 13: 13.
OBJECTS OF;
Salvation. 1 The. 5: 8.
Righteousness. Gal. 5: 5.
Christ's glorious appearing. Tit. 2: 13.
A resurrection. Acts 23: 6. Acts 24: 15.
Eternal life. Tit. 1: 2. Tit. 3: 7.
Glory. Rom. 5: 2. Col. 1: 27.
Leads to purity. 1 Jno. 3: 3.
Leads to patience. Rom. 8: 25. 1 The. 1: 3.
Seek for full assurance of. Heb. 6: 11.
Be ready to give an answer concerning. 1 Pet. 3: 15.
Encouragement to. Hos. 2: 15. Zec. 9: 12.
Encourage others to. Psa. 130: 7.
Happiness of. Psa. 146: 5.
Life is the season of. Ecc. 9: 4. Isa. 38: 18.
The wicked have no ground for. Eph. 2: 12.
OF THE WICKED
Is in their worldly possessions. Job 31: 24.
Shall make them ashamed. Isa. 20: 5, 6. Zec. 9: 5.
Shall perish. Job 8: 13. Job 11: 20. Pro. 10: 28.
Shall be extinguished in death. Job 27: 8.
Illustrated by, *An Anchor*, Heb. 6: 19. *A helmet*, 1 The. 5: 8.
Exemplified. *David*, Psa. 39: 7. *Paul*, Acts 24: 15. *Abraham*, Rom. 4: 18. *Thessalonians*, 1 The. 1: 3.

Horns.

Natural weapons on heads of animals. Dan. 7: 20.
ANIMALS WITH, MENTIONED;
The ox. Psa. 69: 31.
The ram. Gen. 22: 13.
The goat. Dan. 8: 5.
The unicorn. Psa. 22: 21. Psa. 92: 10.
Tusks of the elephant so called. Eze. 27: 15.
Used offensively. Exo. 21: 29. Eze. 34: 21.
WERE USED
For holding oil. 1 Sam. 16: 1. 1 Kin. 1: 39.
As musical instruments. Jos. 6: 4, 5. 1 Chr. 25: 5.
Representations of, placed at the four corners of the altars. Exo. 27: 2. Exo. 30: 2.
Wearing of, alluded to. Psa. 75: 5, 10.
ILLUSTRATIVE
Of power of God. Psa. 18: 2. Hab. 3: 4.
Of power of Christ. Luke 1: 69. Rev. 5: 6.
Of power of Ephraim, &c. Deu. 33: 17.
Of power of the wicked. Psa. 22: 21. Psa. 75: 10.
Of kings. Dan. 7: 7, 8, 24. Dan. 8: 3, 5, 20.
Of antichristian powers. Rev. 13: 1. Rev. 17: 3, 7.
(Budding of,) of the commencement or revival of a nation. Psa. 132: 17. Eze. 29: 21.
(Raising up,) of arrogance. Psa. 75: 4, 5.
(Exalting,) of increase of power and glory. 1 Sam. 2: 1, 10. Psa. 89: 17, 24. Psa. 92: 10. Psa. 112: 9.
(Pushing with,) of conquests. Deu. 33: 17. 1 Kin. 22: 11. Mic. 4: 13.
(Bringing down,) of degradation. Job 16: 15.
(Cutting off,) of destruction of power. Psa. 75: 10. Jer. 48: 25. Lam. 2: 3.

Horse, The.

Endued with strength by God. Job 39: 19.
DESCRIBED AS
Strong. Psa. 33: 17. Psa. 147: 10.
Swift. Isa. 30: 16. Jer. 4: 13. Hab. 1: 8.
Fearless. Job 39: 20, 22.
Fierce and impetuous. Job 39: 21, 24.
Warlike in disposition. Job 39: 21. Jer. 8: 6.
Sure footed. Isa. 63: 13.
Want of understanding in, alluded to. Psa. 32: 9.
Hard hoofs of, alluded to. Isa. 5: 28.
Loud snorting of, alluded to. Jer. 8: 16, with Job 39: 20.
COLORS OF, MENTIONED;
White. Zec. 1: 8. Zec. 6: 3. Rev. 6: 2.
Black. Zec. 6: 2, 6. Rev. 6: 5.

Red. Zec. 1:8. Zec. 6:2. Rev. 6:4.
Speckled. Zec. 1:8.
Bay. Zec. 6:3, 7.
Grisled. Zec. 6:3, 6.
Pale or ash color. Rev. 6:8.
Fed on grain and herbs. 1 Kin. 4:23. 1 Kin. 18:5.
USED FOR
Mounting cavalry. Exo. 14:9. 1 Sam. 13:5.
Drawing chariots. Mic. 1:13. Zec. 6:2.
Bearing burdens. Ezr. 2:66. Neh. 7:68.
Hunting. Job 39:18.
Conveying posts, &c. 2 Kin. 9:17–19. Est. 8:10.
Kings and princes rode on. Est. 6: 8–11. Eze. 23:23.
Governed by bit and bridle. Psa. 32: 9. Jas. 3:3.
Urged on by whips. Pro. 26:3.
Adorned with bells on the neck. Zec. 14:20.
Numbers of, kept for war. Jer. 51:27. Eze. 26:10.
Prepared and trained for war. Pro. 21:31.
In battle protected by armor. Jer. 46:4.
Vanity of trusting to. Psa. 33:17. Amos 2:15.
THE JEWS
Forbidden to multiply. Deu. 17:16.
Imported from Egypt. 1 Kin. 10:28, 29.
Multiplied in Solomon's reign. 1 Kin. 4:26.
Condemned for multiplying. Isa. 2: 7.
Not to trust in. Hos. 14:3.
Condemned for trusting to. Isa. 30: 16. Isa. 31:3.
Brought back many, from Babylon. Ezr. 2:66.
Notice of early traffic in. Gen. 47:17.
Sold in fairs and markets. Eze. 27: 14. Rev. 18:13.
OFTEN SUFFERED
From blindness. Zec. 12:4.
From plague. Zec. 14:15.
From murrain. Exo. 9:3.
From bites of serpents. Gen. 49:17.
In the hoof from prancing. Jud. 5: 22.
In battle. Jer. 51:21. Hag. 2:22.
Dedicated to the sun by idolaters. 2 Kin. 23:11.
ILLUSTRATIVE OF
Beauty of the church. So. of Sol. 1: 9. Zec. 10:3.
Glorious and triumphant deliverance of the church. Isa. 63:13.
A dull headstrong disposition. Psa. 32:9.
Impetuosity of the wicked in sin. Jer. 8:6.

Hospitality.

Commanded. Rom. 12:13. 1 Pet. 4:9.
Required in ministers. 1 Tim. 3:2. Tit. 1:8.
A test of Christian character. 1 Tim. 5:10.
SPECIALLY TO BE SHOWN TO
Strangers. Heb. 13:2.
The poor. Isa. 58:7. Luke 14:13.
Enemies. 2 Kin. 6:22, 23. Rom. 12:20.
Encouragement to. Luke 14:14. Heb. 13:2.
Exemplified. *Melchizedek*, Gen. 14: 18. *Abraham*, Gen. 18:3–8. *Lot*, Gen. 19:2, 3. *Laban*, Gen. 24:31. *Jethro*, Exo. 2:20. *Manoah*, Jud. 13:15. *Samuel*, 1 Sam. 9:22. *David*, 2 Sam. 6:19. *Barzillai*, 2 Sam. 19: 32. *Shunammite*, 2 Kin. 4:8. *Nehemiah*, Neh. 5:17. *Job*, Job 31:17, 32. *Zaccheus*, Luke 19:6. *Samaritans*, Jno. 4:40. *Lydia*, Acts 16:15. *Jason*, Acts 17:7. *Mnason*, Acts 21, 16. *People of Melita*, Acts 28:2. *Publius*, Acts 28:7. *Gaius*, 3 Jno. 5, 6.

Houses.

Antiquity of. Gen. 12:1. Gen. 19:3.
Deep and solid foundations required for. Mat. 7:24. Luke 6:48.
Sometimes built without foundation. Mat. 7:26. Luke 6:49.
BUILT OF
Clay. Job 4:19.
Bricks. Exo. 1:11–14. Isa. 9:10.
Stone and wood. Lev. 14:40, 42. Hab. 2:11.
Hewn or cut stone. Isa. 3:10. Amos 5:11.
In cities, built in streets. Gen. 19:2. Jos. 2:19.
Often built on city walls. Jos. 2:15. 2 Cor. 11:33.
THE FLAT ROOFS OF,
Surrounded with battlements. Deu. 22:8.
Had often booths on them. 2 Sam. 16:22. Neh. 8:16. Pro. 21:9.
Had often idolatrous altars on them. 2 Kin. 23:12. Jer. 19:13. Zep. 1:5.
Used for drying flax, &c. Jos. 2:6.
Used for exercise. 2 Sam. 11:2. Dan. 4:29.
Used for devotion. Acts 10:9.
Used for making proclamations. Luke 12:3.
Used for secret conference. 1 Sam. 9:25, 26.
Resorted to in grief. Isa. 15:3. Jer. 48:38.
Often covered with week grass. Psa. 129:6, 7.
Accessible from the outside. Mat. 24:17.

The courts of, large and used as apartments. Est. 1:5. Luke 5:19.
Entered by a gate or door. Gen. 43:19. Exo. 12:22. Luke 16:20. Acts 10:17.
Doors of, low and small for safety. Pro. 17:19.
Doors of, how fastened. 2 Sam. 13:18. So. of Sol. 5:5. Luke 11:7.
Admission to, gained by knocking at the door. Acts 12:13. Rev. 3:20.
Walls of, plastered. Lev. 14:42, 43.
Serpents often lodged in walls of. Amos 5:19.
Custom of fastening nails, &c. in walls of, alluded to. Ecc. 12:11. Isa. 22:23.
Had often several stories. Eze. 41:16. Acts 20:9.
Divided into apartments. Gen. 43:30. Isa. 26:20.

APARTMENTS OF, WERE OFTEN
- Large and airy. Jer. 22:14.
- Ceiled and painted. Jer. 22:14. Hag. 1:4.
- Inlayed with ivory. 1 Kin. 22:39. Amos 3:15.
- Hung with rich tapestries. Est. 1:6.
- Warmed with fires. Jer. 36:22. Jno. 18:18.

Upper apartments of, the best, and used for entertainments. Mar. 14:15.
Had often detached apartments for secrecy and for strangers. Jud. 3:20–23. 2 Kin. 4:10, 11. 2 Kin. 9:2, 3.
Lighted by windows. 1 Kin. 7:4.
Street windows of, high and dangerous. 2 Kin. 1:2. 2 Kin. 9:30, 33. Acts 20:9.

OF THE RICH,
- Great. Isa. 5:9. Amos 6:11. 2 Tim. 2:20.
- Goodly. Deu. 8:12.
- Pleasant. Eze. 26:12. Mic. 2:9.

OF BRICK OR CLAY,
- Plastered. Eze 13:10, 11.
- Easily broken through. Job 24:16. Eze. 12:5.
- Often swept away by torrents. Eze. 13:13, 14.

When finished were usually dedicated. Deu. 20:5. Psa. 30, (*title*).
For summer residence. Amos 3:15.
Liable to leprosy. Lev. 14:34–53.
Not to be coveted. Exo. 20:17. Mic. 2:2.
Were hired. Acts 28:30.
Were mortgaged. Neh. 5:3.
Were sold. Acts 4:34.
Law respecting the sale of. Lev. 25:29–33.
Of criminals, desolated. Dan. 2:5. Dan. 3:29.
Desolation of, threatened as a punishment. Isa. 5:9. Isa. 13:16, 21, 22. Eze. 16:41. Eze. 26:12.
Often broken down to repair city walls before sieges. Isa. 22:10.

ILLUSTRATIVE
- Of the body. Job 4:19. 2 Cor. 5:1.
- Of the grave. Job 30:23.
- Of the church. Heb. 3:6. 1 Pet. 2:5.
- Of saints' inheritance. Jno. 14:2. 2 Cor. 5:1.
- (On sand,) of the delusive hope of hypocrites. Mat. 7:26, 27.
- (On a rock,) of the hope of saints. Mat. 7:24, 25.
- (Insecurity of,) of earthly trust. Mat. 6:19, 20.
- (Building of,) of great prosperity. Isa. 65:21. Eze. 28:26.
- (Built and not inhabited,) of calamity. Deu. 28:30. Amos 5:11. Zep. 1:13.
- (To inhabit those, built by others,) of abundant blessings. Deu. 6:10, 11.

Human Nature of Christ, The.

Was necessary to His mediatorial office. 1 Tim. 2:5. Heb. 2:17. Gal. 4:4, 5. 1 Cor. 15:21. Rom. 6:15, 19.

IS PROVED BY HIS
- Conception in the Virgin's womb. Mat. 1:18. Luke 1:31.
- Birth. Mat. 1:16, 25. Mat. 2:2. Luke 2:7, 11.
- Partaking of flesh and blood. Jno. 1:14. Heb. 2:14.
- Having a human soul. Mat. 26:38. Luke 23:46. Acts 2:31.
- Circumcision. Luke 2:21.
- Increase in wisdom and stature. Luke 2:52.
- Weeping. Luke 19:41. Jno. 11:35.
- Hungering. Mat. 4:2. Mat. 21:18.
- Thirsting. Jno. 4:7. Jno. 19:28.
- Sleeping. Mat. 8:24. Mar. 4:38.
- Being subject to weariness. Jno. 4:6.
- Being a man of sorrows. Isa. 53:3, 4. Luke 22:44. Jno. 11:33. Jno. 12:27.
- Being buffeted. Mat. 26:67. Luke 22:64.
- Enduring indignities. Luke 23:11.
- Being scourged. Mat. 27:26. Jno. 19:1.
- Being nailed to the cross. Psa. 22:16, with Luke 23:33.
- Death. Jno. 19:30.
- Side being pierced. Jno. 19:34.
- Burial. Mat. 27:59, 60. Mar. 15:46.
- Resurrection. Acts 3:15. 2 Tim. 2:8.

Was like our own in all things except sin. Acts 3:22. Phi. 2:7, 8. Heb. 2:17.
Was without sin. Heb. 7:26, 28. 1 Jno. 3:5. 1 Pet. 2:22. Heb. 4:15. Jno. 18:38. Jno. 8:46.

Was submitted to the evidence of the senses. Luke 24: 39. Jno. 20: 27. 1 Jno. 1: 1, 2.
WAS OF THE SEED OF
The woman. Gen. 3: 15. Isa. 7: 4. Jer. 31: 22. Luke 1: 31. Gal. 4: 4.
Abraham. Gen. 22: 18, with Gal. 3: 16. Heb. 2: 16.
David. 2 Sam. 7: 12, 16. Psa. 89: 35, 36. Jer. 23: 5. Mat. 22: 42. Mar. 10: 47. Acts 2: 30. Acts 13: 23. Rom. 1: 3.
Genealogy of. Mat. 1: 1, &c. Luke 3: 23, &c.
Attested by Himself. Mat. 8: 20. Mat. 16: 13.
Confession of, a test of belonging to God. Jno. 4: 2.
Acknowledged by men. Mar. 6: 3. Jno. 7: 27. Jno. 19: 5. Acts 2: 22.
Denied by Antichrist. 1 Jno. 4: 3. 2 Jno. 7.

Humility.

Necessary to the service of God. Mic. 6: 8.
Christ an example of. Mat. 11: 29. Jno. 13: 14, 15. Phi. 2: 5–8.
A characteristic of saints. Psa. 34: 2.
THEY WHO HAVE,
Regarded by God. Psa. 138: 6. Isa. 66: 2.
Heard by God. Psa. 9: 12. Psa. 10: 17.
Enjoy the presence of God. Isa. 57: 15.
Delivered by God. Job 22: 29.
Lifted up by God. Jas. 4: 10.
Exalted by God. Luke 14: 11. Luke 18: 14.
Are greatest in Christ's kingdom. Mat. 18: 4. Mat. 20: 26–28.
Receive more grace. Pro. 3: 34. Jas. 4: 6.
Upheld by honor. Pro. 18: 12. Pro. 29: 23.
Is before honor. Pro. 15: 33.
Leads to riches, honor, and life. Pro. 22: 4.
SAINTS SHOULD
Put on. Col. 3: 12.
Be clothed with. 1 Pet. 5: 5.
Walk with. Eph. 4: 1, 2.
Beware of false. Col. 2: 18, 23.
Afflictions intended to produce. Lev. 26: 41. Deu. 8: 3. Lam. 3: 20.
Want of, condemned. 2 Chr. 33: 23. 2 Chr. 36: 12. Jer. 44: 10. Dan. 5: 22.
Temporal judgments averted by. 2 Chr. 7: 14. 2 Chr. 12: 6, 7.
Excellency of. Pro. 16: 19.
Blessedness of. Mat. 5: 3.
Exemplified. *Abraham*, Gen. 18: 27. *Jacob*, Gen. 32: 10. *Moses*, Exo. 3: 11. Exo. 4: 10. *Joshua*, Jos. 7: 6. *Gideon*, Jud. 6: 15. *David*, 1 Chr. 29: 14. *Hezekiah*, 2 Chr. 32: 26. *Manasseh*, 2 Chr. 33: 12. *Josiah*, 2 Chr. 34: 27. *Job*, Job 40: 4. Job 42: 6. *Isaiah*, Isa. 6: 5. *Jeremiah*, Jer. 1: 6. *John the Baptist*, Mat. 3: 14. *Centurion*, Mat. 8: 8. *Woman of Canaan*, Mat. 15: 27. *Elizabeth*, Luke 1: 43. *Peter*, Luke 5: 8. *Paul*, Acts 20: 19.

Humility of Christ, The.

Declared by Himself. Mat. 11: 29.
EXHIBITED IN HIS
Taking our nature. Phi. 2: 7. Heb. 2: 16.
Birth. Luke 2: 4–7.
Subjection to His parents. Luke 2: 51.
Station in life. Mat. 13: 55. Jno. 9: 29.
Poverty. Luke 9: 58. 2 Cor. 8: 9.
Partaking of our infirmities. Heb. 4: 15. Heb. 5: 7.
Submitting to ordinances. Mat. 3: 13–15.
Becoming a servant. Mat. 20: 28. Luke 22: 27. Phi. 2: 7.
Associating with the despised. Mat. 9: 10, 11. Luke 15: 1, 2.
Refusing honors. Jno. 5: 41. Jno. 6: 15.
Entry into Jerusalem. Zec. 9: 9, with Mat. 21: 5, 7.
Washing His disciples' feet. Jno. 13: 5.
Obedience. Jno. 6: 38. Heb. 10: 9.
Submitting to sufferings. Isa. 50: 6. Isa. 53: 7, with Acts 8: 32. Mat. 26: 37–39.
Exposing Himself to reproach and contempt. Psa. 22: 6. Psa. 69: 9, with Rom. 15: 3. Isa. 53: 3.
Death. Jno. 10: 15, 17, 18. Phi. 2: 8. Heb. 12: 2.
Saints should imitate. Phi. 2: 5–8.
On account of, He was despised. Mar. 6: 3. Jno. 9: 29.
His exaltation, the result of. Phi. 2: 9.

Husbands.

Should have but one wife. Gen. 2: 24. Mar. 10: 6–8. 1 Cor. 7: 2–4.
Have authority over their wives. Gen. 3: 16. 1 Cor. 11: 3. Eph. 5: 23.
DUTY OF, TO WIVES;
To respect them. 1 Pet. 3: 7.
To love them. Eph. 5: 25, &c. Col. 3: 19.
To regard them as themselves. Gen. 2: 23, with Mat. 19: 5.
To be faithful to them. Pro. 5: 19. Mal. 2: 14, 15.
To dwell with them for life. Gen. 2: 24. Mat. 19: 3–9.
To comfort them. 1 Sam. 1: 8.
To consult with them. Gen. 31: 4–7.

Not to leave them, though unbelieving. 1 Cor. 7: 11, 12, 14, 16.
Duties of, not to interfere with their duties to Christ. Luke 14: 26, with Mat. 19: 29.
Good—Exemplified. *Isaac*, Gen. 24: 67. *Elkanah*, 1 Sam. 1: 4, 5.
Bad—Exemplified. *Solomon*, 1 Kin. 11: 1. *Ahasuerus*, Est. 1: 10, 11.

Hyke or Upper Garment.

Law respecting fringes of. Num. 15: 38. Deu. 22: 12.
Used by the poor as a covering by night. Exo. 22: 26, 27. Deu. 24: 13.
Burdens often bound up in. Exo. 12: 34.
The skirts of, used to hold things in. 2 Kin. 4: 39. Neh. 5: 13. Hag. 2: 12. Luke 6: 38.
Probably used by women as a vail. Ruth 3: 15.
REQUIRED TO BE GIRT UP
For running. 1 Kin. 18: 46.
For labor. Luke 17: 8.
Often laid aside. Mat. 24: 18. Mar. 10: 50.
The Jews said to be naked when without. 2 Sam. 6: 20. Mar. 14: 51, 52. Jno. 21: 7.
WAS THE GARMENT
Rent in token of anger. Mat. 26: 65.
Rent in token of grief. Joel 2: 13.
Of Samuel rent by Saul. 1 Sam. 15: 27.
Of Saul which David cut. 1 Sam. 24: 4, 5.
Of Jeroboam rent by Ahijah. 1 Kin. 11: 30.
Laid aside by Christ. Jno. 13: 4.
Spread before Christ by the Jews. Mat. 21: 8.
The Jews condemned for making broad the borders of. Mat. 23: 5.

Hypocrites.

God knows and detects. Isa. 29: 15, 16.
Christ knew and detected. Mat. 22: 18.
God has no pleasure in. Isa. 9: 17.
Shall not come before God. Job 13: 16.
DESCRIBED AS
Wilfully blind. Mat. 23: 17, 19, 26.
Vile. Isa. 32: 6.
Self-righteous. Isa. 65: 5. Luke 18: 11.
Covetous. Eze. 33: 31. 2 Pet. 2: 3.
Ostentatious. Mat. 6: 2, 5, 16. Mat. 23: 5.
Censorious. Mat. 7: 3—5. Luke 13: 14, 15.
Regarding tradition more than the word of God. Mat. 15: 1—3.
Exact in minor, but neglecting important duties. Mat. 23: 23, 24.
Having but a form of godliness. 2 Tim. 3: 5.
Seeking only outward purity. Luke 11: 39.
Professing but not practising. Eze. 33: 31, 32. Mat. 23: 3. Rom. 2: 17—23.
Using but lip-worship. Isa. 29: 13, with Mat. 15: 8.
Glorying in appearance only. 2 Cor. 5: 12.
Trusting in privileges. Jer. 7: 4. Mat. 3: 9.
Apparently zealous in the things of God. Isa. 58: 2.
Zealous in making proselytes. Mat. 23: 15.
Devouring widows' houses. Mat. 23: 14.
Loving pre-eminence. Mat. 23: 6, 7.
Worship of, not acceptable to God. Isa. 1: 11—15. Isa. 58: 3—5. Mat. 15: 9.
Joy of, but for a moment. Job 20: 5.
Hope of perishes. Job 8: 13. Job 27: 8, 9.
Heap up wrath. Job 36: 13.
Fearfulness shall surprise. Isa. 33: 14.
Destroy others by slander. Pro. 11: 9.
In power, are a snare. Job 34: 30.
The Apostacy to abound with. 1 Tim. 4: 2.
Beware of the principles of. Luke 12: 1.
Spirit of, hinders growth in grace. 1 Pet. 2: 1.
Woe to. Isa. 29: 15. Mat. 23: 13.
Punishment of. Job 15: 34. Isa. 10: 6. Jer. 42: 20, 22. Mat. 24: 51.
Illustrated. Mat. 23: 27, 28. Luke 11: 44.
Exemplified. *Cain*, Gen. 4: 3. *Absalom*, 2 Sam. 15: 7, 8. *The Jews*, Jer. 3: 10. *Pharisees, &c.* Mat. 16: 3. *Judas*, Mat. 26: 49. *Herodians*, Mar. 12: 13, 15. *Ananias*, Acts 5: 1—8. *Simon*, Acts 8: 13—23.

Idleness and Sloth.

Forbidden. Rom. 12: 11. Heb. 6: 12.
Produce apathy. Pro. 12: 27. Pro. 26: 15.
Akin to extravagance. Pro. 18: 9.
Accompanied by conceit. Pro. 26: 16.
LEAD TO
Poverty. Pro. 10: 4. Pro. 20: 13.
Want. Pro. 20: 4. Pro. 24: 34.
Hunger. Pro. 19: 15. Pro. 24: 34.
Bondage. Pro. 12: 24.
Disappointment. Pro. 13: 4. Pro. 21: 25.
Ruin. Pro. 24: 30, 31. Ecc. 10: 18.
Tattling and meddling. 1 Tim. 5: 13.

Effects of, afford instruction to others. Pro. 24: 30—32.
Remonstrance against. Pro. 6: 6, 9.
False excuses for. Pro. 20: 4. Pro. 22: 13.
Illustrated. Pro. 26: 14. Mat. 25: 18, 26.
Exemplified. *Watchmen*, Isa. 56: 10. *Athenians*, Acts 17: 21. *Thessalonians*. 2 The. 3: 11.

Idolatry.

Forbidden. Exo. 20: 2, 3. Deu. 5: 7.
CONSISTS IN
- Bowing down to images. Exo. 20: 5. Deu. 5: 9.
- Worshipping images. Isa. 44: 17. Dan. 3: 5, 10, 15.
- Sacrificing to images. Psa. 106: 38. Acts 7: 41.
- Worshipping other gods. Deu. 30: 17. Psa. 81: 9.
- Swearing by other gods. Exo. 23: 13. Jos. 23: 7.
- Walking after other gods. Deu. 8: 19.
- Speaking in the name of other gods. Deu. 18: 20.
- Looking to other gods. Hos. 3: 1.
- Serving other gods. Deu. 7: 4. Jer. 5: 19.
- Fearing other gods. 2 Kin. 17: 35.
- Sacrificing to other gods. Exo. 22: 20.
- Worshipping the true God by an image, &c. Exo. 32: 4—6, with Psa. 106: 19, 20.
- Worshipping angels. Col. 2: 18.
- Worshipping the host of heaven. Deu. 4: 19. Deu. 17: 3.
- Worshipping devils. Mat. 4: 9, 10. Rev. 9: 20.
- Worshipping dead men. Psa. 106: 28.
- Setting up idols in the heart. Eze. 14: 3, 4.
- Covetousness. Eph. 5: 5. Col. 3: 5.
- Sensuality. Phi. 3: 19.

Is changing the glory of God into an image. Rom. 1: 23, with Acts 17: 29.
Is changing the truth of God into a lie. Rom. 1: 25, with Isa. 44: 20.
Is a work of the flesh. Gal. 5: 19, 20.
Incompatible with the service of God. Gen. 35: 2, 3. Jos. 24: 23. 1 Sam. 7: 3. 1 Kin. 18: 21. 2 Cor. 6: 15, 16.
DESCRIBED AS
- An abomination to God. Deu. 7: 25.
- Hateful to God. Deu. 16: 22. Jer. 44: 4.
- Vain and foolish. Psa. 115: 4—8. Isa. 44: 19. Jer. 10: 3.
- Bloody. Eze. 23: 39.
- Abominable. 1 Pet. 4: 3.
- Unprofitable. Jud. 10: 14. Isa. 46: 7.
- Irrational. Acts 17: 29. Rom. 1: 21—23.
- Defiling. Eze. 20: 7. Eze. 36: 18.

THEY WHO PRACTICE,
- Forget God. Deu. 8: 19. Jer. 18: 15.
- Go astray from God. Eze. 44: 10.
- Pollute the name of God. Eze. 20: 39.
- Defile the sanctuary of God. Eze. 5: 11.
- Are estranged from God. Eze. 14: 5.
- Forsake God. 2 Kin. 22: 17. Jer. 16: 11.
- Hate God. 2 Chr. 19: 2, 3.
- Provoke God. Deu. 31: 20. Isa. 65: 3. Jer. 25: 6.
- Are vain in their imaginations. Rom. 1: 21.
- Are ignorant and foolish. Rom. 1: 21, 22.
- Inflame themselves. Isa. 57: 5.
- Hold fast their deceit. Jer. 8: 5.
- Carried away by it. 1 Cor. 12: 2.
- Go after it in heart. Eze. 20: 16.
- Are mad upon it. Jer. 50: 38.
- Boast of it. Psa. 97: 7.
- Have fellowship with devils. 1 Cor. 10: 20.
- Ask counsel of their idols. Hos. 4: 12.
- Look to idols for deliverance. Isa. 44: 17. Isa. 45: 20.
- Swear by their idols. Amos 8: 14.

Objects of, numerous. 1 Cor. 8: 5.
OBJECTS OF, DESCRIBED AS
- Strange gods. Gen. 35: 2, 4. Jos. 24: 20.
- Other gods. Jud. 2: 12, 17. 1 Kin. 14: 9.
- New gods. Deu. 32: 17. Jud. 5: 8.
- Gods that cannot save. Isa. 45: 20.
- Gods that have not made the heavens. Jer. 10: 11.
- No gods. Jer. 5: 7. Gal. 4: 8.
- Molten gods. Exo. 34: 17. Lev. 19: 4.
- Molten images. Deu. 27: 15. Hab 2: 18.
- Graven images. Isa. 45: 20. Hos. 11: 2.
- Senseless idols. Deu. 4: 28 Psa 115: 5, 7.
- Dumb idols. Hab. 2: 18. 1 Cor. 12: 2.
- Dumb stones. Hab. 2: 19.
- Stocks. Jer. 3: 9. Hos. 4: 12.
- Abominations. Isa. 44: 19. Jer. 32: 34.
- Images of abomination. Eze. 7: 20.
- Idols of abomination. Eze. 16: 36.
- Stumbling blocks. Eze. 14: 3.
- Teachers of lies. Hab. 2: 18.
- Wind and confusion. Isa. 41: 29.
- Nothing. Isa. 41: 24. 1 Cor. 8: 4.
- Helpless. Jer. 10: 5.
- Vanity. Jer. 18: 15.

Vanities of the Gentiles. Jer. 14:22.
Making idols for the purpose of, described and ridiculed. Isa. 44:10—20.
Obstinate sinners judicially given up to. Deu. 4:28. Deu. 28:64. Hos. 4:17.
Warnings against. Deu. 4:15—19.
Exhortations to turn from. Eze. 14:6 Eze. 20:7. Acts 14:15.
Renounced on conversion. 1 The. 1:9.
Led to abominable sins. Rom. 1:26, 27—32. Acts 15:20.
SAINTS SHOULD
Keep from. Jos. 23:7. 1 Jno. 5:21.
Flee from. 1 Cor. 10:14.
Not have any thing connected with, in their houses. Deu. 7:26.
Not partake of any thing connected with. 1 Cor. 10:19, 20.
Not have religious intercourse with those who practice. Jos. 23:7. 1 Cor. 5:11.
Not covenant with those who practice. Exo. 34:12, 15. Deu. 7:2.
Not intermarry with those who practice. Exo. 34:16. Deu. 7:3.
Testify against. Acts 14:15. Acts 19:26.
Refuse to engage in, though threatened with death. Dan. 3:18.
Saints preserved by God from. 1 Kin. 19:18, with Rom. 11:4.
Saints refuse to receive the worship of. Acts 10:25, 26. Acts 14:11—15.
Angels refuse to receive the worship of. Rev. 22:8, 9.
Destruction of, promised. Eze. 36:25. Zec. 13:2.
Every thing connected with, should be destroyed. Exo. 34:13. Deu. 7:5. 2 Sam. 5:21. 2 Kin. 23:14.
Woe denounced against. Hab. 2:19.
Curse denounced against. Deu. 27:15.
PUNISHMENT OF;
Judicial death. Deu. 17:2—5.
Dreadful judgments which end in death. Jer. 8:2. Jer. 16:1—11.
Banishment. Jer. 8:3. Hos. 8:5—8. Amos 5:26, 27.
Exclusion from heaven. 1 Cor. 6:9, 10. Eph. 5:5. Rev. 22:15.
Eternal torments. Rev. 14:9—11. Rev. 21:8.
Exemplified. *Israel*, Exo. 32:1. 2 Kin. 17:12. *Philistines*, Jud. 16:23. *Micah*, Jud. 17:4, 5. *Jeroboam*, 1 Kin. 12:28. *Maachah*, 1 Kin. 15:13. *Ahab*, 1 Kin. 16:31. *Jezebel*, 1 Kin. 18:19. *Sennacherib*, 2 Kin. 19:37. *Manasseh*, 2 Kin. 21:4—7. *Amon*, 2 Kin. 21:21. *Ahaz*, 2 Chr. 28:3. *Judah*, Jer. 11:13. *Nebuchadnezzar*, Dan. 3:1. *Belshazzar*, Dan. 5:23. *People of Lystra*, Acts 14:11, 12. *Athenians*, Acts 17:16. *Ephesians*, Acts 19:28.
Zeal against—Exemplified. *Asa*, 1 Kin. 15:12. *Josiah*, 2 Kin. 23:5. *Jehoshaphat*, 2 Chr. 17:6. *Israel*, 2 Chr. 31:1. *Manasseh*, 2 Chr. 33:15.
All forms of, forbidden by the law of Moses. Exo. 20:4, 5.
All heathen nations given up to. Psa. 96:5. Rom. 1:23, 25. 1 Cor. 12:2.
Led the heathen to think that their gods visited the earth in bodily shapes. Acts 14:11.
Led the heathen to consider their gods to have but a local influence. 1 Kin. 20:23. 2 Kin. 17:26.
OBJECTS OF;
The heavenly bodies. 2 Kin. 23:5. Acts 7:42.
Angels. Col. 2:18.
Departed spirits. 1 Sam. 28:14, 15.
Earthly creatures. Rom. 1:23.
Images. Deu. 29:17. Psa. 115:4. Isa. 44:17.
Temples built for. Hos. 8:14.
Altars raised for. 1 Kin. 18:26. Hos. 8:11.
Accompanied by feasts. 2 Kin. 10:20. 1 Cor. 10:27, 28.
OBJECTS OF, WORSHIPPED
With sacrifices. Num. 22:40. 2 Kin. 10:24.
With libations. Isa. 57:6. Jer. 19:13.
With incense. Jer. 48:35.
With prayer. 1 Kin. 18:26. Isa. 44:17.
With singing and dancing. Exo. 32:18, 19. 1 Kin. 18:26. (*marg.*) 1 Cor. 10:7.
By bowing to them. 1 Kin. 19:18. 2 Kin. 5:18.
By kissing them. 1 Kin. 19:18. Hos. 13:2.
By kissing the hand to them. Job 31:26, 27.
By cutting the flesh. 1 Kin. 18:28.
By burning children. Deu. 12:31. 2 Chr. 33:6. Jer. 19:4, 5. Eze. 16:21.
In temples. 2 Kin. 5:18.
On high places. Num. 22:41. Jer. 2:20.
In groves. Exo. 34:13.
Under trees. Isa. 57:5. Jer. 2:20.
In private houses. Jud. 17:4, 5.
On the tops of houses. 2 Kin. 23:12. Zep. 1:5.
In secret places. Isa. 57:8.
Rites of, obscene and impure. Exo. 32:25. Num. 25:1—3. 2 Kin. 17:9. Isa. 57:6, 8, 9. 1 Pet. 4:3.
Divination connected with. 2 Chr. 33:6.
Victims sacrificed in, often adorned with garlands. Acts 14:13.
IDOLS, &C. MENTIONED IN SCRIPTURE;
Adrammelech. 2 Kin. 17:31.
Anammelech. 2 Kin. 17:31.
Ashima. 2 Kin. 17:30.
Ashtoreth. Jud. 2:13. 1 Kin. 11:33.
Baal. Jud. 2:11—13. Jud. 6:25.

Baal-berith. Jud. 8:33. Jud. 9:4, 46.
Baal-peor. Num. 25:1—3.
Baal-zebub. 2 Kin. 1:2, 16.
Baal-zephon. Exo. 14:2.
Bel. Jer. 50:2. Jer. 51:44.
Chemosh. Num. 21:29. 1 Kin. 11:33.
Chiun. Amos 5:26.
Dagon. Jud. 16:23. 1 Sam. 5:1—3.
Diana. Acts 19:24, 27.
Huzzab. Nah. 2:7.
Jupiter. Acts 14:12.
Mercury. Acts 14:12.
Molech or Milcom. Lev. 18:21. 1 Kin. 11:5, 33.
Merodach. Jer. 50:2.
Nergal. 2 Kin. 17:30.
Nebo. Isa. 46:1.
Nibhaz and Tartak. 2 Kin. 17:31.
Nisroch. 2 Kin. 19:37.
Queen of heaven. Jer. 44:17, 25.
Remphan. Acts 7:43.
Rimmon. 2 Kin. 5:18.
Succoth-benoth. 2 Kin. 17:30.
Tammuz. Eze. 8:14.

Objects of, carried in procession. Isa. 46:7. Amos 5:26. Acts 7:43.
Early notice of, amongst God's professing people. Gen. 31:19, 30. Gen. 35:1—4. Jos. 24:2.

THE JEWS
Practised, in Egypt. Jos. 24:14. Eze. 23:3, 19.
Brought, out of Egypt with them. Eze. 23:8, with Acts 7:39—41.
Forbidden to practice. Exo. 20:1—5. Exo. 23:24.
Often mixed up, with God's worship. Exo. 32:1—5. 1 Kin. 12:27, 28.
Followed the Canaanites in. Jud. 2:11—13. 1 Chr. 5:25.
Followed the Moabites in. Num. 25:1—3.
Followed the Assyrians in. Eze. 16:28—30. Eze. 23:5—7.
Followed the Syrians in. Jud. 10:6.

Adopted by Solomon. 1 Kin. 11:5—8.
Adopted by the wicked kings. 1 Kin. 21:26. 2 Kin. 21:21. 2 Chr. 28:2—4. 2 Chr. 33:3, 7.
Example of the kings encouraged Israel in. 1 Kin. 12:30. 2 Kin. 21:11. 2 Chr. 33:9.
Great prevalence of, in Israel. Isa. 2:8. Jer. 2:28. Eze. 8:10.
A virtual forsaking of God. Jer. 2:9—13.
The good kings of Judah endeavored to destroy. 2 Chr. 15:16. 2 Chr. 34:7.
Captivity of Israel on account of. 2 Kin. 17:6—18.
Captivity of Judah on account of. 2 Kin. 17:19—23.

Ignorance of God.

Ignorance of Christ is. Jno. 8:19.

EVIDENCED BY
Want of love. 1 Jno. 4:8.
Not keeping His commands. 1 Jno. 2:4.
Living in sin. Tit. 1:16. 1 Jno. 3:6.

LEADS TO
Error. Mat. 22:29.
Idolatry. Isa. 44:19. Acts 17:29, 30.
Alienation from God. Eph. 4:18.
Sinful lusts. 1 The. 4:5. 1 Pet. 1:14.
Persecuting saints. Jno. 15:21. Jno. 16:3.

Is no excuse for sin. Lev. 4:2. Luke 12:48.
The wicked, in a state of. Jer. 9:3. Jno. 15:21. Jno. 17:25. Acts 17:30.
The wicked choose. Job 21:14. Rom. 1:28.
Punishment of. Psa. 79:6. 2 The. 1:8.

MINISTERS SHOULD
Compassionate those in. Heb. 5:2. 2 Tim. 2:24, 25.
Labor to remove. Acts 17:23.

Exemplified. *Pharaoh*, Exo. 5:2. *Israelites*, Psa. 95:10. Isa. 1:3. *False prophets*, Isa. 56:10, 11. *Jews*, Luke 23:34. *Nicodemus*, Jno. 3:10. *Gentiles*, Gal. 4:8. *Paul*, 1 Tim. 1:13.

Incense.

Brought from Sheba. Jer. 6:20.
Called frankincense. So. of Sol. 4:6, 14.
An article of extensive commerce. Rev. 18:13.
Common, not to be offered to God. Exo. 30:9.
For God's service mixed with sweet spices. Exo. 25:6. Exo. 37:29.
Receipt for mixing. Exo. 30:34—36.
None but priests to offer. Num. 16:40. Deu. 33:10.

OFFERED
In censers. Lev. 10:1. Num. 16:17, 46.
On the altar of gold. Ex. 30:1, 6. Exo. 40:5.
Morning and evening. Exo. 30:7:8.
Perpetually. Exo. 30:8.
By the high priest in the most holy place on the day of atonement. Lev. 16:12, 13.
With fire from off the altar of burnt-offering. Lev. 16:12. Num. 16:46.

Offering of, allotted to the priests. Luke 1:9.
The Jews prayed at time of offering. Luke 1:10.
Designed for atonement. Num. 16:46, 47.
Put on meat offerings. Lev. 2:1, 2, 15, 16. Lev. 6:15.
Levites had charge of. 1 Chr. 9:29.
Used in idolatrous worship. Jer. 48:35.

THE JEWS
Not accepted in offering, on account of sin. Isa. 1:13. Isa. 66:3.
Offered, to idols on altars of brick. Isa. 65:3.
Punished for offering, to idols. 2 Chr. 34:25.
Nadab and Abihu destroyed for offering, with strange fire. Lev. 10:1, 2.
Korah and his company punished for offering. Num. 16:16—35.
Uzziah punish for offering. 2 Chr. 26:16—21.
Presented to Christ by the wise men. Mat. 2:11.
ILLUSTRATIVE OF
The merits of Christ. Rev. 8:3, 4.
Prayer. Psa. 141: 2. Mal. 1: 11. Rev. 5:8.

Industry.

Commanded. Eph. 4: 28. 1 The. 4:11.
Required of man in a state of innocence. Gen. 2:15.
Required of man after the fall. Gen. 3:23.
To be suspended on the Sabbath. Exo. 20:10.
Characteristic of godly women. Pro. 31:13, &c.
Early rising necessary to. Pro. 31:15.
REQUISITE TO SUPPLY
Our own wants. Acts 20: 34. 1 The. 2:9.
Wants of others. Acts 20: 35. Eph. 4:28.
The slothful devoid of. Pro. 24: 30, 31.
LEADS TO
Increase of substance. Pro. 13:11.
Affection of relatives. Pro. 31:28.
General commendation. Pro. 31:31.
Illustrated. Pro. 6:6—8.
Exemplified. *Rachel*, Gen. 29:9. *Jacob*, Gen. 31: 6. *Jethro's daughters*, Exo. 2:10. *Ruth*, Ruth 2: 2, 3. *Jeroboam*, 1 Kin. 11:28. *David*, 1 Sam. 16: 11. *Jewish elders*, Ezr. 6:14, 15. *Dorcas*, Acts 9: 39. *Paul*, Acts 18:3. 1 Cor. 4: 12

Indwelling of the Holy Ghost, The.

In His Church, as His temple. 1 Cor. 3:16.
In the body of saints, as His temple. 1 Cor. 6:19. 2 Cor. 6:16.
Promised to saints. Eze. 36:27.
Saints enjoy. Isa. 63:11. 2 Tim. 1:14.
Saints full of. Acts 6:5. Eph. 5:18.
IS THE MEANS OF
Quickening. Rom. 8: 11.
Guiding. Jno. 16:13. Gal. 5:18.
Fructifying. Gal. 5:22.
A proof of being Christ's. Rom. 8:9. 1 Jno. 4: 13.
A proof of adoption. Rom. 8: 15. Gal. 4:5.
Is abiding. 1 Jno. 2:27.
THOSE WHO HAVE NOT
Are sensual. Jude 19.
Are without Christ. Rom. 8:9.
Opposed by the carnal nature. Gal. 5:17.

Ingratitude.

A characteristic of the wicked. Psa. 38:20. 2 Tim. 3:2.
OFTEN EXHIBITED
By relations. Job 19:14.
By servants. Job 19:15, 16.
To benefactors. Psa. 109: 5. Ecc. 9: 15.
To friends in distress. Psa. 38: 11.
Saints avoid the guilt of. Psa. 7:4, 5.
SHOULD BE MET WITH
Prayer. Psa. 35:12, 13. Psa. 109:4.
Fathfulness. Gen. 31:38—42.
Persevering love. 2 Cor. 12:15.
Punishment of. Pro. 17:13. Jer. 18:20, 21.
Exemplified. *Laban*, Gen. 31: 6, 7. *Chief butler*, Gen. 40:23. *Israel*, Exo. 17:4. *Men of Keilah*, 1 Sam. 23: 5, 12. *Saul*, 1 Sam. 24: 17. *Nabal*, 1 Sam. 25:5—11, 21. *Absalom*, 2 Sam. 15:6. *Joash*, 2 Chr. 24:22.

Ingratitude to God.

A characteristic of the wicked. Rom. 1:21.
Inexcusable. Isa. 1:2, 3. Rom. 1:21.
Unreasonable. Jer. 2: 5, 6, 31. Mic. 6:2, 3.
Exceeding folly of. Deu. 32:6.
Guilt of. Psa. 106:7, 21. Jer 2:11—13.
Prosperity likely to produce. Deu. 31:20. Deu. 32:15. Jer. 5:7—11.
Warnings against. Deu. 8:11—14. 1 Sam. 12:24, 25.
Punishment of. Neh. 9:20—27. Hos. 2:8, 9.
Illustrated. Isa. 5:1—7. Eze. 16:1—15.
Exemplified. *Israel*, Deu. 32:18. *Saul*, 1 Sam. 15:17—19. *David*, 2 Sam. 12:7—9. *Nebuchadnezzar*, Dan. 5:18—21. *Lepers*, Luke 17:17, 18.

Injustice.

Forbidden. Lev. 19:15, 35. Deu. 16:19.
SPECIALLY TO BE AVOIDED TOWARDS
The poor. Exo. 23: 6. Pro. 22:16, 22, 23.
The stranger and fatherless. Exo. 22:21, 22. Deu. 24:17. Jer. 22:3.
Servants. Job 31: 13, 14. Deu. 24:14. Jer. 22:13.
Of the least kind, condemned. Luke 16:10.

GOD
Regards. Ecc. 5: 8.
Approves not of. Lam. 3: 35, 36.
Abominates. Pro. 17: 15. Pro. 20: 10.
Hears the cry of those who suffer. Jas. 5: 4.
Provoked to avenge. Psa. 12: 5.
Brings a curse. Deu. 27: 17, 19.
A bad example leads to. Exo. 23: 2.
Intemperance leads to. Pro. 31: 5.
Covetousness leads to. Jer. 6: 13. Eze. 22: 12. Mic. 2: 2.
SAINTS SHOULD
Hate. Pro. 29: 27.
Testify against. Psa. 58: 1, 2. Mic. 3: 8, 9.
Bear, patiently. 1 Cor. 6: 7.
Take no vengeance for. Mat. 5: 39.
THE WICKED
Deal with. Isa. 26: 10.
Judge with. Psa. 82: 2. Ecc. 3: 16. Hab. 1: 4.
Practice, without shame. Jer. 6: 13, 15. Zep. 3: 5.
Punishment of. Pro. 11: 7. Pro. 28: 8. Amos 5: 11, 12. Amos 8: 5, 8. 1 The. 4: 6.
Exemplified. *Potiphar*, Gen. 39: 20. *Sons of Samuel*, 1 Sam. 8: 3. *Ahab*, 1 Kin. 21: 10, 15, 16. *Jews*, Isa. 59: 14. *Princes, &c.* Dan. 6: 4. *Judas*, Mat. 27: 4. *Pilate*, Mat. 27: 24—26. *Priests, &c.* Acts 4: 3. *Festus*, Acts 24: 27.

Insects.

Created by God. Gen. 1: 24, 25.
DIVIDED INTO
Clean and fit for food. Lev. 11: 21, 22.
Unclean and abominable. Lev. 11: 23, 24.
MENTIONED IN SCRIPTURE;
Ant. Pro. 6: 6. Pro. 30: 25.
Bee. Jud. 14: 8. Psa. 118: 12. Isa. 7: 18.
Beetle. Lev. 11: 22.
Caterpillar. Psa. 78: 46. Isa. 33: 4.
Cankerworm. Joel 1: 4. Nah. 3: 15, 16.
Earthworm. Job 25: 6. Mic. 7: 17.
Flea. 1 Sam. 24: 14.
Fly. Exo. 8: 22. Ecc. 10: 1. Isa. 7: 18.
Gnat. Mat. 23: 24.
Grasshopper. Lev. 11: 22. Jud. 6: 5. Job 39: 20.
Hornet. Deu. 7: 20.
Locust. Exo. 10: 12, 13.
Bald locust. Lev. 11: 22.
Lice. Exo. 8: 16. Psa. 105: 31.
Maggot. Exo. 16: 20.
Moth. Job 4: 19. Job 27: 18. Isa. 50: 9.
Palmer-worm. Joel 1: 4. Amos 4: 9.
Spider. Job 8: 14. Pro. 30: 28.
Fed by God. Psa. 104: 25, 27. Psa. 145: 9, 15.

Inspiration of the Holy Ghost, The.

Foretold. Joel 2: 28, with Acts 2: 16—18.
All Scripture given by. 2 Sam. 23: 2. 2 Tim. 3: 16. 2 Pet. 1: 21.
DESIGN OF;
To reveal future events. Acts 1: 16. Acts 28: 25. 1 Pet. 1: 11.
To reveal the mysteries of God. Amos 3: 7. 1 Cor. 2: 10.
To give power to ministers. Mic. 3: 8. Acts 1: 8.
To direct ministers. Eze. 3: 24—27. Acts 11: 12. Acts 13: 2.
To control ministers. Acts 16: 6.
To testify against sin. 2 Kin. 17: 13. Neh. 9: 30. Mic. 3: 8. Jno. 16: 8, 9.
MODES OF;
Various. Heb. 1: 1.
By secret impulse. Jud. 13: 25. 2 Pet. 1: 21.
By a voice. Isa. 6: 8. Acts 8: 29. Rev. 1: 10.
By visions. Num. 12: 6. Eze. 11: 24.
By dreams. Num. 12: 6. Dan. 7: 1.
Necessary to prophesying. Num. 11: 25—27. 2 Chr. 20: 14—17.
Is irresistible. Amos 3: 8.
Despisers of, punished. 2 Chr. 36: 15, 16. Zec. 7: 12.

Iron.

Dug out of the earth. Job 28: 2.
DESCRIBED AS
Strong and durable. Job 40: 18. Dan. 2: 40.
Fusible. Eze. 22: 20.
Malleable. Isa. 2: 4.
Of greater gravity than wator. 2 Kin. 6: 5.
Admits of a high polish. Eze. 27: 19.
Hardened into steel. 2 Sam. 22: 35. Job 20: 24.
Of small comparative value. Isa. 60: 17.
The land of Canaan abounded with. Deu. 8: 9. Deu. 33: 25. (*marg.*)
From the north hardest and best. Jer. 15: 12.
Used from the earliest age. Gen. 4: 22.
MADE INTO
Armor. 2 Sam. 23: 7. Rev. 9: 9.
Weapons of war. 1 Sam. 13: 19. 1 Sam. 17: 7.
Chariots. Jud. 4: 3.
Implements for husbandry. 1 Sam. 13: 20, 21. 2 Sam. 12: 31.
Tools for artificers. Jos. 8: 31. 1 Kin. 6: 7.
Graving tools. Job 19: 24. Jer. 17: 1.
Gates. Acts 12: 10.
Nails and hinges. 1 Chr. 22: 3.
Bars. Psa. 107: 16. Isa. 45: 2.

Fetters. Psa. 105: 18. Psa. 149: 8.
Yokes. Deu. 28: 48. Jer. 28: 13, 14.
Idols. Dan. 5: 4, 23.
Bedsteads. Deu. 3: 11.
Pillars. Jer. 1: 18.
Rods. Psa. 2: 9. Rev. 2: 27.

Sharpens things made of it. Pro. 27: 17.
Working in, a trade. 1 Sam. 13: 19. 2 Chr. 2: 7, 14.
An article of commerce. Eze. 27: 12, 19. Rev. 18: 12.
Great quantity of, provided for the temple. 1 Chr. 22: 3, 14, 16. 1 Chr. 29: 2.
Taken in war often dedicated to God. Jos. 6: 19, 24.
Mode of purifying, taken in war. Num. 31: 21—23.
Miraculously made to swim. 2 Kin. 6: 6.

ILLUSTRATIVE

Of strength. Dan. 2: 33, 40.
Of stubbornness. Isa. 48: 4.
Of severe affliction. Deu. 4: 20. Psa. 107: 10.
Of a hard barren soil. Deu. 28: 23.
Of severe exercise of power. Psa. 2: 9. Rev. 2: 27.
(Seared with,) of insensibility of conscience. 1 Tim. 4: 2.

Ishmaelites, The.

Descended from Abraham's son, Ishmael. Gen. 16: 15, 16. 1 Chr. 1: 28.
Divided into twelve tribes. Gen. 25: 16.
Heads of tribes of. Gen. 25: 13—15. 1 Chr. 1: 29—31.

CALLED

Hagarites. 1 Chr. 5: 10.
Hagarenes. Psa. 83: 6.
Arabians. Isa. 13: 20.

Original possessions of. Gen. 25: 18.
Governed by kings. Jer. 25: 24.
Dwelt in tents. Isa. 13: 20.
Rich in cattle. 1 Chr. 5: 21.
Wore ornaments of gold. Jud. 8: 24.
Were the merchants of the east. Gen. 37: 25. Eze. 27: 20, 21.
Traveled in large companies or caravans. Gen. 37: 25. Job 6: 19.
Waylaid and plundered travellers. Jer. 3: 2.
Often confederate against Israel. Psa. 83: 6.

OVERCOME BY

Gideon. Jud. 8: 10—24.
Reubenites and Gadites. 2 Chr. 5: 10, 18—20.
Uzziah. 2 Chr. 26: 7.

Sent presents to Solomon. 1 Kin. 10: 15. 2 Chr. 9: 14.
Sent flocks to Jehoshaphat. 2 Chr. 17: 11.

PREDICTIONS RESPECTING;

To be numerous. Gen. 16: 10. Gen. 17: 20.
To be wild and savage. Gen. 16: 12.
To be warlike and predatory. Gen. 16: 12.
To be divided into twelve tribes. Gen. 17: 20.
To continue independent. Gen. 16: 12.
To be a great nation. Gen. 21: 13, 18.
To be judged with the nations. Jer. 25: 23—25.
Their glory, &c. to be diminished. Isa. 21: 13—17.
Their submission to Christ. Psa. 72: 10, 15.

Probably preached to by St. Paul. Gal. 1: 17.

Issachar, The Tribe of.

Descended from Jacob's fifth son. Gen. 30: 17, 18.
Predictions respecting. Gen. 49: 14, 15. Deu. 33: 18, 19.

PERSONS SELECTED FROM,

To number the people. Num. 1: 8.
To spy out the land. Num. 13: 7.
To divide the land. Num. 34: 26.

Strength of, on leaving Egypt. Num. 1: 28, 29. Num. 2: 6.
Encamped under the standard of Judah east of the tabernacle. Num. 2: 5.
Next to and under standard of Judah in the journeys of Israel. Num. 10: 14, 15.
Offering of, at the dedication. Num. 7: 18—23.
Families of. Num. 26: 23, 24.
Strength of, on entering Canaan. Num. 26: 25.
On Gerizim said amen to the blessings. Deu. 27: 12.
Bounds of their inheritance. Jos. 19: 17—23.
Assisted Deborah against Sisera. Jud. 5: 15.
Officers of, appointed by David. 1 Chr. 27: 18.
Officers of, appointed by Solomon. 1 Kin. 4: 17.
Some of, at David's coronation. 1 Chr. 12: 32.
Number of wariors belonging to, in David's time. 1 Chr. 7: 2, 5.
Many of, at Hezekiah's passover. 2 Chr. 30: 18.
Remarkable persons of. Jud. 10: 1. 1 Kin. 15: 27.

Jerusalem.

The ancient Salem. Gen. 14: 18. Psa. 76: 2.
The ancient Jebusi or Jebus. Jos. 15: 8. Jos. 18: 28. Jud. 19: 10.

The king of, defeated and slain by Joshua. Jos. 10: 5—23.
Allotted to the tribe of Benjamin. Jos. 18: 28.
Partly taken and burned by Judah. Jud. 1: 8.
THE JEBUSITES
Formerly dwelt in. Jud. 19: 10, 11.
Held possession of, with Judah and Benjamin. Jos. 15: 63. Jud. 1: 21.
Finally dispossessed of, by David. 2 Sam. 5: 6—8.
Enlarged by David. 2 Sam. 5: 9.
Made the royal city. 2 Sam. 5: 9. 2 Sam. 20: 3.
Specially chosen by God. 2 Chr. 6: 6. Psa. 135: 21.
The seat of government under the Romans for a time. Mat. 27: 2, 19.
Roman government transferred from, to Caesarea. Acts 23: 23, 24. Acts 25: 1—13.
CALLED
City of God. Psa. 46: 4. Psa. 48: 1.
City of the Lord. Isa. 60: 14.
City of Judah. 2 Chr. 25: 28.
City of the great king. Psa. 48. 2. Mat. 5: 5.
City of solemnities. Isa. 33: 20.
City of righteousness. Isa. 1: 26.
City of truth. Zec. 8: 3.
A city not forsaken. Isa. 62: 12.
Faithful city. Isa. 1: 21, 26.
Holy city. Neh. 11: 1. Isa. 48: 2. Mat. 4: 5.
Throne of the Lord. Jer. 3: 17.
Zion. Psa. 48: 12. Isa. 33: 20.
Zion of the holy one of Israel. Isa. 60: 14.
Surrounded by mountains. Psa. 125: 2.
Surrounded by a wall. 1 Kin. 3: 1.
Protected by forts and bulwarks. Psa. 48: 12, 13.
Entered by gates. Psa. 122: 2. Jer. 17: 19—21.
Hezekiah made an aqueduct for. 2 Kin. 20: 20.
Spoils of war placed in. 1 Sam. 17: 54. 2 Sam. 8: 7.
DESCRIBED AS
Beautiful for situation. Psa. 48: 2.
Compact. Psa. 122: 3.
Comely. So. of Sol. 6: 4.
The perfection of beauty. Lam. 2: 15.
Joy of the whole earth. Psa. 48: 2. Lam. 2: 15.
Princess among the provinces. Lam. 1: 1.
Great. Jer. 22: 8.
Populous. Lam. 1: 1.
Full of business and tumult. Isa. 22: 3.
Wealth, &c. in the time of Solomon. 1 Kin. 10: 26, 27.
Protected by God. Isa. 31: 5.
Instances of God's care and protection of. 2 Sam. 24: 16. 2 Kin. 19: 32—34. 2 Chr. 12: 7.
The temple built in. 2 Chr. 3: 1. Psa. 68: 29.
THE JEWS
Went up to, at the feasts. Luke 2: 42, with Psa. 122: 4.
Loved. Psa. 137: 5, 6.
Lamented the affliction of. Neh. 1: 2—4.
Prayed for prosperity of. Psa. 51: 18. Psa. 122: 6.
Prayed towards. Dan. 6: 10, with 1 Kin. 8: 44.
Wickedness of. Isa. 1: 1—4. Jer. 5: 1—5. Mic. 3: 10.
Idolatry of. 2 Chr. 28: 24. Eze. 8: 7—10.
Wickedness of, the cause of its calamities. 2 Kin. 21: 12—15. 2 Chr. 24: 18. Lam. 1: 8. Eze. 5: 5—8.
Was the tomb of the prophets. Luke 13: 33, 34.
CHRIST
Preached in. Luke 21; 37, 38. Jno. 18: 20.
Did many miracles in. Jno. 4: 45.
Publicly entered, as king. Mat. 21: 9, 10.
Lamented over. Mat. 23: 37. Luke 19: 41.
Put to death at. Luke 9 31. Acts 13: 27, 29.
Gospel first preached at. Luke 24: 47. Acts 2: 14.
Miraculous gift of the Holy Ghost first given at. Acts 1: 4. Acts 2: 1—5.
Persecution of the Christian church commenced at. Acts 4: 1. Acts 8: 1.
First Christian council held at. Acts 15: 4, 6.
CALAMITIES OF, MENTIONED;
Taken and plundered by Shishak. 1 Kin. 14: 25, 26. 2 Chr. 12: 1—4.
Taken and plundered by Jehoash king of Israel. 2 Kin. 14: 13, 14.
Besieged but not taken by Rezin and Pekah. Isa. 7: 1. 2 Kin. 16: 5.
Besieged but not taken by Sennacherib. 2 Kin. 18: 17, and 2 Kin. 19 ch.
Taken and made tributary by Pharaoh-Necho. 2 Kin. 23: 33—35.
Besieged by Nebuchadnezzar. 2 Kin. 24: 10, 11.
Taken and burned by Nebuchadnezzar. 2 Kin. 25 ch. Jer. 39: 1—8.
Threatened by Sanballat. Neh. 4: 7, 8.
Rebuilt after the capivity by order of Cyrus. Ezr. 1: 1—4.

PROPHECIES RESPECTING,
To be taken by king of Babylon. Jer. 20:5.
To be made a heap of ruins. Jer. 9:11. Jer. 26:18.
To be a wilderness. Isa. 64:10.
To be rebuilt by Cyrus. Isa. 44: 26—28.
To be a quiet habitation. Isa. 33: 20.
To be a terror to her enemies. Zec. 12:2, 3.
Christ to enter, as king. Zec. 9:9.
The gospel to go forth from. Isa. 2:3. Isa. 40:9.
To be destroyed by the Romans. Luke 19:42—44.
Its capture accompanied by severe calamities. Mat. 24:21, 29. Luke 21:23, 24.
Signs preceding its destruction. Mat. 24:6—15. Luke 21:7—11, 25, 28.
ILLUSTRATIVE
Of the church. Gal. 4:25, 26. Heb. 12:22.
Of the church glorified. Rev. 3:12. Rev. 21:2, 10.
(Its strong position,) of saints under God's protection. Psa. 125:2.

Jews, The.

Descended from Abraham. Isa. 51:2. Jno. 8:39.
Divided into twelve tribes. Gen. 35: 22. Gen. 49:28.
CALLED
Hebrews. Gen. 14:13. Gen. 40:15. 2 Cor. 11:22.
Israelites. Exo. 9:7. Jos. 3:17.
Seed of Abraham. Psa. 105:6. Isa. 41:8.
Seed of Jacob. Jer. 33:26.
Seed of Israel. 1 Chr. 16:13.
Children of Jacob. 1 Chr. 16:13.
Children of Israel. Gen. 50:25. Isa. 27:12.
Jeshurun. Deu. 32:15.
Chosen and loved by God. Deu. 7: 6, 7.
Circumcised in token of their covenant relation. Gen. 17:10, 11. Acts 7:8.
Separated from all other nations. Exo. 33:16. Lev. 20:24. 1 Kin. 8:53.
DESCRIBED AS
A peculiar people. Deu. 14:2.
A peculiar treasure. Exo. 19:5. Psa. 135:4.
A holy nation. Exo. 19:6.
A holy people. Deu. 7:6. Deu. 14:21.
A kingdom of priests. Exo. 19:6.
A special people. Deu. 7:6.
The Lord's portion. Deu. 32:9.
Sojourned in Egypt. Exo. 12:40, 41.
Brought out of Egypt by God. Exo. 12:42. Deu. 5:15. Deu. 6:12.
In the desert forty years. Num. 14: 33. Jos. 5:6.
Settled in Canaan. Num. 32:88. Jos. 14:1—5.
Under the theocracy until the time of Samuel. Exo. 19:4—6, with 1 Sam. 8:7.
Desired and obtained kings. 1 Sam. 8:5, 22.
Divided into two kingdoms after Solomon. 1 Kin. 11:31, 32. 1 Kin. 12:19, 20.
Often subdued and made tributary. Jud. 2:13, 14. Jud. 4:2. Jud. 6:2, 6. 2 Kin. 23:33.
Taken captive to Assyria and Babylon. 2 Kin. 17:23. 2 Kin. 18:11. 2 Kin. 24:16. 2 Kin. 25:11.
Restored to their own land by Cyrus. Ezr. 1:1—4.
Had courts of justice. Deu. 16:18.
Had an ecclesiastical establishment. Exo. 28:1. Num. 18:6. Mal. 2: 4—7.
Had a series of prophets to promote national reformation. Jer. 7:25. Jer. 26:4, 5. Jer. 35:15. Jer. 44:4. Eze. 38:17.
The only people who had knowledge of God. Psa. 76:1, with 1 The. 4: 5. Psa. 48:3, with Rom. 1:28.
The only people who worshipped God. Exo. 5:17, with Psa. 96:5. Psa. 115:3, 4. Jno. 4:22.
Religion of, according to rites prescribed by God. Lev. 18:4. Deu. 12:8—11. Heb. 9:1.
Religion of, typical. Heb. 9:8—11. Heb. 10:1.
Their national greatness. Gen. 12:2. Deu. 33:29.
Their national privileges. Rom. 3:2. Rom. 9:4, 5.
Their vast numbers. Gen. 22:17. Num. 10:36.
NATIONAL CHARACTER OF;
Pride of descent, &c. Jer. 13:9. Jno. 8:33, 41.
Love of country. Psa. 137:6.
Fondness for their brethren. Exo. 2:11, 12. Rom. 9:1—3.
Attachment to Moses. Jno. 9:28, 29. Acts 6:11.
Attachment to customs of the law Acts 6:14. Acts 21:21. Acts 22:3.
Fondness for traditionary customs. Jer. 44:17. Eze. 20:18, 30, with 21 v. Mar. 7:3, 4.
Stubborn and stiffnecked. Exo. 32: 9. Acts 7:51.
Prone to rebellion. Deu. 9:7, 24. Isa. 1:2.
Prone to backsliding. Jer. 2:11 —13. Jer. 8:5.
Prone to idolatry. Isa. 2:8. Isa. 57:5.

Prone to formality in religion. Isa. 29: 13. Eze. 33: 31. Mat. 15: 7—9.
Self-righteous. Isa. 65: 5. Rom. 10: 3.
Unfaithful to covenant engagements. Jer. 3: 6—8. Jer. 31: 32. Eze. 16: 59.
Ungrateful to God. Deu. 32: 15. Isa. 1: 2.
Ignorant of the true sense of Scripture. Acts 13: 27. 2 Cor. 3: 13—15.
Distrustful of God. Num. 14: 11. Psa. 78: 22.
Covetous. Jer. 6: 13. Eze. 33: 31. Mic. 2: 2.
Cowardly. Exo. 14: 10. Num. 14: 3. Isa. 51: 12.
Trusted to their privileges for salvation. Jer. 7: 4. Mat. 3: 9.
Distinction of castes amongst, noticed. Isa. 65: 5. Luke 7: 39. Luke 15: 2. Acts 26: 5.
Degenerated as they increased in national greatness. Amos 6: 4.
Often displeased God by their sins. Num. 25: 3. Deu. 32: 16. 1 Kin. 16: 2. Isa. 1: 4. Isa. 5: 24, 25.
A spiritual seed of true believers always amongst. 1 Kin. 19: 18. Isa. 6: 13. Rom. 9: 6, 7. Rom. 11: 1, 5.
MODERN, DIVIDED INTO
Hebrews or pure Jews. Acts 6: 1. Phi. 3: 5.
Hellenists or Grecians. Acts 6: 1. Acts 9: 29.
Many sects and parties. Mat. 16: 6. Mar. 8: 15.
An agricultural people. Gen. 46: 32.
A commercial people. Eze. 27: 17.
Obliged to unite against enemies. Num. 32: 20—22. Jud. 19: 29, with 20 ch. 1 Sam. 11: 7, 8.
Often distinguished in war. Jud. 7: 19—23. 1 Sam. 14: 6—13. 1 Sam. 17: 32, 33. Neh. 4: 16—22.
Strengthened By God in war. Lev. 26: 7, 8. Jos. 5: 13, 14. Jos. 8: 1, 2.
Under God's special protection. Deu. 32: 10, 11. Deu. 33: 27—29. Psa. 105: 13—15. Psa. 121: 3—5.
Enemies of, obliged to acknowledge them as divinely protected. Jos. 2: 9—11. Est. 6: 13.
PROHIBITED FROM
Associating with others. Acts 10: 28.
Covenanting with others. Exo. 23: 32. Deu. 7: 2.
Marrying with others. Deu. 7: 3. Jos. 23: 12.
Following practices of others. Deu. 12: 29—31. Deu. 18: 9—14.
Despised all strangers. 1 Sam. 17: 36. Mat. 16: 26, 27. Eph. 2: 11.
Held no intercourse with strangers. Jno. 4: 9. Acts 11: 2, 3.
Condemned for associating with other nations. Jud. 2: 1—3. Jer. 2: 18.
Received proselytes from other nations. Acts 2: 10, with Exo. 12: 44, 48.
Gentiles made one with, under the gospel. Acts 10: 15, 28. Acts 15: 8, 9. Gal. 3: 28. Eph. 2: 14—16.
ALL OTHER NATIONS
Envied. Neh. 4: 1. Isa. 26: 11. Eze. 35: 11.
Hated. Psa. 44: 10. Eze. 35: 5.
Oppressed. Exo. 3: 9. Jud. 2: 18. Jud. 4: 3.
Persecuted. Lam. 1: 3. Lam. 5: 5.
Rejoiced at calamities of. Psa. 44: 13, 14. Psa. 80: 5, 6. Eze. 36: 4.
None hated or oppressed, with impunity. Psa. 137: 8, 9. Eze. 25: 15, 16. Eze. 35: 6. Oba. 10—16 vs.
CHRIST
Promised to. Gen. 49: 10. Dan. 9: 25.
Expected by. Psa. 14: 7. Mat. 11: 3. Luke 2: 25, 38. Jno. 8: 56.
Regarded as the restorer of national greatness. Mat. 20: 21. Luke 24: 21. Acts 1: 6.
Sprang from. Rom. 9: 5. Heb. 7: 14.
Rejected by. Isa. 53: 3. Mar. 6: 3. Jno. 1: 11.
Murdered by. Acts 7: 52. 1 The. 2: 15.
Imprecated the blood of Christ upon themselves and their children. Mat. 27: 25.
Many of, believed the gospel. Acts 21: 20.
Unbelieving, persecuted the Christians. Acts 17: 5, 13. 1 The. 2: 14—16.
Cast off for unbelief. Rom. 11: 17, 20.
Scattered and peeled. Isa. 18: 2, 7. Jas. 1: 1.
Shall finally be saved. Rom. 11: 26, 27.
Punishment of, for rejecting and killing Christ, illustrated. Mat. 21: 37—43.
Descendants of Abraham. Psa. 105: 6. Isa. 51: 2. Jno. 8: 33. Rom. 9: 7.
The people of God. Deu. 32: 9. 2 Sam. 7: 24. Isa. 51: 16.
Separated to God. Exo. 33: 16. Num. 23: 9. Deu. 4: 34.
Beloved for their fathers' sake. Deu. 4: 37. Deu. 10: 15, with Rom. 11: 28.
Christ descended from. Jno. 4: 22. Rom. 9: 5.
THE OBJECTS OF
God's love. Deu. 7: 8. Deu. 23: 5. Jer. 31: 3.
God's choice. Deu. 7: 6.
God's protection. Psa. 105: 15. Zec. 2: 8.
The covenant established with. Exo. 6: 4. Exo. 24: 6—8. Exo. 34: 27.
PROMISES RESPECTING, MADE TO
Abraham. Gen. 12: 1—3. Gen. 13: 14—17. Gen. 15: 18. Gen. 17: 7, 8.
Isaac. Gen. 26: 2—5, 24.
Jacob. Gen. 28: 12—15. Gen. 35: 9—12.
Themselves. Exo. 6: 7, 8. Exo. 19: 5, 6. Deu. 26: 18, 19.

Privileges of. Psa. 76:1, 2. Rom. 3:1, 2. Rom. 9:4, 5.

PUNISHED FOR

Idolatry. Psa. 78:58—64. Isa. 65:3—7.

Unbelief. Rom. 11:20.

Breaking covenant. Isa. 24:5. Jer. 11:10.

Transgressing the law. Isa. 1:4, 7. Isa. 24:5, 6.

Changing the ordinances. Isa. 24:5.

Killing the prophets. Mat. 23:37, 38.

Imprecating upon themselves the blood of Christ. Mat. 27:25.

Scattered among the nations. Deu. 28:64. Eze. 6:8. Eze. 36:19.

Despised by the nations. Eze. 36:3.

Their country trodden under foot by the Gentiles. Deu. 28:49—52. Luke 21:24.

Their house left desolate. Mat. 24:38.

Deprived of civil and religious privileges. Hos. 3:4.

DENUNCIATIONS AGAINST THOSE WHO

Cursed. Gen. 27:29. Num. 24:9.

Contended with. Isa. 41:11. Isa. 49:25.

Oppressed. Isa. 49:26. Isa. 51:21—23.

Hated. Psa. 129:5. Eze. 35:5, 6.

Aggravated the afflictions of. Zec. 1:14, 15.

Slaughtered. Psa. 79:1—7. Eze. 35:5, 6.

God, mindful of. Psa. 98:3. Isa. 49:15, 16.

Christ was sent to. Mat. 15:24. Mat. 21:37. Acts 3:20, 22, 26.

Compassion of Christ for. Mat. 23:37. Luke 19:41.

The gospel preached to, first. Mat. 10:6. Luke 24:47. Acts 1:8.

Blessedness of blessing. Gen. 27:29.

Blessedness of favoring. Gen. 12:3. Psa. 122:6.

Pray importunately for. Psa. 122:6. Isa. 62:1, 6, 7. Jer. 31:7. Rom. 10:1.

Saints remember. Psa. 102:14. Psa. 137:5. Jer. 51:50.

PROMISES RESPECTING,

The pouring out of the Spirit upon them. Eze. 39:29. Zec. 12:10.

The removal of their blindness. Rom. 11:25. 2 Cor. 3:14—16.

Their return and seeking to God. Hos. 3:5.

Their humiliation for the rejection of Christ. Zec. 12:10.

Pardon of sin. Isa. 44:22. Rom. 11:27.

Salvation. Isa. 59:20, with Rom. 11:26.

Sanctification. Jer. 33:8. Eze. 36:25. Zec. 12:1, 9.

Joy occasioned by conversion of. Isa. 44:23. Isa. 49:13. Isa. 52:8, 9. Isa. 66:10.

Blessing to the Gentiles by conversion of. Isa. 2:1—5. Isa. 60:5. Isa. 66:19. Rom. 11:12, 15.

Re-union of. Jer. 3:18. Eze. 37:16, 17, 20—22. Hos. 1:11. Mic. 2:12.

Restoration to their own land. Isa. 11:15, 16. Isa. 14:1—3. Isa. 27:12:13. Jer. 16:14, 15. Eze. 36:24. Eze. 37:21, 25. Eze. 39:25, 28. Luke 21:24.

Gentiles assisting in their restoration. Isa. 49:22, 23. Isa. 60:10, 14. Isa. 61:4—6.

Subjection of Gentiles to. Isa. 60:11, 12, 14.

Future glory of. Isa. 60:19. Isa. 62:3, 4. Zep. 3:19, 20. Zec. 2:5.

Future prosperity of. Isa. 60:6, 7, 9, 17. Isa. 61:4—6. Hos. 14:5, 6.

That Christ shall appear amongst. Isa. 59:20. Zec. 14:4.

That Christ shall dwell amongst. Eze. 43:7, 9. Zec. 2:11.

That Christ shall reign over. Eze. 34:23, 24. Eze. 37:24, 25.

Conversion of, illustrated. Eze. 37:1—14. Rom. 11:24.

Jordan, The River.

Eastern boundary of Canaan. Num. 34:12.

Often overflowed. Jos. 3:15. 1 Chr. 12:15.

Overflowing of, called the swelling of Jordan. Jer. 12:5. Jer. 49:19.

Empties itself into the Dead Sea. Num. 34:12.

THE PLAINS OF,

Thickly wooded. 2 Kin. 6:2.

Exceeding fertile. Gen. 13:10.

Infested with lions. Jer. 49:19. Jer. 50:44.

Afforded clay for molding brass, &c. 1 Kin. 7:46. 2 Chr. 4:17.

Chosen by Lot for a residence. Gen. 13:11.

Fordable in some places. Jos. 2:7. Jud. 12:5, 6.

Ferry boats often used on. 2 Sam. 19:18.

REMARKABLE EVENTS CONNECTED WITH;

Division of its waters to let Israel pass over. Jos. 3:12—16. Jos. 5:1.

Return of its waters to their place. Jos. 4:18.

Slaughter of Moabites. Jud. 3:28, 29.

Slaughter of the Ephraimites. Jud. 12:4—6.

Its division by Elijah. 2 Kin. 2:8.

Its division by Elisha. 2 Kin. 2:14.

Healing of Naaman the leper. 2 Kin. 5:10, 14.

Baptism of multitudes by John the Baptist. Mat. 3:6. Mar. 1:5. Jno. 1:28.

Baptism of our Lord. Mat. 3: 13, 15. Mar. 1:9.

PASSAGE OF ISRAEL OVER,

Promised. Deu. 4:22. Deu. 9: 1. Deu. 11:31.

In an appointed order. Jos. 3:1—8.

Preceded by priests with the ark. Jos. 3:6, 11, 14.

Successfully effected. Jos. 3: 17. Jos. 4:1, 10, 11.

Commemorated by a pillar of stones raised in it. Jos. 4:9.

Commemorated by a pillar of stones in Gilgal. Jos. 4: 2—8, 20—24.

Alluded to. Psa. 74:15. Psa. 114: 3, 5.

A pledge that God would drive the Canaanites, &c. out of their land. Jos. 3:10.

The Jews had great pride in. Zec. 11:3.

Despised by foreigners. 2 Kin. 5:12.

Moses not allowed to cross. Deu. 3: 27. Deu. 31:2.

Joy.

God gives. Ecc. 2:26. Psa. 4:7.

Christ appointed to give. Isa. 61: 3.

Is a fruit of the Spirit. Gal. 5:22.

The gospel, good tidings of. Luke 2: 10, 11.

God's word affords. Neh. 8:12. Jer. 15:16.

The gospel to be received with. 1 The. 1: 6.

Promised to saints. Psa. 132:16. Isa. 35:10. Isa. 55:12. Isa. 56:7.

Prepared for saints. Psa. 97:11.

Enjoined to saints. Psa. 32:11. Phi. 3:1.

Fulness of, in God's presence. Psa. 16:11.

Vanity of seeking, from earthly things. Ecc. 2:10, 11. Ecc. 11:8.

EXPERIENCED BY

Believers. Luke 24:52. Acts 16:34.

Peace-makers. Pro. 12:20.

The just. Pro. 21: 15.

The wise, and discreet. Pro. 15:23.

Parents of good children. Pro. 23: 24.

Increased to the meek. Isa. 29:19.

OF SAINTS IS

In God. Psa. 89: 16. Psa 149: 2. Hab. 3:18. Rom. 5:11.

In Christ. Luke 1:47. Phi. 3:3.

In the Holy Ghost. Rom. 14:17.

For election. Luke 10:20.

For salvation. Psa. 21:1. Isa. 61:10.

For deliverance from bondage. Psa. 105:43. Jer. 31:10—13.

For manifestation of goodness. 2 Chr. 7:10.

For temporal blessings. Joel 2:23, 24.

For supplies of grace. Isa. 12:3.

For divine protection. Psa. 5:11. Psa. 16:8, 9.

For divine support. Psa. 28:7. Psa. 63:7.

For the victory of Christ. Jno. 16: 33.

For the hope of glory. Rom. 5:2.

For the success of the gospel. Acts 15:3.

OF SAINTS, SHOULD BE

Great. Zec. 9:9. Acts 8:8.

Abundant. 2 Cor. 8:2.

Exceeding. Psa. 21:6. Psa. 68:3.

Animated. Psa. 32:11. Luke 6:23.

Unspeakable. 1 Pet. 1:8.

Full of glory. 1 Pet. 1:8.

Constant. 2 Cor. 6:10. Phi. 4:4.

For evermore. 1 The. 5:16.

With awe. Psa. 2:11.

In hope. Rom. 12:12.

In sorrow. 2 Cor. 6:10.

Under trials. Jas. 1:2. 1 Pet. 1:6.

Under persecutions. Mat. 5:11, 12. Luke 6:22, 23. Heb. 10:34.

Under calamities. Hab. 3:17, 18.

Expressed in hymns. Eph. 5:19. Jas. 5:13.

Afflictions of saints succeeded by. Psa. 30:5. Psa. 126:5. Isa. 35:10. Jno. 16:20.

Pray for restoration of. Psa. 51:8, 12. Psa. 85:6.

Promote, in the afflicted. Job 29:13.

OF SAINTS, MADE FULL BY

The favor of God. Acts 2:28.

Faith in Christ. Rom. 15:13.

Abiding in Christ. Jno. 15:10, 11.

The word of Christ. Jno. 17:13.

Answers to prayer. Jno. 16:24.

Communion of saints. 2 Tim. 1:4. 1 Jno. 1:3, 4. 2 Jno. 12.

Saints should afford, to their ministers. Phi. 2:2. Phile. 20.

MINISTERS SHOULD

Esteem their people as their. Phi. 4:1. 1 The. 2:20.

Promote, in their people. 2 Cor. 1: 24. Phi. 1:25.

Pray for, for their people. Rom. 15: 13.

Have, in the faith and holiness of their people. 2 Cor. 7:4. 1 The. 3: 9. 3 Jno. 4.

Come to their people with. Rom. 15:32.

Finish their course with. Acts 20:24.

Desire to render an account with. Phi. 2:16. Heb. 13:17.

Serve God with. Psa. 100:2.

Liberality in God's service should cause. 1 Chr. 29:9, 17.

Is strengthening to saints. Neh 8: 10.

Saints should engage in all religious services with. Ezr. 6:22. Psa. 42:4.

Saints should have, in all their undertakings. Deu. 12:18.

Saints shall be presented to God with exceeding. 1 Pet. 4: 13, with Jude 24.
The coming of Christ will afford to saints, exceeding. 1 Pet. 4: 13.
Shall be the final reward of saints at the judgment-day. Mat. 25: 21.
OF THE WICKED
Is derived from earthly pleasures. Ecc. 2: 10. Ecc. 11: 9.
Is derived from folly. Pro. 15: 21.
Is delusive. Pro. 14: 13.
Is short-lived. Job 20: 5. Ecc. 7: 6.
Should be turned into mourning. Jas. 4: 9.
Shall be taken away. Isa. 16: 10.
Holy—Illustrated. Isa. 9: 3. Mat. 13: 44.
Holy—Exemplified. *Hannah*, 1 Sam. 2: 1. *David*, 1 Chr. 29: 9. *Wise men*, Mat. 2: 10. *The Virgin Mary*, Luke 1: 47. *Zaccheus*, Luke 19: 6. *Converts*, Acts 2: 46. Acts 13: 52. *Peter*, &c. Acts 5: 41. *Samaritans*, Acts 8: 8. *Jailor*, Acts 16: 34.

Joy of God over His People, The.

Greatness of, described. Zep. 3: 17.
ON ACCOUNT OF THEIR
Repentance. Luke 15: 7, 10.
Faith. Heb. 11: 5, 6.
Fear of Him. Psa. 147: 11.
Praying to Him. Pro. 15: 8.
Hope in His mercy. Psa. 147: 11.
Meekness. Psa. 149: 4.
Uprightness. 1 Chr. 29: 17. Pro. 11: 20.
LEADS HIM TO
Prosper them. Deu. 30: 9.
Do them good. Deu. 28: 63. Jer. 32: 41.
Deliver them. 2 Sam. 22: 20.
Comfort them. Isa. 65: 19.
Give them the inheritance. Num. 14: 8.
Illustrated. Isa. 62: 5. Luke 15: 23, 24.
Exemplified. *Solomon*, 1 Kin. 10: 9.

Judah, The tribe of.

Descended from Jacob's fourth son. Gen. 29: 35.
Predictions respecting. Gen. 49: 8—12. Deu. 33: 7.
PERSONS SELECTED FROM,
To number the people. Num. 1: 7.
To spy out the land. Num. 13: 6.
To divide the land. Num. 34: 19.
Strength of, on leaving Egypt. Num. 1: 26, 27. Num. 2: 4.
Encamped with its standard east of the tabernacle. Num. 2: 3.
Led the first division of Israel in their journeys. Num. 10: 14.
Offering of, at dedication. Num. 7: 12—17.
Families of. Num. 26: 19—21.
Strength of on entering Canaan. Num. 26: 22.
On Gerizim said amen to the blessings. Deu. 27: 12.
Bounds of inheritance. Jos. 15: 1—12.
First and most vigorous in driving out the Canaanites. Jud. 1: 3—20.
Went first against Gibeah. Jud. 20: 18.
Furnished to Israel the first judge. Jud. 3: 9.
Aided Saul in his wars. 1 Sam. 11: 8. 1 Sam. 15: 4.
After Saul's rebellion appointed to furnish kings to Israel. 1 Sam. 13: 14. 1 Sam. 15: 28. 1 Sam. 16: 6, 13. 2 Sam. 2: 4. 2 Sam. 7: 16, 17.
The first to submit to David. 2 Sam. 2: 10.
Reigned over alone by David seven years and a half. 2 Sam. 2: 11. 2 Sam. 5: 5.
Officer placed over by David. 1 Chr. 27: 18.
Reproved for tardiness in bringing back David after Absalom's rebellion. 2 Sam. 19: 11—15.
Other tribes jealous of, on account of David. 2 Sam. 19: 41—43. 2 Sam. 20: 1, 2.
With Benjamin alone adhered to the house of David. 1 Kin. 12: 21.
The last tribe carried into captivity. 2 Kin. 17: 18, 20. 2 Kin. 25: 21.
Our Lord sprang from. Mat. 1: 3—16. Luke 3: 23—33. Heb. 7: 14.
Remarkable persons of; *Achan*, Jos. 7: 18. *Elimelech*, Ruth 1: 1, 2. *Boaz*, Ruth 2: 1. *Obed*, Ruth 4: 21. *Jesse*, Ruth 4: 22. 1 Sam. 16: 1. *David*, 1 Sam. 16: 1, 13. *Solomon*, 1 Kin. 1: 32—39. *Elihu*, 1 Chr. 27: 18. *Pethahiah*, Neh. 11: 24. *Bezaleel*, Exo 31: 2. Exo. 35: 30. *Nashon*, Num. 7: 12. *Caleb*, Num. 14: 24. *Absalom*, 2 Sam. 15: 1. *Elhanan*, 2 Sam. 21: 19. 2 Sam. 23: 24. *Adonijah*, 1 Kin. 1: 5, 6. *Jonathan*, 2 Sam. 21: 21. *Kings of Judah*, 1st and 2nd Books of Kings.

Judea, Modern.

One of the divisions of the Holy Land under the Romans. Luke 3: 1.
Comprised the whole of the ancient kingdom of Judah. 1 Kin. 12: 21—24.
CALLED
The land of Judah. Mat. 2: 6.
Jewry. Dan. 5: 13, with Jno. 7: 1.
A mountainous district. Luke 1: 39, 65.
Parts of, desert. Mat. 3: 1. Acts 8: 26.
Jerusalem the capital of. Mat. 4: 25.

TOWNS OF;
Arimathea. Mat. 27:57. Jno. 19:38.
Azotus or Ashdod. Acts 8:40.
Bethany. Jno. 11:1, 18.
Bethlehem. Mat. 2:1, 6, 16.
Bethphage. Mat. 21:1.
Emmaus. Luke 24:13.
Ephraim. Jno 11:54.
Gaza. Acts 8:26.
Jericho. Luke 10:30. Luke 19:1.
Joppa. Acts 9:36. Acts 10:5, 8.
Lydda. Acts 9:32, 35, 38.
John the Baptist preached in. Mat. 3:1.
OUR LORD
Born in. Mat. 2:1, 5, 6.
Tempted in the wilderness of. Mat. 4:1.
Frequently visited. Jno. 11:7.
Often left, to escape persecution. Jno. 4:1—3.
Several Christian churches in. Acts 9:31. 1 The. 2:14.

Judges, Extraordinary.

Raised up to deliver Israel. Jud. 2:16.
Upheld and strengthened by God. Jud. 2:18.
Remarkable for their faith. Heb. 11:32.
NAMES OF;
Othniel. Jud. 3:9, 10.
Ehud. Jud. 3:15.
Shamgar. Jud. 3:31.
Deborah. Jud. 4:4.
Gideon. Jud. 6:11.
Abimelech. Jud. 9:6.
Tola. Jud. 10:1.
Jair. Jud. 10:3.
Jephthah. Jud. 11:1.
Ibzan. Jud. 12:8.
Elon. Jud. 12:11.
Abdon. Jud. 12:13.
Samson. Jud. 13:24, 25. Jud. 16:31.
Eli. 1 Sam. 4:18.
Samuel. 1 Sam. 7:6, 15—17.
During four hundred and fifty years. Acts 13:20.
Not without intermission. Jud. 17:6. Jud. 18:1. Jud. 19:1. Jud. 21:25.
The office of, not always for life, or hereditary. Jud. 8:23, 29.
Israel not permanently or spiritually benefited by. Jud. 2:17—19.

Judgments.

Are from God. Deu. 32:39. Job 12:23. Amos 3:6. Mic. 6:9.
DIFFERENT KINDS OF;
Blotting out the name. Deu. 29:20.
Abandonment by God. Hos. 4:17.
Cursing men's blessings. Mal. 2:2.
Pestilence. Deu. 28:21, 22. Amos 4:10.
Enemies. 2 Sam. 24:13.
Famine. Deu. 28:38—40. Amos 4:7—9.
Famine of hearing the word. Amos 8:11.
The sword. Exo. 22:24. Jer. 19:7.
Captivity. Deu. 28:41. Eze. 39:23.
Continued sorrows. Psa. 32:10. Psa. 78:32, 33. Eze. 24:23.
Desolation. Eze. 33:29. Joel 3:19
Destruction. Job 31:3. Psa. 34 16. Pro. 2:22. Isa. 11:4.
INFLICTED UPON
Nations. Gen. 15:14. Jer. 51:20, 21.
Individuals. Deu. 29:20. Jer. 23:34.
False gods. Exo. 12:12. Num. 33:4.
Posterity of sinners. Exo. 20:5. Psa. 37:28. Lam. 5:7.
All enemies of saints. Jer. 30:16.
Sent for correction. Job 37:13. Jer. 30:11.
Sent for the deliverance of saints. Exo. 6:6.
ARE SENT, AS PUNISHMENT FOR
Disobedience to God. Lev. 26:14—16. 2 Cor. 7:19, 20.
Despising the warnings of God. 2 Chr. 36:16. Pro. 1:24—31. Jer. 44:4—6.
Murmuring against God. Num. 14:29.
Idolatry. 2 Kin. 22:17. Jer. 16:18.
Iniquity. Isa. 26:21. Eze. 24:13, 14.
Persecuting saints. Deu. 32:43.
Sins of rulers. 1 Chr. 21:2, 12.
Manifest the righteous character of God. Exo. 9:14—16. Eze. 39:21. Dan. 9:14.
Are in all the earth. 1 Chr. 16:14.
Are frequently tempered with mercy. Jer. 4:27. Jer. 5:10, 15—18. Amos 9:8.
SHOULD LEAD TO
Humiliation. Jos. 7:6. 2 Chr. 12:6. Lam. 3:1—20. Joel 1:13. Jon. 3:5, 6.
Prayer. 2 Chr. 20:9.
Contrition. Neh. 1:4. Est. 4:3. Isa. 22:12.
Learning righteousness. Isa. 26:9.
Should be a warning to others. Luke 13:3, 5.
MAY BE AVERTED BY
Humiliation. Exo. 33:3, 4, 14. 2 Chr. 7:14.
Prayer. Jud. 3:9—11. 2 Chr. 7:13, 14.
Forsaking iniquity. Jer. 18:7, 8.
Turning to God. Deu. 30:1—3.
SAINTS
Preserved during. Job 5:19, 20. Psa. 91:7. Isa. 26:20. Eze. 9:6. Rev. 7:3.
Provided for, during. Gen. 47:12. Psa. 33:19. Psa. 37:19.

Pray for those under. Exo. 32: 11—13. Num. 11: 2. Dan. 9: 3.
Sympathize with those under. Jer. 9: 1. Jer. 13: 17. Lam. 3: 48.
Acknowledge the justice of. 2 Sam. 24: 17. Ezr. 9: 13. Neh. 9: 33. Jer. 14: 7.

UPON NATIONS—Exemplified. *The old world*, Gen. 6: 7, 17. *Sodom, &c.* Gen. 19: 24. *Egypt*, Exo. 9: 14. *Israel*, Num. 14: 29, 35. Num. 21: 6. *People of Ashdod*, 1 Sam. 5: 6. *People of Bethshemesh*, 1 Sam. 6: 19. *Amalekites*, 1 Sam. 15: 3.

UPON INDIVIDUALS—Exemplified. *Cain*, Gen. 4: 11, 12. *Canaan*, Gen. 9: 25. *Korah, &c.* Num. 16. 33—35. *Achan*, Jos. 7: 25. *Hophni, &c.* 1 Sam. 2: 34. *Saul*, 1 Sam. 15: 23. *Uzzah*, 2 Sam. 6: 7. *Jeroboam*, 1 Kin. 13: 4. *Ahab*, 1 Kin. 22: 38. *Gehazi*, 2 Kin. 5: 27. *Jezebel*, 2 Kin. 9: 35. *Nebuchadnezzar*, Dan. 4: 31. *Belshazzar*, Dan. 5: 30. *Zacharias*, Luke 1: 20. *Ananias, &c.* Acts 5: 1—10. *Herod*, Acts 12: 23. *Elymas*, Acts 13: 11.

PRESERVATION DURING—Exemplified. *Noah*, Gen. 7: 1, 16. *Lot*, Gen. 19: 15—17. *Joseph, &c.* Gen. 45: 7. *Elijah*, 1 Kin. 17: 9. *Elisha, &c.* 2 Kin. 4: 38—41. *Shunammite*, 2 Kin. 8: 1, 2.

Judgment, The.

Predicted in the Old Testament. 1 Chr. 16: 33. Psa. 9: 7. Psa. 96: 13. Ecc. 3: 17.
A first principle of the gospel. Heb. 6: 2.
A day appointed for. Acts 17: 31. Rom. 2: 16.
Time of, unknown to us. Mar. 13: 32.

CALLED THE
- Day of wrath. Rom. 2: 5. Rev. 6: 17.
- Revelation of the righteous judgment of God. Rom. 2: 5.
- Day of judgment and perdition of ungodly men. 2 Pet 3: 7.
- Day of destruction. Job 21: 30.
- Judgment of the great day. Jude 6.

Shall be administered by Christ. Jno. 5: 22, 27. Acts 10: 42. Rom. 14: 10. 2 Cor. 5: 10.
Saints shall sit with Christ in. 1 Cor. 6: 2. Rev. 20: 4.
Shall take place at the coming of Christ. Mat. 25: 31. 2 Tim. 4: 1.
Of Heathens, by the law of conscience. Rom. 2: 12, 14, 15.
Of Jews by the law of Moses. Rom. 2: 12.
Of Christians, by the gospel. Jas. 2: 12.

SHALL BE HELD UPON
- All nations. Mat. 25: 32.
- All men. Heb. 9: 27. Heb. 12: 23.
- Small and great. Rev. 20: 12.
- The righteous and wicked. Ecc. 3: 17.
- Quick and dead. 2 Tim. 4: 1. 1 Pet. 4: 5.

Shall be in righteousness. Psa. 98: 9. Acts 17: 31.
The books shall be opened at. Dan. 7: 10.

SHALL BE OF ALL
- Actions. Ecc. 11: 9. Ecc. 12: 14. Rev. 20: 13.
- Words. Mat. 12: 36, 37. Jude 15.
- Thoughts. Ecc. 12: 14. 1 Cor. 4: 5.

None, by nature, can stand in. Psa. 130: 3. Psa. 143: 2. Rom. 3: 19.
Saints shall, through Christ, be enabled to stand in. Rom. 8: 33, 34.
Christ will acknowledge saints at. Mat. 25: 34—40. Rev. 3: 5.
Perfect love will give boldness in. 1 Jno. 4: 17.
Saints shall be rewarded at. 2 Tim. 4: 8. Rev. 11: 18.
The wicked shall be condemned in. Mat. 7: 22, 23. Mat. 25: 41.
Final punishment of the wicked will succeed. Mat. 13: 40—42. Mat. 25: 46.
The word of Christ shall be a witness against the wicked in. Jno. 12: 48.

THE CERTAINTY OF, A MOTIVE TO
- Repentance. Acts 17: 30, 31.
- Faith. Isa. 28: 16, 17.
- Holiness. 2 Cor. 5: 9, 10. 2 Pet. 3: 11, 14.
- Prayer and watchfulness. Mar. 13: 33.

Warn the wicked of. Acts 24: 25. 2 Cor. 5: 11.
The wicked dread. Acts 24: 25. Heb. 10: 27.
Neglected advantages increase condemnation at. Mat. 11: 20—24. Luke 11: 31, 32.
Devils shall be condemned at. 2 Pet. 2: 4. Jude 6.

Justice.

Commanded. Deu. 16: 20. Isa. 56: 1.
Christ, an example of. Psa. 98: 9. Isa. 11: 4. Jer. 23: 5.
Specially required in rulers. 2 Sam. 23: 3. Eze. 45: 9.

TO BE DONE
- In executing judgment. Deu. 16: 18. Jer. 21: 12.
- In buying and selling. Lev. 19: 36. Deu. 25: 15.
- To the poor. Pro. 29: 14. Pro. 31: 9.
- To the fatherless and widows. Isa. 1: 17.
- To servants. Col. 4: 1.

Gifts impede. Exo. 23: 8.

GOD
- Requires. Mic. 6: 8.
- Sets the highest value on. Pro. 21: 3.

Delights in. Pro. 11: 1.
Gives wisdom to execute. 1 Kin. 3: 11, 12. Pro. 2: 6, 9.
Displeased with the want of. Ecc. 5: 8.
Brings its own reward. Jer. 22: 15.
SAINTS SHOULD
Study the principles of. Phi. 4: 8.
Receive instruction in. Pro. 1: 3.
Pray for wisdom to execute. 1 Kin. 3: 9.
Always do. Psa. 119: 121. Eze. 18: 8, 9.
Take pleasure in doing. Pro. 21: 15.
Teach others to do. Gen. 18: 19.
Promises to. Isa. 33: 15, 16. Jer. 7: 5, 7.
THE WICKED
Scorn. Pro. 19: 28.
Abhor. Mic. 3: 9.
Call not for. Isa. 59: 4.
Banish. Isa. 59: 14.
Pass over. Luke 11: 42.
Afflict those who act with. Job 12: 4. Amos 5: 12.
Exemplified. *Moses*, Num. 16: 15. *Samuel*, 1 Sam. 12: 4. *David*, 2 Sam. 8: 15. *Solomon*, 1 Kin. 3: 16—27. *Josiah*, Jer. 22: 15. *Joseph*, Luke 23: 50, 51. *Apostles*, 1 The. 2: 10.

Justice of God, The.

Is a part of His character. Deu. 32: 4. Isa. 45: 21.
DECLARED TO BE
Plenteous. Job 37: 23.
Incomparable. Job 4: 1.
Incorruptible. Deu. 10: 17. 2 Chr. 19: 7.
Impartial. 2 Chr. 19: 7. Jer. 32: 19.
Unfailing. Zep. 3: 5.
Undeviating. Job 8: 3. Job 34: 12.
Without respect of persons. Rom. 2: 11. Col. 3: 25. 1 Pet. 1: 17.
The habitation of His throne. Psa. 89: 14.
Not to be sinned against. Jer. 50: 7.
Denied by the ungodly. Eze. 33: 17, 20.
EXHIBITED IN
Forgiving sins. 1 Jno. 1: 9.
Redemption. Rom. 3: 26.
His government. Psa. 9: 4. Jer. 9: 24.
His judgments. Gen. 18: 25. Rev. 19: 2.
All His ways. Eze. 18: 25, 29.
The final judgment. Acts 17: 31.
Acknowledge. Psa. 51: 4, with Rom. 3: 4.
Magnify. Psa. 98: 9. Psa. 99: 3, 4.

Justification before God.

Promised in Christ. Isa. 45: 25. Isa. 53: 11.
Is the act of God. Isa. 50: 8. Rom. 8: 33.
UNDER THE LAW
Requires perfect obedience. Lev. 18: 5, with Rom. 10: 5. Rom. 2: 13. Jas. 2: 10.
Man cannot attain to. Job. 9: 2, 3, 20. Job 25: 4. Psa. 130: 3. Psa. 143: 2, with Rom. 3: 20. Rom. 9, 31, 32.
UNDER THE GOSPEL
Is not of works. Acts 13: 39. Rom. 8: 3. Gal. 2: 16. Gal. 3: 11.
Is not of faith and works united. Acts 15: 1—29. Rom. 3: 28. Rom. 11: 6. Gal. 2: 14—21. Gal. 5: 4.
Is by faith alone. Jno. 5: 24. Acts 13: 39. Rom. 3: 30. Rom. 5: 1. Gal. 2: 16.
Is of grace. Rom. 3: 24. Rom. 4: 16. Rom. 5: 17—21.
In the name of Christ. 1 Cor. 6: 11.
By imputation of Christ's righteousness. Isa. 61: 10. Jer. 23: 6. Rom. 3: 22. Rom. 5: 18. 1 Cor. 1: 30. 2 Cor. 5: 21.
By the blood of Christ. Rom. 5: 9.
By the resurrection of Christ. Rom. 4: 25. 1 Cor. 15: 17.
Blessedness of. Psa. 32: 1, 2, with Rom. 4: 6—8.
Frees from condemnation Isa. 50: 8, 9. Isa. 54: 17, with Rom. 8: 33, 34.
Entitles to an inheritance. Tit. 3: 7.
Ensures glorification. Rom. 8: 30.
The wicked shall not attain to. Exo. 23: 7.
BY FAITH
Revealed under the old dispensation. Hab. 2: 4, with Rom. 1: 17.
Excludes boasting. Rom. 3: 27. Rom. 4: 2. 1 Cor. 1: 29, 31.
Does not make void the law. Rom. 3: 30, 31. 1 Cor. 9: 21.
Typified. Zec. 3: 4, 5.
Illustrated. Luke 18: 14.
Exemplified. *Abraham*, Gen. 15: 6. *Paul*, Phi. 3: 8, 9.

Kenites, The.

Originally a people of Canaan. Gen. 15: 19.
Connected with the Midianites. Num. 10: 29, with Jud. 4: 11.
Dwelt in strongholds. Num. 24: 21.
Had many cities. 1 Sam. 30: 29.
MOSES
Intermarried with. Exo. 2: 21, with Jud. 1: 16.
Invited, to accompany Israel. Num. 10: 29—32.
Part of, dwelt with Israel. Jud. 1: 16. Jud. 4: 11.
Part of, dwelt with the Amalekites 1 Sam. 15: 6.

Showed kindness to Israel in the desert. Exo. 18 ch. 1 Sam. 15: 6.
Not destroyed with Amalekites. 1 Sam. 15: 6.
The Rechabites descended from. 1 Chr. 2: 55.
Sisera slain by Jael one of. Jud. 4: 22. Jud. 5: 24.
DAVID
Pretended that he invaded. 1 Sam. 27: 10.
Sent part of the spoil of war to. 1 Sam. 30: 29.
Ruin of, predicted. Num. 24: 21, 22.

Kings.

Israel warned against seeking. 1 Sam. 8: 9–18.
Sin of Israel in seeking. 1 Sam. 12: 17—20.
Israel in seeking, rejected God as their king. 1 Sam. 8: 7. 1 Sam. 10: 19.
Israel asked for, that they might be like the nations. 1 Sam. 8: 5, 19, 20.
First given to Israel in anger. Hos. 13: 11.
God reserved to Himself the choice of. Deu. 17: 14, 15. 1 Sam. 9: 16, 17. 1 Sam. 16: 12.
When first established in Israel, not hereditary. Deu. 17: 20, with 1 Sam. 13: 13, 14. 1 Sam. 15: 28, 29.
Rendered hereditary in the family of David. 2 Sam. 7: 12—16. Psa. 89: 35—37.
Of Israel not to be foreigners. Deu. 17: 15.
Laws for the government of the kingdom by, written by Samuel. 1 Sam. 10: 25.
FORBIDDEN TO MULTIPLY
Horses. Deu. 17: 16.
Wives. Deu. 17: 17.
Treasure. Deu. 17: 17.
Required to write and keep by them, a copy of the divine law. Deu. 17: 18—20.
Had power to make war and peace. 1 Sam. 11: 5—7.
Often exercised power arbitrarily. 1 Sam. 22: 17, 18. 2 Sam. 1: 15. 2 Sam. 4: 9—12. 1 Kin. 2: 23, 25, 31.
CEREMONIES AT INAUGURATION OF;
Anointing. 1 Sam. 10: 1. 1 Sam. 16: 13. Psa. 89: 20.
Crowning. 2 Kin. 11: 12. 2 Chr. 23: 11. Psa. 21: 3.
Proclaiming with trumpets. 2 Sam. 15: 10. 1 Kin. 1: 34. 2 Kin. 9: 13. 2 Kin. 11: 14.
Enthroning. 1 Kin. 1: 35, 46. 2 Kin. 11: 19.
Girding on the sword. Psa. 45: 3.
Putting into their hands the books of the law. 2 Kin. 11: 12. 2 Chr. 23: 11.
Covenanting to govern lawfully. 2 Sam. 5: 3.
Receiving homage. 1 Sam. 10: 1. 1 Chr. 29: 24.
Shouting "God save the king." 1 Sam. 10: 24. 2 Sam. 16: 16. 2 Kin. 11: 12.
Offering sacrifice. 1 Sam. 11: 15.
Feasting. 1 Chr. 12: 38, 39. 1 Chr. 29: 22.
Attended by a body-guard. 1 Sam. 13: 2. 2 Sam. 8: 18. 1 Chr. 11: 25. 2 Chr. 12: 10.
Dwelt in royal palaces. 2 Chr. 9: 11. Psa. 45: 15.
Arrayed in royal apparel. 1 Kin. 22: 30. Mat. 6: 29.
Names of, often changed at their accession. 2 Kin. 23: 34. 2 Kin. 24: 17.
OFFICERS OF;
Prime minister. 2 Chr. 19: 11, with 2 Chr. 28: 7.
First Counseller. 1 Chr. 27: 33.
Confidant or king's special friend. 1 Kin. 4: 5. 1 Chr. 27: 33.
Comptroller of the household. 1 Kin. 4: 6. 2 Chr. 28: 7.
Scribe or secretary. 2 Sam. 8: 17. 1 Kin. 4: 3.
Captain of the host. 2 Sam. 8: 16. 1 Kin. 4: 4.
Captain of the guard. 2 Sam. 8: 18. 2 Sam. 20: 23.
Recorder. 2 Sam. 8: 16. 1 Kin. 4: 3.
Providers for the king's table. 1 Kin. 4: 7—19.
Master of the wardrobe. 2 Kin. 22: 14. 2 Chr. 34: 22.
Treasurer. 1 Chr. 27: 25.
Storekeeper. 1 Chr. 27: 25.
Overseer of the tribute. 1 Kin. 4: 6. 1 Kin. 12: 18.
Overseer of royal farms. 1 Chr. 27: 26.
Overseer of royal vineyards. 1 Chr. 27: 27.
Overseer of royal plantations. 1 Chr. 27: 28.
Overseer of royal herds. 1 Sam. 21: 7. 1 Chr. 27: 29.
Overseer of royal camels. 1 Chr. 27: 30.
Overseer of royal flocks. 1 Chr. 27: 31.
Armor-bearer. 1 Sam. 16: 21.
Cup-bearer. 1 Kin. 10: 5. 2 Chr. 9: 4.
Approached with greatest reverence. 1 Sam. 24: 8. 2 Sam. 9: 8. 2 Sam. 14: 22. 1 Kin. 1: 23.
Presented with gifts by strangers. 1 Kin. 10: 2, 10, 25. 2 Kin. 5: 5. Mat. 2: 11.
Right hand of, the place of honor. 1 Kin. 2: 19. Psa. 45: 9. Psa. 110: 1.
Attendants of, stood in their presence. 1 Kin. 10: 8. 2 Kin. 25: 19.

Exercised great hospitality. 1 Sam. 20: 25—27. 2 Sam. 9: 7—13. 2 Sam. 19: 33. 1 Kin. 4: 22, 23, 28.

THEIR REVENUES DERIVED FROM
- Voluntary contributions. 1 Sam. 10: 27, with 1 Sam. 16: 20. 1 Chr. 12: 39, 40.
- Tribute from foreign nations. 1 Kin. 4: 21, 24, 25. 2 Chr. 8: 8. 2 Chr. 17: 11.
- Tax on produce of the land. 1 Kin. 4: 7—19.
- Tax on foreign merchandise. 1 Kin. 10: 15.
- Their own flocks and herds. 2 Chr. 32: 29.
- Produce of their own lands. 2 Chr. 26: 10.
- Sometimes nominated their successors. 1 Kin. 1: 33, 34. 2 Chr. 11: 22, 23.
- Punished for transgressing the divine law. 2 Sam. 12: 7—12. 1 Kin. 21: 18—24.

WHO REIGNED OVER ALL ISRAEL;
- Saul. 1 Sam. 11: 15, to 1 Sam. 31 ch. 1 Chr. 10 ch.
- David. 2 Sam. 2: 4, to 1 Kin. 2: 11. 1 Chr. 11 ch. to 1 Chr. 29 ch.
- Solomon. 1 Kin. 1: 39, to 1 Kin. 11: 43. 2 Chr. 1 ch. to 2 Chr. 9 ch.
- Rehoboam. (first part of his reign.) 1 Kin. 12: 1—20. 2 Chr. 10: 1—16.

WHO REIGNED OVER JUDAH;
- Rehoboam, (latter part of his reign.) 1 Kin. 12: 21—24. 1 Kin. 14: 21—31. 2 Chr. 10: 17, to 12 ch.
- Abijam or Abijah. 1 Kin. 15: 1—8. 2 Chr. 13 ch.
- Asa. 1 Kin. 15: 9—24. 2 Chr. 14 ch. to 2 Chr. 16: 14.
- Jehoshaphat. 1 Kin. 22: 41—50. 2 Chr. 17 ch. to 2 Chr. 21: 1.
- Jehoram or Joram. 2 Kin. 8: 16—24. 2 Chr. 21 ch.
- Ahaziah. 2 Kin. 8: 25—29. 2 Kin. 9: 16—29. 2 Chr. 22: 1—9.
- Athaliah, mother of Ahaziah (usurper.) 2 Kin. 11: 1—3. 2 Chr. 22: 10—12.
- Joash or Jehoash. 2 Kin. 11: 4, to 2 Kin. 12 ch. 2 Chr. 23 ch. 2 Chr. 24 ch.
- Amaziah. 2 Kin. 14: 1—20. 2 Chr. 25 ch.
- Azariah or Uzziah. 2 Kin. 14: 21, 22. 2 Kin. 15: 1—7. 2 Chr. 26 ch.
- Jotham. 2 Kin. 15: 32—38. 2 Chr. 27 ch.
- Ahaz. 2 Kin. 16 ch. 2 Chr. 28 ch.
- Hezekiah. 2 Kin. 18 ch. to 2 Kin. 20 ch. 2 Chr. 29 ch. to 2 Chr. 32 ch.
- Manasseh. 2 Kin. 21: 1—18. 2 Chr. 33: 1—20.
- Amon. 2 Kin. 21: 19—26. 2 Chr. 33: 21—25.
- Josiah. 2 Kin. 22 ch. 2 Kin. 23: 1—30. 2 Chr. 34 ch. 2 Chr. 35 ch.
- Jehoahaz. 2 Kin. 23: 31—33. 2 Chr. 36: 1—4.
- Jehoiakim. 2 Kin. 23: 34—37. 2 Kin. 24: 1—6. 2 Chr. 36: 5—8.
- Jehoiachin. 2 Kin. 24: 8—16. 2 Chr. 36: 9, 10.
- Zedekiah. 2 Kin. 24: 17—20. 2 Kin. 25: 1—7. 2 Chr. 36: 11—21.

WHO REIGNED OVER ISRAEL;
- Jeroboam. 1 Kin. 12: 20, 25, to 1 Kin. 14: 20.
- Nadab. 1 Kin. 15: 25—27, 31.
- Baasha. 1 Kin. 15: 28—34. 1 Kin. 16: 1—7.
- Elah. 1 Kin. 16: 8—14.
- Zimri. 1 Kin. 16: 11, 12, 15—20.
- Omri. 1 Kin. 16: 23—28.
- Ahab. 1 Kin. 16: 29, to 1 Kin. 22: 40,
- Ahaziah. 1 Kin. 22: 51—53. 2 Kin. 1 ch.
- Jehoram or Joram. 2 Kin. 3 ch. to 2 Kin. 9: 26.
- Jehu. 2 Kin. 9: 3, to 2 Kin. 10: 36.
- Jehoahaz. 2 Kin. 13: 1—9.
- Jehoash or Joash. 2 Kin. 13: 10—25. 2 Kin. 14: 8—16.
- Jeroboam the Second. 2 Kin. 14: 23—29.
- Zachariah. 2 Kin. 15: 8—12.
- Shallum. 2 Kin. 15: 13—15.
- Menahem. 2 Kin. 15: 16—22.
- Pekahiah. 2 Kin. 15: 23—26.
- Pekah. 2 Kin. 15: 27—31. 2 Kin. 16: 5.
- Hoshea. 2 Kin. 17: 1—6.

Called the Lord's anointed. 1 Sam. 16: 6. 1 Sam. 24: 6. 2 Sam. 19: 21.

CONSPIRACIES AGAINST;
- Absalom against David. 2 Sam. 15: 10.
- Adonijah against Solomon. 1 Kin. 1: 5—7.
- Jeroboam against Rehoboam. 1 Kin. 12: 12, 16.
- Baasha against Nadab. 1 Kin. 15: 27.
- Zimri against Elah. 1 Kin. 16: 9, 10.
- Omri against Zimri. 1 Kin. 16: 17.
- Jehu against Joram. 2 Kin. 9: 14.
- Shallum against Zachariah. 2 Kin. 15: 10.
- Menahem against Shallum. 2 Kin. 15: 14.
- Pekah against Menahem. 1 Kin. 15: 25.

God chooses. Deu. 17: 15. 1 Chr. 28: 4—6.

God ordains. Rom. 13: 1.

God anoints. 1 Sam. 16: 12. 2 Sam. 12: 7.

Set up by God. 1 Sam. 12: 13. Dan. 2: 21.

Removed by God. 1 Kin. 11: 11. Dan. 2: 21.

Christ is the Prince of. Rev. 1: 5.

Christ is the King of. Rev. 17: 14.

Reign by direction of Christ. Pro. 8: 15.
Supreme judges of nations. 1 Sam. 8: 5.
Resistance to, is resistance to the ordinance of God. Rom. 13: 2.
Able to enforce their commands. Ecc. 8: 4.
Numerous subjects the honor of. Pro. 14: 28.
Not saved by their armies. Psa. 33: 16.
Dependent on the earth. Ecc. 5: 9.
SHOULD
Fear God. Deu. 17: 19.
Serve Christ. Psa. 2: 10—12.
Keep the law of God. 1 Kin. 2: 3.
Study the Scriptures. Deu. 17: 19.
Promote the interests of the Church. Ezr. 1: 2—4. Ezr. 6: 1—12.
Nourish the Church. Isa. 49: 23.
Rule in the fear of God. 2 Sam. 23: 3.
Maintain the cause of the poor and oppressed. Pro. 31: 8, 9.
Investigate all matters. Pro. 25: 2.
Not pervert judgment. Pro. 31: 5.
Prolong their reign by hating covetousness. Pro. 28: 16.
Throne of, established by righteousness and justice. Pro. 16: 12. Pro. 29: 14.
SPECIALLY WARNED AGAINST
Impurity. Pro. 31: 3.
Lying. Pro. 17: 7.
Hearkening to lies. Pro. 29: 12.
Intemperance. Pro. 31: 4, 5.
The gospel to be preached to. Acts 9: 15. Acts 26: 27, 28.
Without understanding, are oppressors. Pro. 28: 16.
Often reproved by God. 1 Chr. 16: 21.
Judgments upon, when opposed to Christ. Psa. 2: 2, 5, 9.
WHEN GOOD,
Regard God as their strength. Psa. 99: 4.
Speak righteously. Pro. 16: 10.
Love righteous lips. Pro. 16: 13.
Abhor wickedness. Pro. 16: 12.
Discountenance evil. Pro. 20: 8.
Punish the wicked. Pro. 20: 26.
Favor the wise. Pro. 14: 35.
Honor the diligent. Pro. 22: 29.
Befriend the good. Pro. 22: 14.
Are pacified by submission. Pro. 16: 14. Pro. 25: 15.
Evil counsellors should be removed from. 2 Chr. 22: 3, 4, with Pro. 25: 5.
Curse not, even in thought. Exo. 22: 28. Ecc. 10: 20.
Speak no evil of. Job 34: 18. 2 Pet. 2: 10.
Pay tribute to. Mat. 22: 21. Rom. 13: 6, 7
Be not presumptuous before. Pro. 25: 6.
SHOULD BE
Honored. Rom. 13: 7. 1 Pet. 2: 17.
Feared. Pro. 24: 21.
Reverenced. 1 Sam. 24: 8. 1 Kin. 1: 23, 31.
Obeyed. Rom. 13: 1, 5. 1 Pet. 2: 13.
Prayed for. 1 Tim. 2: 1, 2.
Folly of resisting. Pro. 19: 12. Pro. 20: 2.
Punishment for resisting the lawful authority of. Rom. 13: 2.
Guilt and danger of stretching out the hand against. 1 Sam. 26: 9. 2 Sam. 1: 14.
They that walk after the flesh despise. 2 Pet. 2: 10. Jude 8.
Good—Exemplified. *David*, 2 Sam. 8: 15. *Asa*, 1 Kin. 15: 11. *Jehoshaphat*, 1 Kin. 22: 43. *Amaziah, &c.* 2 Kin. 15: 3. *Uzziah, &c.* 2 Kin. 15: 34. *Hezekiah*, 2 Kin. 18: 3. *Josiah*, 2 Kin. 22: 2.

Lamb, The.

The young of the flock. Exo. 12: 5. Eze. 45: 15.
DESCRIBED AS
Patient. Isa. 53: 7.
Playful. Psa. 114: 4, 6.
Exposed to danger from wild beasts. 1 Sam. 17: 34.
The shepherd's care for. Isa. 40: 11.
USED FOR
Food. Deu. 32: 14. 2 Sam. 12: 4.
Clothing. Pro. 27: 26.
Sacrifice. 1 Chr. 29: 21. 2 Chr. 29: 32.
Considered a great delicacy. Amos 6: 4.
OFFERED IN SACRIFICE
Males. Exo. 12: 5.
Females. Num. 6: 14.
While sucking. 1 Sam. 7: 9.
At a year old. Exo. 12: 5. Num. 6: 14.
From the earliest times. Gen. 4: 4. Gen. 22: 7, 8.
Every morning and evening. Exo. 29: 38, 39. Num. 28: 3, 4.
At the passover. Exo. 12: 3, 6, 7.
By the wicked not accepted. Isa. 1: 11. Isa. 66: 3.
Numbers of, given by Josiah to the people for sacrifice. 2 Chr. 35: 7.
The first-born of an ass to be redeemed with. Exo. 13: 13. Exo. 34: 20.
An extensive commerce in. Ezr. 7: 17. Eze. 27: 21.
Tribute often paid in. 2 Kin. 3: 4. Isa. 16: 1.
Covenants confirmed by gift of. Gen. 21: 28—30.
The image of, was the first impression on money. Gen. 33: 19. (*marg.*) Jos. 24: 32. (*marg.*)

ILLUSTRATIVE
- Of purity of Christ. 1 Pet. 1: 19.
- Of Christ as a sacrifice. Jno. 1: 29. Rev. 5: 6.
- Of any thing dear or cherished. 2 Sam. 12: 3, 9.
- Of the Lord's people. Isa. 5: 17. Isa. 11: 6.
- Of weak believers. Isa. 40: 11. Jno. 21: 15.
- (Patience of,) of the patience of Christ. Isa. 53: 7. Acts 8: 32.
- (Among wolves,) of ministers among the ungodly. Luke 10: 3.
- (Deserted and exposed,) of Israel deprived of God's protection. Hos. 4: 16.
- (Brought to slaughter,) of the wicked under judgments. Jer. 51: 40.
- (Consumed in sacrifice,) of complete destruction of the wicked. Psa. 37: 20.

Lamps.

Design of. 2 Pet. 1: 19.
DESCRIBED AS
- Burning. Gen. 15: 17.
- Shining. Jno. 5: 35.

Lighted with oil. Mat. 25: 3, 8.
Oil for, carried in vessels. Mat. 25: 4.
Sometimes supplied with oil from a bowl through pipes. Zec. 4: 2.
Required to be constantly trimmed. Mat. 25: 7.
USED FOR LIGHTING
- The tabernacle. Exo. 25: 37.
- Private apartments. Acts 20: 8.
- Chariots of war by night. Nah. 2: 3, 4.
- Marriage processions. Mat. 25: 1.
- Persons going out at night. Jno. 18: 3.

Often kept lighting all night. Pro. 31: 18.
Placed on a stand to give light to all in the house. Mat. 5: 15.
Illumination of the tents of Arab chiefs by, alluded to. Job 29: 3, 4.
Probable origin of dark lantern. Jud. 7: 16.
ILLUSTRATIVE
- Of the word of God. Psa. 119: 105. Pro. 6: 23.
- Of omniscience of Christ. Dan. 10: 6. Rev. 1: 14.
- Of graces of the Holy Ghost. Rev. 4: 5.
- Of salvation of God. Gen. 15: 17. Isa. 62: 1.
- Of God's guidance. 2 Sam. 22: 29. Psa. 18: 28.
- Of glory of the cherubim. Eze. 1: 13.
- Of spirit of man. Pro. 20: 27.
- Of ministers. Jno. 5: 35.
- Of wise rulers. 2 Sam. 21: 17. (*marg.*)
- Of severe judgments. Rev. 8: 10.
- Of a succession of heirs. 1 Kin. 11: 36. 1 Kin. 15: 4.
- (Put out,) of destruction of the wicked. Job 18: 5, 6. (*marg.*) Job 21: 17. (*marg.*) Pro. 13: 9.
- (Totally quenched,) of complete destruction of those who curse parents. Pro. 20: 20.

Language.

Of all mankind one at first. Gen. 11 1, 6.
CALLED
- Speech. Mar. 14: 70. Acts 14: 11.
- Tongue. Acts 1: 19. Rev. 5: 9.

CONFUSION OF,
- A punishment for presumption, &c. Gen. 11: 2—6.
- Originated the varieties in. Gen. 11: 7.
- Scattered men over the earth. Gen. 11: 8, 9.
- Divided men into separate nations. Gen. 10: 5, 20, 31.

Great variety of, spoken by men. 1 Cor. 14: 10.
Ancient kingdoms often comprehended nations of different. Est. 1: 22. Dan. 3: 4. Dan. 6: 25.
KINDS OF, MENTIONED;
- Hebrew. 2 Kin. 18: 28. Acts 26: 14.
- Chaldee. Dan. 1: 4.
- Syriac. 2 Kin. 18: 26. Ezr. 4: 7.
- Greek. Acts 21: 37.
- Latin. Luke 23: 38.
- Lycaonian. Acts 14: 11.
- Arabic, &c. Acts 2: 11.
- Egyptian. Psa. 81: 5. Psa. 114: 1. Acts 2: 10.

Of some nations difficult. Eze. 3: 5, 6.
The term barbarian applied to those who spoke a strange. 1 Cor. 14: 11.
POWER OF SPEAKING DIFFERENT,
- A gift of the Holy Ghost. 1 Cor. 12: 10.
- Promised. Mar. 16: 17.
- Given on the day of Pentecost. Acts 2: 3, 4.
- Followed receiving the gospel. Acts 10: 44—46.
- Conferred by laying on of the apostles' hands. Acts 8: 17, 18. Acts 19: 6.
- Necessary to spread of the gospel. Acts 2: 7—11.
- A sign to unbelievers. 1 Cor. 14: 22.
- Sometimes abused. 1 Cor. 14: 2—12, 23.

INTERPRETATION OF,
- Antiquity of engaging persons for. Gen. 42: 23.
- A gift of the Holy Ghost. 1 Cor. 12: 10.

Most important in the early church. 1 Cor. 14: 5, 13, 27, 28.
The Jews punished by being given up to people of a strange. Deu. 28: 49. Isa. 28: 11. Jer. 5: 15.

Laver of Brass.

Moses was commanded to make. Exo. 30: 18.
Wisdom given to Bezaleel to make. Exo. 31: 2, 9.
Made of brazen mirrors of the women. Exo. 38: 8.
Was placed in the court between the altar and the tabernacle. Exo. 30: 18. Exo. 40: 7, 30.
Was anointed with holy oil. Exo. 40: 11. Lev. 8: 11.
THE PRIESTS WASHED IN,
Before consecration. Exo. 40: 12.
Before entering the tabernacle. Exo. 30: 19, 20.
Before approaching the altar. Exo. 30: 20.
One made by Solomon for the temple. 1 Kin. 7: 23–26. 2 Kin. 25: 13.
Called the Brazen sea. 2 Kin. 25: 13. Jer. 52: 17.
ILLUSTRATIVE OF
Christ the fountain for sin. Zec. 13: 1. Rev. 1: 5.
Regeneration. Tit. 3: 5, with Eph. 5: 26.

Law of God, The.

Is absolute and perpetual. Mat. 5: 18.
GIVEN
To Adam. Gen. 2: 16, 17, with Rom. 5: 12—14.
To Noah. Gen. 9: 6.
To the Israelites. Exo. 20: 2, &c. Psa. 78: 5.
Through Moses. Exo. 31: 18. Jno. 7: 19.
Through the ministration of angels. Acts 7: 53. Gal. 3: 19. Heb. 2: 2.
DESCRIBED AS
Pure. Psa. 19: 8.
Spiritual. Rom. 7: 14.
Holy, just, and good. Rom. 7: 12.
Exceeding broad. Psa. 119: 96.
Perfect. Psa. 19: 7. Rom. 12: 2.
Truth. Psa. 119: 142.
Not grievous. 1 Jno. 5: 3.
Requires obedience of the heart. Psa. 51: 6. Mat. 5: 28. Mat. 22: 37.
Requires perfect obedience. Deu. 27: 26. Gal. 3: 10. Jas. 2: 10.
Love is the fulfilling of. Rom. 13: 8, 10. Gal. 5: 14. Jas. 2: 8.
It is man's duty to keep. Ecc. 12: 13.
Man, by nature, not in subjection to. Rom. 7: 5. Rom. 8: 7.
Man cannot render perfect obedience to. 1 Kin. 8: 46. Ecc. 7: 20. Rom. 3: 10.
Sin is a transgression of. 1 Jno. 3: 4.
All men have transgressed. Rom. 3: 9, 19.
Man cannot be justified by. Acts 13: 39. Rom. 3: 20, 28. Gal. 2: 16. Gal. 3: 11.
Gives the knowledge of sin. Rom. 3: 20. Rom. 7: 7.
Worketh wrath. Rom. 4: 15.
Conscience testifies to. Rom. 2: 15.
Designed to lead to Christ. Gal. 3: 24.
OBEDIENCE TO
A characteristic of saints. Rev. 12: 17.
A test of love. 1 Jno. 5: 3.
Of prime importance. 1 Cor. 7: 19.
Blessedness of keeping. Psa. 119: 1. Mat. 5: 19. 1 Jno. 3: 22, 24. Rev. 22: 14.
CHRIST
Came to fulfil. Mat. 5: 17.
Magnified. Isa. 42: 21.
Explained. Mat. 7: 12. Mat. 22: 37–40.
The love of, produces peace. Psa. 119: 165.
SAINTS
Freed from the bondage of. Rom. 6: 14. Rom. 7: 4, 6. Gal. 3: 13.
Freed from the curse of. Gal. 3: 13.
Have, written on their hearts. Jer. 31: 33, with Heb. 8: 10.
Love. Psa. 119: 97, 113.
Delight in. Psa. 119: 77. Rom. 7: 22.
Prepare their hearts to seek. Ezr. 7: 10.
Pledge themselves to walk in. Neh. 10: 29.
Keep. Psa. 119: 55.
Pray to understand. Psa. 119: 18.
Pray for power to keep. Psa. 119: 34.
Should remember. Mal. 4: 4.
Should make the subject of their conversation. Exo. 13: 9.
Lament over the violation of, by others. Psa. 119: 136.
THE WICKED
Despise. Amos 2: 4.
Forget. Hos. 4: 6.
Forsake. 2 Chr. 12: 1. Jer. 9: 13.
Refuse to hear. Isa. 30: 9. Jer. 6: 19.
Refuse to walk in. Psa. 78: 10.
Cast away. Isa. 5: 24.
Is the rule of life to saints. 1 Cor. 9: 21. Gal. 5: 13, 14.
Is the rule of the judgment. Rom. 2: 12.
To be used lawfully. 1 Tim. 1: 8.
Established by faith. Rom. 3: 31.
Punishment for disobeying. Neh. 9: 26, 27. Isa. 65: 11—13. Jer. 9: 13–16.

Law of Moses, The.

Is the law of God. Lev. 26: 46.
GIVEN
  In the desert. Eze. 20: 10, 11.
  At Horeb. Deu. 4:10,15. Deu. 5:2.
  From the Mount Sinai. Exo. 19: 11, 20.
  By disposition of angels. Acts 7: 53.
  Through Moses as mediator. Deu. 5:5, 27, 28. Jno. 1: 17. Gal. 3: 19.
  To the Jews. Lev. 26: 46. Psa. 78: 5.
  After the exodus. Deu. 4:45. Psa. 81: 4, 5.
  To no other nation. Deu. 4: 8. Psa. 147: 20.
None to approach the Mount while God gave. Exo. 19: 13, 21—24. Heb. 12: 20.
Remarkable phenomena connected with, at giving of. Exo. 19: 16—19.
Terror of Israel at receiving. Exo. 19: 16. Exo. 20: 18—20. Deu. 5: 5, 23—25.
Additions made to, in the plains of Moab by Jordan. Num. 36: 13.
CALLED
  A fiery law. Deu. 33: 2.
  Word spoken by angels. Heb. 2: 2.
  Ministration of death. 2 Cor. 3: 7.
  Ministration of condemnation. 2 Cor. 3: 9.
  Lively oracles. Acts 7: 38.
  Royal law. Jas. 2: 8.
  Book of the law. Deu. 30: 10. Jos. 1: 8.
  Book of Moses. 2 Chr. 25: 4. 2 Chr. 35: 12.
Rehearsed by Moses. Deu. 1: 1—3.
Entire of, written in a book. Deu. 31: 9.
Book of, laid up in the sanctuary. Deu. 31: 26..
Tables of, laid up in the ark. Deu. 10: 5.
DIVIDED INTO
  Moral, embodied in the ten commandments. Deu. 5: 22. Deu. 10: 4.
  Ceremonial, relating to manner of worshipping God. Lev. 7: 37, 38. Heb. 9: 1—7.
  Civil, relating to administration of justice. Deu. 17: 9—11. Acts 23: 3. Acts 24: 6.
  A covenant of works to the Jews as a nation. Deu. 28: 1, 15, with Jer. 31: 32.
TAUGHT THE JEWS
  To love and fear God. Deu. 6: 5. Deu. 10: 12, 13. Mat. 22: 36, 38.
  To love their neighbor. Lev. 19: 18. Mat. 22: 39.
  Strict justice and impartiality. Lev. 19: 35, 36.
  All punishments awarded according to. Jno. 8: 5. Jno. 19: 7. Heb. 10: 28.
ALL ISRAELITES REQUIRED
  To know. Exo. 18: 16.
  To observe. Deu. 4: 6. Deu. 6: 2.
  To lay up, in their hearts. Deu. 6: 6. Deu. 11: 18.
  To remember. Mal. 4: 4.
  To teach their children. Deu. 6: 7. Deu. 11: 19.
Kings to write out and study. Deu. 17: 18, 19.
Good kings enforced. 2 Kin. 23: 24, 25. 2 Chr. 31: 21.
Priests and Levites to teach. Deu. 33: 8—10. Neh. 8: 7. Mal. 2: 7.
The scribes were learned in, and expounded. Ezr. 7: 6. Mat. 23: 2.
Public instruction given to youth in. Luke 2: 46. Acts 22: 3.
PUBLICLY READ
  At the feast of tabernacles in the sabbatical year. Deu. 31: 10—13.
  By Joshua. Jos. 8: 34, 35.
  By Ezra. Neh. 8: 2, 3.
  In the synagogues every Sabbath day. Acts 13: 15. Acts 15: 21.
A means of national reformation. 2 Chr. 34: 19—21. Neh. 8: 13—18.
A shadow of good things to come. Heb. 10: 1.
Could not give righteousness and life. Gal. 3: 21, with Rom. 8: 3, 4. Heb. 10: 1.
A schoolmaster to lead to Christ. Gal. 3: 24.
CHRIST
  Made under. Gal. 4: 4.
  Circumcised according to. Luke 2: 21. Rom. 15: 8.
  Came not to destroy but to fulfil. Mat. 5: 17, 18.
  Attended all feasts of. Jno. 2: 23. Jno. 7: 2, 10, 37.
  Fulfilled all precepts of. Psa. 40: 7, 8.
  Fulfilled all types and shadows of. Heb. 9: 8, 11—14. Heb. 10: 1, 11—14.
  Magnified and made honorable. Isa. 42: 21.
  Bore the curse of. Deu. 21: 23, with Gal. 3: 13.
  Abrogated, as a covenant of works. Rom. 7: 4.
Was not the manifestation of the grace of God. Jno. 1: 17. *See* Rom. 8: 3, 4.
Could not disannul the covenant of grace made in Christ. Gal. 3: 17.
Primitive Jewish converts would have all Christians observe. Acts 15: 1.
THE JEWS
  Zealous for. Jno. 9: 28, 29. Acts 21: 20.
  Held those ignorant of, accursed. Jno. 7: 49.
  From regard to, rejected Christ. Rom. 9: 31—33.

Accused Christ of breaking. Jno. 19: 7.
Accused Christians of speaking. Acts 6: 11—14. Acts 21: 28.
Broke it themselves. Jno. 7: 19.
Dishonored God by breaking. Rom. 2: 23.
Shall be judged by. Jno. 5: 45. Rom. 2: 12.
Was a burdensome yoke. Acts 15: 10.
Darkness, &c. at giving of, illustrative of obscurity of Mosaic dispensation. Heb. 12: 18–24.

Leaven.

Used in making bread. Hos. 7: 4.
Diffusive properties of. 1 Cor. 5: 6.
FORBIDDEN
During the feast of passover. Exo. 12: 15—20.
To be offered with blood. Exo. 34: 25.
To be offered, &c. with meat-offerings which were burned. Lev. 2: 11. Lev. 10: 12.
Used with thank offerings. Lev. 7: 13. Amos 4: 5.
First fruits of wheat offered with. Lev. 23: 17.
ILLUSTRATIVE OF
The rapid spread of the gospel. Mat. 13: 33. Luke 13: 21.
Doctrines of Pharisees, &c. Mat. 16: 6, 12.
Ungodly professors. 1 Cor. 5: 6, 7.
False teachers. Gal. 5: 8, 9.
Malice and wickedness. 1 Cor. 5: 8.

Lebanon.

Bounded the land of Canaan on the north. Deu. 1: 7. Deu. 11: 24.
Given to Israel. Jos. 13: 5, 6.
CELEBRATED FOR
Cedars. Psa. 29: 5. Psa. 92: 12. Isa. 14: 8.
Flowers. Nah. 1: 4.
Fragrance. So. of Sol. 4: 11.
Fragrance of its wines. Hos. 14: 7.
Glorious appearance. Isa. 35: 2.
Great part of, not conquered by the Israelities. Jos. 13: 2, 5. Jud. 3: 1—4.
CALLED
The mountains. 2 Chr. 2: 2.
Mount Lebanon. Jud. 3: 3.
That goodly mountain. Deu. 3: 25.
Lofty tops of, covered with snow. Jer. 18: 14.
Part of, barren. Isa. 29: 17.
Forests of, infested with wild beasts. So. of Sol. 4: 8. Isa. 40: 16. Hab. 2: 17.
Many streams came from. So. of Sol. 4: 15.
Formerly inhabited by the Hivites. Jud. 3: 3.
Moses anxious to behold. Deu. 3: 25.
FURNISHED
Wood for Solomon's temple. 1 Kin. 5: 5, 6.
Stones for Solomon's temple. 1 Kin. 5: 14, 18.
Wood for second temple. Ezr. 3: 7.
SOLOMON BUILT
The house of the forest of. 1 Kin. 7: 2.
Storehouses in. 1 Kin. 9: 19.
Difficulties of passing, surmounted by Assyrian army. 2 Kin. 19: 23.
ILLUSTRATIVE
Of great and powerful monarchs. Isa. 10: 24, 34.
Of the Gentile world. Isa. 29: 17.
Of the Jewish nation. Jer. 22: 6, 23. Heb. 2: 17.
Of the temple. Zec. 11: 1.
(Glory of,) of the glory of the church. Isa. 35: 2. Isa. 60: 13.
(Fragrance of,) of the graces of the church. So. of Sol. 4: 11. Hos. 14: 6, 7.
(Shaking of its forest,) of prodigious growth of the church. Psa. 72: 16.
(Mourning of,) of deep affliction. Eze. 31: 15.

Leopard.

Inhabited mountains of Canaan. So. of Sol. 4: 8.
DESCRIBED AS
Spotted. Jer. 13: 23.
Fierce and cruel. Jer. 5: 6.
Swift. Hab. 1: 8.
Lies in wait for its prey. Jer. 5: 6. Hos. 13: 7.
ILLUSTRATIVE
Of God in His judgments. Hos. 13: 7.
Of the Macedonian empire. Dan. 7: 6.
Of antichrist. Rev. 13: 2.
(Tamed,) of the wicked subdued by the gospel. Isa. 11: 6.

Leprosy.

A common disease among the Jews. Luke 4: 27.
INFECTED
Men. Luke 17: 12.
Women. Num. 12: 10.
Houses. Lev. 14: 34.
Garments. Lev. 13: 47.
An incurable disease. 2 Kin. 5: 7.
Often sent as a punishment for sin. Num. 12: 9, 10. 2 Chr. 26: 19.
Often hereditary. 2 Sam. 3: 29. 2 Kin. 5: 27.
PARTS AFFECTED BY;
The hand. Exo. 4: 6.
The head. Lev. 13: 44.

The forehead. 2 Chr. 26:19.
The beard. Lev. 13:30.
The whole body. Luke 5:12.
Often began with a bright red spot. Lev. 13:2, 24.
Turned the skin white. Exo. 4:6. 2 Kin. 5:27.
Turned the hair white or yellow. Lev. 13:3, 10, 30.
THE PRIESTS
Judges and directors in cases of. Deu. 24:8.
Examined persons suspected of. Lev. 13:2, 9.
Shut up persons suspected of, seven days. Lev. 13:4.
Had rules for distinguishing. Lev. 13:5—44.
Examined all persons healed of. Lev. 14:2. Mat. 8:4. Luke 17:14.
Ceremonies at cleansing of. Lev. 14:3—32.
THOSE AFFLICTED WITH,
Ceremonially unclean. Lev. 13:8, 11, 22, 44.
Separated from intercourse with others. Num. 5:2. Num. 12:14, 15.
Associated together. 2 Kin. 7:3. Luke 17:12.
Dwelt in a separate house. 2 Kin. 15:5.
Cut off from God's house. 2 Chr. 26:21.
Excluded from priest's office. Lev. 22:2—4.
To have their heads bare, clothes rent, and lip covered. Lev. 13:45.
To cry unclean when approached. Lev. 13:45.
Less inveterate when it covered the whole body. Lev. 13:13.
Power of God manifested in curing. Num. 12:13, 14. 2 Kin. 5:8—14.
Power of Christ manifested in curing. Mat. 8:3. Luke 5:13. Luke 17:13, 14.
Christ gave power to heal. Mat. 10:8.
GARMENTS
Suspected of, shown to priest. Lev. 13:49.
Suspected of, shut up seven days. Lev. 13:50.
Infected with, to have the piece first torn out. Lev. 13:56.
Incurably infected with, burned. Lev. 13:51, 52.
Suspected of, but not having, washed and pronounced clean. Lev. 13:53, 54, 58, 59.
HOUSES
Suspected of, reported to priest. Lev. 14:35.
Suspected of, emptied. Lev. 14:36.
Suspected of, inspected by priest. Lev. 14:37.
Suspected of, shut up seven days. Lev. 14:38.
To have the part infected with, first removed, and the rest scraped, &c. Lev. 14:39, 42.
Incurably infected with, pulled down and removed. Lev. 14:43—45.
Infected with, communicated uncleanness to every one who entered them. Lev. 14:46, 47.
Suspected of, but not infected, pronounced clean. Lev. 14:48.
Ceremonies at cleansing of. Lev. 14:49—53.

Leviathan.

Created by God. Psa. 104:26.
Nature and habits of. Job 41 ch.
God's power, exhibited in destroying. Psa. 74:14.
ILLUSTRATIVE OF
Powerful and cruel kings. Isa. 27:1.
Power and severity of God. Job 41:10.

Levites, The.

Descended from Jacob's third son. Gen. 29:34. Heb. 7:9, 10.
Prophecies respecting. Gen. 49:5, 7. Deu. 33:8—11.
Originally consisted of three families or divisions. Num. 3:17. 1 Chr. 6:16—48.
Not numbered with Israel. Num. 1:47—49.
Numbered separately after the people from a month old. Num. 3:14—16, 39.
FAMILIES, AS NUMBERED,
Of Gershom. Num. 3:18, 21, 22.
Of Kohath. Num. 3:19, 27, 28.
Of Merari. Num. 3:20, 33, 34.
Chosen by God for service of the sanctuary. 1 Chr. 15:2, with Num. 3:6.
Were consecrated. Num. 8:6, 14.
Taken instead of the first-born of Israel. Num. 3:12, 13, 40—45. Num. 8:16—18.
Zeal against idolatry a cause of their appointment. Exo. 32:26—28, with Deu. 33:9, 10.
Entered on their service at twenty-five years of age. Num. 8:24.
Numbered as ministers at thirty. Num. 4:3, 23, &c.
Superannuated at fifty. Num. 8:25.
When superannuated, required to perform the less arduous duties. Num. 8:26.
CEREMONIES AT CONSECRATION OF;
Cleansing and purifying. Num. 8:7.
Making a sin-offering for. Num. 8:8, 12.

Elders of Israel laying their hands on them. Num. 8: 9, 10.
Presenting them to God as an offering for the people. Num. 8: 11, 15.
Setting before the priests and presenting them as their offering to God. Num. 8: 13.
Given to Aaron and sons. Num. 3: 9. Num. 8: 19.
Encamped round the tabernacle. Num. 1: 50, 52, 53. Num. 3: 23, 29, 35.
Marched in the centre of Israel. Num. 2: 17.
SERVICES OF;
Ministering to the Lord. Deu. 10: 8.
Ministering to priests. Num. 3: 6, 7. Num. 18: 2.
Ministering to the people. 2 Chr. 35: 3.
Keeping the charge of the sanctuary. Num. 18: 3. 1 Chr. 23: 32.
Keeping sacred instruments and vessels. Num. 3: 8. 1 Chr. 9: 28, 29.
Keeping sacred oil, flour, &c. 1 Chr. 9: 29, 30.
Keeping sacred treasures. 1 Chr. 26: 20.
Taking charge of the tithes, offerings, &c. 2 Chr. 31: 11—19. Neh. 12: 44.
Doing the service of tabernacle. Num. 8: 19, 22.
Taking down, putting up, and carrying the tabernacle, &c. Num. 1: 50, 51. Num. 4: 5—33.
Preparing the sacrifices for the priests. 1 Chr. 23: 31. 2 Chr. 35: 11.
Preparing the show bread. 1 Chr. 9: 31, 32. 1 Chr. 23: 29.
Purifying the holy things. 1 Chr. 23: 28.
Regulating weights and measures. 1 Chr. 23: 29.
Teaching the people. 2 Chr. 17: 8, 9. 2 Chr. 30: 22. 2 Chr. 35: 3. Neh. 8: 7.
Blessing the people. Deu. 10: 8.
Keeping the gates of the temple. 1 Chr. 9: 17—26. 1 Chr. 23: 5. 2 Chr. 35: 15. Neh. 12: 25.
Conducting the sacred music. 1 Chr. 23: 5—30. 2 Chr. 5: 12, 13. Neh. 12: 24, 27—43.
Singing praises before the army. 2 Chr. 20: 21, 22.
Judging and deciding in controversies. Deu. 17: 9. 1 Chr. 23: 4. 2 Chr. 19: 8.
Guarding king's person and house in time of danger. 2 Kin. 11: 5—9. 2 Chr. 23: 5—7.
Had no inheritance in Israel. Deu. 10: 9. Jos. 13: 33. Jos. 14: 3.
The Jews to be kind and benevolent to. Deu. 12: 12, 18, 19. Deu. 14: 29. Deu. 16: 11, 14.
Eight and forty cities with extensive suburbs, appointed for. Num. 35: 2—8.
The tithes given to, for their support. Num. 18: 21, 24. 2 Chr. 31: 4, 5. Neh. 12: 44, 45. *See* Heb. 7: 5.
Bound to give a tenth of their tithes to the priests. Num. 18: 26—32.
Had a part of the offerings. Deu. 18: 1, 2.
DAVID
Numbered them first from thirty years old. 1 Chr. 23: 2, 3.
Divided them into four classes. 1 Chr. 23: 4—6.
By his last words had them numbered from twenty years old. 1 Chr. 23: 24, 27.
Made them serve from twenty on account of the lightness of their duties. 1 Chr. 23: 26, 28—32.
Subdivided them into twenty-four courses. 1 Chr. 23: 6, with 1 Chr. 25: 8—31.
Made them attend in courses. 2 Chr. 8: 14. 2 Chr. 31: 17.
Served in courses after captivity. Ezr. 6: 18.
Had chiefs or officers over them. Num. 3: 24, 30, 35. 1 Chr. 15: 4—10. 2 Chr. 35: 9. Ezr. 8: 29.
Were all under control of the high priest's deputy. Num. 3: 32. 1 Chr. 9: 20.
While in attendance lodged around the temple. 1 Chr. 9: 27.
Punished with death for encroaching on the priestly office. Num. 18: 3.
Punishment of Korah and others of, for offering incense. Num. 16: 1—35.

Liberality.

Pleasing to God. 2 Cor. 9: 7. Heb. 13: 16.
God never forgets. Heb. 6: 10.
Christ set an example of. 2 Cor. 8: 9.
Characteristic of saints. Psa. 112: 9. Isa. 32: 8.
Unprofitable, without love. 1 Cor. 13: 3.
SHOULD BE EXERCISED
In the service of God. Exo. 35: 21—29.
Toward saints. Rom. 12: 13. Gal. 6: 10.
Toward servants. Deu. 15: 12—14.
Toward the poor. Deu. 15: 11. Isa. 58: 7.
Toward strangers. Lev. 25: 35.
Toward enemies. Pro. 25: 21.
Toward all men. Gal. 6: 10.
In lending to those in want. Mat. 5: 42.
In giving alms. Luke 12: 33.
In relieving the destitute. Isa. 58: 7.

In forwarding missions. Phi. 4:14—16.
In rendering personal services. Phi. 2:30.
Without ostentation. Mat. 6:1—3.
With simplicity. Rom. 12:8.
According to ability. Deu. 16:10, 17. 1 Cor. 16:2.
Willingly. Exo. 25:2. 2 Cor. 8:12.
Abundantly. 2 Cor. 8:7. 2 Cor. 9:11—13.
Exercise of, provokes others to. 2 Cor. 9:2.
Labor to be enabled to exercise. Acts 20:35. Eph. 4:28.
WANT OF,
Brings many a curse. Pro. 28:27.
A proof of not loving God. 1 Jno. 3:17.
A proof of not having faith. Jas. 2:14—16.
Blessings connected with. Psa. 41:1. Pro. 22:9. Acts 20:35.
Promises to. Psa. 112:9. Pro. 11:25. Pro. 28:27. Ecc. 11:1, 2. Isa. 58:10.
Exhortations to. Luke 3:11. Luke 11:41. Acts 20:35. 1 Cor. 16:1. 1 Tim. 6:17, 18.
Exemplified. *Princes of Israel*, Num. 7:2. *Boaz*, Ruth 2:16. *David*, 2 Sam. 9:7, 10. *Barzillai, &c.* 2 Sam. 17:28. *Araunah*, 2 Sam. 24:22. *Shunammite*, 2 Kin. 4:8, 10. *Judah*, 2 Chr. 24:10, 11. *Nehemiah*, Neh. 7:70. *Jews*, Neh. 7:71, 72. *Job*, Job 29:15, 16. *Nebuzaradan*, Jer. 40:4, 5. *Joanna, &c.* Luke 8:3. *Zaccheus*, Luke 19:8. *Primitive Christians*, Acts 2:45. *Barnabas*, Acts 4:36, 37. *Dorcas*, Acts 9:36. *Cornelius*, Acts 16:2. *Church of Antioch*, Acts 11:29, 30. *Lydia*, Acts 16:15. *Paul*, Acts 20:34. *Stephanas, &c.* 1 Cor. 16:17.
Extraordinary—Exemplified. *Israelites*, Exo. 36:5. *Poor widow*, Mar. 12:42—44. *Churches of Macedonia*, 2 Cor. 8:1—5.

Liberty, Christian.

Foretold. Isa. 42:7. Isa. 61:1.
CONFERRED
By God. Col. 1:13.
By Christ. Gal. 4:3—5. Gal. 5:1.
By the Holy Ghost. Rom. 8:15. 2 Cor. 3:17.
Through the gospel. Jno. 8:32.
Confirmed by Christ. Jno. 8:36.
Proclaimed by Christ. Isa. 61:1. Luke 4:18.
The service of Christ is. 1 Cor. 7:22.
IS FREEDOM FROM
The law. Rom. 7:6. Rom. 8:2.
The curse of the law. Gal. 3:13.
The fear of death. Heb. 2:15.
Sin. Rom. 6:7, 18.
Corruption. Rom. 8:21.
Bondage of man. 1 Cor. 9:19.
Jewish ordinances. Gal. 4:3. Col. 2:20.
Called the glorious liberty of the children of God. Rom. 8:21.
Saints are called to. Gal. 5:13.
SAINTS SHOULD
Praise God for. Psa. 116:16, 17.
Assert. 1 Cor. 10:29.
Walk in. Psa. 119:45.
Stand fast in. Gal. 2:5. Gal. 5:1.
Not abuse. Gal. 5:13. 1 Pet. 2:16.
Not offend others by. 1 Cor. 8:9. 1 Cor. 10:29, 32.
The gospel is the law of. Jas. 1:25. Jas. 2:12.
FALSE TEACHERS
Promise, to others. 2 Pet. 2:19.
Abuse. Jude 4.
Try to destroy. Gal. 2:4.
The wicked, devoid of. Jno. 8:34, with Rom. 6:20.
Typified. Lev. 25:10—17. Gal. 4:22—26, 31.

Life, Eternal.

Christ is. 1 Jno. 1:2. 1 Jno. 5:20.
Revealed by Christ. Jno. 6:68. 2 Tim. 1:10.
To know God and Christ is. Jno. 17:3.
GIVEN
By God. Psa. 133:3. Rom. 6:23.
By Christ. Jno. 6:27. Jno. 10:28.
In Christ. 1 Jno. 5:11.
Through Christ. Rom. 5:21. Rom. 6:23.
To all given to Christ. Jno. 17:2.
To those who believe in God. Jno. 5:24.
To those who believe in Christ. Jno. 3:15, 16. Jno. 6:40, 47.
To those who hate life for Christ. Jno. 12:25.
In answer to prayer. Psa. 21:4.
Revealed in the Scriptures. Jno. 5:39.
RESULTS FROM
Drinking the water of life. Jno. 4:14.
Eating the bread of life. Jno. 6:50—58.
Eating of the tree of life. Rev. 2:7.
They who are ordained to, believe the gospel. Acts 13:48.
SAINTS
Have promises of. 1 Tim. 4:8. 2 Tim. 1:1. Tit. 1:2. 1 Jno. 2:25.
Have hope of. Tit. 1:2. Tit. 3:7.
May have assurance of. 2 Cor. 5:1. 1 Jno. 5:13.
Shall reap, through the Spirit. Gal. 6:8.
Shall inherit. Mat. 19:29.
Look for the mercy of God unto. Jude 21.
Should lay hold of. 1 Tim. 6:12, 19.
Are preserved unto. Jno. 10:28, 29.

Shall rise unto. Dan. 12: 2. Jno. 5: 29.
Shall go into. Mat. 25: 46.
Shall reign in. Dan. 7: 18. Rom. 5: 17.
The self-righteous think to inherit, by works. Mar. 10: 17.
Cannot be inherited by works. Rom. 2: 7, with Rom. 3: 10—19.
THE WICKED
Have not. 1 Jno. 3: 15.
Judge themselves unworthy of. Acts 13: 46.
Exhortation to seek. Jno. 6: 27.

Life, Natural.

God is the Author of. Gen. 2: 7. Acts 17: 28.
God preserves. Psa. 36: 6. Psa. 66: 9.
Is in the hand of God. Job 12: 10. Dan. 5: 23.
Forfeited by sin. Gen. 2: 17. Gen. 3: 17—19.
Of others, not to be taken away. Exo. 20: 13.
DESCRIBED AS
Vain. Ecc. 6: 12.
Limited. Job 7: 1. Job 14: 5.
Short. Job 14: 1. Psa. 89: 47.
Uncertain. Jas. 4: 13—15.
Full of trouble. Job 14: 1.
God's loving-kindness better than. Psa. 63: 3.
The value of. Job 2: 4. Mat. 6: 25.
Preserved by discretion. Pro. 13: 3.
Sometimes prolonged, in answer to prayer. Isa. 38: 2—5. Jas. 5: 15.
Obedience to God, tends to prolong. Deu. 30: 20.
Obedience to parents, tends to prolong. Exo. 20: 12. Pro. 4: 10.
Cares and pleasures of, dangerous. Luke 8: 14. Luke 21: 34. 2 Tim. 2: 4.
Saints have true enjoyment of. Psa. 128: 2. 1 Tim. 4: 8.
Of saints, specially protected by God. Job 2: 6. Acts 18: 10. 1 Pet. 3: 13.
Of the wicked, not specially protected by God. Job 36: 6. Psa. 78: 50.
The wicked have their portion of good, during. Psa. 17: 14. Luke 6: 24. Luke 16: 25.
SHOULD BE SPENT IN
The fear of God. 1 Pet. 1: 17.
The service of God. Luke 1: 75.
Living unto God. Rom. 14: 8. Phi. 1: 21.
Peace. Rom. 12: 18. 1 Tim. 2: 2.
Doing good. Ecc. 3: 12.
Should be taken all due care of. Mat. 10: 23. Acts 27: 34.
Should be laid down, if necessary, for Christ. Mat. 10: 39. Luke 14: 26. Acts 20: 24.
Should be laid down, if necessary, for the brethren. Rom. 16: 4. 1 Jno. 3: 16.
BE THANKFUL FOR
The preservation of. Psa. 103: 4. Jno. 2: 6.
The supply of its wants. Gen. 48: 15.
The dissatisfied despise. Ecc. 2: 17.
We know not what is good for us in. Ecc. 6: 12.
Be not over-anxious to provide for its wants. Mat. 6: 25.
The enjoyment of, consists not in abundance of possessions. Luke 12: 15.
IS COMPARED TO
An eagle hasting to the prey. Job 9: 26.
A pilgrimage. Gen. 47: 9.
A tale told. Psa. 90: 9.
A swift post. Job 9: 25.
A swift ship. Job 9: 26.
A hand-breadth. Psa. 39: 5.
A shepherd's tent removed. Isa. 38: 18.
A dream. Psa. 73: 20.
A sleep. Psa. 90: 5.
A vapor. Jas. 4: 14.
A shadow. Ecc. 6: 12.
A thread cut by the weaver. Isa. 38: 12.
A weaver's shuttle. Job 7: 6.
A flower. Job 14: 2.
Grass. 1 Pet. 1: 24.
Water spilt on the ground. 2 Sam. 14: 14.
Wind. Job 7: 7.
Shortness of, should lead to spiritual improvement. Deu. 32: 29. Psa. 90: 12.
Sometimes judicially shortened. 1 Sam. 2: 32, 33. Job 36: 14.
Miraculously restored by Christ. Mat. 9: 18, 25. Luke 7: 15, 22. Jno. 11: 43.

Life, Spiritual.

God is the Author of. Psa. 36: 9. Col. 2: 13.
Christ is the Author of. Jno. 5: 21, 25. Jno. 6: 33, 51—53. Jno. 14: 6. 1 Jno. 4: 9.
The Holy Ghost is the Author of. Eze. 37: 14, with Rom. 8: 9—13.
The word of God is the instrument of. Isa. 55: 3. 2 Cor. 3: 6. 1 Pet. 4: 6.
Is hidden with Christ. Col. 3: 3.
The fear of God is. Pro. 14: 27. Pro. 19: 23.
Spiritual-mindedness is. Rom. 8: 6.
IS MAINTAINED BY
Christ. Jno. 6: 57. 1 Cor. 10: 3, 4.
Faith. Gal. 2: 20.
The word of God. Deu. 8: 3, with Mat. 4: 4.

Prayer. Psa. 69:32.
Has its origin in the new-birth. Jno. 3:3—8.
Has its infancy. Luke 10:21. 1 Cor. 3:1, 2. 1 Jno. 2:12.
Has its youth. 1 Jno. 2:13, 14.
Has its maturity. Eph. 4:13. 1 Jno. 2:13, 14.
IS DESCRIBED AS
A life unto God. Rom. 6:11. Gal. 2:19.
Newness of life. Rom. 6:4.
Living in the Spirit. Gal. 5:25.
Revived by God. Psa. 85:6. Hos. 6:2.
Evidenced by love to the brethren. 1 Jno. 3:14.
All saints have. Eph. 2:1, 5. Col. 2:13.
Should animate the services of saints. Rom. 12:1. 1 Cor. 14:15.
Saints praise God for. Psa. 119:175.
Seek to grow in. Eph. 4:15. 1 Pet. 2:2.
Pray for the increase of. Psa. 119:25. Psa. 143:11.
The wicked alienated from. Eph. 4:18.
Lovers of pleasure destitute of. 1 Tim. 5:6.
Hypocrites destitute of. Jude 12. Rev. 3:1.
Illustrated. Eze. 37:9, 10. Luke 15:24.

Light.

God the only source of. Jas. 1:17.
Created by God. Gen. 1:3. Isa. 45:7.
Separated from darkness. Gen. 1:4.
Sun, moon, and stars appointed to communicate to the earth. Gen. 1:14—17. Jer. 31:35.
DIVIDED INTO
Natural. Job 24:14. Isa. 5:30.
Extraordinary or miraculous. Exo. 14:20. Psa. 78:14. Acts 9:3. Acts 12:7.
Artificial. Jer. 25:10. Acts. 16:29.
Communicated to the body through the eye. Pro. 15:30. Mat. 6:22.
DESCRIBED AS
White and pure. Mat. 17:2.
Bright. Job 37:21.
Shining. 2 Sam. 23:4. Job 41:18.
Diffusive. Job 25:3, with Job 36:30.
Useful and precious. Ecc. 2:13.
Agreeable. Ecc. 11:7.
Manifesting objects. Jno. 3:20, 21. Eph. 5:13.
The theory of, beyond man's comprehension. Job 38:19, 20, 24.
ILLUSTRATIVE OF
Glory of God. Psa. 104:2, with 1 Tim. 6:16.
Purity of God. 1 Jno. 1:5.
Wisdom of God. Dan. 2:22.
Guidance of God. Psa. 27:1. Psa. 36:9.
Favor of God. Psa. 4:6. Isa. 2:5.
Christ the source of all wisdom. Luke 2:32. Jno. 1:4, 9. Jno. 8:12. Jno. 12:46.
Glory of Christ. Acts 9:3, 5. Acts 26:13.
Purity of Christ. Mat. 17:2.
Word of God. Psa. 119:105, 130. 2 Pet. 1:19.
Gospel. 2 Cor. 4:4. 1 Pet. 2:9.
Ministers. Mat. 5:14. Jno. 5:35.
Wise rulers. 2 Sam. 21:17. 2 Sam. 23:4.
The soul of man. Job 18:5, 6.
Saints. Luke 16:8. Eph. 5:8. Phi. 2:15.
Future glory of saints. Psa. 97:11. Col. 1:12.
The path of the just. Pro. 4:18.
The glory of the church. Isa. 60:1—3.
Whatever makes manifest. Jno. 3:21. Eph. 5:13.

Lion, The.

Canaan infested by. 2 Kin. 17:25, 26.
DESCRIBED AS
Superior in strength. Jud. 14:18. Pro. 30:30.
Active. Deu. 33:22.
Courageous. 2 Sam. 17:10.
Fearless even of man. Isa. 31:4. Nah. 2:11.
Fierce. Job 10:16. Job 28:8.
Voracious. Psa. 17:12.
Majestic in movement. Pro. 30:29, 30.
Greatness of its teeth alluded to. Psa. 58:6. Joel 1:6.
God's power exhibited in restraining. 1 Kin. 13:28. Dan. 6:22, 27.
God provides for. Job 38:39. Psa. 104:21, 28.
Lurketh for its prey. Psa. 10:9.
Roars when seeking prey. Psa. 104:21. Isa. 31:4.
Rends its prey. Deu. 33:20. Psa. 7:2.
Often carries its prey to its den. Nah. 2:12.
Conceals itself by day. Psa. 104:22.
Often perishes for lack of food. Job 4:11.
INHABITS
Forests. Jer. 5:6.
Thickets. Jer. 4:7.
Mountains. So. of Sol. 4:8.
Deserts. Isa. 30:6.
Attacks the sheepfolds. 1 Sam. 17:34. Amos 3:12. Mic. 5:8.
Attacks and destroys men. 1 Kin. 13:24. 1 Kin. 20:36.
Universal terror caused by roaring of. Jer. 2:15. Amos 3:8.

Criminals often thrown to. Dan. 6: 7, 16. 24.
Hunting of, alluded to. Job 10: 16.
SLAIN BY
Samson. Jud. 14: 5, 6.
David. 1 Sam. 17: 35, 36.
Benaiah. 2 Sam. 23: 20.
A swarm of bees found in the carcass of, by Samson. Jud. 14: 8.
Disobedient prophet slain by. 1 Kin. 13: 24, 26.
ILLUSTRATIVE
Of Israel. Num. 24: 9.
Of the tribe of Judah. Gen. 49: 9.
Of the tribe of Gad. Deu. 33: 20.
Of Christ. Rev. 5: 5.
Of God in protecting His church. Isa. 31: 4.
Of God in executing judgments. Isa. 38: 13. Lam. 3: 10. Hos. 5: 14. Hos. 13: 8.
Of boldness of saints. Pro. 28: 1.
Of brave men. 2 Sam. 1: 23. 2 Sam. 23: 20.
Of cruel and powerful enemies. Isa. 5: 29. Jer. 49: 19. Jer. 51: 38.
Of persecutors. Psa. 22: 13. 2 Tim. 4: 17.
Of the devil. 1 Pet. 5: 8.
Of imaginary fears of the slothful. Pro. 22: 13. Pro. 26: 13.
(Tamed,) of the natural man subdued by grace. Isa. 11: 7. Isa. 65: 25.
(Roaring of,) of a king's wrath. Pro. 19: 12. Pro. 20: 2.

Locust, The.

A small insect. Pro. 30: 24, 27.
Clean and fit for food Lev. 11: 21, 22.
DESCRIBED AS
Wise. Pro. 30: 24, 27.
Voracious. Exo. 10: 15.
Rapid in movement. Isa. 33: 4.
Like to horses prepared for battle. Joel 2: 4, with Rev. 9: 7.
Carried every way by the wind. Exo. 10: 13, 19.
Immensely numerous. Psa. 105: 34. Nah. 3: 15.
Flies in bands and with order. Pro. 30: 27.
One of the plagues of Egypt. Exo. 10: 4—15.
THE JEWS
Used, as food. Mat. 3: 4.
Threatened with, as a punishment for sin. Deu. 28: 38, 42.
Deprecated the plague of. 1 Kin. 8: 37, 38.
Often plagued by. Joel 1: 4. Joel 2: 25.
Promised deliverance from the plague of, on humiliation, &c. 2 Chr. 7: 13, 14.
ILLUSTRATIVE
Of destructive enemies. Joel 1: 6, 7. Joel 2: 2—9.
Of false teachers of the apostacy. Rev. 9: 3.
Of ungodly rulers. Nah. 3: 17.
(Destruction of,) of destruction of God's enemies. Nah. 3: 15.

Long-suffering of God, The.

Is part of His character. Exo. 34: 6. Num. 14: 18. Psa. 86: 15.
Salvation, the object of. 2 Pet. 3: 15.
Through Christ's intercession. Luke 13: 8.
Should lead to repentance. Rom. 2: 4. 2 Pet. 3: 9.
An encouragement to repent. Joel 2: 13.
Exhibited in forgiving sins. Rom. 3: 25.
EXERCISED TOWARD
His people. Isa. 30: 18. Eze. 20: 17.
The wicked. Rom. 9: 22. 1 Pet. 3: 20.
Plead in prayer. Jer. 15: 15.
Limits set to. Gen. 6: 3. Jer. 44: 22.
THE WICKED
Abuse. Ecc. 8: 11. Mat. 24: 48, 49.
Despise. Rom. 2: 4.
Punished for despising. Neh. 9: 30. Mat. 24: 48—51. Rom. 2: 5.
Illustrated. Luke 13: 6, 9.
Exemplified. *Manasseh*, 2 Chr. 33: 10—13. *Israel*, Psa. 78: 38. Isa. 48: 9. *Jerusalem*, Mat. 23: 37. *Paul*, 1 Tim. 1: 16.

Love of Christ, The.

To the Father. Psa. 91: 14. Jno. 14: 31.
To His church. So. of Sol. 4: 8, 9. So. of Sol. 5: 1. Jno. 15: 9. Eph. 5: 25.
To those who love Him. Pro. 8: 17. Jno. 14: 21.
MANIFESTED IN HIS
Coming to seek the lost. Luke 19: 10.
Praying for His enemies. Luke 23: 34.
Giving Himself for us. Gal. 2: 20.
Dying for us. Jno. 15: 13. 1 Jno. 3: 16.
Washing away our sins. Rev. 1: 5.
Interceding for us. Heb. 7: 25. Heb. 9: 24.
Sending the Spirit. Psa. 68: 18. Jno. 16: 7.
Rebukes and chastisements. Rev. 3: 19.
Passeth knowledge. Eph. 3: 19.
To be imitated. Jno. 13: 34. Jno. 15 12. Eph. 5: 2. 1 Jno. 3: 16.
TO SAINTS, IS
Unquenchable. So. of Sol. 8: 7.
Constraining. 2 Cor. 5: 14.
Unchangeable. Jno. 13: 1.
Indissoluble. Rom 8: 35.
Obedient saints abide in. Jno. 15: 10.
Saints obtain victory through. Rom. 8: 37.

Is the banner over His saints. So. of Sol. 2: 4.
Is the ground of His saints love to Him. Luke 7: 47.
To saints, shall be acknowledged even by enemies. Rev. 3: 9.
Illustrated. Mat. 18: 11—13.
Exemplified towards. *Peter*, Luke 22: 32, 61. *Lazarus, &c.* Jno. 11: 5, 36. *His apostles*, Jno. 13: 1, 34. *John*, Jno. 13: 23.

Love of God, The.

Is a part of His character. 2 Cor. 13: 11. 1 Jno. 4: 8.
Christ, the especial object of. Jno. 15: 9. Jno. 17: 26.
Christ abides in. Jno. 15: 10.
DESCRIBED AS
- Sovereign. Deu. 7: 8. Deu. 10: 15.
- Great. Eph. 2: 4.
- Abiding. Zep. 3: 17.
- Unfailing. Isa. 49: 15, 16.
- Unalienable. Rom. 8: 39.
- Constraining. Hos. 11: 4.
- Everlasting. Jer. 31: 3.

Irrespective of merit. Deu. 7: 7. Job 7: 17.
MANIFESTED TOWARDS
- Perishing sinners. Jno. 3: 16. Tit. 3: 4.
- His saints. Jno. 16: 27. Jno. 17: 23. 2 The. 2: 16. 1 Jno. 4: 16.
- The destitute. Deu. 10: 18.
- The cheerful giver. 2 Cor. 9: 7.

EXHIBITED IN
- The giving of Christ. Jno. 3: 16.
- The sending of Christ. 1 Jno. 4: 9.
- Christ's dying for us while sinners. Rom. 5: 8. 1 Jno. 4: 10.
- Election. Mal. 1: 2, 3. Rom. 9: 11—13.
- Adoption. 1 Jno. 3: 1.
- Redemption. Isa. 43: 3, 4. Isa. 63: 9.
- Freeness of salvation. Tit. 3: 4—7.
- Forgiving sin. Isa. 38: 17.
- Quickening souls. Eph. 2: 4, 5.
- Drawing us to Himself. Hos. 11: 4.
- Temporal blessings. Deu. 7: 13.
- Chastisements. Heb. 12: 6.
- Defeating evil counsels. Deu. 23: 5.

Shed abroad in the heart by the Holy Ghost. Rom. 5: 5.
Saints know and believe. 1 Jno. 4: 16.
Saints should abide in. Jude 21.
PERFECTED IN SAINTS
- By obedience. 1 Jno. 2: 5.
- By brotherly love. 1 Jno. 4: 12.

The source of our love to Him. 1 Jno. 4: 19.
To be sought in prayer. 2 Cor. 13: 14.

Love to Christ.

Exhibited by God. Mat. 17: 5. Jno. 5: 20.
Exhibited by saints. 1 Pet. 1: 8.
His personal excellence is deserving of. So. of Sol. 5: 9—16.
His love to us a motive to. 2 Cor. 5: 14.
MANIFESTED IN
- Seeking Him. So. of Sol. 3: 2.
- Obeying Him. Jno. 14: 15, 21, 23.
- Ministering to Him. Mat. 27: 55, with Mat. 25: 40.
- Preferring Him to all others. Mat. 10: 37.
- Taking up the cross for Him. Mat. 10: 38.

A characteristic of saints. So. of Sol. 1: 4.
An evidence of adoption. Jno. 8: 42.
SHOULD BE
- Sincere. Eph. 6: 24.
- With the soul. So. of Sol. 1: 7.
- In proportion to our mercies. Luke 7: 47.
- Supreme. Mat. 10: 37.
- Ardent. So. of Sol. 2: 5. So. of Sol. 8: 6.
- Unquenchable. So. of Sol. 8: 7.
- Even unto death. Acts 21: 13. Rev. 12: 11.

Promises to. 2 Tim. 4: 8. Jas. 1: 12.
Increase of, to be prayed for. Phi. 1: 9.
Pray for grace to those who have. Eph. 6: 24.
THEY WHO HAVE,
- Are loved by the Father. Jno. 14: 21, 23. Jno. 16: 27.
- Are loved by Christ. Pro. 8: 17. Jno. 14: 21.
- Enjoy communion with God and Christ. Jno. 14: 23.

Decrease of, rebuked. Rev. 2: 4.
Want of, denounced. 1 Cor. 16: 22.
The wicked, destitute of. Psa. 35: 19, with Jno. 15: 18, 25.
Exemplified. *Joseph of Arimathea*, Mat. 27: 57—60. *Penitent woman*, Luke 7: 47. *Certain women*, Luke 23: 28. *Thomas*, Jno. 11: 16. *Mary Magdalene*, Jno. 20: 11. *Peter*, Jno. 21: 15—17. *Paul*, Acts 21: 13.

Love to God.

Commanded. Deu. 11: 1. Jos. 22: 5.
The first great commandment. Mat. 22: 38.
With all the heart. Deu. 6: 5, with Mat. 22: 37.
Better than all sacrifices. Mar. 12: 33.
PRODUCED BY
- The Holy Ghost. Gal. 5: 22. 2 The. 3: 5.
- The love of God to us. 1 Jno. 4: 19.
- Answers to prayer. Psa. 116: 1.

Exhibited by Christ. Jno. 14: 31.
A characteristic of saints. Psa. 5: 11.
SHOULD PRODUCE
- Joy. Psa. 5: 11.

Love to saints. 1 Jno. 5:1.
Hatred of sin. Psa. 97:10.
Obedience to God. Deu. 30:20. 1 Jno. 5:3.
Perfected in obedience. 1 Jno. 2:5.
Perfected, gives boldness. 1 Jno. 4:17, 18.
God, faithful to those who have. Deu. 7:9.
THEY WHO HAVE
Are known of Him. 1 Cor. 8:3.
Are preserved by Him. Psa. 145:20.
Are delivered by Him. Psa. 91:14.
Partake of His mercy. Exo. 20:6. Deu. 7:9.
Have all things working for their good. Rom. 8:28.
Persevere in. Jude 21.
Exhort one another to. Psa. 31:23.
Pray for. 2 The. 3:5.
The love of the world is a proof of not having. 1 Jno. 2:15.
They who love not others, are without. 1 Jno. 4:20.
Hypocrites, without. Luke 11:42. Jno. 5:42.
The uncharitable, without. 1 Jno. 3:17.
God tries the sincerety of. Deu. 13:3.
Promises connected with. Deu. 11:13—15. Psa. 69:36. Isa. 56:6, 7. Jas. 1:12.

Love to Man.

Is of God. 1 Jno. 4:7.
Commanded by God. 1 Jno. 4:21.
Commanded by Christ. Jno. 13:34. Jno. 15:12. 1 Jno. 3:23.
After the example of Christ. Jno. 13:34. Jno. 15:12. Eph. 5:2.
Taught by God. 1 The. 4:9.
Faith worketh by. Gal. 5:6.
A fruit of the Spirit. Gal. 5:22. Col. 1:8.
Purity of heart leads to. 1 Pet. 1:22.
Explained. 1 Cor. 13:4—7.
Is an active principle. 1 The. 1:3. Heb. 6:10.
Is an abiding principle. 1 Cor. 13:8, 13.
Is the second great commandment. Mat. 22:37—39.
Is the end of the commandment. 1 Tim. 1:5.
Supernatural gifts are nothing without. 1 Cor. 13:1, 2.
The greatest sacrifices are nothing without. 1 Cor. 13:3.
Especially enjoined upon ministers. 1 Tim. 4:12. 2 Tim. 2:22.
SAINTS SHOULD
Put on. Col. 3:14.
Follow after. 1 Cor. 14:1.
Abound in. Phi. 1:9. 1 The. 3:12.
Continue in. 1 Tim. 2:15. Heb. 13:1.
Provoke each other to. 2 Cor. 8:7. 2 Cor. 9:2. Heb. 10:24.
Be sincere in. Rom. 12:9. 2 Cor. 6:6. 2 Cor. 8:8. 1 Jno. 3:18.
Be disinterested in. 1 Cor. 10:24. 1 Cor. 13:5. Phi. 2:4.
Be fervent in. 1 Pet. 1:22. 1 Pet. 4:8.
Should be connected with brotherly-kindness. Rom. 12:10. 2 Pet. 1:7.
Should be with a pure heart. 1 Pet. 1:22.
All things should be done with. 1 Cor. 16:14.
SHOULD BE EXHIBITED, TOWARD
Saints. 1 Pet. 2:17. 1 Jno. 5:1.
Ministers. 1 The. 5:13.
Our families. Eph. 5:25. Tit. 2:4.
Fellow-countrymen. Exo. 32:32. Rom. 9:2, 3. Rom. 10:1.
Strangers. Lev. 19:34. Deu. 10:19.
Enemies. Exo. 23:4, 5. 2 Kin. 6:22. Mat. 5:44. Rom. 12:14, 20. 1 Pet. 3:9.
All men. Gal. 6:10.
SHOULD BE EXHIBITED, IN
Ministering to the wants of others. Mat. 25:35. Heb. 6:10.
Loving each other. Gal. 5:13.
Relieving strangers. Lev. 25:35. Mat. 25:35.
Clothing the naked. Isa. 58:7. Mat. 25:36.
Visiting the sick, &c. Job 31:16—22. Jas. 1:27.
Sympathizing. Rom. 12:15. 1 Cor. 12:26.
Supporting the weak. Gal. 6:2. 1 The. 5:14.
Covering the faults of others. Pro. 10:12, with 1 Pet. 4:8.
Forgiving injuries. Eph. 4:32. Col. 3:13.
Forbearing. Eph. 4:2.
Rebuking. Lev. 19:17. Mat. 18:15.
Necessary to true happiness. Pro. 15:17.
The love of God is a motive to. Jno. 13:34. 1 Jno. 4:11.
AN EVIDENCE OF
Being in the light. 1 Jno. 2:10.
Discipleship with Christ. Jno. 13:35.
Spiritual life. 1 Jno. 3:14.
Is the fulfilling of the law. Rom. 13:8—10. Gal. 5:14. Jas. 2:8.
Love to self is the measure of. Mar. 12:33.
Is good and pleasant. Psa. 133:1, 2.
Is a bond of union. Col. 2:2.
Is the bond of perfectness. Col. 3:14.
Hypocrites, devoid of. 1 Jno. 2:9, 11. 1 Jno. 4:20.
The wicked devoid of. 1 Jno. 3:10.
Exemplified. *Joseph*, Gen. 45:15. *Ruth*, Ruth 1:16, 17. *Jonathan*, &c. 1 Sam. 20:17, 41, 42. *Obadiah*, 1 Kin.

18: 4. *Centurion*, Luke 7: 5. *Primitive Church*, Acts 2: 46. Heb. 10: 33, 34. *Lydia*, Acts 16: 15. *Aquila*, &c. Rom. 16: 3, 4. *Paul*, 2 Cor. 6: 11, 12. *Epaphroditus*, Phi. 2: 25, 26, 30. *Philippians*, Phi. 4: 15—19. *Colossians*, Col. 1: 4. *Thessalonians*, 1 The. 3: 6. *Onesiphorus*, 2 Tim. 1: 16—18. *Philemon*, Phile. 7—9. *Moses*, Heb. 11: 25.

Loving-kindness of God, The.

Is through Christ. Eph. 2: 7. Tit. 3: 4—6.

DESCRIBED AS

- Great. Neh. 9: 17.
- Excellent. Psa. 36: 7.
- Good. Psa. 69: 16.
- Marvellous. Psa. 17: 7. Psa. 31: 21.
- Multitudinous. Isa. 63: 7.
- Everlasting. Isa. 54: 8.
- Merciful. Psa. 117: 2.
- Better than life. Psa. 63: 3.

Consideration of the dealings of God gives a knowledge of. Psa. 107: 43.

SAINTS

- Betrothed in. Hos. 2: 19.
- Drawn by. Jer. 31: 3.
- Preserved by. Psa. 40: 11.
- Quickened after. Psa. 119: 88.
- Comforted by. Psa. 119: 76.
- Look for mercy through. Psa. 51: 1.
- Receive mercy through. Isa. 54: 8.
- Are heard according to. Psa. 119: 149.
- Are ever mindful of. Psa. 26: 3. Psa. 48: 9.
- Should expect, in affliction. Psa. 42: 7, 8.
- Crowned with. Psa. 103: 4.

Never utterly taken from saints. Psa. 89: 33. Isa. 54: 10.

Former manifestations of, to be pleaded in prayer. Psa. 25: 6. Psa. 89: 49.

PRAY FOR THE

- Exhibition of. Psa. 17: 7. Psa. 143: 8.
- Continuance of. Psa. 36: 10.
- Extension of. Gen. 24: 12. 2 Sam. 2: 6.

Praise God for. Psa. 92: 2. Psa. 138: 2.

Proclaim, to others. Psa. 40: 10.

Lying.

Forbidden. Lev. 19: 11. Col. 3: 9.

Hateful to God. Pro. 6: 16—19.

An abomination to God. Pro. 12: 22.

A hindrance to prayer. Isa. 59: 2, 3.

The devil, the father of. Jno. 8: 44.

The devil excites men to. 1 Kin. 22: 22. Acts 5: 3.

SAINTS

- Hate. Psa. 119: 163. Pro. 13: 5.
- Avoid. Isa. 63: 8. Zep. 3: 13.
- Respect not those who practice. Psa. 40: 4.
- Reject those who practice. Psa. 101: 7.
- Pray to be preserved from. Psa. 119: 29. Pro. 30: 8.

Unbecoming in rulers. Pro. 17: 7.

The evil of rulers hearkening to. Pro. 29: 12.

False prophets addicted to. Jer. 23: 14. Eze. 22: 28.

False witnesses addicted to. Pro. 14: 5, 25.

Antinomians guilty of. 1 Jno. 1: 6. 1 Jno. 2: 4.

Hypocrites addicted to. Hos. 11: 12.

Hypocrites, a seed of. Isa. 57: 4.

THE WICKED

- Addicted to, from their infancy. Psa. 58: 3.
- Love. Psa. 52: 3.
- Delight in. Psa. 62: 4.
- Seek after. Psa. 4: 2.
- Prepare their tongues for. Jer. 9: 3, 5.
- Bring forth. Psa. 7: 14.
- Give heed to. Pro. 17: 4.

A characteristic of the Apostacy. 2 The. 2: 9. 1 Tim. 4: 2.

LEADS TO

- Hatred. Pro. 26: 28.
- Love of impure conversation. Pro. 17: 4.

Often accompanied by gross crimes. Hos. 4: 1, 2.

Folly of concealing hatred by. Pro. 10: 18.

Vanity of getting riches by. Pro. 21: 6.

Shall be detected. Pro. 12: 19.

Poverty preferable to. Pro. 19: 22.

Excludes from heaven. Rev. 21: 27. Rev. 22: 15.

They who are guilty of, shall be cast into hell. Rev. 21: 8.

Punishment for. Psa. 5: 6. Psa. 120: 3, 4. Pro. 19: 5. Jer. 50: 36.

Exemplified. *The devil*, Gen. 3: 4. *Cain*, Gen. 4: 9. *Sarah*, Gen. 18: 15. *Jacob*, Gen. 27: 19. *Joseph's brethren*, Gen. 37: 31, 32. *Gibeonites*, Jos. 9: 9—13. *Samson*, Jud. 16: 10. *Saul*. 1 Sam. 15: 13. *Michal*, 1 Sam. 19: 14. *David*, 1 Sam. 21: 2. *Prophet of Bethel*, 1 Kin. 13: 18. *Gehazi*, 2 Kin. 5: 22. *Job's friends*, Job 13: 4. *Ninevites*, Nah. 3: 1. *Peter*, Mat. 26: 72. *Ananias, &c.* Acts 5: 5. *Cretans*, Tit. 1: 12.

Macedonian Empire, The.

Called the kingdom of Grecia. Dan. 11: 2.

ILLUSTRATED BY THE,

- Brazen part of the image in Nebuchadnezzar's dream. Dan. 2: 32, 39.

Leopard with four wings and four heads. Dan. 7: 6, 17.
Rough goat with notable horn. Dan. 8: 5, 21.
Philippi the chief city of. Acts 16: 12.
PREDICTIONS RESPECTING,
Conquest of the Medo-Persian kingdom. Dan. 8: 6, 7. Dan. 11: 2, 3.
Power and greatness of Alexander its last king. Dan. 8: 8. Dan. 11: 3.
Division of it into four kingdoms. Dan. 8: 8, 22.
Divisions of it ruled by strangers. Dan. 11: 4.
History of its four divisions. Dan. 11: 4—29.
The little horn to arise out of one of its divisions. Dan. 8: 8—12, 23—25.
Gospel preached in, by God's desire. Acts 16: 9, 10.
Liberality of the churches of. 2 Cor. 8: 1—5.

Magistrates.

Are appointed by God. Rom. 13: 1.
Are ministers of God. Rom. 13: 4, 6.
Purpose of their appointment. Rom. 13: 4. 1 Pet. 2: 14.
Their office to be respected. Acts 23: 5.
Are not a terror to the good, but to the evil. Rom. 13: 3.
To be wisely selected and appointed. Exo. 18: 21. Ezr. 7: 25.
To be prayed for. 1 Tim. 2: 1, 2.
SHOULD
Seek wisdom from God. 1 Kin. 3: 9.
Rule in the fear of God. 2 Sam. 23: 3. 2 Chr. 19: 7.
Know the law of God. Ezr. 7: 25.
Be faithful to the Sovereign. Dan. 6: 4.
Enforce the laws. Ezr. 7: 26.
Judge wisely. 1 Kin. 3: 16—28.
Hate covetousness. Exo. 18: 21.
Not take bribes. Exo. 23: 8. Deu. 16: 19.
Defend the poor, &c. Job 29: 12, 16.
Judge for God, not for man. 2 Chr. 19: 6.
Judge righteously. Deu. 1: 16. Deu. 16: 18. Deu. 25: 1.
Be impartial. Exo. 23: 6. Deu. 1: 17.
Be diligent in ruling. Rom. 12: 8.
Subjection to their authority enjoined. Mat. 23: 2, 3. Rom. 13: 1. 1 Pet. 2: 13, 14.
Wicked—Illustrated. Pro. 28: 15.
Good—Exemplified. *Joseph*, Gen. 41: 46. *Gideon*, Jud. 8: 35. *Samuel*, 1 Sam. 12: 3, 4. Ezr. 10: 1—9. *Nehemiah*, Neh. 3: 15. *Job*, Job 29: 16. *Daniel*, Dan. 6: 3.
Wicked—Exemplified. *Sons of Samuel*, 1 Sam. 8: 3. *Pilate*, Mat. 27: 24, 26. *Magistrates in Philippi*, Acts 16: 22, 23. *Gallio*, Acts 18: 16, 17. *Felix*, Acts 24: 26.

Malice.

Springs from an evil heart. Mat. 15: 19, 20. Gal. 5: 19.
Forbidden. 1 Cor. 14: 20. Col. 3: 8. Eph. 4: 26, 27.
A hindrance to growth in grace. 1 Pet. 2: 1, 2.
Incompatible with the worship of God. 1 Cor. 5: 7, 8.
Christian liberty not to be made a cloak for. 1 Pet. 2: 16.
Saints avoid. Job 31: 29, 30. Psa. 35: 12—14.
THE WICKED
Speak with. 3 Jno. 10.
Live in. Tit. 3: 3.
Conceive. Psa. 7: 14.
Filled with. Rom. 1: 29.
Visit saints with. Psa. 83: 3. Mat. 22: 6.
Pray for those who injure you through. Mat. 5: 44.
Brings its own punishment. Psa. 7: 15, 16.
God requites. Psa. 10: 14. Eze. 36: 5.
Punishment of. Amos 1: 11, 12. Oba. 10—15.
Exemplified. *Cain*, Gen. 4: 5. *Esau*, Gen. 27: 41. *Joseph's brethren*, Gen. 37: 19, 20. *Saul*, 1 Sam. 18: 9—11. *Shimei*, 2 Sam. 16: 5. 1 Kin. 2: 8, 9. *Joab*, 2 Sam. 3: 27. 1 Kin. 2: 5, 28—33. *Sanballat*, &c. Neh. 2: 10. *Haman*, Est. 3: 5, 6. *Edomites*, Eze. 35: 5. *Presidents*, &c. Dan. 6: 4—9. *Herodias*, Mar. 6: 19. *Scribes*, &c. Mar. 11: 18. Luke 11: 54. *Diotrephes*, 3 Jno. 10.

Man.

Made for God. Pro. 16: 4, with Rev. 4: 11.
God's purpose in creation completed by making. Gen. 2: 5, with 7 v.
Cannot profit God. Job 22: 2. Psa. 16: 2.
Unworthy of God's favor. Job 7: 17. Psa. 8: 4.
CREATED
By God. Gen. 1: 27. Isa. 45: 12.
By Christ. Jno. 1: 3. Col. 1: 16.
By the Holy Ghost. Job 33: 4.
After consultation, by the Trinity. Gen. 1: 26.
On the sixth day. Gen. 1: 31.
Upon the earth. Deu. 4: 32. Job 20: 4.
From the dust. Gen. 2: 7. Job 33: 6.
In the image of God. Gen. 1: 26, 27. 1 Cor. 11: 7.

After the likeness of God. Gen. 1: 26. Jas. 3: 9.
Male and female. Gen. 1: 27. Gen. 5: 2.
A living soul. Gen. 2: 7. 1 Cor. 15: 45.
In uprightness. Ecc. 7: 29.
In knowledge (inferred). Col. 3: 10.
Under obligations to obedience. Gen. 2: 16, 17.
A type of Christ. Rom. 5: 14.
pproved of by God. Gen. 1: 31.
lessed by God. Gen. 1: 28. Gen. 5: 2.
laced in the garden of Eden. Gen. 2: 15.
very herb and tree given to, for food. Gen. 1: 29.
llowed to eat flesh after the flood. Gen. 9: 3.
ot good for, to be alone. Gen. 2: 18.
'oman formed to be a help for. Gen. 21: 2—25.
OSSESSED OF
A body. Mat. 6: 25.
A soul. Luke 12: 20. Acts 14: 22. 1 Pet. 4: 19.
A spirit. Pro. 18: 14. Pro. 20: 17. 1 Cor. 2: 11.
Understanding. Eph. 1: 18. Eph. 4: 18.
Will. 1 Cor. 9: 17. 2 Pet. 1: 21.
Affections. 1 Chr. 29: 3. Col. 3: 2.
Conscience. Rom. 2: 15. 1 Tim. 4: 2.
Memory. Gen. 41: 9. 1 Cor. 15: 2.
ade by God in his successive generations. Job 10: 8—11. Job 31: 15.
earfully and wonderfully made. Psa. 139: 14.
f every nation, made of one blood. Acts 17: 26.
uickened by the breath of God. Gen. 2: 7. Gen. 7: 22. Job 33: 4.
'ade wise by the inspiration of the Almighty. Job 32: 8, 9.
ferior to angels. Psa. 8: 5, with Heb. 2: 7.
of the earth earthy. 1 Cor. 15: 47.
ature and constitution of, different from other creatures. 1 Cor. 15: 39.
ore valuable than other creatures. Mat. 6: 26. Mat. 10: 31. Mat. 12: 12.
'iser than other creatures. Job 35: 11.
eceived dominion over other creatures. Gen. 1: 28. Psa. 8: 6—8.
ave names to other creatures. Gen. 2: 19, 20.
tellect of, matured by age. 1 Cor. 13: 11.
ALLED
The potsherd of the earth. Isa. 45: 9.
A worm. Job 25: 6.
Vain man. Job 11: 12. Jas. 2: 20.
Flesh. Gen. 6: 12. Joel 2: 28.
OMPARED TO
Grass. Isa. 40: 6—8. 1 Pet. 1: 24.
Clay in the potter's hands. Isa. 64: 8. Jer. 18: 2, 6.
Vanity. Psa. 144: 4.
A sleep. Psa. 90: 5.
A wild ass's colt. Job 11: 12.
Originally naked and not ashamed. Gen. 2: 25.
Disobeyed God by eating part of the forbidden fruit. Gen. 3: 1—12.
Filled with shame after the fall. Gen. 3: 10.
Covered himself with fig-leaves. Gen. 3: 7.
Clothed by God with skins. Gen. 3: 21.
Punished for disobedience. Gen. 3: 16—19.
Banished from paradise. Gen. 3: 23: 24.
Involved posterity in his ruin. Rom. 5: 12—19.
Has sought out many inventions. Ecc. 7: 29.
Born in sin. Psa. 51: 5.
Born to trouble. Job 5: 7.
Has an appointed time on the earth. Job 7: 1.
Days of, compared to a shadow. 1 Chr. 29: 15.
Days of, as the days of a hireling. Job 7: 1.
Has but few days. Job 14: 1.
Ordinary limit of his life. Psa. 90: 10.
Ignorant of what is good for him. Ecc. 6: 12.
Ignorant of what is to come after him. Ecc. 10 14.
Unprofited by all his labor and travail. Ecc. 2: 22. Ecc. 6: 12.
Cannot direct his ways. Jer. 10: 23. Pro. 20: 24.
Walks in a vain show. Psa. 39: 6.
GOD
Instructs. Psa. 94: 10.
Orders the goings of. Pro. 5: 21. Pro. 20: 24.
Prepares the heart of. Pro. 16: 1.
Enables to speak. Pro. 16: 1.
Preserves. Job 7: 20. Psa. 36: 6.
Provides for. Psa. 145: 15, 16.
Destroys the hopes of. Job 14: 19.
Makes the wrath of, to praise Him. Psa. 76: 10.
Makes his beauty consume away. Psa. 39: 11.
Turns, to destruction. Psa. 90: 3.
Cannot be just with God. Job 9: 2. Job 25: 4. Psa. 143: 2. Rom. 3: 20.
Cannot cleanse himself. Job 15: 14. Jer. 2: 22.
All the ways of, clean in his own eyes. Pro. 16: 2.
CHRIST
Knew what was in. Jno. 2: 25.
Took on Him nature of. Jno. 1: 14. Heb. 2: 14, 16.
Made in the likeness of. Phi. 2: 7.

Was found in fashion as. Phi. 2: 8.
Approved of God as. Acts 2: 22.
Called the second, as covenant head of the church. 1 Cor. 15: 47.
Is the head of every. 1 Cor. 11: 3.
A refuge as, to sinners. Isa. 32: 2.
As such, is the cause of the resurrection. 1 Cor. 15: 21, 22.

Shall be recompensed according to his works. Psa. 62: 12. Rom. 2: 6.
Cannot retain his spirit from death. Ecc. 8: 8.
Would give all his possessions for the preservation of life. Job 2: 4.
Able to sustain bodily affliction. Pro. 18: 14.
Sinks under trouble of mind. Pro. 18: 14.
No trust to be placed in. Psa. 118: 8. Isa. 2: 22.
The help of, vain. Psa. 60: 11.
The whole duty of. Ecc. 12: 13.

Manasseh, The tribe of.

Descended from Joseph's eldest son adopted by Jacob. Gen. 41: 51. Gen. 48: 5.
Predictions respecting. Gen. 48: 20. Gen. 49: 22—26. Deu. 33: 13—17.

PERSONS SELECTED FROM,
To number the people. Num. 1: 10.
To spy out the land. Num. 13: 11.
To divide the land. Num. 34: 23.

Strength of, on leaving Egypt. Num. 1: 34, 35.
Part of third division of Israel in their journeys. Num. 10: 22, 23.
Encamped next to, and under the standard of Ephraim west of tabernacle. Num. 2: 18, 20.
Offering of, at dedication. Num. 7: 54—59.
Families of. Num. 26: 29—33.
Strength of, on entering Canaan. Num. 26: 34.
On Gerizim said amen to the blessings. Deu. 27: 12.
Half of, obtained inheritance east of Jordan. Num. 32: 33, 39—42. Jos. 13: 29—31.
Inheritance of the other half. Jos. 17: 1—11.
Could not drive out the Canaanites but made them tributary. Jos. 17: 12, 13. Jud. 1: 27, 28.

SOME OF
Aided David against Saul. 1 Chr. 12: 19—21.
At coronation of David. 1 Chr. 12: 31—37.
Returned to their allegiance to the house of David in Asa's reign. 2 Chr. 15: 9.
At Hezekiah's passover. 2 Chr. 30: 1, 11, 18.

David appointed rulers and captains over. 1 Chr. 26: 32. 1 Chr. 27: 20, 21.
Often at war with Ephraim. Jud. 12: 1, 6. Isa. 9: 21.
Country of, purified from idols by Hezekiah and Josiah. 2 Chr. 31: 1. 2 Chr. 34: 6.
Remarkable persons of; *Daughters of Zelophehad*, Num. 27: 1—7. *Gideon*, Jud. 6: 15. *Abimelech*, Jud. 9: 1. *Jotham*, Jud. 9: 5, 7, 21. *Jair*, Jud. 10: 3. *Jephthah*, Jud. 11: 1. *Barzillai*, 2 Sam. 17: 27. *Elijah*. 1 Kin. 17: 1.

Manna.

Miraculously given to Israel for food in the wilderness. Exo. 16: 4, 15. Neh. 9: 15.

CALLED
God's manna. Neh. 9: 20.
Bread of heaven. Psa. 105: 40.
Bread from heaven. Exo. 16: 4. Jno. 6: 31.
Corn of heaven. Psa. 78: 24.
Angel's food. Psa. 78: 25.
Spiritual meat. 1 Cor. 10: 3.

Previously unknown. Deu. 8: 3, 16.

DESCRIBED AS,
Like coriander seed. Exo. 16: 31. Num. 11: 7.
White. Exo. 16: 31.
Like in color to bdellium. Num. 11: 7.
Like in taste to wafers made with honey. Exo. 16: 31.
Like in taste to oil. Num. 11: 8.
Like hoar frost. Exo. 16: 14.

Fell after the evening dew. Num. 11: 9.
None fell on the Sabbath day. Exo. 16: 26, 27.
Gathered every morning. Exo. 16: 21.
An omer of, gathered for each person. Exo. 16: 16.
Two portions of, gathered the sixth day on account of the Sabbath. Exo. 16: 5, 22—26.
He that gathered much or little had sufficient and nothing over. Exo. 16: 18.
Melted away by the sun. Exo. 16: 21.

GIVEN
When Israel murmured for bread. Exo. 16: 2, 3.
In answer to prayer. Psa. 105: 40.
Through Moses. Jno. 6: 31, 32.
To exhibit God's glory. Exo. 16: 7.
As a sign of Moses's divine mission. Jno. 6: 30, 31.
For forty years. Neh. 9: 21.
As a test of obedience. Exo. 16: 4.
To teach that man does not live by bread only. Deu. 8: 3, with Mat. 4: 4.
To humble and prove Israel. Deu. 8: 16.

Kept longer than a day (except on the Sabbath) became corrupt. Exo. 16: 19, 20.

THE ISRAELITES
- At first covetous of. Exo. 16:17.
- Ground, made into cakes and baked in pans. Num. 11:8.
- Counted, inferior to food of Egypt. Num. 11:4—6.
- Loathed. Num. 21:5.
- Punished for despising. Num. 11:10—20.
- Punished for loathing. Num. 21:6.

Ceased when Israel entered Canaan. Exo. 16:35. Jos. 5:12.

ILLUSTRATIVE OF
- Christ. Jno. 6:32—35.
- Blessedness given to saints. Rev. 2:17.

A golden pot of, laid up in the holiest for a memorial. Exo. 16:32—34. Heb. 9:4.

Marriage.

Divinely instituted. Gen. 2:24.

A covenant relationship. Mal. 2:4.

DESIGNED FOR
- The happiness of man. Gen. 2:18.
- Increasing the species. Gen. 1:28. Gen. 9:1.
- Raising up a godly seed. Mal. 2:15.
- Preventing fornication. 1 Cor. 7:2.

The expectation of the promised seed of the woman an incentive to, in the early age. Gen. 3:15, with Gen. 4:1. (*marg.*)

Lawful in all. 1 Cor. 7:2, 28. 1 Tim. 5:14.

Honorable for all. Heb. 13:4.

Should be only in the Lord. 1 Cor. 7:39.

EXPRESSED BY
- Joining together. Mat. 19:6.
- Making affinity. 1 Kin. 3:1.
- Taking to wife. Exo. 2:1.
- Giving daughters to sons, and sons to daughters. Deu. 7:3. Ezr. 9:12.

Indissoluble during the joint lives of the parties. Mat. 19:6. Rom. 7:2, 3. 1 Cor. 7:39.

Early introduction of polygamy. Gen. 4:19.

Contracted in patriarchal age with near relations. Gen. 20:12. Gen. 24:24. Gen. 28:2.

Often contracted by parents for children. Gen. 24:49—51. Gen. 34:6, 8.

Should be with consent of parents. Gen. 28:8. Jud. 14:2, 3.

Consent of the parties necessary to. Gen. 24:57, 58. 1 Sam. 18:20. 1 Sam. 25:41.

Parents might refuse to give their children in. Exo. 22:17. Deu. 7:3.

THE JEWS
- Forbidden to contract, with their near relations. Lev. 18:6.
- Forbidden to contract with idolaters. Deu. 7:3, 4. Jos. 23:12. Ezr. 9:11, 12.
- Often contracted with foreigners. 1 Kin. 11:1. Neh. 13:23.
- Sometimes guilty of polygamy. 1 Kin. 11:1, 3.
- Careful in contracting for their children. Gen. 24:2, 3. Gen. 28:1, 2.
- Betrothed themselves some time before. Deu. 20:7. Jud. 14:5, 7, with 8 v. Mat. 1:18.
- Contracted, when young. Pro. 2:17. Joel 1:8.
- Often contracted, in their own tribe. Exo. 2:1. Num. 36:6—13. Luke 1:5, 27.
- Obliged to contract with a brother's wife who died without seed. Deu. 25:5. Mat. 22:24.
- Considered being debarred from, a reproach. Isa. 4:1.
- Considered being debarred from, a cause of grief. Jud. 11:38.
- Often punished by being debarred from. Jer. 7:34. Jer. 16:9. Jer. 25:10.
- Were allowed divorce from, because of hardness of their hearts. Deu. 24:1, with Mat. 19:7, 8.
- Exempted from going to war immediately after. Deu. 20:7.

Priest not to contract, with divorced or improper persons. Lev. 21:7.

The high priest not to contract, with a widow or a divorced or profane person. Lev. 21:14.

Contracted at the gate and before witnesses. Ruth 4:1, 10, 11.

Modes of demanding women in. Gen. 24:3, 4. Gen. 34:6, 8. 1 Sam. 25:39, 40.

Elder daughters usually given in, before the younger. Gen. 29:26.

A dowry given to the woman's parents before. Gen. 29:18. Gen 34:12. 1 Sam. 18:27, 28. Hos. 3:2.

CELEBRATED,
- With great rejoicing. Jer. 33:11. Jno. 3:29.
- With feasting. Gen. 29:22. Jud. 14:10. Mat. 22:2, 3. Jno. 2:1—10.
- For seven days. Jud. 14:12.

A benediction pronounced after. Gen. 24:60. Ruth 4:11, 12.

THE BRIDE
- Received presents before. Gen. 24:53.
- Given a handmaid at. Gen. 24:59. Gen. 29:24, 29.
- Adorned with jewels for. Isa. 49:18. Isa. 61:10.
- Gorgeously apparelled. Psa. 45:13, 14.
- Attended by bridesmaids. Psa. 45:9.
- Stood on the right of bridegroom. Psa. 45:9.

Called to forget her father's house. Psa. 45:10.

THE BRIDEGROOM

Adorned with ornaments. Isa. 61:10.

Attended by many friends. Jud. 14:11. Jno. 3:29.

Presented with gifts. Psa. 45:12.

Crowned with garlands. So. of Sol. 3:11.

Rejoiced over the bride. Isa. 62:5.

Returned with the bride to his house at night. Mat. 25:1—6.

Garments provided for guests at. Mat. 22:12.

Infidelity of those contracted in, punished as if married. Deu. 22:23, 24. Mat. 1:19.

ILLUSTRATIVE OF

God's union with the Jewish nation. Isa. 54:5. Jer. 3:14. Hos. 2:19, 20.

Christ's union with His church. Eph. 5:23, 24, 32.

Martyrdom.

Is death endured for the word of God, and testimony of Christ. Rev. 6:9. Rev. 20:4.

SAINTS

Forewarned of. Mat. 10:21. Mat. 24:9. Jno. 16:2.

Should not fear. Mat. 10:28. Rev. 2:10.

Should be prepared for. Mat. 16:24, 25. Acts 21:13.

Should resist sin unto. Heb. 12:4.

Reward of. Rev. 2:10. Rev. 6:11.

Inflicted at the instigation of the devil. Rev. 2:10, 13.

The Apostacy guilty of inflicting. Rev. 17:6. Rev. 18:24.

Of saints, shall be avenged. Luke 11:50, 51. Rev. 18:20—24.

Exemplified. *Abel*, Gen. 4:8, with 1 Jno. 3:12. *Ahimelech and his fellow priests*, 1 Sam. 22:18, 19. *Prophets and Saints of old*, 1 Kin. 18:4. 1 Kin. 19:10. Luke 11:50, 51, Heb. 11:37. *Urijah*, Jer. 26:23. *John the Baptist*, Mar. 6:27. *Peter*, Jno. 21:18, 19. *Stephen*, Acts 7:58. *Primitive Christians*, Acts 9:1, with Acts 22:4. Acts 26:10. *James*, Acts 12:2. *Antipas*, Rev. 2:13.

Masters.

Authority of, established. Col. 3:22. 1 Pet. 2:18.

SHOULD, WITH THEIR HOUSEHOLDS,

Worship God. Gen. 35:3.

Fear God. Acts 10:2.

Serve God. Jos. 24:15.

Observe the Sabbath. Exo. 20:10. Deu. 5:12—14.

Put away idols. Gen. 35:2.

Should select faithful servants. Ge[n.] 24:2. Psa. 101:6, 7.

Should receive faithful advice fro[m] servants. 2 Kin. 5:13, 14.

DUTY OF, TOWARD SERVANTS;

To act justly. Job 31:13, 15. Co[l.] 4:1.

To deal with them in the fear [of] God. Eph. 6:9. Col. 4:1.

To esteem them highly, if saint[s.] Phile. 16.

To take care of them in sicknes[s.] Luke 7:3.

To forbear threatening them. Ep[h.] 6:9.

Not to defraud them. Gen 31:7.

Not to keep back their wages. Le[v.] 19:13. Deu. 24:15.

Not to rule over them with rigo[r.] Lev. 25:43. Deu. 24:14.

Benevolent, blessed. Deu. 15:18.

Unjust, denounced. Jer. 22:13. Ja[s.] 5:4.

Good—Exemplified. *Abraham*, Ge[n.] 18:19. *Jacob*, Gen. 35:2. *Joshu[a,]* Jos. 24:15. *Centurion*, Luke 7:2, [3.] *Cornelius*, Acts 10:2.

Bad—Exemplified. *Egyptians*, Exo. 1:13, 14. *Nabal*, 1 Sam. 25:17. *Ama[l]ekite*, 1 Sam. 30:13.

Measures.

Unjust, an abomination to Go[d.] Pro. 20:10.

The Jews not to be unjust in. Le[v.] 19:35. Deu. 25:14, 15.

The Jews often used unjust. Mic. 6:10.

OF LIQUIDS AND SOLIDS;

Log. Lev. 14:10, 15.

Cab. 2 Kin. 6:25.

Omer or tenth-deal, (the tenth o[f] an ephah.) Exo. 16:36. Lev. 5:11. Lev. 14:10.

Hin. Exo. 29:40.

Bath or ephah. Isa. 5:10. Eze. 45:11.

Homer or Cor. Isa. 5:10. Eze. 45:14

Firkin. Jno. 2:6.

OF LENGTH;

Handbreadth. Exo. 25:25. Psa. 39:5.

Span. Exo. 28:16. 1 Sam. 17:4.

Cubit. Gen. 6:15, 16. Deu. 3:11.

Fathom. Acts 27:28.

Furlong. Luke 24:13. Jno. 11:18

Mile. Mat. 5:41.

Distances measured by rods an[d] lines. 2 Sam. 8:2. Jer. 31:39. Eze. 40:3. Rev. 21:16.

Were regulated by the standard o[f] the sanctuary. 1 Chr. 23:29.

ILLUSTRATIVE

(Correcting in measure,) of mitigated afflictions. Jer. 30:11.

(Drinking tears in great measure,) of severe afflictions. Psa. 80:5

(Weighing the waters in a measure,) of God's infinite wisdom. Job 28: 23, 25.
(Measuring the dust of the earth,) of God's greatness. Isa. 40: 12.
(The measure of our days,) of the shortness of life. Psa. 39: 4.
(Drinking water, by measure,) of severe famine. Eze. 4: 11, 16.
(The measure of the stature of Christ,) of perfection. Eph. 4: 13:
(Opening the mouth without measure,) of the insatiableness of hell. Isa. 5: 14.

Meat-offerings.

Were most holy. Lev. 6: 17.
CONSISTED OF
Fine flour. Lev. 2: 1.
Unleavened cakes baked in the oven. Lev. 2: 4.
Fine flour baked in a pan. Lev. 2: 5.
Fine flour baked in a frying pan. Lev. 2: 7.
Green ears of corn parched. Lev. 2: 14.
Barley meal. Num. 5: 15.
Oil and incense used with. Lev. 2: 1, 4, 15.
Of jealousy, without oil or incense. Num. 5: 15.
Always seasoned with salt. Lev. 2: 13.
No leaven used with. Lev. 2: 11. Lev. 6: 17.
Not to be offered on altar of incense. Exo. 30: 9.
OFFERED
On the altar of burnt-offering. Exo. 40: 29.
With the daily sacrifices. Exo. 29: 40—42.
With all burnt-sacrifices. Num. 15: 3—12.
By the poor for a trespass-offering. Lev. 5: 11.
By the high priest every day, half in the morning and half in the evening. Lev. 6: 20—22.
A small part of, was consumed on the altar for a memorial. Lev. 2: 2, 9, 16. Lev. 6: 15.
When offered for a priest entirely consumed by fire. Lev. 6: 23.
High priest's deputy had care of. Num. 4: 16.
Laid up in a chamber of the temple. Neh. 10: 39. Neh. 13: 5. Eze. 42: 13.
The priest's portion. Lev. 2: 3. Lev. 6: 17.
To be eaten by the males of the house of Aaron alone. Lev. 6: 18.
To be eaten in the holy place. Lev. 6: 16.
THE JEWS,
Often not accepted in. Amos 5: 22.
Condemned for offering, to idols. Isa. 57: 6.
Often prevented from offering, by judgments. Joel 1: 9, 13.
Materials for public, often provided by the princes. Num. 7: 13, 19, 25. Eze. 45: 17.

Medo-Persian Kingdom.

Extended from India to Ethiopia. Est. 1: 1.
Peopled by descendants of Elam. Gen. 10: 22.
ILLUSTRATED BY
Silver part of image in Nebuchadnezzar's dream. Dan. 2: 32, 39.
A bear. Dan. 7: 5.
A ram with two horns. Dan. 8: 3, 20.
Shusan a chief city of. Est. 1: 2. Est. 8: 15.
Achmetha or Ecbatana a chief city of. Ezr. 6: 2.
Divided into many provinces. Est. 1: 1. Dan. 6: 1.
Laws of, unalterable. Dan. 6: 12, 15.
Ruled by, absolute kings. Est. 3: 8, 11. Est. 7: 9.
KINGS OF, MENTIONED IN SCRIPTURE;
Cyrus. Ezr. 1: 1.
Ahasuerus or Cambyses. Ezr. 4: 6.
Artaxerxes Smerdis (an usurper). Ezr. 4: 7.
Darius Hystaspes. Ezr. 6: 1. Dan. 5: 31.
Xerxes. Dan. 11: 2.
Artaxerxes Longimanus or Ahasuerus. Ezr. 6: 14. Ezr. 7: 1. Est. 1: 1.
KINGS OF,
Called kings of Assyria. Ezr. 6: 22.
Called kings of Babylon. Neh. 13: 6.
Styled themselves kings of kings. Ezr. 7: 12.
Dwelt in royal palaces. Est. 1: 2. Est. 8: 14.
Were exceeding rich. Est. 1: 4. Dan. 12: 2.
Entertained magnificently. Est. 1: 3, 5, 7.
Held in their hand a golden sceptre. Est. 5: 2.
Put to death all who approached them without permission. Est. 4: 11, 16.
Celebrated for wise men. Est. 1: 13. Mat. 2: 1.
People of, warlike. Eze. 27: 10. Eze. 38: 5.
Peculiar customs in. Est. 1: 8. Est. 2: 12, 13.
Babylon taken by the king of. Dan. 5: 30, 31.

The Jews delivered from captivity by means of. 2 Chr. 36: 20, 22, 23. Ezr. 1:1—4.

PREDICTIONS RESPECTING,
- Extensive conquest. Dan. 8: 4.
- Conquest of Babylon. Isa. 21:1, 2. Dan. 5:28.
- Deliverance of the Jews. Isa. 44: 28. Isa. 45: 1—4.
- Invasion of Greece under Xerxes. Dan. 11:2.
- Downfall by Alexander. Dan. 8: 6, 7. Dan. 11:3.

Meekness.

Christ set an example of. Psa. 45: 4. Isa. 53: 7. Mat. 11:29. Mat. 21: 5. 2 Cor. 10: 1. 1 Pet. 2: 21—23.

His teaching. Mat. 5: 38—45.

A fruit of the Spirit. Gal. 5: 22, 23.

SAINTS SHOULD
- Seek. Zep. 2: 3.
- Put on. Col. 3: 12, 13.
- Receive the word of God with. Jas. 1: 21.
- Exhibit, in conduct, &c. Jas. 3: 13.
- Answer for their hope with. 1 Pet. 3: 15.
- Show, to all men. Tit. 3: 2.
- Restore the erring with. Gal. 6: 1.

Precious in the sight of God. 1 Pet. 3: 4.

MINISTERS SHOULD
- Follow after. 1 Tim. 6: 11.
- Instruct opposers with. 2 Tim. 2: 24, 25.
- Urge, on their people. Tit. 3: 1, 2.

A characteristic of wisdom. Jas. 3: 17.

Necessary to a Christian walk. Eph. 4: 1, 2. 1 Cor. 6: 7.

THEY WHO ARE GIFTED WITH,
- Are preserved. Psa. 76: 9.
- Are exalted. Psa. 147: 6. Mat. 23: 12.
- Are guided and taught. Psa. 25: 9.
- Are richly provided for. Psa. 22: 26.
- Are beautified with salvation. Psa. 149: 4.
- Increase their joy. Isa. 29: 19.
- Shall inherit the earth. Psa. 37: 11.

The gospel to be preached to those who possess. Isa. 61: 1.

Blessedness of. Mat. 5: 5

Exemplified. *Moses*, Num. 12: 3. *David*, 1 Sam. 30: 6. 2 Sam. 16: 9—12. *Paul*, 1 Cor. 4: 12. 1 The. 2: 7.

Mercy.

After the example of God. Luke 6: 36.

Enjoined. 2 Kin. 6: 21—23. Hos. 12: 6. Rom. 12: 20, 21. Col. 3: 12.

To be engraved on the heart. Pro. 3: 3.

Characteristic of saints. Psa. 37: 26. Isa. 57: 1.

SHOULD BE SHOWN
- With cheerfulness. Rom. 12: 8.
- To our brethren. Zec. 7: 9.
- To those that are in distress. Luke 10: 37.
- To the poor. Pro. 14: 31. Dan. 4: 27.
- To backsliders. Luke 15: 18—20. 2 Cor. 2: 6—8.
- To animals. Pro. 12: 10.

Upholds the throne of kings. Pro. 20: 28.

Beneficial to those who exercise. Pro. 11: 17.

Blessedness of showing. Pro. 14: 21. Mat. 5: 7.

Hypocrites devoid of. Mat. 23: 23.

Denunciations against those devoid of. Hos. 4: 1, 3. Mat. 18: 23—35. Jas. 2: 13.

Mercy of God, The.

Is part of His character. Exo. 34: 6, 7. Psa. 62: 12. Neh. 9: 17. Jon. 4: 2, 10, 11. 2 Cor. 1: 3.

DESCRIBED AS
- Great. Num. 14: 18. Isa. 54: 7.
- Rich. Eph. 2: 4.
- Manifold. Neh. 9: 27. Lam. 3: 32.
- Plenteous. Psa. 86: 5, 15. Psa. 103: 8.
- Abundant. 1 Pet. 1: 3.
- Sure. Isa. 55: 3. Mic. 7: 20.
- Everlasting. 1 Chr. 16: 34. Psa. 89: 28. Psa. 106: 1. Psa. 107: 1. Psa. 136.
- Tender. Psa. 25: 6. Psa. 103: 4. Luke 1: 78.
- New every morning. Lam. 3: 23.
- High as heaven. Psa. 36: 5. Psa. 103: 11.
- Filling the earth. Psa. 119: 64.
- Over all His works. Psa. 145: 9.

Is His delight. Mic. 7: 18.

MANIFESTED
- In the sending of Christ. Luke 1: 78.
- In salvation. Tit. 3: 5.
- In long-suffering. Lam. 3: 22. Dan. 9: 9.
- To His people. Deu. 32: 43. 1 Kin. 8: 23.
- To them that fear Him. Psa. 103: 17. Luke 1: 50.
- To returning backsliders. Jer. 3: 12. Hos. 14: 4. Joel 2: 13.
- To repentant sinners. Psa. 32: 5. Pro. 28: 13. Isa. 55: 7. Luke 15: 18—20.
- To the afflicted. Isa. 49: 13. Isa. 54: 7.
- To the fatherless. Hos. 14: 3.
- To whom He will. Hos. 2: 23, with Rom. 9: 15, 18.

With everlasting kindness. Isa. 54:8.
A ground of hope. Psa. 130:7. Psa. 147:11.
A ground of trust. Psa. 52:8.
SHOULD BE
Sought for ourselves. Psa. 6:2.
Sought for others. Gal. 6:16. 1 Tim. 1:2. 2 Tim. 1:18.
Pleaded in prayer. Psa. 6:4. Psa. 25:6. Psa. 51:1.
Rejoiced in. Psa. 31:7.
Magnified. 1 Chr. 16:34. Psa. 115:1. Psa. 118:1–4, 29. Jer. 33:11.
Typified. *Mercy-seat*, Exo. 25:17.
Exemplified. *Lot*, Gen. 19:16, 19. *Epaphroditus*, Phi. 2:27. *Paul*, 1 Tim. 1:13.

Mercy-seat.

Moses commanded to make. Exo. 25:17.
Bezaleel given wisdom to make. Exo. 31:2, 3, 7.
Made of pure gold. Exo. 25:17. Exo. 37:6.
The cherubim formed out of, and at each end of it. Exo. 25:18–20. Heb. 9:5.
Placed upon the ark of testimony. Exo. 25:21. Exo. 26:34. Exo. 40:20.
GOD
Appeared over in the cloud. Lev. 16:2.
Dwelt over. Psa. 80:1.
Spake from above. Exo. 25:22. Num. 7:89.
Covered with a cloud of incense on the day of atonement. Lev. 16:13.
The blood of sacrifices on the day of atonement sprinkled upon and before. Lev. 16:14, 15.
ILLUSTRATIVE OF
Christ. Rom. 3:25, with Heb. 9:3. (*Greek.*)
The throne of grace. Heb. 4:16.

Metals.

Dug out of the earth. Job 28:1, 2, 6.
MENTIONED IN SCRIPTURE;
Gold. Gen. 2:11, 12.
Silver. Gen. 44:2.
Brass. Exo. 27:2, 4. 2 Chr. 12:10.
Copper. Ezr. 8:27. 2 Tim. 4:14.
Iron. Num. 35:16. Pro. 27:17.
Lead. Exo. 15:10. Jer. 6:29.
Tin. Num. 31:22.
Comparative value of. Isa. 60:17. Dan. 2:32, &c.
Often mixed with dross. Isa. 1:25.
The holy land abounded in. Deu. 8:9.
Antiquity of the art of working in. Gen. 4:22.
Freed from dross by fire. Eze. 22:18, 20.
Ceremonially cleansed by fire. Num. 31:21–23.
Cast in mold. Jud. 17:4. Jer. 6:29.
Clay of Jordan used for molding. 1 Kin. 7:46.
An extensive commerce in. Eze. 27:12.

Midianites.

Descended from Midian, son of Abraham by Keturah. Gen. 25:1, 2. 1 Chr. 1:32.
Dwelt east of Jordan, beside Moab. Num. 22:1, 4.
A SMALL PART OF
Dwelt near Horeb. Exo. 2:15, with Exo. 3:1.
Retained the knowledge and worship of Jehovah. Exo. 2:16, with Exo. 18:9–12.
Governed by kings. Num. 31:8. Jud. 8:5.
Dwelt in tents. Hab. 3:7.
Engaged in commerce. Gen. 37:28, 36.
Conquered by Hadad. Gen. 36:35. 1 Chr. 1:46.
Excited by Moab against Israel. Num. 22:4.
Terrified at approach of Israel. Hab. 3:3–7.
WITH THE MOABITES,
Sent for Balaam to curse Israel. Num. 22:5–7.
Seduced Israel to idolatry, &c. Num. 25:1–6.
Punished for seducing Israel. Num. 25:16–18. Num. 31:1–12.
Allowed to oppress Israel. Jud. 6:1–6.
Gideon raised up against. Jud. 6:11–14.
With Amalek, &c. opposed Gideon. Jud. 6:33.
Miraculously defeated and destroyed by Gideon. Jud. 7:16–22. Jud. 8:10, 11.
Princes of, slain. Jud. 7:24, 25. Jud. 8:12, 21.
Completeness of their destruction, alluded to. Psa. 83:9–11. Isa. 9:4. Isa. 10:26.
Shall minister to future glory of the church. Isa. 60:6.

Milk.

An animal secretion, of a white color. Lam. 4:7.
Used as food by the Jews. Gen. 18:8. Jud. 5:25.
DIFFERENT KINDS MENTIONED;
Of cows. Deu. 32:14. 1 Sam. 6:7.
Of camels. Gen. 32:15.
Of goats. Pro. 27:27.
Of sheep. Deu. 32:14.
Of sea-monsters. Lam. 4:3.
Flocks and herds fed for supply of. Pro. 27:23, 27. Isa. 7:21, 22. 1 Cor. 9:7.

Canaan abounded with. Exo. 3:8, 17. Jos. 5:6.
MADE INTO
Butter. Pro. 30:33.
Cheese. Job 10:10.
Kept by the Jews in bottles. Jud. 4:19.
Young animals not to be seethed in that of the mother. Exo. 23:19.
ILLUSTRATIVE OF
Temporal blessings. Gen. 49:12.
Blessings of the gospel. Isa. 55:1. Joel 3:18.
First principles of God's word. 1 Cor. 3:2. Heb. 5:12. 1 Pet. 2:2.
Godly and edifying discourses. So. of Sol. 4:11.
Wealth of the Gentiles. Isa. 60:16.
Doctrines of the gospel. So. of Sol. 5:1.

Mills.

Antiquity of. Exo. 11:5.
USED FOR GRINDING
Manna in the wilderness. Num. 11:8.
Corn. Isa. 47:2.
Female servants usually employed at. Exo. 11:5. Mat. 24:41.
Male captives often employed at. Jud. 16:21. Lam. 5:13.
STONES USED IN
Hard. Job 41:24.
Heavy. Mat. 18:6.
Large. Rev. 18:21.
Not to be taken in pledge. Deu. 24:6.
Often thrown down on enemies during sieges. Jud. 9:53. 2 Sam. 11:21.
ILLUSTRATIVE
(Grinding at,) of degradation, &c. Isa. 47:1, 2.
(Ceasing,) of desolation. Jer. 25:10. Rev. 18:22.

Ministers.

Called by God. Exo. 28:1, with Heb. 5:4.
Qualified by God. Isa. 6:5—7. 2 Cor. 3:5, 6.
Commissioned by Christ. Mat. 28:19.
Sent by the Holy Ghost. Acts 13:2, 4.
Have authority from God. 2 Cor. 10:8. 2 Cor. 13:10.
Authority of, is for edification. 2 Cor. 10:8. 2 Cor. 13:10.
Separated unto the gospel. Rom. 1:1.
Entrusted with the gospel. 1 The. 2:4.
DESCRIBED AS
Ambassadors for Christ. 2 Cor. 5:20.
Ministers of Christ. 1 Cor. 4:1.
Stewards of the mysteries of God. 1 Cor. 4:1.
Defenders of the faith. Phi. 1:7.
The servants of Christ's people. 2 Cor. 4:5.
Specially protected by God. 2 Cor. 1:10.
Necessity for. Mat. 9:37, 38. Rom. 10:14.
Excellency of. Rom. 10:15.
Labors of, vain, without God's blessing. 1 Cor. 3:7. 1 Cor. 15:10.
Compared to earthen vessels. 2 Cor. 4:7.
SHOULD BE
Pure. Isa. 52:11. 1 Tim. 3:9.
Holy. Exo. 28:36. Lev. 21:6. Tit. 1:8.
Humble. Acts 20:19.
Patient. 2 Cor. 6:4. 2 Tim. 2:24.
Blameless. 1 Tim. 3:2. Tit. 1:7.
Willing. Isa. 6:8. 1 Pet. 5:2.
Disinterested. 2 Cor. 12:14. 1 The. 2:6.
Impartial. 1 Tim. 5:21.
Gentle. 1 The. 2:7. 2 Tim. 2:24.
Devoted. Acts 20:24. Phi. 1:20, 21.
Strong in grace. 2 Tim. 2:1.
Self-denying. 1 Cor. 9:27.
Sober, just, and temperate. Lev. 10:9. Tit. 1:8.
Hospitable. 1 Tim. 3:2. Tit. 1:8.
Apt to teach. 1 Tim. 3:2. 2 Tim. 2:24.
Studious and meditative. 1 Tim. 4:13, 15.
Watchful. 2 Tim. 4:5.
Prayerful. Eph. 3:14. Phi. 1:4.
Strict in ruling their own families. 1 Tim. 3:4, 12.
Affectionate to their people. Phi. 1:7. 1 The. 2:8, 11.
Ensamples to the flock. Phi. 3:17. 2 The. 3:9. 1 Tim. 4:12. 1 Pet. 5:3.
SHOULD NOT BE
Lords over God's heritage. 1 Pet. 5:3.
Greedy of filthy lucre. Acts 20:33. 1 Tim. 3:3, 8. 1 Pet. 5:2.
Contentious. 1 Tim. 3:3. Tit. 1:7.
Crafty. 2 Cor. 4:2.
Men-pleasers. Gal. 1:10. 1 The. 2:4.
Easily dispirited. 2 Cor. 4:8, 9. 2 Cor. 6:10.
Entangled by cares. Luke 9:60. 2 Tim. 2:4.
Given to wine. 1 Tim. 3:3. Tit. 1:7.
Should seek the salvation of their flock. 1 Cor. 10:33.
Should avoid giving unnecessary offence. 1 Cor. 10:32, 33. 2 Cor. 6:3.
Should make full proof of their ministry. 2 Tim. 4:5.
ARE BOUND, TO
Preach the gospel to all. Mar. 16:15. 1 Cor. 1:17.
Feed the Church. Jer. 3:15. Jno. 21:15—17. Acts 20:28. 1 Pet. 5:2.
Build up the Church. 2 Cor. 12:19. Eph. 4:12.
Watch for souls. Heb. 13:17.

Pray for their people. Joel 2:17. Col. 1:9.
Strengthen the faith of their people. Luke 22:32. Acts 14:22.
Teach. 2 Tim. 2:2.
Exhort. Tit. 1:9. Tit. 2:15.
Warn affectionately. Acts 20:31.
Rebuke. Tit. 1:13. Tit. 2:15.
Comfort. 2 Cor. 1:4—6.
Convince gainsayers. Tit. 1:9.
War a good warfare. 1 Tim. 1:18. 2 Tim. 4:7.
Endure hardness. 2 Tim. 2:3.

SHOULD PREACH
Christ crucified. Acts 8:5, 35. 1 Cor. 2:2.
Repentance and faith. Acts 20:21.
According to the oracles of God. 1 Pet. 4:11.
Everywhere. Mar. 16:20. Acts 8:4.
Not with enticing words of man's wisdom. 1 Cor. 1:17. 1 Cor. 2:1, 4.
Not setting forth themselves. 2 Cor. 4:5.
Without deceitfulness. 2 Cor. 2:17. 2 Cor. 4:2. 1 The. 2:3, 5.
Fully, and without reserve. Acts 5:20. Acts 20:20, 27. Rom. 15:19.
With boldness. Isa. 58:1. Eze. 2:6. Mat. 10:27, 28.
With plainness of speech. 2 Cor. 3:12.
With zeal. 1 The. 2:8.
With constancy. Acts 6:4. 2 Tim. 4:2.
With consistency. 2 Cor. 1:18, 19.
With heedfulness. 1 Tim. 4:16.
With good will and love. Phi. 1:15—17.
With faithfulness. Eze. 3:17, 18.
Without charge, if possible. 1 Cor. 9:18. 1 The. 2:9.

Woe to those who do not preach the gospel. 1 Cor. 9:16.

WHEN FAITHFUL,
Approve themselves as the ministers of God. 2 Cor. 6:4.
Thank God for His gifts to their people. 1 Cor. 1:4. Phi. 1:3. 1 The. 3:9.
Glory in their people. 2 Cor. 7:4.
Rejoice in the faith and holiness of their people. 1 The. 2:19, 20. 1 The. 3:6—9.
Commend themselves to the consciences of men. 2 Cor. 4:2.
Are rewarded. Mat. 24:47. 1 Cor. 3:14. 1 Cor. 9:17, 18. 1 Pet. 5:4.

WHEN UNFAITHFUL,
Described. Isa. 56:10—12. Tit. 1:10, 11.
Deal treacherously with their people. Jno. 10:12.
Delude men. Jer. 6:14. Mat. 15:14.
Seek gain. Mic. 3:11. 2 Pet. 2:3.
Shall be punished. Eze. 33:6—8. Mat. 24:48—51.

THEIR PEOPLE ARE BOUND, TO
Regard them as God's messengers. 1 Cor. 4:1. Gal. 4:14.
Not to despise them. Luke 10:16. 1 Tim. 4:12.
Attend to their instructions. Mal. 2:7. Mat. 23:3.
Follow their holy example. 1 Cor. 11:1. Phi. 3:17.
Imitate their faith. Heb. 13:7.
Hold them in reputation. Phi. 2:29. 1 The. 5:13. 1 Tim. 5:17.
Love them. 2 Cor. 8:7. 1 The. 3:6.
Pray for them. Rom. 15:30. 2 Cor. 1:11. Eph. 6:19. Heb. 13:18.
Obey them. 1 Cor. 16:16. Heb. 13:17.
Give them joy. 2 Cor. 1:14. 2 Cor. 2:3.
Help them. Rom. 16:9. Phi. 4:3.
Support them. 2 Chr. 31:4. 1 Cor. 9:7—11. Gal. 6:6.

Pray for the increase of. Mat. 9:38.
Faithful—Exemplified. *The Eleven Apostles*, Mat. 28:16—19. *The seventy*, Luke 10:1, 17. *Matthias*, Acts 1:26. *Philip*, Acts 8:5. *Barnabas*, Acts 11:23. *Simeon, &c.* Acts 13:1. *Paul*, Acts 28:31. *Tychicus*, Eph. 6:21. *Timothy*, Phi. 2:22. *Epaphroditus*, Phi. 2:25. *Archippus*, Col. 4:17. *Titus*, Tit. 1:5.

Miracles.

Power of God necessary to. Jno. 3:2.

DESCRIBED AS
Marvellous things. Psa. 78:12.
Marvellous works. Isa. 29:14. Psa. 105:5.
Signs and wonders. Jer. 32:21. Jno. 4:48. 2 Cor. 12:12.

MANIFEST
The glory of God. Jno. 11:4.
The glory of Christ. Jno. 2:11. Jno. 11:4.
The works of God. Jno. 9:3.

Were evidences of a divine commission. Exo. 4:1—5. Mar. 16:20.
The Messiah was expected to perform. Mat. 11:2, 3. Jno. 7:31.
Jesus was proved to be the Messiah by. Mat. 11:4—6. Luke 7:20—22. Jno. 5:36. Acts 2:22.
Jesus was followed on account of. Mat. 4:23—25. Mat. 14:35, 36. Jno. 6:2, 26. Jno. 12:18.
A gift of the Holy Ghost. 1 Cor. 12:10.

WERE PERFORMED
By the power of God. Exo. 8:19. Acts 14:3. Acts 15:12. Acts 19:11.
By the power of Christ. Mat. 10:1.
By the power of the Holy Ghost. Mat. 12:28. Rom. 15:19.
In the name of Christ. Mar. 16:17. Acts 3:16. Acts 4:30.

First preaching of the gospel confirmed by. Mar. 16:20. Heb. 2:4.
They who wrought, disclaimed all power of their own. Acts 3:12.
Should produce faith. Jno. 2:23. Jno. 20:30, 31.
Should produce obedience. Deu. 11:1—3. Deu. 29:2, 3, 9.
Instrumental to the early propagation of the gospel. Acts 8:6. Rom. 15:18, 19.
FAITH REQUIRED IN
Those, who performed. Mat. 17:20. Mat. 21:21. Jno. 14:12. Acts 3:16. Acts 6:8.
Those for whom they were performed. Mat. 9:28. Mat. 13:58. Mar. 9:22—24. Acts 14:9.
Should be remembered. 1 Chr. 16:12. Psa. 105:5.
Should be told to future generations. Exo. 10:2. Jud. 6:13.
Insufficient of themselves, to produce conversion. Luke 16:31.
THE WICKED
Desire to see. Mat. 27:42. Luke 11:29. Luke 23:8.
Often acknowledge. Jno. 11:47. Acts 4:16.
Do not understand. Psa. 106:7.
Do not consider. Mar. 6:52.
Forget. Neh. 9:17. Psa. 78:1, 11.
Proof against. Num. 14:22. Jno. 12:37.
Guilt of rejecting the evidence afforded by. Mat. 11:20—24. Jno. 15:24.

Miracles of Christ, The.

Water turned into wine. Jno. 2:6—10.
Nobleman's son healed. Jno. 4:46—53.
Centurion's servant healed. Mat. 8:5—13.
Draughts of fishes. Luke 5:4—6. Jno. 21:6.
Devils cast out. Mat. 8:28—32. Mat. 9:32, 33. Mat. 15:22—28. Mat. 17:14—18. Mark 1:23—27.
Peter's wife's mother healed. Mat. 8:14, 15.
Lepers cleansed. Mat. 8:3. Luke 17:14.
Paralytic healed. Mar. 2:3—12.
Withered hand restored. Mat. 12:10—13.
Impotent man healed. Jno. 5:5—9.
The dead raised to life. Mat. 9:18, 19, 23—25. Luke 7:12—15. Jno. 11:11—44.
Issue of blood stopped. Mat. 9:20—22.
The blind restored to sight. Mat. 9:27—30. Mar. 8:22—25. Jno. 9:1—7.
The deaf and dumb cured. Mar. 7:32—35.
The multitude fed. Mat. 14:15—21. Mat. 15:32—38.
His walking on the sea. Mat. 14:25—27.
Peter walking on the sea. Mat. 14:29.
Tempest stilled. Mat. 8:23—26. Mat. 14:32.
Sudden arrival of the ship. Jno. 6:21.
Tribute-money. Mat. 17:27.
Woman healed of infirmity. Luke 13:11—13.
Dropsy cured. Luke 14:2—4.
Fig-tree blighted. Mat. 21:19.
Malchus healed. Luke 22:50, 51.
Performed before the messengers of John. Luke 7:21, 22.
Many and divers diseases healed. Mat. 4:23, 24. Mat. 14:14. Mat. 15:30. Mar. 1:34. Luke 6:17—19.
His transfiguration. Mat. 17:1—8.
His resurrection. Luke 24:6, with Jno. 10:18.
His appearance to His disciples, the doors being shut. Jno. 20:19.
His ascension. Acts 1:9.

Miracles through Evil Agents.

Performed through the power of the devil. 2 The. 2:9. Rev. 16:14.
WROUGHT
In support of false religions. Deu. 13:1—2.
By false christs. Mat. 24:24.
By false prophets. Mat. 24:24. Rev. 19:20.
A mark of the Apostacy. 2 The. 2:3, 9. Rev. 13:13.
Not to be regarded. Deu. 13:3.
Deceive the ungodly. 2 The. 2:10—12. Rev. 13:14. Rev. 19:20.
Exemplified. *Magicians of Egypt*, Exo. 7:11, 22. Exo. 8:7. *Witch of Endor*, 1 Sam. 28:7—14. *Simon Magus*, Acts 8:9—11.

Miracles wrought through Servants of God.

MOSES AND AARON:
Rod turned into a serpent. Exo. 4:3. Exo. 7:10.
Rod restored. Exo. 4:4.
Hand made leprous. Exo. 4:6.
Hand healed. Exo. 4:7.
Water turned into blood. Exo. 4:9, 30.
River turned into blood. Exo. 7:20.
Frogs brought. Exo. 8:6.
Frogs removed. Exo. 8:13.
Lice brought. Exo. 8:17.
Flies brought. Exo. 8:21—24.
Flies removed. Exo. 8:31.
Murrain of beasts. Exo. 9:3—6.
Boils and blains brought. Exo. 9:10, 11.
Hail brought. Exo. 9:23.
Hail removed. Exo. 9:33.
Locusts brought. Exo. 10:13.

Locusts removed. Exo. 10: 19.
Darkness brought. Exo. 10: 22.
The first-born destroyed. Exo. 12: 29.
The red sea divided. Exo. 14: 21, 22.
Egyptians overwhelmed. Exo. 14: 26—28.
Water sweetened. Exo. 15: 25.
Water from rock in Horeb. Exo. 17: 6.
Amalek vanquished. Exo. 17: 11—13.
Destruction of Korah. Num. 16: 28—32.
Water from rock in Kadesh. Num. 20: 11.
Healing by brazen serpent. Num. 21: 8, 9.

JOSHUA:
Waters of Jordan divided. Jos. 3: 10—17.
Jordan restored to its course. Jos. 4: 18.
Jericho taken. Jos. 6: 6—20.
The sun and moon stayed. Jos. 10: 12—14.
Midianites destroyed. Jud. 7: 16—22.

SAMSON:
A lion killed. Jud. 14: 6.
Philistines killed. Jud. 14: 19. Jud. 15: 15.
The gates of Gaza carried away. Jud. 16: 3.
Dagon's house pulled down. Jud. 16: 30.

SAMUEL:
Thunder and rain in harvest. 1 Sam. 12: 18.

THE PROPHET OF JUDAH:
Jeroboam's hand withered. 1 Kin. 13: 4.
The altar rent. 1 Kin. 13: 5.
The withered hand restored. 1 Kin. 13: 6.

ELIJAH:
Drought caused. 1 Kin. 17: 1. Jas. 5: 17.
Meal and oil multiplied. 1 Kin. 17: 14—16.
A child restored to life. 1 Kin. 17: 22, 23.
Sacrifice consumed by fire. 1 Kin. 18: 36, 38.
Men destroyed by fire. 2 Kin. 1: 10—12.
Rain brought. 1 Kin. 18: 41—45. Jas. 5: 18.
Waters of Jordan divided. 2 Kin. 2: 8.
Taken to heaven. 2 Kin. 2: 11.

ELISHA:
Waters of Jordan divided. 2 Kin. 2: 14.
Waters healed. 2 Kin. 2: 21, 22.
Children torn by bears. 2 Kin. 2: 24.
Oil multiplied. 2 Kin. 4: 1—7.
Child restored to life. 2 Kin. 4: 32—35.
Naaman healed. 2 Kin. 5: 10, 14.
Gehazi struck with leprosy. 2 Kin. 5: 27.
Iron caused to swim. 2 Kin. 6: 6.
Syrians smitten with blindness. 2 Kin. 6: 18.
Syrians restored to sight. 2 Kin. 6: 20.
A man restored to life. 2 Kin. 13: 21.

ISAIAH:
Hezekiah healed. 2 Kin. 20: 7
Shadow put back on the dial 2 Kin. 20: 11.

THE SEVENTY DISCIPLES:
Various miracles. Luke 10: 9, 17.

THE APOSTLES, &C.
Many miracles. Acts 2: 43. Acts 5: 12.

PETER:
Lame man cured. Acts 3: 7.
Death of Ananias. Acts 5: 5.
Death of Sapphira. Acts 5: 10.
The sick healed. Acts 5: 15, 16.
Eneas made whole. Acts 9: 34.
Dorcas restored to life. Acts 9: 40.

STEPHEN:
Great miracles. Acts 6: 8.

PHILIP:
Various miracles. Acts 8: 6, 7, 13.

PAUL:
Elymas smitten with blindness. Acts 13: 11.
Lame man cured. Acts 14: 10.
An unclean spirit cast out. Acts 16: 18.
Special miracles. Acts 19: 11, 12.
Eutychus restored to life. Acts 20: 10—12.
Viper's bite made harmless. Acts 28: 5.
Father of Publius healed. Acts 28: 8.

PAUL AND BARNABAS:
Various miracles. Acts 14: 3.

Miraculous Gifts of the Holy Ghost.

Foretold. Isa. 35: 4—6. Joel 2: 28, 29.
Of different kinds. 1 Cor. 12: 4—6.
Enumerated. 1 Cor. 12: 8—10, 28. 1 Cor. 14: 1.
Christ was endued with. Mat. 12: 28.
Poured out on the day of Pentecost. Acts 2: 1—4.

COMMUNICATED
Upon the preaching of the gospel. Acts 10: 44—46.
By the laying on of the Apostles' hands. Acts 8: 17, 18. Acts 19: 6.

For the confirmation of the gospel. Mar. 16:20. Acts 14:3. Rom. 15:19. Heb. 2:4.
For the edification of the Church. 1 Cor. 12:7. 1 Cor. 14:12, 13.
Dispensed, according to His sovereign will. 1 Cor. 12:11.
Were to be sought after. 1 Cor. 12:31. 1 Cor. 14:1.
Temporary nature of. 1 Cor. 13:8.
WERE NOT TO BE
Neglected. 1 Tim. 4:14. 2 Tim. 1:6.
Despised. 1 The. 5:20.
Purchased. Acts 8:20.
Might be possessed without saving grace. Mat. 7:22, 23. 1 Cor. 13:1, 2.
Counterfeited by Antichrist. Mat. 24:24. 2 The. 2:9. Rev. 13:13, 14.

Missionaries, all Christians should be as.

After the example of Christ. Acts 10:38.
Women and children as well as men. Psa. 8:2. Pro. 31:26. Mat. 21:15, 16. Phi. 4:3. 1 Tim. 5:10. Tit. 2:3—5. 1 Pet. 3:1.
The zeal of idolaters should provoke to. Jer. 7:18.
The zeal of hypocrites should provoke to. Mat. 23:15.
An imperative duty. Jud. 5:23. Luke 19:40.
The principle on which. 2 Cor. 5:14, 15.
However weak they may be. 1 Cor. 1:27.
From their calling as saints. Exo. 19:6. 1 Pet. 2:9.
As faithful stewards. 1 Pet. 4:10, 11.
In youth. Psa. 71:17. Psa. 148:12, 13.
In old age. Deu. 32:7. Psa. 71:18.
In the family. Deu. 6:7. Psa. 78:5—8. Isa. 38:19. 1 Cor. 7:16.
In their intercourse with the world. Mat 5:16. Phi. 2:15, 16. 1 Pet. 2:12.
In first giving their own selves to the Lord. 2 Cor. 8:5.
In declaring what God has done for them. Psa. 66:16. Psa. 116:16—19.
In hating life for Christ. Luke 14:26.
In openly confessing Christ. Mat. 10:32.
In following Christ. Luke 14:27. Luke 18:22.
In preferring Christ above all relations. Luke 14:26. 1 Cor. 2:2.
In joyfully suffering for Christ. Heb. 10:34.
In forsaking all for Christ. Luke 5:11.
In a holy example. Mat. 5:16. Phi. 2:15. 1 The. 1:7.
In holy conduct. 1 Pet. 2:12.
In holy boldness. Psa. 119:46.
In dedicating themselves to the service of God. Jos. 24:15. Psa. 27:4.
In devoting all property to God. 1 Chr. 29:2, 3, 14, 16. Ecc. 11:1. Mat 6:19. 20. Mar. 12:44. Luke 12:33 Luke 18:22, 28. Acts 2:45. Acts 4:32—34.
In holy conversation. Psa. 37:30 with Pro. 10:31. Pro. 15:7. Eph 4:29. Col. 4:6.
In talking of God and His works. Psa. 71:24. Psa. 77:12. Psa. 119:27. Psa. 145:11, 12.
In showing forth God's praises. Isa. 43:21.
In inviting others to embrace the gospel. Psa. 34:8. Isa. 2:3. Jno. 1:46. Jno. 4:29.
In seeking the edification of others. Rom. 14:19. Rom. 15:2. 1 The. 5:11.
In admonishing others. 1 The. 5:14. 2 The. 3:15.
In reproving others. Lev. 19:17. Eph. 5:11.
In teaching and exhorting. Psa. 34:11. Psa. 51:13. Col. 3:16. Heb. 3:13. Heb. 10:25.
In interceding for others. Col. 4:3. Heb. 13:18. Jas. 5:16.
In aiding ministers in their labors. Rom. 16:3, 9. 2 Cor. 11:9. Phi. 4:14—16. 3 Jno. 6.
In giving a reason for their faith. Exo. 12:26, 27. Deu. 6:20, 21. 1 Pet. 3:15.
In encouraging the weak. Isa. 35:3, 4. Rom. 14:1. Rom. 15:1. 1 The. 5:14.
In visiting and relieving the poor, the sick, &c. Lev. 25:35. Psa. 112:9, with 2 Cor. 9:9. Mat. 25:36. Acts 20:35. Jas. 1:27.
With a willing heart. Exo. 35:29. 1 Chr. 29:9, 14.
With a superabundant liberality. Exo. 36:5—7. 2 Cor. 8:3.
Encouragement to. Pro. 11:25, 30. 1 Cor. 1:27. Jas. 5:19, 20.
Blessedness of. Dan. 12:3.
Illustrated. Mat. 25:14. Luke 19:13, &c., &c.
Exemplified. *Hannah*, 1 Sam. 2:1—10. *Captive maid*, 2 Kin. 5:3. *Chief of the Fathers, &c.* Ezr. 1:5. *Shadrach, &c.* Dan. 3:16—18. *Restored demoniac*, Mar. 5:20. *Shepherds*, Luke 2:17. *Anna*, Luke 2:38. *Joanna, &c.* Luke 8:3. *Leper*, Luke 17:15. *Disciples*, Luke 19:37, 38. *Centurion*, Luke 23:47. *Andrew*, Jno. 1:41, 42. *Philip*, Jno. 1:46. *Woman of Samaria*, Jno. 4:29. *Barnabas*, Acts 4:36, 37. *Persecuted Saints*, Acts 8:4. Acts 11:19, 20. *Apollos*, Acts 18:25 *Aquilla, &c.* Acts 18:26. *Various individuals*, Rom. Chap. 16th. *Onesiphorus*, 2 Tim. 1:16. *Philemon*, Phile. 1—6.

Missionary-work by Ministers.

Commanded. Mat. 28:19. Mar. 16:15.
Warranted by predictions concerning the heathen, &c. Isa. 42:10—12. Isa. 66:19.
Is according to the purpose of God. Luke 24:46, 47. Gal. 1:15, 16. Col. 1:25—27.
Directed by the Holy Ghost. Acts 13:2.
Required. Luke 10:2. Rom. 10:14, 15.
The Holy Ghost calls to. Acts 13:2.
Christ engaged in. Mat. 4:17, 23. Mat. 11:1. Mar. 1:38, 39. Luke 8:1.
Christ sent His disciples to labor in. Mar. 3:14. Mar. 6:7. Luke 10:1—11.
Obligations to engage in. Acts 4:19, 20. Rom. 1:13—15. 1 Cor. 9:16.
Excellency of. Isa. 52:7, with Rom. 10:15.
Worldly concerns should not delay. Luke 9:59—62.
God qualifies for. Exo. 3:11, 18. Exo. 4:11, 12, 15. Isa. 6:5—9.
God strengthens for. Jer. 1:7—9.
Guilt and danger of shrinking from. Jon. 1:3, 4.
Requires wisdom and meekness. Mat. 10:16.
Be ready to engage in. Isa. 6:8.
Aid those engaged in. Rom. 16:1, 2. 2 Cor. 11:9. 3 Jno. 5—8.
Harmony should subsist amongst those engaged in. Gal. 2:9.
SUCCESS OF,
  To be prayed for. Eph. 6:18, 19. Col. 4:3.
  A cause of joy. Acts 15:3.
  A cause of praise. Acts 11:18. Acts 21:19, 20.
No limits to the sphere of. Isa. 11:9. Mar. 16:15. Rev. 14:6.
Opportunities for, not to be neglected. 1 Cor. 16:9.
Exemplified. *Levites*, 2 Chr. 17:8, 9. *Jonah*, Jon. 3:2. *The Seventy*, Luke 10:1, 17. *Apostles*, Mar. 6:12. Acts 13:2—5. *Philip*, Acts 8:5. *Paul, &c.* Acts 13:2—4. *Silas*, Acts 15:40, 41. *Timotheus*, Acts 16:3. *Noah*, 2 Pet. 2:5.

Moabites.

Descended from Lot. Gen. 19:37.
CALLED
  Children of Lot. Deu. 2:9.
  People of Chemosh. Num. 21:29. Jer. 48:46.
Are given to, as a possession. Deu. 2:9.
Separated from the Amorites by the river Arnon. Num. 21:13.
Expelled the ancient Emims. Deu. 2:9—11.
Possessed many and great cities. Num. 21:28, 30. Isa. 15:1—4. Jer. 48:21—24.
Governed by kings. Num. 23:7. Jos. 24:9.
DESCRIBED AS
  Proud and arrogant. Isa. 16:6. Jer. 48:29.
  Idolatrous. 1 Kin. 11:7.
  Superstitious. Jer. 27:3, 9.
  Rich and confident. Jer. 48:7.
  Prosperous and at ease. Jer. 48:11.
  Mighty and men of war. Jer. 48:14.
Deprived of a large part of their territories by the Amorites. Num. 21:26.
Refused to let Israel pass. Jud. 11:17, 18.
Alarmed at the number, &c. of Israel. Num. 22:3.
With Midian send for Balaam to curse Israel. Num. 22 ch. to Num. 24 ch.
ISRAELITES
  Enticed to idolatry by. Num. 25:1—3.
  Forbidden to spoil. Deu. 2:9, with Jud. 11:15.
  Forbidden to make leagues with. Deu. 23:6.
  Sometimes intermarried with. Ruth 1:4. 1 Kin. 11:1. 1 Chr. 8:8. Neh. 13:23.
Excluded from the congregation of Israel for ever. Deu. 23:3, 4. Neh. 13:1, 2.
Always hostile to Israel. Psa. 83:6. Eze. 25:8.
Harassed and subdued by Saul. 1 Sam. 14:47.
Gave an asylum to David's family. 1 Sam. 22:4.
Made tributary to David. 2 Sam. 8:2, 12.
Benaiah slew two champions of. 2 Sam. 23:20.
Paid tribute of sheep and wool to the king of Israel. 2 Kin. 3:4. Isa. 16:1.
Revolted from Israel after the death of Ahab. 2. Kin. 1:1. 2 Kin. 3:5.
Israel and Judah joined against. 2 Kin. 3:6, 7.
Miraculously deceived by the color of the water. 2 Kin. 3:21—24.
Conquered by Israel and Judah. 2 Kin. 3:24—26.
King of, sacrificed his son to excite animosity against Israel. 2 Kin. 3:27.
Joined Babylon against Judah. 2 Kin. 24:2.
PROPHESIES RESPECTING;
  Terror on account of Israel. Exo. 15:15.

Desolation and grief. Isa. 15 ch. Isa. 16:2—11.
Inability to avert destruction. Isa. 16:12.
To be destroyed in three years. Isa. 16:13, 14.
To be captives in Babylon. Jer. 27:3, 8. Jer. 48:7.
Their desolation as a punishment for their hatred of Israel. Jer. 48:26, 27. Eze. 25:8, 9.
Restoration from captivity. Jer. 48:47.
Subjugation to Messiah. Num. 24:17. Isa. 25:10.
Subjugation to Israel. Isa. 11:14.

Money.

Gold and silver used as. Gen. 13:2. Num. 22:18.
Brass introduced as, by the Romans. Mat. 10:9.
Originally stamped with the image of a lamb. Gen. 23:15, with Gen. 33:19. (*marg.*)
Of the Romans, stamped with the image of Cæsar. Mat. 22:20, 21.
Usually taken by weight. Gen. 23:16. Jer. 32:10.
PIECES OF, MENTIONED;
Talent of gold. 1 Kin. 9:14. 2 Kin. 23:33.
Talent of silver. 1 Kin. 16:24. 2 Kin. 5:22, 23.
Shekel of silver. Jud. 17:10. 2 Kin. 15:20.
Half shekel or bekah. Exo. 30:15.
Third of a shekel. Neh. 10:32.
Fourth of a shekel. 1 Sam. 9:8.
Gerah the twentieth of a shekel. Num. 3:47.
Pound. Luke 19:13.
Penny. Mat. 20:2. Mar. 6:37.
Farthing. Mat. 5:26. Luke 12:6.
Mite. Mar. 12:42. Luke 21:2.
Of the Jews regulated by the standard of the sanctuary. Lev. 5:15. Num. 3:47.
Was current with the merchants. Gen. 23:16.
Jews forbidden to take usury for. Lev. 25:37.
Changing of, a trade. Mat. 21:12. Jno. 2:15.
WAS GIVEN
For lands. Gen. 23:9. Acts 4:37.
For slaves. Gen. 37:28. Exo. 21:21.
For merchandise. Gen. 43:12. Deu. 2:6.
For tribute. 2 Kin. 23:33. Mat. 22:19.
As wages. Ezr. 3:7. Mat. 20:2. Jas. 5:4.
As offerings. 2 Kin. 12:7—9. Neh. 10:32.
As alms. 1 Sam. 2:36. Acts 3:3, 6.
Custom of presenting a piece of. Job 42:11.
Power and usefulness of. Ecc. 7:12. Ecc. 10: [illegible].
Love of, the root of all evil. 1 Tim. 6:10.

Months.

Sun and moon designed to mark out. Gen. 1:14.
The patriarchs computed time by Gen. 29:14.
The Jews computed time by. Jud. 11:37. 1 Sam. 6:1. 1 Kin. 4:7.
Commenced with first appearance of new moon. Num. 10:10, with Psa. 81:3.
Originally had no names. Gen. 7:11. Gen. 8:4.
The year composed of twelve. 1 Chr. 27:2—15. Est. 2:12. Rev. 22:2.
NAMES OF THE TWELVE;
First, Nisan or Abib. Exo. 13:4. Neh. 2:1.
Second, Zif. 1 Kin. 6:1, 37.
Third, Sivan. Est. 8:9.
Fourth, Thammuz. Zec. 8:19.
Fifth, Ab. Zec. 7:3.
Sixth, Elul. Neh. 6:15.
Seventh, Ethanim. 1 Kin. 8:2.
Eighth, Bul. 1 Kin. 6:38.
Ninth, Chisleu. Zec. 7:1.
Tenth, Tebeth. Est. 2:16.
Eleventh, Sebat. Zec. 1:7.
Twelfth, Adar. Ezr. 6:15. Est. 3:7.
Idolaters prognosticated by. Isa. 47:13.
Observance of, condemned. Gal. 4:10.

Moon, The.

Created by God. Gen. 1:14. Psa. 8:3.
Made to glorify God. Psa. 148:3.
Called the lesser light. Gen. 1:16.
DESCRIBED AS
Fair. So. of Sol. 6:10.
Bright. Job 31:26.
Has a glory of its own. 1 Cor. 15:41
APPOINTED
To divide day from night. Gen. 1 14.
For signs and seasons. Gen. 1: 14. Psa. 104:19.
For a light in the firmament. Gen. 1:15.
To light the earth by night. Jer. 31:35.
To rule the night. Gen. 1:16. Psa. 136:9.
By an ordinance for ever. Psa. 72:5, 7. Psa. 89:37. Jer. 31:36.
For the benefit of all. Deu. 4: 19.
Influences vegetation. Deu. 33:14.
First appearance of, a time of festivity. 1 Sam. 20:5, 6. Psa. 81:3.
MIRACLES CONNECTED WITH;
Standing still in Ajalon. Jos. 10:12, 13.

Signs in, before the destruction of Jerusalem. Luke 21: 25.
Lunacy attributed to the influence of. Psa. 121: 6, with Mat. 4: 24.
Worshipped as the queen of heaven. Jer. 7: 18. Jer. 44: 17—19, 25.
WORSHIPPING OF,
Forbidden to the Jews. Deu. 4: 19.
Condemned as atheism. Job 31: 26, 28.
To be punished with death. Deu. 17: 3—6.
Jews often guilty of. 2 Kin. 23: 5. Jer. 8: 2.
Jews punished for. Jer. 8: 1—3.
ILLUSTRATIVE
Of glory of Christ in the Church. Isa. 60: 20.
Of fairness of the Church. So. of Sol. 6: 10.
Of changeableness of the world. Rev. 12: 1.
(Becoming as blood,) of judgments. Rev. 6: 12.
(Withdrawing her light,) of deep calamities. Isa. 13: 10. Joel 2: 10. Joel 3: 15. Mat. 24: 29.

Morning.

The second part of the day at the creation. Gen. 1: 5, 8, 13, 19, 23, 31.
The first part of the natural day. Mar. 16: 2.
Ordained by God. Job 38: 12.
Began with first dawn. Jos. 6: 15. Psa. 119: 147.
Continued until noon. 1 Kin. 18: 26. Neh. 8: 3.
First dawning of, called the eyelids of the morning. Job 3: 9. (*marg.*) Job 41: 18.
The outgoings of, made to rejoice. Psa. 65: 8.
THE JEWS
Generally rose early in. Gen. 28: 18. Jud. 6: 28.
Eat but little in. Ecc. 10: 16.
Went to the temple in. Luke 21: 38. Jno. 8: 2.
Offered a part of the daily sacrifice in. Exo. 29: 38, 39. Num. 28: 4—7.
Devoted a part of, to prayer and praise. Psa. 5: 3. Psa. 59: 16. Psa. 88: 13.
Gathered the manna in. Exo. 16: 21.
Began their journeys in. Gen. 22: 3.
Held courts of justice in. Jer. 21: 12. Mat. 27: 1.
Contracted covenants in. Gen. 26: 31.
Transacted business in. Ecc. 11: 6. Mat. 20: 1.
Was frequently cloudless. 2 Sam. 23: 4.
A red sky in, a sign of bad weather. Mat. 16: 3.
Ushered in by the morning star. Job 38: 7.
ILLUSTRATIVE
Of the resurrection day. Psa. 49: 14.
(Breaking forth,) of the glory of the church. So. of Sol. 6: 10. Isa. 58: 8.
(Star of,) of the glory of Christ. Rev. 22: 16.
(Star of,) of reward of saints. Rev. 2: 28.
(Clouds in,) of the shortlived profession of hypocrites. Hos. 6: 4.
(Wings of,) of rapid movements. Psa. 139: 9.
(Spread upon the mountains,) of heavy calamities. Joel 2: 2.

Moth, The.

Destructive to garments. Mat. 6: 19. Jas. 5: 2.
Destroyed by the slightest touch. Job 4: 19.
ILLUSTRATIVE
Of God in the execution of His judgments. Hos. 5: 12.
(Eating a garment,) of God's judgments. Isa. 50: 9. Isa. 51: 8.
(Garments eaten by,) of those who have suffered severe judgments. Job 13: 28.
(Making its house in garments,) of man's folly in providing earthly things. Job 27: 18.

Mountains.

The elevated parts of the earth. Gen. 7: 19, 20.
GOD
Formed. Amos 4: 13.
Set fast. Psa. 65: 6.
Gives strength to. Psa. 95: 4.
Weighs, in a balance. Isa. 40: 12.
Waters, from His chambers. Psa. 104: 13.
Parches, with draught. Hag. 1: 11.
Causes, to smoke. Psa. 104: 32. Psa. 144: 5.
Sets the foundations of, on fire. Deu. 32: 22.
Makes waste. Isa. 42: 15.
Causes, to tremble. Nah. 1: 5. Hab. 3: 10.
Causes, to skip. Psa. 114: 4, 6.
Causes, to melt. Jud. 5: 5. Psa. 97: 5. Isa. 64: 1, 3.
Removes. Job 9: 5.
Overturns. Job 9: 5. Job 28: 9.
Scatters. Hab. 3: 6.
Made to glorify God. Psa. 148: 9.
CALLED
God's mountains. Isa. 49: 11.
The ancient mountains. Deu. 33: 15.

The everlasting mountains. Hab. 3: 6.
Perpetual hills. Hab. 3: 6.
Everlasting hills. Gen. 49: 26.
Pillars of heaven. Job 26: 11.
Many exceeding high. Psa. 104: 18. Isa. 2: 14.
Collect the vapors which ascend from the earth. Psa. 104: 6, 8.
Are the sources of springs and rivers. Deu. 8: 7. Psa. 104: 8—10.
Canaan abounded in. Deu. 11: 11.
Volcanic fires of, alluded to. Isa. 64: 1, 2. Jer. 51: 25. Nah. 1: 5, 6.
MENTIONED IN SCRIPTURE;
Ararat. Gen. 8: 4.
Abarim. Num. 33: 47, 48.
Amalek. Jud. 12: 15.
Bashan. Psa. 68: 15.
Bethel. 1 Sam. 13: 2.
Carmel. Jos. 15: 55. Jos. 19: 26. 2 Kin. 19: 23.
Ebal. Deu. 11: 29. Deu. 27: 13.
Ephraim. Jos. 17: 15. Jud. 2: 9.
Gerizim. Deu. 11: 29. Jud. 9: 7.
Gilboa. 1 Sam. 31: 1. 2 Sam. 1: 6, 21.
Gilead. Gen. 31: 21, 25. So. of Sol. 4: 1.
Hachilah. 1 Sam. 23: 19.
Hermon. Jos. 13: 11.
Hor. Num. 20: 22. Num. 34: 7, 8.
Horeb. Exo. 3: 1.
Lebanon. Deu. 3: 25.
Mizar. Psa. 42: 6.
Moreh. Jud. 7: 1.
Moriah. Gen. 22: 2. 2 Chr. 3: 1.
Nebo, (part of Abarim). Num. 32: 3. Deu. 34: 1.
Olives or mount of corruption. 1 Kin. 11: 7, with 2 Kin. 23: 13. Luke 21: 37.
Pisgah, (part of Abarim). Num. 21: 20. Deu. 34: 1.
Seir. Gen. 14: 6. Gen. 36: 8.
Sinai. Exo. 19: 2, 18, 20, 23. Exo. 31: 18.
Sion. 2 Sam. 5: 7.
Tabor. Jud. 4: 6, 12, 14.
A defence to a country. Psa. 125: 2.
Afford refuge in time of danger. Gen. 14: 10. Jud. 6: 2. Mat. 24: 16. Heb. 11: 38.
Afforded pasturage. Exo. 3: 1. 1 Sam. 25: 7. 1 Kin. 22: 17. Psa. 147: 8. Amos 4: 1.
ABOUNDED WITH
Herbs. Pro. 27: 25.
Minerals. Deu. 8: 9.
Precious things. Deu. 33: 15.
Stone for building. 1 Kin. 5: 14, 17. Dan. 2: 45.
Forests. 2 Kin. 19: 23. 2 Chr. 2: 2, 8—10.
Vineyards. 2 Chr. 26: 10. Jer. 31: 5.
Spices. So. of Sol. 4: 6. So. of Sol. 8: 14.
Deer. 1 Chr. 12: 8. So. of Sol. 2: 8
Game. 1 Sam. 26: 20.
Wild beasts. So. of Sol. 4: 8. Hab 2: 17.
Often inhabited. Gen. 36: 8. Jos 11: 21.
Sometimes selected as places for divine worship. Gen. 22: 2, 5. Exo. 3: 12. Isa. 2: 2.
Often selected as places for idolatrous worship. Deu. 12: 2. 2 Chr. 21: 11.
Proclamations often made from. Isa. 40: 9.
Beacons or ensigns often raised upon. Isa. 13: 2. Isa. 30: 17.
ILLUSTRATIVE
Of difficulties. Isa. 40: 4. Zec. 4: 7. Mat. 17: 20.
Of persons in authority. Psa. 72: 3. Isa. 44: 23.
Of the church of God. Isa. 2: 2. Dan. 2: 35, 44, 45.
Of God's righteousness. Psa. 36: 6.
Of proud and haughty persons. Isa. 2: 14.
(Burning,) of destructive enemies. Jer. 51: 25. Rev. 8: 8.
(Breaking forth into singing,) of exceeding joy. Isa. 44: 23. Isa. 55: 12.
(Threshing of,) of heavy judgments. Isa. 41: 15.
(Made waste,) of desolation. Isa. 42: 15. Mal. 1: 3.
(Dropping new wine,) of abundance. Amos 9: 13.

Mule, The.

First mention of. Gen. 36: 24.
Stupid and intractable. Psa. 32: 9.
USED FOR
Riding, by persons of distinction. 2 Sam. 13: 29. 2 Sam. 18: 9. 1 Kin. 1: 33.
Carrying burdens. 2 Kin. 5: 17. 1 Chr. 12: 40.
Conveying posts and messengers. Est. 8: 10, 14.
Liable to the plague. Zec. 14: 15.
Food of. 1 Kin. 4: 28. (*marg.*) 1 Kin. 18: 5.
THE JEWS
Forbidden to breed. Lev. 19: 19.
Set a great value upon. 1 Kin. 18: 5.
Brought many, from Babylon. Ezr. 2: 66.
Shall use, at the restoration. Isa. 66: 20.
Of Togarmah, sold in fairs of Tyre. Eze. 27: 14.
Often given as tribute. 1 Kin. 10: 25.

Murder.

Forbidden by Mosaic law. Exo. 20: 13. Deu. 5: 17.

Why forbidden by God. Gen. 9:6.
The law made to restrain. 1 Tim. 1:9.
DESCRIBED AS KILLING
With premeditation. Exo. 21: 14.
From hatred. Num. 35: 20, 21. Deu. 19: 11.
By lying in wait. Num. 35: 20. Deu. 19:11.
By an instrument of iron. Num. 35:16.
By the blow of a stone. Num. 35: 17.
By a hand weapon of wood. Num. 35:18.
Killing a thief in the day, counted as. Exo. 22:3.
Early introduction of. Gen. 4:8.
Represented as a sin crying unto heaven. Gen. 4: 10, with Heb. 12: 24. Rev. 6: 10.
The Jews often guilty of. Isa. 1:21.
PERSONS GUILTY OF,
Fearful and cowardly. Gen. 4: 14.
Wanderers and vagabonds. Gen. 4: 14.
Flee from God's presence. Gen. 4: 16.
Not protected in refuge cities. Deu. 19: 11, 12.
Had no protection from altars. Exo. 21: 14.
Not to be pitied or spared. Deu. 19: 13.
Often committed by night. Neh. 6: 10. Job 24: 14.
Imputed to the nearest city when the murderer was unknown. Deu. 21:1—3.
Mode of clearing those suspected of. Deu. 21:3—9. *See* Mat. 27: 24.
To be proved by two witnesses at least. Num. 35: 30. Deu. 19: 11, 15.
PUNISHMENT FOR,
The curse of God. Gen. 4:11.
Death. Gen. 9: 5, 6. Exo. 21: 12. Num. 35:16.
Not to be commuted. Num. 35: 32.
Inflicted by the nearest of kin. Num. 35:19, 21.
Forbidden. Gen. 9: 6. Exo. 20: 13. Deu. 5: 17, with Rom. 13: 9.
Explained by Christ. Mat. 5: 21, 22.
Hatred is. 1 Jno. 3:15.
Is a work of the flesh. Gal. 5: 21.
Comes from the heart. Mat. 15: 19.
DEFILES THE
Hands. Isa. 59: 3.
Person and garments. Lam. 4: 13, 14.
Land. Num. 35: 33. Psa. 106: 38.
Not concealed from God. Isa. 26:21. Jer. 2: 34.
Cries for vengeance. Gen. 4: 10.
GOD
Abominates. Pro. 6: 16, 17.
Makes inquisition for. Psa. 9: 12.
Will avenge. Deu. 32: 43. 1 Kin. 21: 19. Hos. 1: 4.
Requires blood for. Gen. 9: 5. Num. 35: 33. 1 Kin. 2: 32.
Rejects the prayers of those guilty of. Isa. 1: 15. Isa. 59: 2, 3.
Curses those guilty of. Gen. 4: 11.
The law made to restrain. 1 Tim. 1: 9.
SAINTS
Specially warned against. 1 Pet. 4: 15.
Deprecate the guilt of. Psa. 51: 14.
Should warn others against. Gen. 37: 22. Jer. 26: 15.
Connected with idolatry. Eze. 22: 3, 4. 2 Kin. 3: 27.
THE WICKED
Filled with. Rom. 1: 29.
Devise. Gen. 27: 41. Gen. 37: 18.
Intent on. Jer. 22:17.
Lie in wait to commit. Psa. 10: 8—10.
Swift to commit. Pro. 1: 16. Rom. 3: 15.
Perpetrate. Job 24: 14. Eze. 22: 3.
Have hands full of. Isa. 1: 15.
Encourage others to commit. 1 Kin. 21: 8—10. Pro. 1: 11.
Characteristic of the devil. Jno. 8: 44.
Punishment of. Gen. 4: 12—15. Gen. 9: 6. Num. 35: 30. 2 Kin. 9: 36, 37. Jer. 19: 4—9.
Punishment of, not commuted under the Law. Num. 35: 31.
Of saints, specially avenged. Deu. 32: 43. Mat. 23: 35. Rev. 18: 20, 24.
Excludes from heaven. Gal. 5: 21. Rev. 22: 15.
Exemplified. *Cain*, Gen. 4: 8. *Esau*, Gen. 27: 41. *Joseph's brethren*, Gen. 37: 20. *Pharaoh*, Exo. 1: 22. *Abimelech*, Jud. 9: 5. *Men of Shechem*, Jud. 9: 24. *Amalekite*, 2 Sam. 1: 16. *Rechab, &c.* 2 Sam. 4: 5—7. *David*, 2 Sam. 12: 9. *Absalom*, 2 Sam. 13: 29. *Joab*, 1 Kin. 2: 31, 32. *Baasha*, 1 Kin. 15: 27. *Zimri*, 1 Kin. 16: 10. *Jezebel*, 1 Kin. 21: 10. *Elders of Jezreel*, 1 Kin. 21: 13. *Ahab*, 1 Kin. 21: 19. *Hazael*, 2 Kin. 8: 12, 15. *Adrammelech, &c.* 2 Kin. 19: 37. *Manasseh*, 2 Kin. 21: 16. *Ishmael*, Jer. 41: 7. *Princes of Israel*, Eze. 11: 6. *People of Gilead*, Hos. 6: 8. *The Herods*, Mat. 2: 16. Mat. 14: 10. Acts 12: 2. *Herodias and her daughter*, Mat. 14: 8—11. *Chief priests*, Mat. 27: 1. *Judas*, Mat. 27: 4. *Barabbas*, Mar. 15: 7. *Jews*, Acts 7: 52. 1 The. 2: 15.

Murmuring.

Forbidden. 1 Cor. 10: 10. Phi. 2: 14.
AGAINST
God. Pro. 19: 3.

The sovereignty of God. Rom. 9: 19, 20.
The service of God. Mal. 3: 14.
Christ. Luke 5: 30. Luke 15: 2. Luke 19: 7. Jno. 6: 41—43, 52.
Ministers of God. Exo. 17: 3. Num. 16: 41.
Disciples of Christ. Mar. 7: 2. Luke 5: 30. Luke 6: 2.
Unreasonableness of. Lam. 3: 39.
Tempts God. Exo. 17: 2.
Provokes God. Num. 14: 2, 11. Deu. 9: 8, 22.
Saints cease from. Isa. 29: 23, 24.
Characteristic of the wicked. Jude 16.
Guilt of encouraging others in. Num. 13: 31—33, with Num. 14: 36, 37.
Punishment of. Num. 11: 1. Num. 14: 27—29. Num. 16: 45, 46. Psa. 106: 25, 26.
Illustrated. Mat. 20: 11. Luke 15: 29, 30.
Exemplified. *Cain*, Gen. 4: 13, 14. *Moses*, Exo. 5: 22, 23. *Israelites*, Exo. 14: 11. Exo. 15: 24. Exo. 16: 2. Exo. 17: 2, 3. Num. 11: 1—4. Num. 21: 5. *Aaron, &c.* Num. 12: 1, 2, 8. *Korah, &c.* Num. 16: 3. *Elijah*, 1 Kin. 19: 4. *Job*, Job 3: 1, &c. *Jeremiah*, Jer. 20: 14—18. *Jonah*, Jon. 4: 8, 9. *Disciples*, Mar. 14: 4, 5. Jno. 6: 61. *Pharisees*, Luke 15: 2. Luke 19: 7. *Jews*, Jno. 6: 41—43. *Grecians*, Acts 6: 1.

Music.

Early invention of. Gen. 4: 21.
DIVIDED INTO,
Vocal. 2 Sam. 19: 35. Acts 16: 25.
Instrumental. Dan. 6: 18.
Designed to promote joy. Ecc. 2: 8, 10.
Vanity of all unsanctified. Ecc. 2: 8, 11.
Considered efficacious in mental disorders. 1 Sam. 16: 14—17, 23.
Effects produced on the prophets of old by. 1 Sam. 10: 5, 6. 2 Kin. 3: 15.
INSTRUMENTS OF,
Cymbals. 1 Chr. 16: 5. Psa. 150: 5.
Cornet. Psa. 98: 6. Hos. 5: 8.
Dulcimer. Dan. 3: 5.
Flute. Dan. 3: 5.
Harp. Psa. 137: 2. Eze. 26: 13.
Organ. Gen. 4: 21. Job 21: 12. Psa. 150: 4.
Pipe. 1 Kin. 1: 40. Isa. 5: 12. Jer. 48: 36.
Psaltery. Psa. 33: 2. Psa. 71: 22.
Sackbut. Dan. 3: 5.
Tabret. 1 Sam. 10: 5. Isa. 24: 8.
Timbrel. Exo. 15: 20. Psa. 68: 25.
Trumpet. 2 Kin. 11: 14. 2 Chr. 29: 27.
Viol. Isa. 14: 11. Amos 5: 23.
Made of fir wood. 2 Sam. 6: 5.
Made of almug wood. 1 Kin. 10: 12.
Made of brass. 1 Cor. 13: 1.
Made of silver. Num. 10: 2.
Made of horns of animals. Jos. 6: 8.
Many, with strings. Psa. 33: 2. Psa. 150: 4.
Early invention of. Gen. 4: 21.
Invented by David. 1 Chr. 23: 5. 2 Chr. 7: 6.
The Jews celebrated for inventing. Amos 6: 5.
Often expensively ornamented. Eze. 28: 13.
Great diversity of. Ecc. 2: 8.
Appointed to be used in the temple. 1 Chr. 16: 4—6. 1 Chr. 23: 5, 6. 1 Chr. 25: 1. 2 Chr. 29: 25.
Custom of sending away friends with. Gen. 31: 27.
THE JEWS USED,
In sacred processions. 2 Sam. 6: 4, 5, 15. 1 Chr. 13: 6—8. 1 Chr. 15: 27, 28.
At laying foundation of temple. Ezr. 3: 9, 10.
At consecration of temple. 2 Chr. 5: 11—13.
At coronation of kings. 2 Chr. 23: 11, 13.
At dedication of city walls. Neh. 12: 27, 28.
To celebrate victories. Exo. 15: 20. 1 Sam. 18: 6, 7.
In religious feasts. 2 Chr. 30: 21.
In private entertainments. Isa. 5: 12. Amos 6: 5.
In dances. Mat. 11: 17. Luke 15: 25.
In funeral ceremonies. Mat. 9: 23.
In commemorating great men. 2 Chr. 35: 25.
Used in idol worship. Dan. 3: 5.
The movements of armies regulated by. Jos. 6: 8. 1 Cor. 14: 8.
Generally put aside in times of affliction. Psa. 137: 2—4. Dan. 6: 18.
ILLUSTRATIVE
Of joy and gladness. Zep. 3: 17. Eph. 5: 19.
Of heavenly felicity. Rev. 5: 8, 9.
(Ceasing of,) of calamities. Isa. 24: 8, 9. Rev. 18: 22.

Naphtali, The Tribe of.

Descended from Jacob's sixth son. Gen. 30: 7, 8.
Predictions respecting. Gen. 49: 21. Deu. 33: 23.
PERSONS SELECTED FROM,
To number the people. Num. 1: 15.
To spy out the land. Num. 13: 14.
To divide the land. Num. 34: 28.
Strength of, on leaving Egypt. Num. 1: 42, 43.
The rear of the fourth division of Israel in their journeys. Num. 10: 25, 27.

Encamped under the standard of Dan north of the tabernacle. Num. 2:25, 29.
Offering of, at the dedication. Num. 7:78—83.
Families of. Num. 26:48, 49.
Strength of, on entering Canaan. Num. 26:50.
On Ebal said amen to the curses. Deu. 27:13.
Bounds of their inheritance. Jos. 19:32—39.
Did not drive out the Canaanites, but make them tributary. Jud. 1:33.
Chosen from Zebulun to go with Barak against Sisera. Jud. 4:6, 10.
Praised for aiding against Sisera. Jud. 5:18.
Joined Gideon in the pursuit and overthrow of the Midianites. Jud. 7:23.
Some of, at David's coronation. 1 Chr. 12:34.
Officer placed over, by David. 1 Chr. 27:19.
Officer placed over, by Solomon. 1 Kin. 4:15.
Land of, ravaged by Benhadad. 1 Kin. 15:20.
Land of, purged of idols by Josiah. 2 Chr. 34:6.
Taken captive by Tiglath-pileser. 2 Kin. 15:29.
Specially favored by our Lord's ministry. Isa. 9:1, 2. Mat. 4:13—15.
Remarkable persons of; *Barak*, Jud. 4:6. *Hiram*, 1 Kin. 7:14.

Nazarites.

Persons separated to the service of God. Num. 6:2.
DIFFERENT KINDS OF;
- From the womb. Jud. 13:5. Luke 1:15.
- By a particular vow. Num. 6:2.

Required to be holy. Num. 6:8.
Esteemed pure. Lam. 4:7.
PROHIBITED FROM
- Wine or strong drink. Num. 6:3. Luke 1:15.
- Grapes or any thing made from the vine. Num. 6:3, 4. Jud. 13:14.
- Cutting or shaving the head. Num. 6:5. Jud. 13:5. Jud. 16:17.
- Defiling themselves by the dead. Num. 6:6, 7.

Raised up for the good of the nation. Amos 2:11.
Ungodly Jews tried to corrupt. Amos 2:12.
DEFILED DURING VOW
- To shave the head the seventh day. Num. 6:9.
- To bring two turtle doves for a burnt offering. Num. 6:10, 11.
- To recommence their vow with a trespass offering. Num. 6:12.

ON COMPLETION OF VOW
- To be brought to tabernacle door. Num. 6:13.
- To offer sacrifices. Num. 6:14—17.
- To shave their heads. Num. 6:18. Acts 18:18. Acts 21:24.
- To have the left shoulder of the ram of the peace offering waved upon their hands by the priest. Num. 6:19, 20, with Lev. 7:32.

ILLUSTRATIVE OF
- Christ. Heb. 7:26.
- Saints. 2 Cor. 6:17. Jas. 1:27.

Nethinim.

Were the servants of the Levites. Ezr. 8:20.
Probably originated in the appointment of the Gibeonites. Jos. 9:27.
The remnant of the Canaanites appointed as, by Solomon. 1 Kin. 9:20, 21, with Ezr. 2:58.
WITH THE PRIESTS AND LEVITES
- Had cities to reside in. 1 Chr. 9:2. Ezr. 2:70.
- Exempted from tribute. Ezr. 7:24.

Had chiefs or captains over them. Neh. 11:21.
A large number of, returned from the captivity. Ezr. 2:43—54. Neh. 7:46—56, 60.
Were zealous for the covenant. Neh. 10:28, 29.

New Birth, The.

The corruption of human nature requires. Jno. 3:6. Rom. 8:7, 8.
None can enter heaven without. Jno. 3:3.
EFFECTED BY
- God. Jno. 1:13. 1 Pet. 1:3.
- Christ. 1 Jno. 2:29.
- The Holy Ghost. Jno. 3:6. Tit. 3:5.

THROUGH THE INSTRUMENTALITY OF
- The word of God. Jas. 1:18. 1 Pet. 1:23.
- The resurrection of Christ. 1 Pet: 1:3.
- The ministry of the gospel. 1 Cor. 4:15.

Is of the will of God. Jas. 1:18.
Is of the mercy of God. Tit. 3:5.
Is for the glory of God. Isa. 43:7.
DESCRIBED AS
- A new creation. 2 Cor. 5:17. Gal. 6:15. Eph. 2:10.
- Newness of life. Rom. 6:4.
- A spiritual resurrection. Rom. 6:4—6. Eph. 2:1, 5. Col. 2:12. Col. 3:1.
- A new heart. Eze. 36:26.
- A new spirit. Eze. 11:19. Rom. 7:6.
- Putting on the new man. Eph. 4:24.

The inward man. Rom. 7: 22. 2 Cor. 4: 16.
Circumcision of the heart. Deu. 30: 6, with Rom. 2: 29. Col. 2: 11.
Partaking of the divine nature. 2 Pet. 1: 4.
The washing of regeneration. Tit. 3: 5.
All saints partake of. Rom. 8: 16, 17. 1 Pet. 2: 2. 1 Jno. 5: 1.
PRODUCES
Likeness to God. Eph. 4: 24. Col. 3: 10.
Likeness to Christ. Rom. 8: 29. 2 Cor. 3: 18. 1 Jno. 3: 2.
Knowledge of God. Jer. 24: 7. Col. 3: 10.
Hatred of sin. 1 Jno. 3: 9. 1 Jno. 5: 18.
Victory over the world. 1 Jno. 5: 4.
Delight in God's law. Rom. 7: 22.
EVIDENCED BY
Faith in Christ. 1 Jno. 5: 1.
Righteousness. 1 Jno. 2: 29.
Brotherly love. 1 Jno. 4: 7.
Connected with adoption. Isa. 43: 6, 7. Jno. 1: 12, 13.
The ignorant cavil at. Jno. 3: 4.
Manner of effecting—Illustrated. Jno. 3: 8.
Preserves from Satan's devices. 1 Jno. 5: 18.

Night.

The darkness first called. Gen. 1: 5.
Caused by God. Psa. 104: 20.
Belongs to God. Psa. 74: 16.
The heavenly bodies designed to separate day from. Gen. 1: 14.
The moon and stars designed to rule and give light by. Gen. 1: 16—18. Jer. 31: 35.
Commenced at sunset. Gen. 28: 11.
Continued until sunrise. Psa. 104: 22. Mat. 28: 1, with Mar. 16: 2.
REGULAR SUCCESSION OF,
Established by covenant. Gen. 8: 22. Jer. 33: 20.
Ordained for the glory of God. Psa. 19: 2.
Originally divided into three watches. Lam. 2: 19, with Jud. 7: 19. Exo. 14: 24.
Divided into four watches by the Romans. Luke 12: 38, with Mat. 14: 25. Mar. 13: 35.
FREQUENTLY
Exceeding dark. Pro. 7: 9.
Cold and frosty. Gen. 31: 40. Jer. 36: 30.
Accompanied by heavy dews. Num. 11: 9. Jud. 6: 38, 40. Job 29: 19. So. of Sol. 5: 2.
Unsuitable for labor. Jno. 9: 4.
Unsuitable for traveling. Jno. 11: 10.
Designed for rest. Psa. 104: 23.
Wearisome to the afflicted. Job 7: 3, 4.
Favorable to the purposes of the wicked. Gen. 31: 39. Job 24: 14, 15. Oba. 5 v. 1 The. 5: 2.
Wild beasts go forth in search of prey during. 2 Sam. 21: 10. Psa. 104: 21, 22.
THE JEWS
Forbidden to keep the wages of servants during. Lev. 19: 13.
Forbidden to allow malefactors to hang during. Deu. 21: 23.
In affliction spent, in sorrow and humiliation. Psa. 6: 6. Psa. 30: 5. Joel 1: 13.
In affliction spent, in prayer. Psa. 22: 2.
Often kept lamps burning during. Pro. 31: 18.
Eastern shepherds watched over their flocks during. Gen. 31: 40. Luke 2: 8.
Eastern fishermen continued their employment during. Luke 5: 5. Jno. 21: 3.
GOD FREQUENTLY
Revealed His will in. Gen. 31: 24. Gen. 46: 2. Num. 22: 20. Dan. 7: 2.
Visited His people in. 1 Kin. 3: 5. Psa. 17: 3.
Executed His judgments in. Exo. 12: 12. 2 Kin. 19: 35. Job 27: 20. Dan. 5: 30.
ILLUSTRATIVE OF
Spiritual darkness. Rom. 13: 12.
Seasons of severe calamities. Isa. 21: 12. Amos 5: 8.
Seasons of spiritual desertion. So. of Sol. 3: 1.
Death. Jno. 9: 4.

Nile, The River.

Empties itself into the Mediterranean Sea by seven streams. Isa. 11: 15.
CALLED
The river. Gen. 41: 1, 3.
The Egyptian sea. Isa. 11: 15.
The stream of Egypt. Isa. 27: 12.
Sihor. Jos. 13: 3. Jer. 2: 18.
ABOUNDED IN
Crocodiles. Eze. 29: 3.
Fish. Exo. 7: 21. Eze. 29: 4.
Reeds and flags. Isa. 19: 6, 7.
Annual overflow of its banks alluded to. Jer. 46: 8. Amos 8: 8. Amos 9: 5.
THE EGYPTIANS
Took great pride in. Eze. 29: 9.
Carried on extensive commerce by. Isa. 23: 3.
Bathed in. Exo. 2: 5.
Drank of. Exo. 7: 21, 24.
Punished by failure of its waters. Isa. 19: 5, 6.

Punished by destruction of its fish. Isa. 19: 8.

REMARKABLE EVENTS CONNECTED WITH;

Male children drowned in. Exo. 1: 22.

Moses exposed on its banks. Exo. 2: 3.

Its waters turned into blood. Exo. 7: 15, 20.

Miraculous generation of frogs. Exo. 8: 3.

Nineveh.

Origin and antiquity of. Gen. 10: 11.

Situated on the river Tigris. Nah. 2: 6, 8.

The ancient capital of Assyria. 2 Kin. 19: 36. Isa. 37: 37.

Called the bloody city. Nah. 3: 1.

DESCRIBED AS

Great. Jon. 1: 2. Jon. 3: 2.

Extensive. Jon. 3: 3.

Rich. Nah. 2: 9.

Strong. Nah. 3: 12.

Commercial. Nah. 3: 16.

Populous. Jon. 4: 11.

Vile. Nah. 1: 14.

Wicked. Jon. 1: 2.

Idolatrous. Nah. 1: 14.

Full of joy and carelessness. Zep. 2: 15.

Full of lies and robbery. Nah. 3: 1.

Full of witchcraft, &c. Nah. 3: 4.

Jonah sent to proclaim the destruction of. Jon. 1: 2. Jon. 3: 1, 2, 4.

Inhabitants of, repented at Jonah's preaching. Jon. 3: 5—9. Mat. 12: 41. Luke 11: 32.

Destruction of, averted. Jon. 3: 10. Jon. 4: 11.

PREDICTIONS RESPECTING;

Coming up of the Babylonish armies against. Nah. 2: 1—4. Nah. 3: 2.

Destruction of its people. Nah. 1: 12. Nah. 3: 3.

Spoiling of its treasures. Nah. 2: 9.

Destruction of its idols. Nah. 1: 14. Nah. 2: 7.

Degradation and contempt put on. Nah. 3: 5—7. Zep. 2: 15.

Utter destruction. Nah. 1: 8, 9.

Complete desolation. Zep. 2: 13—15.

Feebleness of its people. Nah. 3: 13.

Being taken while the people were drunk. Nah. 1: 10. Nah. 3: 11.

Captivity of its people. Nah. 3: 10.

Oak-tree, The.

The hill of Bashan celebrated for. Isa. 2: 13.

DESCRIBED AS

Strong. Amos 2: 9.

Thick spreading. 2 Sam. 18: 9. Eze. 6: 13.

Casting its leaves in winter. Isa. 6: 13.

The Tyrians made oars of. Eze. 27: 6.

Idolaters often made idols of. Isa. 44: 14.

THE ANCIENTS OFTEN

Rested under. Jud. 6: 11, 19. 1 Kin. 13: 14.

Buried their dead under. Gen. 35: 8. 1 Chr. 10: 12.

Erected monuments under. Jos. 24: 26.

Performed idolatrous rites under. Isa. 1: 29. Isa. 57: 5. (*marg.*) Eze. 6: 13. Hos. 4: 13.

Absalom in his flight intercepted by, and suspended from. 2 Sam. 18: 9, 10, 14.

Jacob buried his family idols under. Gen. 35: 4.

ILLUSTRATIVE

Of the church. Isa. 6: 13.

Of strong and powerful men. Amos 2: 9.

Of wicked rulers. Isa. 2: 13. Zec. 11: 2.

(Fading,) of the wicked under judgments. Isa. 1: 30.

Oaths.

The lawful purpose of, explained. Heb. 6: 16.

Antiquity of. Gen. 14: 22. Gen. 24: 3, 8.

USED FOR

Confirming covenants. Gen. 26: 28. Gen. 31: 44, 53. 1 Sam. 20: 16, 17.

Deciding controversies in courts of law. Exo. 22: 11. Num. 5: 19. 1 Kin. 8: 31.

Pledging allegiance to sovereigns. 2 Kin. 11: 4. Ecc. 8: 2.

Binding to performance of sacred duties. Num. 30: 2. 2 Chr. 15: 14, 15. Neh. 10: 29. Psa. 132: 2.

Binding to performance of any particular act. Gen. 24: 3, 4. Gen. 50: 25. Jos. 2: 12.

Judicial form of administering. 1 Kin. 22: 16. Mat. 26: 63.

Often accompanied by raising up the hand. Gen. 14: 22. Dan. 12: 7. Rev. 10: 5, 6.

Often accompanied by placing the hand under the thigh of the person sworn to. Gen. 24: 2, 9. Gen. 47: 29.

To be taken in fear and reverence. Ecc. 9: 2.

THE JEWS

Forbidden to take, in name of idols. Jos. 23: 7.

Forbidden to take in the name of any created thing. Mat. 5: 34—36. Jas. 5: 12.

Forbidden to take false. Lev. 6:3. Zec. 8:17.
Forbidden to take rash, or unholy. Lev. 5:4.
To use God's name alone in. Deu. 6:13. Deu. 10:20. Isa. 65:16.
To take, in truth, judgment, &c. Jer. 4:2.
Generally respected the obligation of. Jos. 9:19, 20. 2 Sam. 21:7. Psa. 15:4. Mat. 14:9.
Fell into many errors respecting. Mat. 23:16—22.
Often guilty of rashly taking. Jud. 21:7. Mat. 14:7. Mat. 26:72.
Often guilty of falsely taking. Lev. 6:3. Jer. 5:2. Jer. 7:9.
Condemned for false. Zec. 5:4. Mal. 3:5.
Condemned for profane. Jer. 23:10. Hos. 4:2.

INSTANCES OF RASH, &c.;
Joshua, &c. Jos. 9:15, 16.
Jephthah. Jud. 11:30—36.
Saul. 1 Sam. 14:27, 44.
Herod. Mat. 14:7—9.
The Jews who sought to kill Paul. Acts 23:21.

Custom of swearing by the life of the king. Gen. 42:15, 16.

EXPRESSIONS USED AS;
By the fear of Isaac. Gen. 31:53.
As the Lord liveth. Jud. 8:19. Ruth 3:13.
The Lord do so to me, and more also. Ruth 1:17.
God do so to thee, and more also. 1 Sam. 3:17.
By the Lord. 2 Sam. 19:7. 1 Kin. 2:42.
Before God I lie not. Gal. 1:20.
I call God for a record. 2 Cor. 1:23.
God is witness. 1 The. 2:5.
I charge you by the Lord. 1 The. 5:27.
As thy soul liveth. 1 Sam. 1:26. 1 Sam. 25:26.

God used, to show the immutability of His counsel. Gen. 22:16. Num. 14:28. Heb. 6:17.

Obedience to God.

Commanded. Deu. 13:4.
Without faith, is impossible. Heb. 11:6.

INCLUDES
Obeying His voice. Exo. 19:5. Jer. 7:23.
Obeying His law. Deu. 11:27. Isa. 42:24.
Obeying Christ. Exo 23:21. 2 Cor. 10:5.
Obeying the gospel. Rom. 1:5. Rom. 6:17. Rom. 10:16, 17.
Keeping His commandments. Ecc. 12:13.
Submission to higher powers. Rom. 13:1.

Better than sacrifice. 1 Sam. 15:22.
Justification obtained by that of Christ. Rom. 5:19.
Christ, an example of. Mat. 3:15. Jno. 15:10. Phi. 2:5—8. Heb. 5:8.
Angels engaged in. Psa. 103:20.
A characteristic of saints. 1 Pet. 1:14.
Saints elected to. 1 Pet. 1:2.
Obligations to. Acts 4:19, 20. Acts 5:29.
Exhortations to. Jer. 26:13. Jer. 38:20.

SHOULD BE
From the heart. Deu. 11:13. Rom. 6:17.
With willingness. Psa. 18:44. Isa. 1:19.
Unreserved. Jos. 22:2, 3.
Undeviating. Deu. 28:14.
Constant. Phi. 2:12.

Resolve upon. Exo. 24:7. Jos. 24:24.
Confess your failure in. Dan. 9:10.
Prepare the heart for. 1 Sam. 7:3. Ezr. 7:10.
Pray to be taught. Psa. 119:35. Psa. 143:10.
Promises to. Exo. 23:22. 1 Sam. 12:14. Isa. 1:19. Jer. 7:23.
To be universal in the latter days. BDan. 7:27.
lessedness of. Deu. 11:27. Deu. 28:1—13. Luke 11:28. Jas. 1:25.
The wicked refuse. Exo. 5:2. Neh. 9:17.
Punishment of refusing. Deu. 11:28. Deu. 28:15—68. Jos. 5:6. Isa. 1:20.
Exemplified. *Noah*, Gen. 6:22. *Abram*, Gen. 12:1—4, with Heb. 11:8. Gen. 22:3, 12. *Israelites*, Exo. 12:28. Exo. 24:7. *Caleb, &c.* Num. 32:12. *Asa*, 1 Kin. 15:11. *Elijah*, 1 Kin. 17:5. *Hezekiah*, 2 Kin. 18:6. *Josiah*, 2 Kin. 22:2. *David*, Psa. 119:106. *Zerubbabel, &c.* Hag. 1:12. *Joseph*, Mat. 1:24. *Wise men*, Mat. 2:12. *Zacharias, &c.* Luke 1:6. *Paul*, Acts 26:19. *Saints of Rome*, Rom. 16:19.

Offence.

Occasions of, must arrive. Mat. 18:7.
Occasions of, forbidden. 1 Cor. 10:32. 2 Cor. 6:3.
Persecution, a cause of, to mere professors. Mat. 13:21. Mat. 24:10. Mat. 26:31.

THE WICKED TAKE, AT
The low station of Christ. Isa. 53:1—3. Mat. 13:54—57.
Christ, as the corner-stone. Isa. 8:14, with Rom. 9:33. 1 Pet. 2:8.
Christ, as the bread of life. Jno. 6:58—61.
Christ crucified. 1 Cor. 1:23. Gal. 5:11.

The righteousness of faith. Rom. 9:32.
The necessity of inward purity. Mat. 15:11, 12.
Blessedness of not taking, at Christ. Mat. 11:6.
Saints warned against taking. Jno. 16:1.
SAINTS SHOULD
Be without. Phi. 1:10.
Be cautious of giving. Psa. 73:15. Rom. 14:13. 1 Cor. 8:9.
Have a conscience void of. Acts 24:16.
Cut off what causes, to themselves. Mat. 5:29, 30. Mar. 9:43—47.
Not let their liberty occasion, to others. 1 Cor. 8:9.
Use self-denial rather than occasion. Rom. 14:21. 1 Cor. 8:13.
Avoid those who cause. Rom. 16:17.
Reprove those who cause. Exo. 32:21. 1 Sam. 2:24.
MINISTERS SHOULD
Be cautious of giving. 2 Cor. 6:3.
Remove that which causes. Isa. 57:14.
All things that cause, shall be gathered out of Christ's kingdom. Mat. 13:41.
Denunciation against those who cause. Mat. 18:7. Mar. 9:42.
Punishment for occasioning. Eze. 44:12. Mal. 2:8, 9. Mat. 18:6, 7.
Exemplified. *Aaron*, Exo. 32:2—6. *Balaam, &c.* Num. 31:16, with Rev. 2:14. *Gideon*, Jud. 8:27. *Sons of Eli*, 1 Sam. 2:12—17. *Jeroboam*, 1 Kin. 12:26—30. *Old Prophet*, 1 Kin. 13:18—26. *Priests*, Mal. 2:8. *Peter*, Mat. 16:23.

Offences Against the Holy Ghost.

Exhortations against. Eph. 4:30. 1 The. 5:19.
EXHIBITED IN
Tempting Him. Acts 5:9.
Vexing Him. Isa. 63:10.
Grieving Him. Eph. 4:30.
Quenching Him. 1 The. 5:19.
Lying to Him. Acts 5:3, 4.
Resisting Him. Acts 7:51.
Undervaluing His gifts. Acts 8:19, 20.
Danger of trifling with the Holy Ghost. Heb. 6:4—6.
Doing despite unto Him. Heb. 10:29.
Disregarding His testimony. Neh. 9:30.
Blasphemy against Him, unpardonable. Mat. 12:31, 32. 1 Jno. 5:16.

Offerings.

To be made to God alone. Exo. 22:20. Jud. 13:16.
Antiquity of. Gen. 4:3, 4.
DIFFERENT KINDS OF;
Burnt. Lev. 1:3—17. Psa. 66:15.
Sin. Lev. 4:3—35. Lev. 6:25. Lev. 10:17.
Trespass. Lev. 5:6—19. Lev. 6:6. Lev. 7:1.
Peace. Lev. 3:1—17. Lev. 7:11.
Heave. Exo. 29:27, 28. Lev. 7:14. Num. 15:19.
Wave. Exo. 29:26. Lev. 7:30.
Meat. Lev. 2 ch. Num. 15:4.
Drink. Gen. 35:14. Exo. 29:40. Num. 15:5.
Thank. Lev. 7:12. Lev. 22:29. Psa. 50:14.
Free-will. Lev. 23:38. Deu. 16:10. Deu. 23:23.
Incense. Exo. 30:8. Mal. 1:11. Luke 1:9.
First-fruits. Exo. 22:29. Deu. 18:4.
Tithe. Lev. 27:30. Num. 18:21. Deu. 14:22.
Gifts. Exo. 35:22. Num. 7:2—88.
Jealousy. Num. 5:15.
Personal, for redemption. Exo. 30:13, 15.
Declared to be most holy. Num. 18:9.
REQUIRED TO BE
Perfect. Lev. 22:21.
The best of their kind. Mal. 1:14.
Offered willingly. Lev. 22:19.
Offered in righteousness. Mal. 3:3.
Offered in love and charity. Mat. 5:23, 24.
Brought in a clean vessel. Isa. 66:20.
Brought to the place appointed of God. Deu. 12:6. Psa. 27:6. Heb. 9:9.
Laid before the altar. Mat. 5:23, 24.
Presented by the priest. Heb. 5:1.
Brought without delay Exo. 22:29, 30.
Unacceptable without gratitude. Psa. 50:8, 14.
Could not make the offerer perfect. Heb. 9:9.
THINGS FORBIDDEN AS;
The price of fornication. Deu. 23:18.
The price of a dog. Deu. 23:18.
Whatever was blemished. Lev. 22:20.
Whatever was imperfect. Lev. 22:24.
Whatever was unclean. Lev, 27:11, 27.
Laid up in the temple. 2 Chr. 31:12. Neh. 10:37.
Hezekiah prepared chambers for. 2 Chr. 31:11.
THE JEWS OFTEN
Slow in presenting. Neh. 13:10—12.
Defrauded God of. Mal. 3:8.

Gave the worst they had as. Mal. 1: 8, 13.
Rejected in, because of sin. Isa. 1: 13. Mal. 1: 10.
Abhorred, on account of the sins of the priests. 1 Sam. 2: 17.
Presented to idols. Eze. 20: 28.
Made by strangers, to be the same as by the Jews. Num. 15: 14—16.
Many offences under the law, beyond the efficacy of. 1 Sam. 3: 14. Psa. 51: 16.
ILLUSTRATIVE OF
Christ's offering of Himself. Eph. 5: 2.
The conversion of the Gentiles. Rom. 15: 16.
The conversion of the Jews. Isa. 66: 20.

Oil.

Given by God. Psa. 104: 14, 15. Jer. 31: 12. Joel 2: 19, 24.
Comes from the earth. Psa. 104: 14, 15. Hos. 2: 22.
KINDS OF, MENTIONED;
Olive. Exo. 30: 24. Lev. 24: 2.
Myrrh. Est. 2: 12.
Extracted by presses. Hag. 2: 16, with Mic. 6: 15.
The poor employed in extracting. Job 24: 11.
Canaan abounded in. Deu. 8: 8.
DESCRIBED AS
Soft. Psa. 55: 21.
Smooth. Pro. 5: 3.
Penetrating. Psa. 109: 18.
Healing. Isa. 1: 6, with Luke 10: 34.
The ointments of the Jews made of perfumes mixed with. Exo. 30: 23—25. Jno. 12: 3.
Jews often extravagant in the use of. Pro. 21: 17.
Was titheable by the law. Deu. 12: 17.
First-fruits of, given to God. Deu. 18: 4. 2 Chr. 31: 5. Neh. 10: 37.
USED
For food. 1 Kin. 17: 12. Eze. 16: 13.
For anointing the person. Psa. 23: 5. Psa. 104: 15. Luke 7: 46.
For anointing to offices of trust. Exo. 29: 7. 1 Sam. 10: 1. 1 Kin. 19: 16.
For anointing the sick. Mar. 6: 13. Jas. 5: 14.
In God's worship. Lev. 7: 10. Num. 15: 4—10.
In idolatrous worship. Hos. 2: 5, 8.
For lamps. Exo. 25: 6. Exo. 27: 20. Mat. 25: 3.
When fresh especially esteemed. Psa. 92: 10.
Dealing in, a trade. 2 Kin. 4: 7.
Exported. 1 Kin. 5: 11. Eze. 27: 17. Hos. 12: 1.
Sold by measure. 1 Kin. 5: 11. Luke 16: 6.
KEPT IN
Boxes. 2 Kin. 9: 1.
Horns. 1 Kin. 1: 39.
Pots. 2 Kin. 4: 2.
Cruises. 1 Kin. 17: 12.
Cellars. 1 Chr. 27: 28.
Storehouses. 2 Chr. 32: 28.
Stores of, laid up in fortified cities. 2 Chr. 11: 11.
Failure of, a severe calamity. Hag. 1: 11.
Miraculous increase of. 2 Kin. 4: 2—6.
ILLUSTRATIVE OF
The unction of the Holy Spirit. Psa. 45: 7. Psa. 89: 20. Zec. 4: 12.
The consolation of the gospel. Isa. 61: 3.
Kind reproof. Psa. 141: 5.

Olive-tree, The.

Often grew wild. Rom. 11: 17.
CULTIVATED
In olive yards. 1 Sam. 8: 14. Neh. 5: 11.
Among rocks. Deu. 32: 13.
On the sides of mountains. Mat. 21: 1.
Canaan abounded in. Deu. 6: 11. Deu. 8: 8. (*marg.*)
Assyria abounded in. 2 Kin. 18: 32.
Kings of Israel largely cultivated. 1 Chr. 27: 28.
DESCRIBED AS
Green. Jer. 11: 16.
Fair and beautiful. Jer. 11: 16, with Hos. 14: 6.
Fat and unctuous. Jud. 9: 9. Rom. 11: 17.
Bearing goodly fruit. Jer. 11: 16, with Jas. 3: 12.
Grafting of, alluded to. Rom. 11: 24.
Pruning of, alluded to. Rom. 11: 18, 19.
Often cast its flowers. Job 15: 33.
Often cast its fruit. Deu. 28: 40.
Often suffered from caterpillars. Amos 4: 9.
Good for the service of God and man. Jud. 9: 9.
Oil procured from. Exo. 27: 20. Deu. 8: 8.
USED FOR MAKING
The cherubim in the temple. 1 Kin. 6: 23.
The doors and posts of the temple. 1 Kin. 6: 31—33.
Booths at feast of tabernacles. Neh. 8: 15.
Beaten to remove the fruit. Deu. 24: 20.
Shaken when fully ripe. Isa. 17: 6.

Gleaning of, left for the poor. Deu. 24:20.
Fruit of, during sabbatical year left for the poor, &c. Exo. 23:11.
The fruit of, trodden in presses to extract the oil. Mic. 6:15, with Hag. 2:16.
Failure of, a great calamity. Hab. 3:17, 18.
ILLUSTRATIVE
Of Christ. Rom. 11:17, 24. Zec. 4:3, 12.
Of the Jewish church. Jer. 11:16.
Of the righteous. Psa. 52:8. Hos. 14:6.
Of children of pious parents. Psa. 128:3.
Of the two witnesses. Rev. 11:3, 4.
(When wild,) of the Gentiles. Rom. 11:17, 24.
(Gleaning of,) of the remnant of grace. Isa. 17:6. Isa. 24:13.
Probable origin of its being the emblem of peace. Gen. 8:11.

Ostrich, The.

Unclean and unfit for food. Lev. 11:13.
Furnished with wings and feathers. Job 39:13.
Lays her eggs in the sand. Job 39:14.
DESCRIBED AS
Void of wisdom. Job 39:17.
Imprudent. Job 39:15.
Cruel to her young. Job 39:16.
Rapid in movement. Job 39:18.
ILLUSTRATIVE
Of the unnatural cruelty of the Jews in their calamities. Lam. 4:3.
(Companionship with,) of extreme desolation. Job 30:29. (*marg.*)

Owl, The.

Varieties of. Lev. 11:16, 17. Deu. 14:15, 16.
Unclean and not to be eaten. Lev. 11:13, with 16 v.
DESCRIBED AS
Mournful in voice. Mic. 1:8.
Solitary in disposition. Psa. 102:6.
Careful of its young. Isa. 34:15.
Inhabits deserted cities and houses. Isa. 13:21. Isa. 34:11—14. Jer. 50:39.
Illustrative of mourners. Psa. 102:6.

Ox, The.

Often found wild. Deu. 14:5.
INCLUDES THE
Bull. Gen. 32:15. Job 21:10.
Bullock. Psa. 50:9. Jer. 46:21.
Cow. Num. 18:17. Job 21:10.
Heifer. Gen. 15:9. Num. 19:2.
Was clean and fit for food. Deu. 14:4.
DESCRIBED AS
Strong. Psa. 144:14. Pro. 14:4.
Beautiful. Jer. 46:20. Hos. 10:11.
Not without sagacity. Isa. 1:3.
Horns and hoofs of, alluded to. Psa. 69:31.
Lowing of, alluded to. 1 Sam. 15:14. Job 6:5.
WAS FED
With grass. Job 40:15. Psa. 106: 20. Dan. 4:25.
With corn. Isa. 30:24.
With straw. Isa. 11:7.
On the hills. Isa. 7:25.
In the valleys. 1 Chr. 27:29. Isa. 65 10.
In stalls. Hab. 3:17.
Rapid manner of collecting its food alluded to. Num. 22:4.
Formed a part of the patriarchal wealth. Gen. 13:2, 5. Gen. 26:14. Job 1:3.
Formed a part of the wealth of Israel in Egypt. Gen. 50:8. Exo. 10:9. Exo. 12:32.
Formed a part of the wealth of the Jews. Num. 32:4. Psa. 144:14.
Required great care and attention. Pro. 27:23.
Herdmen appointed over. Gen. 13:7. 1 Sam. 21:7.
Urged on by the goad. Jud. 3:31.
USED FOR
Drawing wagons, &c. Num. 7:3. 1 Sam. 6:7.
Carrying burdens. 1 Chr. 12:40.
Plowing. 1 Kin. 19:19. Job 1:14. Amos 6:12.
Earing the ground. Isa. 30:24. Isa. 32:20.
Treading out the corn. Hos. 10:11.
Sacrifice. Exo. 20:24. 2 Sam. 24:22.
Food. 1 Kin. 1:9. 1 Kin. 19:21. 2 Chr. 18:2.
Often stall-fed for slaughter. Pro. 15:17.
Goes to the slaughter unconscious. Pro. 7:22.
Young of, considered a great delicacy. Gen. 18:7. Amos 6:4.
Male firstlings of, belonged to God. Exo. 34:19.
Tithe of, given to the priests. 2 Chr. 31:6.
LAWS RESPECTING;
To rest on the Sabbath. Exo. 23:12. Deu. 5:14.
Not to be yoked with an ass in the same plow. Deu. 22:10.
Not to be muzzled when treading out the corn. Deu. 25:4. 1 Cor. 9:9.
If stolen to be restored double. Exo. 22:4.
Of others not to be coveted. Exo. 20:17. Deu. 5:21.
Of others if lost or hurt through neglect, to be made good. Exo. 22:9—13.

Killing a man, to be stoned. Exo. 21:28—32.
Mode of reparation for one, killing another. Exo. 21:35, 36.
Straying to be brought back to its owner. Exo. 23:4. Deu. 22:1, 2.
Fallen under its burden to be raised up again. Deu. 22:4.
Fat of, not to be eaten. Lev. 7:23.
Increase of, promised. Deu. 7:13. Deu. 28:4.
Publicly sold. 2 Sam. 24:24. Luke 14:19.
Often given as a present. Gen. 12:16. Gen. 20:14.
The wicked often took, in pledge from the poor. Job 24:3.
Custom of sending the pieces of, to collect the people to war. 1 Sam. 11:7.
Sea of brass rested on figures of. 1 Kin. 7:25.
ILLUSTRATIVE
(Engaged in husbandry,) of Ministers. Isa. 30:24. Isa. 32:20.
(Not muzzled in treading corn,) of Minister's right to support. 1 Cor. 9:9, 10.
(Prepared for a feast,) of the provision of the gospel. Pro. 9:2. Mat. 22:4.
(Led to slaughter,) of a rash youth. Pro. 7:22.
(Led to slaughter,) of saints under persecution. Jer. 11:19.
(Stall fed,) of sumptuous living. Pro. 15:17.
BULL OR BULLOCK ILLUSTRATIVE
Of fierce enemies. Psa. 22:12. Psa. 68:30.
(Firstling of,) of the glory of Joseph. Deu. 33:17.
(In a net,) of the impatient under judgment. Isa. 51:20.
(Fatted,) of greedy mercenaries. Jer. 46:21.
(Unaccustomed to the yoke,) of intractable sinners. Jer. 31:18.
KINE ILLUSTRATIVE
Of proud and wealthy rulers. Amos 4:1.
(well favored,) of years of plenty. Gen. 41:2, 26, 29.
(Lean,) of years of scarcity. Gen. 41:3, 27. 30.
HEIFER ILLUSTRATIVE
Of a beloved wife. Jud. 14:18.
(Sliding back,) of backsliding Israel. Hos. 4:16.
(Taught, &c.) of Israel's fondness for ease in preference to obedience. Hos. 10:11.
(Of three years old,) of Moab in affliction. Isa. 15:5. Jer. 48:34.
(Fair,) of the beauty and wealth of Egypt. Jer. 46:20.
(At grass,) of the luxurious Chaldees. Jer. 50:11.

Palaces.

Jerusalem celebrated for. Psa. 48:3, 13.
THE TERM APPLIED TO
Residences of kings. Dan. 4:4. Dan. 6:18.
Houses of great men. Amos 3:9. Mic. 5:5.
The temple of God. 1 Chr. 29:1, 19.
The house of the high priest. Mat. 26:58.
DESCRIBED AS
High. Psa. 78:69.
Polished. Psa. 144:12.
Pleasant. Isa. 13:22.
OF KINGS
Called the king's house. 2 Kin. 25:9. 2 Chr. 7:11.
Called the house of the kingdom. 2 Chr. 2:1, 12.
Called the king's palace. Est. 1:5.
Called the royal house. Est. 1:9.
Splendidly furnished. Est. 1:6.
Surrounded with gardens. Est. 1:5.
Surrounded with terraces. 2 Chr. 9:11.
Under governors. 1 Kin. 4:6. Neh. 7:2.
Often attended by eunuchs as servants. 2 Kin. 20:18. Dan. 1:3, 4.
Were strictly guarded. 2 Kin. 11:5.
Afforded support to all the King's retainers. Ezr. 4:14. Dan. 1:5.
Royal decrees issued from. Est. 3:15. Est. 8:14.
Royal decrees laid up in. Ezr. 6:2.
Contained treasures of the king. 1 Kin. 15:18. 2 Chr. 12:9. 2 Chr. 25:24.
Gorgeous apparel suited to, alone. Luke 7:25.
Were entered by gates. Neh. 2:8.
Often the storehouses of rapine. Amos 3:10.
OFTEN AS A PUNISHMENT
Spoiled. Amos 3:11.
Forsaken. Isa. 32:14.
Desolate. Psa. 69:25. (*marg.*) Eze. 19:7.
Scenes of bloodshed. Jer. 9:21.
Burned with fire. 2 Chr. 36:19. Jer. 17:27.
Overgrown with thorns, &c. Isa. 34:13.
The habitation of dragons, &c. Isa. 13:22.
The spider makes its way even into. Pro. 30:28.
ILLUSTRATIVE OF
The splendor of the church. So. of Sol. 8:9.
The godly children of saints. Psa. 144:12.
The place of Satan's dominion. Luke 11:21.

Palm-tree, The.

First mention of, in Scripture. Exo. 15: 27.
Jericho celebrated for. Deu. 34: 3. Jud. 1: 16.
DESCRIBED AS
- Tall. So. of Sol. 7: 7.
- Upright. Jer. 10: 5.
- Flourishing. Psa. 92: 12.
- Fruitful to a great age. Psa. 92: 14.

The fruit of, called dates. 2 Chr. 31: 5. (*marg.*)
Requires a moist and fertile soil. Exo. 15: 27.
Tents often pitched under the shade of. Jud. 4: 5.
THE BRANCHES OF, WERE
- The emblem of victory. Rev. 7: 9.
- Carried at feast of tabernacles. Lev. 23: 40.
- Used for constructing booths. Neh. 8: 15.
- Spread before Christ. Jno. 12: 13.

Blasted as a punishment. Joel 1: 12.
Represented in carved work on the walls and doors of the temple of Solomon. 1 Kin. 6: 29, 32, 35. 2 Chr. 3: 5.
ILLUSTRATIVE OF
- The church. So. of Sol. 7: 7, 8.
- The righteous. Psa. 92: 12.
- The upright appearance of idols. Jer. 10: 5.

Parables.

REMARKABLE PARABLES OF THE OLD TESTAMENT.
- Judges 9: 8—15.
- 2 Sam. 12: 1—4.
- 2 Sam. 14: 5—7.

PARABLES OF CHRIST.
- Wise and foolish builders. Mat. 7: 24—27.
- Children of the bride-chamber. Mat. 9: 15.
- New cloth and old garment. Mat. 9: 16.
- New wine and old bottles. Mat. 9: 17.
- Unclean spirit. Mat. 12: 43.
- Sower. Mat. 13: 3, 18. Luke 8: 5, 11.
- Tares. Mat. 13: 24—30, 36—43.
- Mustard-seed. Mat. 13: 31, 32. Luke 13: 19.
- Leaven. Mat. 13: 33.
- Treasure hid in a field. Mat. 13: 44.
- Pearl of great price. Mat. 13: 45, 46.
- Net cast into the sea. Mat. 13: 47—50.
- Meats defiling not. Mat. 15: 10—15.
- Unmerciful servant. Mat. 18: 23—35.
- Laborers hired. Mat. 20: 1—16.
- Two sons. Mat. 21: 28—32.
- Wicked husbandmen. Mat. 21: 33—45.
- Marriage-feast. Mat. 22: 2—14.
- Fig-tree leafing. Mat. 24: 32—34.
- Man of the house watching. Mat. 24: 43.
- Faithful, and evil servants. Mat. 24: 45—51.
- Ten virgins. Mat. 25: 1—13.
- Talents. Mat. 25: 14—30.
- Kingdom, divided against itself. Mar. 3: 24.
- House, divided against itself. Mar. 3: 25.
- Strong man armed. Mar. 3: 27. Luke 11: 21.
- Seed growing secretly. Mar. 4: 26—29.
- Lighted candle. Mar. 4: 21. Luke 11: 33—36.
- Man taking a far journey. Mar. 13: 34—37.
- Blind leading the blind. Luke 6: 39.
- Beam and mote. Luke 6: 41, 42.
- Tree and its fruit. Luke 6: 43—45.
- Creditor and debtors. Luke 7: 41—47.
- Good Samaritan. Luke 10: 30—37.
- Importunate friend. Luke 11: 5—9.
- Rich fool. Luke 12: 16—21.
- Cloud and wind. Luke 12: 54—57.
- Barren fig-tree. Luke 13: 6—9.
- Men bidden to a feast. Luke 14: 7—11.
- Builder of a tower. Luke 14: 28—30, 33.
- King going to war. Luke 14: 31—33.
- Savor of salt. Luke 14: 34, 35.
- Lost sheep. Luke 15: 3—7.
- Lost piece of silver. Luke 15: 8—10.
- Prodigal son. Luke 15: 11—32.
- Unjust steward. Luke 16: 1—8.
- Rich man and Lazarus. Luke 16: 19—31.
- Importunate widow. Luke 18: 1—8.
- Pharisee and Publican. Luke 18: 9—14.
- Pounds. Luke 19: 12—27.
- Good Shepherd. Jno. 10: 1—6.
- Vine and branches. Jno. 15: 1—5.

Pardon.

Promised. Isa. 1: 18. Jer. 31: 34, with Heb. 8: 12. Jer. 50: 20.
None without shedding of blood. Lev. 17: 11, with Heb. 9: 22.
Legal sacrifices, ineffectual for. Heb. 10: 4.
Outward purifications, ineffectual for. Job 9: 30, 31. Jer. 2: 22.

The blood of Christ, alone, is efficacious for. Zec. 13:1, with 1 Jno. 1:7.

IS GRANTED

By God alone. Dan. 9:9. Mar. 2:7.
By Christ. Mar. 2:5. Luke 7:48.
Through Christ. Luke 1:69, 77. Acts 5:31. Acts 13:38.
Through the blood of Christ. Mat. 26:28. Rom. 3:25. Col. 1:14.
For the name's sake of Christ. 1 Jno. 2:12.
According to the riches of grace. Eph. 1:7.
On the exaltation of Christ. Acts 5:31.
Freely. Isa. 43:25.
Readily. Neh. 9:17. Psa. 86:5.
Abundantly. Isa. 55:7. Rom. 5:20.
To those who confess their sins. 2 Sam. 12:13. Psa. 32:5. 1 Jno. 1:9.
To those who repent. Acts 2:38.
To those who believe. Acts 10:43.

Should be preached in the name of Christ. Luke 24:47.

EXHIBITS THE

Compassion of God. Mic. 7:18, 19.
Grace of God. Rom. 5:15, 16.
Mercy of God. Exo. 34:7. Psa. 51:1.
Goodness of God. 2 Chr. 30:18. Psa. 86:5.
Forbearance of God. Rom. 3:25.
Loving-kindness of God. Psa. 51:1.
Justice of God. 1 Jno. 1:9.
Faithfulness of God. 1 Jno. 1:9.

EXPRESSED BY

Forgiving transgression. Psa. 32:1.
Removing transgression. Psa. 103:12.
Blotting out transgression. Isa. 44:22.
Covering sin. Psa. 32:1.
Blotting out sin. Acts 3:19.
Casting sins into the sea. Mic. 7:19.
Not imputing sin. Rom. 4:8.
Not mentioning transgression. Eze. 18:22.
Remembering sins no more. Heb. 10:17.

All saints enjoy. Col. 2:13. 1 Jno. 2:12.

Blessedness of. Psa. 32:1, with Rom. 4:7.

SHOULD LEAD TO

Returning to God. Isa. 44:22.
Loving God. Luke 7:47.
Fearing God. Psa. 130:4.
Praising God. Psa. 103:2, 3.

Ministers are appointed to proclaim. Isa. 40:1, 2. 2 Cor. 5:19.

PRAY FOR,

For yourselves. Psa. 25:11, 18. Psa. 51:1. Mat. 6:12. Luke 11:4.
For others. Jas. 5:15. 1 Jno. 5:16.

Encouragement to pray for. 2 Chr. 7:14.

WITHHELD FROM

The unforgiving. Mar. 11:26. Luke 6:37.
The unbelieving. Jno. 8:21, 24.
The impenitent. Luke 13:2—5.
Blasphemers against the Holy Ghost. Mat. 12:32. Mar. 3:28, 29.
Apostates. Heb. 10:26, 27. 1 Jno. 5:16.

Illustrated. Luke 7:42. Luke 15:20—24.

Exemplified. *Israelites*, Num. 14:20. *David*, 2 Sam. 12:13. *Manasseh*, 2 Chr. 33:13. *Hezekiah*, Isa. 38:17. *The Paralytic*, Mat. 9:2. *The Penitent*, Luke 7:47.

Parents.

Receive their children from God. Gen. 33:5. 1 Sam. 1:27. Psa. 127:3.

THEIR DUTY TO THEIR CHILDREN IS

To love them. Tit. 2:4.
To bring them to Christ. Mat. 19:13, 14.
To train them up for God. Pro. 22:6. Eph. 6:4.
To instruct them in God's word. Deu. 4:9. Deu. 11:19. Isa. 38:19.
To tell them of God's judgments. Joel 1:3.
To tell them of the miraculous works of God. Exo. 10:2. Psa. 78:4.
To command them to obey God. Deu. 32:46. 1 Chr. 28:9.
To bless them. Gen. 48:15. Heb. 11:20.
To pity them. Psa. 103:13.
To provide for them. Job 42:15. 2 Cor. 12:14. 1 Tim. 5:8.
To rule them. 1 Tim. 3:4, 12.
To correct them. Pro. 13:24. Pro. 19:18. Pro. 23:13. Pro. 29:17. Heb. 12:7.
Not to provoke them. Eph. 6:4. Col. 3:21.
Not to make unholy connections for them. Gen. 24:1—4. Gen. 28:1, 2.

Wicked children, a cause of grief to. Pro. 10:1. Pro. 17:25.

SHOULD PRAY FOR THEIR CHILDREN,

For their spiritual welfare. Gen. 17:18. 1 Chr. 29:19.
When in temptation. Job 1:5.
When in sickness. 2 Sam. 12:16. Mar. 5:23. Jno. 4:46, 49.

WHEN FAITHFUL,

Are blessed by their children. Pro. 31:28.
Leave a blessing to their children. Psa. 112:2. Pro. 11:21. Isa. 65:23.

Sins of, visited on their children. Exo. 20:5. Isa. 14:20. Lam. 5:7.

Negligence of, sorely punished. 1 Sam. 3:13.

WHEN WICKED,

Instruct their children in evil. Jer. 9:14. 1 Pet. 1:18.

Set a bad example to their children. Eze. 20: 18. Amos 2: 4.
Good—Exemplified. *Abraham*, Gen. 18: 19. *Jacob*, Gen. 44: 20, 30. *Joseph*, Gen. 48: 13—20. *Mother of Moses*, Exo. 2: 2, 3. *Manoah*, Jud. 13: 8. *Hannah*, 1 Sam. 1: 28. *David*, 2 Sam. 18: 5, 33. *Shunammite*, 2 Kin. 4: 19, 20. *Job*, Job 1: 5. *Mother of Lemuel*, Pro. 31: 1. *Nobleman*, Jno. 4: 49. *Lois and Eunice*, 2 Tim. 1: 5.
Bad—Exemplified. *Mother of Micah*, Jud. 17: 3. *Eli*, 1 Sam. 3: 13. *Saul*, 1 Sam. 20: 33. *Athaliah*, 2 Chr. 22: 3. *Manasseh*, 2 Chr. 33: 6. *Herodias*, Mar. 6: 24.

Paschal Lamb, Typical Nature of.

A type of Christ. Exo. 12: 3. 1 Cor. 5: 7.
A male of the first year. Exo. 12: 5. Isa. 9: 6.
Without blemish. Exo. 12: 5. 1 Pet. 1: 19.
Taken out of the flock. Exo. 12: 5. Heb. 2: 14, 17.
Chosen before-hand. Exo. 12: 3. 1 Pet. 2: 4.
Shut up four days that it might be closely examined. Exo. 12: 6. Jno. 8: 46. Jno. 18: 38.
Killed by the people. Exo. 12: 6. Acts 2: 23.
Killed at the place where the Lord put His name. Deu. 16: 2, 5—7. 2 Chr. 35: 1. Luke 13: 33.
Killed in the evening. Exo. 12: 6. Mar. 15: 34, 37.
Its blood to be shed. Exo. 12: 7. Luke 22: 20.
Blood of, sprinkled on lintel and door-posts. Exo. 12: 22. Heb. 9: 13, 14. Heb. 10: 22. 1 Pet. 1: 2.
Blood of, not sprinkled on threshhold. Exo. 12: 7. Heb. 10: 29.
Not a bone of, broken. Exo. 12: 46. Jno. 19: 36.
Not eaten raw. Exo. 12: 9. 1 Cor. 11: 28, 29.
Roasted with fire. Exo. 12: 8. Psa. 22: 14, 15.
Eaten with bitter herbs. Exo. 12: 8. Zec. 12: 10.
Eaten with unleavened bread. Exo. 12: 39. 1 Cor. 5: 7, 8. *See* 2 Cor. 1: 12.
Eaten in haste. Exo. 12: 11. Heb. 6: 18.
Eaten with the loins girt. Exo. 12: 11. Luke 12: 35. Eph. 6: 14. 1 Pet. 1: 13.
Eaten with staff in hand. Exo. 12: 11. Psa. 23: 4.
Eaten with shoes on. Exo. 12: 11. Eph. 6: 15.
Not taken out of the house. Exo. 12: 46. Eph. 3: 17.
What remained of it till morning to be burned. Exo. 12: 10. Mat. 7: 6. Luke 11: 3.

Patience.

God, is the God of. Rom. 15: 5.
Christ, an example of. Isa. 53: 7, with Acts 8: 32. Mat. 27: 14.
Enjoined. Tit. 2: 2. 2 Pet. 1: 6.
Should have its perfect work. Jas. 1: 4.
Trials of saints lead to. Rom. 5: 3. Jas. 1: 3.
PRODUCES
- Experience. Rom. 5: 4.
- Hope. Rom. 15: 4.

Suffering with, for well-doing, is acceptable with God. 1 Pet. 2: 20.
TO BE EXERCISED IN
- Running the race set before us. Heb. 12: 1.
- Bringing forth fruits. Luke 8: 15.
- Well-doing. Rom. 2: 7. Gal. 6: 9.
- Waiting for God. Psa. 37: 7. Psa. 40: 1.
- Waiting for Christ. 1 Cor. 1: 7. 2 The. 3: 5.
- Waiting for the hope of the gospel. Rom. 8: 25. Gal. 5: 5.
- Waiting for God's salvation. Lam. 3: 26.
- Bearing the yoke. Lam. 3: 27.
- Tribulation. Luke 21: 19. Rom. 12: 12.

Necessary to the inheritance of the promises. Heb. 6: 12. Heb. 10: 36.
Exercise, towards all. 1 The. 5: 14.
They who are in authority, should exercise. Mat. 18: 26. Acts 26: 3.
Ministers should follow after. 1 Tim. 6: 11.
Ministers approved by. 2 Cor. 6: 4.
SHOULD BE ACCOMPANIED BY
- Godliness. 2 Pet. 1: 6.
- Faith. 2 The. 1: 4. Heb. 6: 12. Rev. 13: 10.
- Temperance. 2 Pet. 1: 6.
- Long-suffering. Col. 1: 11.
- Joyfulness. Col. 1: 11.

Saints strengthened unto all. Col. 1: 11.
Commended. Ecc. 7: 8. Rev. 2: 2, 3.
Illustrated. Jas. 5: 7.
Exemplified. *Job*, Job 1: 21. Jas. 5: 11. *Simeon*, Luke 2: 25. *Paul*, 2 Tim. 3: 10. *Abraham*, Heb. 6: 15. *Prophets*, Jas. 5: 10. *John*, Rev. 1: 9.

Patriarchal Government.

Vested in the heads of families. Gen. 18: 19.
EXERCISED IN
- Training, &c. their servants for war. Gen. 14: 14.
- Vindicating their wrongs. Gen. 14: 12, 15, 16.

Forming treaties and alliances. Gen. 14:13. Gen. 21:22—32. Gen. 26:28—33.
Acting as priests. Gen. 8:20. Gen. 12: 7, 8. Gen. 35:1—7. Job 1:5.
Acting as judges. Gen. 38:24.
Arbitrarily disinheriting and putting away servants and children. Gen. 21:14. 1 Chr. 5:1.
Blessing and cursing their children. Gen. 9: 25, 26. Gen. 27: 28, 29. Gen. 49 ch.
The authority of heads of families for, acknowledged. Gen. 23: 6.

Peace.

God is the author of. Psa. 147:14. Isa. 45:7. 1 Cor. 14:33.
RESULTS FROM
Heavenly wisdom. Jas. 3:17.
The government of Christ. Isa. 2: 4.
Praying for rulers. 1 Tim. 2:2.
Seeking the peace of those with whom we dwell. Jer. 29:7.
Necessary to the enjoyment of life. Psa. 34:12, 14, with 1 Pet. 3:10, 11.
GOD BESTOWS UPON THOSE WHO
Obey Him. Lev. 26:6.
Please Him. Pro. 16:7.
Endure His chastisements. Job 5: 17, 23, 24.
Is a bond of union. Eph. 4:3.
The fruit of righteousness should be sown in. Jas. 3:18.
The church shall enjoy. Psa. 125:5. Psa 128:6. Isa. 2:4. Hos. 2:18.
SAINTS SHOULD
Love. Zec. 8:19.
Seek. Psa. 34:14, with 1 Pet. 3:11.
Follow. 2 Tim. 2:22.
Follow the things which make for. Rom. 14:19.
Cultivate. Psa. 120:7.
Speak. Est. 10:3.
Live in. 2 Cor. 13:11.
Have, with each other. Mar. 9:50. 1 The. 5:13.
Endeavor to have with all men. Rom. 12:18. Heb. 12:14.
Pray for that of the church. Psa. 122:6—8.
Exhort others to. Gen. 45:24.
Ministers should exhort to. 2 The. 3:12.
Advantages of. Pro. 17:1. Ecc. 4:6.
Blessedness of. Psa. 133:1.
Blessedness of promoting. Mat. 5:9.
THE WICKED
Hypocritically speak. Psa. 28:3.
Speak not. Psa. 35:20.
Enjoy not. Isa. 48:22. Eze. 7:25.
Opposed to. Psa. 120:7.
Hate. Psa. 120:6.
Shall abound in the latter days. Isa. 2:4. Isa. 11:13. Isa. 32:18.
Exemplified. *Abraham*, Gen. 13:8, 9. *Abimelech*, Gen. 26: 29. *Mordecai*, Est. 10:3. *David*, Psa. 120:7.

Peace-offerings.

A male or female of herd or flock. Lev. 3:1, 6, 12.
THE OFFERER REQUIRED
To give it freely. Lev. 19:5.
To bring it himself. Lev. 7:29, 30.
To lay his hand upon its head. Lev. 3:2, 8, 13.
To kill it at tabernacle door. Lev. 3:2, 8, 13.
Required to be perfect and free from blemish. Lev. 3:1, 6. Lev. 22:21.
THE PRIEST
Prepared. Eze. 46:2.
Sprinkled the blood on the altar. Lev. 3:2, 8, 13.
Offered the inside fat, &c. by fire. Lev. 3:3, 4, 9, 10.
Laid it upon the daily burnt-offering to be consumed with it. Lev. 3:5, with Lev. 6:12, 13.
Waved the breast as a wave-offering. Exo. 29: 26, 28. Lev. 7:29, 30.
Heaved the right shoulder as an heave-offering. Exo. 29:22—27.
Had the shoulder and breast as his portion. Exo. 29: 28. Lev. 7:31—34.
An offering most acceptable. Lev. 3:5, 16.
Generally accompanied by a burnt-offering. Jud. 21: 4. 1 Sam. 10: 8. 1 Kin. 3:15.
Often accompanied by a sin-offering. Lev. 23: 19.
WAS OFFERED
As a thanksgiving-offering. Lev. 7:12, 13.
As a votive offering. Lev. 7:16.
For reconciliation. Eze. 45: 15. Eph. 2:13, 14.
For confirming the legal covenant. Exo. 24:5.
At consecration of priests. Exo. 29:22, 29.
For the people at large. Lev. 9:4.
At expiration of Nazarite's vow. Num. 6:14.
At all the festivals. Num. 10:10.
At dedication of tabernacle. Num. 7:17, 23, &c.
At dedication of temple. 1 Kin. 8: 62—64.
At coronation of kings. 1 Sam. 11: 15.
By Joshua after his victories. Jos. 8:31.
By Israel after their defeat. Jud. 20:26.
By David on bringing up the ark. 2 Sam. 6:17.
By David after the plague. 2 Sam. 24:25.

By Solomon three times a year. 1 Kin. 9:25.
By Manasseh on repairing and restoring the altar. 2 Chr. 33:15, 16.
If a thanksgiving offering to be eaten the day offered. Lev. 7:15.
If a votive offering to be eaten the same day or the next. Lev. 7:16, 17. Lev. 19:6—8.
To be eaten before the Lord. Deu. 12:17, 18.
No unclean person to eat of. Lev. 7:20, 21.

Peace, Spiritual.

God is the God of. Rom. 15:33. 2 Cor. 13:11. 1 The. 5:23. Heb. 13:20.
God ordains. Isa. 26:12.
God speaks, to His saints. Psa. 85:8.
Christ is the Lord of. 2 The. 3:16.
Christ is the prince of. Isa. 9:6.
Christ gives. 2 The. 3:16.
Christ guides into the way of. Luke 1:79.
Christ is our. Eph. 2:14.
Is through the atonement of Christ. Isa. 53:5. Eph. 2:14, 15. Col. 1:20.
Bequeathed by Christ. Jno. 14:27.
PREACHED
By Christ. Eph. 2:17.
Through Christ. Acts 10:36.
By ministers. Isa. 52:7, with Rom. 10:15.
Announced by angels. Luke 2:14.
Follows upon justification. Rom. 5:1.
A fruit of the Spirit. Rom. 14:17. Gal. 5:22.
Divine wisdom is the way of. Pro. 3:17.
ACCOMPANIES
Faith. Rom. 15:13.
Righteousness. Isa. 32:17.
Acquaintance with God. Job 22:21.
The love of God's law. Psa. 119:165.
Spiritual-mindedness. Rom. 8:6.
Established by covenant. Isa. 54:10. Eze. 34:25. Mal. 2:5.
PROMISED TO
The Church. Isa. 66:12.
The Gentiles. Zec. 9:10.
Saints. Psa. 72:3, 7. Isa. 55:12.
The meek. Psa. 37:11.
Those who confide in God. Isa. 26:3.
Returning backsliders. Isa. 57:18, 19.
We should love. Zec. 8:19.
The benediction of ministers should be. Num. 6:26. Luke 10:5.
SAINTS
Have in Christ. Jno. 16:33.
Have, with God. Isa. 27:5. Rom. 5:1.
Enjoy. Psa. 119:165.
Repose in. Psa. 4:8.
Blessed with. Psa. 29:11.
Kept in perfect. Isa. 26:3.
Ruled by. Col. 3:15.
Kept by. Phi. 4:7.
Die in. Psa. 37:37. Luke 2:29.
Wish, to each other. Gal. 6:16. Phi. 1:2. Col. 1:2. 1 The. 1:1.
OF SAINTS
Great. Psa. 119:165. Isa. 54:13.
Abundant. Psa. 72:7. Jer. 33:6.
Secure. Job 34:29.
Passeth all understanding. Phi. 4:7.
Consummated after death. Isa. 57:2.
The gospel is good tidings of. Rom. 10:15.
THE WICKED
Know not the way of. Isa. 59:8. Rom. 3:17.
Know not the things of. Luke 19:42.
Promise, to themselves. Deu. 29:19.
Are promised, by false teachers. Jer. 6:14.
There is none for. Isa. 48:22. Isa. 57:21.
Supports under trials. Jno. 14:27. Jno. 16:33.

Perfection.

Is of God. Psa. 18:32. Psa. 138:8.
All saints have, in Christ. 1 Cor. 2:6. Phi. 3:15. Col 2:10.
God's perfection the standard of. Mat. 5:48.
IMPLIES
Entire devotedness. Mat. 19:21.
Purity and holiness in speech. Jas. 3:2.
Saints commanded to aim at. Gen. 17:1. Deu. 18:13.
Saints claim not. Job 9:20. Phi. 3:12.
Saints follow after. Pro. 4:18. Phi. 3:12.
Ministers appointed to lead saints to. Eph. 4:12. Col. 1:28.
Exhortation to. 2 Cor. 7:1. 2 Cor. 13:11.
Impossibility of attaining to. 2 Chr. 6:36. Psa. 119:96.
THE WORD OF GOD IS
The rule of. Jas. 1:25.
Designed to lead us to. 2 Tim. 3:16, 17.
Charity is the bond of. Col. 3:14.
Patience leads to. Jas. 1:4.
Pray for. Heb. 13:20, 21. 1 Pet. 5:10.
The Church shall attain to. Jno. 17:23. Eph. 4:13.
Blessedness of. Psa. 37:37. Pro. 2:21.

Persecution.

Christ suffered. Psa. 69:26. Jno. 5:16.

Christ voluntarily submitted to. Isa. 50:6.
Christ was patient under. Isa. 53:7.
Saints may expect. Mar. 10:30. Luke 21:12. Jno. 15:20.
Saints suffer, for the sake of God. Jer. 15:15.
Of saints, is a persecution of Christ. Zec. 2:8, with Acts 9:4, 5.
All that live godly in Christ, shall suffer. 2 Tim. 3:12.
ORIGINATES IN
Ignorance of God and Christ. Jno. 16:3.
Hated to God and Christ. Jno. 15: 20, 24.
Hatred to the gospel. Mat. 13:21.
Pride. Psa. 10:2.
Mistaken zeal. Acts 13:50. Acts 26:9—11.
Is inconsistent with the spirit of the gospel. Mat. 26:52.
Men by nature addicted to. Gal. 4:29.
Preachers of the gospel subject to. Gal. 5:11.
Is sometimes unto death. Acts 22:4.
God forsakes not His saints under. 2 Cor. 4:9.
God delivers out of. Dan. 3:25, 28. 2 Cor. 1:10. 2 Tim. 3:11.
Cannot separate from Christ. Rom. 8:35.
Lawful means may be used to escape. Mat. 2:13. Mat. 10:23. Mat. 12: 14, 15.
SAINTS SUFFERING, SHOULD
Commit themselves to God. 1 Pet. 4:19.
Exhibit patience. 1 Cor. 4:12.
Rejoice. Mat. 5:12. 1 Pet. 4:13.
Glorify God. 1 Pet. 4:16.
Pray for deliverance. Psa. 7:1. Psa. 119:86.
Pray for those who inflict. Mat. 5: 44.
Return blessing for. Rom. 12:14.
The hope of future blessedness supports under. 1 Cor. 15:19, 32. Heb. 10:34, 35.
Blessedness of enduring, for Christ's sake. Mat. 5:10. Luke 6:22.
Pray for those suffering. 2 The. 3:2.
Hypocrites cannot endure. Mar. 4:17.
False teachers shrink from. Gal. 6: 12.
THE WICKED
Addicted to. Psa. 10:2. Psa. 69:26.
Active in. Psa. 143:3. Lam. 4:19.
Encourage each other in. Psa. 71: 11.
Rejoice in its success. Psa. 13:4. Rev. 11:10.
Punishment for. Psa. 7:13. 2 The. 1: 6.
Illustrated. Mat. 21:33—39.
Spirit of—Exemplified. *Pharaoh, &c.* Exo. 1:8—14. *Saul*, 1 Sam. 26:18. *Jezebel*, 1 Kin. 19:2. *Zedekiah, &c.* Jer. 38:4—6. *Chaldeans*, Dan. 3:8, &c. *Pharisees*, Mat. 12:14. *Jews*, Jno. 5:16. 1 The. 2:15. *Herod*, Acts 12:1. *Gentiles*, Acts 14:5. *Paul*, Phi. 3:6. 1 Tim. 1:13.
Suffering of—Exemplified. *Micaiah*, 1 Kin. 22:27. *David*, Psa. 119:161. *Jeremiah*, Jer. 32:2. *Daniel*, Dan. 6: 5—17. *Peter, &c.* Acts 4:3. *Apostles*, Acts 5:18. *The Prophets*, Acts 7:52. *Primitive Church*, Acts 8:1. *Paul and Barnabas*, Acts 13:50. *Paul and Silas*, Acts 16:23. *Hebrews*, Heb. 10:33. *Saints of old*, Heb. 11:36.

Perseverance.

An evidence of reconciliation with God. Col. 1:21—23.
An evidence of belonging to Christ. Jno. 8:31. Heb. 3:6, 14.
A characteristic of saints. Pro. 4:18.
TO BE MANIFESTED IN
Seeking God. 1 Chr. 16:11.
Waiting upon God. Hos. 12:6.
Prayer. Rom. 12:12. Eph. 6:18.
Well-doing. Rom. 2:7. 2 The. 3:13.
Continuing in the faith. Acts 14: 22. Col. 1:23. 2 Tim. 4:7.
Holding fast hope. Heb. 3:6.
MAINTAINED THROUGH
The power of God. Psa. 37:24. Phi. 1:6.
The power of Christ. Jno. 10:28.
The intercession of Christ. Luke 22:31, 32. Jno. 17:11.
The fear of God. Jer. 32:40.
Faith. 1 Pet. 1:5.
Promised to saints. Job 17:9.
Leads to increase of knowledge. Jno. 8:31, 32.
IN WELL-DOING
Leads to assurance of hope. Heb. 6:10, 11.
Is not in vain. 1 Cor. 15:58. Gal. 6:9.
Ministers should exhort to. Acts 13: 43. Acts 14:22.
Encouragement to. Heb. 12:2, 3.
Promises to. Mat. 10:22. Mat. 24: 13. Rev. 2:26–28.
Blessedness of. Jas. 1:25.
WANT OF,
Excludes from the benefits of the gospel. Heb. 6:4–6.
Punished. Jno. 15:6. Rom. 11:22.
Illustrated. Mar. 4:5, 17.

Pharisees, The.

A sect of the Jews. Acts 15:5.
The strictest observers of the Mosaic ritual. Acts 26:5.
By descent, especially esteemed. Acts 23:6.
CHARACTER OF;
Zealous of the law. Acts 15:5. Phi. 3:5.

Zealous of tradition. Mar. 7:3, 5—8. Gal. 1:14.
Outwardly moral. Luke 18:11. Phi. 3:5, 6.
Rigid in fasting. Luke 5:33. Luke 18:12.
Active in proselytizing. Mat. 23:15.
Self-righteous. Luke 16:15. Luke 18:9.
Avaricious. Mat. 23:14. Luke 16:14.
Ambitious of precedence. Mat 23:6.
Fond of public salutations. Mat. 23:7.
Fond of distinguished titles. Mat. 23:7—10.
Particular in paying all dues. Mat. 23:23.
Oppressive. Mat. 23:4.
Cruel in persecuting. Acts 9:1, 2.

Believed in the resurrection, &c. Acts 23:8.
Made broad their phylacteries, &c. Mat. 23:5.
Their opinions, a standard to others. Jno. 7:48.
Many priests and Levites were of. Jno. 1:19, 24.
Many rulers, lawyers, and scribes were of. Jno. 3:1. Acts 5:34. Acts 23:9.
Had disciples. Luke 5:33. Acts 22:3.
Some came to John for baptism. Mat. 3:7.
As a body, rejected John's baptism. Luke 7:30.

CHRIST
Often invited by. Luke 7:36. Luke 11:37.
Condemned by, for associating with sinners. Mat. 9:11. Luke 7:39. Luke 15:1, 2.
Asked for signs by. Mat. 12:38. Mat. 16:1.
Tempted by, with questions about the law. Mat. 19:3. Mat. 22:15, 16, 35.
Watched by, for evil. Luke 6:7.
Offended, by His doctrine. Mat. 15:12. Mat. 21:45. Luke 16:14.
Declared the imaginary righteousness of, to be insufficient for salvation. Mat. 5:20.
Declared the doctrines of, to be hypocrisy. Mat. 16:6, 11, 12. Luke 12:1.
Denounced woes against. Mat. 23:13, &c.
Called, an evil and adulterous generation. Mat. 12:39.
Called, serpents and generation of vipers. Mat. 23:33.
Called fools and blind guides. Mat. 23:17, 24.
Compared, to whited sepulchres. Mat. 23:27.
Compared, to graves that appear not. Luke 11:44.

Left Judea for a time on account of. Jno. 4:1—3.
Imputed Christ's miracles to Satan's power. Mat 9:34. Mat. 12:24.
Sent officers to apprehend Christ. Jno. 7:32, 45.
Often sought to destroy Christ. Mat. 12:14. Mat. 21:46. Jno. 11:47, 53, 57.

Philistines, The.

Descended from Casluhim. Gen. 10:13, 14.
Originally dwelt in the land of Caphtor. Jer. 47:4. Amos 9:7.
Conquered the Avims and took from them the west coast of Canaan. Deu. 2:23.

CALLED
The Caphtorims. Deu. 2:23.
The Cherethites. 1 Sam. 30:14. Zep. 2:5.

COUNTRY OF,
Called Philistia. Psa. 87:4. Psa. 108:9.
Divided into five states or lordships. Jos. 13:3. Jud. 3:3. 1 Sam. 6:16.
Had many flourishing cities. 1 Sam. 6:17.
Given by God to the Israelites. Jos. 13:2, 3. Jos. 15:45, 47.

Were a great people and governed by kings in the patriarchal age. Gen. 21:22, 34. Gen. 26:8.

CHARACTER OF;
Proud. Zec. 9:6.
Idolatrous. Jud. 16:23. 1 Sam. 5:2.
Superstitious. Isa. 2:6.
Warlike. 1 Sam. 17:1. 1 Sam. 28:1.

Men of great strength and stature amongst. 1 Sam. 17:4—7. 2 Sam. 21:16, 18—20.
Some of, left to prove Israel. Jud. 3:1—3.
Always confederated with the enemies of Israel. Psa. 83:7. Isa. 9:11, 12.
Shamgar slew six hundred of, and delivered Israel. Jud. 3:31.
Oppressed Israel after the death of Jair for eighteen years. Jud. 10:7, 8.
Oppressed Israel after the death of Abdon forty years. Jud. 13:1.

SAMSON
Promised as a deliverer from. Jud. 13:5.
Intermarried with. Jud. 14:1, 10.
Slew thirty, near Askelon. Jud. 14:19.
Burned vineyards, &c. of. Jud. 15:3—5.
Slew many for burning his wife. Jud. 15:7, 8.

Slew a thousand with the jawbone of an ass. Jud. 15: 15, 16.
Blinded and imprisoned by. Jud. 16: 21.
Pulled down the house of Dagon and destroyed immense numbers of. Jud. 16: 29, 30.
Defeated Israel at Ebenezer. 1 Sam. 4: 1, 2.
Defeated Israel and took the ark. 1 Sam. 4: 3—11.
Put the ark into Dagon's house. 1 Sam. 5: 1—4.
Plagued for retaining the ark. 1 Sam. 5: 6—12.
Sent back the ark and were healed. 1 Sam. 6: 1—18.
Miraculously routed at Mizpeh. 1 Sam. 7: 7—14.
Jonathan smote a garrison of, at Geba and provoked them. 1 Sam. 13: 3, 4.
Invaded the land of Israel with a great army. 1 Sam. 13: 5, 17—23.
Jonathan and his armor-bearer smote a garrison of, at the passages. 1 Sam. 14: 1—14.
Miraculously discomfited. 1 Sam. 14: 15—23.
Saul constantly at war with. 1 Sam. 14: 52.
Defied Israel by their champion. 1 Sam. 17: 4—10.
Defeated by Israel at Ephes-dammin and pursued to Ekron. 1 Sam. 17: 1, 52.
DAVID
Slew Goliath the champion of. 1 Sam. 17: 40—50.
Procured Saul's daughter for an hundred foreskins of. 1 Sam. 18: 25—27.
Often defeated during Saul's reign. 1 Sam. 19: 8. 1 Sam. 23: 1—5.
Fled to, for safety. 1 Sam. 27: 1—7.
Gained the confidence of Achish king of. 1 Sam. 28: 2. 1 Sam. 29: 9.
Distrusted by. 1 Sam. 29: 2—7.
Often defeated in the course of his reign. 2 Sam. 5: 17—23. 2 Sam. 8: 1. 2 Sam. 21: 15—22. 2 Sam. 23: 8—12.
Had a guard composed of. 2 Sam. 8: 18, with Eze. 25: 16. Zep. 2: 5.
Gathered all their armies to Aphek against Israel. 1 Sam. 28: 1. 1 Sam. 29: 1.
Ziklag a town of, taken and plundered by the Amalekites. 1 Sam. 30: 1, 2, 16.
Israel defeated by, and Saul slain. 1 Sam. 31: 1—10.
Besieged in Gibbethon by Nadab. 1 Kin. 15: 27.
Sent by God against Jehoram. 2 Chr. 21: 16, 17.
Defeated by Uzziah. 2 Chr. 26: 6, 7.
Distressed Judah under Ahaz. 2 Chr. 28: 18, 19.
Defeated by Hezekiah. 2 Kin. 18: 8.
Israel condemned for imitating. Jud. 10: 6. Amos 6: 2. Amos 9: 7.
PROPHECIES RESPECTING;
Union with Syria against Israel. Isa. 9: 11, 12.
Punishment with other nations. Jer. 25: 20.
Dismay at ruin of Tyre. Zec. 9: 3, 5.
Base men to be their rulers. Zec. 9: 6.
Hatred and revenge against Israel to be fully recompensed. Eze. 25: 15—17. Amos 1: 6—8.
Utter destruction by Pharaoh king of Egypt. Jer. 47: 1—4. Zep. 2: 5, 6.
Destruction and desolation of their cities. Jer. 47: 5. Zep. 2: 4.
Their country to be a future possession to Israel. Oba. 19 v. Zep. 2: 7.
To help in Israel's restoration. Isa. 11: 14.

Pilgrims and Strangers.

Described. Jno. 17: 16.
Saints are called to be. Gen. 12: 1, with Acts 7: 3. Luke 14: 26, 27, 33.
All saints are. Psa. 39: 12. 1 Pet. 1: 1.
Saints confess themselves. 1 Chr. 29: 15. Psa. 39: 12. Psa. 119: 19. Heb. 11: 13.
AS SAINTS THEY
Have the example of Christ. Luke 9: 58.
Are strengthened by God. Deu. 33: 25. Psa. 84: 6, 7.
Are actuated by faith. Heb. 11: 9.
Have their faces toward Zion. Jer. 50: 5.
Keep the promises in view. Heb. 11: 13.
Forsake all for Christ. Mat. 19: 27.
Look for a heavenly country. Heb. 11: 16.
Look for a heavenly city. Heb. 11: 10.
Pass their sojourning in fear. 1 Pet. 1: 17.
Rejoice in the statutes of God. Psa. 119: 54.
Pray for direction. Psa. 43: 3. Jer. 50: 5.
Have a heavenly conversation. Phi. 3: 20.
Hate worldly fellowship. Psa. 120: 5, 6.
Are not mindful of this world. Heb. 11: 15.
Are not at home in this world. Heb. 11: 9.
Shine as lights in the world. Phi. 2: 15.

Invite others to go with them. Num. 10: 29.
Are exposed to persecution. Psa. 120: 5—7. Jno. 17: 14.
Should abstain from fleshly lusts. 1 Pet. 2: 11.
Should have their treasure in heaven. Mat. 6: 19. Luke 12: 33. Col. 3: 1, 2.
Should not be over anxious about worldly things. Mat. 6: 25.
Long for their pilgrimage to end. Psa. 55: 6. 2 Cor. 5: 1—8.
Die in faith. Heb. 11: 13.
The world is not worthy of. Heb. 11: 38.
God is not ashamed to be called their God. Heb. 11: 16.
Typified. *Israel*, Exo. 6: 4. Exo. 12: 11.
Exemplified. *Abraham*, Gen. 23: 4. Acts 7: 4, 5. *Jacob*, Gen. 47: 9. *Saints of old*, 1 Chr. 29: 15. Heb. 11: 13, 38. *David*, Psa. 39: 12. *The Apostles*, Mat. 19: 27.

Pillars.

The supports of a building. Jud. 16: 29.
Things raised up as memorials. Gen. 31: 51.
MADE OF
Marble. Est. 1: 6.
Wood. 1 Kin. 10: 12.
Iron. Jer. 1: 18.
Brass. 1 Kin. 7: 15
Silver. So. of Sol. 3: 10.
The vail and hangings of the tabernacle supported by. Exo. 26: 32, 37. Exo. 36: 36, 38.
Two, placed in the temple porch. 1 Kin. 7: 15—21.
OF MEMORIAL
Sometimes of a single stone. Gen. 28: 18.
Sometimes of a heap of stones. Jos. 4: 8, 9, 20.
To witness vows. Gen. 28: 18. Gen. 31: 13.
To witness covenants. Gen. 31: 52.
To mark the graves of the dead. Gen. 35: 20.
To commemorate remarkable events. Exo. 24: 4. Jos. 4: 20, 24.
To perpetuate names. 2 Sam. 18: 18.
In honor of idols. Lev. 26: 1. (*marg.*) Deu. 7: 5. (*marg.*)
Often anointed. Gen. 28: 18. Gen. 31: 13.
Often had inscriptions. Job 19: 24.
The divine glory appeared to Israel in the form of. Exo. 13: 21, 22. Num. 12: 5.
Lot's wife became a pillar of salt. Gen. 19: 26.
ILLUSTRATIVE OF
Stability of the heavens. Job 26: 11.
Stability of the earth. 1 Sam. 2: 8. Psa. 75: 3.
The church. 1 Tim. 3: 15.
Stability of Christ. So. of Sol. 5: 15. Rev. 10: 1.
Ministers. Jer. 1: 18. Gal. 2: 9.
Saints who overcome in Christ. Rev. 3: 12.

Plague or Pestilence, The.

Inflicted by God. Eze. 14: 19. Hab. 3: 5.
One of God's four sore judgments. Eze. 14: 21.
Described as noisome. Psa. 91: 3.
Israel threatened with, as a punishment for disobedience. Lev. 26: 24, 25. Deu. 28: 21.
Desolating effects of. Psa. 91: 7. Jer. 16: 6, 7. Amos 6: 9, 10.
Equally fatal day and night. Psa. 91: 5, 6.
Fatal to man and beast. Psa. 78: 50. (*marg.*) Jer. 21: 6.
SENT UPON
The Egyptians. Exo. 12: 29: 30.
Israel for making golden calf. Exo. 32: 35.
Israel for despising manna. Num. 11: 33.
Israel for murmuring at destruction of Korah. Num. 16: 46—50.
Israel for worshipping Baal-peor. Num. 25: 18.
David's subjects for his numbering the people. 2 Sam. 24: 15.
Often broke out suddenly. Psa. 106: 29.
Often followed war and famine. Jer. 27: 13. Jer. 28: 8. Jer. 29: 17, 18.
Egypt often afflicted with. Jer. 42: 17, with Amos 4: 10.
Specially fatal in cities. Lev. 26: 25. Jer. 21: 6, 9.
Was attributed to a destroying angel. Exo. 12: 23, with 2 Sam. 24: 16.
The Jews sought deliverance from, by prayer. 1 Kin. 8: 37, 38. 2 Chr. 20: 9.
Predicted to happen before destruction of Jerusalem. Mat. 24: 7. Luke 21: 11.
ILLUSTRATIVE OF
God's judgments upon the apostacy. Rev. 18: 4, 8.
The diseased state of man's heart. 1 Kin. 8: 38.

Plowing.

The breaking up or tilling of the earth. Jer. 4: 3. Hos. 10: 12.
Noah the supposed inventor of. Gen. 5: 29.
PERFORMED
By a plow. Luke 9: 62.

With oxen. 1 Sam. 14: 14. Job 1: 14.
During the cold winter season. Pro. 20: 4.
In long and straight furrows. Psa. 129: 3.
Generally by servants. Isa. 61: 5. Luke 17: 7.
Sometimes by the owner of the land himself. 1 Kin. 19: 19.
With an ox and an ass yoked together forbidden to the Jews. Deu. 22: 10.
Difficulty of, on rocky ground. Amos 6: 12.
Followed by harrowing and sowing. Isa. 28: 24, 25.
ILLUSTRATIVE
Of repentance and reformation. Jer. 4: 3.
Of peace and prosperity. Isa. 2: 4. Mic. 4: 3.
Of a severe course of affliction. Hos. 10: 11.
Of a course of sin. Job 4: 8. Hos. 10: 13.
Of the labor of ministers. 1 Cor. 9: 10.
(Attention and constancy required in,) of continued devotedness. Luke 9: 62.

Pomegranate-tree, The.

Egypt abounded with. Num. 20: 5.
Canaan abounded with. Num. 13: 23. Deu. 8: 8.
THE JEWS
Cultivated, in orchards. So. of Sol. 4: 13.
Often dwelt under shade of. 1 Sam. 14: 2.
Drank the juice of. So. of Sol. 8: 2.
The blasting of, a great calamity. Joel 1: 12.
God's favor exhibited, in making fruitful. Hag. 2: 19.
REPRESENTATIONS OF ITS FRUIT
On the high priest's robe. Exo. 39: 24—26.
On the pillars of the temple. 1 Kin. 7: 18.
ILLUSTRATIVE.
Of saints. So. of Sol. 6: 11. So. of Sol. 7: 12.
(An orchard of,) of the church. So. of Sol. 4: 13.
(Fruit of,) of the graces of the church. So. of Sol. 4: 3. So. of Sol. 6: 7.

Pools and Ponds.

Made by God. Isa. 35: 7.
Made by man. Isa. 19: 10.
ARTIFICIAL, DESIGNED FOR
Supplying cities with water. 2 Kin. 20: 20.
Supplying gardens, &c. with water. Ecc. 2: 6.
Preserving fish. Isa. 19: 10.
Water of, brought into the city by a ditch or conduit. Isa. 22: 11, with 2 Kin. 20: 20.
Filled by the rain. Psa. 84: 6.
MENTIONED IN SCRIPTURE;
Bethesda. Jno. 5: 2.
Gibeon. 2 Sam. 2: 13.
Hebron. 2 Sam. 4: 12.
Samaria. 1 Kin. 22: 38.
Siloam. Jno. 9: 7.
The upper pool. 2 Kin. 18: 17. Isa 7: 3.
The lower pool. Isa. 22: 9.
The king's pool. Neh. 2: 14.
The old pool. Isa. 22: 11.
The land of Egypt abounded in. Exo. 7: 19.
ILLUSTRATIVE
Of Nineveh. Nah. 2: 8.
(In the wilderness,) of the gifts of the Spirit. Isa. 35: 7. Isa. 41: 18.
(Turning cities into,) of great desolation. Isa. 14: 23.

Poor, The.

Made by God. Job 34: 19. Pro. 22: 2.
Are such by God's appointment. 1 Sam. 2: 7. Job 1: 21.
CONDITION OF, OFTEN RESULTS FROM
Sloth. Pro. 20: 13.
Bad company. Pro. 28: 19.
Drunkenness and gluttony. Pro. 23: 21.
GOD
Regards, equally with the rich. Job 34: 19.
Forgets not. Psa. 9: 18.
Hears. Psa. 69: 33. Isa. 41: 17.
Maintains the right of. Psa. 140: 12.
Delivers. Job 36: 15. Psa. 35: 10.
Protects. Psa. 12: 5. Psa. 109: 31.
Exalts. 1 Sam. 2: 8. Psa. 107: 41.
Provides for. Psa. 68: 10. Psa. 146: 7.
Despises not the prayer of. Psa 102: 17.
Is the refuge of. Psa. 14: 6.
Shall never cease out of the land. Deu. 15: 11. Zep. 3: 12. Mat. 26: 11
MAY BE
Rich in faith. Jas. 2: 5.
Liberal. Mar. 12: 42. 2 Cor. 8: 2.
Wise. Pro. 28: 11.
Upright. Pro. 19: 1.
Christ lived as one of. Mat. 8: 20.
Christ preached to. Luke 4: 18.
Christ delivers. Psa. 72: 12.
Offerings of, acceptable to God. Mar. 12: 42—44. 2 Cor. 8: 2, 12.
SHOULD
Rejoice in God. Isa. 29: 19.
Hope in God. Job 5: 16.
Commit themselves to God. Psa. 10: 14.

When converted, rejoice in their exaltation. Jas. 1:9.
Provided for under the Law. Exo. 23:11. Lev. 19:9, 10.
NEGLECT TOWARDS, IS
A neglect of Christ. Mat. 25:42—45.
Inconsistent with love to God. 1 Jno. 3:17.
A proof of unbelief. Jas. 2:15—17.
Rob not. Pro. 22:22.
Wrong not in judgment. Exo. 23:6.
Take no usury from. Lev. 25:36.
Harden not the heart against. Deu. 15:7.
Shut not the hand against. Deu. 15:7.
Rule not, with rigor. Lev. 25:39, 43.
Oppress not. Deu. 24:14. Zec. 7:10.
Despise not. Pro. 14:21. Jas. 2:2—4.
Relieve. Lev. 25:35. Mat. 19:21.
Defend. Psa. 82:3, 4.
Do justice to. Psa. 82:3. Jer. 22:3, 16.
A CARE FOR,
Is characteristic of saints. Psa. 112:9, with 2 Cor. 9:9. Pro. 29:7.
Is a fruit of repentance. Luke 3:11.
Should be urged. 2 Cor. 8:7, 8. Gal. 2:10.
GIVE TO,
Not grudgingly. Deu. 15:10. 2 Cor. 9:7.
Liberally. Deu. 14:29. Deu. 15:8, 11.
Cheerfully. 2 Cor. 8:12. 2 Cor. 9:7.
Without ostentation. Mat. 6:1.
Specially if saints. Rom. 12:13. Gal. 6:10.
Pray for. Psa. 74:19, 21.
THEY WHO IN FAITH, BELIEVE,
Are happy. Pro. 14:21.
Are blessed. Deu. 15:10. Psa. 41:1. Pro. 22:9. Acts 20:35.
Have the favor of God. Heb. 13:16.
Have promises. Pro. 28:27. Luke 14:13, 14.
By oppressing, God is reproached. Pro. 14:31.
By mocking, God is reproached. Pro. 17:5.
THE WICKED
Care not for. Jno. 12:6.
Oppress. Job 24:4—10. Eze. 18:12.
Vex. Eze. 22:20.
Regard not the cause of. Pro. 29:7.
Sell. Amos 2:6.
Crush. Amos 4:1.
Tread down. Amos 5:11.
Grind the faces of. Isa. 3:15.
Devour. Hab. 3:14.
Persecute. Psa. 10:2.
Defraud. Amos 8:5, 6.
Despise the counsel of. Psa. 14:6.
Guilt of defrauding. Jas. 5:4.
PUNISHMENT FOR
Oppressing. Pro. 22:16. Eze. 22:29, 31.
Spoiling. Isa. 3:13—15. Eze. 18:13.
Refusing to assist. Job 22:7, 10. Pro. 21:13.
Acting unjustly towards. Job 20:19, 29. Job 22:6, 10. Isa. 10:1—3. Amos 5:11, 12.
Oppression of—Illustrated. 2 Sam. 12:1—6.
Care for—Illustrated. Luke 10:33—35.
Exemplified. *Gideon*, Jud. 6:15. *Ruth*, Ruth 2:2. *Widow of Zarephath*, 1 Kin. 17:12. *Prophet's Widow*, 2 Kin. 4:2. *Saints of old*, Heb. 11:37.
Regard for—Exemplified. *Boaz*, Ruth 2:14. *Job*, Job 29:12—16. *Nebuzaradan*, Jer. 39:10. *Zaccheus*, Luke 19:8. *Peter and John*, Acts 3:6. *Dorcas*, Acts 9:36, 39. *Cornelius*, Acts 10:2. *Church at Antioch*, Acts 11:29, 30. *Paul*, Rom. 15:25. *Churches of Macedonia and Achaia*, Rom. 15:26. 2 Cor. 8:1—5.

Power of Christ, The.

As the Son of God, is the power of God. Jno. 5:17—19. Jno. 10:28—30.
As man, is from the Father. Acts 10:38.
DESCRIBED AS
Supreme. Eph. 1:20, 21. 1 Pet. 3:22.
Unlimited. Mat. 28:18.
Over all flesh. Jno. 17:2.
Over all things. Jno. 3:35. Eph. 1:22.
Glorious. 2 The. 1:9.
Everlasting. 1 Tim. 6:16.
Is able to subdue all things. Phi. 3:21.
EXHIBITED IN
Creation. Jno. 1:3, 10. Col. 1:16.
Upholding all things. Col. 1:17. Heb. 1:3.
Salvation. Isa. 63:1. Heb. 7:25.
His teaching. Mat 7:28, 29. Luke 4:32.
Working miracles. Mat. 8;27. Luke 5:17.
Enabling others to work miracles. Mat. 10:1. Mar. 16:17, 18. Luke 10:17.
Forgiving sins. Mat. 9:6. Acts 5:31.
Giving spiritual life. Jno. 5:21, 25, 26.
Giving eternal life. Jno. 17:2.
Raising the dead. Jno. 5:28, 29.
Raising Himself from the dead. Jno. 2:19—21. Jno. 10:18.
Overcoming the world. Jno. 16:33.
Overcoming Satan. Col. 2:15. Heb. 2:14.
Destroying the works of Satan. 1 Jno. 3:8.

Ministers should make known. 2 Pet. 1:16.

SAINTS

Made willing by. Psa. 110:3.
Succored by. Heb. 2:18.
Strengthened by. Phi. 4:13. 2 Tim. 4:17.
Preserved by. 2 Tim. 1:12. 2 Tim. 4:18.
Bodies of, shall be changed by. Phi. 3:21.

Rests upon saints. 2 Cor. 12:9.
Present in the assembly of saints. 1 Cor. 5:4.
Shall be specially manifested at His second coming. Mar. 13:26. 2 Pet. 1:16.
Shall subdue all power. 1 Cor. 15:24.
The wicked shall be destroyed by. Psa. 2:9. Isa. 11:4. Isa. 63:3. 2 The. 1:9.

Power of God, The.

Is one of His attributes. Psa. 62:11.

EXPRESSED BY THE

Voice of God. Psa. 29:3, 5. Psa. 68:33.
Finger of God. Exo. 8:19. Psa. 8:3.
Hand of God. Exo. 9:3, 15. Isa. 48:13.
Arm of God. Job 40:9. Isa. 52:10.
Thunder of His power, &c. Job 26:14.

DESCRIBED AS

Great. Psa. 79:11. Nah. 1:3.
Strong. Psa. 89:13. Psa. 136:12.
Glorious. Exo. 15:6. Isa. 63:12.
Mighty. Job 9:4. Psa. 89:13.
Everlasting. Isa. 26:4. Rom. 1:20.
Sovereign. Rom. 9:21.
Effectual. Isa. 43:13. Eph. 3:7.
Irresistible. Deu. 32:39. Dan. 4:35.
Incomparable. Exo. 15:11, 12. Deu. 3:24. Job 40:9. Psa. 89:8.
Unsearchable. Job 5:9. Job 9:10.
Incomprehensible. Job 26:14. Ecc. 3:11.

All things possible to. Mat. 19:26.
Nothing too hard for. Gen. 18:14. Jer. 32:27.
Can save by many or by few. 1 Sam. 14:6.
Is the source of all strength. 1 Chr. 29:12. Psa. 68:35.

EXHIBITED IN

Creation. Psa. 102:25. Jer. 10:12.
Establishing and governing all things. Psa. 65:6. Psa. 66:7.
The miracles of Christ. Luke 11:20.
The resurrection of Christ. 2 Cor. 13:4. Col. 2:12.
The resurrection of saints. 1 Cor. 6:14.
Making the gospel effectual. Rom. 1:16. 1 Cor. 1:18, 24.
Delivering His people. Psa. 106:8.
The destruction of the wicked. Exo. 9:16. Rom. 9:22.

SAINTS

Long for exhibitions of. Psa. 63:1, 2.
Have confidence in. Jer. 20:11.
Receive increase of grace by. 2 Cor. 9:8.
Strengthened by. Eph. 6:10. Col. 1:11.
Upheld by. Psa. 37:17. Isa. 41:10.
Supported in affliction by. 2 Cor. 6:7. 2 Tim. 1:8.
Delivered by. Neh. 1:10. Dan. 3:17.
Exalted by. Job 36:22.
Kept by, unto salvation. 1 Pet. 1:5.

Exerted in behalf of saints. 2 Chr. 16:9.
Works in, and for saints. 2 Cor. 13:4. Eph. 1:19. Eph. 3:20.
The faith of saints stands in. 1 Cor. 2:5.

SHOULD BE

Acknowledged. 1 Chr. 29:11. Isa. 33:13.
Pleaded in prayer. Psa. 79:11. Mat. 6:13.
Feared. Jer. 5:22. Mat. 10:28.
Magnified. Psa. 21:13. Jude 25.

Efficiency of ministers is through. 1 Cor. 3:6—8. Gal. 2:8. Eph. 3:7.
Is a ground of trust. Isa. 26:4. Rom. 4:21.

THE WICKED

Know not. Mat 22:29.
Have against them. Ezr. 8:22.
Shall be destroyed by. Luke 12:5.

The heavenly host magnify. Rev. 4:11. Rev. 5:13. Rev. 11:17.

Power of the Holy Ghost, The.

Is the power of God. Mat. 12:28, with Luke 11:20.
Christ commenced His ministry in. Luke 4:14.
Christ wrought His miracles by. Mat. 12:28.

EXHIBITED IN

Creation. Gen. 1:2. Job 26:13. Psa. 104:30.
The conception of Christ. Luke 1:35.
Raising Christ from the dead. 1 Pet. 3:18.
Giving spiritual life. Eze. 37:11—14, with Rom. 8:11.
Working miracles. Rom. 15:19.
Making the gospel efficacious. 1 Cor. 2:4. 1 The. 1:5.
Overcoming all difficulties. Zec. 4:6, 7.

Promised by the Father. Luke 24: 49.
Promised by Christ. Acts 1: 8.
SAINTS
Upheld by. Psa. 51: 12.
Strengthened by. Eph. 3: 16.
Enabled to speak the truth boldly by. Mic. 3: 8. Acts 6: 5, 10. 2 Tim. 1: 7, 8.
Helped in prayer by. Rom. 8: 26.
Abound in hope by. Rom. 15: 13.
Qualifies ministers. Luke 24: 49. Acts 1: 8.
God's word the instrument of. Eph. 6: 17.

Praise.

God is worthy of. 2 Sam. 22: 4.
Christ is worthy of. Rev. 5: 12.
God is glorified by. Psa. 22: 23. Psa. 50: 23.
Offered to Christ. Jno. 12: 13.
Acceptable through Christ. Heb. 13: 15.
IS DUE TO GOD ON ACCOUNT OF
His majesty. Psa. 96: 1, 6. Isa. 24: 14.
His glory. Psa. 138: 5. Eze. 3: 12.
His excellency. Exo. 15: 7. Psa. 148: 13.
His greatness. 1 Chr. 16: 25. Psa. 145: 3.
His holiness. Exo. 15: 11. Isa. 6: 3.
His wisdom. Dan. 2: 20. Jude 25.
His power. Psa. 21: 13.
His goodness. Psa. 107: 8. Psa. 118: 1. Psa. 136: 1. Jer. 33: 11.
His mercy. 2 Chr. 20: 21. Psa. 89: 1. Psa. 118: 1—4. Psa. 136th.
His loving-kindness and truth. Psa. 138: 2.
His faithfulness and truth. Isa. 25: 1.
His salvation. Psa. 18: 46. Isa. 35: 10. Isa. 61: 10. Luke 1: 68, 69.
His wonderful works. Psa. 89: 5. Psa. 150: 2. Isa. 25: 1.
His consolation. Psa. 42: 5. Isa. 12: 1.
His judgment. Psa. 101: 1.
His counsel. Psa. 16: 7. Jer. 32: 19.
Fulfilling of His promises. 1 Kin. 8: 56.
Pardon of sin. Psa. 103: 1—3. Hos. 14: 2.
Spiritual health. Psa. 103: 3.
Constant preservation. Psa. 71: 6—8.
Deliverance. Psa. 40: 1—3. Psa. 124: 6.
Protection. Psa. 28: 7. Psa. 59: 17.
Answering prayer. Psa. 28: 6. Psa. 118: 21.
The hope of glory. 1 Pet. 1: 3, 4.
All spiritual blessings. Psa. 103: 2. Eph. 1: 3.
All temporal blessings. Psa. 104: 1, 14. Psa. 136: 25.
The continuance of blessings. Psa. 68: 19.
IS OBLIGATORY UPON
Angels. Psa. 103: 20. Psa. 148: 2.
Saints. Psa. 30: 4. Psa. 149: 5.
Gentiles. Psa. 117: 1, with Rom. 15: 11.
Children. Psa. 8: 2, with Mat. 21: 16.
High and low. Psa. 148: 1, 11.
Young and old. Psa. 148: 1, 12.
Small and great. Rev. 19: 5.
All men. Psa. 107: 8. Psa. 145: 21.
All creation. Psa. 148: 1—10. Psa. 150: 6.
Is good and comely. Psa. 33: 1. Psa. 147: 1.
SHOULD BE OFFERED
With the understanding. Psa. 47: 7, with 1 Cor. 14: 15.
With the soul. Psa. 103: 1. Psa. 104: 1, 35.
With the whole heart. Psa. 9: 1. Psa. 111: 1. Psa. 138: 1.
With uprightness of heart. Psa. 119: 7.
With the lips. Psa. 63: 3. Psa. 119: 171.
With the mouth. Psa. 51: 15. Psa. 63: 5.
With joy. Psa. 63: 5. Psa. 98: 4.
With gladness. 2 Chr. 29: 30. Jer. 33: 11.
With thankfulness. 1 Chr. 16: 4. Neh. 12: 24. Psa. 147: 7.
Continually. Psa. 35: 28. Psa. 71: 6.
During life. Psa. 104: 33.
More and more. Psa. 71: 14.
Day and night. Rev. 4: 8.
Day by day. 2 Chr. 30: 21.
For ever and ever. Psa. 145: 1, 2.
Throughout the world. Psa. 113: 3.
In psalms and hymns, &c. Psa. 105: 2. Eph. 5: 19. Col. 3: 16.
Accompanied with musical instruments. 1 Chr. 16: 41, 42. Psa. 150: 3, 5.
Is a part of public worship. Psa. 9: 14. Psa. 100: 4. Psa. 118: 19, 20. Heb. 2: 12.
SAINTS SHOULD
Show forth. Isa. 43: 21. 1 Pet. 2: 9.
Be endued with the spirit of. Isa. 61: 3.
Render, under affliction. Acts 16: 25.
Glory in. 1 Chr. 16: 35.
Triumph in. Psa. 106: 47.
Express their joy by. Jas. 5: 13.
Declare. Isa. 42: 12.
Invite others to. Psa. 34: 3. Psa. 95: 1.
Pray for ability to offer. Psa. 51: 15. Psa. 119: 175.

Posture suited to. 1 Chr. 23:30. Neh. 9:5.

CALLED THE
- Fruit of the lips. Heb. 13:15.
- Voice of praise. Psa. 66:8.
- Voice of triumph. Psa. 47:1.
- Voice of melody. Isa. 51:3.
- Voice of a psalm. Psa. 98:5.
- Garment of praise. Isa. 61:3.
- Sacrifice of praise. Heb. 13:15.
- Sacrifices of joy. Psa. 27:6.
- Calves of the lips. Hos. 14:2.

The heavenly host engage in. Isa. 6:3. Luke 2:13. Rev. 4:9—11. Rev. 5:12.

Exemplified. *Melchizedek*, Gen. 14:20. *Moses, &c.* Exo. 15:1—21. *Jethro*, Exo. 18:10. *Israelites*, 1 Chr. 16:36. *David*, 1 Chr. 29:10—13. Psa. 119:164. *Priests and Levites*, Ezr. 3:10—11. *Ezra*, Neh. 8:6. *Hezekiah*, Isa. 38:19. *Zacharias*, Luke 1:64. *Shepherds*. Luke 2:20. *Simeon*, Luke 2:28. *Anna*, Luke 2:38. *Multitudes*, Luke 18:43. *Disciples*, Luke 19:37, 38. *The Apostles*, Luke 24:53. *First Converts*, Acts 2:47. *Lame man*, Acts 3:8. *Paul and Silas*, Acts 16:25.

Prayer.

Commanded. Isa. 55:6. Mat. 7:7. Phi. 4:6.

TO BE OFFERED
- To God. Psa. 5:2. Mat. 4:10.
- To Christ. Luke 23:42. Acts 7:59.
- To the Holy Ghost. 2 The. 3:5.
- Through Christ. Eph. 2:18. Heb. 10:19.

God hears. Psa. 10:17. Psa. 65:2.

God answers. Psa. 99:6. Isa. 58:9.

IS DESCRIBED AS
- Bowing the knees. Eph. 3:14.
- Looking up. Psa. 5:3.
- Lifting up the soul. Psa. 25:1.
- Lifting up the heart. Lam. 3:41.
- Pouring out the heart. Psa. 62:8.
- Pouring out the soul. 1 Sam. 1:15.
- Calling upon the name of the Lord. Gen. 12:8. Psa. 116:4. Acts 22:16.
- Crying unto God. Psa. 27:7. Psa. 34:6.
- Drawing near to God. Psa. 73:28. Heb. 10:22.
- Crying to heaven. 2 Chr. 32:20.
- Beseeching the Lord. Exo. 32:11.
- Seeking unto God. Job 8:5.
- Seeking the face of the Lord. Psa. 27:8.
- Making supplication. Job 8:5. Jer. 36:7.

Acceptable through Christ. Jno. 14:13, 14. Jno. 15:16. Jno. 16:23, 24.

Ascends to heaven. 2 Chr. 30:27. Rev. 5:8.

Quickening grace necessary to. Psa. 80:18.

THE HOLY GHOST
- Promised as a Spirit of. Zec. 12:10.
- As the Spirit of adoption, leads to. Rom. 8:15. Gal. 4:6.
- Helps our infirmities in. Rom. 8:26.

An evidence of conversion. Acts 9:11.

Of the righteous, availeth much. Jas. 5:16.

Of the upright, a delight to God Pro. 15:8.

SHOULD BE OFFERED UP
- In the Holy Ghost. Eph. 6:18. Jude 20.
- In faith. Mat. 21:22. Jas. 1:6.
- In full assurance of faith. Heb. 10:22.
- In a forgiving spirit. Mat. 6:12.
- With the heart. Jer. 29:13. Lam. 3:41.
- With the whole heart. Psa. 119:58, 145.
- With preparation of heart. Job 11:13.
- With a true heart. Heb. 10:22.
- With the soul. Psa. 42:4.
- With the spirit and understanding. Jno. 4:22—24. 1 Cor. 14:15.
- With confidence in God. Psa. 56:9. Psa. 86:7. 1 Jno. 5:14.
- With submission to God. Luke 22:42.
- With unfeigned lips. Psa. 17:1.
- With deliberation. Ecc. 5:2.
- With holiness. 1 Tim. 2:8.
- With humility. 2 Chr. 7:14. 2 Chr. 33:12.
- With truth. Psa. 145:18. Jno. 4:24.
- With desire to be heard. Neh. 1:6. Psa. 17:1. Psa. 55:1, 2. Psa. 61:1.
- With desire to be answered. Psa. 27:7. Psa. 102:2. Psa. 108:6. Psa. 143:1.
- With boldness. Heb. 4:16.
- With earnestness. 1 The. 3:10. Jas. 5:17.
- With importunity. Gen. 32:26. Luke 11:8, 9. Luke 18:1—7.
- Night and day. 1 Tim. 5:5.
- Without ceasing. 1 The. 5:17.
- Everywhere. 1 Tim. 2:8.
- In everything. Phi. 4:6.

For temporal blessings. Gen. 28:20. Pro. 30:8. Mat. 6:11.

For spiritual blessings. Mat. 6:33.

For mercy and grace to help in time of need. Heb. 4:16.

Model for. Mat. 6:9—13.

Vain repetitions in, forbidden. Mat. 6:7.

Ostentation in, forbidden. Mat. 6:5.

ACCOMPANIED WITH
- Repentance. 1 Kin. 8:33. Jer. 36:7.
- Confession. Neh. 1:4, 7. Dan. 9:4—11.
- Self-abasement. Gen. 18:27.
- Weeping. Jer. 31:9. Hos. 12:4.

Fasting. Neh. 1: 4. Dan. 9: 3. Acts 13: 3.
Watchfulness. Luke 21: 36. 1 Pet. 4: 7.
Praise. Psa. 66: 17.
Thanksgiving. Phi. 4: 6. Col. 4: 2.
PLEAD IN THE
Promises of God. Gen. 32: 9—12. Exo. 32: 13. 1 Kin. 8: 26. Psa. 119: 49.
Covenant of God. Jer. 14: 21.
Faithfulness of God. Psa. 143: 1.
Mercy of God. Psa. 51: 1. Dan. 9: 18.
Righteousness of God. Dan. 9: 16.
Rise early for. Psa. 5: 3. Psa. 119: 147.
Seek divine teaching for. Luke 11: 1.
Faint not in. Luke 18: 1.
Continue instant in. Rom. 12: 12.
Avoid hindrances in. 1 Pet. 3: 7.
Suitable in affliction. Isa. 26: 16. Jas. 5: 13.
Shortness of time a motive to. 1 Pet. 4: 7.
POSTURES IN;
Standing. 1 Kin. 8: 22. Mar. 11: 25.
Bowing down. Psa. 95: 6.
Kneeling. 2 Chr. 6: 13. Psa. 95: 6. Luke 22: 41. Acts 20: 36.
Falling on the face. Num. 16: 22. Jos. 5: 14. 1 Chr. 21: 16. Mat. 26: 39.
Spreading forth the hands. Isa. 1: 15.
Lifting up the hands. Psa. 28: 2. Lam. 2: 19. 1 Tim. 2: 8.
The promises of God encourage to. Isa. 65: 24. Amos 5: 4. Zec. 13: 9.
The promises of Christ encourage to. Luke 11: 9, 10. Jno. 14: 13, 14.
Experience of past mercies an incentive to. Psa. 4: 1. Psa. 116: 2.

Prayer, Answers to.

God gives. Psa. 99: 6. Psa. 118: 5. Psa. 138: 3.
Christ gives. Jno. 4: 10, 14. Jno. 14: 14.
Christ received. Jno. 11: 42. Heb. 5: 7.
GRANTED
Through the grace of God. Isa. 30: 19.
Sometimes immediately. Isa. 65: 24. Dan. 9: 21, 23. Dan. 10: 12.
Sometimes after delay. Luke 18: 7.
Sometimes differently from our desire. 2 Cor. 12: 8, 9.
Beyond expectation. Jer. 33: 3. Eph. 3: 20.
Promised. Isa. 58: 9. Jer. 29: 12. Mat. 7: 7.
Promised especially in times of trouble. Psa. 50: 15. Psa. 91: 15.
RECEIVED BY THOSE WHO
Seek God. Psa. 34: 4.
Seek God with all the heart. Jer. 29: 12, 13.
Wait upon God. Psa. 40: 1.
Return to God. 2 Chr. 7: 14. Job 22: 23, 27.
Ask in faith. Mat. 21: 22. Jas. 5: 15.
Ask in the name of Christ. Jno. 14: 13.
Ask according to God's will. 1 Jno. 5: 14.
Call upon God in truth. Psa. 145: 18.
Fear God. Psa. 145: 19.
Set their love upon God. Psa. 91: 14, 15.
Keep God's commandments. 1 Jno. 3: 22.
Call upon God under oppression. Isa. 19: 20.
Call upon God under affliction. Psa. 18: 6. Psa. 106: 44. Isa. 30: 19, 20.
Abide in Christ. Jno. 15: 7.
Humble themselves. 2 Chr. 7: 14. Psa. 9: 12.
Are righteous. Psa. 34: 15. Jas. 5: 16.
Are poor and needy. Isa. 41: 17.
SAINTS
Are assured of. 1 Jno. 5: 15.
Love God for. Psa. 116: 1.
Bless God for. Psa. 66: 20.
Praise God for. Psa. 116: 17. Psa 118: 21.
A motive for continued prayer. Psa. 116: 2.
DENIED TO THOSE WHO
Ask amiss. Jas. 4: 3.
Regard iniquity in the heart. Psa. 66: 18.
Live in sin. Isa. 59: 2. Jno. 9: 31.
Offer unworthy service to God. Mal. 1: 7—9.
Forsake God. Jer. 14: 10, 12.
Reject the call of God. Pro. 1: 24, 25, 28.
Hear not the law. Pro. 28: 9. Zec. 7: 11—13.
Are deaf to the cry of the poor. Pro. 21: 13.
Are blood-shedders. Isa. 1: 15. Isa. 59: 3.
Are idolaters. Jer. 11: 11—14. Eze. 8: 15—18.
Are wavering. Jas. 1: 6, 7.
Are hypocrites. Job 27: 8, 9.
Are proud. Job 35: 12, 13.
Are self-righteous. Luke 18: 11, 12, 14.
Are the enemies of saints. Psa. 18: 40, 41.
Cruelly oppress saints. Mic. 3: 2—4.
Exemplified.—*Abraham*, Gen. 17: 20. *Lot*, Gen. 19: 19—21. *Abraham's servant*, Gen. 24: 15—27. *Jacob*, Gen.

32: 24—30. *Israelites*, Exo. 2: 23, 24. *Moses*, Exo. 17: 4—6, 11—13. Exo. 32: 11—14. *Samson*, Jud. 15: 18, 19. *Hannah*, 1 Sam. 1: 27. *Samuel*, 1 Sam. 7: 9. *Solomon*, 1 Kin. 3: 9, 12. *Man of God*, 1 Kin. 13: 6. *Elijah*, 1 Kin. 18: 36—38. Jas. 5: 17, 18. *Elisha*, 2 Kin. 4: 33—35. *Jehoahaz*, 2 Kin. 13: 4. *Hezekiah*, 2 Kin. 19: 20. *Jabez*, 1 Chr. 4: 10. *Asa*, 2 Chr. 14: 11, 12. *Jehoshaphat*, 2 Chr. 20: 6—17. *Manasseh*, 2 Chr. 33: 13, 19. *Ezra*, &c. Ezr. 8: 21—23. *Nehemiah*, Neh. 4: 9, 15. *Job*, Job 42: 10. *David*, Psa. 18: 6. *Jeremiah*, Lam. 3: 55, 56. *Daniel*, Dan. 9: 20—23. *Jonah*, Jon. 2: 2, 10. *Zacharias*, Luke 1: 13. *Blind man*, Luke 18: 38, 41—43. *Thief on the Cross*, Luke 23: 42, 43. *Apostles*, Acts 4: 29—31. *Cornelius*, Acts 10: 4, 31. *Primitive Christians*, Acts 12: 5, 7. *Paul and Silas*, Acts 16: 25, 26. *Paul*, Acts 28: 8.

Refusal of, exemplified. *Saul*, 1 Sam. 28: 15. *Elders of Israel*, Eze. 20: 3. *Pharisees*, Mat. 23: 14.

Prayer, Intercessory.

Christ set an example of. Luke 22: 32. Luke 23: 34. Jno. 17: 9—24.
Commanded. 1 Tim. 2: 1. Jas. 5: 14, 16.
SHOULD BE OFFERED UP FOR
- Kings. 1 Tim. 2: 2.
- All in authority. 1 Tim. 2: 2.
- Ministers. 2 Cor. 1: 11. Phi. 1: 19.
- The Church. Psa. 122: 6. Isa. 62: 6, 7.
- All saints. Eph. 6: 18.
- All men. 1 Tim. 2: 1.
- Masters. Gen. 24: 12—14.
- Servants. Luke 7: 2, 3.
- Children. Gen. 17: 18. Mat. 15: 22.
- Friends. Job 42: 8.
- Fellow-countrymen. Rom. 10: 1.
- The sick. Jas. 5: 14.
- Persecutors. Mat. 5: 44.
- Enemies among whom we dwell. Jer. 29: 7.
- Those who envy us. Num. 12: 13.
- Those who forsake us. 2 Tim. 4: 16.
- Those who murmur against God. Num. 11: 1, 2. Num. 14: 13, 19.

By ministers for their people. Eph. 1: 16. Eph. 3: 14—19. Phi. 1: 4.
Encouragement to. Jas. 5: 16. 1 Jno. 5: 16.
Beneficial to the offerer. Job 42: 10.
Sin of neglecting. 1 Sam. 12: 23.
Seek an interest in. 1 Sam. 12: 19. Heb. 13: 18.
Unavailing for the obstinately-impenitent. Jer. 7: 13—16. Jer. 14: 10, 11.
Exemplified. *Abraham*, Gen. 18: 23—32. *Abraham's servant*, Gen. 24: 12—14. *Moses*, Exo. 8: 12. Exo. 32: 11—13. *Samuel*, 1 Sam. 7: 5. *Solomon*, 1 Kin. 8: 30—36. *Elisha*, 2 Kin. 4: 33. *Hezekiah*, 2 Chr. 30: 18. *Isaiah*, 2 Chr. 32: 20. *Nehemiah*, Neh. 1: 4—11. *David*, Psa. 25: 22. *Ezekiel*, Eze. 9: 8. *Daniel*, Dan. 9: 3—19. *Stephen*, Acts 7: 60. *Peter and John*, Acts 8: 15. *Church of Jerusalem*, Acts 12: 5. *Paul*, Col. 1: 9—12. 2 The. 1: 11. *Epaphras*, Col. 4: 12. *Philemon*, Phile. 22.

Prayer, Private.

Christ was constant in. Mat. 14: 23. Mat. 26: 36, 39. Mar. 1: 35. Luke 9: 18, 29.
Commanded. Mat. 6: 6.
SHOULD BE OFFERED
- At evening, morning, and noon. Psa. 55: 17.
- Day and night. Psa. 88: 1.
- Without ceasing. 1 The. 5: 17.

Shall be heard. Job 22: 27.
Rewarded openly. Mat. 6: 6.
An evidence of conversion. Acts 9: 11.
Nothing should hinder. Dan. 6: 10.
Exemplified. *Lot*, Gen. 19: 20. *Eliezer*, Gen. 24: 12. *Jacob*, Gen. 32: 9—12. *Gideon*, Jud. 6: 22, 36, 39. *Hannah*, 1 Sam. 1: 10. *David*, 2 Sam. 7: 18—29. *Hezekiah*, 2 Kin. 20: 2. *Isaiah*, 2 Kin. 20: 11. *Manasseh*, 2 Chr. 33: 18, 19. *Ezra*, Ezr. 9: 5, 6. *Nehemiah*, Neh. 2: 4. *Jeremiah*, Jer. 32: 16—25. *Daniel*, Dan. 9: 3, 17. *Jonah*, Jon. 2: 1. *Habakkuk*, Hab. 1: 2. *Anna*, Luke 2: 37. *Paul*, Acts 9: 11. *Peter*, Acts 9: 40. Acts 10: 9. *Cornelius*, Acts 10: 30.

Prayer, Public.

Acceptable to God. Isa. 56: 7.
God promises to hear. 2 Chr. 7: 14, 16.
God promises to bless in. Exo. 20: 24.
CHRIST
- Sanctifies by His presence. Mat. 18: 20.
- Attended. Mat. 12: 9. Luke 4: 16.
- Promises answers to. Mat. 18: 19.

Instituted form of. Luke 11: 2.
Should not be made in an unknown tongue. 1 Cor. 14: 14—16.
Saints delight in. Psa. 42: 4. Psa. 122: 1.
Exhortation to. Heb. 10: 25.
Urge others to join in. Psa. 95: 6. Zec. 8: 21.
Exemplified. *Joshua, &c.* Jos. 7: 6—9. *David*, 1 Chr. 29: 10—19. *Solomon*, 2 Chr. 6th chap. *Jehoshaphat, &c.* 2 Chr. 20: 5—13. *Jeshua, &c.* Neh. 9th chap. *Jews*, Luke 1: 10. *Primitive Christians*, Acts 2: 46. Acts 4: 24. Acts 12: 5, 12. *Peter, &c.* Acts 3: 1. *Teachers and Prophets, at Antioch*, Acts 13: 3. *Paul, &c.* Acts 16: 16.

Prayer, Social and Family.

Promise of answers to. Mat. 18:19.
Christ promises to be present at. Mat. 18:20.
Punishment for neglecting. Jer. 10:25.
Exemplified. *Abram*, Gen. 12:5, 8. *Jacob*, Gen. 35:2, 3, 7. *Joshua*, Jos. 24:15. *David*, 2 Sam. 6:20. *Job*, Job 1:5. *The Disciples*, Acts 1:13, 14. *Cornelius*, Acts 10:2. *Paul and Silas*, Acts 16:25. *Paul, &c.* Acts 20:36. Acts 21:5.

Precious Stones.

Dug out of the earth. Job 28:5, 6.
Brought from Ophir. 1 Kin. 10:11. 2 Chr. 9:10.
Brought from Sheba. 1 Kin. 10:1, 2. Eze. 27:22.
CALLED
- Stones of fire. Eze. 28:14, 16.
- Stones to be set. 1 Chr. 29:2.
- Jewels. Isa. 61:10. Eze. 16:12.
- Precious jewels. 2 Chr. 20:25. Pro. 20:15.

Of great variety. 1 Chr. 29:2.
Of divers colors. 1 Chr. 29:2.
Brilliant and glittering. 1 Chr. 29:2. Rev. 21:11.
MENTIONED IN SCRIPTURE;
- Agate. Exo. 28:19. Isa. 54:12.
- Amethyst. Exo. 28:19. Rev. 21:20.
- Beryl. Dan. 10:6. Rev. 21:20.
- Carbuncle. Exo. 28:17. Isa. 54:12.
- Coral. Job 28:18.
- Chalcedony. Rev. 21:19.
- Chrysolyte. Rev. 21:20.
- Chrysoprasus. Rev. 21:20.
- Diamond. Exo. 28:18. Jer. 17:1. Eze. 28:13.
- Emerald. Eze. 27:16. Rev. 4:3.
- Jacinth. Rev. 9:17. Rev. 21:20.
- Jasper. Rev. 4:3. Rev. 21:11, 19.
- Onyx. Exo. 28:20. Job 28:16.
- Pearl. Job 28:18. Mat. 13:45, 46. Rev. 21:21.
- Ruby. Job 28:18. Lam. 4:7.
- Sapphire. Exo. 24:10. Eze. 1:26.
- Sardine or Sardius. Exo. 28:17. Rev. 4:3.
- Sardonyx. Rev. 21:20.
- Topaz. Job 28:19. Rev. 21:20.

Highly prized by the ancients. Pro. 17:8.
Extensive commerce in. Eze. 27:22. Rev. 18:12.
Often given as presents. 1 Kin. 10:2, 10.
Art of engraving upon, early known to the Jews. Exo. 28:9, 11, 21.
Art of setting, known to the Jews. Exo. 28:20.
USED FOR
- Adorning the high priest's ephod. Exo. 28:12.
- Adorning the breastplate of judgment. Exo. 28:17—20. Exo. 39:10—14.
- Decorating the person. Eze. 28:13.
- Ornamenting royal crowns. 2 Sam. 12:30.
- Setting in seals and rings. So. of Sol. 5:12.
- Adorning the temple. 2 Chr. 3:6.
- Honoring idols. Dan. 11:38.

A part of the treasure of kings. 2 Chr. 32:27.
Given by the Jews for the tabernacle Exo. 25:7.
Prepared by David for the temple. 1 Chr. 29:2.
Given by chief men for the temple 1 Chr. 29:8.
ILLUSTRATIVE OF
- Preciousness of Christ. Isa. 28:16. 1 Pet. 2:6.
- Beauty and stability of the church. Isa. 54:11, 12.
- Saints. Mal. 3:17. 1 Cor. 3:12.
- Seductive splendor and false glory of the apostacy. Rev. 17:4. Rev. 18:16.
- Wordly glory of nations. Eze. 28:13—16.
- Glory of heavenly Jerusalem. Rev. 21:11.
- Stability of heavenly Jerusalem. Rev. 21:19.

Preciousness of Christ.

To God. Mat. 3:17. 1 Pet. 2:4.
To Saints. So. of Sol. 5:10. Phi. 3:8. 1 Pet. 2:7.
ON ACCOUNT OF HIS
- Goodness and beauty. Zec. 9:17.
- Excellence and grace. Psa. 45:2.
- Name. So. of Sol. 1:3. Heb. 1:4.
- Atonement. 1 Pet. 1:19, with Heb. 12:24.
- Words. Jno. 6:68.
- Promises. 2 Pet. 1:4.
- Care and tenderness. Isa. 40:11.

As the corner-stone of the Church. Isa. 28:16, with 1 Pet. 2:6.
As the source of all grace. Jno. 1:14. Col. 1:19.
Unsearchable. Eph. 3:8.
Illustrated. So. of Sol. 2:3. So. of Sol. 5:10—16. Mat. 13:44—46.

Presents.

Antiquity of. Gen. 32:13. Gen. 43:15.
WERE GIVEN
- To judges to secure a favorable hearing. Pro. 17:23. Amos 2:6.
- To kings to engage their aid. 1 Kin. 15:18.
- By kings to each other in token of inferiority. 1 Kin. 10:25. 2 Chr. 9:23, 24. Psa. 72:10.

To appease the angry feelings of others. Gen. 32: 20. 1 Sam. 25: 27, 28, 35.
To confirm covenants. Gen. 21: 28—30.
To reward service. 2 Sam. 18: 12. Dan. 2: 6, 48.
To show respect. Jud. 6: 18.
In token of friendship. 1 Sam. 18: 3, 4.
As tribute. Jud. 3: 15. 2 Sam. 8: 2. 2 Chr. 17: 5.
On occasions of visits. 2 Kin. 8: 8.
On all occasions of public rejoicing. Neh. 8: 12. Est. 9: 19.
At marriages. Gen. 24: 53. Psa. 45: 12.
On recovering from sickness. 2 Kin. 20: 12.
On restoration to prosperity. Job 42: 10, 11.
On sending away friends. Gen. 45: 22. Jer. 40: 5.

Considered essential on all visits of business. 1 Sam. 9: 7.
Not bringing, considered a mark of disrespect and disaffection. 1 Sam. 10: 27. 2 Kin. 17: 4.
Generally procured a favorable reception. Pro. 18: 16. Pro. 19: 6.
When small or defective, refused. Mal. 1: 8.
Of persons of rank, of great value and variety. 2 Kin. 5: 5. 2 Chr. 9: 1.
Receiving of, a token of good will. Gen. 33: 10, 11.

THINGS GIVEN AS;
Cattle. Gen. 32: 14, 15, 18.
Horses and mules. 1 Kin. 10: 25.
Money. Gen. 45: 22. 1 Sam. 9: 8. Job 42: 11.
Eatables. Gen. 43: 11. 1 Sam. 25: 18. 1 Kin. 14: 3.
Garments. Gen. 45: 22. 1 Sam. 18: 4.
Weapons of war. 1 Sam. 18: 4.
Ornaments. Gen. 24: 22, 47. Job 42: 11.
Gold and silver vessels. 1 Kin. 10: 25.
Precious stones. 1 Kin. 10: 2.
Servants. Gen. 20: 14. Gen. 29: 24, 29.

Often borne by servants. Jud. 3: 18.
Often conveyed on camels, &c. 1 Sam. 25: 18. 2 Kin. 8: 9. 2 Chr. 9: 1.
Sometimes sent before the giver. Gen. 32: 21.
Generally presented in person. Gen. 43: 15, 26. Jud. 3: 17. 1 Sam. 25: 27.
Laid out and presented with great ceremony. Gen. 43: 25. Jud. 3: 18. Mat. 2: 11.

Presumption.

A characteristic of the wicked. 2 Pet. 2: 10.
A characteristic of Antichrist. 2 The. 2: 4.

EXHIBITED IN
Opposing God. Job 15: 25, 26.
Wilful commission of sin. Rom. 1: 32.
Self-righteousness. Hos. 12: 8. Rev. 3: 17.
Spiritual pride. Isa. 65: 5. Luke 18: 11.
Esteeming our own ways right. Pro. 12: 15.
Seeking precedence. Luke 14: 7—11.
Planning for futurity. Luke 12: 18. Jas. 4: 13.
Pretending to prophecy. Deu. 18: 22.

Pray to be kept from sins of. Psa. 19: 13.
Saints avoid. Psa. 131: 1.
Punishment for. Num. 15: 30. Rev. 18: 7, 8.
Exemplified. *Builders of Babel*, Gen. 11: 4. *Israelites*, Num. 14: 44. *Korah &c.* Num. 16: 3, 7. *Men of Bethshemesh*, 1 Sam. 6: 19. *Uzzah*, 2 Sam. 6: 6. *Jeroboam*, 1 Kin. 13: 4. *Benhadad*, 1 Kin. 20: 19. *Uzziah*, 2 Chr. 26: 16. *Sennacherib*, 2 Chr. 32: 13, 14. *Theudas*, Acts 5: 36. *Sons of Sceva*, Acts 19: 13, 14. *Diotrephes*, 3 Jno. 9.

Pride.

Is sin. Pro. 21: 4.
Hateful to God. Pro. 6: 16, 17. Pro. 16: 5.
Hateful to Christ. Pro. 8: 12, 13.

OFTEN ORIGINATES IN
Self-righteousness. Luke 18: 11, 12.
Religious privileges. Zep. 3: 11.
Unsanctified knowledge. 1 Cor. 8: 1.
Inexperience. 1 Tim. 3: 6.
Possession of power. Lev. 26: 19. Eze. 30: 6.
Possession of wealth. 2 Kin. 20: 13.

Forbidden. 1 Sam. 2: 3. Rom. 12: 3, 16.
Defiles a man. Mar. 7: 20, 22.
Hardens the mind. Dan. 5: 20.

SAINTS
Give not way to. Psa. 131: 1.
Respect not, in others. Psa. 40: 4.
Mourn over, in others. Jer. 13: 17.
Hate, in others. Psa. 101: 5.

A hindrance to seeking God. Psa. 10: 4. Hos. 7: 10.
A hindrance to improvement. Pro. 26: 12.

A CHARACTERISTIC OF
The devil. 1 Tim. 3: 6.
The world. 1 Jno. 2: 16.
False teachers. 1 Tim. 6: 3, 4.
The wicked. Hab. 2: 4, 5. Rom. 1: 30.

Comes from the heart. Mar. 7: 21—23.
The wicked encompassed with. Psa. 73: 6.
LEADS MEN TO
Contempt and rejection of God's word and ministers. Jer. 43: 2.
A persecuting spirit. Psa. 10: 2.
Wrath. Pro. 21: 24.
Contention. Pro. 13: 10. Pro. 28: 25.
Self-deception. Jer. 49: 16. Oba. 3.
Exhortation against. Jer. 13: 15.
IS FOLLOWED BY
Shame. Pro. 11: 2.
Debasement. Pro. 29: 23. Isa. 28: 3.
Destruction. Pro. 16: 18. Pro. 18: 12.
Shall abound in the last days. 2 Tim. 3: 2.
Woe to. Isa. 28: 1, 3.
THEY WHO ARE GUILTY OF, SHALL BE
Resisted. Jas. 4: 6.
Brought into contempt. Isa. 23: 9.
Recompensed. Psa. 31: 23.
Marred. Jer. 13: 9.
Subdued. Exo. 18: 11. Isa. 13: 11.
Brought low. Psa. 18: 27. Isa. 2: 12.
Abased. Dan. 4: 37, with Mat. 23: 12.
Scattered. Luke 1: 51.
Punished. Zep. 2: 10, 11. Mal. 4: 1.
Exemplified. *Ahithophel*, 2 Sam. 17: 23. *Hezekiah*, 2 Chr. 32: 25. *Pharaoh*, Neh. 9: 10. *Haman*, Est. 3: 5. *Moab*, Isa. 16: 6. *Tyre*, Isa. 23: 9. *Israel*, Isa. 28: 1. Hos. 5: 5, 9. *Judah*, Jer. 13: 9. *Babylon*, Jer. 50: 29, 32. *Assyria*, Eze. 31: 3, 10. *Nebuchadnezzar*, Dan. 4: 30. Dan. 5: 20. *Belshazzar*. Dan. 5: 22, 23. *Edom*, Oba. 3. *Scribes*, Mar. 12: 38, 39. *Herod*, Acts 12: 21—23. *Laodiceans*, Rev. 3: 17.

Priests.

First notice of persons acting as. Gen. 4: 3, 4.
During patriarchal age heads of families acted as. Gen. 8: 20. Gen. 12: 8. Gen. 35: 7.
After the exodus young men (first-born) deputed to act as. Exo. 24: 5, with Exo. 19: 22.
The sons of Aaron appointed as, by perpetual statute. Exo. 29: 9. Exo. 40: 15.
All except seed of Aaron excluded from being. Num. 3: 10. Num. 16: 40. Num. 18: 7.
Sanctified by God for the office. Exo. 29: 44.
Publicly consecrated. Exo. 28: 3. Num. 3: 3.
CEREMONIES AT CONSECRATION OF;
Washing in water. Exo. 29: 4. Lev. 8: 6.
Clothing with the holy garments. Exo. 29: 8, 9. Exo. 40: 14. Lev. 8: 13.
Anointing with oil. Exo. 30: 30. Exo. 40: 13.
Offering sacrifices. Exo. 29: 10—19. Lev. 8: 14—23.
Purification by blood of the consecration-ram. Exo. 29: 20, 21. Lev. 8: 23, 24.
Placing in their hands the wave-offering. Exo. 29: 22—24. Lev. 8: 25—27.
Partaking of the sacrifices of consecration. Exo. 29: 31—33. Lev. 8: 31, 32.
Lasted seven days. Exo. 29: 35—37. Lev. 8: 33.
Required to remain in the tabernacle seven days after consecration. Lev. 8: 33—36.
No blemished or defective persons could be consecrated. Lev. 21: 17—23.
Required to prove their genealogy before they exercised the office. Ezr. 2: 62. Neh. 7: 64.
GARMENTS OF,
The coat or tunic. Exo. 28: 40. Exo. 39: 27.
The girdle. Exo. 28: 40.
The bonnet. Exo. 28: 40. Exo. 39: 28.
The linen breeches. Exo. 28: 42. Exo. 39: 28.
Worn at consecration. Exo. 29: 9. Exo. 40: 15.
Worn always while engaged in the service of the tabernacle. Exo. 28: 43. Exo. 39: 41.
Worn by the high priest on the day of atonement. Lev. 16: 4.
Purified by sprinkling of blood. Exo. 29: 21.
Laid up in holy chambers. Eze. 44: 19.
Often provided by the people. Ezr. 2: 68, 69. Neh. 7: 70, 72.
Required to wash in the brazen laver before they performed their services. Exo. 30: 18—21.
SERVICES OF;
Keeping the charge of the tabernacle, &c. Num. 18: 1, 5, 7.
Covering the sacred things of the sanctuary before removal. Num. 4: 5—15.
Offering sacrifices. Lev. 1 ch. to Lev. 6 ch. 2 Chr. 29: 34. 2 Chr. 35: 11.
Lighting and trimming the lamps of the sanctuary. Exo. 27: 20, 21. Lev. 24: 3, 4.
Keeping the sacred fire always burning on the altar. Lev. 6: 12, 13.

Burning incense. Exo. 30: 7, 8. Luke 1: 9.
Placing and removing show-bread. Lev. 24: 5—9.
Offering first-fruits. Lev. 23: 10, 11. Deu. 26: 3, 4.
Blessing the people. Num. 6: 23—27.
Purifying the unclean. Lev. 15: 30, 31.
Deciding in cases of jealousy. Num. 5: 14, 15.
Deciding in cases of leprosy. Lev. 13: 2—59. Lev. 14: 34—45.
Judging in cases of controversy. Deu. 17: 8—13. Deu. 21: 5.
Teaching the law. Deu. 33: 8, 10. Mal. 2: 7.
Blowing the trumpets on various occasions. Num. 10: 1—10. Jos. 6: 3, 4.
Carrying the ark. Jos. 3: 6, 17. Jos. 6: 12.
Encouraging the people when they went to war. Deu. 20: 1—4.
Valuing things devoted. Lev. 27: 8.
Were to live by the altar as they had no inheritance. Deu. 18: 1, 2. 1 Cor. 9: 13.
REVENUES OF;
Tenth of the tithes paid to the Levites. Num. 18: 26, 28. Neh. 10: 37, 38. Heb. 7: 5.
First-fruits. Num. 18: 8, 12, 13. Deu. 18: 4.
Redemption-money of the first-born. Num. 3: 48, 51. Num. 18: 15, 16.
First-born of animals or their substitutes. Num. 18: 17, 18, with Exo. 13: 12, 13.
First of the wool of sheep. Deu. 18: 4.
Show-bread after its removal. Lev. 24: 9. 1 Sam. 21: 4—6. Mat. 12: 4.
Part of all sacrifices. Lev. 7: 6—10, 31—34. Num. 6: 19, 20. Num. 18: 8—11. Deu. 18: 3.
All devoted things. Num. 18: 14.
All restitutions when the owner could not be found. Num. 5: 8.
A fixed portion of the spoil taken in war. Num. 31: 29, 41.
Thirteen of the Levitical cities given to, for residence. 1 Chr. 6: 57—60, with Num. 35: 1—8.
Might purchase and hold other lands in possession. 1 Kin. 2: 26. Jer. 32: 8, 9.
SPECIAL LAWS RESPECTING;
Not to marry divorced or improper persons. Lev. 21: 7.
Not to defile themselves for the dead except the nearest of kin. Lev. 21: 1—6.
Not to drink wine, &c. while attending in the tabernacle. Lev. 10: 9. Eze. 44: 21.
Not to defile themselves by eating what died or was torn. Lev. 22: 8.
While unclean could not perform any service. Lev. 22: 1, 2, with Num. 19: 6, 7.
While unclean could not eat of the holy things. Lev. 22: 3—7.
No sojourner or hired servant to eat of their portion. Lev. 22: 10.
All bought and home-born servants to eat of their portion. Lev. 22: 11.
Children of, married to strangers, not to eat of their portion. Lev. 22: 12.
Restitution to be made to, by persons ignorantly eating of their holy things. Lev. 22: 14—16.
Divided by David into twenty-four courses. 1 Chr. 24: 1—19. 2 Chr. 8: 14. 2 Chr. 35: 4, 5.
The four courses which returned from Babylon subdivided into twenty-four. Ezr. 2: 36—39, with Luke 1: 5.
Each course of, had its president or chief. 1 Chr. 24: 6, 31. 2 Chr. 36: 14.
Services of, divided by lot. Luke 1: 9.
Punishment for invading the office of. Num. 16: 1—35. Num. 18: 7. 2 Chr. 26: 16—21.
On special occasions persons not of Aaron's family acted as. Jud. 6: 24—27. 1 Sam. 7: 9. 1 Kin. 18: 33.
WERE SOMETIMES
Greedy. 1 Sam. 2: 13—17.
Drunken. Isa. 28: 7.
Profane and wicked. 1 Sam. 2: 22—24.
Unjust. Jer. 6: 13.
Corrupters of the law. Isa. 28: 7, with Mal. 2: 8.
Slow to sanctify themselves for God's service. 2 Chr. 29: 34.
Generally participated in punishment of the people. Jer. 14: 18. Lam. 2: 20.
Made of the lowest of the people by Jeroboam and others. 1 Kin. 12 31. 2 Kin. 17: 32.
Services of, ineffectual for removing sin. Heb. 7: 11. Heb. 10: 11.
ILLUSTRATIVE OF
Christ. Heb. 10: 11, 12.
Saints. Exo. 19: 6. 1 Pet. 2: 9.

Prisons.

Antiquity of. Gen. 39: 20.
KINDS OF, MENTIONED;
State. Jer. 37: 21, with Gen. 39: 20.
Common. Acts 5: 18.
Dungeons attached to. Jer. 38: 6. Zec. 9: 11.
Were under the care of a keeper. Gen. 39: 21.

USED FOR CONFINING
- Persons accused of crimes. Luke 23:19.
- Persons accused of heresy. Acts 4:3. Acts 5:18. Acts 8:3.
- Suspected persons. Gen. 42:19.
- Condemned criminals till executed. Lev. 24:12. Acts 12:4, 5.
- Enemies taken captive. Jud. 16:21. 2 Kin. 17:4. Jer. 52:11.
- Debtors till they paid. Mat. 5:26. Mat. 18:30.
- Persons under the king's displeasure. 1 Kin. 22:27. 2 Chr. 16:10. Mar. 6:17.

Confinement in, often awarded as a punishment. Ezr. 7:26.

Confinement in, considered a severe punishment. Luke 22:33.

PLACES USED AS;
- Court of the king's house. Jer. 32:2.
- House of the king's scribe. Jer. 37:15.
- House of the captain of the guard. Gen. 40:3.
- Prisoner's own house, where he was kept bound to a soldier. Acts 28:16, 30, with 2 Tim. 1:16—18.

The king had power to commit to. 1 Kin. 22:27.

Magistrates had power to commit to. Mat. 5:25.

PERSONS CONFINED IN,
- Said to be in ward. Lev. 24:12.
- Said to be in hold. Acts 4:3.
- Often placed in dungeons. Jer. 38:6. Acts 16:24.
- Often bound with fetters. Gen. 42:19. Eze. 19:9. Mar. 6:17.
- Often chained to two soldiers. Acts 12:6.
- Often fastened in stocks. Jer. 29:26. Acts 16:24.
- Often kept to hard labor. Jud. 16:21.
- Often subjected to extreme suffering. Psa. 79:11. Psa. 102:20. Psa. 105:18. (*marg.*)
- Fed on bread and water. 1 Kin. 22:27.
- Clothed in prison dress. 2 Kin. 25:29.
- Sometimes allowed to be visited by their friends. Mat. 11:2. Mat. 25:36. Acts 24:23.
- Might have their condition ameliorated by the king. Jer. 37:20, 21.
- Often executed in. Gen. 40:22. Mat. 14:10.

The king had power to release from. Gen. 40:21.

Magistrates had power to release from. Acts 16:35, 36.

KEEPERS OF,
- Strictly guarded the doors. Acts 12:6.
- Responsible for the prisoners. Acts 16:23, 27.
- Put to death if prisoners escaped. Acts 12:19.
- Often used severity. Jer. 37:16, 20. Acts 16:24.
- Sometimes acted kindly. Gen. 39:21. Acts 16:33, 34.
- Sometimes entrusted the care of the prison to well-conducted prisoners. Gen. 39:22, 23.

ILLUSTRATIVE OF
- Deep afflictions. Psa. 142:7.
- Hell. Rev. 20:7.
- Bondage to sin and Satan. Isa 42 7. Isa. 49:9. Isa. 61:1.

Privileges of Saints.

Abiding in Christ. Jno. 15:4, 5.

Partaking of the divine nature. 2 Pet. 1:4.

Access to God by Christ. Eph. 3:12.

Being of the household of God. Eph. 2:19.

Membership with the Church of the first-born. Heb. 12:23.

HAVING
- Christ for their Shepherd. Isa. 40:11, with Jno. 10:14, 16.
- Christ for their Intercessor. Rom. 8:34. Heb. 7:25. 1 Jno. 2:1.
- The promises of God. 2 Cor. 7:1. 2 Pet. 1:4.

The possession of all things. 1 Cor. 3:21, 22.

All things working together for their good. Rom. 8:28. 2 Cor. 4:15—17.

Their names written in the book of life. Rev. 13:8. Rev. 20:15.

HAVING GOD FOR THEIR
- King. Psa. 5:2. Psa. 44:4. Isa. 44:6.
- Glory. Psa. 3:3. Isa. 60:19.
- Salvation. Psa. 18:2. Psa. 27:1. Isa. 12:2.
- Father. Deu. 32:6. Isa. 63:16. Isa. 64:8.
- Redeemer. Psa. 19:14. Isa. 43:14.
- Friend. 2 Chr. 20:7, with Jas. 2:23.
- Helper. Psa. 33:20. Heb. 13:6.
- Keeper. Psa. 121:4, 5.
- Deliverer. 2 Sam. 22:2. Psa. 18:2.
- Strength. Psa. 18:2. Psa. 27:1. Psa. 46:1.
- Refuge. Psa. 46:1, 11. Isa. 25:4.
- Shield. Gen. 15:1. Psa. 84:11.
- Tower. 2 Sam. 22:3. Psa. 61:3.
- Light. Psa. 27:1. Isa. 60:19. Mic. 7:8.
- Guide. Psa. 48:14. Isa. 58:11.
- Law-giver. Neh. 9:13, 14. Isa. 33:22.
- Habitation. Psa. 90:1. Psa. 91:9.
- Portion. Psa. 73:26. Lam. 3:24.

Union in God and Christ. Jno. 17:21.

Committing themselves to God. Psa. 31:5. Acts 7:59. 2 Tim. 1:12.
Calling upon God in trouble. Psa. 50:15.
Suffering for Christ. Acts 5:41. Phi 1:29.
Profiting by chastisement. Psa. 119:67. Heb. 12:10, 11.
Secure during public calamities. Job 5:20, 23. Psa. 27:1—5. Psa. 91:5—10.
Interceding for others. Gen. 18:23—33. Jas. 5:16.

Procrastination.

Condemned by Christ. Luke 9:59—62.
Saints avoid. Psa. 27:8. Psa. 119:60.
TO BE AVOIDED IN
- Hearkening to God. Psa. 95:7, 8, with Heb. 3:7, 8.
- Seeking God. Isa. 55:6.
- Glorifying God. Jer. 13:16.
- Keeping God's commandments. Psa. 119:60.
- Making offerings to God. Exo. 22:29.
- Performance of vows. Deu. 23:21. Ecc. 5:4.

MOTIVES FOR AVOIDING;
- The present the accepted time. 2 Cor. 6:2.
- The present the best time. Ecc. 12:1.
- The uncertainty of life. Pro. 27:1.

Danger of, illustrated. Mat. 5:25. Luke 13:25.
Exemplified. *Lot*, Gen. 19:16. *Felix*, Acts 24:25.

Promises of God, The.

Contained in the Scriptures. Rom. 1:2.
Made in Christ. Eph. 3:6. 2 Tim. 1:1.
MADE TO
- Christ. Gal. 3:16, 19.
- Abraham. Gen. 12:3, 7, with Gal. 3:16.
- Isaac. Gen. 26:3, 4.
- Jacob. Gen. 28:14.
- David. 2 Sam. 7:12. Psa. 89:3, 4, 35, 36.
- The Israelites. Rom. 9:4.
- The Fathers. Acts 13:32. Acts 26:6, 7.
- All who are called of God. Acts 2:39.
- Those who love Him. Jas. 1:12. Jas. 2:5.

Confirmed by an oath. Psa. 89:3, 4. Heb. 6:17.
The covenant established upon. Heb. 8:6.
God is faithful to. Tit. 1:2. Heb. 10:23.
God remembers. Psa. 105:42. Luke 1:54, 55.
ARE
- Good. 1 Kin. 8:56.
- Holy. Psa. 105:42.
- Exceeding great and precious. 2 Pet. 1:4.
- Confirmed in Christ. Rom. 15:8.
- Yea and amen in Christ. 2 Cor. 1:20.
- Fulfilled in Christ. 2 Sam. 7, 12, with Acts 13:23. Luke 1:69—73.
- Through the righteousness of faith. Rom. 4:13, 16.
- Obtained through faith. Heb. 11:33.
- Given to those who believe. Gal. 3:22.
- Inherited through faith and patience. Heb. 6:12, 15. Heb. 10:36.
- Performed in due season. Jer. 33:14. Acts 7:17. Gal. 4:4.

Not one shall fail. Jos. 23:14. 1 Kin. 8:56.
The law not against. Gal. 3:21.
The law could not disannul. Gal. 3:17.
SUBJECTS OF;
- Christ. 2 Sam. 7:12, 13, with Acts 13:22, 23.
- The Holy Ghost. Acts 2:33. Eph. 1:13.
- The gospel. Rom. 1:1, 2.
- Life in Christ. 2 Tim. 1:1.
- A crown of life. Jas. 1:12.
- Eternal life. Tit. 1:2. 1 Jno. 2:25.
- The life that now is. 1 Tim. 4:8.
- Adoption. 2 Cor. 6:18, with 2 Cor. 7:1.
- Preservation in affliction. Isa. 43:2.
- Blessing. Deu. 1:11.
- Forgiveness of sins. Isa. 1:18. Heb. 8:12.
- Putting the law into the heart. Jer. 31:33, with Heb. 8:10.
- Second coming of Christ. 2 Pet. 3:4.
- New heavens and earth. 2 Pet. 3:13.
- Entering into rest. Jos. 22:4, with Heb. 4:1.

Should lead to perfecting holiness. 2 Cor. 7:1.
The inheritance of the saints is of. Rom. 4:13. Gal. 3:18.
SAINTS
- Children of. Rom. 9:8. Gal. 4:28.
- Heirs of. Gal. 3:29. Heb. 6:17. Heb. 11:9.
- Stagger not at. Rom. 4:20.
- Have implicit confidence in. Heb. 11:11.
- Expect the performance of. Luke 1:38, 45. 2 Pet. 3:13.
- Sometimes, through infirmity, tempted to doubt. Psa. 77:8, 10.

Plead, in prayer. Gen. 32:9,12. 1 Chr. 17:23, 26. Isa. 43:26.
Should wait for the performance of. Acts 1:4.
Gentiles shall be partakers of. Eph. 3:6.
Man, by nature, has no interest in. Eph. 2:12.
Scoffers despise. 2 Pet. 3:3, 4.
Fear, lest ye come short of. Heb. 4:1.

Prophecies Respecting Christ.

As the Son of God. Psa. 2:7. Fulfilled, Luke 1:32, 35.
As the seed of the woman. Gen. 3:15. Fulfilled, Gal. 4:4.
As the seed of Abraham. Gen. 17:7. Gen. 22:18. Fulfilled, Gal. 3:16.
As the seed of Isaac. Gen. 21:12. Fulfilled, Heb. 11:17—19.
As the seed of David. Psa. 132:11. Jer. 23:5. Fulfilled, Acts 13:23. Rom. 1:3.
His coming at a set time. Gen. 49:10. Dan. 9:24, 25. Fulfilled, Luke 2:1.
His being born of a virgin. Isa. 7:14. Fulfilled, Mat. 1:18. Luke 2:7.
His being called Immanuel. Isa. 7:14. Fulfilled, Mat. 1:22, 23.
His being born in Bethlehem of Judea. Mic. 5:2. Fulfilled, Mat. 2:1. Luke 2:4—6.
Great persons coming to adore Him. Psa. 72:10. Fulfilled, Mat. 2:1—11.
The slaying of the children of Bethlehem. Jer. 31:15. Fulfilled, Mat. 2:16—18.
His being called out of Egypt. Hos. 11:1. Fulfilled, Mat. 2:15.
His being preceded by John the Baptist. Isa. 40:3. Mal. 3:1. Fulfilled. Mat. 3:1, 3. Luke 1:17.
His being anointed with the Spirit. Psa. 45:7. Isa. 11:2. Isa. 61:1. Fulfilled, Mat. 3:16. Jno. 3:34. Acts 10:38.
His being a Prophet like unto Moses. Deu. 18:15—18. Fulfilled, Acts 3:20—22.
His being a Priest after the order of Melchizedek. Psa. 110:4. Fulfilled, Heb. 5:5, 6.
His entering on His public ministry. Isa. 61:1, 2. Fulfilled, Luke 4:16—21, 43.
His ministry commencing in Galilee. Isa. 9:1, 2. Fulfilled, Mat. 4:12—16, 23.
His entering publicly into Jerusalem. Zec. 9:9. Fulfilled, Mat. 21:1—5.
His coming into the temple. Hag. 2:7, 9. Mal. 3:1. Fulfilled, Mat. 21:12. Luke 2:27—32. Jno. 2:13—16.
His poverty. Isa. 53:2. Fulfilled, Mar. 6:3. Luke 9:58.
His meekness and want of ostentation. Isa. 42:2. Fulfilled, Mat. 12:15, 16, 19.
His tenderness and compassion. Isa. 40:11. Isa. 42:3. Fulfilled, Mat. 12:15, 20. Heb. 4:15.
His being without guile. Isa. 53:9. Fulfilled, 1 Pet. 2:22.
His zeal. Psa. 69:9. Fulfilled, Jno. 2:17.
His preaching by parables. Psa. 78:2. Fulfilled, Mat. 13:34, 35.
His working miracles. Isa. 35:5, 6. Fulfilled, Mat. 11:4—6. Jno. 11:47.
His bearing reproach. Psa. 22:6. Psa. 69:7, 9, 20. Fulfilled, Rom. 15:3.
His being rejected by His brethren. Psa. 69:8. Isa. 63:3. Fulfilled, Jno. 1:11. Jno. 7:3.
His being a stone of stumbling to the Jews. Isa. 8:14. Fulfilled, Rom. 9:32. 1 Pet. 2:8.
His being hated by the Jews. Psa. 69:4. Isa. 49:7. Fulfilled, Jno. 15:24, 25.
His being rejected by the Jewish rulers. Psa. 118:22. Fulfilled, Mat. 21:42. Jno. 7:48.
That the Jews and Gentiles should combine against Him. Psa. 2:1, 2. Fulfilled, Luke 23:12. Acts 4:27.
His being betrayed by a friend. Psa. 41:9. Psa. 55:12—14. Fulfilled, Jno. 13:18, 21.
His disciples forsaking Him. Zec. 13:7. Fulfilled, Mat. 26:31, 56.
His being sold for thirty pieces of silver. Zec. 11:12. Fulfilled, Mat. 26:15.
His price being given for the potter's field. Zec. 11:13. Fulfilled, Mat. 27:7.
The intensity of His sufferings. Psa. 22:14, 15. Fulfilled, Luke 22:42, 44.
His sufferings being for others. Isa. 53:4—6, 12. Dan. 9:26. Fulfilled, Mat. 20:28.
His patience and silence under sufferings. Isa. 53:7. Fulfilled, Mat. 26:63. Mat. 27:12—14.
His being smitten on the cheek. Mic. 5:1. Fulfilled, Mat. 27:30.
His visage being marred. Isa. 52:14. Isa. 53:3. Fulfilled, Jno. 19:5.
His being spitted on and scourged. Isa. 50:6. Fulfilled, Mar. 14:65. Jno. 19:1.
His hands and feet being nailed to the cross. Psa. 22:16. Fulfilled, Jno. 19:18. Jno. 20:25.
His being forsaken by God. Psa. 22:1. Fulfilled, Mat. 27:46.
His being mocked. Psa. 22:7, 8. Fulfilled, Mat. 27:39—44.
Gall and vinegar being given Him to drink. Psa. 69:21. Fulfilled, Mat. 27:34.

His garments being parted, and lots cast for His vesture. Psa. 22: 18. Fulfilled, Mat. 27: 35.
His being numbered with the transgressors. Isa. 53: 12. Fulfilled, Mar. 15: 28.
His intercession for His murderers. Isa. 53: 12. Fulfilled, Luke 23: 34.
His death. Isa. 53: 12. Fulfilled. Mat. 27: 50.
That a bone of Him should not be broken. Exo. 12: 46.. Psa. 34: 20. Fulfilled, Jno. 19: 33, 36.
His being pierced. Zec. 12: 10. Fulfilled, Jno. 19: 34, 37.
His being buried with the rich. Isa. 53: 9. Fulfilled, Mat. 27: 57–60.
His flesh not seeing corruption. Psa. 16: 10. Fulfilled, Acts 2: 31.
His resurrection. Psa. 16: 10. Isa. 26: 19. Fulfilled, Luke 24: 6, 31, 34.
His ascension. Psa. 68: 18. Fulfilled, Luke 24: 51. Acts 1: 9.
His sitting on the right hand of God. Psa. 110: 1. Fulfilled, Heb. 1: 3.
His exercising the priestly office in heaven. Zec. 6: 13. Fulfilled, Rom. 8: 34.
His being the chief corner-stone of the Church. Isa. 28: 16. Fulfilled, 1 Pet. 2: 6, 7.
His being King in Zion. Psa. 2: 6. Fulfilled, Luke 1: 32. Jno. 18: 33—37.
The conversion of the Gentiles to Him. Isa. 11: 10. Isa. 42: 1. Fulfilled, Mat. 1: 17, 21. Jno. 10: 16. Acts 10: 45, 47.
His righteous government. Psa. 45: 6, 7. Fulfilled, Jno. 5: 30. Rev. 19: 11.
His universal dominion. Psa. 72: 8. Dan. 7: 14. Fulfilled, Phi. 2: 9, 11.
The perpetuity of His kingdom. Isa. 9: 7. Dan. 7: 14. Fulfilled, Luke 1: 32, 33.

Prophecy.

Is the foretelling of future events. Gen. 49: 1. Num. 24: 14.
God is the Author of. Isa. 44: 7. Isa. 45: 21.
God gives, through Christ. Rev. 1: 1.
A gift of Christ. Eph. 4: 11. Rev. 11: 3.
A gift of the Holy Ghost. 1 Cor. 12: 10.
Came not by the will of man. 2 Pet. 1: 21.
Given from the beginning. Luke 1: 70.
Is a sure word. 2 Pet. 1: 19.
THEY WHO UTTERED,
  Raised up by God. Amos 2: 11.
  Ordained by God. 1 Sam. 3: 20. Jer. 1: 5.
  Sent by God. 2 Chr. 36: 15. Jer, 7 25.
  Sent by Christ. Mat. 23: 34.
  Filled with the Holy Ghost. Luk 1: 67.
  Moved by the Holy Ghost. 2 Pet 1: 21.
  Spake by the Holy Ghost. Acts 1 16. Acts 11: 28. Acts 28: 25.
  Spake in the name of the Lord. Chr. 33: 18. Jas. 5: 10.
  Spake with authority. 1 Kin. 17: 1
God accomplishes. Isa. 44: 26. Act 3: 18.
Christ the great subject of. Acts 3 22—24. Acts 10: 43. 1 Pet. 1: 10, 11
Fulfilled respecting Christ. Luke 24 44.
Gift of, promised. Joel 2: 28, with Acts 2: 16, 17.
Is for the benefit of after ages, 1 Pet. 1: 12.
Is as a light in a dark place. 2 Pet 1: 19.
Is not of private interpretation. 2 Pet. 1: 20.
Despise not. 1 The. 5: 20.
Give heed to. 2 Pet. 1: 19.
Receive in faith. 2 Chr. 20: 20. Luke 24: 25.
Blessedness of reading, hearing, and keeping. Rev. 1: 3. Rev. 22: 7.
Guilt of pretending to the gift of Jer. 14: 14. Jer. 23: 13, 14. Eze. 13 2, 3.
PUNISHMENT FOR
  Not giving ear to. Neh 9: 30.
  Adding to, or taking from. Rev. 22: 18, 19.
  Pretending to the gift of. Deu. 18 20. Jer. 14: 15. Jer. 23: 15.
Gift of, sometimes possessed by unconverted men. Num. 24: 2—9. 1 Sam. 19: 20, 23. Mat. 7: 22. Jno. 11: 49—51. 1 Cor. 13: 2.
How tested. Deu. 13: 1—3. Deu. 18 22.

Prophets.

God spake of old by. Hos. 12: 10. Heb. 1: 1.
The messengers of God. 2 Chr. 36: 15. Isa. 44: 26.
The servants of God. Jer. 35: 15.
The watchmen of Israel. Eze. 3: 17.
WERE CALLED
  Men of God. 1 Sam. 9: 6.
  Prophets of God. Ezr. 5: 2.
  Holy prophets. Luke 1: 70. Rev. 18: 20. Rev. 22: 6.
  Holy men of God. 2 Pet. 1: 21.
  Seers. 1 Sam. 9: 9.
Were esteemed as holy men. 2 Kin. 4: 9.
Women sometimes endowed as. Joel 2: 28.

GOD COMMUNICATED TO,
His secret things. Amos 3:7.
At sundry times and in divers ways. Heb. 1:1.
By an audible voice. Num. 12:8. 1 Sam. 3:4—14.
By angels. Dan. 8:15—26. Rev. 22:8, 9.
By dreams and visions. Num. 12:6. Joel 2:28.
Were under the influence of the Holy Ghost while prophesying. Luke 1:67. 2 Pet. 1:21.
Spake in the name of the Lord. 2 Chr. 33:18. Eze. 3:11. Jas. 5:10.
Frequently spake in parables and riddles. 2 Sam. 12:1—6. Isa. 5:1—7. Eze. 17:2—10.
Frequently in their actions, &c. were made signs to the people. Isa. 20:2—4. Jer. 19:1, 10, 11. Jer. 27:2, 3. Jer. 43:9. Jer. 51:63. Eze. 4:1—13. Eze. 5:1—4. Eze. 7:23. Eze. 12:3—7. Eze. 21:6, 7. Eze. 24:1—24. Hos. 1:2—9.
Frequently left without divine communications on account of sins of the people. 1 Sam. 28:6. Lam. 2:9. Eze. 7:26.
WERE REQUIRED
To be bold and undaunted. Eze. 2:6. Eze. 3:8, 9.
To be vigilant and faithful. Eze. 3:17—21.
To receive with attention all God's communications. Eze. 3:10.
Not to speak anything but what they received from God. Deu. 18:20.
To declare everything that the Lord commanded. Jer. 26:2.
Sometimes received divine communications and uttered predictions under great bodily and mental excitement. Jer. 23:9. Eze. 3:14, 15. Dan. 7:28. Dan. 10:8. Hab. 3:2, 16.
Sometimes uttered their predictions in verse. Deu. 32:44. Isa. 5:1.
Often accompanied by music while predicting. 1 Sam. 10:5. 2 Kin. 3:15.
Often committed their predictions to writing. 2 Chr. 21:12. Jer. 36:2.
Writings of, read in the synagogues every Sabbath. Luke 4:17. Acts 13:15.
ORDINARY,
Numerous in Israel. 1 Sam. 10:5. 1 Kin. 18:4.
Trained up and instructed in schools. 2 Kin. 2:3, 5, with 1 Sam. 19:20.
The sacred bards of the Jews. Exo. 15:20, 21. 1 Sam. 10:5, 10. 1 Chr. 25:1.
EXTRAORDINARY,
Specially raised up on occasions of emergency. 1 Sam. 3:19—21. Isa. 6:8, 9. Jer. 1:5.
Often endued with miraculous power. Exo. 4:1—4. 1 Kin. 17:23. 2 Kin. 5:3—8.
Frequently married men. 2 Kin. 4:1. Eze. 24:18.
Wore a coarse dress of hair-cloth. 2 Kin. 1:8. Zec. 13:4. Mat. 3:4. Rev. 11:3.
Often led a wandering and unsettled life. 1 Kin. 18:10—12. 1 Kin. 19:3, 8, 15. 2 Kin. 4:10.
Simple in their manner of life. Mat. 3:4.
The historiographers of the Jewish nation. 1 Chr. 29:29. 2 Chr. 9:29.
The interpreters of dreams, &c. Dan. 1:17.
Were consulted in all difficulties. 1 Sam. 9:6. 1 Sam. 28:15. 1 Kin. 14:2—4. 1 Kin. 22:7.
Presented with gifts by those who consulted them. 1 Sam. 9:7, 8. 1 Kin. 14:3.
Sometimes thought it right to reject presents. 2 Kin. 5:15, 16.
WERE SENT TO
Reprove the wicked and exhort to repentance. 2 Kin. 17:13. 2 Chr. 24:19. Jer. 25:4, 5.
Denounce the wickedness of kings. 1 Sam. 15:10, 16—19. 2 Sam. 12:7—12. 1 Kin. 18:18. 1 Kin. 21:17—22.
Exhort to faithfulness and constancy in God's service. 2 Chr. 15:1, 2, 7.
Predict the coming, &c. of Christ. Luke 24:44. Jno. 1:45. Acts 3:24. Acts 10:43.
Predict the downfall of nations. Isa. 15:1. Isa. 17:1, &c. Jer. 47 ch. to Jer. 51 ch.
Felt deeply on account of the calamities which they predicted. Isa. 16:9—11. Jer. 9:1—7.
PREDICTIONS OF,
Frequently proclaimed at the gate of the Lord's house. Jer. 7:2.
Proclaimed in the cities and streets. Jer. 11:6.
Written on tables and fixed up in some public place. Hab. 2:2.
Written on rolls and read to the people. Isa. 8:1. Jer. 36:2.
Were all fulfilled. 2 Kin. 10:10. Isa. 44:26. Acts 3:18. Rev. 10:7.
Assisted the Jews in their great national undertakings. Ezr. 5:2.
MENTIONED IN SCRIPTURE;
Enoch. Gen. 5:21—24, with Jude 14 v.
Noah. Gen. 9:25—27.
Jacob. Gen. 49:1.

Aaron. Exo. 7:1.
Moses. Deu. 18:18.
Miriam. Exo. 15:20.
Deborah. Jud. 4:4.
Prophet sent to Israel. Jud. 6:8.
Prophet sent to Eli. 1 Sam. 2:27.
Samuel. 1 Sam. 3:20.
David. Psa. 16:8—11, with Acts 2:25:30.
Nathan. 2 Sam. 7:2. 2 Sam. 12:1. 1 Kin. 1:10.
Zadok. 2 Sam. 15:27.
Gad. 2 Sam. 24:11. 1 Chr. 29:29.
Ahijah. 1 Kin. 11:29. 1 Kin. 12:15. 2 Chr. 9:29.
Prophet of Judah. 1 Kin. 13:1.
Iddo. 2 Chr. 9:29. 2 Chr. 12:15.
Shemaiah. 1 Kin. 12:22. 2 Chr. 12:7, 15.
Azariah the son of Oded. 2 Chr. 15:2, 8.
Hanani. 2 Chr. 16:7.
Jehu the son of Hanani. 1 Kin. 16:1, 7, 12.
Elijah. 1 Kin. 17:1.
Elisha. 1 Kin. 19:16.
Micaiah the son of Imlah. 1 Kin. 22:7, 8.
Jonah. 2 Kin. 14:25. Jon. 1:1. Mat. 12:39.
Isaiah. 2 Kin. 19:2. 2 Chr. 26:22. Isa. 1:1.
Hosea. Hos. 1:1.
Amos. Amos 1:1. Amos 7:14, 15.
Micah. Mic. 1:1.
Oded. 2 Chr. 28:9.
Nahum. Nah. 1:1.
Joel. Joel 1:1. Acts 2:16.
Zephaniah. Zep. 1:1.
Huldah. 2 Kin. 22:14.
Jeduthun. 2 Chr. 35:15.
Jeremiah. 2 Chr. 36:12, 21. Jer. 1:1, 2.
Habakkuk. Hab. 1:1.
Obadiah. Oba. 1 v.
Ezekiel. Eze. 1:3.
Daniel. Dan. 12:11, with Mat. 24:15.
Haggai. Ezr. 5:1. Ezr. 6:14. Hag. 1:1.
Zechariah son of Iddo. Ezr. 5:1. Zec. 1:1.
Malachi. Mal. 1:1.
Zacharias the father of John. Luke 1:67.
Anna. Luke 2:36.
Agabus. Acts 11:28. Acts 21:10.
Daughters of Philip. Acts 21:9.
Paul. 1 Tim. 4:1.
Peter. 2 Pet. 2:1, 2.
John. Rev. 1:1.

One generally attached to the king's household. 2 Sam. 24:11. 2 Chr. 29:25. 2 Chr. 35:15.

THE JEWS
Require to hear and believe. Deu. 18:15, with 2 Chr. 20:20.
Often tried to make them speak smooth things. 1 Kin. 22:13. Isa. 30:10. Amos 2:12.
Persecuted them. 2 Chr. 36:16. Mat. 5:12.
Often imprisoned them. 1 Kin. 22:27. Jer. 32:2. Jer. 37:15, 16.
Often put them to death. 1 Kin. 18:13. 1 Kin. 19:10. Mat. 23:34—37.
Often left without, on account of sin. 1 Sam. 3:1. Psa. 74:9. Amos 8:11, 12.

Were mighty through faith. Heb. 11:32—40.
Great patience of, under suffering. Jas. 5:10.
God avenged all injuries done to. 2 Kin. 9:7. 1 Chr. 16:21, 22. Mat. 23:35—38. Luke 11:50.
Christ predicted to exercise the office of. Deu. 18:15, with Acts 3:22.
Christ exercised the office of. Mat. 24 ch. Mar. 10:32—34.

Prophets, False.

Pretended to be sent by God. Jer. 23:17, 18, 31.
Not sent or commissioned by God. Jer. 14:14. Jer. 23:21. Jer. 29:31.
Made use of by God to prove Israel. Deu. 13:3.

DESCRIBED AS
Light and treacherous. Zep. 3:4.
Covetous. Mic. 3:11.
Crafty. Mat. 7:15.
Drunken. Isa. 28:7.
Immoral and profane. Jer. 23:11, 14.

Women sometimes acted as. Neh. 6:14. Rev. 2:20.
Called foolish prophets. Eze. 13:3.
Compared to foxes in the desert. Eze. 13:4.
Compared to wind. Jer. 5:13.
Influenced by evil spirits. 1 Kin. 22:21, 22.

PROPHESIED
Falsely. Jer. 5:31.
Lies in the name of the Lord. Jer. 14:14.
Out of their own heart. Jer. 23:16, 26. Eze. 13:2.
In the name of false gods. Jer. 2:8.
Peace, when there was no peace. Jer. 6:14. Jer. 23:17. Eze. 13:10. Mic. 3:5.

Often practised divination and witchcraft. Jer. 14:14. Eze. 22:28. Acts 13:6.
Often pretended to dreams, &c. Jer. 23:28, 32.
Often deceived by God as a judgment. Eze. 14:9.

THE PEOPLE
Led into error by. Jer. 23:13. Mic. 3:5.

Made to forget God's name by. Jer. 23:27.
Deprived of God's word by. Jer. 23:30.
Taught profaneness and sin by. Jer. 23:14, 15.
Oppressed and defrauded by. Eze. 22:25.
Warned not to listen to. Deu. 13:3. Jer. 23:16. Jer. 27:9, 15, 16.
Encouraged and praised. Jer. 5:31. Luke 6:26.
Mode of trying and detecting. Deu. 13:1, 2. Deu. 18:21, 22. 1 Jno. 4:1—3.
PREDICTED TO ARISE
Before destruction of Jerusalem. Mat. 24:11, 24.
In the latter times. 2 Pet. 2:1.
Judgments denounced against. Jer. 8:1, 2. Jer. 14:15. Jer. 28:16, 17. Jer. 29:32.
Involved the people in their own ruin. Isa. 9:15, 16. Jer. 20:6. Eze. 14:10.

Proselytes.

Described. Est. 8:17. Isa. 56:3.
REQUIRED
To give up all heathen practices. Ezr. 6:21.
To give up all heathen associates. Ruth 1:16. Ruth 2:11. Psa. 45:10. Luke 14:26.
To be circumcised. Gen. 17:13, with Exo. 12:48.
To enter into convenant to serve the Lord. Deu. 29:10—13, with Neh. 10:28, 29.
To observe the law of Moses as Jews. Exo. 12:49.
Unfaithfulness in, punished. Eze. 14:7.
From the Ammonites and Moabites restricted forever from holding office in the congregation. Deu. 23:3.
From the Egyptians and Edomites restricted to the third generation from holding office in the congregation. Deu. 23:7, 8.
Were entitled to all privileges. Exo. 12:48. Isa. 56:3—7.
Went up to the feasts. Acts 2:10. Acts 8:27.
Pharisees, &c. zealous in making. Mat. 23:15.
Many, embraced the gospel. Acts 6:5. Acts 13:43.
Latterly called devout Greeks. Jno. 12:20, with Acts 17:4.

Protection.

God is able to afford. 1 Pet. 1:5. Jude 24.
God is faithful to afford. 1 The. 5:23, 24. 2 The. 3:3.
OF GOD, IS
Indispensable. Psa. 127:1.
Seasonable. Psa. 46:1.
Unfailing. Deu. 31:6, Jos. 1:5.
Effectual. Jno. 10:28—30. 2 Cor. 12:9.
Uninterrupted. Psa. 121:3.
Encouraging. Isa. 41:10. Isa. 50:7.
Perpetual. Psa. 121:8.
Often afforded through means inadequate in themselves. Jud. 7:7. 1 Sam. 17:45, 50. 2 Chr. 14:11.
IS AFFORDED TO
Those who hearken to God. Pro. 1:33.
Returning sinners. Job 22:23, 25.
The perfect in heart. 2 Chr. 16:9.
The poor. Psa. 14:6. Psa. 72:12—14.
The oppressed. Psa. 9:9.
The Church. Psa. 48:3. Zec. 2:4, 5.
IS VOUCHSAFED TO SAINTS, IN
Preserving them. Psa. 145:20.
Strengthening them. 2 Tim. 4:17.
Upholding them. Psa. 37:17, 24. Psa. 63:8.
Keeping their feet. 1 Sam. 2:9. Pro. 3:26.
Keeping them from evil. 2 The. 3:3.
Keeping them from falling. Jude 24.
Keeping them in the way. Exo. 23:20.
Keeping them from temptation. Rev. 3:10.
Providing a refuge for them. Pro. 14:26. Isa. 4:6. Isa. 32:2.
Defending them against their enemies. Deu. 20:1—4. Deu. 33:27. Isa. 59:19.
Defeating the counsels of enemies. Isa. 8:10.
Temptation. 1 Cor. 10:13. 2 Pet. 2:9.
Persecution. Luke 21:18.
Calamities. Psa. 57:1. Psa. 59:16.
All dangers. Psa. 91:3—7.
All places. Gen. 28:15. 2 Chr. 16:9.
Sleep. Psa. 3:5. Psa. 4:8. Pro. 3:24.
Death. Psa. 23:4.
SAINTS
Acknowledge God as their. Psa. 18:2. Psa. 62:2. Psa. 89:18.
Pray for. Psa. 17:5, 8. Isa. 51:9.
Praise God for. Psa. 5:11.
WITHDRAWN FROM THE
Disobedient. Lev. 26:14—17.
Backsliding. Jos. 23:12, 13. Jud. 10:13.
Presumptuous. Num. 14:40—45.
Unbelieving. Isa. 7:9.
Obstinately impenitent. Mat. 23:38.
NOT TO BE FOUND IN
Idols. Deu. 32:37—39. Isa. 46:7.
Man. Psa. 146:3. Isa. 30:7.
Riches. Pro. 11:4, 28. Zep. 1:18.
Hosts. Jos. 11:4—8, with Psa. 33:16
Horses. Psa. 33:17. Pro. 21:31.

Illustrated. Deu. 32:11. Psa. 125:1, 2. Pro. 18:10. Isa. 25:4. Isa. 31:5. Luke 13:34.
Exemplified. *Abraham*, Gen. 15:1. *Jacob*, Gen. 48:16. *Joseph*, Gen. 49:23—25. *Israel*, Jos. 24:17. *David*, Psa. 18:1, 2. *Shadrach, &c.* Dan. 3:28. *Daniel*, Dan. 6:22. *Peter*, Acts 12:4—7. *Paul*, Acts 18:10. Acts 26:17.

Providence of God, The.

Is His care over His works. Psa. 145:9.
Is exercised in
- Preserving His creatures. Neh. 9:6. Psa. 36:6. Mat. 10:29.
- Providing for His creatures. Psa. 104:27, 28. Psa. 136:25. Psa. 147:9. Mat. 6:26.
- The special preservation of saints. Psa. 37:28. Psa. 91:11. Mat. 10:30.
- Prospering saints. Gen. 24:48, 56.
- Protecting saints. Psa. 91:4. Psa. 140:7.
- Delivering saints. Psa. 91:3. Isa. 31:5.
- Leading saints. Deu. 8:2, 15. Isa. 63:12.
- Bringing His words to pass. Num. 26:65. Jos. 21:45. Luke 21:32, 33.
- Ordering the ways of men. Pro. 16:9. Pro. 19:21. Pro. 20:24.
- Ordaining the conditions and circumstances of men. 1 Sam. 2:7, 8. Psa. 75:6, 7.
- Determining the period of human life. Psa. 31:15. Psa. 39:5. Acts 17:26.
- Defeating wicked designs. Exo. 15:9—19. 2 Sam. 17:14, 15. Psa. 33:10.
- Overruling wicked designs for good. Gen. 45:5—7. Gen. 50:20. Phi. 1:12.
- Preserving the course of nature. Gen. 8:22. Job 26:10. Psa. 104:5—9.
- Directing all events. Jos. 7:14. 1 Sam. 6:7—10, 12. Pro. 16:33. Isa. 44:7. Acts 1:26.
- Ruling the elements. Job 37:9—13. Isa. 50:2. Jno. 1:4, 15. Nah. 1:4.
- Ordering the minutest matters. Mat. 10:29, 30. Luke 21:18.

Is righteous. Psa. 145:17. Dan. 4:37.
Is ever watchful. Psa. 121:4. Isa. 27:3.
Is all pervading. Psa. 139:1—5.
Sometimes dark and mysterious. Psa. 36:6. Psa. 73:16. Psa. 77:19. Rom. 11:33.
All things are ordered by,
- For His glory. Isa. 63:14.
- For good to saints. Rom. 8:28.

The wicked made to promote the designs of. Isa. 10:5—12. Acts 3:17, 18.
To be acknowledged
- In prosperity. Deu. 8:18. 1 Chr. 29:12.
- In adversity. Job 1:21. Psa. 119:75.
- In public calamities. Amos 3:6.
- In our daily support. Gen. 48:15.
- In all things. Pro. 3:6.

Cannot be defeated. 1 Kin. 22:30, 34. Pro. 21:30.
Man's efforts are vain without. Psa. 127:1, 2. Pro. 21:31.
Saints should
- Trust in. Mat. 6:33, 34. Mat. 10:9, 29—31.
- Have full confidence in. Psa. 16:8. Psa. 139:10.
- Commit their works unto. Pro. 16:3.
- Encourage themselves in. 1 Sam. 30:6.
- Pray in dependence upon. Acts 12:5.
- Pray to be guided by. Gen. 24:12—14. Gen. 28:20, 21. Acts 1:24.

Result of depending upon. Luke 22:35.
Connected with the use of means. 1 Kin. 21:19, with 1 Kin. 22:37, 38. Mic. 5:2, with Luke 2:1—4. Acts 27:22, 31, 32.
Danger of denying. Isa. 10:13—17. Eze. 28:2—10. Dan. 4:29—31. Hos. 2:8, 9.

Prudence.

Exhibited in the manifestation of God's grace. Eph. 1:8.
Exemplified by Christ. Isa. 52:13. Mat. 21:24—27. Mat. 22:15—21.
Intimately connected with wisdom. Pro. 8:12.
The wise celebrated for. Pro. 16:21.
They who have,
- Get knowledge. Pro. 18:15.
- Deal with knowledge. Pro. 13:16.
- Look well to their goings. Pro. 14:15.
- Understand the ways of God. Hos. 14:9.
- Understand their own ways. Pro. 14:8.
- Crowned with knowledge. Pro. 14:18.
- Not ostentatious of knowledge. Pro. 12:23.
- Foresee and avoid evil. Pro. 22:3.
- Are preserved by it. Pro. 2:11.
- Suppress angry feelings, &c. Pro. 12:16. Pro. 19:11.
- Regard reproof. Pro. 15:5.
- Keep silence in the evil time. Amos 5:13.

Saints act with. Psa. 112:5.
Saints should specially exercise, in their intercourse with unbelievers. Mat. 10:16. Eph. 5:15. Col. 4:5.

Virtuous wives act with. Pro. 31: 16, 26.
The young should cultivate. Pro. 3: 21.
OF THE WICKED
 Fails in the times of perplexity. Jer. 49: 7.
 Keeps them from the knowledge of the gospel. Mat. 11: 25.
 Denounced by God. Isa. 5: 21. Isa. 29: 15.
 Defeated by God. Isa. 29: 14. 1 Cor. 1: 19.
Necessity for—Illustrated. Mat. 25: 3, 9. Luke 14: 28—32.
Exemplified. *Jacob*, Gen. 32: 3—23. *Joseph*, Gen. 41: 39. *Jethro*, Exo. 18: 19, &c. *Gideon*, Jud. 8: 1—3. *David*, 1 Sam. 16: 18. *Abigail*, 1 Sam. 25: 23—31. 2 Sam. 15: 32—34, with 2 Sam. 17: 6—14. *Aged Counsellors of Rehoboam*, 1 Kin. 12: 7. *Solomon*, 2 Chr. 2: 12. *Nehemiah*, Neh. 2: 12—16. Neh. 4: 13—18. *The Poor Wise Man*, Ecc. 9: 15. *The Scribe*, Mar. 12: 32—34. *Gamaliel*, Acts 5: 34—39. *Sergius Paulus*, Acts 13: 7. *Paul*, Acts 23: 6.

Publicans, The.

The collectors of the public taxes. Luke 5: 27.
Suspected of extortion. Luke 3: 13.
Often guilty of extortion. Luke 19: 8.
Chiefs of, were very rich. Luke 19: 2.
THE JEWS
 Despised. Luke 18: 11.
 Classed with the most infamous characters. Mat. 11: 19. Mat. 21: 32.
 Despised our Lord for associating with. Mat. 9: 11. Mat. 11: 19.
Often kind to their friends. Mat. 5: 46, 47.
Often hospitable. Luke 5: 29. Luke 19: 6.
MANY OF,
 Believed the preaching of John. Mat. 21: 32.
 Received John's baptism. Luke 3: 12. Luke 7: 29.
 Attended the preaching of Christ. Mar. 2: 15. Luke 15: 1.
 Embraced the gospel. Mat. 21: 31.
Matthew the apostle was of. Mat. 10: 3.

Punishment of the Wicked, The.

Is from God. Lev. 26: 18. Isa. 13: 11.
ON ACCOUNT OF THEIR
 Sin. Lam. 3: 39.
 Iniquity. Jer. 36: 31. Eze. 3: 17—18. Eze. 18: 4, 13, 20. Amos 3: 2.
 Idolatry. Lev. 26: 30. Isa. 10: 10, 11.
 Rejection of the law of God. 1 Sam. 15: 23. Hos. 4: 6—9.
 Ignorance of God. 2 The. 1: 8.
 Evil ways and doings. Jer. 21: 14. Hos. 4: 9. Hos. 12: 2.
 Pride. Isa. 10: 12. Isa. 24: 21. Luke 14: 11.
 Unbelief. Mark 16: 16. Rom. 11: 20. Heb. 3: 18, 19. Heb. 4: 2.
 Covetousness. Isa. 57: 17. Jer. 51: 13.
 Oppressing. Isa. 49: 26. Jer. 30: 16, 20.
 Persecuting. Jer. 11: 21, 22. Mat. 23: 34—36.
 Disobeying God. Neh. 9: 26, 27. Eph. 5: 6.
 Disobeying the gospel. 2 The. 1: 8.
Is the fruit of their sin. Job 4: 8. Pro. 22: 8. Rom. 6: 21. Gal. 6: 8.
Is the reward of their sins. Psa. 91: 8. Isa. 3: 11. Jer. 16: 18. Rom. 6: 23. Heb. 2: 2.
Often brought about by their evil designs. Est. 7: 10. Psa. 37: 15. Psa. 57: 6.
Often commences in this life. Pro. 11: 31.
IN THIS LIFE BY
 Sickness. Lev. 26: 16. Psa. 78: 50.
 Famine. Lev. 26: 19, 20, 26, 29. Psa. 107: 34.
 Noisome beasts. Lev. 26: 22.
 War. Lev. 26: 25, 32, 33. Jer. 6: 4.
 Deliverance unto enemies. Neh. 9: 27.
 Fear. Lev. 26: 36, 37. Job 18: 11.
 Reprobate mind. Rom. 1: 28.
 Put in slippery places. Psa. 73: 3—19.
 Trouble and distress. Isa. 8: 22. Zep. 1: 15.
 Cutting off. Psa. 94: 23.
 Bringing down their pride. Isa. 13: 11.
Future, shall be awarded by Christ. Mat. 16: 27. Mat. 25: 31, 41.
FUTURE, DESCRIBED AS
 Hell. Psa. 9: 17. Mat. 5: 29. Luke 12: 5. Luke 16: 23.
 Darkness. Mat. 8: 12. 2 Pet. 2: 17.
 Death. Rom. 5: 12—17. Rom. 6: 23.
 Resurrection of damnation. Jno. 5: 29.
 Rising to shame and everlasting contempt. Dan. 12: 2.
 Everlasting destruction. Psa. 52: 5. Psa. 92: 7. 2 The. 1: 9.
 Everlasting fire. Mat. 25: 41. Jude 7.
 Second death. Rev. 2: 11. Rev. 21: 8.
 Damnation of hell. Mat. 23: 33.
 Eternal damnation. Mar. 3: 29.
 Blackness of darkness. 2 Pet. 2: 17. Jude 13.
 Everlasting burnings. Isa. 33: 14.

The wrath of God. Jno. 3:36.
Wine of the wrath of God. Rev. 14:10.
Torment with fire. Rev. 14:10.
Torment for ever and ever. Rev. 14:11.
The righteousness of God requires. 2 The. 1:6.
Often sudden and unexpected. Psa. 35:8. Psa. 64:7. Pro. 29:1. Luke 12:20. 1 The. 5:3.

SHALL BE
According to their deeds. Mat. 16:27. Rom. 2:6, 9. 2 Cor. 5:10.
According to the knowledge possessed by them. Luke 12:47, 48.
Increased by neglect of privileges. Mat. 11:21–24. Luke 10:13–15.
Without mitigation. Luke 16:23–26.
Accompanied by remorse. Isa. 66:24, with Mar. 9:44.

No combination avails against. Pro. 11:21.
Deferred, emboldens them in sin. Ecc. 8:11.
Should be a warning to others. Num. 26:10. 1 Cor. 10:6–11. Jude 7.
Consummated at the day of judgment. Mat. 25:31, 46. Rom. 2:5, 16. 2 Pet. 2:9.

Punishments.

Antiquity of. Gen. 4:13, 14.
Power of inflicting, given to magistrates. Job 31:11. Rom. 13:4.
Designed to be a warning to others. Deu. 13:11. Deu. 17:13. Deu. 19:20.

WERE INFLICTED
On the guilty. Deu. 24:16. Pro. 17:26.
Without pity. Deu. 19:13, 21.
Without partiality. Deu. 13:6–8.
By order of magistrates. Acts 16:22.
By order of kings. 2 Sam. 1:13–16. 1 Kin. 2:23–46.
Immediately after sentence was passed. Deu. 25:2. Jos. 7:25.
By the witnesses. Deu. 13:9, with Deu. 17:7. Jno. 8:7. Acts 7:58, 59.
By the people. Num. 15:35, 36. Deu. 13:9.
By soldiers. 2 Sam. 1:15. Mat. 27:27–35.

Sometimes deferred until God was consulted. Num. 15:34.
Sometimes deferred for a considerable time. 1 Kin. 2:5, 6, 8, 9.

SECONDARY KINDS OF;
Imprisonment. Ezr. 7:26. Mat. 5:25.
Confinement in a dungeon. Jer. 38:6. Zec. 9:11.
Confinement in stocks. Jer. 20:2. Acts 16:24.
Fine, or giving of money. Exo. 21:22. Deu. 22:19.
Restitution. Exo. 21:36. Exo. 22:1–4. Lev. 6:4, 5. Lev. 24:18.
Retaliation or injuring according to the injury done. Exo. 21:24. Deu. 19:21.
Binding with chains and fetters. Psa. 105:18.
Scourging. Deu. 25:2, 3. Mat. 27:26. Acts 22:25. 2 Cor. 11:24.
Selling the criminal, &c. Mat. 18:25.
Banishment. Ezr. 7:26. Rev. 1:9.
Torturing. Mat. 18:34. Heb. 11:37.
Putting out the eyes. Jud. 16:21. 1 Sam. 11:2.
Cutting off hands and feet. 2 Sam. 4:12.
Mutilating the hands and feet. Jud. 1:5–7.
Cutting off nose and ears. Eze. 23:25.
Plucking out the hair. Neh. 13:25. Isa. 50:6.
Confiscating the property. Ezr. 7:26.

Inflicting of capital, not permitted to the Jews by the Romans. Jno. 18:31.

CAPITAL KINDS OF;
Burning. Gen. 38:24. Lev. 20:14. Dan. 3:6.
Hanging. Num. 25:4. Deu. 21:22, 23. Jos. 8:29. 2 Sam. 21:12. Est. 7:9, 10.
Crucifying. Mat. 20:19. Mat. 27:35.
Beheading. Gen. 40:19. Mar. 6:16, 27.
Slaying with the sword. 1 Sam. 15:33. Acts 12:2.
Stoning. Lev. 24:14. Deu. 13:10. Acts 7:59.
Cutting in pieces. Dan. 2:5. Mat. 24:51.
Sawing asunder. Heb. 11:37.
Exposing to wild beasts. Dan. 6:16, 24. *See* 1 Cor. 15:32.
Bruising in mortars. Pro. 27:22.
Casting headlong from a rock. 2 Chr. 25:12.
Casting into the sea. Mat. 18:6.

Strangers not exempted from. Lev. 20:2.
Were sometimes commuted. Exo. 21:29, 30.
For murder not to be commuted. Num. 35:31, 32.

Purifications or Baptisms.

Of Israel at the exodus. Exo. 14:22. 1 Cor. 10:2.

Of Israel before receiving the law. Exo. 19: 10.
Of priests before consecration. Exo. 29: 4.
Of Levites before consecration. Num. 8: 6, 7.
Of high priest on day of atonement. Lev. 16: 4, 24.
Of things for burnt-offerings. 2 Chr. 4: 6.
Of individuals who were ceremonially unclean. Lev. 15: 2—13. Lev. 17: 15. Lev. 22: 4—7. Num. 19: 7—12, 21.
Of the healed leper. Lev. 14: 8, 9.
Of Nazarites after vow expired. Acts 21: 24, 26.
Used by the devout before entering God's house. Psa. 26: 6. Heb. 10: 22.
Multiplied by traditions. Mat. 15: 2. Mar. 7: 3, 4.
MEANS USED FOR;
 Water of separation. Num. 19: 9.
 Running water. Lev. 15: 13.
 Water mixed with blood. Exo. 24: 5—8, with Heb. 9: 19.
WAS BY
 Sprinkling. Num. 19: 13, 18. Heb. 9: 19.
 Washing parts of the body. Exo. 30: 19.
 Washing the whole body. Lev. 8: 6. Lev. 14: 9.
Of priests performed in the brazen laver. Exo. 30: 18. 2 Chr. 4: 6.
Vessels in the houses of the Jews for. Jno. 2: 6.
Consequence of neglecting those prescribed by law. Lev. 17: 16. Num. 19: 13, 20.
Availed to sanctifying the flesh. Heb. 9: 13.
Insufficient for spiritual purification. Job 9: 30, 31. Jer. 2: 22.
The Jews laid great stress on. Jno. 3: 25.
ILLUSTRATIVE OF
 Purification by the blood of Christ. Heb. 9: 9—12.
 Regeneration. Eph. 5: 26. 1 Jno. 1: 7.

Rain.

Occasioned by the condensing of the clouds. Job 36: 27, 28. Psa. 77: 17. Ecc. 11: 3.
GOD
 Made a decree for. Job 28: 26.
 Prepares. Psa. 147: 8.
 Gives. Job 5: 10.
 Causes, to come down. Joel 2: 23.
 Exhibits goodness in giving. Acts 14: 17.
 Exhibits greatness in giving. Job 36: 26, 27.
 Sends upon the evil and good. Mat. 5: 45.
 Should be praised for. Psa. 147: 7, 8.
 Should be feared on account of. Jer. 5: 24.
Impotence of idols exhibited in not being able to give. Jer. 14: 22.
Not sent upon the earth immediately after creation. Gen. 2: 5.
Rarely falls in Egypt. Deu. 11: 10. Zec. 14: 18.
Canaan abundantly supplied with. Deu. 11: 11.
DESIGNED FOR
 Refreshing the earth. Psa. 68: 9. Psa. 72: 6.
 Making fruitful the earth. Heb. 6: 7.
 Replenishing the springs and fountains of the earth. Psa. 104: 8.
Promised in due season to the obedient. Lev. 26: 4. Deu. 11: 14. Eze. 34: 26, 27.
Frequently withheld on account of iniquity. Deu. 11: 17. Jer. 3: 3. Jer. 5: 25. Amos 4: 7.
THE WANT OF,
 Causes the earth to open. Job 29: 23. Jer. 14: 4.
 Dries up springs and fountains. 1 Kin. 17: 7.
 Occasions famine. 1 Kin. 18: 1, 2.
 Removed by prayer. 1 Kin. 8: 35, 36. Jas. 5: 18.
Withheld for three years and six months in the days of Elijah. 1 Kin. 17: 1. Jas. 5: 17.
DIVIDED INTO
 Great. Ezr. 10: 9.
 Plentiful. Psa. 68: 9.
 Overflowing. Eze. 38: 22.
 Sweeping. Pro. 28: 3.
 Small. Job 37: 6.
The former, after harvest, to prepare for sowing. Deu. 11: 14. Jer. 5: 24.
The latter, before harvest. Joel 2: 23. Zec. 10: 1.
The rainbow often appears during. Gen. 9: 14, with Eze. 1: 28.
Often succeeded by heat and sunshine. 2 Sam. 23: 4. Isa. 18: 4. (*marg.*)
The appearance of a cloud from the west indicated. 1 Kin. 18: 44. Luke 12: 54.
The north wind drives away. Pro. 25: 23.
Unusual in harvest time. Pro. 26: 1.
Thunder and lightning often with. Psa. 135: 7.
Storm and tempest often with. Mat. 7: 25, 27.
INSTANCES OF EXTRAORDINARY;
 Time of the flood. Gen. 7: 4, 12.
 Plague of, upon Egypt. Exo. 9: 18, with 23 v.

During wheat harvest in the days of Samuel. 1 Sam. 12: 17, 18.
After long drought in Ahab's reign. 1 Kin. 18: 45.
After the captivity. Ezr. 10: 9, 13.
Often impeded traveling in the east. 1 Kin. 18: 44, with Isa. 4: 6.
Often destroyed houses, &c. Eze. 13: 13—15. Mat. 7: 27.
ILLUSTRATIVE
Of the word of God. Isa. 55: 10, 11.
Of the doctrine of faithful ministers. Deu. 32: 2.
Of Christ in the communication of His graces. Psa. 72: 6. Hos. 6: 3.
Of spiritual blessings. Psa. 68: 9. Psa. 84: 6. Eze. 34: 26.
Of righteousness. Hos. 10: 12.
(Destructive,) of God's judgments. Job 20: 23. Psa. 11: 6. Eze. 38: 22.
(Destructive,) of a poor man oppressing the poor. Pro. 28: 3.

Raven, The.

Unclean and not to be eaten. Lev. 11: 15. Deu. 14: 14.
Called the raven of the valley. Pro. 30: 17.
DESCRIBED AS
Black. So. of Sol. 5: 11.
Solitary in disposition. Isa. 34: 11.
Improvident. Luke 12: 24.
Carnivorous. Pro. 30: 17.
God provides food for. Job 38: 41. Psa. 147: 9. Luke 12: 24.
Sent by Noah from the ark. Gen. 8: 7.
Elijah fed by. 1 Kin. 17: 4—6.
Plumage of, illustrative of the glory of Christ. So. of Sol. 5: 11.

Reaping.

Is the cutting of the corn in harvest, Job 24: 6, with Lev. 23: 10.
The sickle used for. Deu. 16: 9. Mar. 4: 29.
Both men and women engaged in. Ruth 2: 8, 9.
THE JEWS NOT TO REAP
The corners of their fields. Lev. 19: 9, with Lev. 23: 22.
During the Sabbatical year. Lev. 25: 5.
During the year of jubilee. Lev. 25: 11.
The fields of others. Deu. 23: 25.
Mode of gathering the corn for, alluded to. Psa. 129: 7. Isa. 17: 5.
Corn after, was bound up into sheaves. Gen. 37: 7. Psa. 129: 7.
PERSONS ENGAGED IN,
Under the guidance of a steward. Ruth 2: 5, 6.
Visited by the master. Ruth 2: 4. 2 Kin. 4: 18.
Fed by the master who himself presided at their meals. Ruth 2: 14.
Received wages. Jno. 4: 36. Jas. 5: 4.
A time of great rejoicing. Psa. 126: 5, 6.
The Jews often hindered from, on account of their sins. Mic. 6: 15.
Often unprofitable on account of sin. Jer. 12: 13.
ILLUSTRATIVE OF
Receiving the reward of wickedness. Job 4: 8. Pro. 22: 8. Hos. 8: 7. Gal. 6: 8.
Receiving the reward of righteousness. Hos. 10: 12. Gal. 6: 8, 9.
Ministers receiving temporal provision for spiritual labors. 1 Cor. 9: 11.
Gathering in souls to God. Jno. 4: 38.
The judgments of God on the antichristian world. Rev. 14: 14—16.
The final judgment. Mat. 13: 30, 39—43.

Rebellion against God.

Forbidden. Num. 14: 9. Jos. 22: 19.
Provokes God. Num. 16: 30. Neh. 9: 26.
Provokes Christ. Exo. 23: 20, 21, with 1 Cor. 10: 9.
Vexes the Holy Spirit. Isa. 63: 10.
EXHIBITED IN
Unbelief. Deu. 9: 23. Psa. 106: 24, 25.
Rejecting His government. 1 Sam. 8: 7. 1 Sam. 15: 23.
Revolting from Him. Isa. 1: 5. Isa. 31: 6.
Despising His law. Neh. 9: 26.
Despising His counsels. Psa. 107: 11.
Distrusting His power. Eze. 17: 15
Murmuring against Him. Num. 20: 3, 10.
Refusing to hearken to Him. Deu. 9: 23. Eze. 20: 8. Zec. 7: 11.
Departing from Him. Isa. 59: 13.
Rebelling against governors appointed by Him. Jos. 1: 18.
Departing from His precepts. Dan. 9: 5.
Departing from His instituted worship. Exo. 32: 8, 9. Jos. 22: 16—19.
Sinning against light. Job 24: 13. Jno. 15: 22. Acts 13: 41.
Walking after our own thoughts. Isa. 65: 2.
CONNECTED WITH
Stubbornness. Deu. 31: 27.
Injustice and corruption. Isa. 1: 23.
Contempt of God. Psa. 107: 11

Man is prone to. Deu. 31: 27. Rom. 7: 14—18.
The heart is the seat of. Jer. 5: 23. Mat. 15: 18, 19. Heb. 3: 12.
THEY WHO ARE GUILTY OF,
Aggravate their sin by. Job 34: 37.
Practice hypocrisy to hide. Hos. 7: 14.
Persevere in. Deu. 9: 7, 24.
Increase in, though chastised. Isa. 1: 5.
Warned not to exalt themselves. Psa. 66: 7.
Denounced. Isa. 30: 1.
Have God as their enemy. Isa. 63: 10.
Have God's hand against them. 1 Sam. 12: 15, with Psa. 106: 26, 27.
Impoverished for. Psa. 68: 6.
Brought low for. Psa. 107: 11, 12.
Delivered into the hands of enemies on account of. Neh. 9: 26, 27.
Cast out in their sins for. Psa. 5: 10.
Cast out of the Church for. Eze. 20: 38.
Restored through Christ alone. Psa. 68: 18.
Heinousness of. 1 Sam. 15: 23.
GUILT OF,
Aggravated by God's fatherly care. Isa. 1: 2.
Aggravated by God's unceasing invitations to return to Him. Isa. 65: 2.
To be deprecated. Jos. 22: 29.
To be confessed. Lam. 1: 18, 20. Dan. 9: 5.
God alone can forgive. Dan. 9: 9.
God is ready to forgive. Neh. 9: 17.
Religious instruction designed to prevent. Psa. 78: 5, 8.
Promises to those who avoid. Deu. 28: 1—13. 1 Sam. 12: 14.
Forgiven upon repentance. Neh. 9: 26, 27.
MINISTERS
Cautioned against. Eze. 2: 8.
Sent to those guilty of. Eze. 2: 3—7. Eze. 3: 4—9. Mar. 12: 4—8.
Should warn against. Num. 14: 9.
Should testify against. Isa. 30: 8, 9. Eze. 17: 12. Eze. 44: 6.
Should remind their people of past. Deu. 9: 7. Deu. 31: 27.
Punishment for. Lev. 26: 14—39. 1 Sam. 12: 15. Isa. 1: 20. Jer. 4: 16—18. Eze. 20: 8, 38.
Punishment for teaching. Jer. 28: 16.
Ingratitude of—Illustrated. Isa. 1: 2, 3.
Exemplified. *Pharaoh*. Exo. 5: 1, 2. *Korah, &c*. Num. 16: 11. *Moses and Aaron*, Num. 20: 12, 24. *Israelites*, Deu. 9: 23, 24. *Saul*, 1 Sam. 15: 9, 23. *Jeroboam*, 1 Kin. 12: 28—33. *Zedekiah*, 2 Chr. 36: 13. *Kingdom of Israel*, Hos. 7: 14. Hos. 13: 16.

Rechabites.

Descended from Hemath. 1 Chr. 2: 55.
The head of, assisted Jehu in his conspiracy against the house of Ahab. 2 Kin. 10: 15—17.
Prohibited by Jonadab from forming settlements or drinking wine. Jer. 35: 6—8.
Obedience of, a sign to Israel. Jer. 35: 12—17.
Perpetuity to, promised. Jer. 35: 18, 19.

Reconciliation with God.

Predicted. Dan. 9: 24, with Isa. 53: 5.
Proclaimed by angels at the birth of Christ. Luke 2: 14.
Blotting out the hand-writing of ordinances is necessary to. Eph. 2: 16. Col. 2: 14.
EFFECTED FOR MEN
By God in Christ. 2 Cor. 5: 19.
By Christ as High Priest. Heb. 2: 17.
By the death of Christ. Rom. 5: 10. Eph. 2: 16. Col. 1: 21, 22.
By the blood of Christ. Eph. 2: 13. Col. 1: 20.
While alienated from God. Col. 1: 21.
Without strength. Rom. 5: 6.
Yet sinners. Rom. 5: 8.
While enemies to God. Rom. 5: 10.
The ministry of, committed to ministers. 2 Cor. 5: 18, 19.
Ministers, in Christ's stead, should beseech men to seek. 2 Cor. 5: 20.
EFFECTS OF;
Peace of God. Rom. 5: 1. Eph. 2: 16, 17.
Access to God. Rom. 5: 2. Eph. 2: 18.
Union of Jews and Gentiles. Eph. 2: 14.
Union of things in heaven and earth. Col. 1: 20, with Eph. 1: 10.
A pledge of final salvation. Rom. 5: 10.
Necessity for—Illustrated. Mat. 5: 24—26.
Typified. Lev. 8: 15. Lev. 16: 20

Redemption.

Defined. 1 Cor. 6: 20. 1 Cor. 7: 23.
Is of God. Isa. 44: 21—23. Isa. 43: 1, with Luke 1: 68.
Is by Christ. Mat. 20: 28. Gal. 3: 13.
Is by the blood of Christ. Acts 20: 28. Heb. 9: 12. 1 Pet. 1: 19. Rev. 5: 9.
Christ sent to effect. Gal. 4: 4, 5.
Christ is made, unto us. 1 Cor. 1: 30.

IS FROM
The bondage of the law. Gal. 4:5.
The curse of the law. Gal. 3:13.
The power of sin. Rom. 6:18, 22.
The power of the grave. Psa. 49:15.
All troubles. Psa. 25:22.
All iniquity. Psa. 130:8. Tit. 2:14.
All evil. Gen. 48:16.
This present evil world. Gal. 1:4.
Vain conversation. 1 Pet. 1:18.
Enemies. Psa. 106:10, 11. Jer. 15:21.
Death. Hos. 13:14.
Destruction. Psa. 103:4.

Man cannot effect. Psa. 49:7.
Corruptible things cannot purchase. 1 Pet. 1:18.

PROCURES FOR US
Justification. 3:24.
Forgiveness of sin. Eph. 1:7. Col. 1:14.
Adoption. Gal. 4:4, 5.
Purification. Tit. 2:14.

The present life, the only season for. Job 36:18, 19.

DESCRIBED AS
Precious. Psa. 49:8.
Plenteous. Psa. 130:7.
Eternal. Heb. 9:12.

SUBJECTS OF.
The soul. Psa. 49:15.
The body. Rom. 8:23.
The life. Psa. 103:4. Lam. 3:58.
The inheritance. Eph. 1:14.

MANIFESTS THE
Power of God. Isa. 50:2.
Grace of God. Isa. 52:3.
Love and pity of God. Isa. 63:9. Jno. 3:16. Rom. 6:8. 1 Jno. 4:10.

A subject for praise. Isa. 44:22, 23. Isa. 51:11.
Old Testament saints partakers of. Heb. 9:15.

THEY WHO PARTAKE OF,
Are the property of God. Isa. 43:1. 1 Cor. 6:20.
Are first-fruits unto God. Rev. 14:4.
Are a peculiar people. 2 Sam. 7:23. Tit. 2:14, with 1 Pet. 2:9.
Are assured of. Job 19:25. Psa. 31:5.
Are sealed unto the day of. Eph. 4:30.
Are Zealous of good works. Eph. 2:10. Tit. 2:14. 1 Pet. 2:9.
Walk safely in holiness. Isa. 35:8, 9.
Shall return to Zion with joy. Isa. 35:10.
Alone can learn the songs of heaven. Rev. 14:3, 4.
Commit themselves to God. Psa. 31:5.
Have an earnest of the completion of. Eph. 1:14, with 2 Cor. 1:22.
Wait for the completion of. Rom. 8:23. Phi. 3:20, 21. Tit. 2:11—13.
Pray for the completion of. Psa. 26:11. Psa. 44:26.
Praise God for. Psa. 71:23. Psa. 103:4. Rev. 5:9.
Should glorify God for. 1 Cor. 6:20.
Should be without fear. Isa. 43:1.

Typified. *Israel*, Exo. 6:6. *First-born*, Exo. 13:11—15. Num. 18:15. *Atonement-money*, Exo. 30:12—15. *Bond-servant*, Lev. 25:47—54.

Red Heifer, The.

To be without spot or blemish. Num. 19:2.
To be given to Eleazar the second priest to offer. Num. 19:3.
To be slain without the camp. Num. 19:3.
Entire of, to be burned. Num. 19:5.
Blood of, sprinkled seven times before the tabernacle. Num. 19:4.
Cedar, hyssop, &c. burned with. Num. 19:6.
Ashes of, collected and mixed with water for purification. Num. 19:9, 11—22.

COMMUNICATED UNCLEANNESS TO
The priest that offered her. Num. 19:7.
The man that burned her. Num. 19:8.
The man who gathered the ashes. Num. 19:10.

Could only purify the flesh. Heb. 9:13.
A type of Christ. Heb. 9:12—14.

Repentance.

What it is. Isa. 45:22. Mat. 6:19—21. Acts 14:15. 2 Cor. 5:17. Col. 3:2. 1 The. 1:9. Heb. 12:1, 2.
Commanded to all by God. Eze. 18:30—32. Acts 17:30.
Commanded by Christ. Rev. 2:5, 16. Rev. 3:3.
Given by God. Acts 11:18. 2 Tim. 2:25.
Christ came to call sinners to. Mat. 9:13.
Christ exalted to give. Acts 5:31.
By the operation of the Holy Ghost. Zec. 12:10.
Called repentance unto life. Acts 11:18.
Called repentance unto salvation. 2 Cor. 7:10.

WE SHOULD BE LED TO, BY
The long-suffering of God. Gen. 6:3, with 1 Pet. 3:20. 2 Pet. 3:9.
The goodness of God. Rom. 2:4.
The chastisements of God. 1 Kin. 8:47. Rev. 3:19.

Godly sorrow works. 2 Cor. 7:10.

Necessary to the pardon of sin. Acts 2:38. Acts 3:19. Acts 8:22.
Conviction of sin necessary to. 1 Kin. 8:38. Pro. 28:13. Acts 2:37, 38. Acts 19:18.
PREACHED
By Christ. Mat. 4:17. Mar. 1:15.
By John the Baptist. Mat. 3:2.
By the Apostles. Mar. 6:12. Acts 20:21.
In the name of Christ. Luke 24:47.
Not to be repented of. 2 Cor. 7:10.
The present time the season for. Psa. 95:7, 8, with Heb. 3:7, 8. Pro. 27:1. Isa. 55:6. 2 Cor. 6:2. Heb. 4:7.
There is joy in heaven over one sinner brought to. Luke 15:7, 10.
Ministers should rejoice over their people on their. 2 Cor. 7:9.
Should be evidenced by fruits. Isa. 1:16, 17. Dan. 4:27. Mat. 3:8. Acts 26:20.
SHOULD BE ACCOMPANIED BY
Humility. 2 Chr. 7:14. Jas. 4:9, 10.
Shame and confusion. Ezr. 9:6—15. Jer. 31:19. Eze. 16:61, 63. Dan. 9:7, 8.
Self-abhorrence. Job 42:6.
Confession. Lev. 26:40. Job 33:27.
Faith. Mat. 21:32. Mar. 1:15. Acts 20:21.
Prayer. 1 Kin. 8:33. Acts 8:22.
Conversion. Acts 3:19. Acts 26:20.
Turning from sin. 2 Chr. 6:26.
Turning from idolatry. Eze. 14:6. 1 The. 1:9.
Greater zeal in the path of duty. 2 Cor. 7:11.
Exhortations to. Eze. 14:6. Eze. 18:30. Acts 2:38. Acts 3:19.
THE WICKED
Averse to. Jer. 8:6. Mat. 21:32.
Not led to, by the judgments of God. Rev. 9:20, 21. Rev. 16:9.
Not led to, by miraculous interference. Luke 16:30, 31.
Neglect the time given for. Rev. 2:21.
Condemned for neglecting. Mat. 11:20.
Danger of neglecting. Mat. 11:20—24. Luke 13:3, 5. Rev. 2:22.
Neglect of, followed by swift judgment. Rev. 2:5, 16.
Denied to apostates. Heb. 6:4—6.
Illustrated. Luke 15:18—21. Luke 18:13. *The Prodigal Son*, Luke 15:17—19. *The Repentant Son*. Mat. 21:29. *Paul*, Gal. 1:23.
True—Exemplified. *Israelites*, Jud. 10:15, 16. *David*, 2 Sam. 12:13. *Manasseh*, 2 Chr. 33:12, 13. *Job*, Job 42:6. *Nineveh*, Jon. 3:5—8. Mat. 12:41. *Peter*, Mat. 26:75. *Zaccheus*, Luke 19:8. *Thief on the cross*, Luke 23:40, 41. *Corinthians*, 2 Cor. 7:9, 10.
False—Exemplified. *Saul*, 1 Sam. 15:24—30. *Ahab*, 1 Kin. 21:27—29. *Judas*, Mat. 27:3—5.

Rephaim, or Giants, The.

Subdued by Chedorlaomer. Gen. 14:5.
Dwelt in Canaan. Jos. 17:15. (*marg.*)
Og the king of Bashan was of. Jos. 13:12.
THE VALLEY OF,
A border of Judah. Jos. 15:8.
Was exceedingly fruitful. Isa. 17:5.
David obtained victories over the Philistines in. 2 Sam. 5:18, 25.
The last of, destroyed by David and his warriors. 1 Sam. 17:4, 49, 50. 2 Sam. 21:15—22.

Reproof.

God gives reproof to His own children. 2 Sam. 7:14. Job 5:17. Psa. 94:12. Psa. 119:67, 71, 75. Heb. 12:6, 7.
God gives, to the wicked. Psa. 50:21. Isa. 51:20.
Christ sent to give. Isa. 2:4. Isa. 11:3.
The Holy Spirit gives. Jno. 16:7, 8.
Christ gives, in love. Rev. 3:19.
ON ACCOUNT OF
Impenitence. Mat. 11:20—24.
Not understanding. Mat. 16:9, 11. Mar. 7:18. Luke 24:25. Jno. 8:43. Jno. 13:7, 8.
Hardness of heart. Mar. 8:17. Mar. 16:14.
Fearfulness. Mar. 4:40. Luke 24:37, 38.
Unbelief. Mat. 17:17, 20. Mar. 16:14.
Vain boasting. Luke 22:34.
Hypocrisy. Mat. 15:7. Mat. 23:13, &c.
Reviling Christ. Luke 23:40.
Unruly conduct. 1 The. 5:14.
Oppressing our brethren. Neh. 5:7.
Sinful practices. Mat. 21:13. Luke 3:19. Jno. 2:16.
The Scriptures are profitable for. Psa. 19:7—11. 2 Tim. 3:16.
WHEN FROM GOD,
Is for correction. Psa. 39:11.
Is despised by the wicked. Pro. 1:30.
Should not discourage saints. Heb. 12:5.
Pray that it be not in anger. Psa. 6:1.
Should be accompanied by exhortation to repentance. 1 Sam. 12:20—25.
DECLARED TO BE
Better than secret love. Pro. 27:5.
Better than the praise of fools. Ecc. 7:5.

An excellent oil. Psa. 141: 5.
More profitable to saints, than stripes to a fool. Pro. 17: 10.
A proof of faithful friendship. Pro. 27: 6.
LEADS TO
Understanding. Pro. 15: 32.
Knowledge. Pro. 19: 25.
Wisdom. Pro. 15: 31. Pro. 29: 15.
Honor. Pro. 13: 18.
Happiness. Pro. 6: 23.
Eventually brings more respect than flattery. Pro. 28: 23.
Of those who offend, a warning to others. Lev. 19: 17. Acts 5: 3, 4, 9. 1 Tim. 5: 20. Tit. 1: 10, 13.
Hypocrites not qualified to give. Mat. 7: 5.
Ministers are sent to give. Jer. 44: 4. Eze. 3: 17.
Ministers are empowered to give. Mic. 3: 8.
MINISTERS SHOULD GIVE,
Openly. 1 Tim. 5: 20.
Fearlessly. Eze. 2: 3—7.
With all authority. Tit. 2: 15.
With long-suffering, &c. 2 Tim. 4: 2.
Unreservedly. Isa. 58: 1.
Sharply, if necessary. Tit. 1: 13.
With Christian love. 2 The. 3: 15.
They who give, are hated by scorners. Pro. 9: 8. Pro. 15: 12.
Hatred of, a proof of brutishness. Pro. 12: 1.
Hatred of, leads to destruction. Pro. 15: 10. Pro. 29: 1.
Contempt of, leads to remorse. Pro. 5: 12.
Rejection of, leads to error. Pro. 10: 17.
SAINTS SHOULD
Give. Lev. 19: 17. Eph. 5: 11.
Give no occasion for. Phi. 2: 15.
Receive kindly. Psa. 141: 5.
Love those who give. Pro. 9: 8.
Delight in those who give. Pro. 24: 25.
Attention to a proof of prudence. Pro. 15: 5.
Exemplified. *Samuel*, 1 Sam. 13: 13. *Nathan*, 2 Sam. 12: 7—9. *Ahijah*, 1 Kin. 14: 7—11. *Elijah*, 1 Kin. 21: 20. *Elisha*, 2 Kin. 5: 26. *Joab*, 1 Chr. 21: 3. *Shemaiah*, 2 Chr. 12: 5. *Hanani*, 2 Chr. 16: 7. *Zechariah*, 2 Chr. 24: 20. *Daniel*, Dan. 5: 22, 23. *John the Baptist*, Mat. 3: 7. Luke 3: 19. *Stephen*, Acts 7: 51. *Peter*, Acts 8: 20. *Paul*, 1 Cor. 1: 10—13. 1 Cor. 5: 1—5. 1 Cor. 6: 1—8. 1 Cor. 11: 17—22. Gal. 2: 11.

Reptiles.

Created by God. Gen. 1: 24, 25.
Made for praise and glory of God. Psa. 148: 10.
Placed under the dominion of man. Gen. 1: 26.
Unclean and not eaten. Lev. 11: 31, 40—43. Acts 10: 11—14.
MENTIONED IN SCRIPTURE;
Chameleon. Lev. 11: 30.
Lizard. Lev. 11: 30.
Tortoise. Lev. 11: 29.
Snail. Lev. 11: 30. Psa. 58: 8.
Frog. Exo. 8: 2. Rev. 16: 13.
Horse-leech. Pro. 30: 15.
Scorpion. Deu. 8: 15.
Serpent. Job 26: 13. Mat. 7: 10.
Flying fiery serpent. Deu. 8: 15. Isa. 30: 6.
Dragon. Deu. 32: 33. Job 30: 29. Jer. 9: 11.
Viper. Acts 28: 3.
Adder or asp. Psa. 58: 4. Psa. 91: 13. Pro. 23: 32.
Cockatrice or basilisk. Isa. 11: 8. Isa. 59: 5.
Solomon wrote a history of. 1 Kin. 4: 33.
Worshipped by the Gentiles. Rom. 1: 23.
No image or similitude of, to be made for worshipping. Deu. 4: 16, 18.
Jews condemned for worshipping. Eze. 8: 10.

Resignation.

Christ set an example of. Mat. 26: 39—44. Jno. 12: 27. Jno. 18: 11.
Commanded. Psa. 37: 7. Psa. 46: 10.
SHOULD BE EXHIBITED IN
Submission to the will of God. 2 Sam. 15: 26. Psa. 42: 5, 11. Mat. 6: 10.
Submission to the sovereignty of God in His purposes. Rom. 9: 20, 21.
The prospect of death. Acts 21: 13. 2 Cor. 4: 16, to 2 Cor. 5: 1.
Loss of goods. Job 1: 15, 16, 21.
Loss of children. Job 1: 18, 19, 21.
Chastisements. Heb. 12: 9.
Bodily suffering. Job 2: 8—10.
The wicked are devoid of. Pro. 19: 3.
Exhortation to. Psa. 37: 1—11.
MOTIVES TO;
God's greatness. Psa. 46: 10.
God's love. Heb. 12: 6.
God's justice. Neh. 9: 33.
God's wisdom. Rom. 11: 32, 33.
God's faithfulness. 1 Pet. 4: 19.
Our own sinfulness. Lam. 3: 39. Mic. 7: 9.
Exemplified. *Jacob*, Gen. 43: 14. *Aaron*, Lev. 10: 3. *Israelites*, Jud. 10: 15. *Eli*, 1 Sam. 3: 18. *David*, 2 Sam. 12: 23. *Hezekiah*, 2 Kin. 20: 19. *Job*, Job 2: 10. *Stephen*, Acts 7: 59. *Paul*, Acts 21: 13. *Disciples*, Acts 21: 14. *Peter*, 2 Pet. 1: 14.

Resurrection, The.

A doctrine of the Old Testament. Job 19: 26. Psa. 16: 10. Psa. 49: 15. Isa. 26: 19. Dan. 12: 2. Hos. 13: 14.
A first principle of the gospel. 1 Cor. 15: 13, 14. Heb. 6: 1, 2.
Expected by the Jews. Jno. 11: 24. Heb. 11: 35.
Denied by the Sadducees. Mat. 22: 23. Luke 20: 27. Acts 23: 8.
Explained away by false teachers. 2 Tim. 2: 18.
Called in question by some in the primitive church. 1 Cor. 15: 12.
Is not incredible. Mar. 12: 24. Acts 26: 8.
Is not contrary to reason. Jno. 12: 24. 1 Cor. 15: 35—49.
Assumed and proved by our Lord. Mat. 22: 29—32. Luke 14: 14. Jno. 5: 28, 29.
Preached by the Apostles. Acts 4: 2. Acts 17: 18. Acts 24: 15.
Credibility of, shown by the resurrection of individuals. Mat. 9: 25. Mat. 27: 53. Luke 7: 14. Jno. 11: 44. Heb. 11: 35.
Certainty of, proved by the resurrection of Christ. 1 Cor. 15: 12—20.
EFFECTED BY THE POWER OF
God. Mat. 22: 29.
Christ. Jno. 5: 28, 29. Jno. 6: 39, 40, 44.
The Holy Ghost. Rom. 8: 11.
Shall be of all the dead. Jno. 5: 28. Acts 24: 15. Rev. 20: 13.
SAINTS IN, SHALL
Rise through Christ. Jno. 11: 25. Acts 4: 2. 1 Cor. 15: 21, 22.
Rise first. 1 Cor. 15: 23. 1 The. 4: 16.
Rise to eternal life. Dan. 12: 2. Jno. 5: 29.
Be glorified with Christ. Col. 3: 4.
Be as the angels. Mat. 22: 30.
Have incorruptible bodies. 1 Cor. 15: 42.
Have glorious bodies. 1 Cor. 15: 43.
Have powerful bodies. 1 Cor. 15: 43.
Have spiritual bodies. 1 Cor. 15: 44.
Have bodies like Christ's. Phi. 3: 21. 1 Jno. 3: 2.
Be recompensed. Luke 14: 14.
Saints should look forward to. Dan. 12: 13. Phi. 3: 11. 2 Cor. 5: 1.
Of saints shall be followed by the change of those then alive. 1 Cor. 15: 51, with 1 The. 4: 17.
THE PREACHING OF, CAUSED
Mocking. Acts 17: 32.
Persecution. Acts 23: 6. Acts 24: 11—15.
Blessedness of those who have part in the first. Rev. 20: 6.
OF THE WICKED, SHALL BE TO
Shame and everlasting contempt. Dan. 12: 2.
Damnation. Jno. 5: 29.
Illustrative of the new birth. Jno. 5: 25.
Illustrated. Eze. 37: 1—10. 1 Cor. 15: 36, 37.

Resurrection of Christ, The.

Foretold by the prophets. Psa. 16: 10, with Acts 13: 34, 35. Isa. 26: 19.
Foretold by Himself. Mat. 20: 19. Mar. 9: 9. Mar. 14: 28. Jno. 2: 19—22.
WAS NECESSARY TO
The fulfilment of Scripture. Luke 24: 45, 46.
Forgiveness of sins. 1 Cor. 15: 17.
Justification. Rom. 4: 25. Rom. 8: 34.
Hope. 1 Cor. 15: 19.
The efficacy of preaching. 1 Cor. 15: 14.
The efficacy of faith. 1 Cor. 15: 14, 17.
A proof of His being the Son of God. Psa. 2: 7, with Acts 13: 33. Rom. 1: 4.
EFFECTED BY
The power of God. Acts 2: 24. Acts 3: 15. Rom. 8: 11. Eph. 1: 20. Col. 2: 12.
His own power. Jno. 2: 19. Jno. 10: 18.
The power of the Holy Ghost. 1 Pet. 3: 18.
On the first day of the week. Mar. 16: 9.
On the third day after His death. Luke 24: 46. Acts 10: 40. 1 Cor. 15: 4.
THE APOSTLES
At first did not understand the predictions respecting. Mar. 9: 10. Jno. 20: 9.
Very slow to believe. Mar. 16: 13. Luke 24: 9, 11, 37, 38.
Reproved for their unbelief of. Mar. 16: 14.
HE APPEARED AFTER, TO
Mary Magdalene. Mar. 16: 9. Jno. 20: 18.
The women. Mat. 28: 9.
Simon Peter. Luke 24: 34.
Two disciples. Luke 24: 13—31.
Apostles, except Thomas. Jno. 20: 19, 24.
Apostles, Thomas being present Jno. 20: 26.
Apostles at the sea of Tiberias. Jno. 21: 1.
Apostles in Galilee. Mat. 28: 16, 17.
Above five hundred brethren. 1 Cor. 15: 6.
James. 1 Cor. 15: 7.
All the Apostles. Luke 24: 51. Acts 1: 9. 1 Cor. 15: 7.
Paul. 1 Cor. 15: 8.
Fraud impossible in. Mat. 27: 63—66.
He gave many infallible proofs of. Luke 24: 35, 39, 43. Jno. 20: 20, 27. Acts 1: 3.

WAS ATTESTED BY
Angels. Mat. 28: 5—7. Luke 24: 4—7, 23.
Apostles. Acts 1: 22. Acts 2: 32. Acts 3: 15. Acts 4: 33.
His enemies. Mat. 28: 11—15.
Asserted and preached by the Apostles. Acts 25: 19. Acts 26: 23.
SAINTS
Begotten to a lively hope by. 1 Pet. 1: 3, 21.
Desire to know the power of. Phi. 3: 10.
Should keep, in remembrance. 2 Tim. 2: 8.
Shall rise in the likeness of. Rom. 6: 5. 1 Cor. 15: 49, with Phi. 3: 21.
Is an emblem of the new birth. Rom. 6: 4. Col. 2: 12.
The first-fruits of our resurrection. Acts 26: 23. 1 Cor. 15: 20, 23.
The truth of the gospel involved in. 1 Cor. 15: 14, 15.
Followed by His exaltation. Acts 4: 10, 11. Rom. 8: 34. Eph. 1: 20. Phi. 2: 9, 10. Rev. 1: 18.
An assurance of the judgment. Acts 17: 31.
Typified. *Isaac*, Gen. 22: 13, with Heb. 11: 19. *Jonah*, Jon. 2: 10, with Mat. 12: 40.

Reuben, The Tribe of.

Descended from Jacob's first son. Gen. 29: 32.
Predictions respecting. Gen. 49: 4. Deu. 33: 6.
PERSONS SELECTED FROM,
To number the people. Num. 1: 5.
To spy out the land. Num. 13: 4.
Strength of, on leaving Egypt. Num. 1: 20, 21.
Led the second division of Israel in their journeys. Num. 10: 18.
Encamped with its standard south of the tabernacle. Num. 2: 10.
Offering of, at the dedication. Num. 7: 30—35.
Families of. Num. 26: 5, 6, 8, 9.
Obtained inheritance east of Jordan on condition of helping to conquer Canaan. Num. 32: 1—33. Deu. 3: 18—20.
Bounds of their inheritance. Deu. 3: 16, 17. Jos. 13: 15—23.
Strength of, at the time of receiving their inheritance. Num. 26: 7.
Cities built by. Num. 32: 37, 38.
On Ebal said amen to the curses. Deu. 27: 13.
Dismissed by Joshua after the conquest of Canaan. Jos. 22: 1—9.
Assisted in building the altar of witness which offended the other tribes. Jos. 22: 10—29.
Did not assist against Sisera. Jud. 5: 15, 16.
Some of, at David's coronation. 1 Chr. 12: 37, 38.
Officers appointed over, by David. 1 Chr. 26: 32. 1 Chr. 27: 16.
Took land, &c. of the Hagarites. 1 Chr. 5: 10, 18—22.
Invaded and conquered by Hazael king of Syria. 2 Kin. 10: 32, 33.
Carried away by Tiglath Pilezer. 2 Kin. 15: 29, with 1 Chr. 5: 6, 26.
Remarkable persons of; *Dathan*, *Abiram*, and *On*. Num. 16: 1. Num. 26: 9, 10. *Adina*, *&c.* 1 Chr. 11: 42.

Revenge.

Forbidden, by our Lord. Lev. 19: 18. Pro. 24: 17, 29. Mat. 5: 39—41. Rom. 12: 17, 19. 1 The. 5: 15. 1 Pet. 3: 9.
Christ an example of forbearing. Isa. 53: 7. 1 Pet. 2: 23.
Rebuked by Christ. Luke 9: 54, 55.
Inconsistent with Christian spirit. Luke 9: 55.
Proceeds from a spiteful heart. Eze. 25: 15.
INSTEAD OF TAKING, WE SHOULD
Trust in God. Pro. 20: 22. Rom. 12: 16.
Exhibit love. Lev. 19: 18. Luke 6: 35.
Give place unto wrath. Rom. 12: 19.
Exercise forbearance. Mat. 5: 38—41.
Bless. Rom. 12: 14.
Overcome others by kindness. Pro. 25: 21, 22, with Rom. 12: 20.
Keep others from taking. 1 Sam. 24: 10. 1 Sam. 25: 24—31. 1 Sam. 26: 9.
Be thankful for being kept from taking. 1 Sam. 25: 32, 33.
The wicked are earnest after. Jer. 20: 10.
Punishment for. Eze. 25: 15—17. Amos 1: 11, 12.
Exemplified. *Simon and Levi*, Gen. 34: 25. *Samson*, Jud. 15: 7, 8. Jud. 16: 28—30. *Joab*, 2 Sam. 3: 27. *Absalom*, 2 Sam. 13: 23—29. *Jezebel*, 1 Kin. 19: 2. *Ahab*, 1 Kin. 22: 26. *Haman*, Est. 3: 8—15. *Edomites*, Eze. 25: 12. *Philistines*, Eze. 25: 15. *Herodias*, Mar. 6: 19—24. *James and John*, Luke 9: 54. *Chief priests*, Acts 5: 33. *Jews*, Acts 7: 54, 59. Acts 23: 12.

Reviling and Reproaching.

Forbidden. 1 Pet. 3: 9.
Of rulers specially forbidden. Exo. 22: 28, with Acts 23: 4, 5.
THE WICKED UTTER, AGAINST
God. Psa. 74: 22. Psa. 79: 12.
God, by oppressing the poor. Pro. 14: 31.
Christ. Mat. 27: 39. Luke 7: 34.
Saints. Psa. 102: 8. Zep. 2: 8,

Rulers. 2 Pet. 2: 10, 11. Jude 8, 9.
Of Christ, predicted. Psa. 69: 9, with Rom. 15: 3. Psa. 89: 51.
The conduct of Christ under. 1 Pet. 2: 23.
SAINTS
Endure. 1 Tim. 4: 10. Heb. 10: 33.
Endure for God's sake. Pro. 69: 7.
Endure for Christ's sake. Luke 6: 22.
Should expect. Mat. 10: 25.
Should not fear. Isa. 51: 7.
Sometimes depressed by. Psa. 42: 10, 11. Psa. 44: 16. Psa. 69: 20.
May take pleasure in. 2 Cor. 12: 10.
Supported under. 2 Cor. 12: 10.
Trust in God under. Psa. 57: 3. Psa. 119: 42.
Pray under. 2 Kin. 19: 4, 16. Psa. 89: 50.
Return blessings for. 1 Cor. 4: 12. 1 Pet. 3: 9.
Ministers should not fear. Eze. 2: 6.
Happiness of enduring, for Christ's sake. 1 Pet. 4: 14.
Blessedness of enduring, for Christ's sake. Mat. 5: 11. Luke 6: 22.
Excludes from heaven. 1 Cor. 6: 10.
Punishment for. Zep. 2: 8, 9. Mat. 5: 22.
Exemplified. *Joseph's brethren*. Gen. 37: 19. *Goliath*, 1 Sam. 17: 43. *Michal*, 2 Sam. 6: 20. *Shimei*, 2 Sam. 16: 7, 8. *Sennacherib*, Isa. 37: 17, 23, 24. *Moabites and Ammonites*, Zep. 2: 8. *Pharisees*, Mat. 12: 24. *Jews*, Mat. 27: 39, 40. Jno. 8: 48. *Malefactor*, Luke 23: 39. *Athenian philosophers*, Acts 17: 18.

Reward of Saints, The.

Is from God. Rom. 2: 7. Col. 3: 24. Heb. 11: 6.
Is of grace, through faith alone. Rom. 4: 4, 5, 16. Rom. 11: 6.
Is of God's good pleasure. Mat. 20: 14, 15. Luke 12: 32.
Prepared by God. Heb. 11: 16.
Prepared by Christ. Jno. 14: 2.
As servants of Christ. Col. 3: 24.
Not on account of their merits. Rom. 4: 4, 5.
DESCRIBED AS
Being with Christ. Jno. 12: 26. Jno. 14: 3. Phi. 1: 23. 1 The. 4: 17.
Beholding the face of God. Psa. 17: 15. Mat. 5: 8. Rev. 22: 4.
Beholding the glory of Christ. Jno. 17: 24.
Being glorified with Christ. Rom. 8: 17, 18. Col. 3: 4. Phi. 3: 21. 1 Jno. 3: 2.
Sitting in judgment with Christ. Dan. 7: 22. Mat. 19: 28. Luke 22: 30, with 1 Cor. 6: 2.
Reigning with Christ. 2 Tim. 2: 12. Rev. 3: 21. Rev. 5: 10. Rev. 20: 4.
Reigning for ever and ever. Rev. 22: 5.
A crown of righteousness. 2 Tim. 4: 8.
A crown of glory. 1 Pet. 5: 4.
A crown of life. Jas. 1: 12. Rev. 2: 10.
An incorruptible crown. 1 Cor. 9: 25.
Joint heirship with Christ. Rom. 8: 17.
Inheritance of all things. Rev. 21: 7.
Inheritance with saints in light. Acts 20: 32. Acts 26: 18. Col. 1: 12.
Inheritance eternal. Heb. 9: 15.
Inheritance incorruptible, &c. 1 Pet. 1: 4.
A kingdom. Mat. 25: 34. Luke 22: 29.
A kingdom immovable. Heb. 12: 28.
Shining as the stars. Dan. 12: 3.
Everlasting light. Isa. 60: 19.
Everlasting life. Luke 18: 30. Jno. 6: 40. Jno. 17: 2, 3. Rom. 2: 7. Rom. 6: 23. 1 Jno. 5: 11.
An enduring substance. Heb. 10: 34.
A house, eternal in the heavens. 2 Cor. 5: 1.
A city which had foundation. Heb. 11: 10.
Entering into the joy of the Lord. Mat. 25: 21, with Heb. 12: 2.
Rest. Heb. 4: 9. Rev. 14: 13.
Fulness of joy. Psa. 16: 11.
The prize of the high calling of God in Christ. Phi. 3: 14.
Treasure in heaven. Mat. 19: 21. Luke 12: 33.
An eternal weight of glory. 2 Cor. 4: 17.
Is great. Mat. 5: 12. Luke 6: 35. Heb. 10: 35.
Is full. 2 Jno. 8.
Is sure. Pro. 11: 18.
Is satisfying. Psa. 17: 15.
Is inestimable. Isa. 64: 4, with 1 Cor. 2: 9.
Saints may feel confident of. Psa. 73: 24. Isa. 25: 8, 9. 2 Cor. 5: 1. 2 Tim. 4: 8.
Hope of, a cause of rejoicing. Rom. 5: 2.
Be careful not to lose. 2 Jno. 8.
THE PROSPECT OF, SHOULD LEAD TO
Diligence. 2 Jno. 8.
Pressing forward. Phi. 3: 14.
Enduring suffering for Christ. 2 Cor. 4: 16—18. Heb. 11: 26.
Faithfulness unto death. Rev. 2: 10.
Present afflictions not to be compared with. Rom. 8: 18. 2 Cor. 5: 17.

Shall be given at the second coming of Christ. Mat. 16:27. Rev. 22:12.

Riches.

The true riches. Eph. 3:8. 1 Cor. 1 30. Col. 2:3. 1 Pet. 2:7.
God gives. 1 Sam. 2:7. Ecc. 5:19.
To God belongs this world's riches. Hag. 2:8.
God gives power to obtain. Deu. 8:18.
The blessing of the Lord brings. Pro. 10:22.
Give worldly power. Pro. 22:7.
DESCRIBED AS
- Temporary. Pro. 27:24.
- Uncertain. 1 Tim. 6:17.
- Unsatisfying. Ecc. 4:8. Ecc. 5:10.
- Corruptible. Jas. 5:2. 1 Pet. 1:18.
- Fleeting. Pro. 23:5. Rev. 18:16, 17.
- Deceitful. Mat. 13:22.
- Liable to be stolen. Mat. 6:19.
- Perishable. Jer. 48:36.
- Thick clay. Hab. 2:6.

Often an obstruction to the reception of the gospel. Mar. 10:23–25.
Deceitfulness of, chokes the word. Mat. 13:22.
The love of, the root of all evil. 1 Tim. 6:10.
OFTEN LEAD TO
- Pride. Eze. 28:5. Hos. 12:8.
- Forgetting God. Deu. 8:13, 14.
- Denying God. Pro. 30:8, 9.
- Forsaking God. Deu. 32:15.
- Rebelling against God. Neh. 9:25, 26.
- Rejecting Christ. Mat. 19:22. Mat. 10:22.
- Self-sufficiency. Pro. 28:11.
- Anxiety. Ecc. 5:12.
- An overbearing spirit. Pro. 18:23.
- Violence. Mic. 6:12.
- Oppression. Jas. 2:6.
- Fraud. Jas. 5:4.
- Sensual indulgence. Luke 16:19. Jas. 5:5.

Life consists not in abundance of. Luke 12:15.
Be not over-anxious for. Pro. 30:8.
Labor not for. Pro. 23:4.
THEY WHO COVET,
- Fall into temptation and a snare. 1 Tim. 6:9.
- Fall into hurtful lusts. 1 Tim. 6:9.
- Err from the faith. 1 Tim. 6:10.
- Use unlawful means to acquire. Pro. 28:20.
- Bring trouble on themselves. 1 Tim. 6:10.
- Bring trouble on their families. Pro. 15:27.

Profit not in the day of wrath. Pro. 11:4.
Cannot secure prosperity. Jas. 1:11.
Cannot redeem the soul. Psa. 49:6–9. 1 Pet. 1:18.
Cannot deliver in the day of God's wrath. Zep. 1:18. Rev. 6:15–17.
THEY WHO POSSESS, SHOULD
- Ascribe them to God. 1 Chr. 29:12.
- Not trust in them. Job 31:24. 1 Tim. 6:17.
- Not set the heart on them. Psa. 62:10.
- Not boast of obtaining them. Deu. 8:17.
- Not glory in them. Jer. 9:23.
- Not hoard them up. Mat. 6:19.
- Devote them to God's service. 1 Chr. 29:3. Mar. 12:42–44.
- Give of them to the poor. Mat. 19:21. 1 Jno. 3:17.
- Use them in promoting the salvation of others. Luke 16:9.
- Be liberal in all things. 1 Tim. 6:18.
- Esteem it a privilege to be allowed to give. 1 Chr. 29:14.
- Not to be high-minded. 1 Tim. 6:17.
- When converted, rejoice in being humbled. Jas. 1:9, 10.

Heavenly treasures superior to. Mat. 6:19, 20.
Of the wicked laid up for the just. Pro. 13:22.
THE WICKED
- Often increase in. Psa. 73:12.
- Often spend their days in. Job 21:13.
- Swallow down. Job 20:15.
- Trust in the abundance of. Psa. 52:7.
- Heap up. Job 27:16. Psa. 39:6. Ecc. 2:26.
- Keep, to their hurt. Ecc. 5:13.
- Boast themselves in. Psa. 49:6. Psa. 52:7.
- Profit not by. Pro. 11:4. Pro. 13:7. Ecc. 5:11.
- Have trouble with. Pro. 15:6. 1 Tim. 6:9, 10.
- Must leave, to others. Psa. 49:10.

Vanity of heaping up. Psa. 39:6. Ecc. 5:10, 11.
Guilt of trusting in. Job 31:24, 28. Eze. 28:4, 5, 8.
Guilt of rejoicing in. Job 31:25, 28.
DENUNCIATIONS AGAINST THOSE WHO
- Get, by vanity. Pro. 13:11. Pro. 21:6.
- Get, unlawfully. Jer. 17:11.
- Increase, by oppression. Pro. 22:16. Hab. 2:6–8. Mic. 2:2, 3.
- Hoard up. Ecc. 5:13, 14. Jas. 5:3.
- Trust in. Pro. 11:28.
- Receive their consolation from. Luke 6:24.
- Abuse. Jas. 5:1, 5.
- Spend, upon their appetite. Job 20:15–17.

Folly and danger of trusting to—Illustrated. Luke 12:16–21.

Danger of misusing — Illustrated. Luke 16: 19—25.
Examples of saints possessing. *Abram*, Gen. 13: 2. *Lot*, Gen. 13: 5, 6. *Isaac*, Gen. 26: 13, 14. *Jacob*, Gen. 32: 5, 10. *Joseph*, Gen. 45: 8, 13. *Boaz*, Ruth 2: 1. *Barzillai*, 2 Sam. 19: 32. *Shunammite*, 2 Kin. 4: 8. *David*, 1 Chr. 29: 28. *Jehoshaphat*, 2 Chr. 17: 5. *Hezekiah*, 2 Chr. 32: 27—29. *Job*, Job 1: 3. *Joseph of Arimathea*, Mat. 27: 57. *Zaccheus*, Luke 19: 2. *Dorcas*, Acts 9: 36.
Examples of those truly rich. Mat. 5: 8. Mat. 8: 10. Mat. 13: 45, 46. Luke 10: 42. Jno. 1: 45. Phi. 3: 8. Jas. 2: 5. 1 Pet. 2: 7. Rev. 3: 18.
Examples of wicked men possessing. *Laban*, Gen. 30: 30. *Esau*, Gen. 36: 7. *Nabal*, 1 Sam. 25: 2. *Haman*, Est. 5: 11. *Ammonites*, Jer. 49: 4. *Tyrians*, Eze. 28: 5. *Young man*, Mat. 19: 22.

Righteousness.

Is obedience to God's law. Deu. 6: 25, with Rom. 10: 5. Luke 1: 6, with Psa. 1: 2.
God loves. Psa. 11: 7.
God looks for. Isa. 5: 7.
CHRIST
Is the Son of. Mal. 4: 2.
Loves. Psa. 45: 7, with Heb. 1: 9.
Was girt with. Isa. 11: 5.
Put on, as a breast-plate. Isa. 59: 17.
Was sustained by. Isa. 59: 16.
Preached. Psa. 40: 9.
Fulfilled all. Mat. 3: 15.
Is made unto His people. 1 Cor. 1: 30.
Is the end of the law for. Rom. 10: 4.
Has brought in everlasting. Dan. 9: 24.
Shall judge with. Psa. 72: 2. Isa. 11: 4. Acts 17: 31. Rev. 19: 11.
Shall reign in. Psa. 45: 6. Isa. 32: 1. Heb. 1: 8.
Shall execute. Psa. 99: 4. Jer. 23: 6.
None, by nature have. Job 15: 14. Psa. 14: 3, with Rom. 3: 10.
Cannot come by the law. Gal. 2: 21. Gal. 3: 21.
No justification by works of. Rom. 3: 20. Rom. 9: 31, 32. Gal. 2: 16.
No salvation by works of. Eph. 2: 8, 9. 2 Tim. 1: 9. Tit. 3: 5.
Unregenerate man seeks justification by works of. Luke 18: 9. Rom. 10: 3.
The blessing of God is not to be attributed to our works of. Deu. 9: 5.
SAINTS
Have, in Christ. Isa. 45: 24. Isa. 54: 17. 2 Cor. 5: 21.
Have, imputed. Rom. 4: 11, 22.
Are covered with the robe of. Isa. 61: 10.
Receive, from God. Psa. 24: 5.
Are renewed in. Eph. 4: 24.
Are led in the paths of. Psa. 23: 3.
Are servants of. Rom. 6: 16, 18.
Characterized by. Gen. 18: 25. Psa. 1: 5, 6.
Know. Isa. 51: 7.
Do. 1 Jno. 2: 29. 1 Jno. 3: 7.
Work, by faith. Heb. 11: 33.
Follow after. Isa. 51: 1.
Put on. Job 29: 14.
Wait for the hope of. Gal. 5: 5.
Pray for the spirit of. Psa. 51: 10.
Hunger and thirst after. Mat. 5: 6.
Walk before God in. 1 Kin. 3: 6.
Offer the sacrifice of. Psa. 4: 5. Psa. 51: 19.
Put no trust in their own. Phi. 3: 6—8.
Count their own, as filthy rags. Isa. 64: 6.
Should seek. Zep. 2: 3.
Should live in. Tit. 2: 12. 1 Pet. 2: 24.
Should serve God in. Luke 1: 75.
Should yield their members as instruments of. Rom. 6: 13.
Should yield their members servants to. Rom. 6: 19.
Should have on the breast-plate of. Eph. 6: 14.
Shall receive a crown of. 2 Tim. 4: 8.
Shall see God's face in. Psa. 17: 15.
Of saints endures forever. Psa. 112: 3, 9, with 2 Cor. 9: 9.
An evidence of the new birth. 1 Jno. 2: 29.
The kingdom of God is. Rom. 14: 17.
The fruit of the Spirit is in all. Eph. 5: 9.
The Scriptures instruct in. 2 Tim. 3: 16.
Judgments designed to lead to. Isa. 26: 9.
Chastisements yield the fruit of. Heb. 12: 11.
Has no fellowship with unrighteousness. 2 Cor. 6: 14.
MINISTERS SHOULD
Be preachers of. 2 Pet. 2: 5.
Reason of. Acts 24: 25.
Follow after. 1 Tim. 6: 11. 2 Tim. 2: 22.
Be clothed with. Psa. 132: 9.
Be armed with. 2 Cor. 6: 7.
Pray for fruit of, in their people. 2 Cor. 9: 10. Phi. 1: 11.
Keeps saints in the right way. Pro. 11: 5. Pro. 13: 6.
Judgment should be executed in. Lev. 19: 15.
THEY WHO WALK IN, AND FOLLOW,
Are righteous. 1 Jno. 3: 7.

Are the excellent of the earth. Psa. 16:3, with Pro. 12:26.
Are accepted with God. Acts 10:35.
Are loved by God. Psa. 146:8. Pro. 15:9.
Are blessed by God. Psa. 5:12.
Are heard by God. Luke 18:7. Jas. 5:16.
Are objects of God's watchful care. Job 36:7. Psa. 34:15. Pro. 10:3. 1 Pet. 3:12.
Are tried by God. Psa. 11:5.
Are exalted by God. Job 36:7.
Dwell in security. Isa. 33:15, 16.
Are bold as a lion. Pro. 28:1.
Are delivered out of all troubles. Psa. 34:19. Pro. 11:8.
Are never forsaken by God. Psa. 37:25.
Are abundantly provided for. Pro. 13:25. Mat. 6:25—33.
Are enriched. Psa. 112:3. Pro. 15:6.
Think and desire good. Pro. 11:23. Pro. 12:5.
Know the secret of the Lord. Psa. 25:14. Pro. 3:32.
Have their prayers heard. Psa. 34:17. Pro. 15:29. 1 Pet. 3:12.
Have their desires granted. Pro. 10:24.
Find it with life and honor. Pro. 21:21.
Shall hold on their way. Job 17:9.
Shall never be moved. Psa. 15:2, 5. Psa. 55:22. Pro. 10:30. Pro. 12:3.
Shall be ever remembered. Psa. 112:6.
Shall flourish as a branch. Pro. 11:28.

Shall be glad in the Lord. Psa. 64:10.
Brings its own reward. Pro. 11:18. Isa. 3:10.
Tends to life. Pro. 11:19. Pro. 12:28.
The work of, shall be peace. Isa. 32:17.
The effect of, shall be quietness and assurance for ever. Isa. 32:17.
Is a crown of glory to the aged. Pro. 16:31.

THE WICKED
Are far from. Psa. 119:150. Isa. 46:12.
Are free from. Rom. 6:20.
Are enemies of. Acts 13:10.
Leave off. Amos 5:7, with Psa. 36:3.
Follow not after. Rom. 9:30.
Do not. 1 Jno. 3:10.
Do not obey. Rom. 2:8, with 2 The. 2:12.
Love lying rather than. Psa. 52:3.
Make mention of God, not in. Isa. 48:1.
Though favored, will not learn. Isa. 26:10, with Psa. 106:43.
Speak contemptuously against those who follow. Psa. 31:18. Mat. 27:39—44.
Hate those who follow. Psa. 34:21.
Slay those who follow. Psa. 37:32. 1 Jno. 3:12, with Mat. 23:35.
Should break off their sins by. Dan. 4:27.
Should awake to. 1 Cor. 15:34.
Should sow to themselves in. Hos. 10:12.
Vainly wish to die as those who follow. Num. 23:10.

The throne of kings established by. Pro. 16:12. Pro. 25:5.
Nations exalted by. Pro. 14:34.

BLESSEDNESS OF
Having imputed, without works. Rom. 4:6.
Doing. Psa. 106:3.
Hungering and thirsting after. Mat. 5:6.
Suffering for. 1 Pet. 3:14.
Being persecuted for. Mat. 5:10.
Turning others to. Dan. 12:3.

Promised to the Church. Isa. 32:16. Isa. 45:8. Isa. 61:11. Isa. 62:1.
Promised to saints. Isa. 60:21. Isa. 61:3.
Exemplified. *Jacob*, Gen. 30:33. *David*, 2 Sam. 22:21. *Zacharias, &c.* Luke 1:6. *Abel*, Heb. 11:4. *Lot*, 2 Pet. 2:8.

Righteousness Imputed.

Predicted. Isa. 56:1. Eze. 16:14.
Revealed in the gospel. Rom. 1:17.
Is of the Lord. Isa. 54:17.

DESCRIBED AS
The righteousness of faith. Rom. 4:13. Rom. 9:30. Rom. 10:6.
The righteousness of God, without the law. Rom. 3:21.
The righteousness of God by faith in Christ. Rom. 3:22.
Christ being made righteousness unto us. 1 Cor. 1:30.
Our being made the righteousness of God, in Christ. 2 Cor. 5:21.

Christ is the end of the law for. Rom. 10:4.
Christ called THE LORD OUR RIGHTEOUSNESS. Jer. 23:6.
Christ brings in an everlasting righteousness. Dan. 9:24.
Is a free gift. Rom. 5:17.
God's righteousness never to be abolished. Isa. 51:6.
The promises made through. Rom. 4:13.

SAINTS
Have, on believing. Rom. 4:5, 11, 24.
Clothed with the robe of righteousness. Isa. 61:10.

Exalted in righteousness. Psa. 89: 16.
Desire to be found in. Phi. 3: 9.
Glory in having. Isa. 45: 24, 25.
Exhortation to seek righteousness. Mat. 6: 33.
The Gentiles attained to. Rom. 9: 30.
Blessedness of those who have. Rom. 4: 6.
THE JEWS
Ignorant of. Rom. 10: 3.
Stumble at righteousness by faith. Rom. 9: 32.
Submit not to. Rom. 10: 3.
Exemplified. *Abraham*, Rom. 4: 9, 22. Gal. 3: 6. *Paul*, Phi. 3: 7—9.

Righteousness of God, The.

Is part of His character. Psa. 7: 9. Psa. 116: 5. Psa. 119: 137.
DESCRIBED AS
Very high. Psa. 71: 19.
Abundant. Psa. 48: 10.
Beyond computation. Psa. 71: 15.
Everlasting. Psa. 119: 142.
Enduring for ever. Psa. 111: 3.
The habitation of His throne. Psa. 97: 2.
Christ acknowledged. Jno. 17: 25.
Christ committed His cause to. 1 Pet. 2: 23.
Angels acknowledge. Rev. 16: 5.
EXHIBITED IN
His testimonies. Psa. 119: 138, 144.
His commandments. Deu. 4: 8. Psa. 119: 172.
His judgments. Psa. 19: 9. Psa. 119: 7, 62.
His word. Psa. 119: 123.
His ways. Psa. 145: 17.
His acts. Jud. 5: 11. 1 Sam. 12: 7.
His government. Psa. 96: 13. Psa. 98: 9.
The gospel. Psa. 85: 10, with Rom. 3: 25, 26.
The final judgment. Acts 17: 31.
The punishment of the wicked. Rom. 2: 5. 2 The. 1: 6. Rev. 16: 7. Rev. 19: 2.
Shown to the posterity of saints. Psa. 103: 17.
Shown openly before the heathen. Psa. 98: 2.
God delights in the exercise of. Jer. 9: 24.
The heavens shall declare. Psa. 50: 6. Psa. 97: 6.
SAINTS
Ascribe, to Him. Job 36: 3. Dan. 9: 7.
Acknowledge, in His dealings. Ezr. 9: 15.
Acknowledge, though the wicked prosper. Jer. 12: 1, with Psa. 73: 12—17.
Recognize, in the fulfilment of His promises. Neh. 9: 8.
Confident of beholding. Mic. 7: 9.
Upheld by. Isa. 41: 10.
Do not conceal. Psa. 40: 10.
Mention, only. Psa. 71: 16.
Talk of. Psa. 35: 28. Psa. 71: 15, 24.
Declare to others. Psa. 22: 31.
Magnify. Psa. 7: 17. Psa. 51: 14. Psa. 145: 7.
Plead, in prayer. Psa. 143 11. Dan. 9: 16.
Leads Him to love righteouness. Psa. 11: 7.
WE SHOULD PRAY
To be led in. Psa. 5: 8.
To be quickened in. Psa. 119: 40.
To be delivered in. Psa. 31: 1. Psa. 71: 2.
To be answered in. Psa. 143: 1.
To be judged according to. Psa. 35: 24.
For its continued manifestation. Psa. 36: 10.
His care and defence of His people designed to teach. Mic. 6: 4, 5.
The wicked have no interest in. Psa. 69: 27.
Illustrated. Psa. 36: 6.

Rings.

Antiquity of. Gen. 24: 22. Gen. 38: 18.
Made of gold and set with precious stones. Num. 31: 50, 51. So. of Sol. 5: 14.
WERE WORN
On the hands. Gen. 41: 42.
On the arms. 2 Sam. 1: 10.
In the ears. Job 42: 11. Hos. 2: 13. Eze. 16: 12.
In the nose. Isa. 3: 21.
Rich men distinguished by. Jas. 2: 2.
Women of rank adorned with. Isa. 3: 16, 21.
OF KINGS
Used for sealing decrees. Est. 3: 12. Est. 8: 8, 10.
Given to favorites as a mark of honor. Gen. 41: 42. Est. 3: 10. Est. 8: 2.
Numbers of, taken from Midianites. Num. 31: 50.
ILLUSTRATIVE
Of the glory of Christ. So. of Sol. 5: 14.
(Put on the hands,) of favor. Luke 15: 22.

Rivers.

Source of. Job 28: 10. Psa. 104: 8, 10.
Enclosed within banks. Dan. 12: 5.
Flow through valleys. Psa. 104: 8, 10.
SOME OF
Great and mighty. Gen. 15: 18. Psa. 74: 15.
Deep. Eze. 47: 5. Zec. 10: 11.
Broad. Isa. 33: 21.
Rapid. Jud. 5: 21.

Parted into many streams. Gen. 2: 10. Isa. 11: 15.
Run into the sea. Ecc. 1: 7. Eze. 47: 8.
God's power over, unlimited. Isa. 50: 2. Nah. 1: 4.
USEFUL FOR
Supplying drink to the people. Jer. 2: 18.
Commerce. Isa. 23: 3.
Promoting vegetation. Gen. 2: 10.
Bathing. Exo. 2: 5.
Baptism often performed in. Mat. 3: 6.
Of Canaan abounded with fish. Lev. 11: 9, 10.
BANKS OF,
Covered with flags. Exo. 2: 3, 5.
Planted with trees. Eze. 47: 7.
Frequented by doves. So. of Sol. 5: 12.
Frequented by wild beasts. Jer. 49: 19.
Places of common resort. Psa. 137: 1.
Frequently overflowed. Jos. 3: 15. 1 Chr. 12: 15.
Peculiarly fruitful. Psa. 1: 3. Isa. 32: 20.
Gardens often made beside. Num. 24: 6.
Cities often built beside. Psa. 46: 4. Psa. 137: 1.
Often the boundaries of kingdoms, &c. Jos. 22: 25. 1 Kin. 4: 24.
MENTIONED IN SCRIPTURE;
Of Eden. Gen. 2: 10.
Of Jotbath. Deu. 10: 7.
Of Ethiopia. Isa. 18: 1.
Of Babylon. Psa. 137: 1.
Of Egypt. Gen. 15: 18.
Of Damascus. 2 Kin. 5: 12.
Of Ahava. Ezr. 8: 15.
Of Judah. Joel 3: 18.
Of Philippi. Acts 16: 13.
Abana. 2 Kin. 5: 12.
Arnon. Deu. 2: 36. Jos. 12: 1.
Chebar. Eze. 1: 1, 3. Eze. 10: 15, 20.
Euphrates. Gen. 2: 14.
Gihon. Gen. 2: 13.
Gozan. 2 Kin. 17: 6. 1 Chr. 5: 26.
Hiddekel. Gen. 2: 14.
Jabbok. Deu. 2: 37. Jos. 12: 2.
Jordan. Jos. 3: 8. 2 Kin. 5: 10.
Kanah. Jos. 16: 8.
Kishon. Jud. 5: 21.
Pharpar. 2 Kin. 5: 12.
Pison. Gen. 2: 11.
Ulai. Dan. 8: 16.
Many, fordable in some places. Gen. 32: 22. Jos. 2: 7. Isa. 16: 2.
ILLUSTRATIVE
Of the abundance of grace in Christ. Isa. 32: 2, with Jno. 1: 16.
Of the gifts and graces of the Holy Spirit. Psa. 46: 4. Isa. 41: 18. Isa. 43: 19, 20. Jno. 7: 38, 39.
Of heavy afflictions. Psa. 69: 2. Isa. 43: 2.
Of abundance. Job 20: 17. Job 29: 6.
Of people flying from judgments. Isa. 23: 10.
(Steady course of,) of peace of saints. Isa. 66: 12.
(Fruitfulness of trees planted by,) of the permanent prosperity of saints. Psa. 1: 3. Jer. 17: 8.
(Drying up of,) of God's judgments. Isa. 19: 1—8. Jer. 51: 36. Nah. 1: 4. Zec. 10: 11.
(Overflowing of,) of God's judgments. Isa. 8: 7, 8. Isa. 28: 2, 18. Jer. 47: 2.

Rocks.

Often composed of flint. Deu. 8: 15. Deu. 32: 13.
DESCRIBED AS
Hard. Jer. 5: 3.
Durable. Job 19: 24.
Barren. Eze. 26: 4, 14. Amos 6: 12. Luke 8: 6.
Often sharp-pointed and craggy. 1 Sam. 14: 4.
Often had holes and clefts. Exo 33: 22.
Were a defence to a country. Isa. 33: 16.
Dreaded by mariners. Acts 27: 29.
INHABITED BY
Wild goats. Job 39: 1.
Conies. Psa. 104: 18. Pro. 30: 26.
Doves. So. of Sol. 2: 14. Jer. 48: 28.
Eagles. Job 39: 28. Jer. 49: 16.
The olive tree flourished amongst. Deu. 32: 13. Job 29: 6.
Bees often made their honey amongst. Deu. 32: 13. Psa. 81: 16.
USED AS
Altars. Jud. 6: 20, 21, 26. Jud. 13: 19.
Places for idolatrous worship. Isa. 57: 5.
Places of Observation. Exo. 33: 21. Num. 23: 9.
Places of safety in danger. 1 Sam. 13: 6. Isa. 2: 19. Jer. 16: 16. Rev. 6: 15.
Places for shelter by the poor in their distress. Job 24: 8. Job 30: 3, 6.
The shadow of, grateful to travelers during the heat of the day. Isa. 32: 2.
Houses often built on. Mat. 7: 24, 25.
Tombs often hewn out of. Isa. 22: 16. Mat. 27: 60.
Important events often engraved upon. Job 19: 24.
MENTIONED IN SCRIPTURE;
Adullam. 1 Chr. 11: 15.
Bozez. 1 Sam. 14: 4.
Engedi. 1 Sam. 24: 1, 2.
Etam. Jud. 15: 8.
Horeb in Rephidim. Exo. 17: 1—6.

Meribah in Kadesh. Num. 20: 1—11.
Oreb. Jud. 7: 25. Isa. 10: 26.
Rimmon. Jud. 20: 45.
Seneh. 1 Sam. 14: 4.
Sela-hammahlekoth in the wilderness of Maon. 1 Sam. 23: 25, 28.
Selah in the valley of salt. 2 Kin. 14: 7. (*marg.*) 2 Chr. 25: 11, 12.

Man's industry in cutting through. Job 28: 9, 10.
Hammers used for breaking. Jer. 23: 29.
Casting down from, a punishment. 2 Chr. 25: 12.

MIRACLES CONNECTED WITH;
Water brought from. Exo. 17: 6. Num. 20: 11.
Fire ascended out of. Jud. 6: 21.
Broken in pieces by the wind. 1 Kin. 19: 11.
Rent at the death of Christ. Mat. 27: 51.

God's power exhibited in removing, &c. Job 14: 18. Nah. 1: 6.

ILLUSTRATIVE OF
God as creator of His people. Deu. 32: 18.
God as the strength of His people. Psa. 18: 1, 2. Psa. 62: 7. Isa. 17: 10.
God as defence of His people. Psa. 31: 2, 3.
God as refuge of His people. Psa. 94: 22.
God as salvation of His people. Deu. 32: 15. Psa. 89: 26. Psa. 95: 1.
Christ as refuge of His people. Isa. 32: 2.
Christ as foundation of His church. Mat. 16: 18, with 1 Pet. 2: 6.
Christ as source of spiritual gifts. 1 Cor. 10: 4.
Christ as a stumbling-stone to the wicked. Isa. 8: 14. Rom. 9: 33. 1 Pet. 2: 8.
A place of safety. Psa. 27: 5. Psa. 40: 2.
Whatever we trust in. Deu. 32: 31, 37.
The ancestor of a nation. Isa 51: 1.

Roe, The.

Clean and fit for food. Deu. 12: 15. Deu. 14: 5.
Male of, called the roebuck. 1 Kin. 4: 23.

DESCRIBED AS
Cheerful. Pro. 5: 19.
Wild. 2 Sam. 2: 18.
Swift. 1 Chr. 12: 8.

Inhabits the mountains. 1 Chr. 12: 8.
Often hunted by men. Pro. 6: 5.

ILLUSTRATIVE OF
Christ. So. of Sol. 2: 9, 17.
The church. So. of Sol. 4: 5. So. of Sol. 7: 3.
A good wife. Pro. 5: 19.
The swift of foot. 2 Sam. 2: 18.

Roman Empire, The.

Called the world from its extent. Luke 2: 1.

REPRESENTED BY THE
Legs of iron in Nebuchadnezzar's vision. Dan. 2: 33, 40.
Terrible beast in Daniel's vision. Dan. 7: 7, 19.

Rome the capitol of. Acts 18: 2. Acts 19: 21.
Judea a province of, under a procurator or a governor. Luke 3: 2. Acts 23: 24, 26. Acts 25: 1.

ALLUSIONS TO MILITARY AFFAIRS OF;
Strict obedience to superiors. Mat. 8: 8, 9.
Use of the panoply or defensive armor. Rom. 13: 12. 2 Cor. 6: 7. Eph. 6: 11—17.
Soldiers not allowed to entangle themselves with earthly cares. 2 Tim. 2: 4.
Hardship endured by soldiers. 2 Tim. 2: 3.
The soldier's special comrade who shared his toils and dangers. Phi. 2: 25.
Danger of sentinels' sleeping. Mat. 28: 13, 14.
Expunging from the muster roll names of soldiers guilty of crimes. Rev. 3: 5.
Crowning of soldiers who distinguished themselves. 2 Tim. 4: 7, 8.
Triumph of victorious generals. 2 Cor. 2: 14—16. Col. 2: 15.
Different military officers, &c. Acts 21: 31. Acts 23: 23, 24.
Italian and Augustus' band. Acts 10: 1. Acts 27: 1.

ALLUSIONS TO JUDICIAL AFFAIRS OF;
Persons accused, examined by scourging. Acts 22: 24, 29.
Criminals delivered over to the soldiers for execution. Mat. 27: 26, 27.
Accusation in writing placed over the head of those executed. Jno. 19: 19.
Garments of those executed given to the soldiers. Mat. 27: 35. Jno. 19: 23.
Prisoners chained to soldiers for safety. Acts 21: 33, with Acts 12: 6. 2 Tim. 1: 16, with Acts 28: 16.
Accusers and accused confronted together. Acts 23: 35. Acts 25: 16—19.
Accused persons protected from popular violence. Acts 23: 20, 24—27.
Power of life and death vested in its authorities. Jno. 18: 31, 39, 40. Jno. 19: 10.

All appeals made to the emperor. Acts 25:11, 12.
Those who appealed to Cæsar, to be brought before him. Acts 26:32.

ALLUSIONS TO CITIZENSHIP OF;
Obtained by purchase. Acts 22:28.
Obtained by birth. Acts 22:28.
Exempted from the degradation of scourging. Acts 16:37, 38. Acts 22:25.

ALLUSIONS TO GRECIAN GAMES ADOPTED BY;
Gladiatorial fights. 1 Cor. 4:9. 1 Cor. 15:32.
Foot races. 1 Cor. 9:24. Phi. 2:16. Phi. 3:11—14. Heb. 12:1, 2.
Wrestling. Eph. 6:12.
Training of combatants. 1 Cor. 9:25, 27.
Crowning of conquerors. 1 Cor. 9:25. Phi. 3:14. 2 Tim. 4:8.
Rules observed in conducting. 2 Tim. 2:5.

EMPERORS OF, MENTIONED;
Tiberius. Luke 3:1.
Augustus. Luke 2:1.
Claudius. Acts 11:28.
Nero. Phi. 4:22. 2 Tim. 4:17.

PREDICTIONS RESPECTING;
Its universal dominion. Dan. 7:23.
Its division into ten parts. Dan. 2:41—43. Dan. 7:20, 24.
Origin of papal power in. Dan. 7:8, 20—25.

Sabbath, The.

Instituted by God. Gen. 2:3.
Grounds of its institution. Gen. 2:2, 3. Exo. 20:11.
The seventh day observed as. Exo. 20:9, 10, 11.
Made for man. Mar. 2:27.

GOD
Blessed. Gen. 2:3. Exo. 20:11.
Sanctified. Gen. 2:3. Exo. 31:15
Hallowed. Exo. 20:11.
Commanded, to be kept. Lev. 19:3:30.
Commanded, to be sanctified. Exo. 20:8.
Will have His goodness commemorated in the observance of. Deu. 5:15.
Shows favor in appointing. Neh. 9:14.
Shows considerate kindness in appointing. Exo. 23:12.

A sign of the covenant. Exo. 31:13, 17.
A type of the heavenly rest. Heb. 4:4, 9.

CHRIST
Is Lord of. Mar. 2:28.
Was accustomed to observe. Luke 4:16.
Taught on. Luke 4:31. Luke 6:6.

Servants and cattle should be allowed to rest upon. Exo. 20:10. Deu. 5:14.
No manner of work to be done on. Exo. 20:10. Lev. 23:3.
No purchases to be made on. Neh. 10:31. Neh. 13:15—17.
No burdens to be carried on. Neh. 13:19. Jer. 17:21.
Divine worship to be celebrated on. Eze. 46:3. Acts 16:13.
The Scriptures to be read on. Acts 13:27. Acts 15:21.
The word of God to be preached on. Acts 13:14, 15, 44. Acts 17:2. Acts 18:4.
Works connected with religious service lawful on. Num. 28:9. Mat. 12:5. Jno. 7:23.
Works of mercy lawful on. Mat. 12:12. Luke 13:16. Jno. 9:14.
Necessary wants may be supplied on. Mat. 12:1. Luke 13:15. Luke 14:1.

CALLED
The Sabbath of the Lord. Exo. 20:10. Lev. 23:3. Deu. 5:14.
The Sabbath of rest. Exo. 31:15.
The rest of the holy Sabbath. Exo. 16:23.
God's holy day. Isa. 58:13.
The Lord's day. Rev. 1:10.

First day of the week kept as, by primitive church. Jno. 20:26, Acts 20:7. 1 Cor. 16:2.

SAINTS
Observe. Neh. 13:22.
Honor God in observing. Isa. 58:13.
Rejoice in. Psa. 118:24. Isa. 58:13.
Testify against those who desecrate. Neh. 13:15, 20, 21.

Observance of, to be perpetual. Exo. 31:16, 17, with Mat. 5:17, 18.
Blessedness of honoring. Isa. 58:13, 14.
Blessedness of keeping. Isa. 56:2, 6.
Denunciations against those who profane. Neh. 13:18. Jer. 17:27.
Punishment of those who profane. Exo. 31:14, 15. Num. 15:32—36.

THE WICKED
Mock at. Lam. 1:7.
Pollute. Isa. 56:2. Eze. 20:13, 16.
Profane. Neh. 13:17. Eze. 22:8.
Wearied by. Amos 8:5.
Hide their eyes from. Eze. 22:26.
Do their own pleasure on. Isa. 58:13.
Bear burdens on. Neh. 13:15.
Work on. Neh. 13:15.
Traffic on. Neh. 10:31. Neh. 13:15, 16.
Sometimes pretend to be zealous for. Luke 13:14. Jno. 9:16.
May be judicially deprived of. Lam. 2:6. Hos. 2:11.

Honoring of—Exemplified. *Moses, &c.* Num. 15:32—34. *Nehemiah*, Neh. 13:15, 21. *The women*, Luke 23:56. *Paul*, Acts 13:14. *Disciples*, Acts 16:13. *John*, Rev. 1:10.
Dishonoring of—Exemplified. *Gatherers of manna*, Exo. 16:27. *Gatherers of sticks*, Num. 15:32. *Men of Tyre*, Neh. 13:16. *Inhabitants of Jerusalem*, Jer. 17:21—23.

Sackcloth.

Made of coarse hair. Mat. 3:4, with Rev. 6:12.
Rough and unsightly. Zec. 13:4.
Of a black color. Rev. 6:12.
WAS WORN
By God's prophets. 2 Kin. 1:8. Isa. 20:2. Mat. 3:4. Rev. 11:3.
By persons in affliction. Neh. 9:1. Psa. 69:11. Jon. 3:5.
Girt about the loins. Gen. 37:34. 1 Kin. 20:31.
Frequently next the skin in deep affliction. 1 Kin. 21:27. 2 Kin. 6:30. Job 16:15.
Often over the whole person. 2 Kin. 19:1, 2.
With ashes on the head. Est. 4:1.
Often with ropes on the head. 1 Kin. 20:31.
In the streets. Isa. 15:3.
At funerals. 2 Sam. 3:31.
The Jews lay in, when in deep affliction. 2 Sam. 21:10. 1 Kin. 21:27. Joel 1:13.
No one clothed in, allowed into the palaces of kings. Est. 4:2.
ILLUSTRATIVE
(Girding with,) of heavy afflictions. Isa. 3:24. Isa. 22:12. Isa. 32:11.
(Covering the heavens with,) of severe judgments. Isa. 50:3.
(Heavens becoming black as,) of severe judgments. Rev. 6:12.
(Putting off,) of joy and gladness. Psa. 30:11.

Sacrifices.

Divine institution of. Gen. 3:21, with Gen. 1:29 and Gen. 9:3. Gen. 4:4, 5, with Heb. 11:4.
To be offered to God alone. Exo. 22:20. Jud. 13:16. 2 Kin. 17:36.
When offered to God, an acknowledgment of His being the supreme God. 2 Kin. 5:17. Jon. 1:16.
CONSISTED OF
Clean animals or bloody sacrifices. Gen. 8:20.
The fruits of the earth or unbloody sacrifices. Gen. 4:4. Lev. 2:1.
Always offered upon altars. Exo. 20:24.
The offering of, an acknowledgment of sin. Heb. 10:3.
WERE OFFERED
From the earliest age. Gen. 4:3, 4.
By the patriarchs. Gen. 22:2, 13. Gen. 31:54. Gen. 46:1. Job 1:5.
After the departure of Israel from Egypt. Exo. 5:3, 17. Exo. 18:12. Exo. 24:5.
Under the Mosaic dispensation. Lev. 1 ch. to 7 ch. Heb. 10:1—3.
Daily. Exo. 29:38, 39. Num. 28:3, 4.
Weekly. Num. 28:9, 10.
Monthly. Num. 28:11.
Yearly. Lev. 16:3. 1 Sam. 1:3, 21. 1 Sam. 20:6.
At all the feasts. Num. 10:10.
For the whole nation. Lev. 16:15—30. 1 Chr. 29:21.
For individuals. Lev. 1:2. Lev. 17:8.
In faith of a coming Saviour. Heb. 11:4, 17, 28.
Required to be perfect and without blemish. Lev. 22:19. Deu. 15:21. Deu. 17:1. Mal. 1:8, 14.
Generally the best of their kind. Gen. 4:4. 1 Sam. 15:22. Psa. 66:15. Isa. 1:11.
DIFFERENT KINDS OF;
Burnt offering wholly consumed by fire. Lev. 1 ch. 1 Kin. 18:38.
Sin offering for sins of ignorance. Lev. 4 ch.
Trespass offering for intentional sins. Lev. 6:1—7. Lev. 7:1—7.
Peace offering. Lev. 3 ch.
To be brought to the place appointed by God. Deu. 12:6. 2 Chr. 7:12.
Were bound to the horns of the altar. Psa. 118:27.
Were salted with salt. Lev. 2:13. Mar. 9:49.
Often consumed by fire from heaven. Lev. 9:24. 1 Kin. 18:38. 2 Chr. 7:1.
When bloody, accompanied with meat and drink offering. Num. 15:3—12.
No leaven offered with, except for thanksgiving. Exo. 23:18, with Lev. 7:13.
Fat of, not to remain until morning. Exo. 23:8.
THE PRIESTS
Appointed to offer. 1 Sam. 2:28. Eze. 44:11, 15. Heb. 5:1. Heb. 8:3.
Had a portion of, and lived by. Exo. 29:27, 28. Deu. 18:3. Jos. 13:14. 1 Cor. 9:13.
Were typical of Christ's sacrifice. 1 Cor. 5:7. Eph. 5:2. Heb. 10:1, 11, 12.
Were accepted when offered in sincerity and faith. Gen. 4:4, with Heb. 11:4. Gen. 8:21.
Imparted a legal purification. Heb. 9:13, 22.
Could not take away sin. Psa. 40:6. Heb. 9:9. Heb. 10:1—11.

Without obedience, worthless. 1 Sam. 15: 22. Pro. 21: 3. Mar. 12: 33.
The covenants of God confirmed by. Gen. 15: 9—17. Exo. 24: 5—8, with Heb. 9: 19, 20. Psa. 50: 5.
THE JEWS
  Condemned for not treating, with respect. 1 Sam. 2: 29. Mal. 1: 12.
  Condemned for bringing defective and blemished. Mal. 1: 13, 14.
  Condemned for not offering. Isa. 43: 23, 24.
  Unaccepted in, on account of sin. Isa. 1: 11, 15. Isa. 66: 3. Hos. 8: 13.
  Condemned for offering, to idols. 2 Chr. 34: 25. Isa. 65: 3, 7. Eze. 20: 28, 31.
Offered to false gods, are offered to devils. Lev. 17: 7. Deu. 32: 17. Psa. 106: 37. 1 Cor. 10: 20.
On great occasions, very numerous. 2 Chr. 5: 6. 2 Chr. 7: 5.
For public use often provided by the state. 2 Chr. 31: 3.
ILLUSTRATIVE OF
  Prayer. Psa. 141: 2.
  Thanksgiving. Psa. 27: 6. Psa. 107: 22. Psa. 116: 17. Heb. 13: 15.
  Devotedness. Rom. 12: 1. Phi. 2: 17.
  Benevolence. Phi. 4: 18. Heb. 13: 16.
  Righteousness. Psa. 4: 5. Psa 51: 19.
  A broken spirit. Psa. 51: 17.
  Martyrdom. Phi. 2: 7. 2 Tim. 4: 6.

Sadducees, The.

A sect of the Jews. Acts 5: 17.
Denied the resurrection and a future state. Mat. 22: 23. Luke 20: 27.
The resurrection a cause of dispute between them and the Pharisees. Acts 23: 6—9.
Were refused baptism by John. Mat. 3: 7.
CHRIST
  Tempted by. Mat. 16: 1.
  Cautioned His disciples against their principles. Mat. 16: 6, 11, 12.
  Vindicated the resurrection against Mat. 22: 24—32. Mar. 12: 19—27.
  Silenced. Mat. 22: 34.
Persecuted the early Christians. Acts 4: 1. Acts 5: 17, 18, 40.

Saints, Compared to.

The sun. Jud. 5: 31. Mat. 13: 43.
Stars. Dan. 12: 3.
Lights. Mat. 5: 14. Phi. 2: 15.
Mount Zion. Psa. 125: 1, 2.
Lebanon. Hos. 14: 5—7.
Treasure. Exo. 19: 5. Psa. 135: 4.
Jewels. Mal. 3: 17.
Gold. Job 23: 10. Lam. 4: 2.
Vessels of gold and silver. 2 Tim. 2: 20.
Stones of a crown. Zec. 9: 16.
Lively stones. 1 Pet. 2: 5.
Babes. Mat. 11: 25. 1 Pet. 2: 2.
Little children. Mat. 18: 3. 1 Cor. 14: 20.
Obedient children. 1 Pet. 1: 14.
Members of the body. 1 Cor. 12: 20, 27.
Soldiers. 2 Tim. 2: 3, 4.
Runners in a race. 1 Cor. 9: 24. Heb. 12: 1.
Wrestlers. 2 Tim. 2: 5.
Good servants. Mat. 25: 21.
Strangers and pilgrims. 1 Pet. 2: 11.
Sheep. Psa. 78: 52. Mat. 25: 33. Jno. 10: 4.
Lambs. Isa. 40: 11. Jno. 21: 15.
Calves of the stall. Mal. 4: 2.
Lions. Pro. 28: 1. Mic. 5: 8.
Eagles. Psa. 103: 5. Isa. 40: 31.
Doves. Psa. 68: 13. Isa. 60: 8.
Thirsting deer. Psa. 42: 1.
Good fishes. Mat. 13: 48.
Dew and showers. Mic. 5: 7.
Watered gardens. Isa. 58: 11.
Unfailing springs. Isa. 58: 11.
Vines. So. of Sol. 6: 11. Hos. 14: 7.
Branches of a vine. Jno. 15: 2, 4, 5.
Pomegranates. So. of Sol. 4: 13.
Good figs. Jer. 24: 2—7.
Lilies. So. of Sol. 2: 2. Hos. 14: 5.
Willows by the water-courses. Isa. 44: 4.
Trees planted by rivers. Psa. 1: 3.
Cedars in Lebanon. Psa. 92: 12.
Palm trees. Psa. 92: 12.
Green olive trees. Psa. 52: 8. Hos. 14: 6.
Fruitful trees. Psa. 1: 3. Jer. 17: 8.
Corn. Hos. 14: 7.
Wheat. Mat. 3: 12. Mat. 13: 29, 30.
Salt. Mat. 5: 13.

Salt.

Characterized as good and useful. Mar. 9: 50.
USED FOR
  Seasoning food. Job 6: 6.
  Seasoning sacrifices. Lev. 2: 13. Eze. 43: 24.
  Ratifying covenants. Num. 18: 19. 2 Chr. 13: 5.
  Strengthening new-born infants. Eze. 16: 4.
Partaking of another's, a bond of friendship. Ezr. 4: 14. (*marg.*)
Lost its savor when exposed to the air. Mat. 5: 13. Mar. 9: 50.
OFTEN FOUND
  In pits. Jos. 11: 8. (*marg.*) Zep. 2. 9.
  In springs. Jas. 3: 12.
  Near the Dead Sea. Num. 34: 12. Deu. 3: 17.
Places where it abounded barren and unfruitful. Jer. 17: 6. Eze. 47: 11.

The valley of, celebrated for victories. 2 Sam. 8: 13. 2 Kin. 14: 7. 1 Chr. 18: 12.

MIRACLES CONNECTED WITH;
- Lot's wife turned into a pillar of. Gen. 19: 26.
- Elisha healed the bad water with. 1 Kin. 2: 21.

Places sown with, to denote perpetual desolation. Jud. 9: 45.

Liberally afforded to the Jews after the captivity. Ezr. 6: 9. Ezr. 7: 22.

ILLUSTRATIVE
- Of saints. Mat. 5: 13.
- Of grace in the heart. Mar. 9: 50.
- Of wisdom in speech. Col. 4: 6.
- (Without savor,) of graceless professors. Mat. 5: 13. Mar. 9: 50.
- (Pits of,) of desolation. Zep. 2: 9.
- (Salted with fire,) of preparation of the wicked for destruction. Mar. 9: 49.

Salutations.

Antiquity of. Gen. 18: 2. Gen. 19: 1.

WERE GIVEN
- By brethren to each other. 1 Sam. 17: 22.
- By inferiors to their superiors. Gen. 47: 7.
- By superiors to inferiors. 1 Sam. 30: 21.
- By all passers-by. 1 Sam. 10: 3, 4. Psa. 129: 8.
- On entering a house. Jud. 18: 15. Mat. 10: 12. Luke 1: 40, 41, 44.

Often sent through messengers. 1 Sam. 25: 5, 14. 2 Sam. 8: 10.

Often sent by letter. Rom. 16: 21—23. 1 Cor. 16: 21. Col. 4: 18. 2 The. 3: 17.

Denied to persons of bad character. 2 Jno. 10 v.

Persons in haste excused from giving or receiving. 2 Kin. 4: 29. Luke 10: 24.

EXPRESSIONS USED AS;
- Peace be with thee. Jud. 19: 20.
- Peace to thee, and peace to thine house, and peace unto all that thou hast. 1 Sam. 25: 6.
- Peace be to this house. Luke 10: 5.
- The Lord be with you. Ruth 2: 4.
- The Lord bless thee. Ruth 2: 4.
- The blessing of the Lord be upon you, we bless you in the name of the Lord. Psa. 129: 8.
- Blessed be thou of the Lord. 1 Sam. 15: 13.
- God be gracious unto thee. Gen. 43: 29.
- Art thou in heath? 2 Sam. 20: 9.
- Hail. Mat. 26: 49. Luke 1: 28.
- All hail. Mat. 28: 9.

Often perfidious. 2 Sam. 20: 9. Mat. 26: 49.

Given to Christ in derision. Mat. 27: 29, with Mar. 15: 18.

OFTEN ACCOMPANIED BY
- Falling on the neck and kissing. Gen. 33: 4. Gen. 45: 14, 15. Luke 15: 20.
- Laying hold of the beard with the right hand, &c. 2 Sam. 20: 9.
- Bowing frequently to the ground. Gen. 33: 3.
- Embracing and kissing the feet. Mat. 28: 9. Luke 7: 38, 45.
- Touching the hem of the garment. Mat. 14: 36.
- Falling prostrate on the ground. Est. 8: 3. Mat. 2: 11. Luke 8: 41.
- Kissing the dust. Psa. 72: 9. Isa. 49: 23.

The Jews condemned for giving, only to their own countrymen. Mat. 5: 47.

The Pharisees condemned for seeking, in public. Mat. 23: 7. Mar. 12: 38.

Salvation.

Is of God. Psa. 3: 8. Psa. 37: 39. Jer. 3: 23.

Is of the purpose of God. 2 Tim. 1: 9.

Is of the appointment of God. 1 The. 5: 9.

God is willing to give. 1 Tim. 2: 4.

Is by Christ. Isa. 63: 9. Eph. 5: 23.

Is by Christ alone. Isa. 45: 21, 22. Isa. 59: 16. Acts 4: 12.

Announced after the fall. Gen. 3: 15.

Of Israel, predicted. Isa. 35: 4. Isa. 45: 17. Zec. 9: 16. Rom. 11: 26.

Of the Gentiles, predicted. Isa. 45: 22. Isa. 49: 6. Isa. 52: 10.

Revealed in the gospel. Eph. 1: 13. 2 Tim. 1: 10.

Came to the Gentiles through the fall of the Jews. Rom. 11: 11.

CHRIST
- The Captain of. Heb. 2: 10.
- The Author of. Heb. 5: 9.
- Appointed for. Isa. 49: 6.
- Raised up for. Luke 1: 69.
- Has. Zec. 9: 9.
- Brings, with Him. Isa. 62: 11. Luke 19: 9.
- Mighty to effect. Isa. 63: 1. Heb. 7: 25.
- Came to effect. Mat. 18: 11. 1 Tim. 1: 15.
- Died to effect. Jno. 3: 14, 15. Gal. 1: 4.
- Exalted to give. Acts 5: 31.

Is not by works. Rom. 11: 6. Eph. 2: 9. 2 Tim. 1: 9. Tit. 3: 5.

Is of grace. Eph. 2: 5, 8. 2 Tim. 1: 9. Tit. 2: 11.

Is of love. Rom. 5: 8. 1 Jno. 4: 9, 10.

Is of mercy. Psa. 6: 4. Tit. 3: 5.

Is of the long-suffering of God. 2 Pet. 3: 15.

Is through faith in Christ. Mar. 16: 16. Acts 16: 31. Rom. 10: 9. Eph. 2: 8. 1 Pet. 1: 5.

Reconciliation to God, a pledge of. Rom. 5: 10.

IS DELIVERANCE FROM
- Sin. Mat. 1: 21, with 1 Jno. 3: 5.
- Uncleanness. Eze. 36: 29.
- The devil. Col. 2: 15. Heb. 2: 14, 15.
- Wrath. Rom. 5: 9. 1 The 1: 10.
- This present evil world. Gal. 1: 4.
- Enemies. Luke 1: 71, 74.
- Eternal death. Jno. 3: 16, 17.

Confession of Christ necessary to. Rom. 10: 10.

Regeneration necessary to. Jno. 3: 3.

Final perseverance necessary to. Mat. 10: 22.

DESCRIBED AS
- Great. Heb. 2: 3.
- Glorious. 2 Tim. 2: 10.
- Common. Jude 3.
- From generation to generation. Isa. 51: 8.
- To the uttermost. Heb. 7: 25.
- Eternal. Isa. 45: 17. Isa. 51: 6. Heb. 5: 9.

Searched into and exhibited by the prophets. 1 Pet. 1: 10,

The gospel is the power of God unto. Rom. 1: 16. 1 Cor. 1: 18.

Preaching the word is the appointed means of. 1 Cor. 1: 21.

The Scriptures are able to make wise unto. 2 Tim. 3: 15. Jas. 1: 21.

Now is the day of. Isa. 49: 8. 2 Cor. 6: 2.

From sin, to be worked out with fear and trembling. Phi. 2: 12.

SAINTS
- Chosen to. 2 The. 2: 13. 2 Tim. 1: 9.
- Appointed to obtain. 1 The. 5: 9.
- Are heirs of. Heb. 1: 14.
- Have, through grace. Acts 15: 11.
- Have a token of, in their patient suffering for Christ. Phi. 1: 28, 29.
- Kept by the power of God unto. 1 Pet. 1: 5.
- Beautified with. Psa. 149: 4.
- Clothed with. Isa. 61: 10.
- Satisfied by. Luke 2: 30.
- Love. Psa. 40: 16.
- Hope for. Lam. 3: 26. Rom. 8: 24.
- Wait for. Gen. 49: 18. Lam. 3: 26.
- Long for. Psa. 119: 81, 174.
- Earnestly look for. Psa. 119: 123.
- Daily approach nearer to. Rom. 13: 11.
- Receive, as the end of their faith. 1 Pet. 1: 9.
- Welcome the tidings of. Isa. 52: 7, with Rom. 10: 15.
- Pray to be visited with. Psa. 85: 7. Psa. 106: 4. Psa. 119: 41.
- Pray for assurance of. Psa. 35: 3.
- Pray for a joyful sense of. Psa. 51: 12.
- Evidence, by works. Heb. 6: 9, 10.
- Ascribe, to God. Psa. 25: 5. Isa. 12: 2.
- Praise God for. 1 Chr. 16: 23. Psa. 96: 2.
- Commemorate, with thanks. Psa. 116: 13.
- Rejoice in. Psa. 9: 14. Psa. 21: 1. Isa. 25: 9.
- Glory in. 1 Cor. 1: 31. Gal. 6: 14.
- Declare. Psa. 40: 10. Psa. 71: 15.

Godly sorrow worketh repentance unto. 2 Cor. 7: 10.

All the earth shall see. Isa. 52: 10. Luke 3: 6.

MINISTERS
- Give the knowledge of. Luke 1: 77.
- Show the way of. Acts 16: 17.
- Should exhort to. Eze. 3: 18, 19. Acts 2: 40.
- Should labor to lead others to. Rom. 11: 14.
- Should be clothed with. 2 Chr. 6: 41. Psa. 132: 16.
- Should use self-denial to lead others to. 1 Cor. 9: 22.
- Should endure suffering that the elect may obtain. 2 Tim. 2: 10.
- Are a sweet savor of Christ, unto God, in those who obtain. 2 Cor. 2: 15.

The heavenly host ascribe, to God. Rev. 7: 10. Rev. 19: 1.

SOUGHT IN VAIN FROM
- Idols. Isa. 45: 20. Jer. 2: 28.
- Earthly power. Jer. 3: 23.

No escape for those who neglect. Heb. 2: 3.

Is far off from the wicked. Psa. 119: 155. Isa. 59: 11.

ILLUSTRATED BY
- A rock. Deu. 32: 15. 2 Sam. 22: 47. Psa. 95: 1.
- A horn. Psa. 18: 2. Luke 1: 69.
- A tower. 2 Sam. 22: 51.
- A helmet. Isa. 59: 17. Eph. 6: 17.
- A shield. 2 Sam. 22: 36.
- A lamp. Isa. 62: 1.
- A cup. Psa. 116: 13.
- Clothing. 2 Chr. 6: 41. Psa. 132: 16. Psa. 149: 4. Isa. 61: 10.
- Wells. Isa. 12: 3.
- Walls and bulwarks. Isa. 26: 1. Isa. 60: 18.
- Chariots. Hab. 3: 8.
- A victory. 1 Cor. 15: 57.

Typified. Num. 21: 4—9, with Jno. 3: 14, 15.

Samaria, Ancient.

The territory of Ephraim and Manasseh properly so called. Jos. 17: 17, 18. Isa. 28: 1.

The whole kingdom of Israel sometimes called. Eze. 16: 46, 51. Hos. 8: 5, 6.

Had many cities. 1 Kin. 13: 32.

SAMARIA THE CAPITAL OF,
Built by Omri king of Israel. 1 Kin. 16: 23, 24.
Called after Shemer the owner of the hill on which it was built. 1 Kin. 16: 24.
Called the mountain of Samaria. Amos 4: 1. Amos 6: 1.
Called the head of Ephraim. Isa. 7: 9.
Kings of Israel sometimes took their titles from. 1 Kin. 21: 1. 2 Kin. 1: 3.
The residence of the kings of Israel. 1 Kin. 16: 29. 2 Kin. 1: 2. 2 Kin. 3: 1, 6.
The burial place of the kings of Israel. 1 Kin. 16: 28. 1 Kin. 22: 37. 2 Kin. 13: 13.
Was a fenced city, and well provided with arms. 2 Kin. 10: 2.
The pool of Samaria near to. 1 Kin. 22: 38.
The prophet Elisha dwelt in. 2 Kin. 2: 25. 2 Kin. 5: 3. 2 Kin. 6: 32.
Besieged by Benhadad. 1 Kin. 20: 1—12.
Deliverance of, predicted. 1 Kin. 20: 13, 14.
Deliverance of, effected. 1 Kin. 20: 15—21.
Besieged again by Benhadad. 2 Kin. 6: 24.
Suffered severely from famine. 2 Kin. 6: 25—29.
Elisha predicted plenty in. 2 Kin. 7: 1, 2.
Delivered by miraculous means. 2 Kin. 7: 6, 7.
Remarkable plenty in, as foretold by Elisha. 2 Kin. 7: 16—20.
Besieged and taken by Shalmaneser. 2 Kin. 17: 5, 6. 2 Kin. 18: 9, 10.
A mountainous country. Jer. 31: 5. Amos 3: 9.
PEOPLE OF, CHARACTERIZED AS
Proud and arrogant. Isa. 9: 9.
Corrupt and wicked. Eze. 16: 46, 47. Hos. 7: 1. Amos 3: 9, 10.
Idolatrous. Eze. 23: 5. Amos 8: 14. Mic. 1: 7.
Predictions respecting its destruction. Isa. 8: 4. Isa. 9: 11, 12. Hos. 13: 16. Amos 3: 11, 12. Mic. 1: 6.
Inhabitants of, carried captive to Assyria. 2 Kin. 17: 6, 23. 2 Kin. 18: 11.
Repeopled from Assyria. 2 Kin. 17: 24, 25.

Samaria, Modern.

Situated between Judea and Gali Luke 17: 11. Jno. 4: 3, 4.
Had many cities, &c. Mat. 10: 5. Luke 9: 52.
CITIES OF, MENTIONED IN SCRIPTURE;
Samaria. Acts 8: 5.
Sychar. Jno. 4: 5.
Antipatris. Acts 23: 31.
Christ preached in. Jno. 4: 39—42.
Christ at first forbade His disciples to visit. Mat. 10: 5.
Christ after His resurrection commanded the gospel to be preached in. Acts 1: 8.
INHABITANTS OF,
Their true descent. 2 Kin. 17: 24. Ezr. 4: 9, 10.
Boasted descent from Jacob. Jno. 4: 12.
Professed to worship God. Ezr. 4: 2.
Their religion mixed with idolatry 2 Kin. 17: 41, with Jno. 4: 22
Worshipped on Mount Gerizim. Jno. 4: 20.
Opposed the Jews after their return from captivity. Neh. 4: 1—18.
Expected the Messiah. Jno. 4: 25, 29.
Were superstitious. Acts 8: 9—11.
More humane and grateful than the Jews. Luke 10: 33—36. Luke 17: 16—18.
Abhorred by the Jews. Jno. 8: 48.
Had no intercourse or dealings with the Jews. Luke 9: 52, 53. Jno. 4: 9.
Ready to hear and embrace the gospel. Jno. 4: 39—42. Acts 8: 6—8.
The persecuted Christians fled to. Acts 8: 1.
The gospel first preached in, by Philip. Acts 8: 5.
Many Christian churches in. Acts 9: 31.

Sanctification.

Is separation to the service of God. Psa. 4: 3. 2 Cor. 6: 17.
EFFECTED BY
God. Eze. 37: 28. 1 The. 5: 23. Jude 1.
Christ. Heb. 2: 11. Heb. 13: 12.
The Holy Ghost. Rom. 15: 16. 1 Cor. 6: 11.
In Christ. 1 Cor. 1: 2.
Through the atonement of Christ. Heb. 10: 10. Heb. 13: 12.
Through the word of God. Jno. 17: 17, 19. Eph. 5: 26.
Christ made, of God, unto us. 1 Cor. 1: 30.
Saints elected to salvation through. 2 The. 2: 13. 1 Pet. 1: 2.
All saints are in a state of. Acts 20: 32. Acts 26: 18. 1 Cor. 6: 11.
The Church made glorious by. Eph. 5: 26, 27.

SHOULD LEAD TO
Mortification of sin. 1 The. 4: 3, 4.
Holiness. Rom. 6: 22. Eph. 5: 7—9.
Offering up of saints acceptable through. Rom. 15: 16.
Saints fitted for the service of God by. 2 Tim. 2: 21.
God wills all saints to have. 1 The. 4: 3.
MINISTERS
Set apart to God's service by. Jer. 1: 5.
Should pray that their people may enjoy complete. 1 The. 5: 23.
Should exhort their people to walk in. 1 The. 4: 1, 3.
None can inherit the kingdom of God without. 1 Cor. 6: 9—11.
Typified. Gen. 2: 3. Exo. 13: 2. Exo. 19: 14. Exo. 40: 9—15. Lev. 27: 14—16.

Scape-goat, The.

Part of the sin-offering on the day of atonement. Lev. 16: 5, 7.
Chosen by lot. Lev. 16: 8.
The high priest transferred the sins of Israel to, by confessing them with both hands upon its head. Lev. 16: 21.
Sent into the wilderness by the hands of a fit person. Lev. 16: 21, 22.
COMMUNICATED UNCLEANNESS TO
The high priest. Lev. 16: 24.
The man who led him away. Lev. 16: 26.
Typical of Christ. Isa. 53: 6, 11, 12.

Sciences.

Architecture. Deu. 8: 12. 1 Chr. 29: 19.
Arithmetic. Gen. 15: 5. Lev. 26: 8. Job 29: 18.
Astronomy. Job 38: 31, 32. Isa. 13: 10.
Astrology. Isa. 47: 13.
Botany. 1 Kin. 4: 33.
Geography. Gen. 10: 1—30. Isa. 11: 11.
History and Chronology. 1 Kin. 22: 39. 2 Kin. 1: 18. 1 Chr. 9: 1. 1 Chr. 29: 29.
Mechanics. Gen. 6: 14—16. Gen. 11: 4. Exo. 14: 6, 7.
Medicine. Jer. 8: 22. Mar. 5: 26.
Music. 1 Chr. 16: 4—7. 1 Chr. 25: 6.
Navigation. 1 Kin. 9: 27. Psa. 107: 23.
Surveying. Jos. 18: 4—9. Neh. 2: 12—16. Eze. 40: 5, 6. Zec. 2: 2.
Zoology. 1 Kin. 4: 33.

Scorning and Mocking.

The sufferings of Christ by, predicted. Psa. 22: 6—8. Isa. 53: 3. Luke 18: 32.
Christ endured. Mat. 9: 24. Mat. 27: 29.
SAINTS ENDURE, ON ACCOUNT OF
Being children of God. Gen. 21: 9, with Gal. 4: 29.
Their uprightness. Job 12: 4.
Their faith. Heb. 11: 36.
Their faithfulness in declaring the word of God. Jer. 20: 7, 8.
Their zeal for God's house. Neh. 2: 19.
THE WICKED INDULGE IN, AGAINST
The second coming of Christ. 2 Pet. 3: 3, 4.
The gifts of the Spirit. Acts 2: 13.
God's threatenings. Isa. 5: 19. Jer. 17: 15.
God's ministers. 2 Chr. 36: 16.
God's ordinances. Lam. 1: 7.
Saints. Psa. 123: 4. Lam. 3: 14, 63.
The resurrection of the dead. Acts 17: 32.
All solemn admonitions. 2 Chr. 30: 6—10.
Idolaters addicted to. Isa. 57: 3—6.
Drunkards addicted to. Psa. 69: 12. Hos. 7: 5.
THEY WHO ARE ADDICTED TO,
Delight in. Pro. 1: 22.
Are contentious. Pro. 22: 10.
Are scorned by God. Pro. 3: 34.
Are hated by men. Pro. 24: 9.
Are avoided by saints. Psa. 1: 1. Jer. 15: 17.
Walk after their own lusts. 2 Pet. 3: 3.
Are proud and haughty. Pro. 21: 24.
Hear not rebuke. Pro. 13: 1.
Love not those who reprove. Pro. 15: 12.
Hate those who reprove. Pro. 9: 8.
Go not to the wise. Pro. 15: 12.
Bring others into danger. Pro. 29: 8.
Shall themselves endure. Eze. 23: 32.
Characteristic of the latter days. 2 Pet. 3: 3. Jude 18.
Woe denounced against. Isa. 5: 18, 19.
Punishment for. 2 Chr. 36: 17. Pro. 19: 29. Isa. 29: 20. Lam. 3: 64—66.
Exemplified. *Ishmael*, Gen. 21: 9. *Children at Bethel*, 2 Kin. 2: 23. *Ephraim and Manasseh*, 2 Chr. 30: 10, *Chiefs of Judah*, 2 Chr. 36: 16. *Sanballat*, Neh. 4: 1. *Enemies of Job*, Job 30: 1, 9. *Enemies of David*, Psa. 35: 15, 16. *Rulers of Israel*, Isa. 28: 14. *Ammonites*, Eze. 25: 3. *Tyrians*, Eze. 26: 2. *Heathen*, Eze. 36: 2, 3. *Soldiers*, Mat. 27: 28—30. Luke 23: 36. *Chief Priests, &c.* Mat. 27: 41. *Pharisees*, Luke 16: 14. *The men who held Jesus*, Luke 22: 63, 64. *Herod, &c.* Luke 23: 11. *People and rulers*, Luke 23: 35. *Some of the multitude*, Acts 2: 13. *Athenians*, Acts 17: 32.

Scorpion, The.

Armed with a sharp sting in its tail. Rev. 9: 10.
Sting of, venomous and caused torment. Rev. 9: 5.

Abounded in the great desert. Deu. 8: 15.
Unfit for food. Luke 11: 12.
ILLUSTRATIVE OF,
 Wicked men. Eze. 2: 6.
 Ministers of Antichrist. Rev. 9: 3, 5, 10.
 Severe scourges. 1 Kin. 12: 11.
Christ gave His disciples power over. Luke 10: 19.

Scribes.

Antiquity of. Jud. 5: 14.
Wore an inkhorn at their girdles. Eze. 9: 2, 3.
FAMILIES CELEBRATED FOR FURNISHING;
 Kenites. 1 Chr. 2: 55.
 Zebulun. Jud. 5: 14.
 Levi. 1 Chr. 24: 6. 2 Chr. 34: 13.
Generally men of great wisdom. 1 Chr. 27: 32.
Often learned in the law. Ezr. 7: 6.
Were ready writers. Psa. 45: 1.
ACTED AS
 Secretaries to kings. 2 Sam. 8: 17. 2 Sam. 20: 25. 2 Kin. 12: 10. Est. 3: 12.
 Secretaries to prophets. Jer. 36: 4, 26.
 Notaries in courts of justice. Jer. 32: 11, 12.
 Religious teachers. Neh. 8: 2—6.
 Writers of public documents. 1 Chr. 24: 6.
 Keepers of the muster-rolls of the host. 2 Kin. 25: 19. 2 Chr. 26: 11. Jer. 52: 25.
MODERN,
 Were doctors of the law. Mar. 12: 28, with Mat. 22: 35.
 Wore long robes and loved pre-eminence. Mar. 12: 38, 39.
 Sat in Moses' seat. Mat. 23: 2.
 Were frequently Pharisees. Acts 23: 9.
 Esteemed wise and learned. 1 Cor. 1: 20.
 Regarded as interpreters of Scripture. Mat. 2: 4. Mat. 17: 10. Mar. 12: 35.
 Their manner of teaching contrasted with that of Christ. Mat. 7: 29. Mar. 1: 22.
 Condemned by Christ for hypocrisy. Mat. 23: 15.
 Often offended at our Lord's conduct and teaching. Mat. 21: 15. Mar. 2: 6, 7, 16. Mar. 3: 22.
 Tempted our Lord. Jno. 8: 3.
 Active in procuring our Lord's death. Mat. 26: 3. Luke 23: 10.
 Persecuted the early Christians. Acts 4: 5, 18, 21. Acts 6: 12.
Illustrative of well-instructed ministers of the gospel. Mat. 13: 52.

Scriptures, The.

Given by inspiration of God. 2 Tim. 3: 16.
Given by inspiration of the Holy Ghost. Acts 1: 16. Heb. 3: 7. 2 Pet. 1: 21.
Christ sanctioned, by appealing to them. Mat. 4: 4. Mar. 12: 10. Jno. 7: 42.
Christ taught out of. Luke 24: 27.
ARE CALLED THE
 Word. Jas. 1: 21—23. 1 Pet. 2: 2.
 Word of God. Luke 11: 28. Heb. 4: 12.
 Word of Christ. Col. 3: 16.
 Word of truth. Jas. 1: 18.
 Holy Scriptures. Rom. 1: 2. 2 Tim. 3: 15.
 Scripture of truth. Dan. 10: 21.
 Book. Psa. 40: 7. Rev. 22: 19.
 Book of the Lord. Isa. 34: 16.
 Book of the law. Neh. 8: 3. Gal. 3: 10.
 Law of the Lord. Psa. 1: 2. Isa. 30: 9.
 Sword of the Spirit. Eph. 6: 17.
 Oracles of God. Rom. 3: 2. 1 Pet. 4: 11.
Contain the promises of the gospel. Rom. 1: 2.
Reveal the laws, statutes, and judgments of God. Deu. 4: 5, 14, with Exo. 24: 3, 4.
Record divine prophecies. 2 Pet. 1: 19—21.
Testify of Christ. Jno. 5: 39. Acts 10: 43. Acts 18: 28. 1 Cor. 15: 3.
Are full and sufficient. Luke 16: 29, 31.
Are an unerring guide. Pro. 6: 23. 2 Pet. 1: 19.
Are able to make wise unto salvation through faith in Christ Jesus. 2 Tim. 3: 15.
Are profitable both for doctrine and practice. 2 Tim. 3: 16, 17.
DESCRIBED AS
 Pure. Psa. 12: 6. Psa. 119: 140. Pro. 30: 5.
 True. Psa. 119: 160. Jno. 17: 17.
 Perfect. Psa. 19: 7.
 Precious. Psa. 19: 10.
 Quick and powerful. Heb. 4: 12.
Written for our instruction. Rom. 15: 4.
Intended for the use of all men. Rom. 16: 26.
Nothing to be taken from, or added to. Deu. 4: 2. Deu. 12: 32.
One portion of, to be compared with another. 1 Cor. 2: 13.
DESIGNED FOR
 Regenerating. Jas. 1: 18. 1 Pet. 1: 23.
 Quickening. Psa. 119: 50, 93.
 Illuminating. Psa. 119: 130.

Converting the soul. Psa. 19: 7.
Making wise the simple. Psa. 19: 7.
Sanctifying. Jno. 17: 17. Eph. 5: 26.
Producing faith. Jno. 20: 31.
Producing hope. Psa. 119: 49. Rom. 15: 4.
Producing obedience. Deu. 17: 19, 20.
Cleansing the heart. Jno. 15: 3. Eph. 5: 26.
Cleansing the ways. Psa. 119: 9.
Keeping from destructive paths. Psa. 17: 4.
Supporting life. Deu. 8: 3, with Mat. 4: 4.
Promoting growth in grace. 1 Pet. 2: 2.
Building up in the faith. Acts 20: 32.
Admonishing. Psa. 19: 11. 1 Cor. 10: 11.
Comforting. Psa. 119: 82. Rom. 15: 4.
Rejoicing the heart. Psa. 19: 8. Psa. 119: 111.

Work effectually in them that believe. 1 The. 2: 13.
The letter of, without the spirit, killeth. Jno. 6: 63, with 2 Cor. 3: 6.
Ignorance of, a source of error. Mat. 22: 29. Acts 13: 27.
Christ enables us to understand. Luke 24: 45.
The Holy Ghost enables us to understand. Jno. 16: 13. 1 Cor. 2: 10—14.
No prophecy of, is of any private interpretation. 2 Pet. 1: 20.
Everything should be tried by. Isa. 8: 20. Acts 17: 11.

SHOULD BE

The standard of teaching. 1 Pet. 4: 11.
Believed. Jno. 2: 22.
Appealed to. 1 Cor. 1: 31. 1 Pet. 1: 16.
Read. Deu. 17: 19. Isa. 34: 16.
Read publicly to ALL. Deu. 31: 11—13. Neh. 8: 3. Jer. 36: 6. Acts 13: 15.
Known. 2 Tim. 3: 15.
Received, not as the word of men, but as the word of God. 1 The. 2: 13.
Received with meekness. Jas. 1: 21.
Searched. Jno. 5: 39. Jno. 7: 52.
Searched daily. Acts 17: 11.
Laid up in the heart. Deu. 6: 6. Deu. 11: 18.
Taught to children. Deu. 6: 7. Deu. 11: 19. 2 Tim. 3: 15.
Taught to ALL. 2 Chr. 17: 7—9. Neh. 8: 7, 8.
Talked of continually. Deu. 6: 7.
Not handled deceitfully. 2 Cor. 4: 2.
Not only heard, but obeyed. Mat. 7: 24, with Luke 11: 28. Jas. 1: 22.
Used against our spiritual enemies. Mat. 4: 4, 7, 10, with Eph. 6: 11, 17.

All should desire to hear. Neh. 8: 1.
Mere hearers of, deceive themselves. Jas. 1: 22.
Advantage of possessing. Rom. 3: 2.

SAINTS

Love exceedingly. Psa. 119: 97, 113, 159, 167.
Delight in. Psa. 1: 2.
Regard, as sweet. Psa. 119: 103.
Esteem, above all things. Job 23: 12.
Long after. Psa. 119: 82.
Stand in awe of. Psa. 119: 161. Isa. 66: 2.
Keep, in remembrance. Psa. 119: 16.
Grieve when men disobey. Psa. 119: 158.
Hide, in their hearts. Psa. 119: 11.
Hope in. Psa. 119: 74, 81, 147.
Meditate in. Psa. 1: 2. Psa. 119: 99, 148.
Rejoice in. Psa. 119: 162. Jer. 15: 16.
Trust in. Psa. 119: 42.
Obey. Psa. 119: 67. Luke 8: 21. Jno. 17: 6.
Speak of. Psa. 119: 172.
Esteem, as a light. Psa. 119: 105.
Pray to be taught. Psa. 119: 12, 18, 33, 66.
Pray to be conformed to. Psa. 119: 133.
Plead the promises of, in prayer. Psa. 119: 25, 28, 41, 76, 169.

They who search, are truly noble. Acts 17: 11.
Blessedness of hearing and obeying. Luke 11: 28. Jas. 1: 25.
Let them dwell richly in you. Col. 3: 16.

THE WICKED

Corrupt. 2 Cor. 2: 17.
Make, of none effect through their traditions. Mar. 7: 9—13.
Reject. Jer. 8: 9.
Stumble at. 1 Pet. 2: 8.
Obey not. Psa. 119: 158.
Frequently wrest, to their own destruction. 2 Pet. 3: 16.

Denunciations against those who add to, or take from. Rev. 22: 18, 19.
Destruction of, punished. Jer. 36: 29—31.

Sea, The.

The gathering together of the waters originally called. Gen. 1: 10.
Great rivers often called. Isa. 11: 15. Jer. 51: 36.
Lakes often called. Deu. 3: 17. Mat. 8: 24, 27, 32.

GOD

Created. Exo. 20: 11. Psa. 95: 5. Acts 14: 15.

Made the birds and fishes out of. Gen. 1: 20—22.
Founded the earth upon. Psa. 24: 2.
Set bounds to, by a perpetual decree. Job 26: 10. Job 38: 8, 10, 11. Pro. 8: 27, 29.
Measures the waters of. Isa. 40: 12.
Does what He pleases in. Psa. 135: 6.
Dries up, by His rebuke. Isa. 50: 2. Nah. 1: 4.
Shakes, by His word. Hag. 2: 6.
Stills, by His power. Psa. 65: 7. Psa. 89: 9. Psa. 107: 29.

Of immense extent. Job 11: 9. Psa. 104: 25.
Of great depth. Psa. 68: 22.
Rivers supplied by exhalations from. Ecc. 1: 7.
Replenished by rivers. Ecc. 1: 7. Eze. 47: 8.

CALLED THE

Deep. Job 41: 31. Psa. 107: 24. 2 Cor. 11: 25.
Great waters. Psa. 77: 19.
Great and wide sea. Psa. 104: 25.

The clouds the garment of. Job 38: 9.
Darkness the swaddling band of. Job 38: 9.
Sand the barrier of. Jer. 5: 22.
Inhabited by innumerable creatures great and small. Psa. 104: 25, 26.
The wonders of God seen in. Psa. 107: 24.
Made to glorify God. Psa. 69: 34. Psa. 148: 7.

SEAS MENTIONED IN SCRIPTURE;

The Adriatic or sea of Adria. Acts 27: 27.
Mediterranean or great sea. Num. 34: 6. Deu. 11: 24. Deu. 34: 2. Zec. 14: 8.
Red Sea. Exo. 10: 19. Exo. 13: 18. Exo. 23: 31.
Sea of Joppa or sea of the Philistines. Ezr. 3: 7, with Exo. 23: 31.
Salt or Dead Sea. Gen. 14: 3. Num. 34: 12.
Sea of Galilee. Mat. 4: 18. Mat. 8: 32. Jno. 6: 1.
Sea of Jazer. Jer. 48: 32.

Raised by the wind. Psa. 107: 25, 26. Jon. 1: 4.
Caused to foam by Leviathan. Job 41: 31, 32.

THE WAVES OF,

Raised upon high. Psa. 93: 3. Psa. 107: 25.
Tossed to and fro. Jer. 5: 22.
Multitudinous. Jer. 51: 42.
Mighty. Psa. 93: 4. Acts 27: 41.
Tumultuous. Luke 21: 25. Jude 13 v.

The shore of, covered with sand. Gen. 22: 17. 1 Kin. 4: 29. Job 6: 3. Psa. 78: 27.
Numerous islands in. Eze. 26: 18.
Passed over in ships. Psa. 104: 26. Psa. 107: 23.
Sailing on, dangerous. Acts 27: 9, 20. 2 Cor. 11: 26.

COMMERCIAL NATIONS

Often built cities on the borders of. Gen. 49: 13. Eze. 27: 3. Nah. 3: 8.
Derived great wealth from. Deu. 33: 19.

Shall give up its dead at the last day. Rev. 20: 13.
The renewed earth shall be without. Rev. 21: 1.

ILLUSTRATIVE

Of heavy afflictions. Isa. 43: 2. Lam. 2: 13.
(Troubled,) of the wicked. Isa. 57: 20.
(Roaring,) of hostile armies. Isa. 5: 30. Jer. 6: 23.
(Waves of,) of righteousness. Isa. 48: 18.
(Waves of,) of devastating armies. Eze. 26: 3, 4.
(Waves of,) of the unsteady. Jas. 1: 6.
(Covered with waters,) of the diffusion of spiritual knowledge over the earth in the latter days. Isa. 11: 9. Hab. 2: 14.
(Smooth as glass,) of the peace of heaven. Rev. 4: 6. Rev. 15: 2.

Sealing of the Holy Ghost.

Christ received. Jno. 6: 27.
Saints receive. 2 Cor. 1: 22. Eph. 1: 13.
Is unto the day of redemption. Eph. 4: 30.
The wicked do not receive. Rev. 9: 4.
Judgment suspended until all saints receive. Rev. 7: 3.
Typified. Rom. 4: 11.

Seals.

Called signets. Gen. 38: 18, 25.
Precious stones set in gold used as. Exo. 28: 11.
Inscriptions upon, alluded to. 2 Tim. 2: 19.
Generally worn as rings or bracelets. Jer. 22: 24.

IMPRESSIONS OF,

Frequently taken in clay. Job 38: 14.
Used for security. Dan. 6: 17. Mat. 27: 66.
Attached to all royal decrees. 1 Kin. 21: 8. Est. 3: 12. Est. 8: 8.
Attached to covenants. Neh. 9: 38. Neh. 10: 1.
Attached to leases and transfers of property. Jer. 32: 9 12, 44.
Set upon treasures. Deu. 32: 34.

Attached to the victims approved for sacrifice, alluded to. Jno. 6: 27.
Were given by kings as a badge of authority. Gen. 41: 41, 42.

ILLUSTRATIVE OF
Circumcision. Rom. 4: 11.
Converts. 1 Cor. 9: 2.
What is dear or valued. So. of Sol. 8: 6. Jer. 22: 24. Hag. 2: 23.
Secrecy Dan. 12: 4. Rev. 5: 1. Rev. 10: 4.
Security. So. of Sol. 4: 12. 2 Tim. 2: 19. Rev. 7: 2—8. Rev. 20: 3.
Full approval. Jno. 3: 33.
Appropriation of saints to God by the Spirit. 2 Cor. 1: 22. Eph. 1: 13. Eph. 4: 30.
Restraint. Job 9: 7. Job 37: 7. Rev. 20: 3.

Second Coming of Christ, The.

Time of, unknown. Mat. 24: 36. Mar. 13: 32.

CALLED THE
Times of refreshing from the presence of the Lord. Acts 3: 19.
Times of restitution of all things. Acts 3: 21, with Rom. 8: 21.
Last time. 1 Pet. 1: 5.
Appearing of Jesus Christ. 1 Pet. 1: 7.
Revelation of Jesus Christ. 1 Pet. 1: 13.
Glorious appearing of the great God and our Saviour. Tit. 2: 13.
Coming of the day of God. 2 Pet. 3: 12.
Day of our Lord Jesus Christ. 1 Cor. 1: 8.

FORETOLD BY
Prophets. Dan. 7: 13. Jude 14.
Himself. Mat. 25: 31. Jno. 14: 3.
Apostles. Acts 3: 20. 1 Tim. 6: 14.
Angels. Acts 1: 10, 11.

Signs preceding. Mat. 24: 3, &c.

THE MANNER OF;
In clouds. Mat. 24: 30. Mat. 26: 64. Rev. 1: 7.
In the glory of His Father. Mal. 16: 27.
In His own glory. Mat. 25: 31.
In flaming fire. 2 The. 1: 8.
With power and great glory. Mat. 24: 30.
As He ascended. Acts 1: 9, 11.
With a shout and the voice of the Archangel, &c. 1 The. 4: 16.
Accompanied by Angels. Mat. 16: 27. Mat. 25: 31. Mar. 8: 38. 2 The. 1: 7.
With His saints. 1 The. 3: 13. Jude 14.
Suddenly. Mar. 13: 36.
Unexpectedly. Mat. 24: 44. Luke 12: 40.
As a thief in the night. 1 The. 5: 2. 2 Pet. 3: 10. Rev. 16: 15.
As the lightning. Mat. 24: 27.

The heavens and earth shall be dissolved, &c. at. 2 Pet. 3: 10, 12.
They who shall have died in Christ shall rise first at. 1 The. 4: 16.
The saints alive at, shall be caught up to meet Him. 1 The. 4: 17.
Is not to make atonement. Heb. 9 28, with Rom. 6: 9, 10, and Heb. 10 14.

THE PURPOSES OF, ARE TO
Complete the salvation of saints. Heb. 9: 28. 1 Pet. 1: 5.
Be glorified in His saints. 2 The. 1: 10.
Be admired in them that believe. 2 The. 1: 10.
Bring to light the hidden things of darkness, &c. 1 Cor. 4: 5.
Judge. Psa. 50: 3, 4, with Jno. 5: 22. 2 Tim. 4: 1. Jude 15. Rev. 20: 11—13.
Reign. Isa. 24: 23. Dan. 7: 14. Rev. 11: 15.
Destroy death. 1 Cor. 15: 25, 26.

Every eye shall see Him at. Rev. 1: 7.
Should be always considered as at hand. Rom. 13: 12. Phi. 4: 5. 1 Pet. 4: 7.
Blessedness of being prepared for. Mat. 24: 46. Luke 12: 37, 38.

SAINTS
Assured of. Job 19: 25, 26.
Love. 2 Tim. 4: 8.
Look for. Phi. 3: 20. Tit. 2: 13.
Wait for. 1 Cor. 1: 7. 1 The. 1: 10.
Haste unto. 2 Pet. 3: 12.
Pray for. Rev. 22: 20.
Should be ready for. Mat. 24: 44. Luke 12: 40.
Should watch for. Mat. 24: 42. Mar. 13: 35—37. Luke 21: 36.
Should be patient unto. 2 The. 3: 5. Jas. 5: 7, 8.

Shall be preserved unto. Phi. 1: 6. 2 Tim. 4: 18. 1 Pet. 1: 5. Jude 24.
Shall not be ashamed at. 1 Jno. 2: 28 1 Jno. 4: 17.
Shall be blameless at. 1 Cor. 1: 8. 1 The. 3: 13. 1 The. 5: 23. Jude 24.
Shall be like Him at. Phi. 3: 21. 1 Jno. 3: 2.
Shall see Him as He is, at. 1 Jno. 3: 2.
Shall appear with Him in glory at. Col. 3: 4.
Shall receive a crown of glory at. 2 Tim. 4: 8. 1 Pet. 5: 4.
Shall reign with Him at. Dan. 7: 27. 2 Tim. 2: 12. Rev. 5: 10. Rev. 20: 6. Rev. 22: 5.
Faith of, shall be found unto praise at. 1 Pet. 1: 7.

THE WICKED
Scoff at. 2 Pet. 3: 3, 4.

Presume upon the delay of. Mat. 24: 48.
Shall be surprised by. Mat. 24: 37—39. 1 The. 5: 3. 2 Pet. 3: 10.
Shall be punished at. 2 The. 1: 8, 9.
The man of sin to be destroyed at. 2 The. 2: 8.
Illustrated. Mat. 25: 6. Luke 12: 36, 39. Luke 19: 12, 15.

Seed.

Every herb, tree and grass yields its own. Gen. 1; 11, 12, 29.
Each kind of, has its own body. 1 Cor. 15: 38.
SOWING OF,
Time for, called seed-time. Gen. 8: 22.
Necessary to its productiveness. Jno. 12: 24. 1 Cor. 15: 36.
Required constant diligence. Ecc. 11: 4, 6.
Often attended with great waste. Mat. 13: 4, 5, 7.
Often attended with danger. Psa. 126: 5, 6.
Yearly return of time of sowing, secured by covenant. Gen. 8: 21, 22.
The ground carefully plowed, and prepared for. Isa. 28: 24, 25.
Often sown beside rivers. Ecc. 11: 1. Isa. 32: 20.
Often trodden into the ground, by the feet of oxen, &c. Isa. 32: 20.
Required to be watered by the rain. Isa. 55: 10.
In Egypt required to be artificially watered. Deu. 11: 10.
Yielded an abundant increase in Canaan. Gen. 26: 12. *See* Mat. 13: 23.
MOSAIC LAWS RESPECTING;
Different kinds of, not to be sown in the same field. Lev. 19: 19. Deu. 22: 9.
If dry, exempted from uncleanness though touched by an unclean thing. Lev. 11: 37.
If wet, rendered unclean by contact with an unclean thing. Lev. 11: 38.
The tithe of, to be given to God. Lev. 27: 30.
Not to be sown during the sabbatical year. Lev. 25: 4, 20.
Not to be sown in year of jubilee. Lev. 25: 11.
Difference between, and the plant which grows from it, noticed. 1 Cor. 15: 37, 38.
THE JEWS PUNISHED BY
Its rotting in the ground. Joel 1: 17. Mal. 2: 3.
Its yielding but little increase. Isa. 5: 10. Hag. 1: 6.
Its increase being consumed by locusts, &c. Deu. 28: 38. Joel 1: 4.
Its increase being consumed by enemies. Lev. 26: 16. Deu. 28: 33, 51.
Its being choked by thorns. Jer. 12: 13, with Mat. 13: 7.
ILLUSTRATIVE OF
The word of God. Luke 8: 11. 1 Pet. 1: 23.
Spiritual life. 1 Jno. 3: 9.
SOWING, ILLUSTRATIVE OF
Preaching the gospel. Mat. 13: 3, 32. 1 Cor. 9: 11.
Scattering or dispersing a people. Zec. 10: 9.
Christian liberality. Ecc. 11: 6. 2 Cor. 9: 6.
Men's works producing a corresponding recompense. Job 4: 8. Hos. 10: 12. Gal. 6: 7, 8.
The death of Christ and its effects. Jno. 12: 24.
The burial of the body. 1 Cor. 15: 36—38.

Seeking God.

Commanded. Isa. 55: 6. Mat. 7: 7.
INCLUDES SEEKING
His name. Psa. 83: 16.
His word. Isa. 34: 16.
His face. Psa. 27: 8. Psa. 105: 4.
His strength. 1 Chr. 16: 11. Psa. 105: 4.
His commandments. 1 Chr. 28: 8. Mal. 2: 7.
His precepts. Psa. 119: 45, 94.
His kingdom. Mat. 6: 33. Luke 12: 31.
His righteousness. Mat. 6: 33.
Christ. Mal. 3: 1. Luke 2: 15, 16.
Honor which comes from Him. Jno. 5: 44.
Justification by Christ. Gal. 2: 16, 17.
The city which God has prepared. Heb. 11: 10, 16. Heb. 13: 14.
By prayer. Job 8: 5. Dan. 9: 3.
In His house. Deu. 12: 5. Psa. 27: 4.
SHOULD BE
Immediate. Hos. 10: 12.
Evermore. Psa. 105: 4.
While He may be found. Isa. 55: 6.
With diligence. Heb. 11: 6.
With the heart. Deu. 4: 29. 1 Chr. 22: 19.
In the day of trouble. Psa. 77: 2.
ENSURES
His being found. Deu. 4: 29. 1 Chr. 28: 9. Pro. 8: 17. Jer. 29: 13.
His favor. Lam. 3: 25.
His protection. Ezr. 8: 22.
His not forsaking us. Psa. 9: 10.
Life. Psa. 69: 32. Amos 5: 4, 6.
Prosperity. Job 8: 5, 6. Psa. 34: 10.
Being heard of Him. Psa. 34: 4.
Understanding all things. Pro. 28: 5.

Gifts of righteousness. Hos. 10: 12.
Imperative upon all. Isa. 8: 19.
Afflictions designed to lead to. Psa. 78: 33, 34. Hos. 5: 15.
None, by nature, are found to be engaged in. Psa. 14: 2, with Rom. 3: 11. Luke 12: 23, 30.
SAINTS
Specially exhorted to. Zep. 2: 3.
Desirous of. Job 5: 8.
Purpose, in heart. Psa. 27: 8.
Prepare their hearts for. 2 Chr. 30: 19.
Set their hearts to. 2 Chr. 11: 16.
Engage in, with the whole heart. 2 Chr. 15: 12. Psa. 119: 10.
Early in. Job 8: 5. Psa. 63: 1. Isa. 26: 9.
Earnest in. So. of Sol. 3: 2, 4.
Characterized by. Psa. 24: 6.
Is never in vain. Isa. 45: 19.
Blessedness of. Psa. 119: 2.
Leads to joy. Psa. 70: 4. Psa. 105: 3.
Ends in praise. Psa. 22: 26.
Promise connected with. Psa. 69: 32.
Shall be rewarded. Heb. 11: 6.
THE WICKED
Are gone out of the way of. Psa. 14: 2, 3, with Rom. 3: 11, 12.
Prepare not their hearts for. 2 Chr. 12: 14.
Refuse, through pride. Psa. 10: 4.
Not led to, by affliction. Isa. 9: 13.
Sometimes pretend to. Ezr. 4: 2. Isa. 58: 2.
Rejected, when too late in. Pro. 1: 28.
They who neglect denounced. Isa. 31: 1.
Punishment of those who neglect. Zep. 1: 4—6.
Exemplified. *Asa*, 2 Chr. 14: 7. *Jehoshaphat*, 2 Chr. 17: 3, 4. *Uzziah*, 2 Chr. 26: 5. *Hezekiah*, 2 Chr. 31: 21. *Josiah*, 2 Chr. 34: 3. *Ezra*, Ezr. 7: 10. *David*, Psa, 34: 4. *Daniel*, Dan. 9: 3, 4.

Self-delusion.

A characteristic of the wicked. Psa. 49: 18.
Prosperity frequently leads to. Psa. 30: 6. Hos. 12: 8. Luke 12: 17—19.
Obstinate sinners often given up to. Psa. 81: 11, 12. Hos. 4: 17. 2 The. 2: 10, 11.
EXHIBITED IN THINKING THAT
Our own ways are right. Pro. 14: 12.
We should adhere to established wicked practices. Jer. 44: 17.
We are pure. Pro. 30: 12.
We are better than others. Luke 18: 11.
We are rich in spiritual things. Rev. 3: 17.
We may have peace while in sin. Deu. 29: 19.
We are above adversity. Psa. 10: 6.
Gifts entitle us to heaven. Mat. 7: 21, 22.
Privileges entitle us to heaven. Mat. 3: 9. Luke 13: 25, 26.
God will not punish our sins. Psa. 10: 11. Jer. 5: 12.
Christ shall not come to judge. 2 Pet. 3: 4.
Our lives shall be prolonged. Isa 56: 12. Luke 12: 19. Jas. 4: 13.
Frequently persevered in, to the last. Mat. 7: 22. Mat. 25: 11, 12. Luke 13: 24, 25.
Fatal consequences of. Mat. 7: 23. Mat. 24: 48—51. Luke 12: 20. 1 The. 5: 3.
Exemplified. *Ahab*, 1 Kin. 20: 27, 34. *Israelites*, Hos. 12: 8. *Jews*, Jno. 8: 33, 41. *Church of Laodicea*, Rev. 3: 17. *Babylon*, Isa. 47: 7—11.

Self-denial.

Christ set an example of. Mat. 4: 8—10. Mat. 8: 20. Jno. 6: 38. Rom. 15: 3. Phi. 2: 6—8.
A test of devotedness to Christ. Mat. 10: 37, 38. Luke 9: 23, 24.
NECESSARY
In following Christ. Luke 14: 27—33.
In the warfare of saints. 2 Tim. 2: 4.
To the triumph of saints. 1 Cor. 9: 25—27.
Ministers especially called to exercise. 2 Cor. 6: 4, 5.
SHOULD BE EXERCISED IN
Denying ungodliness and worldly lusts. Rom. 6: 12. Tit. 2: 12.
Controlling the appetite. Pro. 23: 2.
Abstaining from fleshly lusts. 1 Pet. 2: 11.
No longer living to lusts of men. 1 Pet. 4: 2.
Mortifying sinful lusts. Mar. 9: 43. Col. 3: 5.
Mortifying deeds of the body. Rom. 8: 13.
Not pleasing ourselves. Rom. 15: 1—3.
Not seeking our own profit. 1 Cor. 10: 24, 33. 1 Cor. 13: 5. Phi. 2: 4.
Preferring the profit of others. Rom. 14: 20, 21. 1 Cor. 10: 24, 33.
Assisting others. Luke 3: 11.
Even lawful things. 1 Cor. 10: 23.
Forsaking all. Luke 14: 33.
Taking up the cross and following Christ. Mat. 10: 38. Mat. 16: 24.
Crucifying the flesh. Gal. 5: 24.
Being crucified with Christ. Rom. 6: 6.
Being crucified unto the world. Gal. 6: 14.

Putting off the old man which is corrupt. Eph. 4: 22. Col. 3: 9.
Preferring Christ to all earthly relations. Mat. 8: 21, 22. Luke 14: 26.
Becomes strangers and pilgrims. Heb. 11: 13—15. 1 Pet. 2: 11.
Danger of neglecting. Mat. 16: 25, 26. 1 Cor. 9: 27.
Reward of. Mat. 19: 28, 29. Rom. 8: 13.
Happy result of. 2 Pet. 1: 4.
Exemplified. *Abraham*, Gen. 13: 9. Heb. 11: 8, 9. *Widow of Zarephath*, 1 Kin. 17: 12—15. *Esther*, Est. 4: 16. *Rechabites*, Jer. 35: 6, 7. *Daniel*, Dan. 1: 8—16. *Apostles*, Mat. 19: 27. *Simon, Andrew, James and John*, Mar. 1: 16—20. *Poor Widow*, Luke 21: 4. *Primitive Christians*, Acts 2: 45. Acts 4: 34. *Barnabas*, Acts 4: 36, 37. *Paul*, Acts 20: 24. 1 Cor. 9: 19, 27. *Moses*, Heb. 11: 24, 25.

Self-examination.

Enjoined. 2 Cor. 13: 5.
Necessary before the communion. 1 Cor. 11: 28.
Cause of difficulty in. Jer. 17: 9.
SHOULD BE ENGAGED IN
With holy awe. Psa. 4: 4.
With diligent search. Psa. 77: 6. Lam. 3: 40.
With prayer for divine searching. Psa. 26: 2. Psa. 139: 23, 24.
With purpose of amendment. Psa. 119: 59. Lam. 3: 40.
Advantages of. 1 Cor. 11: 31. Gal. 6: 4. 1 Jno. 3: 20—22.

Selfishness.

Contrary to the law of God. Lev. 19: 18. Mat. 22: 39. Jas. 2: 8.
The example of Christ condemns. Jno. 4: 34. Rom. 15: 3. 2 Cor. 8: 9.
God hates. Mal. 1: 10.
EXHIBITED IN
Being lovers of ourselves. 2 Tim. 3: 2.
Pleasing ourselves. Rom. 15: 1.
Seeking our own. 1 Cor. 10: 33. Phi. 2: 21.
Seeking after gain. Isa. 56: 11.
Seeking undue precedence. Mat. 20: 21.
Living to ourselves. 2 Cor. 5: 15.
Neglect of the poor. 1 Jno. 3: 17.
Serving God for reward. Mal. 1: 10.
Performing duty for reward. Mic. 3: 11.
Inconsistent with Christian love. 1 Cor. 13: 5.
Inconsistent with the communion of saints. Rom. 12: 4, 5, with 1 Cor. 12: 12—27.
Especially forbidden to saints. 1 Cor. 10: 24. Phi. 2: 4.
The love of Christ should constrain us to avoid. 2 Cor. 5: 14, 15.
Ministers should be devoid of. 1 Cor. 9: 19—23. 1 Cor. 10: 33.
All men addicted to. Eph. 2: 3. Phi. 2: 21.
Saints falsely accused of. Job 1: 9—11.
Characteristic of the last days. 2 Tim. 3: 1, 2.
Exemplified. *Cain*, Gen. 4: 9. *Nabal*, 1 Sam. 25: 3, 11. *Haman*, Est. 6: 6. *Priests*, Isa. 56: 11. *Jews*, Zec. 7: 6. *James and John*, Mar. 10: 37. *Multitude*, Jno. 6: 26.

Self-righteousness.

Man is prone to. Pro. 20: 6. Pro. 30: 12.
Hateful to God. Luke 16: 15.
IS VAIN BECAUSE OUR RIGHTEOUSNESS IS
But external. Mat. 23: 25—28. Luke 11: 39—44.
But partial. Mat. 23: 25. Luke 11: 42.
No better than filthy rags. Isa. 64: 6.
Ineffectual for salvation. Job 9: 30, 31. Mat. 5: 20, with Rom. 3: 20.
Unprofitable. Isa. 57: 12.
Is boastful. Mat. 23: 30.
THEY WHO ARE GIVEN TO
Audaciously approach God. Luke 18: 11.
Seek to justify themselves. Luke 10: 29.
Seek to justify themselves before men. Luke 16: 15.
Reject the righteousness of God. Rom. 10: 3.
Condemn others. Mat. 9: 11—13. Luke 7: 39.
Consider their own way right. Pro. 21: 2.
Despise others. Isa. 65: 5. Luke 18: 9.
Proclaim their own goodness. Pro. 20: 6.
Are pure in their own eyes. Pro. 30: 12.
Are abominable before God. Isa. 65: 5.
Folly of. Job 9: 20.
Saints renounce. Phi. 3: 7—10.
Warning against. Deu. 9: 4.
Denunciation against. Mat. 23: 27, 28.
Illustrated. Luke 18: 10—12.
Exemplified. *Saul*, 1 Sam. 15: 13. *Young man*, Mat. 19, 20. *Lawyer*, Luke 10: 25, 29. *Pharisees*, Luke 11: 39. Jno. 8: 33. Jno. 9: 28. *Israel*, Rom. 10: 3. *Church of Laodicea*, Rev. 3: 17.

Self-will and Stubbornness.

Forbidden. 2 Chr. 30: 8. Psa. 75: 5. Psa. 95: 8.

PROCEED FROM
 Unbelief. 2 Kin. 17:14.
 Pride. Neh. 9:16, 29.
 An evil heart. Jer. 7:24.
God knows. Isa. 48:4.
EXHIBITED IN
 Refusing to hearken to God. Pro. 1:24.
 Refusing to hearken to the messengers of God. 1 Sam. 8:19. Jer. 44:16. Zec. 7:11.
 Refusing to walk in the ways of God. Neh. 9:17. Psa. 78:10. Isa. 42:24. Jer. 6:16.
 Refusing to hearken to parents. Deu. 21:18, 19.
 Refusing to receive correction. Deu. 21:18. Jer. 5:3. Jer. 7:28.
 Rebelling against God. Deu. 31:27. Psa. 78:8.
 Resisting the Holy Ghost. Acts 7:51.
 Walking in the counsels of an evil heart. Jer. 7:24, with Jer. 23:17.
 Hardening the neck. Neh. 9:16.
 Hardening the heart. 2 Chr. 36:13.
 Going backward and not forward. Jer. 7:24.
Heinousness of. 1 Sam. 15:23.
MINISTERS SHOULD
 Be without. Tit. 1:7.
 Warn their people against. Heb. 3:7—12.
 Pray that their people may be forgiven for. Exo. 34:9. Deu. 9:27.
Characteristic of the wicked. Pro. 7:11. 2 Pet. 2:10.
The wicked cease not from. Jud. 2:19.
Punishment for. Deu. 21:21. Pro. 29:1.
Illustrated. Psa. 32:9. Jer. 31:18.
Exemplified. *Simeon and Levi*, Gen. 49:6. *Israelites*, Exo. 32:9. Deu. 9:6, 13. *Saul*, 1 Sam. 15:19—23. *David*, 2 Sam. 24:4. *Josiah*, 2 Chr. 35:22. *Zedekiah*, 2 Chr. 36:13.

Serpents.

Created by God. Job 26:13.
Characterized as subtle. Gen. 3:1. Mat. 10:16.
Called crooked. Job 26:13. Isa. 27:1.
Unclean and unfit for food. Mat. 7:10.
INFEST
 Hedges. Ecc. 10:8.
 Holes in walls. Amos 5:19.
 Deserts. Deu. 8:15.
Produced from eggs. Isa. 59:5.
Cursed above all creatures. Gen. 3:14.
Doomed to creep on their belly. Gen. 3:14.
Doomed to eat their food mingled with dust. Gen. 3:14. Isa. 65:25. Mic. 7:17.
Many kinds of, poisonous. Deu. 32:24. Psa. 58:4.
All kinds of, can be tamed. Jas. 3:7.
Were often enchanted or fascinated. Ecc. 10:11.
Dangerous to travelers. Gen. 49:17.
Man's aversion and hatred to. Gen. 3:15.
Often sent as a punishment. Num. 21:6. Deu. 32:24. 1 Cor. 10:9.
MIRACLES CONNECTED WITH;
 Moses' rod turned into. Exo. 4:3. Exo. 7:9, 15.
 Israelites cured by looking at one of brass. Num. 21:8, 9. Jno. 3:14, 15.
 Power over, given to the disciples. Mar. 16:18. Luke 10:19.
ILLUSTRATIVE
 Of the devil. Gen. 3:1, with 2 Cor. 11:3. Rev. 12:9. Rev. 20:2.
 Of hypocrites. Mat. 23:33.
 Of the tribe of Dan. Gen. 49:17.
 Of enemies who harass and destroy. Isa. 14:29. Jer. 8:17.
 (Sharp tongue of,) of malice of the wicked. Psa. 140:3.
 (Poisonous bite of,) of baneful effects of wine. Pro. 23:31, 32.

Servants.

Early mention of. Gen. 9:25, 26.
DIVIDED INTO
 Male. Gen, 24:34. Gen. 32:5.
 Female. Gen. 16:6. Gen. 32:5.
 Bond. Gen. 43:18. Lev. 25:46.
 Hired. Mar. 1:20. Luke 15:17.
Persons devoted to the service of another so called. Exo. 24:13. 1 Kin. 19:21.
The subjects of a prince or king so called. Exo. 9:20. Exo. 11:8.
Persons of low condition so called. Ecc. 10:7.
Persons devoted to God so called. Psa. 119:49. Isa. 56:6. Rom. 1:1.
The term often used to express humility. Gen. 18:3. Gen. 33:5. 1 Sam. 20:7. 1 Kin. 20:32.
HIRED,
 Called hirelings. Job 7:1. Jno. 10:12, 13.
 Engaged by the year. Lev. 25:53. Isa. 16:14.
 Engaged by the day. Mat. 20:2.
 Not to be oppressed. Deu. 24:14.
 To be paid without delay at the expiration of their service. Lev. 19:13. Deu. 24:15.
 To be esteemed worthy of their hire. Luke 10:7.
 To partake of the produce of the land the sabbatical year. Lev. 25:6.

If foreigners not allowed to partake of the passover or holy things. Exo. 12:45. Lev. 22:10.
Anxiety of, for the end of their daily toil, alluded to. Job 7:2.
Hebrew slaves serving their brethren to be treated as. Lev. 25:39, 40.
Hebrew slaves serving strangers to be treated as. Lev. 25:47, 53.
Often stood in the market place waiting for employment. Mat. 20:1—3.
Often well fed and taken care of. Luke 15:17.
Often oppressed and their wages kept back. Mal. 3:5. Jas. 5:4.

SLAVES OR BOND,
Called bondmen. Gen. 43:18. Gen. 44:9.
By birth. Gen. 14:14. Psa. 116:16. Jer. 2:14.
By purchase. Gen. 17:27. Gen. 37:36.
Captives taken in war often kept as. Deu. 20:14. 2 Kin. 5:2.
Strangers sojourning in Israel might be purchased as. Lev. 25:45.
Persons belonging to other nations might be purchased as. Lev. 25:44.
Persons unable to pay their debts liable to be sold as. 2 Kin. 4:1. Neh. 5:4, 5. Mat. 18:25.
Thieves unable to make restitution were sold as. Exo. 22:3.
More valuable than hired servants. Deu. 15:18.
When Israelites not to be treated with rigor. Lev. 25:39, 40, 46.
When Israelites to have their liberty after six years' service. Exo. 21:2. Deu. 15:12.
Israelites sold as, refusing their liberty, to have their ears bored to the door. Exo. 21:5, 6. Deu. 15:16, 17.
Israelites sold to strangers as, might be redeemed by their nearest of kin. Lev. 25:47—55.
All Israelites sold as, to be free at the jubilee. Lev. 25:10, 40, 41, 54.
Could not when set free demand wives or children procured during servitude. Exo. 21:3, 4.
To be furnished liberally, when their servitude expired. Deu. 15:13, 14.
When foreigners to be circumcised. Gen. 17:13, 27. Exo. 12:44.
To be allowed to rest on the Sabbath. Exo. 20:10.
To participate in all national rejoicings. Deu. 12:18. Deu. 16:11, 14.
Persons of distinction had many. Gen. 14:14. Ecc. 2:7.
Engaged in the most menial offices. 1 Sam. 25:41. Jno. 13:4, 5.
Maimed or injured by masters, to have their freedom. Exo. 21:26, 27.
Masters to be recompensed for injury done to. Exo. 21:32.
Laws respecting the killing of. Exo. 21:20, 21.
Of others not to be coveted or enticed away. Exo. 20:17. Deu. 5:21.
Seeking protection not to be delivered up to masters. Deu. 23:15.
Custom of branding, alluded to. Gal. 6:17.
Sometimes rose to rank and station. Ecc. 10:7.
Sometimes intermarried with their master's family. 1 Chr. 2:34, 35.
Laws respecting marriage with female. Exo. 21:7—11.
Seizing and stealing of men for, condemned and punished by the law. Exo. 21:16. Deu. 24:7. 1 Tim. 1:10.
Laws respecting, often violated. Jer. 34:8—16.

BOND, ILLUSTRATIVE
Of Christ. Psa. 40:6, with Heb. 10:5. Phi. 2:7, 8.
Of saints. 1 Cor. 6:20. 1 Cor. 7:23.
Of the wicked. 2 Pet. 2:19, with Rom. 6:16, 19.

Christ condescended to the office of. Mat. 20:28. Luke 22:27. Jno. 13:5. Phi. 2:7.
Are inferior to their masters. Luke 22:27.
Should follow Christ's example. 1 Pet. 2:21.

DUTIES OF, TO MASTERS;
To pray for them. Gen. 24:12.
To honor them. Mal. 1:6. 1 Tim. 6:1.
To revere them the more, when they are believers. 1 Tim. 6:2.
To be subject to them. 1 Pet. 2:18.
To obey them. Eph. 6:5. Tit. 2:9.
To attend to their call. Psa. 123:2.
To please them well in all things. Tit. 2:9.
To sympathize with them. 2 Sam 12:18.
To prefer their business to their own necessary food. Gen. 24:33.
To bless God for mercies shown to them. Gen. 24:27, 48.
To be faithful to them. Luke 16:10—12. 1 Cor. 4:2. Tit. 2:10.
To be profitable to them. Luke 19:15, 16, 18. Phile. 11.
To be anxious for their welfare. 1 Sam. 25:14—17. 2 Kin. 5:2, 3.
To be earnest in transacting their business. Gen. 24:54—56.
To be prudent in the management of their affairs. Gen. 24:34—49.

To be industrious in laboring for them. Neh. 4:16, 23.
To be kind and attentive to their guests. Gen. 43:23, 24.
To be submissive even to the froward. Gen. 16:6, 9. 1 Pet. 2:18.
Not to answer them rudely. Tit. 2:9.
Not to serve them with eye-service, as men-pleasers. Eph. 6:6. Col. 3:22.
Not to defraud them. Tit. 2:10.
Should be contented in their situation. 1 Cor. 7:20, 21.
Should be compassionate to their fellows. Mat. 18:33.
SHOULD SERVE
For conscience towards God. 1 Pet. 2:19.
In the fear of God. Eph. 6:5. Col. 3:22.
As the servants of Christ. Eph. 6:5, 6.
Heartily, as to the Lord, and not unto men. Eph. 6:7. Col. 3:23.
As doing the will of God from the heart. Eph. 6:6.
In singleness of heart. Eph. 6:5. Col. 3:22.
With good will. Eph. 6:7.
When patient under injury are acceptable to God. 1 Pet. 2:19, 20.
WHEN GOOD
Are the servants of Christ. Col. 3:24.
Are brethren beloved in the Lord. Phile. 16.
Are the Lord's freemen. 1 Cor. 7:22.
Are partakers of gospel privileges. 1 Cor. 12:13. Gal. 3:28. Eph. 6:8. Col. 3:11.
Deserve the confidence of their masters. Gen. 24:2, 4, 10. Gen. 39:4.
Often exalted. Gen. 41:40. Pro. 17:2.
Often advanced by masters. Gen. 39:4, 5.
To be honored. Gen. 24:31. Pro. 27:18.
Bring God's blessing upon their masters. Gen. 30:27, 30. Gen. 39:3.
Adorn the doctrine of God their Saviour in all things. Tit. 2:10.
Have God with them. Gen. 31:42. Gen. 39:21. Acts. 7:9, 10.
Are prospered by God. Gen. 39:3.
Are protected by God. Gen. 31:7.
Are guided by God. Gen. 24:7, 27.
Are blessed by God. Mat. 24:46.
Are mourned over after death. Gen. 35:8. (*See marginal note.*)
Shall be rewarded. Eph. 6:8. Col. 3:24.
The property of masters increased by faithful. Gen. 30:29, 30.

CHARACTERISTICS OF WICKED SERVANTS:
Eye-servants. Eph. 6:6. Col. 3:22.
Men-pleasers. Eph. 6:6. Col. 3:22.
Deceit. 2 Sam. 19:26. Psa. 101:6, 7.
Quarrelsomeness. Gen. 13:7. Gen. 26:20.
Covetousness. 2 Kin. 5:20..
Lying. 2 Kin. 5:22, 25.
Stealing. Tit. 2:10.
Gluttony, &c. Mat. 24:49.
Unmerciful to their fellows. Mat. 18:30.
Will not submit to correction. Pro. 29:19.
Do not bear to be exalted. Pro. 30:21, 22, with Isa. 3:5.
Shall be punished. Mat. 24:50.
Good—Exemplified. *Eliezer*, Gen. 24th Chapter. *Deborah*, Gen. 24:59, with Gen. 35:8. *Jacob*, Gen. 31:36—40. *Joseph*, Gen. 39:3. Acts 7:10. *Servants of Boaz*, Ruth 2:4. *Jonathan's armor-bearer*, 1 Sam. 14:6, 7. *David's servants*, 2 Sam. 12:18. *Captive maid*, 2 Kin. 5:2—4. *Servants of Naaman*, 2 Kin. 5:13. *Servants of Centurion*, Mat. 8:9. *Servants of Cornelius*, Acts 10:7. *Onesimus after his conversion*, Phile. 11.
Bad—Exemplified. *Servants of Abraham and Lot*, Gen. 13:7. *Servants of Abimelech*, Gen. 21:25. *Absalom's servants*, 2 Sam. 13:28, 29. 2 Sam. 14:30. [*Absalom's servants obeyed a bad master; they were bad men rather than bad servants.*] *Ziba*, 2 Sam. 16:1—4. *Servants of Shimei*, 1 Kin. 2:39. *Jeroboam*, 1 Kin. 11:26. *Zimri*, 1 Kin. 16:9. *Gehazi*, 2 Kin. 5:20. *Servants of Amon*, 2 Kin. 21:23. *Job's servants*, Job 19:16. *Servants of the High Priest*, Mar. 14:65. *Onesimus before his conversion*, Phile. 11.

Sheep.

Clean and used as food. Deu. 14:4.
DESCRIBED AS
Innocent. 2 Sam. 24:17.
Sagacious. Jno. 10:4, 5.
Agile. Psa. 114:4, 6.
Being covered with a fleece. Job 31:20.
Remarkably prolific. Psa. 107:41. Psa. 144:13. So. of Sol. 4:2. Eze. 36:37.
Bleating of, alluded to. Jud. 5:16. 1 Sam. 15:14.
Under man's care from the earliest age. Gen. 4:4.
Constituted a great part of patriarchal wealth. Gen. 13:5. Gen. 24:35. Gen. 26:14.
Males of, called rams. 1 Sam. 15:22. Jer. 51:40.
Females of, called ewes. Psa. 78:71.

Young of, called lambs. Exo. 12:3. Isa. 11:6.

PLACES CELEBRATED FOR;
- Kedar. Eze. 27:21.
- Bashan. Deu. 32:14.
- Nebaioth. Isa. 60:7.
- Bozra. Mic. 2:12.

Flesh of, extensively used as food. 1 Sam. 25:18. 1 Kin. 1:19. 1 Kin. 4:23. Neh. 5:18. Isa. 22:13.

Milk of, used as food. Deu. 32:14. Isa. 7:21, 22. 1 Cor. 9:7.

Skins of, worn as clothing by the poor. Heb. 11:37.

Skins of, made into a covering for the tabernacle. Exo. 25:5. Exo. 36:19. Exo. 39:34.

Wool of, made into clothing. Job 31:20. Pro. 31:13. Eze. 34:3.

Offered in sacrifice from the earliest age. Gen. 4:4. Gen. 8:20. Gen. 15:9, 10.

Offered in sacrifice under the law. Exo. 20:24. Lev. 1:10. 1 Kin. 8:5, 63.

FLOCKS OF,
- Attended by members of the family. Gen. 29:6. Exo. 2:16. 1 Sam. 16:11.
- Attended by servants. 1 Sam. 17:20. Isa. 61:5.
- Guarded by dogs. Job 30:1.
- Kept in folds or cotes. 1 Sam. 24:3. 2 Sam. 7:8. Jno. 10:1.
- Conducted to the richest pastures. Psa. 23:2.
- Fed on the mountains. Exo. 3:1. Eze. 34:6, 13.
- Fed in the valleys. Isa. 65:10.
- Frequently covered the pastures. Psa. 65:13.
- Watered every day. Gen. 29:8—10. Exo. 2:16, 17.
- Made to rest at noon. Psa. 23:2, with So. of Sol. 1:7.
- Followed the shepherd. Jno. 10:4, 27.
- Fled from strangers. Jno. 10:5.

Washed and shorn every year. So. of Sol. 4:2.

Firstlings of, not to be shorn. Deu. 15:19.

Firstlings of, not to be redeemed. Num. 18:17.

Firstlings of, could not be dedicated as a free-will offering. Lev. 27:26.

Tithe of, given to the Levites. 2 Chr. 31:4—6.

First wool of, given to the priests. Deu. 18:4.

Time of shearing, a time of rejoicing. 1 Sam. 25:2, 11, 36. 2 Sam. 13:23.

WERE FREQUENTLY
- Given as presents. 2 Sam. 17:29. 1 Chr. 12:40.
- Given as tribute. 2 Kin. 3:4. 2 Chr. 17:11.
- Destroyed by wild beasts. Jer. 50:17. Mic. 5:8. Jno. 10:12.
- Taken in great numbers in war. Jud. 6:4. 1 Sam. 14:32. 1 Chr. 5:21. 2 Chr. 14:15.
- Cut off by disease. Exo. 9:3.

False prophets assume the simple appearance of. Mat. 7:15.

ILLUSTRATIVE
- Of the Jews. Psa. 74:1. Psa. 78:52. Psa. 79:13.
- Of the people of Christ. Jno. 10:7—26. Jno. 21:16, 17. Heb. 13:20. 1 Pet. 5:2.
- Of the wicked in their death. Psa. 49:14.
- Of those under God's judgment. Psa. 44:11.
- (In patience and simplicity,) of patience, &c. of Christ. Isa. 53:7.
- (In proneness to wander,) of those who depart from God. Psa. 119:176. Isa. 53:6. Eze. 34:16.
- (Lost,) of the unregenerate. Mat. 10:6.
- (When found,) of restored sinners. Luke 15:5, 7.
- (Separated from the goats,) of the separation of saints from the wicked. Mat. 25:32, 33.

Shepherds.

Early mention of. Gen. 4:2.

Usually carried a scrip or bag. 1 Sam. 17:40.

Carried a staff or rod. Lev. 27:32. Psa. 23:4.

Dwelt in tents while tending their flocks. So. of Sol. 1:8. Isa. 38:12.

Members of the family both male and female acted as. Gen. 29:6. 1 Sam. 16:11. 1 Sam. 17:15.

Had hired keepers under them. 1 Sam. 17:20.

The unfaithfulness of hireling, alluded to. Jno. 10:12.

CARE OF THE SHEEP BY, EXHIBITED IN
- Knowing them. Jno. 10:14.
- Going before and leading them. Psa. 77:20. Psa 78:52. Psa. 80:1.
- Seeking out good pasture for them. 1 Chr. 4:39—41. Psa. 23:2.
- Numbering them when they return from pasture. Jer. 33:13.
- Watching over them by night. Luke 2:8.
- Tenderness to the ewes in lamb, and to the young. Gen. 33:13, 14. Psa. 78:71.
- Defending them when attacked by wild beasts. 1 Sam. 17:34—36. Amos 3:12.
- Searching them out when lost and straying. Eze. 34:12. Luke 15:4, 5.

Attending them when sick. Eze. 34:16.
An abomination to the Egyptians. Gen. 46:34.
ILLUSTRATIVE
Of God as leader of Israel. Psa. 77:20. Psa. 80:1.
Of Christ as the good shepherd. Eze. 34:23. Zec. 13:7. Jno. 10:14. Heb. 13:20.
Of kings as the leaders of the people. Isa. 44:28. Jer. 6:3. Jer. 49:19.
Of ministers of the gospel. Jer. 23:4.
(Searching out straying sheep,) of Christ seeking the lost. Eze. 34:12. Luke 15:2—7.
(Their care and tenderness,) of tenderness of Christ. Isa. 40:11. Eze. 34:13—16.
(Ignorant and foolish,) of bad ministers. Isa. 56:11. Jer. 50:6. Eze. 34:2, 10. Zec. 11:7, 8, 15—17.

Showbread.

Twelve cakes of fine flour. Lev. 24:5.
Called hallowed bread. 1 Sam. 21:4.
Materials for, provided by the people. Lev. 24:8. Neh. 10:32:33.
Prepared by Levites. 1 Chr. 9:32. 1 Chr. 23:29.
Placed in two rows on the table by the priests. Exo. 25:30. Exo. 40:23. Lev. 24:6.
TABLE OF,
Dimensions, &c. of. Exo. 25:23.
Covered with gold. Exo. 25:24.
Had an ornamental border. Exo. 25:25.
Had staves of shittim wood covered with gold. Exo. 25:28.
Had rings of gold in the corners for the staves. Exo. 25:26, 27.
Had dishes, spoons, covers, and bowls of gold. Exo. 25:29.
Placed in the north side of the tabernacle. Exo. 40:22. Heb. 9:2.
Directions for removing. Num. 4:7.
Pure frankincense placed on. Lev. 24:7.
Was changed every Sabbath day. Lev. 24:8.
After removal from the table given to the priests. Lev. 24:9.
Not lawful for any but priests to eat, except in extreme cases. 1 Sam. 21:4—6, with Mat. 12:4.
ILLUSTRATIVE OF
Christ as the bread of life. Jno. 6:48.
The Church. 1 Cor. 5:7. 1 Cor. 10:17.

Shields.

A part of defensive armor. Psa. 115:9, with Psa. 140:7.
FREQUENTLY MADE OF, OR COVERED WITH
Gold. 2 Sam. 8:7. 1 Kin. 10:17.
Brass. 1 Kin. 14:27.
Said to belong to God. Psa. 47:9.
KINDS OF;
The buckler or target. 2 Chr. 9:15, with 1 Chr. 5:18. Eze. 26:8.
The small shield. 2 Cor. 9:16.
Often borne by an armor-bearer. 1 Sam. 17:7.
BEFORE WAR
Gathered together. Jer. 51:11.
Uncovered. Isa. 22:6.
Repaired. Jer. 46:3.
Anointed. 2 Sam. 1:21, with Isa. 21:5.
Often made red. Nah. 2:3.
Provided by the kings of Israel in great abundance. 2 Chr. 11:12. 2 Chr. 26:14. 2 Chr. 32:5.
A disgrace to lose, or throw away. 2 Sam. 1:21.
Of the vanquished, often burned. Eze. 39:9.
In times of peace were hung up in towers of armories. Eze. 27:10, with So. of Sol. 4:4.
Were scarce in Israel in the days of Deborah and Barak. Jud. 5:8.
Many of the Israelites used, with expertness. 1 Chr. 12:8, 24, 34. 2 Chr. 14:8. 2 Chr. 25:5.
ILLUSTRATIVE OF
Protection of God. Gen. 15:1. Psa. 33:20.
Favor of God. Psa. 5:12.
Truth of God. Psa. 91:4.
Salvation of God. 2 Sam. 22:36. Psa. 18:35.
Faith. Eph. 6:16.

Ships.

Probably originated from the ark made by Noah. Gen. 7:17, 18.
Antiquity of, among the Jews. Gen. 49:13. Jud. 5:17.
DESCRIBED AS
Gallant. Isa. 33:21.
Large. Jas. 3:4.
Strong. Isa. 23:14.
Swift. Job 9:26.
Solomon built a navy of. 1 Kin. 9:26.
MENTIONED IN SCRIPTURE;
Of Chittim. Num. 24:24. Dan. 11:30.
Of Tarshish. Isa. 23:1. Isa. 60:9.
Of Adramyttium. Acts 27:2.
Of Alexandria. Acts 27:6.
Of Chaldea. Isa. 43:14.
Of Tyre. 2 Chr. 8:18.
Generally made of the fir tree. Eze. 27:5.
Sometimes made of bulrushes. Isa. 18:2.
The seams of, were calked. Eze. 27:9, 27.

PARTS OF MENTIONED;
The forepart or foreship. Acts 27: 30, 41.
The hinder part or stern. Acts 27: 29, 41.
The hold or between the sides. Jon. 1: 5.
The mast. Isa. 33: 23. Eze. 27: 5.
The sails. Isa. 33: 23. Eze. 27: 7.
The tackling. Isa. 33: 23. Acts 27: 19.
The rudder or helm. Jas. 3: 4.
The rudder-bands. Acts 27: 40.
The anchors. Acts 27: 29, 40.
The boats. Acts 27: 30, 32.
The oars. Isa. 33: 21. Eze. 27: 6.
Often the property of individuals. Acts 27: 11.
Commanded by a master. Jon. 1: 6. Acts 27: 11.
Guided in their course by pilots. Eze. 27: 8, 27—29.
Governed and directed by the helm. Jas. 3: 4.
Course of frequently directed by the heavenly bodies. Acts 27: 20.
Worked by mariners or sailors. Eze. 27: 9, 27. Jon. 1: 5. Acts 27: 30.
Generally impelled by sails. Acts 27: 2—7.
Often impelled by oars. Jon. 1: 13. Jno. 6: 19.
NAVIGATED
Rivers. Isa. 33: 21.
Lakes. Luke 5: 1, 2.
The ocean. Psa. 104: 26. Psa. 107: 23.
Soundings usually taken for, in dangerous places. Acts 27: 28.
Usually distinguished by signs or figure heads. Acts 28: 11.
Course of, through the midst of the sea, wonderful. Pro. 30: 18, 19.
EMPLOYED IN
Trading. 1 Kin. 22: 48. 2 Chr. 8: 18. 2 Chr. 9: 21.
Fishing. Mat. 4: 21. Luke 5: 4—9. Jno. 21: 3—8.
War. Num. 24: 24. Dan. 11: 30, 40.
Carrying passengers. Jon. 1: 3. Acts 27: 2, 6. Acts 28: 11.
The hinder part of, occupied by the passengers. Mar. 4: 38.
ENDANGERED BY
Storms. Jon. 1: 4. Mar. 4: 37, 38.
Quicksands. Acts 27: 17.
Rocks. Acts 27: 29.
When damaged were sometimes undergirded with cables. Acts 27: 17.
Were often wrecked. 1 Kin. 22: 48. Psa. 48: 7. Acts 27: 41—44. 2 Cor. 11: 25.
ILLUSTRATIVE
Of industrious women. Pro. 31: 14.
(Wrecked,) of departure from the faith. 1 Tim. 1: 19.

Shoes.

Early use of. Gen. 14: 23.
Called sandals. Mar. 6: 9. Acts 12: 8.
Soles of, sometimes plated with brass or iron. Deu. 33: 25.
Bound round the feet with latchets or strings. Jno. 1: 27. Acts 12: 8.
OF LADIES OF DISTINCTION
Often made of badgers' skins. Eze. 16: 10.
Often highly ornamental. So. of Sol. 7: 1.
Probably often adorned with tinkling ornaments. Isa. 3: 18.
Loosing of, for another a degrading office. Mar. 1: 7. Jno. 1: 27.
Bearing, for another a degrading office, only performed by slaves. Mat. 3: 11.
THE JEWS
Put on, before beginning a journey. Exo. 12: 11.
Never wore, in mourning. 2 Sam. 15: 30. Isa. 20: 2, 3. Eze. 24: 17, 23.
Put off, when they entered sacred places. Exo. 3: 5. Jos. 5: 15.
Worn out by a long journey. Jos. 9: 5, 13.
Of Israel preserved for forty years, while journeying in the wilderness. Deu. 29: 5.
Often given as bribes. Amos 2: 6. Amos 8: 6.
CUSTOMS CONNECTED WITH;
A man who refused to marry a deceased brother's wife disgraced by her pulling off his shoes. Deu. 25: 9, 10.
The right of redemption resigned by a man's giving one of his shoes to the next of kin. Ruth 4: 7, 8.
The Apostles prohibited from taking for their journey more, than the pair they had on. Mat. 10: 10. Mar. 6: 9. Luke 10: 4.
ILLUSTRATIVE
Of the preparation of the gospel. Eph. 6: 15.
Of the beauty conferred on saints. So. of Sol. 7: 1, with Luke 15: 22.
(Having blood on,) of being engaged in war and slaughter. 1 Kin. 2: 5.
(Taken off,) of an ignominious and servile condition. Isa. 47: 2. Jer. 2: 25.
(Thrown over a place,) of subjection. Psa. 60: 8. Psa. 108: 9.

Sickness.

Sent by God. Deu. 28: 59—61. Deu. 32: 39. 2 Sam. 12: 15. Acts 12: 23.
The devil sometimes permitted to inflict. Job 2: 6, 7. Luke 9: 39. Luke 13: 16.

Often brought on by intemperance. Hos. 7: 5.
Often sent as a punishment of sin. Lev. 26: 14—16. 2 Chr. 21: 12--15. 1 Cor. 11: 30.
One of God's four sore judgments on a guilty land. Eze. 14: 19—21.
GOD
Promises to heal. Exo. 23: 25. 2 Kin. 20: 5.
Heals. Deu. 32: 39. Psa. 103: 3. Isa. 38: 5, 9.
Exhibits His mercy in healing. Phi. 2: 27.
Exhibits His power in healing. Luke 5: 17.
Exhibits His love in healing. Isa. 38: 17.
Often manifests saving grace to sinners during. Job 33: 19—24. Psa. 107: 17—21.
Permits saints to be tried by. Job 2: 5, 6.
Strengthens saints in. Psa. 41: 3.
Comforts saints in. Psa. 41: 3.
Hears the prayers of those in. Psa. 30: 2. Psa. 107: 18—20.
Preserves saints in time of. Psa. 91: 3—7.
Abandons the wicked to. Jer. 34: 17.
Persecutes the wicked by. Jer. 29: 18.
Healing of, lawful on the Sabbath. Luke 13: 14—16.
Christ compassionated those in. Isa. 53: 4, with Mat. 8: 16, 17.
CHRIST HEALED,
Being present. Mar. 1: 31. Mat. 4: 23.
Not being present. Mat. 8: 13.
By imposition of hands. Mar. 6: 5. Luke 13: 13.
With a touch. Mat. 8: 3.
Through the touch of His garment. Mat. 14: 35, 36. Mar. 5: 27—34.
With a word. Mat. 8: 8, 13.
Faith required in those healed of, by Christ. Mat. 9: 28, 29. Mar. 5: 34. Mar. 10: 52..
Often incurable by human means. Deu. 28: 27. 2 Chr. 21: 18.
The Apostles were endued with power to heal. Mat. 10: 1. Mar. 16: 18, 20.
THE POWER OF HEALING
One of the miraculous gifts bestowed on the early Church. 1 Cor. 12: 9, 30. Jas. 5: 14, 15.
SAINTS
Acknowledge that, comes from God. Psa. 31: 1—8. Isa. 38: 12, 15.
Are resigned under. Job 2: 10.
Mourn under, with prayer. Isa. 38: 14.
Pray for recovery from. Isa. 38: 2, 3.
Ascribe recovery from, to God. Isa. 38: 20.
Praise God for recovery from. Psa. 103: 1—3. Isa. 38: 19. Luke 17: 15.
Thank God publicly for recovery from. Isa. 38: 20. Acts 3: 8.
Feel for others in. Psa. 35: 13.
Visit those in. Mat. 25: 36.
Visiting those in, an evidence of belonging to Christ. Mat. 25: 34, 36, 40.
Pray for those afflicted with. Acts 28: 8. Jas. 5: 14, 15.
God's aid should be sought in. 2 Chr. 16: 12.
THE WICKED
Have much sorrow, &c. with. Ecc. 5: 17.
Forsake those in. 1 Sam. 30: 13.
Visit not those in. Mat. 25: 43.
Not visiting those in, an evidence of not belonging to Christ. Mat. 25: 43, 45.
Illustrative of sin. Lev. 13: 45, 46. Isa. 1: 5. Jer. 8: 22. Mat. 9: 12.

Sidonians, The.

Descended from Sidon, son of Canaan. Gen. 10: 15. 1 Chr. 1: 13.
Formerly a part of the Phœnician nation. Mat. 15: 21, 22, with Mar. 7: 24, 26.
Dwelt on the sea coast. Luke 6: 17. Acts 27: 3.
CITIES OF MENTIONED;
Zidon. Jos. 11: 8. Jos. 19: 28.
Zarephath or Sarepta. 1 Kin. 17: 9. Luke 4: 26.
Governed by kings. Jer. 25: 22. Jer. 27: 3.
CHARACTER OF;
Careless and secure. Jud. 18: 7.
Idolatrous. 1 Kin. 11: 5.
Superstitious. Jer. 27: 3, 9.
Wicked and impenitent. Mat. 11: 21, 22.
Engaged in extensive commerce. Isa. 23: 2.
Were skilful sailors. Eze. 27: 8.
Supplied the Jews with timber. 1 Chr. 22: 4. Ezr. 3: 7.
Supplied from Judea with provisions. Acts 12: 20, with Eze. 27: 17.
TERRITORY OF,
Bordered on the land of Canaan. Gen. 10: 19.
Given by God to Israel. Gen. 49: 13. Jos. 13: 6.
Allotted to the tribe of Asher. Jos. 19: 24, 28.
Visited by our Lord. Mat. 15: 21.
Israel unable to expel. Jud. 1: 31. Jud. 3: 3.
Hostile and oppressive to God's people. Jud. 10: 12. Eze. 28: 22, 24. Joel 3: 5, 6.
Solomon intermarried with. 1 Kin. 11: 1.

Ahab intermarried with. 1 Kin. 16: 31.
Israel followed the idolatry of. Jud. 10: 6. 1 Kin. 11: 33.
PREDICTIONS RESPECTING;
Territory of, to be given to Nebuchadnezzar, king of Babylon. Jer. 27: 3, 6.
Partaking with the other nations of God's judgments. Jer. 25: 22—28. Eze. 32: 30.
All their helpers to be cut off. Jer. 47: 4.
That God should be glorified in the judgments upon them. Eze. 28: 21—23.
Their spoliation and oppression of the Jews to be fully recompensed. Joel 3: 4, 8.
Many of, attended Christ's ministry. Mar. 3: 8.
Having revolted from Herod, were obliged to propitiate him. Acts 12: 20.

Sieges.

Fenced cities invested by. 2 Kin. 18: 13.
Threatened as a punishment. Deu. 28: 52.
DESCRIBED AS
Encamping against. 2 Sam. 12: 28. 2 Chr. 32: 1.
Pitching against. 2 Kin. 25: 1.
Compassing about with armies. 2 Kin. 6: 14. Luke 21: 20.
Setting in array against. Jer. 50: 9.
Being against round about. Jer. 51: 2.
Often lasted for a long time. 2 Kin. 17: 5.
Great noise and tumult of, alluded to. Joel 2: 5.
THOSE ENGAGED IN,
Built forts and mounts. Eze. 4: 2. Eze. 26: 8.
Dug a trench round the city. |Luke 19: 43.
Invested the city on every side. Eze. 23: 24.
Cut off all supplies. 2 Kin. 19: 24.
Frequently laid ambushes. Jud. 9: 34.
Called upon the city to surrender. 1 Kin. 20: 2, 3. 2 Kin. 18: 18, 20.
Employed battering rams, &c. against the walls. Eze. 4: 2. Eze. 26: 9.
Cast arrows and other missiles into the city. 2 Kin. 19: 32.
Often suffered much during. Eze. 29: 18.
The Jews forbidden to cut down fruit trees for purposes of. Deu. 20: 19, 20.
Extreme difficulty of taking cities by, alluded to. Pro. 18: 19.
CITIES INVESTED BY,
Repaired and newly fortified beforehand. 2 Chr. 32: 5. Isa. 22: 9, 10. Nah. 3: 14.
Supplied with water beforehand. Nah. 3: 14.
The inhabitants of, cut off beforehand supplies of water outside, useful to besiegers. 2 Chr. 32: 3, 4.
Were strictly shut up. Jos. 6: 1.
Walls of, defended by the inhabitants. 2 Sam. 11: 20, 21. 2 Kin. 18: 26. 2 Chr. 32: 18.
Sometimes used ambushes or sorties. Jer. 51: 12.
Often suffered from famine. 2 Kin. 6: 26—29. 2 Kin. 25: 3. Eze. 6: 12.
Often suffered from pestilence. Jer. 21: 6. Jer. 32: 24.
Often demanded terms of peace. 1 Sam. 11: 1—3.
Frequently taken by ambush. Jud. 9: 43, 44.
Frequently taken by assault. Jos. 10: 35. 2 Sam. 12: 29.
Frequently succored by allies. 1 Sam. 11: 11. 1 Sam. 23: 5.
Inhabitants of, exhorted to be courageous. 2 Chr. 32: 6—8.
CITIES TAKEN BY,
Given up to pillage. Jer. 50: 26, 27.
Inhabitants of, often put to the sword. Jos. 10: 28, 30, 32, 35. Jer. 50: 30.
Frequently broken down. Jud. 9: 45.
Frequently destroyed by fire. Jos. 8: 19.
Sometimes sown with salt. Jud. 9: 45.
Sometimes called after the name of the captor. 2 Sam. 12: 28.
MENTIONED IN SCRIPTURE;
Jericho. Jos. 6: 2—20.
Ai. Jos. 7: 2—4. Jos. 8: 1—19.
Makkedah. Jos. 10: 28.
Libnah. Jos. 10: 29, 30.
Lachish. Jos. 10: 31, 32.
Eglon. Jos. 10: 34, 35.
Hebron. Jos. 10: 36, 37.
Debir. Jos. 10: 38, 39.
Shechem. Jud. 9: 34, 45.
Thebez. Jud. 9: 50.
Jabesh-gilead. 1 Sam. 11: 1.
Keilah. 1 Sam. 23: 1.
Ziklag. 1 Sam. 30: 1, 2.
Rabbah. 2 Sam. 11: 1. 2 Sam. 12: 26—29.
Gibbethon. 1 Kin. 16: 15.
Tirzah. 1 Kin. 16: 17.
Samaria. 1 Kin. 20: 1. 2 Kin. 6: 24. 2 Kin 17: 5.
Ramoth-gilead. 1 Kin. 22: 4, 29.
Cities of Israel in Galilee. 2 Kin. 15: 29.
Cities of Judah. 2 Kin. 18: 13.
Jerusalem. 2 Kin. 24: 10, 11. 2 Kin. 25: 1, 2.

ILLUSTRATIVE OF
The omnipresence of God. Psa. 139: 5.
The judgments of God. Mic. 5: 1.
Zion in her affliction. Isa. 1: 8.

Silver.

Veins of, found in the earth. Job 28: 1.
Generally found in an impure state. Pro. 25: 4.
Comparative value of. Isa. 60: 17.
DESCRIBED AS
White and shining. Psa. 68: 13, 14.
Fusible. Eze. 22: 20, 22.
Malleable. Jer. 10: 9.
Purified by fire. Pro. 17: 3. Zec. 13: 9.
PURIFIED, CALLED
Refined silver. 1 Chr. 29: 4.
Choice silver. Pro. 8: 19.
Tarshish carried on extensive commerce in. Jer. 10: 9. Eze. 27: 12.
The patriarchs rich in. Gen. 13: 2. Gen. 24: 35.
Used as money from the earliest age. Gen. 23: 15, 16. Gen. 37: 28. 1 Kin. 16: 24.
Very abundant in the reign of Solomon. 1 Kin. 10: 21, 22, 27. 2 Chr. 9: 20, 21, 27.
The working in, a trade. Acts 19: 24.
MADE INTO
Cups. Gen. 44: 2.
Dishes. Num. 7: 13, 84, 85.
Bowls. Num. 7: 13, 84.
Thin plates. Jer. 10: 9.
Chains. Isa. 40: 19.
Wires (alluded to). Ecc. 12: 6.
Sockets for the boards of the tabernacle. Exo. 26: 19, 25, 32. Exo. 36: 24, 26, 30, 36.
Ornaments and hooks for the pillars of the tabernacle. Exo. 27: 17. Exo. 38: 19.
Candlesticks. 1 Chr. 28: 15.
Tables. 1 Chr. 28: 16.
Beds or couches. Est. 1: 6.
Vessels. 2 Sam. 8: 10. Ezr. 6: 5.
Idols. Psa. 115: 4. Isa. 2: 20. Isa. 30: 22.
Ornaments for the person. Exo. 3: 22.
Given by the Israelites for making the tabernacle. Exo. 25: 3. Exo. 35: 24.
Given by David and his subjects for making the temple. 1 Chr. 28: 14. 1 Chr. 29: 2, 6—9.
Taken in war often consecrated to God. Jos. 6: 19. 2 Sam. 8: 11. 1 Kin. 15: 15.
Taken in war purified by fire. Num. 31: 22, 23.
Often given as presents. 1 Kin. 10: 25. 2 Kin. 5: 5, 23.
Tribute often paid in. 2 Chr. 17: 11. Neh. 5: 15.
ILLUSTRATIVE
Of the words of the Lord. Psa. 12: 6.
Of the tongue of the just. Pro. 10: 20.
Of good rulers. Isa. 1: 22, 23.
Of the Medo-Persian kingdom. Dan. 2: 32, 39.
Of saints purified by affliction. Psa. 66: 10. Zec. 13: 9.
(Labor of seeking for,) of diligence required for attaining knowledge Pro. 2: 4.
(Reprobate,) of the wicked. Jer. 6: 30.
(Dross of,) of the wicked. Isa. 1: 22. Eze. 22: 18.
Wisdom to be esteemed more than. Job 28: 15. Pro. 3: 14. Pro. 8: 10, 19. Pro. 16: 16.

Simeon, The Tribe of.

Descended from Jacob's second son by Leah. Gen. 29: 33
Prediction respecting. Gen. 49: 5—7.
PERSONS SELECTED FROM,
To number the people. Num. 1: 6.
To spy out the land. Num. 13: 5.
To divide the land. Num. 34: 20.
Formed part of the second division of Israel in their journeys. Num. 10: 18, 19.
Encamped under the standard of Reuben south of the tabernacle. Num. 2: 12.
Strength of, on leaving Egypt. Num. 1: 22, 23. Num. 2: 13.
Offering of, at the dedication. Num. 7: 36—41.
Families of. Num. 26: 12, 13.
Strength of, on entering Canaan. Num. 26: 14.
Plagued for following the idolatry, &c. of Midian, which accounts for their decrease. Num. 25: 9, 14. Num. 26: 14, with Num. 1: 23.
On Mount Gerizim said amen to the blessings. Deu. 27: 12.
Inheritance of, within Judah. Jos. 19: 1—8.
Bounds of their inheritance with cities and villages. Jos. 19: 2—8. 1 Chr. 4: 28—33.
United with Judah in expelling the Canaanites from their inheritance. Jud. 1: 3, 17.
Many of, at the coronation of David. 1 Chr. 12: 25.
Officer appointed over, by David. 1 Chr. 27: 16.
Part of, united with Judah under Asa. 2 Chr. 15: 9.

Josiah purged their land of idols. 2 Chr. 34: 6.
Part of, destroyed the remnant of the Amalekites, and dwelt in their land. 1 Chr. 4: 39—43.

Simplicity.

Is opposed to fleshly wisdom. 2 Cor. 1: 12.
Necessity for. Mat. 18: 2, 3.
SHOULD BE EXHIBITED
In preaching the gospel. 1 The. 2: 3—7.
In acts of benevolence. Rom. 12: 8.
In all our conduct. 2 Cor. 1: 12.
Concerning our own wisdom. 1 Cor. 3: 18.
Concerning evil. Rom. 16: 19.
Concerning malice. 1 Cor. 14: 20.
Exhortation to. Rom. 16: 19. 1 Pet. 2: 2.
THEY WHO HAVE THE GRACE OF,
Are made wise by God. Mat. 11: 25.
Are made wise by the word of God. Psa. 19: 7. Psa. 119: 130.
Are preserved by God. Psa. 116: 6.
Made circumspect by instruction. Pro. 1: 4.
Profit by the correction of others. Pro. 19: 25. Pro. 21: 11.
Beware of being corrupted from that, which is in Christ. 2 Cor. 11: 3.
Illustrated. Mat. 6: 22.
Exemplified. *David*, Psa. 131: 1, 2. *Jeremiah*, Jer. 1: 6. *Primitive Christians*, Acts 2: 46. Acts 4: 32. *Paul*, 2 Cor. 1: 12.

Sin.

Is the transgression of the law. 1 Jno. 3: 4.
Is of the devil. 1 Jno. 3: 8, with Jno. 8: 44.
All unrighteousness is. 1 Jno. 5: 17.
Omission of what we know to be good is. Jas. 4: 17.
Whatever is not of faith is. Rom. 14: 23.
The thought of foolishness is. Pro. 24: 9.
All the imaginations of the unrenewed heart are. Gen. 6: 5. Gen. 8: 21.
DESCRIBED AS
Coming from the heart. Mat. 15: 19.
The fruit of lust. Jas. 1: 15.
The sting of death. 1 Cor. 15: 56.
Rebellion against God. Deu. 9: 7. Jos. 1: 18.
Works of darkness. Eph. 5: 11.
Dead works. Heb. 6: 1. Heb. 9: 14.
The abominable thing that God hates. Pro. 15: 9. Jer. 44: 4, 11.
Reproaching the Lord. Num. 15: 30. Psa. 74: 18.
Defiling. Pro. 30: 12. Isa. 59: 3.
Deceitful. Heb. 3: 13.
Disgraceful. Pro. 14: 34.
Often very great. Exo. 32: 30. 1 Sam. 2: 17.
Often mighty. Amos 5: 12.
Often manifold. Amos 5: 12.
Often presumptuous. Psa. 19: 13.
Sometimes open and manifest. 1 Tim. 5: 24.
Sometimes secret. Psa. 90: 8. 1 Tim. 5: 24.
Besetting. Heb. 12: 1.
Like scarlet and crimson. Isa. 1: 18.
Reaching unto heaven. Rev. 18: 5.
Entered into the world by Adam. Gen. 3: 6, 7, with Rom. 5: 12.
All men are conceived and born in. Gen. 5: 3. Job 15: 14. Job 25: 4. Psa. 51: 5.
All men are shapen in. Psa. 51: 5.
Scripture concludes all under. Gal. 3: 22.
No man is without. 1 Kin. 8: 46. Ecc. 7: 20.
Christ alone was without. 2 Cor. 5: 21. Heb. 4: 15. Heb. 7: 26. 1 Jno. 3: 5.
GOD
Abominates. Deu. 25: 16. Pro. 6: 16—19.
Marks. Job 10: 14.
Remembers. Rev. 18: 5.
Is provoked to jealousy by. 1 Kin. 14: 22.
Is provoked to anger by. 1 Kin. 16: 2.
Alone can forgive. Exo. 34: 7. Dan. 9: 9. Mic. 7: 18. Mar. 2: 7.
Recompenses. Jer. 16: 18. Rev. 18: 6.
Punishes. Isa. 13: 11. Amos 3: 2.
THE LAW
Is transgressed by every. Jas. 2: 10, 11, with 1 Jno. 3: 4.
Gives knowledge of. Rom. 3: 20. Rom. 7: 7.
Shows exceeding sinfulness of. Rom. 7: 13.
Made to restrain. 1 Tim. 1: 9, 10.
By its strictness stirs up. Rom. 7: 5, 8, 11.
Is the strength of. 1 Cor. 15: 56.
Curses those guilty of. Gal. 3: 10.
No man can cleanse himself from. Job 9: 30, 31. Pro. 20: 9. Jer. 2: 22.
No man can atone for. Mic. 6: 7.
God has opened a fountain for. Zec. 13: 1.
Christ was manifested to take away. Jno. 1: 29. 1 Jno. 3: 5.
Christ's blood redeems from. Eph. 1: 7.
Christ's blood cleanses from. 1 Jno. 1: 7.
SAINTS
Made free from. Rom. 6: 18.
Dead to. Rom. 6: 2, 11. 1 Pet. 2: 24.
Profess to have ceased from. 1 Pet 4: 1.

Cannot live in. 1 Jno. 3: 9. 1 Jno. 5: 18.
Resolve against. Job 34: 32.
Ashamed of having committed. Rom. 6: 21.
Abhor themselves on account of. Job 42: 6. Eze. 20: 43.
Have yet the remains of, in them. Rom. 7: 17, 23, with Gal. 5: 17.
The fear of God restrains. Exo. 20: 20. Psa. 4: 4. Pro. 16: 6.
The word of God keeps from. Psa. 17: 4. Psa. 119: 11.
The Holy Ghost convinces of. Jno. 16: 8, 9.
If we say that we have no, we deceive ourselves, and the truth is not in us. 1 Jno. 1: 8.
If we say that we have no, we make God a liar. 1 Jno. 1: 10.
Confusion of face belongs to those guilty of. Dan. 9: 7, 8.
SHOULD BE
Confessed. Job 33: 27. Pro. 28: 13.
Mourned over. Psa. 38: 18. Jer. 3: 21.
Hated. Psa. 97: 10. Pro. 8: 13. Amos 5: 15.
Abhorred. Rom. 12: 9.
Put away. Job 11: 14.
Departed from. Psa. 34: 14. 2 Tim. 2: 19.
Avoided even in appearance. 1 The. 5: 22.
Guarded against. Psa. 4: 4. Psa. 39: 1.
Striven against. Heb. 12: 4.
Mortified. Rom. 8: 13. Col. 3: 5.
Wholly destroyed. Rom. 6: 6.
Specially strive against besetting. Heb. 12: 1.
Aggravated by neglected advantages. Luke 12: 47. Jno. 15: 22.
Guilt of concealing. Job 31: 33. Pro. 28: 13.
WE SHOULD PRAY TO GOD
To search for, in our hearts. Psa. 139: 23, 24.
To make us know our. Job 13: 23.
To forgive our. Exo. 34: 9. Luke 11: 4.
To keep us from. Psa. 19: 13.
To deliver us from. Mat. 6: 13.
To cleanse us from. Psa. 51: 2.
Prayer hindered by. Psa. 66: 18. Isa. 59: 2.
Blessings withheld on account of. Jer. 5: 25.
THE WICKED
Servants to. Jno. 8: 34. Rom. 6: 16.
Dead in. Eph. 2: 1.
Guilty of, in everything they do. Pro. 21: 4. Eze. 21: 24.
Plead necessity for. 1 Sam. 13: 11, 12.
Excuse. Gen. 3: 12, 13. 1 Sam. 15: 13—15.
Encourage themselves in. Psa. 64: 5.
Defy God in committing. Isa. 5: 18, 19.
Boast of. Isa. 3: 9.
Make a mock at. Pro. 14: 9.
Expect impunity in. Psa. 10: 11. Psa. 50: 21. Psa. 94: 7.
Cannot cease from. 2 Pet. 2: 14.
Heap up. Psa. 78: 17. Isa. 30: 1.
Encouraged in, by prosperity. Job 21: 7—15. Pro. 10: 16.
Led by despair to continue in. Jer. 2: 25. Jer. 18: 12.
Try to conceal, from God. Gen. 3: 8, 10, with Job 31: 33.
Throw the blame of, on God. Gen. 3: 12. Jer. 7: 10.
Throw the blame of, on others. Gen. 3: 12, 13. Exo. 32: 22—24.
Tempt others to. Gen. 3: 6. 1 Kin. 16: 2. 1 Kin. 21: 25. Pro. 1: 10—14.
Delight in those who commit. Psa. 10: 3. Hos. 7: 3. Rom. 1: 32.
Shall bear the shame of. Eze. 16: 52.
Shall find out the wicked. Num. 32: 23.
Ministers should warn the wicked to forsake. Eze. 33: 9. Dan. 4: 27.
LEADS TO
Shame. Rom. 6: 21.
Disquiet. Psa. 38: 3.
Disease. Job 20: 11.
The ground was cursed on account of. Gen. 3: 17, 18.
Toil and sorrow originated in. Gen. 3: 16, 17, 19, with Job 14: 1.
Excludes from heaven. 1 Cor. 6: 9, 10. Gal. 5: 19—21. Eph. 5: 5. Rev. 21: 27.
When finished brings forth death. Jas. 1: 15.
Death, the wages of. Rom. 6: 23.
Death, the punishment of. Gen. 2: 17. Eze. 18: 4.

Sincerity.

Christ was an example of. 1 Pet. 2: 22.
Ministers should be examples of. Tit. 2: 7.
Opposed to fleshly wisdom. 2 Cor. 1: 12.
SHOULD CHARACTERIZE
Our love to God. 2 Cor. 8: 8, 24.
Our love to Christ. Eph. 6: 24.
Our service to God. Jos. 24: 14. Jno. 4: 23, 24.
Our faith. 1 Tim. 1: 5.
Our love to one another. Rom. 12: 9. 1 Pet. 1: 22. 1 Jno. 3: 18.
Our whole conduct. 2 Cor. 1: 12.
The preaching of the gospel. 2 Cor. 2: 17. 1 The. 2: 3—5.
A characteristic of the doctrines of the gospel. 1 Pet. 2: 2.
The gospel sometimes preached without. Phi. 1: 16.

The wicked devoid of. Psa. 5:9. Psa. 55:21.
Exhortations to. Psa. 34:13. 1 Cor. 5:8. 1 Pet. 2:1.
Pray for, on behalf of others. Phi. 1:10.
Blessedness of. Psa. 32:2.
Exemplified. *Men of Zebulun*, 1 Chr. 12:33. *Hezekiah*, Isa. 38:3. *Nathanael*, Jno. 1:47. *Paul*, 2 Cor. 1:12. *Timothy*, 2 Tim. 1:5. *Lois and Eunice*, 2 Tim. 1:5. *The Redeemed*, Rev. 14:5.

Sin-offering.

Probable origin of. Gen. 4:4, 7.
WAS OFFERED
- For sins of ignorance. Lev. 4:2, 13, 22, 27.
- At the consecration of priests. Exo. 29:10, 14. Lev. 8:14.
- At the consecration of Levites. Num. 8:8.
- At the expiration of a Nazarite's vow. Num. 6:14.
- On the day of atonement. Lev. 16:3, 9.

Was a most holy sacrifice. Lev. 6:25, 29.
CONSISTED OF
- A young bullock for priests. Lev. 4:3. Lev. 9:2, 8. Lev. 16:3, 6.
- A young bullock or he-goat for the congregation. Lev. 4:14. Lev. 16:9. 2 Chr. 29:23.
- A male kid for a ruler. Lev. 4:23.
- A female kid or female lamb for a private person. Lev. 4:28, 32.

Sins of the offerer transferred to, by imposition of hands. Lev. 4:4, 15, 24, 29. 2 Chr. 29:23.
Was killed in the same place as the burnt-offering. Lev. 4:24. Lev. 6:25.
THE BLOOD OF,
- For a priest or for the congregation, brought by the priest into the tabernacle. Lev. 4:5, 16.
- For a priest or for the congregation, sprinkled seven times before the Lord, outside the vail, by the priest with his finger. Lev. 4:6, 17.
- For a priest or for the congregation, put upon the horns of the altar of incense. Lev. 4:7, 18.
- For a ruler or for a private person put upon the horns of the altar of burnt-offering by the priest with his finger. Lev. 4:25, 30.
- In every case poured at the foot of the altar of burnt-offering. Lev. 4:7, 18, 25, 30. Lev. 9:9.

Fat of the inside, kidneys, &c. burned on the altar of burnt-offering. Lev. 4:8--10, 19, 26, 31. Lev. 9:10.
When for a priest or the congregation, the skin, carcass, &c. burned without the camp. Lev. 4:11, 12, 21. Lev. 6:30. Lev. 9:11.
Was eaten by the priests in a holy place, when its blood had not been brought into the tabernacle. Lev. 6:26, 29, with 30 v.
Aaron, &c. rebuked for burning and not eating that of the congregation, its blood not having been brought into the tabernacle. Lev. 10:16—18, with Lev. 9:9, 15.
Whatever touched the flesh of, was rendered holy. Lev. 6:27.
Garments sprinkled with the blood of, to be washed. Lev. 6:27.
Laws respecting the vessels used for boiling the flesh of. Lev. 6:28.
Was typical of Christ's sacrifice. 2 Cor. 5:21. Heb. 13:11—13.

Sins, National.

Pervade all ranks. Isa. 1:5. Jer. 5:1—5. Jer. 6:13.
Often caused and encouraged by rulers. 1 Kin. 12:26—33. 1 Kin. 14:16. 2 Chr. 21:11—13. Pro. 29:12.
Often caused by prosperity. Deu. 32:15. Neh. 9:28. Jer. 48:11. Eze. 16:49. Eze. 28:5.
DEFILE
- The land. Lev. 18:25. Num. 35:33, 34. Psa. 106:38. Isa. 24:5. Mic. 2:10.
- The people. Lev. 18:24. Eze. 14:11.
- National worship. Isa. 1:10—15. Amos 5:21, 22. Hag. 2:14.

Aggravated by privileges. Isa. 5:4—7. Eze. 20:11—13. Amos 2:4. Amos 3:1, 2. Mat. 11:21—24.
Lead the heathen to blaspheme. Eze. 36:20, 23. Rom. 2:24.
Are a reproach to a people. Pro. 14:34.
SHOULD BE
- Repented of. Jer. 18:8. Jon. 3:5.
- Mourned over. Joel 2:12.
- Confessed. Lev. 26:40. Deu. 30:2. Jud. 10:10. 1 Kin. 8:47, 48.
- Turned from. Isa. 1:16. Hos. 14:1, 2. Jon. 3:10.

Saints especially mourn over. Psa. 119:136. Eze. 9:4.
MINISTERS SHOULD
- Mourn over. Ezr. 10:6, Jer. 13:17. Eze. 6:11. Joel 2:17.
- Testify against. Isa. 30:8, 9. Isa. 58:1. Eze. 2:3—5. Eze. 22:2. Jon. 1:2.
- Try to turn the people from. Jer. 23:22.
- Pray for forgiveness of. Exo. 32:31, 32. Joel 2:17.

National prayer rejected on account of. Isa. 1:15. Isa. 59:2.
National worship rejected on account of. Isa. 1:10—14. Jer. 6:19, 20. Jer. 7:9—14.

Cause the withdrawal of privileges. Lam. 2:9. Amos 8:11. Mat. 23: 37—39.
Bring down national judgments. Mat. 23:35, 36. Mat. 27:25.
Denunciations against. Isa. 1:24. Isa. 30:1. Jer. 5:9. Jer. 6:27—30.
Punishment for. Isa. 3:8. Jer. 12: 17. Jer. 25:12. Eze. 28:7—10.
Punishment for, averted on repentance. Jud. 10:15, 16. 2 Chr. 12:6, 7. Psa. 106:43—46. Jon. 3:10.
Exemplified. *Sodom and Gomorrah*, Gen. 18:20. 2 Pet. 2:6. *Children of Israel*, Exo. 16:8. Exo. 32:31. *Nations of Canaan*, Deu. 9:4. *Kingdom of Israel*, 2 Kin. 17:8—12. Hos. 4:1, 2. *Kingdom of Judah*, 2 Kin. 17:19. Isa. 1:2—7. *Moab*, Jer. 48:29, 30. *Babylon*, Jer. 51:6, 13, 52. *Tyre*, Eze. 28:2. *Nineveh*, Nah. 3:1.

Slander.

An abomination unto God. Pro. 6: 16, 19.
Forbidden. Exo. 23:1. Eph. 4:31. Jas. 4:11.
INCLUDES
- Whispering. Rom. 1:29. 2 Cor. 12:20.
- Backbiting. Rom. 1: 30. 2 Cor. 12:20.
- Evil surmising. 1 Tim. 6:4.
- Tale-bearing. Lev. 19:16.
- Babbling. Ecc. 10:11.
- Tattling. 1 Tim. 5:13.
- Evil speaking. Psa. 41: 5. Psa. 109:20.
- Defaming. Jer. 20:10. 1 Cor. 4:13.
- Bearing false witness. Exo. 20:16. Deu. 5:20. Luke 3:14.
- Judging uncharitably. Jas. 4:11, 12.
- Raising false reports. Exo. 23:1.
- Repeating matters. Pro. 17:9.

Is a deceitful work. Psa. 52:2.
Comes from the evil heart. Mat. 15: 19. Luke 6:45.
Often arises from hatred. Psa. 41:7. Psa. 109:3.
Idleness leads to. 1 Tim. 5:13.
The wicked addicted to. Psa. 50:20. Jer. 6:28. Jer. 9:4.
Hypocrites addicted to. Pro. 11:9.
A characteristic of the devil. Rev. 12: 10.
The wicked love. Psa. 52:4.
They who indulge in, are fools. Pro. 10:18.
They who indulge in, not to be trusted. Jer. 9:4.
Women warned against. Tit. 2:3.
Ministers' wives should avoid. 1 Tim. 3:11.
Christ was exposed to. Psa. 35:11. Mat. 26:60.
Rulers exposed to. 2 Pet. 2:10. Jude 8.
Ministers exposed to. Rom. 3:8. 2 Cor. 6:8.
The nearest relations exposed to. Psa. 50:20.
Saints exposed to. Psa. 38:12. Psa. 109:2. 1 Pet. 4:4.
SAINTS
- Should keep their tongue from Psa. 34:13, with 1 Pet. 3:10.
- Should lay aside. Eph. 4:31. 1 Pet. 2:1.
- Should be warned against. Tit. 3: 1, 2.
- Should give no occasion for. 1 Pet. 2:12. 1 Pet. 3:16.
- Should return good for. 1 Cor. 4: 13.
- Blessed in enduring. Mat. 5:11.
- Characterized as avoiding. Psa. 15:1, 3.

Should not be listened to. 1 Sam. 24:9.
Should be discountenanced with anger. Pro. 25:23.
EFFECTS OF;
- Separating friends. Pro. 16:28. Pro. 17:9.
- Deadly wounds. Pro. 18:8. Pro. 26:22.
- Strife. Pro. 26:20.
- Discord among brethren. Pro. 6: 19.
- Murder. Psa. 31:13. Eze 22:9.

The tongue of, is a scourge. Job 5: 21.
Is venomous. Psa. 140:3. Ecc. 10:11.
Is destructive. Pro. 11:9.
End of, is mischievous madness. Ecc. 10:13.
Men shall give account for. Mat. 12: 36. Jas. 1:26.
Punishment for. Deu. 19:16—21: Psa. 101:5.
Illustrated. Pro. 12:18. Pro. 25:18.
Exemplified. *Laban's Sons*, Gen. 31: 1. *Doeg*, 1 Sam. 22:9—11. *Princes of Ammon*, 2 Sam. 10:3. *Ziba*, 2 Sam. 16:3. *Children of Belial*, 1 Kin. 21: 13. *Enemies of the Jews*, Ezr. 4:7—16. *Gashmu*, Neh. 6:6. *Haman*, Est. 3:8. *David's enemies*, Psa. 31: 13. *Jeremiah's enemies*, Jer. 38:4. *Jews*, Mat. 11:18, 19. *Witnesses against Christ*, Mat. 26:59—61. *Priests*, Mar. 15:3. *Enemies of Stephen*, Acts 6:11. *Enemies of Paul, &c.* Acts 17:7. *Tertullus*, Acts 24:2, 5.

Sobriety.

Commanded. 1 Pet. 1:13. 1 Pet. 5:8.
The gospel designed to teach. Tit. 2:11, 12.
With watchfulness. 1 The. 5:6.
With prayer. 1 Pet. 4:7.

REQUIRED IN
- Ministers. 1 Tim. 3:2, 3. Tit. 1:8.
- Wives of ministers. 1 Tim. 3:11.
- Aged men. Tit. 2:2.
- Young men. Tit. 2:6.
- Young women. Tit. 2:4.
- All saints. 1 The. 5:6, 8.

Women should exhibit, in dress. 1 Tim. 2:9.
We should estimate our character and talents with. Rom. 12:3.
We should live in. Tit. 2:12.
Motives to. 1 Pet. 4:7. 1 Pet. 5:8.

Spear, The.

An offensive weapon. 2 Sam. 23:8, 18.
First mention of, in Scripture. Jos. 8:18.

PARTS OF, MENTIONED;
- The staff of wood. 1 Sam. 17:7.
- The head of iron or brass. 1 Sam. 17:7, with 2 Sam. 21:16.

Probably pointed at both ends. 2 Sam. 2:23.
Called the glittering spear. Job 39:23. Hab. 3:11.

DIFFERENT KINDS OF;
- Lances. Jer. 50:42.
- Javelins. Num. 25:7. 1 Sam. 18:10.
- Darts. 2 Sam. 18:14. Job 41:26, 29.

Those who used, called spearmen. Psa. 68:30. Acts 23:23.
Frequently used by horse soldiers. Nah. 3:3.
Furbished before war. Jer. 46:4.
Pruning-hooks made into, before war. Joel 3:10.
Made into pruning-hooks in peace. Isa. 2:4. Mic. 4:3.

THE ISRAELITES
- Acquainted with the making of. 1 Sam. 13:19.
- Frequently used. Neh. 4:13, 16.
- Ill provided with, in the times of Deborah and of Saul. Jud. 5:8. 1 Sam. 13:22.

Provided by the kings of Israel in great abundance. 2 Chr. 11:12. 2 Chr. 32:5.
Frequently thrown from the hand. 1 Sam. 18:11. 1 Sam. 19:10.
Often retained in the hand of the person using. Num. 25:7. 2 Sam. 2:23.
Stuck in the ground beside the bolster during sleep. 1 Sam. 26:7—11.
Illustrative of the bitterness of the wicked. Psa. 57:4.

Stars, The.

Infinite in number. Gen. 15:5. Jer. 33:22.

GOD
- Created. Gen. 1:16. Psa. 8:3. Psa. 148:5.
- Set, in the firmament of heaven. Gen. 1:17.
- Appointed to give light by night. Gen. 1:16, with 14 v. Psa. 136:9. Jer. 31:35.
- Numbers and names. Psa. 147:4.
- Established, for ever. Psa. 148:3, 6. Jer. 31:36.
- Obscures. Job 9:7.

Revolve in fixed orbits. Jud. 5:20.
Shine in the firmament of heaven. Dan. 12:3.
Appear of different magnitudes. 1 Cor. 15:41.
Appear after sunset. Neh. 4:21, with Job 3:9.

CALLED
- The host of heaven. Deu. 17:3. Jer. 33:22.
- Stars of light. Psa. 148:3.
- Stars of heaven. Isa. 13:10.

When grouped together called constellations. 2 Kin. 23:5. (*marg.*) Isa. 13:10.
Exhibit the greatness of God's power. Psa. 8:3, with Isa. 40:26.
Made to praise God. Psa. 148:3.
Impure in the sight of God. Job 25:5.

MENTIONED IN SCRIPTURE;
- Morning star. Rev. 2:28.
- Arcturus. Job 9:9. Job 38:32.
- Pleiades. Job 9:9. Job 38:31. Amos 5:8.
- Orion. Job 9:9. Job 38:31. Amos 5:8.
- Mazzaroth. Job 38:32.

One of extraordinary brightness (a meteor) appeared at Christ's birth. Mat. 2:2, 9.
Idolaters worshipped. Jer. 8:2. Jer. 19:13.
The Israelites forbidden to worship. Deu. 4:19. Deu. 17:2—4.
Punishment for worshipping. Deu. 17:5—7.
False gods frequently worshipped under the representation of. Amos 5:26. Acts 7:43.
Astrology and star-gazing practised by the Babylonians, &c. Isa. 47:13.
Use of, in navigation alluded to. Acts 27:20.

ILLUSTRATIVE
- Of Christ. Num. 24:17.
- Of angels. Job 38:7.
- Of ministers. Rev. 1:16, 20. Rev. 2:1.
- Of princes and subordinate governors. Dan. 8:10. Rev. 8:12.
- (Bright and morning star,) of Christ. Rev. 22:16.
- (Morning star,) of glory to be given to faithful saints. Rev. 2:28.
- (Shining of,) of the reward of faithful ministers. Dan. 12:3.
- (Withdrawing their light,) of severe judgments. Isa. 13:10. Eze. 32:7. Joel 2:10. Joel 3:15.
- (Setting the nest amongst,) of pride and carnal security. Oba. 4 v.

(Wandering,) of false teachers. Jude 13 v.

Steadfastness.

Exhibited by God in all His purposes and ways. Num. 23: 19. Dan. 6: 26. Jas. 1: 17.
Commanded. Phi. 4: 1. 2 The. 2: 15. Jas. 1: 6—8.
Godliness necessary to. Job 11: 13—15.
SECURED BY
The power of God. Psa. 55: 22. Psa. 62: 2. 1 Pet. 1: 5. Jude 24.
The presence of God. Psa. 16: 8.
Trust in God. Psa. 26: 1.
The intercession of Christ. Luke 22: 31, 32.
A characteristic of saints. Job 17: 9. Jno. 8: 31.
SHOULD BE MANIFESTED
In cleaving to God. Deu. 10: 20. Acts 11: 23.
In the work of the Lord. 1 Cor. 15: 58.
In continuing in the Apostles' doctrine and fellowship. Acts 2: 42.
In holding fast our profession. Heb. 4: 14. Heb. 10: 23.
In holding fast the confidence and rejoicing of the hope. Heb. 3: 6, 14.
In keeping the faith. Col. 2: 5. 1 Pet. 5: 9.
In standing fast in the faith. 1 Cor. 16: 13.
In holding fast what is good. 1 The. 5: 21.
In maintaining Christian liberty. Gal. 5: 1.
In striving for the faith of the gospel. Phi. 1: 27. with Jude 3.
Even under affliction. Psa. 44: 17—19. Rom. 8: 35—37. 1 The. 3: 3.
Saints pray for. Psa. 17: 5.
Saints praise God for. Psa. 116: 8.
MINISTERS
Exhorted to. 2 Tim. 1: 13, 14. Tit. 1: 9.
Should exhort to. Acts 13: 43. Acts 14: 22.
Should pray for, in their people. 1 The. 3: 13. 2 The. 2: 17.
Encouraged by, in their people. 1 The. 3: 8.
Rejoiced by, in their people. Col. 2: 5.
The wicked devoid of. Psa. 78: 8, 37.
Principle of—Illustrated. Mat. 7: 24, 25. Jno. 15: 4. Col. 2: 7.
Want of—Illustrated. Luke 8: 6, 13. Jno. 15: 6. 2 Pet. 2: 17. Jude 12.
Exemplified. *Caleb*, Num. 14: 24. *Joshua*, Jos. 24: 15. *Josiah*, 2 Kin. 22: 2. *Job*, Job 2: 3. *David*, Psa. 18: 21, 22. *Shadrach, &c.* Dan. 3: 18. *Daniel*, Dan. 6: 10. *Primitive Christians*, Acts 2: 42. *Corinthians*, 1 Cor. 15: 1. *Colossians*, Col. 2: 5. *Those who overcame Satan*, Rev. 12: 11.

Strangers in Israel.

All foreigners sojourning in Israel were counted as. Exo. 12: 49.
Under the care and protection of God. Deu. 10: 18. Psa. 146: 9.
Very numerous in Solomon's reign. 2 Chr. 2: 17.
CHIEFLY CONSISTED OF
The remnant of the mixed multitude who came out of Egypt. Exo. 12: 38.
The remnant of the nations of the land. 1 Kin. 9: 20. 2 Chr. 8: 7.
Captives taken in war. Deu. 21: 10.
Foreign servants. Lev. 25: 44, 45.
Persons who sought employment among the Jews. 1 Kin. 7: 13. 1 Kin. 9: 27.
Persons who came into Israel for the sake of religious privileges. 1 Kin. 8: 41.
LAWS RESPECTING;
Not to practice idolatrous rites. Lev. 20: 2.
Not to blaspheme God. Lev. 24: 16.
Not to eat blood. Lev. 17: 10—12.
Not to eat of the passover while uncircumcised. Exo. 12: 43, 44.
Not to work on the Sabbath. Exo. 20: 10. Exo. 23: 12. Deu. 5: 14.
Not to be vexed or oppressed. Exo. 22: 21. Exo. 23: 9. Lev. 19: 33.
Not to be chosen as kings in Israel. Deu. 17: 15.
To be loved. Lev. 19: 34. Deu. 10: 19.
To be relieved in distress. Lev. 25: 35.
Subject to the civil law. Lev. 24: 22.
To have justice done to them in all disputes. Deu. 1: 16. Deu. 24: 17.
To enjoy the benefit of the cities of refuge. Num. 35: 15.
To have the gleaning of the harvest. Lev. 19: 10. Lev. 23: 22. Deu. 24: 19—22.
To participate in the rejoicings of the people. Deu. 14: 29. Deu. 16: 11, 14. Deu. 26: 11.
To have the law read to them. Deu. 31: 12. Jos. 8: 32—35.
The Jews might purchase and have them as slaves. Lev. 25: 44, 45.
The Jews might take usury from. Deu. 23: 20.
Might purchase Hebrew servants subject to release. Lev. 25: 47, 48.
Might offer their burnt-offerings on the altar of God. Lev. 17: 8. Lev. 22: 18. Num. 15: 14.

Allowed to eat what died of itself. Deu. 14: 21.
Motives urged on the Jews for being kind to. Exo. 22: 21. Exo. 23: 9.
Admitted to worship in the outer court of the temple. 1 Kin. 8: 41—43, with Rev. 11: 2. *See* Eph. 2: 14.
Were frequently employed in public works. 1 Chr. 22: 2. 2 Chr. 2: 18.
The Jews condemned for oppressing. Psa. 94: 6. Eze. 22: 7, 29.

Strife.

Christ, an example of avoiding. Isa. 42: 2, with Mat. 12: 15—19. Luke 9: 52—56. 1 Pet. 2: 23.
Forbidden. Pro. 3: 30. Pro. 25: 8.
A work of the flesh. Gal. 5: 20.
An evidence of a carnal spirit. 1 Cor. 3: 3.
Existed in primitive church. 1 Cor. 1: 11.
EXCITED BY
Hatred. Pro. 10: 12.
Pride. Pro. 13: 10. Pro. 28: 25.
Wrath. Pro. 15: 18. Pro. 30: 33.
Frowardness. Pro. 16: 28.
A contentious disposition. Pro. 26: 21.
Tale-bearing. Pro. 26: 20.
Drunkenness. Pro. 23: 29, 30.
Lusts. Jas. 4: 1.
Curious questions. 1 Tim. 6: 4. 2 Tim. 2: 23.
Scorning. Pro. 22: 10.
Difficulty of stopping, a reason for avoiding it. Pro. 17: 14.
Shameful in saints. 2 Cor. 12: 20. Jas. 3: 14.
SAINTS SHOULD
Avoid. Gen. 13: 8. Eph. 4: 3.
Avoid questions that lead to. 2 Tim. 2: 14.
Not walk in. Rom. 13: 13.
Not act from. Phi. 2: 3.
Do all things without. Phi. 2: 14.
Submit to wrong rather than engage in. Pro. 20: 22. Mat. 5: 39, 40. 1 Cor. 6: 7.
Seek God's protection from. Psa. 35: 1. Jer. 18: 19.
Praise God for protection from. 2 Sam. 22: 44. Psa. 18: 43.
Saints kept from tongues of. Psa. 31: 20.
MINISTERS SHOULD
Avoid. 1 Tim. 3: 3. 2 Tim. 2: 24.
Avoid questions that lead to. 2 Tim. 2: 23. Tit. 3: 9.
Not preach through. Phi. 1: 15, 16.
Warn against. 1 Cor. 1: 10. 2 Tim. 2: 14.
Reprove. 1 Cor. 1: 11, 12. 1 Cor. 3: 3. 1 Cor. 11: 17, 18.
Appeased by slowness to anger. Pro. 15: 18.
It is honorable to cease from. Pro. 20: 3.
Hypocrites make religion a pretence for. Isa. 58: 4.
Fools engage in. Pro. 18: 6.
Evidences a love of transgression. Pro. 17: 19.
LEADS TO
Blasphemy. Lev. 24: 10, 11.
Injustice. Hab. 1: 3, 4.
Confusion and every evil work. Jas. 3: 16.
Violence. Exo. 21: 18, 22.
Mutual destruction. Gal. 5: 15.
Temporal blessings embittered by. Pro. 17: 1.
Excludes from heaven. Gal. 5: 20, 21.
Promoters of, should be expelled. Pro. 22: 10.
Punishment for. Psa. 55: 9.
Strength and violence of—Illustrated. Pro. 17: 14. Pro. 18: 19.
Danger of joining in—Illustrated. Pro. 26: 17.
Exemplified. *Herdmen of Abram and of Lot*, Gen. 13: 7. *Herdmen of Gerar and of Isaac*, Gen. 26: 20. *Laban and Jacob*, Gen. 31: 36. *Two Hebrews*, Exo. 2: 13. *Israelites*, Deu. 1: 12. *Judah and Israel*, 2 Sam. 19: 41—43. *Disciples*, Luke 22: 24. *Judaizing Teachers*, Acts 15: 2. *Paul and Barnabas*, Acts 15: 39. *Pharisees and Sadducees*, Acts 23: 7. *Corinthians*, 1 Cor. 1: 11. 1 Cor. 6: 6.

Summer.

Made by God. Psa. 74: 17.
Yearly return of, secured by covenant. Gen. 8: 22.
CHARACTERIZED BY
Excessive heat. Jer. 17: 8.
Excessive drought. Psa. 32: 4.
Approach of, indicated by shooting out of leaves on trees. Mat. 24: 32.
Many kinds of fruit were ripe and used during. 2 Sam. 16: 1. Jer. 40: 10. Jer. 48: 32.
The ancients had houses or apartments suited to. Jud. 3: 20, 24. Amos 3: 15.
The ant provided her winter food during. Pro. 6: 8. Pro. 30: 25.
The wise are diligent during. Pro. 10: 5.
Illustrative of seasons of grace. Jer. 8: 20.

Sun, The.

Called the greater light. Gen. 1: 16.
GOD
Created. Gen. 1: 14, 16. Psa. 74: 16.
Placed, in the firmament. Gen. 1: 17.
Appointed to rule the day. Gen. 1: 16. Psa. 136: 8. Jer. 31: 35.

Appointed to divide seasons, &c. Gen. 1:14.
Exercises sovereign power over. Job 9:7.
Causes, to rise both on evil and good. Mat. 5:45.
Causes, to know its time of setting. Psa. 104:19.
Made to praise and glorify God. Psa. 148:3.
The power and brilliancy of its rising alluded to. Jud. 5:31. 2 Sam. 23:4.
Clearness of its light alluded to. So. of Sol. 6:10.
Compared to a bridegroom coming forth from his chamber. Psa. 19:5.
Compared to a strong man rejoicing to run a race. Psa. 19:5.
Diffuses light and heat to all the earth. Psa. 19:6.
THE RAYS OF,
Pleasant to man. Job 30:28, with Ecc. 11:7.
Produce and ripen fruits. Deu. 33:14.
Soften and melt some substances. Exo. 16:21.
Wither and burn up the herbs of the field. Mar. 4:6. Jas. 1:11.
Change the color of the skin. So. of Sol. 1:6.
Frequently destructive to human life. 2 Kin. 4:18—20. Psa. 121:6. Isa. 49:10.
Indicates the hours of the day by the shadow on the dial. 2 Kin. 20:9.
THE JEWS
Commenced their day with the rising of. Gen. 19:23, 24, with 27, 28 vs. Jud. 9:33.
Commenced their evening with the setting of. Gen. 28:11. Deu. 24:13. Mar. 1:32.
Expressed the east by rising of. Num. 21:11. Deu. 4:41, 47. Jos. 12:1.
Expressed the west by setting of. Jas. 1:4.
Expressed the whole earth by, from rising of, to setting of. Psa. 50:1. Psa. 113:3. Isa. 45:6.
Forbidden to worship. Deu. 4:19. Deu. 17:3.
Made images of. 2 Chr. 14:5. (*marg.*) 2 Chr. 34:4. (*marg.*)
Consecrated chariots and horses, as symbols of. 2 Kin. 23:11.
Worshipped. 2 Kin. 23:5. Jer. 8:2.
Worshippers of, turned their faces towards the east. Eze. 8:16.
MIRACLES CONNECTED WITH;
Standing still for a whole day in the valley of Ajalon. Jos. 10:12, 13.
Shadow put back on the dial. 2 Kin. 20:11.
Darkened at the crucifixion. Luke 23:44, 45.
ILLUSTRATIVE
Of God's favor. Psa. 84:11.
Of Christ's coming. Mal. 4:2.
Of the glory of Christ. Mat. 17:2. Rev. 1:16. Rev. 10:1.
Of supreme rulers. Gen. 37:9. Isa. 13:10.
(Its clearness,) of the purity of the church. So. of Sol. 6:10.
(Its brightness,) of the future glory of saints. Dan. 12:3, with Mat. 13:43.
(Its power,) of the triumph of saints. Jud. 5:31.
(Darkened,) of severe calamities. Eze. 32:7. Joel 2:10, 31, with Mat. 24:29. Rev. 9:2.
(Going down at noon,) of premature destruction. Jer. 15:9. Amos 8:9.
(No more going down,) of perpetual blessedness. Isa. 60:20.
(Before or in sight of,) of public ignominy. 2 Sam. 12:11, 12. Jer. 8:2.

Swearing Falsely.

Forbidden. Lev. 19:12. Num. 30:2. Mat. 5:33.
Hateful to God. Zec. 8:17.
We should not love. Zec. 8:17.
Fraud often leads to. Lev. 6:2, 3.
Saints abstain from. Jos. 9:20. Psa. 15:4.
Blessedness of abstaining from. Psa. 24:4, 5.
THE WICKED
Addicted to. Jer. 5:2. Hos. 10:4.
Plead excuses for. Jer. 7:9, 10.
Shall be judged on account of. Mal. 3:5.
Shall be cut off for. Zec. 5:3.
Shall have a curse upon their houses for. Zec. 5:4.
False witnesses guilty of. Deu. 19:16, 18.
Exemplified. *Saul*, 1 Sam. 19:6, 10. *Shimei*, 1 Kin. 2:41—43. *Jews*, Eze. 16:59. *Zedekiah*, Eze. 17:13—19. *Peter*, Mat. 26:72, 74.

Swearing, Profane.

Of all kinds is desecration of God's name and is forbidden. Exo. 20:7. Mat. 5:34—36. Mat. 23:21, 22. Jas. 5:12.
THE WICKED
Addicted to. Psa. 10:7. Rom. 3:14.
Love. Psa. 109:17.
Clothe themselves with. Psa. 109:18.
Guilt of. Exo. 20:7. Deu. 5:11.
Woe denounced against. Mat. 23:16.
Nations visited for. Jer. 23:10. Hos. 4:1—3.

Punishment for. Lev. 24:16, 23. Psa. 59:12. Psa. 109:17, 18.
Exemplified: *Son of Israelitish woman*, Lev. 24:11. *Gehazi*, 2 Kin. 5:20. *Peter*, Mat. 26:74.

Swine.

When wild inhabited the woods. Psa. 80:13.
Unclean and not to be eaten. Lev. 11:7, 8.
DESCRIBED AS
  Fierce and ungenerous. Mat. 7:6.
  Filthy in its habits. 2 Pet. 2:22.
  Destructive to agriculture. Psa. 80:13.
Fed upon husks. Luke 15:16.
Sacrificing of, an abomination. Isa. 66:3.
Kept in large herds. Mat. 8:30.
Herding of, considered as the greatest degradation to a Jew. Luke 15:15.
The Gergesenes punished for having. Mat. 8:31, 32. Mar. 5:11, 14.
The ungodly Jews condemned for eating. Isa. 65:4. Isa. 66:17.
ILLUSTRATIVE OF
  The wicked. Mat. 7:6.
  Hypocrites. 2 Pet. 2:22.

Sword, The.

Probable origin of. Gen. 3:24.
Was pointed. Eze. 21:15.
Frequently had two edges. Psa. 149:6.
DESCRIBED AS
  Sharp. Psa. 57:4.
  Bright. Nah. 3:3.
  Glittering. Deu. 32:41. Job 20:25.
  Oppressive. Jer. 46:16.
  Hurtful. Psa. 144:10.
Carried in a sheath or scabbard. 1 Chr. 21:27. Jer. 47:6. Eze. 21:3—5.
Suspended from the girdle. 1 Sam. 17:39. 2 Sam. 20:8. Neh. 4:18. Psa. 45:3.
WAS USED
  By the patriarchs. Gen. 34:25. Gen. 48:22.
  By the Jews. Jud. 20:2. 2 Sam. 24:9.
  By heathen nations. Jud. 7:22. 1 Sam. 15:33.
  For self-defence. Luke 22:36.
  For destruction of enemies. Num. 21:24. Jos. 6:21.
  For punishing criminals. 1 Sam. 15:33. Acts 12:2.
  Sometimes for self-destruction. 1 Sam. 31:4, 5. Acts 16:27.
Hebrews early acquainted with making of. 1 Sam. 13:19.
In time of war plowshares made into. Joel 3:10.
In time of peace made into plowshares. Isa. 2:4. Mic. 4:3.
Sharpened and furbished before going to war. Psa. 7:12. Eze. 21:9.
Was brandished over the head. Eze. 32:10.
Was thrust through enemies. Eze. 16:40.
Often threatened as a punishment. Lev. 26:25, 33. Deu. 32:25.
Often sent as a punishment. Ezr. 9:7. Psa. 78:62.
Was one of God's four sore judgments. Eze. 14:21.
Those slain by, communicated ceremonial uncleanness. Num. 19:16.
ILLUSTRATIVE
  Of the word of God. Eph. 6:17, with Heb. 4:12.
  Of the word of Christ. Isa. 49:2, with Rev. 1:16.
  Of the justice of God. Deu. 32:41. Zec. 13:7.
  Of the protection of God. Deu. 33:29.
  Of war and contention. Mat. 10:34.
  Of severe and heavy calamities. Eze. 5:2, 17. Eze. 14:17. Eze. 21:9.
  Of deep mental affliction. Luke 2:35.
  Of the wicked. Psa. 17:13.
  Of the tongue of the wicked. Psa. 57:4. Psa. 64:3. Pro. 12:18.
  Of persecuting spirit of the wicked. Psa. 37:14.
  Of the end of the wicked. Pro. 5:4.
  Of false witnesses. Pro. 25:18.
  Of judicial authority. Rom. 13:4.
  (Drawing of,) of war and destruction. Lev. 26:33. Eze. 21:3—5.
  (Putting, into its sheath,) of peace and friendship. Jer. 47:6.
  (Living by,) of rapine. Gen. 27:40.
  (Not departing from one's house,) of perpetual calamity. 2 Sam. 12:10.

Synagogues.

Places in which the Jews assembled for worship. Acts 13:5, 14.
Early notice of their existence. Psa. 74:8.
Probably originated in the schools of the prophets. 1 Sam. 19:18—24. 2 Kin. 4:23.
Revival of, after the captivity. Neh. 8:1—8.
SERVICE OF, CONSISTED OF
  Prayer. Mat. 6:5.
  Reading the word of God. Neh. 8:18. Neh. 9:3. Neh. 13:1. Acts 15:21.
  Expounding the word of God. Neh. 8:8. Luke 4:21.
  Praise and thanksgiving. Neh. 9:5.
Service in, on the Sabbath day. Luke 4:16. Acts 13:14.

GOVERNED BY
A president or chief ruler. Acts 18: 8, 17.
Ordinary rulers. Mar. 5: 22. Acts 13: 15.
Provided with a chazan or minister, who had charge of the sacred books. Luke 4: 17, 20.
Had seats for the congregation. Acts 13: 14.
Chief seats in, reserved for elders. Mat. 23: 6.
The portion of Scripture for the day sometimes read by one of the congregation. Luke 4: 16.
Strangers were invited to address the congregation in. Acts 13: 15.
CHRIST OFTEN
Attended. Luke 4: 16.
Preached and taught in. Mat. 4: 23. Mar. 1: 39. Luke 13: 10.
Performed miracles in. Mat. 12: 9, 10. Mar. 1: 23. Luke 13: 11.
The Apostles frequently taught and preached in. Acts 9: 20. Acts 13: 5. Acts 17: 1, 17.
Often used as courts of justice. Acts 9: 2. Jas. 2: 2. (*marg.*)
OFFENDERS WERE OFTEN
Given up to, for trial. Luke 12: 11. Luke 21: 12.
Punished in. Mat. 10: 17. Mat. 23: 34. Acts 22: 19.
Expelled from. Jno. 9: 22, 34. Jno. 12: 42. Jno. 16: 2.
The building of, considered a noble and meritorious work. Luke 7: 5.
Sometimes several, in the same city. Acts 6: 9. Acts 9: 2.
Each sect had its own. Acts 6: 9.

Syria.

Originally included Mesopotamia. Gen. 25: 20. Gen. 28: 5. Deu. 26: 5, with Acts 7: 2.
More properly the country around Damascus. 2 Sam. 8: 6.
Damascus the capital of. Isa. 7: 8.
Abana and Pharpar rivers of. 2 Kin. 5: 12.
Governed by kings. 1 Kin. 22: 31. 2 Kin. 5: 1.
INHABITANTS OF,
Called Syrians. 2 Sam. 10: 11. 2 Kin. 5: 20.
Called Syrians of Damascus. 2 Sam. 8: 5.
An idolatrous people. Jud. 10: 6. 2 Kin. 5: 18.
A warlike people. 1 Kin. 20 : 23, 25.
A commercial people. Eze. 27: 18.
Spoke the Syriac language. 2 Kin. 18: 26. Ezr. 4: 7. Dan. 2: 4.
Israel followed the idolatry of. Jud. 10: 6.
DAVID
Destroyed the army of, which assisted Hadadezer. 2 Sam. 8: 5.
Garrisoned and made tributary. 2 Sam. 8: 6.
Dedicated the spoils of. 2 Sam. 8: 11, 12.
Obtained renown by his victory over. 2 Sam. 8: 13.
Sent Joab against the armies of, hired by the Ammonites. 2 Sam. 10: 6—14.
Destroyed a second army of. 2 Sam. 10: 15—19.
Asa sought aid of, against Israel. 1 Kin. 15: 18—20.
Elijah anointed Hazael king over, by divine direction. 1 Kin. 19: 15.
Benhadad king of, besieged Samaria. 1 Kin. 20: 1—12.
THE ISRAELITES
Under Ahab encouraged and assisted by God, overcame. 1 Kin. 20: 13—20.
Forewarned of invasion by, at the return of the year. 1 Kin. 20: 22—25.
Insignificant before. 1 Kin. 20: 26, 27.
Encouraged and assisted by God overcame, a second time. 1 Kin. 20: 28—30.
Craftily drawn into a league with. 1 Kin. 20: 31—43.
At peace with, for three years. 1 Kin. 22: 1.
Under Ahab sought to recover Ramoth-gilead from. 1 Kin. 22: 3—29.
Defeated by, and Ahab slain. 1 Kin. 22: 30—36.
Harassed by frequent incursions of. 2 Kin. 5: 2. 2 Kin. 6: 23.
Heard the secrets of, from Elisha. 2 Kin. 6: 8 -12.
God smote with blindness those sent against Elisha by the king of. 2 Kin. 6: 14, 18—20.
Besieged Samaria again. 2 Kin. 6: 24—29.
Army of, miraculously routed. 2 Kin. 7: 5, 6.
Death of the king of, and the cruelty of his successor foretold by Elisha. 2 Kin. 8: 7, 15.
Joram king of Israel in seeking to recover Ramoth-gilead from, severely wounded. 2 Kin. 8: 28, 29. 2 Kin. 9: 15.
Israel delivered into the hands of, for the sins of Jehoahaz. 2 Kin. 13: 3, 7, 22.
A savior raised up for Israel against. 2 Kin. 13: 5, 23—25.
Elisha predicted to Joash his three victories over. 2 Kin. 13: 14—19.
Joined with Israel against Ahaz and besieged Jerusalem. 2 Kin. 16: 5. Isa. 7: 12.

Retook Elath and drove out the Jews. 2 Kin. 16: 6.
Subdued and its inhabitants taken captive by Assyria. 2 Kin. 16: 9.
PROPHECIES RESPECTING;
Destruction of Rezin king of. Isa. 7: 8, 16.
Ceasing to be a kingdom. Isa. 17: 1—3.
Terror and dismay in, occasioned by its invasion. Jer. 49: 23, 24.
Destruction of its inhabitants. Jer. 49: 26.
Spoliation of Damascus. Isa. 8: 4.
Burning of Damascus. Jer. 49: 27. Amos 1: 4.
Its calamities, the punishments of its sins. Amos 1: 3.
Its inhabitants to be captives. Amos 1: 5.
Its history in connection with the Macedonian empire. Dan. 11: 6, &c.
Subdued and governed by the Romans. Luke 2: 2.
Gospel preached and many churches founded in. Acts 15: 23, 41.

Tabernacle, The.

Moses was commanded to make, after a divine pattern. Exo. 25: 9. Exo. 26: 30. Heb. 8: 5.
Made of the free-will offerings of the people. Exo. 25: 1—8. Exo. 35: 4, 5, 21—29.
Divine wisdom given to Bezaleel, &c. to make. Exo. 31: 2—7. Exo. 35: 30—35. Exo. 36: 1.
CALLED THE
Tabernacle of the Lord. Jos. 22: 19. 1 Kin. 2: 28. 1 Chr. 16: 39.
Tabernacle of testimony or witness. Exo. 38: 21. Num. 1: 50. Num. 17: 7, 8. 2 Chr. 24: 6. Acts 7: 44.
Tabernacle of the congregation. Exo. 27: 21. Exo. 33: 7. Exo. 40: 26.
Tabernacle of Shiloh. Psa. 78: 60.
Tabernacle of Joseph. Psa. 78: 67.
Temple of the Lord. 1 Sam. 1: 9. 1 Sam. 3: 3.
House of the Lord. Jos. 6: 24. 1 Sam. 1: 7, 24.
Was a moveable tent suited to the unsettled condition of Israel. 2 Sam. 7: 6, 7.
Designed for manifestation of God's presence and for His worship. Exo. 25: 8. Exo. 29: 42, 43.
THE BOARDS OF,
Made of shittim wood. Exo. 26: 15. Exo. 36: 20.
Ten cubits high by one and a half broad. Exo. 26: 16. Exo. 36: 21.
Had each two tenons fitted into sockets of silver. Exo. 26: 17, 19. Exo. 36: 22—24.
Twenty on south side. Exo. 26: 18. Exo. 36: 23.
Twenty on north side. Exo. 26: 20. Exo. 36: 25.
Six, and two corner boards for west side. Exo. 26: 22—25. Exo. 36: 27—30.
Supported by bars of shittim wood resting in rings of gold. Exo. 26: 26—29. Exo. 36: 31—33.
With the bars, covered with gold. Exo. 26: 29. Exo. 36: 34.
The door of, a curtain of blue and purple suspended by gold rings from five pillars of shittim wood, &c. Exo. 26: 36, 37. Exo. 36: 37, 38.
COVERINGS OF,
The first or inner, ten curtains of blue, purple, &c. joined with loops and golden taches. Exo. 26: 1—6. Exo. 36: 8—13.
The second, eleven curtains of goats' hair, &c. Exo. 26: 7—13. Exo. 36: 14—18.
The third of rams' skins dyed red. Exo. 26: 14. Exo. 36: 19.
The fourth or outward of badgers' skins. Exo. 26: 14. Exo. 36: 19.
Divided by a vail of blue, purple, &c. suspended from four pillars of shittim wood by gold hooks. Exo. 26: 31—33. Exo. 36: 35, 36. Exo. 40: 21.
DIVIDED INTO
The holy place. Exo. 26: 33. Heb. 9: 2—6.
The most holy place. Exo. 26: 34. Heb. 9: 3, 7.
Had a court round about. Exo. 40: 8.
The table of show-bread, the golden candlestick, and the altar of incense were placed in the holy place. Exo. 26: 35. Exo. 40: 22, 24, 26. Heb. 9: 2.
The ark and mercy-seat put in the most holy place. Exo. 26: 33, 34. Exo. 40: 20, 21. Heb. 9: 4.
COURT OF,
One hundred cubits long and fifty cubits wide. Exo. 27: 18.
Surrounded by curtains of fine linen suspended from pillars in sockets of brass. Exo. 27: 9—15. Exo. 38: 9—16.
The gate of, a hanging of blue, purple, &c. twenty cubits wide, suspended from four pillars, &c. Exo. 27: 16. Exo. 38: 18.
Contained the brazen altar and laver of brass. Exo. 40: 29, 30.
All the pillars of, filletted with silver, &c. Exo. 27: 17. Exo. 38: 17.
All the vessels of, made of brass. Exo. 27: 19.
First reared, on the first day of the second year after the exodus. Exo. 40: 2, 17.

WAS SET UP
By Moses at Mount Sinai. Exo. 40: 18, 19, with Num. 10: 11, 12.
At Gilgal. Jos. 5: 10, 11.
In Shiloh. Jos. 18: 1. Jos. 19: 51.
In Nob. 1 Sam. 21: 1—6.
Finally at Gibeon. 1 Chr. 16: 39. 1 Chr. 21: 29.
Anointed and consecrated with oil. Exo. 40: 9. Lev. 8: 10. Num. 7: 1.
Sprinkled and purified with blood. Heb. 9: 21.
Sanctified by the glory of the Lord. Exo. 29: 43. Exo. 40: 34. Num. 9: 15.
The Lord appeared in, over the mercy-seat. Exo. 25: 22. Lev. 16: 2. Num. 7: 89.
The cloud of glory rested on, by night and day during its abode in the wilderness. Exo. 40: 38. Num. 9: 15, 16.
The journeys of Israel regulated by the cloud on. Exo. 40: 36, 37.
THE PRIESTS
Alone could enter. Num. 18: 3, 5.
Performed all services in. Num. 3: 10. Num. 18: 1, 2. Heb. 9: 6.
Were the ministers of. Heb. 8: 2.
THE LEVITES
Appointed over, and had charge of. Num. 1: 50. Num. 8: 24. Num. 18: 2—4.
Did the inferior service of. Num. 3: 6—8.
Took down, and put up. Num. 1: 51.
Carried. Num. 4: 15, 25, 31.
Pitched their tents around. Num. 1: 53. Num. 3: 23, 29, 35.
Free-will offerings made at the first rearing of. Num. 7: 1—9.
Free-will offerings made at the dedication of the altar of. Num. 7: 10—87.
All offerings to be made at. Lev. 17: 4. Deu. 12: 5, 6, 11, 13, 14.
Punishment for defiling. Lev. 15: 31. Num. 19: 13.
A permanent house substituted for, when the kingdom was established. 2 Sam. 7: 5—13.
ILLUSTRATIVE
Of Christ. Isa. 4: 6. Jno. 1: 14. (*Greek.*) Heb. 9: 8, 9, 11.
Of the church. Psa. 15: 1. Isa. 16: 5. Isa. 54: 2. Heb. 8: 2. Rev. 21: 2, 3.
Of the body. 2 Cor. 5: 1. 2 Pet. 1: 13.
(The holy of holies,) of heaven. Heb. 6: 19, 20. Heb. 9: 12, 24. Heb. 10: 19.
(The vail,) of Christ's body. Heb. 10: 20.
(The vail,) of the obscurity of the Mosaic dispensation. Heb. 9: 8, 10, with Rom. 16: 25, 26. Rev. 11: 19.

Temple, The First.

Built on Mount Moriah on the threshing-floor of Ornan or Araunah. 1 Chr. 21: 28—30, with 1 Chr. 22: 1. 2 Chr. 3: 1.
DAVID
Anxious to build. 2 Sam. 7: 2. 1 Chr. 22: 7. 1 Chr. 29: 3. Psa. 132: 2—5.
Being a man of war not permitted to build. 2 Sam. 7: 5—9, with 1 Kin. 5: 3. 1 Chr. 22: 8.
Told by the prophet that Solomon should build. 2 Sam. 7: 12, 13. 1 Chr. 17: 12.
Made preparations for building. 1 Chr. 22: 2—5, 14—16, 1 Chr. 29: 2—5.
Charged Solomon to build. 1 Chr. 22: 6, 7, 11.
Prayed that Solomon might have wisdom to build. 1 Chr. 29: 19.
Charged his princes to assist in building. 1 Chr. 22: 17—19.
Free-will offerings of the people for building. 1 Chr. 29: 6—9.
SOLOMON
Determined to build. 2 Chr. 2: 1.
Specially instructed for. 2 Chr. 3: 3.
Employed all the strangers in preparing for. 2 Chr. 2: 2, 17, 18, with 1 Kin. 5: 15.
Applied to Hiram for a skilful workman to superintend, &c. the building of. 2 Chr. 2: 7, 13, 14.
Employed thirty thousand Israelites in the work. 1 Kin. 5: 13, 14.
Contracted with Hiram for wood, stone, and labor. 1 Kin. 5: 6—12. 2 Chr. 2: 8—10.
Commenced second day of second month of fourth year of Solomon. 1 Kin. 6: 1, 37. 2 Chr. 3: 2
Built without the noise of hammers, ax, or any tool. 1 Kin. 6: 7
DIVIDED INTO
The sanctuary or greater house. 2 Chr. 3: 5.
The oracle or most holy place. 1 Kin. 6: 19.
The porch. 2 Chr. 3: 4.
Surrounded with three stories of chambers communicating with the interior on the right side. 1 Kin. 6: 5, 6, 8, 10.
Surrounded with spacious courts. 1 Kin. 6: 36. 2 Chr. 4: 9.
Was three score cubits long, twenty broad, and thirty high. 1 Kin. 6: 2. 2 Chr. 3: 3.
Was lighted by narrow windows. 1 Kin. 6: 4.
Was roofed with cedar. 1 Kin. 6: 9.
THE GREATER OR OUTER HOUSE
Was forty cubits long. 2 Kin. 6: 17.

Had folding doors of fir wood carved and gilded. 1 Kin. 6:34, 35.
Had door posts of olive-wood carved and gilded. 1 Kin. 6:33. 2 Chr. 3:7.

THE ORACLE OR MOST HOLY PLACE
Was twenty cubits every way. 1 Kin. 6:16, 20.
Two cherubims of gilded olive-wood made within. 1 Kin. 6:23—28. 2 Chr. 3:11—13.
A partition of chains of gold between it and outer house. 1 Kin. 6:21.
The doors and posts of, of olive-wood carved and gilded. 1 Kin. 6:31, 32.
Separated from the outer house by a vail. 2 Chr. 3:14.

The floor and walls of, covered with cedar and fir wood. 1 Kin. 6:15.
Cedar of, carved with flowers, &c. 1 Kin. 6:18.
Ceiled with fir wood and gilt. 2 Chr. 3:5.
The whole inside and outside covered with gold. 1 Kin. 6:21, 22. 2 Chr. 3:7.
Garnished with precious stones. 2 Chr. 3:6.

THE PORCH OF,
Twenty cubits long and ten broad. 1 Kin. 6:3.
One hundred and twenty cubits high. 2 Chr. 3:4.
Pillars of, with their chapiters described. 1 Kin. 7:15—22. 2 Chr. 3:15—17.

Its magnificence. 2 Chr. 2:5, 9.
Was seven years in building. 1 Kin. 6:38.
Was finished in the eighth month of the eleventh year of Solomon. 1 Kin. 6:38.

WAS CALLED
The house of the Lord. 2 Chr. 23:5, 12.
The mountain of the Lord's house. Isa. 2:2.
House of the God of Jacob. Isa. 2:3.
Zion. Psa. 84:1—7.
Mount Zion. Psa. 74:2.

Appointed as a house of sacrifice. 2 Chr. 7:12.
Appointed as a house of prayer. Isa. 56:7, with Mat. 21:13.
God promised to dwell in. 1 Kin. 6:12, 13.
All dedicated things placed in. 2 Chr. 5:1.
The ark of God brought into with great solemnity. 1 Kin. 8:1—9. 2 Chr. 5:2—10.
Filled with the cloud of glory. 1 Kin. 8:10, 11. 2 Chr. 5:13. 2 Chr. 7:2.
Solemnly dedicated to God by Solomon. 1 Kin. 8:12—66. 2 Chr. 6 ch.
Sacred fire sent down from heaven at its dedication. 2 Chr. 7:3.
Was but a temple built with hands. Acts 7:47, 48.
Complete destruction of, predicted. Jer. 26:18, with Mic. 3:12.

HISTORICAL NOTICES OF;
Pillaged by Shishak king of Egypt. 1 Kin. 14:25, 26. 2 Chr. 12:9.
Repaired by Jehoash at the instigation of Jehoiada. 2 Kin. 12:4—14. 2 Chr. 24:4—13.
Treasures of given by Jehoash to propitiate the Syrians. 2 Kin. 12:17, 18.
Defiled and its treasures given by Ahaz to the king of Assyria. 2 Kin. 16:14, 18. 2 Chr. 28:20, 21.
Purified and divine worship restored under Hezekiah. 2 Chr. 29:3—35.
Its treasures, &c. given by Hezekiah to the Assyrians, to procure a treaty. 2 Kin. 18:13—16.
Polluted by the idolatrous worship of Manasseh. 2 Kin. 21:4—7. 2 Chr. 33:4, 5, 7.
Repaired by Josiah in the eighteenth year of his reign. 2 Kin. 22:3—7. 2 Chr. 34:8—13.
Purified by Josiah. 2 Kin. 23:4—7, 11, 12.
Pillaged and burned by the Babylonians. 2 Kin. 25:9, 13—17. 2 Chr. 36:18, 19.

ILLUSTRATIVE OF
Christ. Jno. 2:19, 21.
The spiritual church. 1 Cor. 3:16. 2 Cor. 6:16. Eph. 2:20—22.
The bodies of saints. 1 Cor. 6:19.

Temple, The Second.

Built on the site of the first temple. Ezr. 2:6, &c.

CYRUS
His decree for building, predicted. Isa. 44:28.
Gave a decree for building, in the first year of his reign. Ezr. 1:1, 2. Ezr. 6:3.
Gave permission to the Jews to go to Jerusalem to build. Ezr. 1:3.
Furnished means for building. Ezr. 6:4.
Ordered those who remained in Babylon to contribute to the building of. Ezr. 1:4.
Gave the vessels of the first temple for. Ezr. 1:7—11. Ezr. 6:5.

Divine worship commenced before the foundation was laid. Ezr. 3:1—6.
Materials for building, procured from Tyre and Sidon. Ezr. 3:7.
Foundation of, laid the second month of second year after the captivity. Ezr. 3:8.

Solemnities connected with laying the foundation of. Ezr. 3:9-11.
Its dimensions. Ezr. 6:3, 4.
Grief of those who had seen the first temple. Ezr. 3:12. Hag. 2:3.
Joy of those who had not seen the first temple. Ezr. 3:13.
THE SAMARITANS, &c.
  Proposed to assist in building. Ezr. 4:1, 2.
  Their help refused by the Jews. Ezr. 4:3.
  Weakened the hands of the Jews in building. Ezr. 4:4, 5.
  Wrote to Artaxerxes Smerdis to interrupt the building. Ezr. 4:6—16.
  Procured its interruption for fifteen years. Ezr. 4:24.
The Jews reproved for not building. Hag. 1:1—5.
The Jews punished for not persevering in building. Hag. 1: 6, 9—11. Hag. 2:15, 17. Zec. 8:10.
The Jews encouraged to proceed in building. Hag. 1: 8. Hag. 2: 19. Zec. 8:9.
Resumed by Zerubbabel and Jeshua. Ezr. 5:2.
Its completion by Zerubbabel foretold, to encourage the Jews. Zec. 4:4—10.
Future glory of, predicted. Hag. 2: 7—9.
Tatnai the governor wrote to Darius to know if the building had his sanction. Ezr. 5:3—17.
The decree of Cyrus found and confirmed by Darius. Ezr. 6:1, 2, 6—12.
Finished the third of the twelfth month in the sixth year of Darius. Ezr. 6:15.
Dedication of, celebrated with joy and thankfulness. Ezr. 6:16—18.
Repaired and beautified by Herod, which occupied forty-six years. Jno. 2:20.
The magnificence of its building and ornaments. Jno. 2:20. Mar. 13:1. Luke 21:5.
Beautiful gate of, mentioned. Acts 3:2.
Solomon's porch connected with. Jno. 10:23. Acts 3:11.
CHRIST
  To appear in. Hag. 2: 7, with Mal. 3:1.
  Presented in. Luke 2:22, 27.
  Miraculously transported to a pinnacle of. Mat. 4:5. Luke 4:9.
  Frequently taught in. Mar. 14:49.
  Purified, at the commencement of His ministry. Jno. 2:15—17.
  Purified, at the close of His ministry. Mat. 21:12, 13.
  Predicted its destruction. Mat. 24: 2. Mar. 13:2. Luke 21:6.
The vail of, rent at our Lord's death. Mat. 27:51.
Separation between the outer or Gentile court and that of the Jews, alluded to. Eph. 2:13, 14.
No Gentile allowed to enter the inner courts of. Acts 21:27--30.
THE JEWS
  Prayed without, while the priest offered incense within. Luke 1: 10. *See* Luke 18:10.
  Considered it blasphemy to speak against. Mat. 26:61. Acts 6:13. Acts 21:28.
  Desecrated by selling oxen, &c. in. Jno. 2:14.
Desecration of, foretold. Dan. 9:27. Dan. 11:31.
Cleansed and re-dedicated by Judas Maccabæus after its desecration by Antiochus Epiphanes. Jno. 10:22.
Desecrated by the Romans. Dan. 9: 27, with Mat. 24:15.

Temptation.

God cannot be the subject of. Jas. 1:13.
Does not come from God. Jas. 1:13.
COMES FROM
  Lusts. Jas. 1:14.
  Covetousness. Pro. 28:20. 1 Tim. 6:9, 10.
The devil is the author of. 1 Chr. 21: 1. Mat. 4:1. Jno. 13:2. 1 The. 3:5.
Evil associates, the instruments of. Pro. 1:10. Pro. 7:6. Pro. 16:29.
OFTEN ARISES THROUGH
  Poverty. Pro. 30:9. Mat. 4:2, 3.
  Prosperity. Pro. 30:9. Mat. 4:8.
  Worldly glory. Num. 22:17. Dan. 4:30. Dan. 5:2. Mat. 4:8.
To distrust of God's providence. Mat. 4:3.
To presumption. Mat. 4:6.
To worshipping the god of this world. Mat. 4:9.
Often strengthened by the perversion of God's word. Mat. 4:6.
PERMITTED AS A TRIAL OF
  Faith. 1 Pet. 1:7. Jas, 1:2, 3.
  Disinterestedness. Job 1:9—12.
Always comformable to the nature of man. 1 Cor. 10:13.
Often ends in sin and perdition. 1 Tim. 6:9. Jas. 1:15.
CHRIST
  Endured, from the devil. Mar. 1: 13.
  Endured, from the wicked. Mat. 16:1. Mat. 22:18. Luke 10:25.
  Resisted by the word of God. Mat. 4:4, 7, 10.
  Overcame. Mat. 4:11.
  Sympathizes with those under. Heb. 4:15.

Is able to succor those under. Heb. 2:18.
Intercedes for His people under. Luke 22:31, 32. Jno. 17:15.
God will not suffer saints to be exposed to, beyond their powers to bear. 1 Cor. 10:13.
God will make a way for saints to escape out of. 1 Cor. 10:13.
God enables the saints to bear. 1 Cor. 10:13.
God knows how to deliver saints out of. 2 Pet. 2:9.
Christ keeps faithful saints from the hour of. Rev. 3:10.
Saints may be in heaviness through. 1 Pet. 1:6.
SAINTS SHOULD
Resist, in faith. Eph. 6:16. 1 Pet. 5:9.
Watch against. Mat. 26:41. 1 Pet. 5:8.
Pray to be kept from. Mat. 6:13. Mat. 26:41.
Not to occasion, to others. Rom. 14:13.
Restore those overcome by. Gal. 6:1.
Avoid the way of. Pro. 4:14, 15.
The devil will renew. Luke 4:13.
Has strength through the weakness of the flesh. Mat. 26:41.
Mere professors fall away in time of. Luke 8:13.
Blessedness of those who meet and overcome. Jas. 1:2—4, 12.
Exemplified. *Eve*, Gen. 3:1, 4, 5. *Joseph*, Gen. 39:7. *Balaam*, Num. 22:17. *Achan*, Jos. 7:21. *David*, 2 Sam. 11:2. *Jeroboam*, 1 Kin. 15:30. *Peter*, Mar. 14:67—71. *Paul*, 2 Cor. 12:7, with Gal. 4:14.

Tents.

Origin and antiquity of. Gen. 4:20.
CALLED
Tabernacles. Num. 24:5. Job 12:6. Heb. 11:9.
Curtains. Isa. 54:2. Heb. 3:7.
Were spread out. Isa. 40:22.
Fastened by cords to stakes or nails. Isa. 54:2. Jer. 10:20, with Jud. 4:21.
WERE USED BY
Patriarchs. Gen. 13:5. Gen. 25:27. Heb. 11:9.
Israel in the desert. Exo. 33:8. Num. 24:2.
The people of Israel in all their wars. 1 Sam. 4:3, 10. 1 Sam. 29:1. 1 Kin. 16:16.
The Rechabites. Jer. 35:7, 10.
The Arabs. Isa. 13:20.
Shepherds while tending their flocks. So. of Sol. 1:8. Isa. 38:12.
All eastern nations. Jud. 6:5. 1 Sam. 17:4. 2 Kin. 7:7. 1 Chr. 5:10.
Separate, for females of the family. Gen. 24:67.
Separate, for the servants. Gen. 31:33.
WERE PITCHED
With order and regularity. Num. 1:52.
In the neighborhood of wells, &c. Gen. 13:10, 12. Gen. 26:17, 18. 1 Sam. 29:1.
Under trees. Gen. 18:1, 4. Jud. 4:5.
On the tops of houses. 2 Sam. 16:22.
Sending persons to seek a convenient place for, alluded to. Deu. 1:33.
Ease and rapidity of their removal, alluded to. Isa. 38:12.
Of the Jews contrasted with those of the Arabs. Num. 24:5, with So. of Sol. 1:5.
Custom of sitting and standing at the door of. Gen. 18:1. Jud. 4:20.
ILLUSTRATIVE
(Spread out,) of the heavens. Isa. 40:22.
(Enlarging of,) of the great extension of the Church. Isa. 54:2.

Thanksgiving.

Christ set an example of. Mat. 11:25. Mat. 26:27. Jno. 6:11. Jno. 11:41.
The heavenly host engaged in. Rev. 4:9. Rev. 7:11, 12. Rev. 11:16, 17.
Commanded. Psa. 50:14. Phi. 4:6.
Is a good thing. Psa. 92:1.
SHOULD BE OFFERED
To God. Psa. 50:14.
To Christ. 1 Tim. 1:12.
Through Christ. Rom. 1:8. Col. 3:17. Heb. 13:15.
In the name of Christ. Eph. 5:20.
In behalf of ministers. 2 Cor. 1:11.
In private worship. Dan. 6:10.
In public worship. Psa. 35:18.
In everything. 1 The. 5:18.
Upon the completion of great undertakings. Neh. 12:31, 40.
Before taking food. Jno. 6:11. Acts 27:35.
Always. Eph. 1:16. Eph. 5:20. 1 The. 1:2.
At the remembrance of God's holiness. Psa. 30:4. Psa. 97:12.
For the goodness and mercy of God. Psa. 106:1. Psa. 107:1. Psa. 136:1—3.
For the gift of Christ. 2 Cor. 9:15.
For Christ's power and reign. Rev. 11:17.
For the reception and effectual working of the word of God in others. 1 The. 2:13.
For deliverance through Christ from in-dwelling sin. Rom. 7:23—25.

For victory over death and the grave. 1 Cor. 15: 57.
For wisdom and might. Dan. 2: 23.
For the triumph of the gospel. 2 Cor. 2: 14.
For the conversion of others. Rom. 6: 17.
For faith exhibited by others. Rom. 1: 8. 2 The. 1: 3.
For love exhibited by others. 2 The. 1: 3.
For the grace bestowed on others. 1 Cor. 1: 4. Phi. 1: 3—5. Col. 1: 3—6.
For the zeal exhibited by others. 2 Cor. 8: 16.
For the nearness of God's presence. Psa. 75: 1.
For appointment to the ministry. 1 Tim. 1: 12.
For willingness to offer our property for God's service. 1 Chr. 29: 6—14.
For the supply of our bodily wants. Rom. 14: 6, 7. 1 Tim. 4: 3, 4.
For all men. 1 Tim. 2: 1.
For all things. 2 Cor. 9: 11. Eph. 5: 20.

Should be accompanied by intercession for others. 1 Tim. 2: 1. 2 Tim. 1: 3. Phile. 4.
Should always accompany prayer. Neh. 11: 17. Phi. 4: 6. Col. 4: 2.
Should always accompany praise. Psa. 92: 1. Heb. 13: 15.
Expressed in psalms. 1 Chr. 16: 7.
Ministers appointed to offer, in public. 1 Chr. 16: 4, 7. 1 Chr. 23: 30. 2 Chr. 31: 2.

SAINTS
Exhorted to. Psa. 105: 1. Col. 3: 15.
Resolved to offer. Psa. 18: 49. Psa. 30: 12.
Habitually offer. Dan. 6: 10.
Offer sacrifices of. Psa. 116: 17.
Abound in the faith with. Col. 2: 7.
Magnify God by. Psa. 69: 30.
Come before God with. Psa. 95: 2.
Should enter God's gate with. Psa. 100: 4.

Of hypocrites, full of boasting. Luke 18: 11.
The wicked averse to. Rom. 1: 21.
Exemplified. *David*, 1 Chr. 29: 13. *Levites*, 2 Chr. 5: 12, 13. *Daniel*, Dan. 2: 23. *Jonah*, Jon. 2: 9. *Simeon*, Luke 2: 28. *Anna*, Luke 2: 38. *Paul*, Acts 28: 15.

Theft.

Is an abomination. Jer. 7: 9, 10.
Forbidden. Exo. 20: 15, with Mar. 10: 19. Rom. 13: 9.
From the poor specially forbidden. Pro. 22: 22.
Includes fraud in general. Lev. 19: 13.
Includes fraud concerning wages. Lev. 19: 13. Mal. 3: 5. Jas. 5: 4.
Proceeds from the heart. Mat. 15: 19.
Defiles a man. Mat. 15: 20.

THE WICKED
Addicted to. Psa. 119: 61.
Store up the fruits of. Amos 3: 10.
Lie in wait to commit. Hos. 6: 9.
Commit, under shelter of the night. Job 24: 14. Oba. 5.
Consent to those who commit. Psa. 50: 18.
Associate with those who commit Isa. 1: 23.
May, for a season, prosper in. Job 12: 6.
Plead excuses for. Jer. 7: 9, 10.
Repent not of. Rev. 9: 21.
Destroy themselves by. Pro. 21: 7.

Connected with murder. Jer. 7: 9. Hos. 4: 2.
Shame follows the detection of. Jer. 2: 26.
Brings a curse on those who commit it. Hos. 4: 2, 3. Zec. 5: 3, 4. Mal. 3: 5.
Brings the wrath of God upon those who commit it. Eze. 22: 29, 31.
Excludes from heaven. 1 Cor. 6: 10.

THEY WHO CONNIVE AT,
Hate their own souls. Pro. 29: 24.
Shall be reproved of God. Psa. 50: 18, 21.

Mosaic law respecting. Exo. 22: 1—8.

SAINTS
Warned against. Eph. 4: 28. 1 Pet. 4: 15.

All earthly treasure exposed to. Mat. 6: 19.
Heavenly treasure secure from. Mat. 6: 20. Luke 12: 33.
Woe denounced against. Isa. 10: 2. Nah. 3: 1.
Illustrates the guilt of false teachers. Jer. 23: 30. Jno. 10: 1, 8, 10.
Exemplified. *Rachel*, Gen. 31: 19. *Achan*, Jos. 7: 21. *Shechemites*, Jud. 9: 25. *Micah*, Jud. 17: 2.

Theocracy, The, or Immediate Government by God.

Lasted from the deliverance out of Egypt until the appointment of kings. Exo. 19: 4—6, with 1 Sam. 8: 7.

WAS ESTABLISHED ON
The right of redemption. Exo. 6: 6, 7. 2 Sam. 7: 23. Isa. 43: 3.
The right of covenant. Deu. 26: 17—19.

CONSISTED IN HIS
Promulgating laws. Exo. 20 ch. to Exo. 23 ch. Deu. 5: 22, 23.
Directing the movements of the nation. Exo. 40: 36, 37. Num. 9: 17—23.

Proclaiming war. Exo. 17:14—16. Num. 31:1, 2. Jos. 6:2, 3. Jos. 8:1.
Appointing civil officers. Exo. 3:10. Num. 27:18, 20.
Appointing ecclesiastical officers. Exo. 28:1. Exo. 40:12—15.
Being the supreme judge. Num. 9:8—11. Num. 15:34, 35. Num. 27:5—11.
Exercise of the prerogative of mercy. Num. 14:20. Deu. 9:18—20.
Distribution of conquered lands. Jos. 13:1—7.
Exacting tribute. Exo. 35:4—29. Lev. 27:30. Deu. 16:16. Deu. 26:1—4.

The tabernacle designed as a royal residence for God during. Exo. 25:8. Lev. 26:11, 12.
The emblem of the divine presence appeared over the tabernacle during. Num. 9:15, 16.
Guilt of Israel in rejecting. 1 Sam. 12:17.

Threshing.

The removing or separating corn, &c. from the straw. 1 Chr. 21:20.

WAS PERFORMED
By a rod or staff. Isa. 28:27.
By cart wheels. Isa. 27:27, 28.
By instruments with teeth. Isa. 41:15. Amos 1:3.
By the feet of horses and oxen. Isa. 28:28. Hos. 10:11. *See* 2 Sam. 24:22.

Cattle employed in, not to be muzzled. Deu. 25:4. 1 Cor. 9:9. 1 Tim. 5:18.
Continued until the vintage in years of abundance. Lev. 26:5.

THE PLACE FOR,
Called the floor. Jud. 6:37. Isa. 21:10.
Called the threshing-floor. Num. 18:27. 2 Sam. 24:18.
Called the barn-floor. 2 Kin. 6:27.
Called the corn-floor. Hos. 9:1.
Was large and roomy. Gen. 50:10.
Generally on high ground. 1 Chr. 21:18, with 2 Chr. 3:1.
Sometimes beside the wine-press for concealment. Jud. 6:11.
Used also for winnowing the corn. Ruth 3:2.
Often robbed. 1 Sam. 23:1.
The Jews slept on, during the time of. Ruth 3:7.
Fulness of, promised as a blessing. Joel 2:24.
Scarcity in, a punishment. Hos. 9:2.

Followed by a winnowing with a shovel or fan. Isa. 30:24. Isa. 41:16. Mat. 3:12.

ILLUSTRATIVE
Of the judgments of God. Isa. 21:10. Jer. 51:33. Hab. 3:12.
Of the labors of ministers. 1 Cor. 9:9, 10.
Of the Church in her conquests. Isa. 41:15, 16. Mic. 4:13.
(Gathering the sheaves for,) of preparing the enemies of the Church for judgments. Mic. 4:12.
(Dust made by,) of complete destruction. 2 Kin. 13:7. Isa. 41:15. (*marg.*)
(An instrument for, with teeth,) of the Church overcoming opposition. Isa. 41:15.

Time.

The duration of the world. Job 22:16. Rev. 10:6.
The measure of the continuance of anything. Jud. 18:31.
An appointed season. Neh. 2:6. Ecc. 3:1, 17.

COMPUTED BY
Years. Gen. 15:13. 2 Sam. 21:1. Dan. 9:2.
Months. Num. 10:10. 1 Chr. 27:1. Job 3:6.
Weeks. Dan. 10:2. Luke 18:12.
Days. Gen. 8:3. Job 1:4. Luke 11:3.
Hours, after the captivity. Dan. 5:5. Jno. 11:9.
Moments. Exo. 33:5. Luke 4:5. 1 Cor. 15:52.

The heavenly bodies, appointed as a means for computing. Gen. 1:14.
The sun-dial early invented for pointing out. 2 Kin. 20:9—11.

ERAS FROM WHICH, COMPUTED;
Nativity of the patriarchs during the patriarchial age. Gen. 7:11. Gen. 8:13. Gen. 17:1.
The exodus from Egypt. Exo. 19:1. Exo. 40:17. Num. 9:1. Num. 33:38. 1 Kin. 6:1.
The jubilee. Lev. 25:15.
Accession of kings. 1 Kin. 6:1. 1 Kin. 15:1. Isa. 36:1. Jer. 1:2. Luke 3:1.
Building of the temple. 1 Kin. 9:10. 2 Chr. 8:1.
The captivity. Eze. 1:1. Eze. 33:21. Eze. 40:1.

Part of a period of, usually counted as the whole. 1 Sam. 13:1. Est. 4:16, with Est. 5:1.
In prophetic language, means a prophetic year, or 365 natural years. Dan. 12:7. Rev. 12:14.
Shortness of man's portion of. Psa. 89:47.
Should be redeemed. Eph. 5:16. Col. 4:5.
Should be spent in the fear of God. 1 Pet. 1:17.

PARTICULAR PERIODS OF, MENTIONED;
The ancient time. Isa. 45:21.

The accepted time. Isa. 49: 8. 2 Cor. 6: 2.
The time of visitation. Jer. 46: 21. Jer. 50: 27.
The time of refreshing. Acts 3: 19.
The time of restitution of all things. Acts 3: 21.
The time of reformation. Heb. 9: 10.
The time of healing. Jer. 14: 19.
The time of need. Heb. 4: 16.
The time of temptation. Luke 8: 13.
The evil time. Psa. 37: 19. Ecc. 9: 12.
The time of trouble. Psa. 27: 5. Jer. 14: 8.
All events of, predetermined by God. Acts 17: 26.
All God's purposes fulfilled in due time. Mar. 1: 15. Gal. 4: 4.

Tithe.

The tenth of anything. 1 Sam. 8: 15, 17.
Antiquity of the custom of giving to God's ministers. Gen. 14: 20. Heb. 7: 6.
Considered a just return to God for His blessings. Gen. 28: 22.
Under the law belonged to God. Lev. 27: 30.
CONSISTED OF A TENTH,
Of all the produce of the land. Lev. 27: 30.
Of all cattle. Lev. 27: 32.
Of holy things dedicated. 2 Chr. 31: 6.
Given by God to the Levites for their services. Num. 18: 21, 24. Neh. 10: 37.
The tenth of, offered by the Levites as an heave offering to God. Num. 18: 26, 27.
The tenth of, given by the Levites to the priests as their portion. Num. 18: 26, 28. Neh. 10: 38.
Reasonableness of appointing, for the Levites. Num 18: 20, 23, 24. Jos. 13: 33.
When redeemed to have a fifth part of the value added. Lev. 27: 31.
Punishment for changing. Lev. 27: 33.
The Jews slow in giving. Neh. 13: 10.
The Jews reproved for withholding. Mal. 3: 8.
The pious governors of Israel caused the payment of. 2 Chr. 31: 5. Neh. 13: 11, 12.
Rulers appointed over, for distributing. 2 Chr. 31: 12. Neh. 13: 13.
The Pharisees scrupulous in paying. Luke 11: 42. Luke 18: 12.
A SECOND,
Or its value yearly brought to the tabernacle and eaten before the Lord. Deu. 12: 6, 7, 17—19. Deu. 14: 22—27.
To be consumed at home every third year to promote hospitality and charity. Deu. 14: 28, 29. Deu. 26: 12—15.

Titles and Names of Christ.

Adam, Second. 1 Cor. 15: 45.
Almighty. Rev. 1: 8.
Amen. Rev. 3: 14.
Alpha and Omega. Rev. 1: 8. Rev. 22: 13.
Advocate. 1 Jno. 2: 1.
Angel. Gen. 48: 16. Exo. 23: 20, 21.
Angel of the Lord. Exo. 3: 2. Jud. 13: 15—18.
Angel of God's presence. Isa. 63: 9.
Apostle. Heb. 3: 1.
Arm of the Lord. Isa. 51: 9. Isa. 53: 1.
Author and Finisher of our faith. Heb. 12: 2.
Blessed and only Potentate. 1 Tim. 6: 15.
Beginning of the creation of God. Rev. 3: 14.
Branch. Jer. 23: 5. Zec. 3: 8. Zec. 6: 12.
Bread of Life. Jno. 6: 35, 48.
Captain of the Lord's hosts. Jos. 5: 14, 15.
Captain of salvation. Heb. 2: 10.
Chief Shepherd. 1 Pet. 5: 4.
Christ of God. Luke 9: 20.
Consolation of Israel. Luke 2: 25.
Chief Corner-stone. Eph. 2: 20. 1 Pet. 2: 6.
Commander. Isa. 55: 4.
Counsellor. Isa. 9: 6.
David. Jer. 30: 9. Eze. 34: 23.
Day-spring. Luke 1: 78.
Deliverer. Rom. 11: 26.
Desire of all nations. Hag. 2: 7.
Door. Jno. 10: 7.
Elect of God. Isa. 42: 1.
Emmanuel. Isa. 7: 14, with Mat. 1: 23.
Eternal life. 1 Jno. 1: 2. 1 Jno. 5: 20.
Everlasting Father. Isa. 9: 6.
Faithful witness. Rev. 1: 5. Rev. 3: 14.
First and Last. Rev. 1: 17. Rev. 2: 8.
First-begotten of the dead. Rev. 1: 5.
First-born of every creature. Col. 1: 15.
Forerunner. Heb. 6: 20.
God. Isa. 40: 9. Jno. 20: 28.
God blessed for ever. Rom. 9: 5.
God's fellow. Zec. 13: 7.
Glory of the Lord. Isa. 40: 5.
Good Shepherd. Jno. 10: 14.
Great High Priest. Heb. 4: 14.
Governor. Mat. 2: 6.
Head of the Church. Eph. 5: 23. Col. 1: 18.

Heir of all things. Heb. 1:2.
Holy One. Psa. 16:10, with Acts 2:27, 31.
Holy One of God. Mar. 1:24.
Holy One of Israel. Isa. 41:14.
Horn of salvation. Luke 1:69.
I AM. Exo. 3:14, with Jno. 8:58.
JEHOVAH. Isa. 26:4.
Jesus. Mat. 1:21. 1 The. 1:10.
Judge of Israel. Mic. 5:1.
Just One. Acts 7:52.
King. Zec. 9:9, with Mat. 21:5.
King of Israel. Jno. 1:49.
King of the Jews. Mat. 2:2.
King of saints. Rev. 15:3.
King of Kings. 1 Tim. 6:15. Rev. 17:14.
Law-giver. Isa. 33:22.
Lamb. Rev. 5:6, 12. Rev. 13:8. Rev. 21:22. Rev. 22:3.
Lamb of God. Jno. 1:29, 36.
Leader. Isa. 55:4.
Life. Jno. 14:6. Col. 3:4. 1 Jno. 1:2.
Light of the world. Jno. 8:12.
Lion of the tribe of Judah. Rev. 5:5.
Lord of glory. 1 Cor. 2:8.
Lord of all. Acts 10:36.
LORD OUR RIGHTEOUSNESS. Jer. 23:6.
Lord God of the holy prophets. Rev. 22:6.
Lord God Almighty. Rev. 15:3.
Mediator. 1 Tim. 2:5.
Messenger of the covenant. Mal. 3:1.
Messiah. Dan. 9:25. Jno. 1:41.
Mighty God. Isa. 9:6.
Mighty One of Jacob. Isa. 60:16.
Morning-star. Rev. 22:16.
Nazarene. Mat. 2:23.
Offspring of David. Rev. 22:16.
Only-begotten. Jno. 1:14.
Our Passover. 1 Cor. 5:7.
Plant of renown. Eze. 34:29.
Prince of life. Acts 3:15.
Prince of peace. Isa. 9:6.
Prince of the kings of the earth. Rev. 1:5.
Prophet. Luke 24:19. Jno. 7:40.
Ransom. 1 Tim. 2:6.
Redeemer. Job 19:25. Isa. 59:20. Isa. 60:16.
Resurrection and life. Jno. 11:25.
Rock. 1 Cor. 10:4.
Root of David. Rev. 22:16.
Root of Jesse. Isa. 11:10.
Ruler of Israel. Mic. 5:2.
Saviour. 2 Pet. 2:20. 2 Pet. 3:18.
Servant. Isa. 42:1. Isa. 52:13.
Shepherd and Bishop of Souls. 1 Pet. 2:25.
Shiloh. Gen. 49:10.
Son of the blessed. Mar. 14:61.
Son of God. Luke 1:35. Jno. 1:49.
Son of the Highest. Luke 1:32.
Son of David. Mat. 9:27.
Son of man. Jno. 5:27. Jno. 6:37.
Star. Num. 24:17.
Sun of righteousness. Mal. 4:2.
Surety. Heb. 7:22.
True God. 1 Jno. 5:20.
True Light. Jno. 1:9.
True Vine. Jno. 15:1.
Truth. Jno. 14:6.
Way. Jno. 14:6.
Wisdom. Pro. 8:12.
Witness. Isa. 55:4.
Wonderful. Isa. 9:6.
Word. Jno. 1:1. 1 Jno. 5:7.
Word of God. Rev. 19:13.
Word of Life. 1 Jno. 1:1.

Titles and Names of the Church.

Assembly of the saints. Psa. 89:7.
Assembly of the upright. Psa. 111:1.
Body of Christ. Eph. 1:22, 23. Col. 1:24.
Branch of God's planting. Isa. 60:21.
Bride of Christ. Rev. 21:9.
Church of God. Acts 20:28.
Church of the Living God. 1 Tim. 3:15.
Church of the first-born. Heb. 12:23.
City of the Living God. Heb. 12:22.
Congregation of saints. Psa. 149:1.
Congregation of the Lord's poor. Psa. 74:19.
Dove. So. of Sol. 2:14. So. of Sol. 5:2.
Family in heaven and earth. Eph. 3:15.
Flock of God. Eze. 34:15. 1 Pet 5:2.
Fold of Christ. Jno. 10:16.
General assembly of the first-born. Heb. 12:23.
Golden candlestick. Rev. 1:20.
God's building. 1 Cor. 3:9.
God's husbandry. 1 Cor. 3:9.
God's heritage. Joel 3:2. 1 Pet. 5:3.
Habitation of God. Eph. 2:22.
Heavenly Jerusalem. Gal. 4:26. Heb. 12:22.
Holy city. Rev. 21:2.
Holy mountain. Zec. 8:3.
Holy hill. Psa. 15:1.
House of God. 1 Tim. 3:15. Heb. 10:21.
House of the God of Jacob. Isa. 2:3.
House of Christ. Heb. 3:6.
Household of God. Eph. 2:19.
Inheritance. Psa. 28:9. Isa. 19:25.
Israel of God. Gal. 6:16.
King's daughter. Psa. 45:13.
Lamb's wife. Rev. 19:7. Rev. 21.
Lot of God's inheritance. Deu. 32:9.
Mount Zion. Psa. 2:6. Heb. 12:22.
Mountain of the Lord's house. Isa. 2:2.
New Jerusalem. Rev. 21:2.
Pillar and ground of the truth. 1 Tim. 3:15.
Sanctuary of God. Psa. 114:2.
Spiritual house. 1 Pet. 2:5.
Spouse of Christ. So. of Sol. 4:12. So. of Sol. 5:1.

Sought out, a city not forsaken. Isa. 62:12.
Temple of God. 1 Cor. 3:16, 17.
Temple of the Living God. 2 Cor. 6: 16.
Vineyard. Jer. 12:10. Mat. 21:41.

Titles and Names of the Devil.

Abaddon. Rev. 9:11.
Accuser of our brethren. Rev. 12:10.
Adversary. 1 Pet. 5:8.
Angel of the bottomless pit. Rev. 9: 11.
Apollyon. Rev. 9:11.
Beelzebub. Mat. 12:24.
Belial. 2 Cor. 6:15.
Crooked serpent. Isa. 27:1.
Dragon. Isa. 27:1. Rev. 20:2.
Enemy. Mat. 13:39.
Evil spirit. 1 Sam. 16:14.
Father of lies. Jno. 8:44.
Great red dragon. Rev. 12:3.
Leviathan. Isa. 27:1.
Liar. Jno. 8:44.
Lying spirit. 1 Kin. 22:22.
Murderer. Jno. 8:44.
Old serpent. Rev. 12:9. Rev. 20:2.
Piercing serpent. Isa. 27:1.
Power of darkness. Col. 1:13.
Prince of this world. Jno. 14:30.
Prince of the devils. Mat. 12:24.
Prince of the power of the air. Eph. 2:2.
Ruler of the darkness of this world. Eph. 6:12.
Satan. 1 Chr. 21:1. Job 1:6.
Serpent. Gen. 3:4, 14. 2 Cor. 11:3.
Spirit that worketh in the children of disobedience. Eph. 2:2.
Tempter. Mat. 4:3. 1 The. 3:5.
The god of this world. 2 Cor. 4:4.
Unclean spirit. Mat. 12:43.
Wicked-one. Mat. 13:19, 38.

Titles and Names of the Holy Ghost.

Breath of the Almighty. Job 33:4.
Comforter. Jno. 14:16, 26. Jno. 15:26.
Eternal Spirit. Heb. 9:14.
Free Spirit. Psa. 51: 12.
God. Acts 5:3, 4.
Good Spirit. Neh. 9:20. Psa. 143:10.
Holy Spirit. Psa. 51:11. Luke 11:13. Eph. 1:13. Eph. 4:30.
Lord, The. 2 The. 3:5.
Power of the Highest. Luke 1:35.
Spirit, The. Mat. 4:1. Jno. 3:6. 1 Tim. 4:1.
Spirit of the Lord God. Isa. 61:1.
Spirit of the Lord. Isa. 11:2. Acts 5: 9.
Spirit of God. Gen. 1:2. 1 Cor. 2: 11. Job 33:4.
Spirit of the Father. Mat. 10:20.
Spirit of Christ. Rom. 8:9. 1 Pet. 1: 11.
Spirit of the Son. Gal. 4:6.
Spirit of life. Rom. 8:2. Rev. 11:11.
Spirit of grace. Zec. 12:10. Heb. 10: 29.
Spirit of prophecy. Rev. 19:10.
Spirit of adoption. Rom. 8:15.
Spirit of wisdom. Isa. 11:2. Eph. 1:17.
Spirit of counsel. Isa. 11:2.
Spirit of might. Isa. 11:2.
Spirit of understanding. Isa. 11:2.
Spirit of knowledge. Isa. 11:2.
Spirit of the fear of the Lord. Isa. 11:2.
Spirit of truth. Jno. 14:17. Jno. 15:26
Spirit of holiness. Rom. 1:4.
Spirit of revelation. Eph. 1:17.
Spirit of judgment. Isa. 4:4. Isa. 28: 6.
Spirit of burning. Isa. 4:4.
Spirit of glory. 1 Pet. 4:14.
Seven Spirits of God. Rev. 1:4.

Titles and Names of Ministers.

Ambassadors for Christ. 2 Cor. 5:20.
Angels of the Church. Rev. 1:20. Rev. 2:1.
Apostles. Luke 6:13. Eph. 4:11. Rev. 18:20.
Apostles of Jesus Christ. Tit. 1:1.
Bishops. Phi. 1:1. 1 Tim. 3:1. Tit. 1:7.
Deacons. Acts 6:1. 1 Tim. 3:8. Phi. 1:1.
Elders. 1 Tim. 5:17. 1 Pet. 5:1.
Evangelists. Eph. 4:11. 2 Tim. 4:5.
Fishers of men. Mat. 4:19. Mar. 1:17.
Laborers. Mat. 9:38, with Phile. 1. 1 The. 2:2.
Messengers of the Church. 2 Cor. 8: 23.
Messengers of the Lord of hosts. Mal. 2:7.
Ministers of God. 2 Cor. 6:4.
Ministers of the Lord. Joel 2:17.
Ministers of Christ. Rom. 15:16. 1 Cor. 4:1.
Ministers of the sanctuary. Eze. 45:4.
Ministers of the gospel. Eph. 3:7. Col. 1:23.
Ministers of the word. Luke 1:2.
Ministers of the New Testament. 2 Cor. 3:6.
Ministers of the Church. Col. 1:24,25.
Ministers of righteousness. 2 Cor 11:15.
Overseers. Acts 20:28.
Pastors. Jer. 3:15. Eph. 4:11.
Preachers. Rom. 10:14. 1 Tim. 2:7.
Servants of God. Tit. 1:1. Jas. 1:1
Servants of the Lord. 2 Tim. 2:24.
Servants of Jesus Christ. Phi. 1:1. Jude 1.
Servants of the Church. 2 Cor. 4:5.
Shepherds. Jer. 23:4.
Soldiers of Christ. Phi. 2:25. 2 Tim. 2:3.
Stars. Rev. 1:20. Rev. 2:1.

Stewards of God. Tit. 1:7.
Stewards of the grace of God. 1 Pet. 4:10.
Stewards of the mysteries of God. 1 Cor. 4:1.
Teachers. Isa. 30:20. Eph. 4:11.
Watchmen. Isa. 62:6. Eze. 33:7.
Witnesses. Acts 1:8. Acts 5:32. Acts 26:16.
Workers together with God. 2 Cor. 6:1.

Titles and Names of Saints.

Believers. Acts 5:14. 1 Tim. 4:12.
Beloved of God. Rom. 1:7.
Beloved brethren. 1 Cor. 15:58. Jas. 2:5.
Blessed of the Lord. Gen. 24:31. Gen. 26:29.
Blessed of the Father. Mat. 25:34.
Brethren. Mat. 23:8. Acts 12:17.
Brethren of Christ. Luke 8:21. Jno. 20:17.
Called of Jesus Christ. Rom. 1:6.
Children of the Lord. Deu. 14:1.
Children of God. Jno. 11:52. 1 Jno. 3:10.
Children of the Living God. Rom. 9: 26.
Children of the Father. Mat. 5:45.
Children of the Highest. Luke 6:35.
Children of Abraham. Gal. 3:7.
Children of Jacob. Psa. 105:6.
Children of promise. Rom. 9:8. Gal. 4:28.
Children of the free-woman. Gal. 4: 31.
Children of the kingdom. Mat. 13:38.
Children of Zion. Psa. 149:2. Joel 2:23.
Children of the bride-chamber. Mat. 9:15.
Children of light. Luke 16:8. Eph. 5:8. 1 The. 5:5.
Children of the day. 1 The. 5:5.
Children of the resurrection. Luke 20:36.
Chosen generation. 1 Pet. 2:9.
Chosen ones. 1 Chr. 16:13.
Chosen vessels. Acts 9:15.
Christians. Acts 11:26. Acts 26:28.
Dear children. Eph. 5:1.
Disciples of Christ. Jno. 8:31. Jno. 15:8.
Elect of God. Col. 3:12. Tit. 1:1.
Epistles of Christ. 2 Cor. 3:3.
Excellent, The. Psa. 16:3.
Faithful brethren in Christ. Col. 1:2.
Faithful, The. Psa. 12:1.
Faithful of the land, The. Psa. 101:6.
Fellow-citizens with the saints. Eph. 2:19.
Fellow-heirs. Eph. 3:6.
Fellow-servants. Rev. 6:11.
Friends of God. 2 Chr. 20:7. Jas. 2:23.
Friends of Christ. Jno. 15:15.
Godly, The. Psa. 4:3. 2 Pet. 2:9.
Heirs of God. Rom. 8:17. Gal. 4:7.
Heirs of the grace of life. 1 Pet. 3:7.
Heirs of the kingdom. Jas. 2:5.
Heirs of promise. Heb. 6:17. Gal. 3:29.
Heirs of salvation. Heb. 1:14.
Holy brethren. 1 The. 5:27. Heb. 3:1.
Holy nation. Exo. 19:6. 1 Pet. 2:9.
Holy people. Deu. 26:19. Isa. 62:12.
Holy priesthood. 1 Pet. 2:5.
Joint-heirs with Christ. Rom. 8:17.
Just, The. Hab. 2:4.
Kings and priests unto God. Rev. 1:6.
Kingdom of priests. Exo. 19:6.
Lambs. Isa. 40:11. Jno. 21:15.
Lights of the world. Mat. 5:14.
Little children. Jno. 13:33. 1 Jno. 2:1.
Lively stones. 1 Pet. 2:5.
Members of Christ. 1 Cor. 6:15. Eph. 5:30.
Men of God. Deu. 33:1. 1 Tim. 6:11. 2 Tim. 3:17.
Obedient children. 1 Pet. 1:14.
Peculiar people. Deu. 14:2. Tit. 2:14. 1 Pet. 2:9.
Peculiar treasure. Exo. 19:5. Psa. 135:4.
People of God. Heb. 4:9. 1 Pet. 2:10.
People near unto God. Psa. 148:14.
People saved by the Lord. Deu. 33: 29.
Pillars in the temple of God. Rev. 3:12.
Ransomed of the Lord. Isa. 35:10.
Redeemed of the Lord. Isa. 51:11.
Royal priesthood. 1 Pet. 2:9.
Salt of the earth. Mat. 5:13.
Servants of Christ. 1 Cor. 7:22. Eph. 6:6.
Servants of righteousness. Rom. 6: 18.
Sheep of Christ. Jno. 10:1—16. Jno. 21:16.
Sojourners with God. Lev. 25:23. Psa. 39:12.
Sons of God. Jno. 1:12. Phi. 2:15. 1 Jno. 3:1, 2.
The Lord's freemen. 1 Cor. 7:22.
Trees of righteousness. Isa. 61:3.
Vessels unto honor. 2 Tim. 2:21.
Vessels of mercy. Rom. 9:23.
Witnesses for God. Isa. 44:8.

Titles and Names of the Wicked.

Adversaries of the Lord. 1 Sam. 2:10.
Children of Belial. Deu. 13:13. 2 Chr. 13:7.
Children of the devil. Acts 13:10. 1 Jno. 3:10.
Children of the wicked one. Mat 13: 38.
Children of hell. Mat. 23:15.
Children of base men. Job 30:8.
Children of fools. Job 30:8.

Children of strangers. Isa. 2:6.
Children of transgression. Isa. 57:4.
Children of disobedience. Eph. 2:2. Col. 3:6.
Children in whom is no faith. Deu. 32:20.
Children of the flesh. Rom. 9:8.
Children of iniquity. Hos. 10:9.
Children that will not hear the law of the Lord. Isa. 30:9.
Children of pride. Job 41:34.
Children of this world. Luke 16:8.
Children of wickedness. 2 Sam. 7:10.
Children of wrath. Eph. 2:3.
Children that are corrupters. Isa. 1:4.
Cursed children. 2 Pet. 2:14.
Enemies of God. Psa. 37:20. Jas. 4:4.
Enemies of the cross of Christ. Phi. 3:18.
Enemies of all righteousness. Acts 13:10.
Evil doers. Psa. 37:1. 1 Pet. 2:14.
Evil men. Pro. 4:14. 2 Tim. 3:13.
Evil generation. Deu. 1:35.
Evil and adulterous generation. Mat. 12:39.
Fools. Pro. 1:7. Rom. 1:22.
Froward generation. Deu. 32:20.
Generation of vipers. Mat. 3:7. Mat. 12:34.
Grievous revolters. Jer. 6:28.
Haters of God. Psa. 81:15. Rom. 1:30.
Impudent children. Eze. 2:4.
Inventors of evil things. Rom. 1:30.
Lying children. Isa. 30:9.
Men of the world. Psa. 17:14.
People laden with iniquity. Isa. 1:4.
Perverse and crooked generation. Deu. 32:5. Mat. 17:17. Phi. 2:15.
Rebellious children. Isa. 30:1.
Rebellious people. Isa. 30:9. Isa. 65:2.
Rebellious house. Eze. 2:5, 8. Eze. 12:2.
Reprobates. 2 Cor. 13:5—7.
Scornful, The. Psa. 1:1.
Seed of falsehood. Isa. 57:4.
Seed of the wicked. Psa. 37:28.
Seed of evil doers. Isa. 1:4. Isa. 14:20.
Serpents. Mat. 23:33.
Servants of corruption. 2 Pet. 2:19.
Servants of sin. Jno. 8:34. Rom. 6:20.
Sinful generation. Mar. 8:28.
Sinners. Psa. 26:9. Pro. 1:10.
Sons of Belial. 1 Sam. 2:12. 1 Kin. 21:10.
Sottish children. Jer. 4:22.
Strange children. Psa. 144:7.
Stubborn and rebellious generation. Psa. 78:8.
Transgressors. Psa. 37:38. Psa. 51:13.
Ungodly, The. Psa. 1:1.
Ungodly men. Jude 4.
Unprofitable servants. Mat. 25:30.
Untoward generation. Acts 2:40.
Vessels of wrath. Rom. 9:22.
Wicked of the earth. Psa. 75:8.
Wicked transgressors. Psa. 59:5.
Wicked servants. Mat. 25:26.
Wicked generation. Mat. 12:45. Mat. 16:4.
Wicked-ones. Jer. 2:33.
Wicked-doers. Psa. 101:8. Pro. 17:4.
Workers of iniquity. Psa. 28:3. Psa. 36:12.

Towers.

Origin and antiquity of. Gen. 11:4.
WERE BUILT
 In cities. Jud. 9:51.
 On the walls of cities. 2 Chr. 14:7. 2 Chr. 26:9.
 In the forests. 2 Chr. 27:4.
 In the deserts. 2 Chr. 26:10.
 In vineyards. Isa. 5:2. Mat. 21:33.
Frequently very high. Isa. 2:15.
Frequently strong and well fortified. Jud. 9:51, with 2 Chr. 26:9.
Were used as armories. So. of Sol. 4:4.
Were used as citadels in times of war. Jud. 9:51. Eze. 27:11.
Watchmen posted on, in times of danger. 2 Kin. 9:17. Hab. 2:1.
MENTIONED IN SCRIPTURE;
 Babel. Gen. 11:9.
 Edar. Gen. 35:21.
 Penuel. Jud. 8:17.
 Shechem. Jud. 9:46.
 Thebez. Jud. 9:50, 51.
 David. So. of Sol. 4:4.
 Lebanon. So. of Sol. 7:4.
 Of the furnaces. Neh. 3:11.
 Meah. Neh. 12:39.
 Jezreel. 2 Kin. 9:17.
 Hananeel. Jer. 31:38. Zec. 14:10.
 Syene. Eze. 29:10. Eze. 30:6.
 Siloam. Luke 13:4.
Of Jerusalem remarkable for number, strength and beauty. Psa. 48:12.
Frequently thrown down in war. Jud. 8:17. Jud. 9:49. Eze. 26:4.
Frequently left desolate. Isa. 32:14. Zep. 3:6.
ILLUSTRATIVE OF
 God as the protector of His people. 2 Sam. 22:3, 51. Psa. 18:2. Psa. 61:3.
 The name of the Lord. Pro. 18:10.
 Ministers. Jer. 6:27.
 Mount Sion. Mic. 4:8.
 The grace and dignity of the church. So. of Sol. 4:4. So. of Sol. 7:4. So. of Sol. 8:10.
 The proud and haughty. Isa. 2:15. Isa. 30:25.

Travelers.

Called way-faring men. Jud. 19:17. Isa. 35:8.

Preparations made by, alluded to Eze. 12: 3, 4.
Often collected together and formed caravans. Gen. 37: 25. Isa. 21: 13. Luke 2: 44.
Often engaged persons acquainted with the country as guides. Num. 10: 31, 32. Job 29: 15.
FRIENDS OF,
Often supplied them with provision. Gen. 21: 14. Gen. 44: 1. Jer. 40: 5.
Sometimes accompanied them a short way. 2 Sam. 19: 31. Acts 20: 38. Acts 21: 5.
Frequently commended them to protection of God. Gen. 43: 13, 14. Acts 21: 5.
Frequently took leave of them with sorrow. Acts 20: 37. Acts 21: 6.
Often sent them away with music. Gen. 31: 27.
Generally commenced their journey early in the morning. Jud. 19: 5.
Generally rested at noon. Gen. 18: 1, 3. Jno. 4: 6.
Halted at even. Gen. 24: 11.
Generally halted at wells or streams. Gen. 24: 11. Gen. 32: 21, 23. Exo. 15: 27. 1 Sam. 30: 21. Jno. 4: 6.
CARRIED WITH THEM
Provisions for the way. Jos. 9: 11, 12. Jud. 19: 19.
Provender for their beasts of burden. Gen. 42: 27. Jud. 19: 19.
Skins filled with water, wine, &c. Gen. 21: 14, 15. Jos. 9: 13.
Presents for those who entertained them. Gen. 43: 15. 1 Kin. 10: 2. 2 Kin. 5: 5. Mat. 2: 11.
Often traveled on foot. Gen. 28: 10, with Gen. 32: 10. Exo. 12: 37. Acts 20: 13.
On foot, how attired. Exo. 12: 11.
After a long journey, described. Jos. 9: 4, 5, 13.
OF DISTINCTION
Rode on asses, camels, &c. Gen. 22: 3. Gen. 24: 64. Num. 22: 21.
Rode in chariots. 2 Kin. 5: 9. Acts 8: 27, 28.
Generally attended by running footmen. 1 Sam. 25: 27. (*marg.*) 1 Kin. 18: 46. 2 Kin. 4: 24. Ecc. 10: 7.
Often preceded by heralds, &c. to have the roads prepared. Isa. 40: 3, 4, with Mar. 1: 2, 3.
Generally performed their journey in great state. 1 Kin. 10: 2. 2 Kin. 5: 5, 9, &c.
Frequently extorted provisions by the way. Jud. 8: 5, 8. 1 Sam. 25: 4—13.
Before setting out gave employment, &c. to their servants. Mat. 25: 14.
Strangers civil to. Gen. 18: 2. Gen. 24: 18, 19.
Generally treated with great hospitality. Gen. 18: 3—8. Gen. 19: 2. Gen. 24: 25, 32, 33. Exo. 2: 20. Jud. 19: 20, 21. Job 31: 32. *See* Heb. 13: 2.
The caravansera or public inn for, noticed. Gen. 42: 27. Exo. 4: 24. Luke 2: 7. Luke 10: 34.
Were frequently asked whence they came and whither they went. Jud. 19: 17.
Protected by those who entertained them. Gen. 19: 6—8. Jud. 19: 23.
For security often left the highways. Jud. 5: 6.
Tessaræ hospitales or pledges of hospitality, alluded to. Rev. 2: 17.
ON ERRANDS REQUIRING DESPATCH
Went with great speed. Est. 8: 10. Job 9: 25.
Saluted no man by the way. 2 Kin. 4: 29. Luke 10: 4.
Estimated the length of their journey by the number of days which it occupied. Gen. 31: 23. Deu. 1: 2. 2 Kin. 3: 9.
The Jews prohibited from taking long journeys on the Sabbath. Exo. 20: 10, with Acts 1: 12.
Ceasing of, threatened as a calamity. Isa. 33: 8.

Trees.

Originally created by God. Gen. 1: 11, 12. Gen. 2: 9.
Made for the glory of God. Psa. 148: 9.
DIFFERENT KINDS OF, MENTIONED;
Of the wood. So. of Sol. 2: 3.
Of the forest. Isa. 10: 19.
Bearing fruit. Neh. 9: 25. Ecc. 2: 5. Eze. 47: 12.
Evergreen. Psa. 37: 35. Jer. 17: 2.
Deciduous or casting the leaves. Isa. 6: 13.
Of various sizes. Eze. 17: 24.
Given as food to the animal creation. Gen. 1: 29, 30. Deu. 20: 19.
Designed to beautify the earth. Gen. 2: 9.
PARTS OF, MENTIONED;
The roots. Jer. 17: 8.
The stem or trunk. Isa. 11: 1. Isa. 44: 19.
The branches. Lev. 23: 40. Dan. 4: 14.
The tender shoots. Luke 21: 29, 30.
The leaves. Isa. 6: 13. Dan. 4: 12. Mat. 21: 19.
The fruit or seeds. Lev. 27: 30. Eze. 36: 30.
Each kind has its own seed for propagating its species. Gen. 1: 11, 12.
Often propagated by birds who carry the seeds along with them. Eze. 17: 3, 5.
Planted by man. Lev. 19: 23.

Each kind of, known by its fruit. Mat. 12: 33.

NOURISHED

By the earth. Gen. 1: 12. Gen. 2: 9.

By the rain from heaven. Isa. 44: 14.

Through their own sap. Psa. 104: 16.

Specially flourished beside the rivers and streams of water. Eze. 47: 12.

When cut down often sprouted from their roots again. Job 14: 7.

Were sold with the land on which they grew. Gen. 23: 17.

OFTEN SUFFERED FROM

Locusts. Exo. 10: 5, 15. Deu. 28: 42.

Hail and frost. Exo. 9: 25. Psa. 78: 47.

Fire. Joel 1: 19.

Desolating armies. 2 Kin. 19: 23. Isa. 10: 34.

Afford an agreeable shade in eastern countries during the heat of the day. Gen. 18: 4. Job 40: 21.

WERE CUT DOWN

With axes. Deu. 19: 5. Psa. 74: 5. Mat. 3: 10.

For building. 2 Kin. 6: 2. 2 Chr. 2: 8, 10.

By besieging armies for erecting forts. Deu. 20: 20. Jer. 6: 6.

For making idols. Isa. 40: 20. Isa. 44: 14, 17.

For fuel. Isa. 44: 14—16. Mat. 3: 10.

God increases and multiples the fruit of, for His people. Lev. 26: 4. Eze. 34 · 27. Joel 2: 22.

God often renders, barren as a punishment. Lev. 26: 20.

Early custom of planting, in consecrated grounds. Gen. 21: 33. (*marg.*)

THE JEWS

Prohibited from planting in consecrated places. Deu. 16: 21.

Prohibited from cutting down fruit-bearing, for sieges. Deu. 20: 19.

Often pitched their tents under. Gen. 18: 1, 4. Jud. 4: 5. 1 Sam. 22: 6.

Often buried under. Gen. 35: 8. 1 Sam. 31: 13.

Often executed criminals on. Deu. 21: 22, 23. Jos. 10: 26. Gal. 3: 13. *See* Gen. 40: 19.

Considered trees on which criminals were executed abominable. Isa. 14: 19.

MENTIONED IN SCRIPTURE;

Almond. Gen. 43: 11. Ecc. 12: 5. Jer. 1: 11.

Almug or algum. 1 Kin. 10: 11, 12. 2 Chr. 9: 10, 11.

Apple. So. of Sol. 2: 3. So. of Sol. 8: 5. Joel 1: 12.

Ash. Isa. 44: 14.

Bay. Psa. 37: 35.

Box. Isa. 41: 19.

Cedar. 1 Kin. 10: 27.

Chestnut. Eze. 31: 8.

Cyprus. Isa. 44: 14.

Fig. Deu. 8: 8.

Fir. 1 Kin. 5: 10. 2 Kin. 19: 23. Psa. 104: 17.

Juniper. 1 Kin. 19: 4, 5.

Lign-aloes. Num. 24: 6.

Mulberry. 2 Sam. 5: 23, 24.

Myrtle. Isa. 41: 19. Isa. 55: 13. Zec. 1: 8.

Mustard. Mat. 13: 32.

Oak. Isa. 1: 30.

Oil-tree. Isa. 41: 19.

Olive. Deu. 6: 11.

Palm. Exo. 15: 27.

Pine. Isa. 41: 19.

Pomegranate. Deu. 8: 8. Joel 1: 12.

Shittah or shittim. Exo. 36: 20. Isa. 41: 19.

Sycamore. 1 Kin. 10: 27. Psa. 78: 47. Amos 7: 14. Luke 19: 4.

Teil. Isa. 6: 13.

Vine. Num. 6: 4. Exe. 15: 2.

Willow. Isa. 44: 4. Eze. 17: 5.

Solomon wrote the history of. 1 Kin. 4: 33.

ILLUSTRATIVE

Of Christ. Rom. 11: 24. Rev. 2: 7. Rev. 22: 2, 14.

Of wisdom. Pro. 3: 18.

Of kings, &c. Isa. 10: 34. Eze. 17: 24. Eze. 31: 7—10. Dan. 4: 10—14.

Of the life and conversation of the righteous. Pro. 11: 30. Pro. 15: 4.

(Green,) of the innocence of Christ. Luke 23: 31.

(Good and fruitful,) of saints. Num. 24: 6. Psa. 1: 3. Isa. 61: 3. Jer. 17: 8. Mat. 7: 17, 18.

(Evergreen,) of saints. Psa. 1: 1—3.

(Duration of,) of continued prosperity of saints. Isa. 65: 22.

(Casting their leaves yet retaining their substance,) of the elect remnant in the church. Isa. 6: 13.

(Barren,) of the wicked. Hos. 9: 16.

(Shaking of the leaves off,) of the terror of the wicked. Isa. 7: 2.

(Producing evil fruit,) of the wicked. Mat. 7: 17—19.

(Dry,) of useless persons. Isa. 56: 3.

(Dry,) of the wicked ripe for judgment. Luke 23: 31.

Trespass offering.

Esteemed as a sin offering, and frequently so called. Lev. 5: 6, 9.

TO BE OFFERED

For concealing knowledge of a crime. Lev. 5: 1.

For involuntarily touching unclean things. Lev. 5: 2, 3.

For rash swearing. Lev. 5: 4.

For sins of ignorance in holy things. Lev. 5: 15.

For any sin of ignorance. Lev. 5: 17.
For breach of trust, or fraud. Lev. 6: 2—5.
Was a most holy offering. Lev. 14: 13.
CONSISTED OF
A she lamb or kid. Lev. 5: 6.
A ram without blemish. Lev. 5: 15. Lev. 6: 6.
Two turtle doves by those unable to bring a lamb. Lev. 5: 7—10.
A meat offering by the very poor. Lev. 5: 11—13.
Being for minor offences was lessened for the poor, not so the sin offering. Lev. 5 ch. with Lev. 4 ch.
Atonement made by. Lev. 5: 6, 10, 13, 16, 18. Lev. 6: 7. Lev. 19: 22.
Accompanied by confession. Lev. 5: 5.
Generally accompanied by restitution. Lev. 5: 16. Lev. 6: 5.
To be slain where the sin offering and burnt offering were slain. Lev. 14: 13. Eze. 40: 39.
Sometimes waved alive before the Lord. Lev. 14: 12, with 13 v.
SPECIAL OCCASIONS OF OFFERING;
Cleansing of a leper. Lev. 14: 2, 12—14, 21, 22.
Purification of women. Lev. 12: 6—8.
Purification of those with issues. Lev. 15: 14, 15.
Purification of Nazarites who had broken their vow. Num. 6: 12.
For connection with a betrothed bondmaid. Lev. 19: 20—22.
Was the perquisites of the priest. Lev. 14: 13. Eze. 44: 29.
Illustrative of Christ. Isa. 53: 10. Eze. 46: 20.

Tribes of Israel, The.

Were twelve in number. Gen. 49: 28. Acts 26: 12. Jas. 1: 1.
Descended from Jacob's sons. Gen. 35: 22—26.
Manasseh and Ephraim numbered among, instead of Joseph and Levi. Gen. 48: 5. Jos. 14: 3, 4.
Predictions respecting each of. Gen. 49: 3—27. Deu. 33: 6—35.
EACH OF,
Under a president or chief. Num. 1: 4—16.
Divided into families. Num. 1: 2. Num. 26: 5—50. Jos. 7: 14.
Usually furnished an equal number of men for war. Num. 31: 4.
Each family of, had a chief or head. Num. 36: 1. 1 Chr. 4: 38.
Total strength of, on leaving Egypt. Exo. 12: 37. Num. 1: 44—46. Num. 2: 32
Divided into four divisions while in the wilderness. Num. 10: 14—28.
Encamped in their divisions and by their standards round the tabernacle. Num. 2: 2—31.
Canaan to be divided amongst according to their numbers. Num. 33: 54.
REUBEN, GAD AND HALF MANASSEH
Settled on east side of Jordan. Deu. 3: 12—17. Jos. 13: 23—32.
Were required to assist in subduing Canaan. Num. 32: 6—32. Deu. 3: 18—20.
Total strength of, on entering the land of Canaan. Num. 26: 51.
Canaan divided amongst nine and a half of, by lot. Jos. 14: 1—5.
Situation of, and bounds of the inheritance of each. Jos. 15 ch. to Jos. 17 ch.
All inheritance to remain in the tribe and family to which allotted. Num. 36: 3—9.
Names of, engraven on the breastplate of the high priest. Exo. 28: 21. Exo. 39: 14.
Divided on mounts Ebal and Gerizim to hear the law. Deu. 27: 12, 13.
Remained as one people until the reign of Rehoboam. 1 Kin. 12: 16—20.

Tribute.

Sometimes exacted by kings from their own subjects. 1 Sam. 8: 10—17.
Exacted from all conquered nations. Jos. 16: 10. Jud. 1: 30, 33, 35. 2 Kin. 23: 33, 35.
OFTEN EXACTED IN
Labor. 1 Kin. 5: 13, 14. (*marg.*) 1 Kin. 9: 15: 21.
Produce of land, &c. 1 Sam. 8: 15. 1 Kin. 4: 7.
Gold and silver. 2 Kin. 23: 33, 35.
The Jews required to pay half a shekel to God as. Exo. 30: 12—16.
Christ to avoid offence wrought a miracle to pay, for Himself and Peter. Mat. 17: 24—27.
KINGS OF ISRAEL
Forbidden to levy unnecessary or oppressive. Deu. 17: 17.
Set officers over. 2 Sam. 20: 24. 1 Kin. 4: 6, 7.
Often oppressed the people with. 1 Kin. 12: 4, 11.
When oppressive frequently led to rebellion. 1 Kin. 12: 14—20.
Priests and Levites exempted from. Ezr. 7: 24.
ROMAN,
Decree of Augustus for. Luke 2: 1.
First levied in Judea when Cyrenius was governor. Luke 2: 2.

Persons enrolled for, in the native place of their tribe and family. Luke 2:3—5.
Collected by the Publicans. Luke 3:12, 13. Luke 5:27.
Was paid in Roman coin. Mat. 22:19, 20.
Was resisted by the Galileans under Judas of Galilee. Acts 5:37, with Luke 13:1.
Christ showed to the Pharisees and Herodians the propriety of paying. Mat. 22:15—22. Mar. 12:13—17.
Our Lord falsely accused of forbidding to pay. Luke 23:2.

All saints exhorted to pay. Rom. 13:6, 7.

Trinity, The.

Doctrine of proved from Scripture. Mat. 3:16, 17. Mat. 28:19. Rom. 8:9. 1 Cor. 12:3—6. 2 Cor. 13:14. Eph. 4:4—6. 1 Pet. 1:2. Jude 20, 21. Rev. 1:4, 5.

Divine titles applied to the three Persons in. Exo. 20:2 with Jno. 20:28, and Acts 5:3, 4.

EACH PERSON IN, DESCRIBED AS
- Eternal. Rom. 16:26, with Rev. 22:13, and Heb. 9:14.
- Holy. Rev. 4:8. Rev. 15:4, with Acts 3:14, and 1 Jno. 2:20.
- True. Jno. 7:28, with Rev. 3:7.
- Omnipresent. Jer. 23:24, with Eph. 1:23, and Psa. 139:7.
- Omnipotent. Gen. 17:1, with Rev. 1:8, and Rom. 15:19. Jer. 32:17, with Heb. 1:3, and Luke 1:35.
- Omniscient. Acts 15:18, with Jno. 21:17, and 1 Cor. 2:10, 11.
- Creator. Gen. 1:1, with Col. 1:16, and Job 33:4. Psa. 148:5, with Jno. 1:3, and Job 26:13.
- Sanctifier. Jude 1, with Heb. 2:11, and 1 Pet. 1:2.
- Author of all spiritual operations. Heb. 13:21, with Col. 1:29, and 1 Cor. 12:11.
- Source of eternal life. Rom. 6:23, with Jno. 10:28, and Gal. 6:8.
- Teacher. Isa. 54:13, with Luke 21:15, and Jno. 14:26. Isa. 48:17, with Gal. 1:12, and 1 Jno. 2:20.
- Raising Christ from the dead. 1 Cor. 6:14, with Jno. 2:19, and 1 Pet. 3:18.
- Inspiring the prophets, &c. Heb. 1:1, with 2 Cor. 13:3, and Mar. 13:11.
- Supplying ministers to the Church. Jer. 3:15, with Eph. 4:11, and Acts 20:28. Jer. 26:5, with Mat. 10:5, and Acts 13:2.

Salvation the work of. 2 The. 2:13, 14. Tit. 3:4—6. 1 Pet. 1:2.

Baptism administered in name of. Mat. 28:19.

Benediction given in name of. 2 Cor. 13:14.

Trumpet.

An instrument of music. 1 Chr. 13:8.

Called the trump. 2 Cor. 15:52.

MADE OF
- Rams' horns. Jos. 6:4.
- Silver. Num. 10:2.

Required to give an intelligible and understood sound. 1 Cor. 14:8.

USED FOR
- Regulating the journeys of the children of Israel. Num. 10:2, 5, 6.
- Calling assemblies. Num. 10:2, 3, 7.
- Blowing over the sacrifices on feast day. Num. 10:10. Psa. 81:3.
- Blowing at all religious processions and ceremonies. 1 Chr. 13:8. 1 Chr. 15:24, 28. 2 Chr. 5:13. 2 Chr. 15:14.
- Assembling the people to war. Jud. 3:27.
- Sounding for a memorial when the people went into battle. Num. 10:9. Num. 31:6, 7.
- Proclaiming kings. 2 Kin. 9:13. 2 Kin. 11:14.
- Giving alarm in cases of danger. Eze. 33:2—6.

Moses commanded to make two, for the tabernacle. Num. 10:2.

Solomon made a great many, for the service of the temple. 2 Chr. 5:12.

The priests to blow the sacred. Num. 10:8. 2 Chr. 5:12. 2 Chr. 7:6.

The feast of trumpets celebrated by blowing of. Lev. 23:24. Num. 29:1.

The jubilee introduced by blowing of. Lev. 25:9.

MIRACLES CONNECTED WITH
- Falling of the walls of Jericho. Jos. 6:20.
- Heard at Mount Sinai at giving of the law. Exo. 19:16. Exo. 20:18.
- Confusion produced in the camp of the Midianites by sound of. Jud. 7:16, 22.

The war-horse acquainted with the sound of. Job 39:24, 25.

SOUNDING OF, ILLUSTRATIVE OF
- God's power to raise the dead. 1 Cor. 15:52. 1 The. 4:16.
- The proclamation of the gospel. Psa. 89:15.
- The bold and faithful preaching of ministers. Isa. 58:1. Hos. 8:1. Joel 2:1.
- The latter day judgments. Rev. 8:2, 13.

Trust.

God is the true object of. Psa. 65:5.

The fear of God leads to. Pro. 14:26.

ENCOURAGEMENTS TO;
The everlasting strength of God. Isa. 26:4.
The goodness of God. Nah. 1:7.
The loving-kindness of God. Psa. 36:7.
The rich bounty of God. 1 Tim. 6:17.
The care of God for us. 1 Pet. 5:7.
Former deliverances. Psa. 9:10. 2 Cor. 1:10.
Should be with the whole heart. Pro. 3:5.
Should be from youth up. Psa. 71:5.
OF SAINTS IS
Not in the flesh. Phi. 3:3, 4.
Not in themselves. 2 Cor. 1:9.
Not in carnal weapons. 1 Sam. 17:38, 39, 45. Psa. 44:6. 2 Cor. 10:4.
In God. Psa. 11:1. Psa. 31:14. 2 Cor. 1:9.
In the word of God. Psa. 119:42.
In the mercy of God. Psa. 13:5. Psa. 52:8.
In Christ. Eph. 3:12.
Through Christ. 2 Cor. 3:4.
Grounded on the covenant. 2 Sam. 23:5.
Strong in the prospect of death. Psa. 23:4.
Fixed. 2 Sam. 22:3. Psa. 112:7.
Unalterable. Job 13:15.
Despised by the wicked. Isa. 36:4, 7.
For ever. Psa. 52:8. Psa. 62:8. Isa. 26:4.
Saints plead, in prayer. Psa. 25:20. Psa. 31:1. Psa. 141:8.
The Lord knows those who have. Nah. 1:7.
Exhortations to. Psa. 4:5. Psa. 115:9—11.
LEADS TO
Being compassed with mercy. Psa. 32:10.
Enjoyment of perfect peace. Isa. 26:3.
Enjoyment of all temporal and spiritual blessings. Isa. 57:13.
Enjoyment of happiness. Pro. 16:20.
Rejoicing in God. Psa. 5:11. Psa. 33:21.
Fulfilment of all holy desires. Psa. 37:5.
Deliverance from enemies. Psa. 37:40.
Safety in times of danger. Pro. 29:25.
Stability. Psa. 125:1.
Prosperity. Pro. 28:25.
KEEPS FROM
Fear. Psa. 56:11. Isa. 12:2. Heb. 13:6.
Sliding. Psa. 26:1.
Desolation. Psa. 34:22.
To be accompanied by doing good. Psa. 37:3.
Blessedness of placing, in God. Psa. 2:12. Psa. 34:8. Psa. 40:4. Jer. 17:7.
OF THE WICKED
Is not in God. Psa. 78:22. Zep. 3:2.
Is in idols. Isa. 42:17. Hab. 2:18.
Is in man. Jud. 9:26. Psa. 118:8, 9.
Is in their own heart. Pro. 28:26.
Is in their own righteousness. Luke 18:9, 12.
Is in vanity. Job 15:31. Isa. 59:4.
Is in falsehood. Isa. 28:15. Jer. 13:25.
Is in earthly alliances. Isa. 30:2. Eze. 17:15.
Is in wealth. Psa. 49:6. Psa. 52:7. Pro. 11:28. Jer. 48:7. Mar. 10:24.
Is vain and delusive. Isa. 30:7. Jer. 2:37.
Shall make them ashamed. Isa. 20:5. Isa. 30:3, 5. Jer. 48:13.
Shall be destroyed. Job 18:14. Isa. 28:18.
Woe and curse of false. Isa. 30:1, 2. Isa. 31:1—3. Jer. 17:5.
Of saints—Illustrated. Psa. 91:12. Pro. 18:10.
Of the wicked—Illustrated. 2 Kin. 18:21. Job 8:14.
Of saints—Exemplified. *David*, 1 Sam. 17:45. 1 Sam. 30:6. *Hezekiah*, 2 Kin. 18:5. *Jehoshaphat*, 2 Chr. 20:12. *Shadrach, &c.* Dan. 3:28. *Paul*, 2 Tim. 1:12.
Of the wicked—Exemplified. *Goliath*, 1 Sam. 17:43—45. *Benhadad*, 1 Kin. 20:10, *Sennacherib*, 2 Chr. 32:8. *Israelites*, Isa. 31:1.

Truth.

God is a God of. Deu. 32:4. Psa. 31:5.
Christ is. Jno. 14:6, with Jno. 7:18.
Christ was full of. Jno. 1:14.
Christ spake. Jno. 8:45.
The Holy Ghost is the Spirit of. Jno 14:17.
The Holy Ghost guides into all. Jno 16:13.
The word of God is. Dan. 10:21. Jno. 17:17.
God regards, with favor. Jer. 5:3.
The judgments of God are according to. Psa. 96:13. Rom. 2:2.
SAINTS SHOULD
Worship God in. Jno. 4:24, with Psa. 145:18.
Serve God in. Jos. 24:14. 1 Sam. 12:24.
Walk before God in. 1 Kin. 2:4. 2 Kin. 20:3.
Keep religious feasts with. 1 Cor. 5:8.
Esteem, as inestimable. Pro. 23:23.
Rejoice in. 1 Cor. 13:6.
Speak, to one another. Zec. 8:16. Eph. 4:25.
Meditate upon. Phi. 4:8.

Write, upon the tables of the heart. Pro. 3:3.
God desires in the heart. Psa. 51:6.
The fruit of the Spirit is in. Eph. 5:9.
MINISTERS SHOULD
Speak. 2 Cor. 12:6. Gal. 4:16.
Teach in. 1 Tim. 2:7.
Approve themselves by. 2 Cor. 4:2. 2 Cor. 6:7, 8. 2 Cor. 7:14.
Magistrates should be men of. Exo. 18:21.
Kings are preserved by. Pro. 20:28.
THEY WHO SPEAK,
Show forth righteousness. Pro. 12:17.
Shall be established. Pro. 12:19.
Are the delight of God. Pro. 12:22.
THE WICKED
Destitute of. Hos. 4:1.
Speak not. Jer. 9:5.
Uphold not. Isa. 59:14, 15.
Plead not for. Isa. 59:4.
Are not valiant for. Jer. 9:3.
Punished for want of. Jer. 9:5, 9. Hos. 4:1.
THE GOSPEL AS,
Came by Christ. Jno. 1:17.
Christ bear witness to. Jno. 18:37.
Is in Christ. Rom. 9:1. 1 Tim. 2:7.
John bear witness to. Jno. 5:33.
Is according to godliness. Tit. 1:1.
Is sanctifying. Jno. 17:17, 19.
Is purifying. 1 Pet. 1:22.
Is part of the Christian armor. Eph. 6:14.
Revealed abundantly to saints. Jer. 33:6.
Abides continually with saints. 2 Jno. 2.
Should be acknowledged. 2 Tim. 2:25.
Should be believed. 2 The. 2:12, 13. 1 Tim. 4:3.
Should be obeyed. Rom. 2:8. Gal. 3:1.
Should be loved. 2 The. 2:10.
Should be manifested. 2 Cor. 4:2.
Should be rightly divided. 2 Tim. 2:15.
The wicked turn away from. 2 Tim. 4:4.
The wicked resist. 2 Tim. 3:8.
The wicked destitute of. 1 Tim. 6:5.
The church is the pillar and ground of. 1 Tim. 3:15.
The devil is devoid of. Jno. 8:44.

Truth of God, The.

Is one of His attributes. Deu. 32:4. Isa. 65:16.
Always goes before His face. Psa. 89:14.
He keeps, for ever. Psa. 146:6.
DESCRIBED AS
Great. Psa. 57:10.
Plenteous. Psa. 86:15.
Abundant. Exo. 34:6.
Inviolable. Num. 23:19. Tit. 1:2.
Reaching to the clouds. Psa. 57:10.
Enduring to all generations. Psa. 100:5.
United with mercy in redemption. Psa. 85:10.
EXHIBITED IN HIS
Counsels of old. Isa. 25:1.
Ways. Rev. 15:3.
Works. Psa. 33:4. Psa. 111:7. Dan. 4:37.
Judicial statutes. Psa. 19:9.
Administration of justice. Psa. 96:13.
Word. Psa. 119:160. Jno. 17:17.
Fulfilment of promises in Christ 2 Cor. 1:20.
Fulfilment of His covenant. Mic. 7:20.
Dealings with saints. Psa. 25:10.
Deliverance of saints. Psa. 57:3.
Punishment of the wicked. Rev. 16:7.
Remembered toward saints. Psa. 98:3.
Is a shield and buckler to saints. Psa. 91:4.
WE SHOULD
Confide in. Psa. 31:5. Tit. 1:2.
Plead, in prayer. Psa. 89:49.
Pray for its manifestation to ourselves. 2 Chr. 6:17.
Pray for its exhibition to others. 2 Sam. 2:6.
Make known to others. Isa. 38:19.
Magnify. Psa. 71:22. Psa. 138:2.
IS DENIED BY
The devil. Gen. 3:4, 5.
The self-righteous. 1 Jno. 1:10.
Unbelievers. 1 Jno. 5:10.
Exemplified towards *Abraham*, Gen. 24:27. *Jacob*, Gen. 32:10. *Israel*, Psa. 98:3.

Types of Christ.

Adam. Rom. 5:14. 1 Cor. 15:45.
Abel. Gen. 4:8, 10. Heb. 12:24.
Abraham. Gen. 17:5, with Eph. 3:15.
Aaron. Exo. 28:1, with Heb. 5:4, 5. Lev. 16:15, with Heb. 9:7, 24.
Ark. Gen. 7:16, with 1 Pet. 3:20, 21.
Ark of the covenant. Exo. 25:16, with Psa. 40:8. Isa. 42:6.
Atonement, sacrifices offered on the day of. Lev. 16:15, 16, with Heb. 9:12, 24.
Brazen serpent. Num. 21:9, with Jno. 3:14, 15.
Brazen altar. Exo. 27:1, 2, with Heb. 13:10.
Burnt offering. Lev. 1:2, 4, with Heb. 10:10.
Cities of refuge. Num. 35:6, with Heb. 6:18.
David. 2 Sam. 8:15, with Eze. 37:24. Psa. 89:19, 20, with Phi. 2:9.

Eliakim. Isa. 22: 20—22, with Rev. 3: 7.
First-fruits. Exo. 22: 29, with 1 Cor. 15: 20.
Golden candlestick. Exo. 25: 31, with Jno. 8: 12.
Golden altar. Exo. 40: 5, 26, 27, with Rev. 8: 3, and Heb. 13: 15.
Isaac. Gen. 22: 1, 2, with Heb. 11: 17—19.
Jacob. Gen. 32: 28, with Jno. 11: 42. Heb. 7: 25.
Jacob's ladder. Gen. 28: 12, with Jno. 1: 51.
Joseph. Gen. 50: 19, 20, with Heb. 7: 52.
Joshua. Jos. 1: 5, 6, with Heb. 4: 8, 9. Jos. 11: 23, with Acts 20: 32.
Jonah. Jon. 1: 17, with Mat. 12: 40.
Laver of brass. Exo. 30: 18—20, with Zec. 13: 1. Eph. 5: 26, 27.
Leper's offering. Lev. 14: 4—7, with Rom. 4: 25.
Manna. Exo. 16: 11—15, with Jno. 6: 32—35.
Melchizedek. Gen. 14: 18—20, with Heb. 7: 1—17.
Mercy-seat. Exo. 25: 17—22, with Rom. 3: 25. Heb. 4: 16.
Morning and evening sacrifices. Exo. 29: 38—41, with Jno. 1: 29, 36.
Moses. Num. 12: 7, with Heb. 3: 2. Deu. 18: 15, with Acts 3: 20—22.
Noah. Gen. 5: 29. 2 Cor. 1: 5.
Paschal lamb. Exo. 12: 3—6, 46, with Jno. 19: 36. 1 Cor. 5: 7.
Peace-offering. Lev. 3: 1, with Eph. 2: 14, 16.
Red heifer. Num. 19: 2—6, with Heb. 9: 13, 14.
Rock of Horeb. Exo. 17: 6, with 1 Cor. 10: 4.
Samson. Jud. 16: 30, with Col. 2: 14, 15.
Scape-goat. Lev. 16: 20—22, with Isa. 53: 6, 12.
Sin-offering. Lev. 4: 2, 3, 12, with Heb. 13: 11, 12.
Solomon. 2 Sam. 7: 12, 13, with Luke 1: 32, 33. 1 Pet. 2: 5.
Tabernacle. Exo. 40: 2, 34, with Heb. 9: 11. Col. 2: 9.
Table and show-bread. Exo. 25: 23—30, with Jno. 1: 16. Jno. 6: 48.
Temple. 1 Kin. 6: 1, 38, with Jno. 2: 19, 21.
Tree of life. Gen. 2: 9, with Jno. 1: 4. Rev. 22: 2.
Trespass-offering. Lev. 6: 1—7, with Isa. 53: 10.
Vail of the tabernacle and temple. Exo. 40: 21. 2 Chr. 3: 14, with Heb. 10: 20.
Zerubbabel. Zec. 4: 7—9, with Heb. 12: 2, 3.

Tyre.

Antiquity of. Isa. 23: 7, with Jos. 19: 29.

CALLED
- The daughter of Zidon. Isa. 23: 12.
- The daughter of Tarshish. Isa. 23: 10.
- The joyous city. Isa. 23: 7.
- The crowning city. Isa. 23: 8.
- The renowned city. Eze. 26: 17.

Insular position of. Eze. 26: 17. Eze. 27: 4, 25.
Strongly fortified. Jos. 19: 29. 2 Sam. 24: 7. Eze. 26: 17. Zec. 9: 3.
Governed by kings. 1 Kin. 5: 1. Jer. 25: 22.

CELEBRATED FOR
- Its beauty. Eze. 27: 3, 4.
- Its commerce. Isa. 23: 2, 3. Eze. 27: 3, 12—25.
- Its wealth. Eze. 27: 33. Eze. 28: 4, 5. Zec. 9: 3.
- Strength and beauty of its ships. Eze. 27: 5—7.

Soldiers of, supplied by Persia, &c. Eze. 27: 10, 11.

INHABITANTS OF,
- Sea-faring men. Eze. 26: 17.
- Mercantile men. Isa. 23: 8.
- Proud and haughty. Isa. 23: 9. Eze. 28: 2, 17.
- Self-conceited. Eze. 28: 3—5.
- Superstitious. Jer. 27: 2, 3, 9.
- Wicked. Eze. 28: 18.

Often confederated against the Jews and rejoiced in their calamities. Psa. 83: 7. Eze. 26: 2. Amos 1: 9.
David and Solomon formed alliances with. 1 Kin. 5: 1. 2 Chr. 2: 3.

SUPPLIED
- Seamen for Solomon's navy. 1 Kin. 9: 27. 2 Chr. 8: 18.
- A master-builder for the temple. 2 Chr. 2: 7, 13.
- Stones and timber for building the temple, &c. 1 Kin. 5: 6, 9. 2 Chr. 2: 8, 9, 16.
- Timber for rebuilding the temple and city. Ezr. 3: 7.

The Jews condemned for purchasing from the people of, on the Sabbath. Neh. 13: 16.

CHRIST
- Alluded to the depravity of. Mat. 11: 21, 22.
- Visited the coasts of. Mat. 15: 21. Mar. 7: 24.
- Was followed by many from. Mar. 3: 8. Luke 6: 17.
- Saint Paul found disciples at. Acts 21: 3, 4.
- Depended for provision upon Galilee. Acts 12: 20.

Propitiated the favor of Herod. Acts 12: 20.

PROPHECIES RESPECTING;
- Envy against the Jews a cause of its destruction. Eze. 26: 2.
- Pride a cause of its destruction. Eze. 28: 2—6.

To be destroyed by the king of Babylon. Isa. 23: 13, 14. Jer. 27: 3, 6. Eze. 26: 7—13.
Inhabitants of, to emigrate to other countries, &c. Isa. 23: 6, 12.
To be scraped as the top of a rock, and to be a place for spreading nets. Eze. 26: 3—5, 14.
The king of Babylon to be rewarded with the spoil of Egypt for his service against. Eze. 29: 18—20.
To lie waste and be forgotten for seventy years. Isa. 23: 15.
Its restoration to commercial greatness after seventy years. Isa. 23: 16, 17.
Its second destruction by the Macedonians. Eze. 27: 32. Eze. 28: 7, 8, 18. Zec. 9: 2—4.
The ruins of the first city to be employed in making a causeway to effect the destruction of insular Tyre. Eze. 26: 12.
Never to recover its greatness. Eze. 26: 21.
Its inhabitants to be sold as slaves, as a recompense for their selling the Jews. Joel 3: 4—8.
All nations to be terrified at its destruction. Eze. 26: 15—18. Eze. 27: 29—36. Zec. 9: 5.
To participate in the blessings of the gospel. Psa. 45: 12. Isa. 23: 18.

Unbelief.

Is sin. Jno. 16: 9.
Defilement inseparable from. Tit. 1: 15.
All, by nature, concluded in. Rom. 11: 32.
PROCEEDS FROM
An evil heart. Heb. 3: 12.
Slowness of heart. Luke 24: 25.
Hardness of heart. Mar. 16: 14. Acts 19: 9.
Disinclination to the truth. Jno. 8: 45, 46.
Judicial blindness. Jno. 12: 39, 40.
Not being Christ's sheep. Jno. 10: 26.
The devil blinding the mind. 2 Cor. 4: 4.
The devil taking away the word out of the heart. Luke 8: 12.
Seeking honor from men. Jno. 5: 44.
Impugns the veracity of God. 1 Jno. 5: 10.
EXHIBITED IN
Rejecting Christ. Jno. 16: 9.
Rejecting the word of God. Psa. 106: 24.
Rejecting the gospel. Isa. 53: 1. Jno. 12: 38.
Rejecting evidence of miracles. Jno. 12: 37.
Departing from God. Heb. 3: 12.
Questioning the power of God. 2 Kin. 7: 2. Psa. 78: 19, 20.
Not believing the works of God. Psa. 78: 32.
Staggering at the promise of God. Rom. 4: 20.
Rebuked by Christ. Mat. 17: 17. Jno. 20: 27.
Was an impediment to the performance of miracles. Mat. 17: 20. Mar. 6: 5.
Miracles designed to convince those in. Jno. 10: 37, 38. 1 Cor. 14: 22.
The Jews rejected for. Rom. 11: 20.
Believers should hold no communion with those in. 2 Cor. 6: 14.
THEY WHO ARE GUILTY OF,
Have not the word of God in them. Jno. 5: 38.
Cannot please God. Heb. 11: 6.
Malign the gospel. Acts 19: 9.
Persecute the ministers of God. Rom. 15: 31.
Excite others against saints. Acts 14: 2.
Persevere in it. Jno. 12: 37.
Harden their necks. 2 Kin. 17: 14.
Are condemned already. Jno. 3: 18.
Have the wrath of God abiding upon. Jno. 3: 36.
Shall not be established. Isa. 7: 9.
Shall die in their sins. Jno. 8: 24.
Shall not enter rest. Heb. 3: 19. Heb. 4: 11.
Shall be condemned. Mar. 16: 16. 2 The. 2: 12.
Shall be destroyed. Jude 5.
Shall be cast into the lake of fire. Rev. 21: 8.
Warnings against. Heb. 3: 12. Heb. 4: 11.
Pray for help against. Mar. 9: 24.
The portion of, awarded to all unfaithful servants. Luke 12: 46.
Exemplified. *Eve*, Gen. 3: 4—6. *Moses and Aaron*, Num. 20: 12. *Israelites*, Deu. 9: 23. *Naaman*, 2 Kin. 5: 12. *Samaritan lord*, 2 Kin. 7: 2. *Disciples*, Mat. 17: 17. Luke 24: 11, 25. *Zacharias*, Luke 1: 20. *Chief Priests*, Luke 22: 67. *The Jews*, Jno. 5: 38. *Brethren of Christ*, Jno. 7: 5. *Thomas*, Jno 20: 25. *Jews of Iconium*, Acts 14: 2. *Thessalonian Jews*, Acts 17: 5. *Ephesians*, Acts 19: 9. *Saul*, 1 Tim. 1: 13. *People of Jericho*, Heb. 11: 31.

Unicorn, The.

Generally had a single horn. Psa. 92: 10.
Sometimes found with two horns. Deu. 33: 17.
DESCRIBED AS
Intractable in disposition. Job 39: 9, 10, 12.
Of vast strength. Job 39: 11.

The young of, remarkable for agility. Psa. 29: 6.

ILLUSTRATIVE

Of God as the strength of Israel. Num. 23: 22. Num. 24: 8.

Of the wicked. Isa. 34: 7.

(Horns of,) of the strength of the descendants of Joseph. Deu. 33: 17.

(Horns of,) of the strength of powerful enemies. Psa. 22: 21.

(The position of its horns,) of the exaltation of saints. Psa. 92: 10.

Union with Christ.

As Head of the Church. Eph. 1: 22, 23. Eph. 4: 15, 16. Col. 1: 18.

Christ prayed that all saints might have. Jno. 17: 21, 23.

DESCRIBED AS

Christ being in us. Eph. 3: 17. Col. 1: 27.

Our being in Christ. 2 Cor. 12: 2. 1 Jno. 5: 20.

Includes union with the Father. Jno. 17: 21. 1 Jno. 2: 24.

Is of God. 1 Cor. 1: 30.

MAINTAINED BY

Faith. Gal. 2: 20. Eph. 3: 17.

Abiding in Him. Jno. 15: 4, 7.

His word abiding in us. Jno. 15: 7. 1 Jno. 2: 24. 2 Jno. 9.

Feeding on Him. Jno. 6: 56.

Obeying Him. 1 Jno. 3: 24.

The Holy Ghost witnesses. 1 Jno. 3: 24.

The gift of the Holy Ghost is an evidence of. 1 Jno. 4: 13.

SAINTS

Have, in mind. 1 Cor. 2: 16. Phi. 2: 5.

Have, in spirit. 1 Cor. 6: 17.

Have, in love. So. of Sol. 2: 16. So. of Sol. 7: 10.

Have, in sufferings. Phi. 3: 10. 2 Tim. 2: 12.

Have, in His death. Rom. 6: 3—8. Gal. 2: 20.

Have assurance of. Jno. 14: 20.

Enjoy, in the Lord's supper. 1 Cor. 10: 16, 17.

Identified with Christ by. Mat. 25: 40, 45. Acts 9: 4, with Acts 8: 1.

Are complete through. Col. 2: 10.

Exhorted to maintain. Jno. 15: 4. Acts 11: 23. Col. 2: 7.

Necessary to growth in grace. Eph. 4: 15, 16. Col. 2: 19.

Necessary to fruitfulness. Jno. 15: 4, 5.

BENEFICIAL RESULTS OF;

Righteousness imputed. 2 Cor. 5: 21. Phi. 3: 9.

Freedom from condemnation. Rom. 8: 1.

Freedom from dominion of sin. 1 Jno. 3: 6.

Being created anew. 2 Cor. 5: 17.

The spirit alive to righteousness. Rom. 8: 10.

Confidence at His coming. 1 Jno. 2: 28.

Abundant fruitfulness. Jno. 15: 5.

Answers to prayer. Jno. 15: 7.

They who have, ought to walk as He walked. 1 Jno. 2: 6.

False teachers have not. Col. 2: 18 19.

Is indissoluble. Rom. 8: 35.

Punishment of those who have not. Jno. 15: 6.

Illustrated. *Vine and branches*. Jno. 15: 1, 5. *Foundation and building*, 1 Cor. 3: 10, 11. Eph. 2: 20, 21. 1 Pet. 2: 4—6. *Body and members*, 1 Cor. 12: 12, 27. Eph. 5: 30. *Husband and wife*, Eph. 5: 25—32.

Unity of God.

A ground for obeying Him exclusively. Deu. 4: 39, 40.

A ground for loving Him supremely. Deu. 6: 4, 5, with Mar. 12: 29, 30.

ASSERTED BY

God Himself. Isa. 44: 6, 8. Isa. 45: 18, 21.

Christ. Mar. 12: 29. Jno. 17: 3.

Moses. Deu. 4: 39. Deu. 6: 4.

Apostles. 1 Cor. 8: 4, 6. Eph. 4: 6. 1 Tim. 2: 5.

Consistent with the deity of Christ and of the Holy Ghost. Jno. 10: 30, with 1 Jno. 5: 7. Jno. 14: 9—11.

EXHIBITED IN

His greatness and wonderful works. 2 Sam. 7: 22. Psa. 86: 10.

His works of creation and providence. Isa. 44: 24. Isa. 45: 5—8.

His being alone possessed of foreknowledge. Isa. 46: 9—11.

His exercise of uncontrolled sovereignty. Deu. 32: 39.

His being the sole object of worship in heaven and earth. Neh. 9: 6. Mat. 4: 10.

His being alone good. Mat. 19: 17.

His being the only Saviour. Isa. 45: 21, 22.

His being the only source of pardon. Mic. 7: 18, with Mar. 2: 7.

His unparalleled election and care of His people. Deu. 4: 32—35.

The knowledge of, necessary to eternal life. Jno. 17: 3.

All saints acknowledge, in worshipping Him. 2 Sam. 7: 22. 2 Kin. 19: 15. 1 Chr. 17: 20.

All should know and acknowledge. Deu. 4: 35. Psa. 83: 18.

May be acknowledged without saving faith. Jas. 2: 19, 20.

Uprightness.

God is perfect in. Isa. 26: 7.

God has pleasure in. 1 Chr. 29: 17.
God created man in. Ecc. 7: 29.
Man has deviated from. Ecc. 7: 29.
SHOULD BE IN
Heart. 2 Chr. 29: 34. Psa. 125: 4.
Speech. Isa. 33: 15.
Walk. Pro. 14: 2.
Judging. Psa. 58: 1. Psa. 75: 2.
Ruling. Psa. 78: 72.
The being kept from presumptuous sins is necessary to. Psa. 19: 13.
With poverty, is better than sin with riches. Pro. 28: 6.
With poverty, is better than folly. Pro. 19: 1.
THEY WHO WALK IN,
Fear God. Pro. 14: 2.
Love Christ. So. of Sol. 1: 4.
Countenanced by God. Psa. 11: 7.
Delighted in by God. Pro. 11: 20.
Their prayer delighted in by God. Pro. 15: 8.
Prospered by God. Job 8: 6. Pro. 14: 11.
Defended by God. Pro. 2: 7.
Upheld in it by God. Psa. 41: 12.
Recompensed by God. Psa. 18: 23, 24.
Find strength in God's way. Pro. 10: 29.
Obtain good from God's word. Mic. 2: 7.
Obtain light in darkness. Psa. 112: 4.
Guided by integrity. Pro. 11: 3.
Walk surely. Pro. 10: 9.
Direct their way. Pro. 21: 29.
Kept by righteousness. Pro. 13: 6.
Scorned by the wicked. Job 12: 4.
Hated by the wicked. Pro. 29: 10. Amos 5: 10.
Abominated by the wicked. Pro. 29: 21.
Persecuted by the wicked. Psa. 37: 14.
Praise is comely for. Psa. 33: 1.
A blessing to others. Pro. 11: 11.
The truly wise walk in. Pro. 15: 21.
The way of, is to depart from evil. Pro. 16: 17.
THEY WHO WALK IN, SHALL
Possess good things. Pro. 28: 10.
Have nothing good withheld. Psa. 84: 11.
Dwell in the land. Pro. 2: 21.
Dwell on high and be provided for. Isa. 33: 16.
Dwell with God. Psa. 15: 2. Psa. 140: 13.
Be blessed. Psa. 112: 2.
Be delivered by righteousness. Pro. 11: 6.
Be delivered by their wisdom. Pro. 12: 6.
Be saved. Pro. 28: 18.
Enter into peace. Psa. 37: 37. Isa. 57: 2.
Have dominion over the wicked. Psa. 49: 14.
Have an inheritance for ever. Psa. 37: 18.
A characteristic of saints. Psa. 111: 1. Isa. 26: 7.
Saints should resolve to walk in. Psa. 26: 11.
THE WICKED
Have not, in heart. Hab. 2: 4.
Leave the path of. Pro. 2: 13.
Do not act with. Mic. 7: 2, 4.
Pray for those who walk in. Psa. 125: 4.
Reprove those who deviate from. Gal. 2: 14.

Urim and Thummtn.

Placed in the breastplate of the high priest. Exo. 28: 30. Lev. 8: 8.
God to be consulted by. Num. 27: 21.
Instances of consulting God by. Jud. 1: 1. Jud. 20: 18, 28. 1 Sam. 23: 9—11. 1 Sam. 30: 7, 8.
Sometimes no answer by, in consequence of the sin of those consulting. 1 Sam. 28: 6.
Were wanting in the second temple. Ezr. 2: 63. Neh. 7: 65.
Illustrative of the light and perfection of Christ, the true high priest. Deu. 33: 8. *See* Jno. 1: 4, 9, 17. Col. 2: 3.

Usury or Interest.

The lending of money or other property for increase. Lev. 25: 37.
Those enriched by unlawful, not allowed to enjoy their gain. Psa. 28: 8.
The curse attending the giving or receiving of unlawful, alluded to. Jer. 15: 10.
THE JEWS
Forbidden to take, from brethren. Deu. 23: 19.
Forbidden to take, from brethren specially when poor. Exo. 22: 25. Lev. 25: 35—37.
Often guilty of taking. Neh. 5: 6, 7. Eze. 22: 12.
Required to restore. Neh. 5: 9—13.
Allowed to take, from strangers. Deu. 23: 20.
True and faithful Israelites never took, from their brethren. Psa. 15: 5. Eze. 18: 8, 9.
Judgments denounced against those who exacted unlawful. Isa. 24: 1, 2. Eze. 18: 13.
Illustrative of the improvement of talents received from God. Mat. 25: 27. Luke 19: 23.

Vail or Veil.

A covering for the head usually worn by women. Gen. 38: 14.

WAS WORN
As a token of modesty. Gen. 24: 65.
As a token of subjection. 1 Cor. 11: 3, 6, 7, 10.
For concealment. Gen. 38: 14.
The removing of, considered rude and insolent. So. of Sol. 5: 7.
Removing of, threatened as a punishment to ungodly women. Isa. 3: 23.
Moses put one on to conceal the glory of his face. Exo. 34: 33, with 2 Cor. 3: 13.
ILLUSTRATIVE
Of the spiritual blindness of the Gentile nations. Isa. 25: 7.
Of the spiritual blindness of the Jewish nation. 2 Cor. 3: 14—16.

Vail, the Sacred.

Moses commanded to make. Exo. 26: 31.
Made by Bezaleel for the tabernacle. Exo. 36: 35.
Suspended from four pillars of shittim wood overlaid with gold. Exo. 26: 32.
Hung between the holy and most holy place. Exo. 26: 33. Heb. 9: 3.
Designed to conceal the ark, mercy-seat, and the symbol of the divine presence. Exo. 40: 3.
THE HIGH PRIEST
Alone allowed to enter within. Heb. 9: 6, 7.
Allowed to enter but once a year. Lev. 16: 2. Heb. 9: 7.
Could not enter without blood. Lev. 16: 3, with Heb. 9: 7.
Made by Solomon for the temple. 2 Chr. 3: 14.
Was rent at the death of our Lord. Mat. 27: 51. Mar. 15: 38. Luke 23: 45.
ILLUSTRATIVE
Of the obscurity of the Mosaic dispensation. Heb. 9: 8.
Of the flesh of Christ which concealed His divinity. Heb. 10: 20. *See* Isa. 53: 2.
(Rending of,) of the death of Christ which opened heaven to saints. Heb. 10: 19, 20, with Heb. 9: 24.

Valleys.

Tracts of land between mountains. 1 Sam. 17: 3.
CALLED
Vales. Deu. 1: 7. Jos. 10: 40.
Dales. Gen. 14: 17. 2 Sam. 18: 18.
Fat valleys, when fruitful. Isa. 28: 1, 4.
Rough valleys, when uncultivated and barren. Deu. 21: 4.
Watered by mountain streams. Psa. 104: 8, 10.
Canaan abounded in. Deu. 11: 11.
ABOUNDED WITH
Fountains and springs. Deu. 8: 7. Isa. 41: 18.
Rocks and caves. Job 30: 6. Isa. 57: 5.
Trees. 1 Kin. 10: 27.
Lily of the valley. So. of Sol. 2: 1.
Ravens. Pro. 30: 17.
Doves. Eze. 7: 16.
Of Israel well tilled and fruitful. 1 Sam. 6: 13. Psa. 65: 13.
Often the scenes of idolatrous rites. Isa. 57: 5.
The heathen supposed that certain deities presided over. 1 Kin. 20: 23, 28.
The Canaanites held possession of, against Judah. Jud. 1: 19.
Often the scenes of great contests Jud. 5: 15. Jud. 7: 8, 22. 1 Sam. 17: 19.
MENTIONED IN SCRIPTURE;
Achor. Jos. 7: 24. Isa. 65: 10. Hos. 2: 15.
Ajalon. Jos. 10: 12.
Baca. Psa. 84: 6.
Berachah. 2 Chr. 20: 26.
Bochim. Jud. 2: 5.
Charashim. 1 Chr. 4: 14.
Elah. 1 Sam. 17: 2. 1 Sam. 21: 9.
Eshcol. Num. 32: 9. Deu. 1: 24.
Gad. 2 Sam. 24: 5. (*marg.*)
Gerar. Gen. 26: 17.
Gibeon. Isa. 28: 21.
Hebron. Gen. 37: 14.
Hinnom or Tophet. Jos. 18: 16. 2 Kin. 23: 10. 2 Chr. 28: 3. Jer. 7: 32.
Jehoshaphat or decision. Joel 3: 2, 14.
Jericho. Deu. 34: 3.
Jezreel. Hos. 1: 5.
Jiphthah-el. Jos. 19: 14, 27.
Keziz. Jos. 18: 21.
Lebanon. Jos. 11: 17.
Megiddo. 2 Chr. 35: 22. Zec. 12: 11.
Moab where Moses was buried. Deu. 34: 6.
Passengers or Hamon-gog. Eze. 39: 11.
Rephaim or giants. Jos. 15: 8. Jos. 18: 16. 2 Sam. 5: 18. Isa. 17: 5.
Salt. 2 Sam. 8: 13. 2 Kin. 14: 17.
Shaveh or king's dale. Gen. 14: 17 2 Sam. 18: 18.
Shittim. Joel 3: 18.
Siddim. Gen. 14: 3, 8.
Sorek. Jud. 16: 4.
Succoth. Psa. 60: 6.
Zared. Num. 21: 12.
Zeboim. 1 Sam. 13: 18.
Zephathah. 2 Chr. 14: 10.
To be filled with hostile chariots, threatened as a punishment. Isa. 22: 7.
MIRACLES CONNECTED WITH;
The moon made to stand still over Ajalon. Jos. 10: 12.

Ditches in, filled with water. 2 Kin. 3:16, 17.
Water in, made to appear to the Moabites like blood. 2 Kin. 3:22, 23.

ILLUSTRATIVE
Of the church of Christ. So. of Sol. 6:11.
(Fruitful and well watered,) of the tents of Israel. Num. 24:6.
(Dark,) of affliction and death. Psa. 23:4.
(Filling up of,) of removing all obstructions to the gospel. Isa. 40:4. Luke 3:5.

Vanity.

A consequence of the fall. Rom. 8:20.
Every man is. Psa. 39:11.
Every state of man is. Psa. 62:9.
Man at his best estate is. Psa. 39:5.
Man is like to. Psa. 144:4.
The thoughts of man are. Psa. 94:11.
The days of man are. Job 7:16. Ecc. 6:12.
Childhood and youth are. Ecc. 11:10.
The beauty of man is. Psa. 39:11. Pro. 31:30.
The help of man is. Psa. 60:11. Lam. 4:17.
Man's own righteousness is. Isa. 57:12.
Worldly wisdom is. Ecc. 2:15, 21. 1 Cor. 3:20.
Worldly pleasure is. Ecc. 2:1.
Worldly anxiety is. Psa. 39:6. Psa. 127:2.
Worldly labor is. Ecc. 2:11. Ecc. 4:4.
Worldly enjoyment is. Ecc. 2:3, 10, 11.
Worldly possessions are. Ecc. 2:4—11.
Treasures of wickedness are. Pro. 10:2.
Heaping up riches is. Ecc. 2:26. Ecc. 4:8.
Love of riches is. Ecc. 5:10.
Unblessed riches are. Ecc. 6:2.
Riches gotten by falsehood are. Pro. 21:6.
All earthly things are. Ecc. 1:2.
Foolish questions, &c. are. 1 Tim. 1:6, 7. 1 Tim. 6:20. 2 Tim. 2:14, 16. Tit. 3:9.
The conduct of the ungodly is. 1 Pet. 1:18.
The religion of hypocrites is. Jas. 1:26.
The worship of the wicked is. Isa. 1:13. Mat. 6:7.
Lying words are. Jer. 7:8.
False teaching is but. Jer. 23:32.
Mere external religion is. 1 Tim. 4:8. Heb. 13:9.
Almsgiving without charity is. 1 Cor. 13:3.
Faith without works is. Jas. 2:14.
Idolatry is. 2 Kin. 17:15. Psa. 31:6. Isa. 44:9, 10. Jer. 10:8. Jer. 18:15.
Wealth gotten by, diminishes. Pro. 13:11.

SAINTS
Hate the thoughts of. Psa. 119:113.
Pray to be kept from. Psa. 119:37. Pro. 30:8.
Avoid. Psa. 24:4.
Avoid those given to. Psa. 26:4.

THE WICKED
Especially characterized by. Job 11:11.
Though full of, affect to be wise. Job 11:12.
Love. Psa. 4:2.
Imagine. Psa. 2:1. Acts 4:25. Rom. 1:21.
Devise. Psa. 36:4. (*See marg.*)
Speak. Psa. 10:7. Psa. 12:2. Psa. 41:6.
Count God's service as. Job 21:15. Mal. 3:14.
Allure others by words of. 2 Pet. 2:18.
Walk after. Jer. 2:5.
Walk in. Psa. 39:6. Eph. 4:17.
Inherit. Jer. 16:19.
Reap. Pro. 22:8. Jer. 12:13.
Judicially given up to. Psa. 78:33. Isa. 57:13.
Fools follow those given to. Pro. 12:11.
Following those given to, leads to poverty. Pro. 28:19.
They who trust in, rewarded with. Job 15:31.

Vine, The.

Often found wild. 2 Kin. 4:39. Hos. 9:10.

CULTIVATED
In vineyards from the time of Noah. Gen. 9:20.
On the sides of hills. Jer. 31:5.
In the valleys. So. of Sol. 6:11.
By the walls of houses. Psa. 128:3.
Required to be dressed and pruned to increase its fruitfulness. Lev. 25:3. 2 Chr. 26:10. Isa. 18:5.
Canaan abounded in. Deu. 6:11. Deu. 8:8.

PLACES CELEBRATED FOR;
Eshcol. Num. 13:23, 24.
Sibmah. Isa. 16:8, 9.
Lebanon. Hos. 14:7.
Egypt. Psa. 78:47. Psa. 80:8.
The dwarf and spreading vine particularly esteemed. Eze. 17:6.
Of Sodom bad and unfit for use. Deu. 32:32.

Often degenerated. Isa. 5:2. Jer. 2:21.
Frequently injured by hail and frost. Psa. 78:47. Psa. 105:32, 33.
Foxes destructive to. So. of Sol. 2:15.
The wild boar destructive to. Psa. 80:13.
THE FRUIT OF,
Called grapes. Gen. 40:10.
Peculiarly sour when unripe. Jer. 31:30.
Eaten fresh from the tree. Deu. 23:24.
Eaten dried. 1 Sam. 25:18. 1 Sam. 30:12.
Sold in the markets. Neh. 13:15.
Made into wine. Deu. 32:14. Mat. 26:29.
The wood of, fit only for burning. Eze. 15:2—5.
Young cattle fed on its leaves and tender shoots. Gen. 49:11.
Probably produced two crops of fruit in the year. Num. 13:20.
Perfumed the air with the fragrance of its flowers, &c. So. of Sol. 2:13. Hos. 14:7. (*marg.*)
God made, fruitful for His people when obedient. Joel 2:22. Zec. 8:12.
Frequently made unfruitful as a punishment. Jer. 8:13. Hos. 2:12. Joel 1:7, 12. Hag. 2:19.
Sometimes cast its fruit before it came to perfection. Job 15:33. Mal. 3:11.
Nazarites prohibited eating any part of, &c. Num. 6:3, 4.
ILLUSTRATIVE
Of Christ. Jno. 15:1, 2.
Of Israel. Psa. 80:8. Isa. 5:2, 7.
(Its fruitful branches,) of saints. Jno. 15:5.
(Its unfruitful branches,) of mere professors. Jno. 15:2, 6.
(Its quick growth,) of the growth of saints in grace. Hos. 14:7.
(Its rich clusters,) of the graces of the Church. So. of Sol. 7:8.
(Pruning of,) of God's purifying His people by afflictions. Jno. 15:2.
(Worthlessness of its wood,) of the unprofitableness, of the wicked. Eze. 15:6, 7.
(Unfruitful,) of the wicked. Hos. 10:1.
(Sitting under one's own,) of peace and prosperity. 1 Kin. 4:25. Mic. 4:4. Zec. 3:10.
Proverbial allusion to fathers eating the unripe fruit of. Jer. 31:29, 30. Eze. 18:2.

Vineyards.

Origin and antiquity of. Gen. 9:20.
The design of planting. Psa. 107:37. 1 Cor. 9:7.
Frequently walled or fenced with hedges. Num. 22:24. Pro. 24:31. Isa. 5:2, 5.
Cottages built in, for the keepers. Isa. 1:8.
Provided with the apparatus for making wine. Isa. 5:2. Mat. 21:33.
The stones carefully gathered out of. Isa. 5:2.
LAWS RESPECTING;
Not to be planted with different kinds of seed. Deu. 22:9.
Not to be cultivated during the sabbatical year. Exo. 23:11. Lev. 25:4.
The spontaneous fruit of, not to be gathered the sabbatical or jubilee year. Lev. 25:5, 11.
Compensation in kind to be made for injury done to. Exo. 22:5.
Strangers entering, allowed to eat fruit of, but not to take any away. Deu. 23:24.
The gleaning of, to be left for the poor. Lev. 19:10. Deu. 24:21.
The fruit of new, not to be eaten for three years. Lev. 19:23.
The fruit of new, to be holy to the Lord in the fourth year. Lev. 19:24.
The fruit of new, to be eaten by the owners from the fifth year. Lev. 19:25.
Planters of, not liable to military service till they had eaten of the fruit. Deu. 20:6.
Frequently let out to husbandmen. So. of Sol. 8:11. Mat. 21:33.
Rent of, frequently paid by part of the fruit. Mat. 21:34.
Were often mortgaged. Neh. 5:3, 4.
Estimated rent of. So. of Sol. 8:11. Isa. 7:23.
Estimated profit arising from, to the cultivators. So. of Sol. 8:12.
The poor engaged in the culture of. 2 Kin. 25:12. Isa. 61:5.
Members of the family often wrought in. So. of Sol. 1:6. Mat. 21:28—30.
Mode of hiring and paying laborers for working in. Mat. 20:1, 2.
Of the kings of Israel superintended by officers of state. 1 Chr. 27:27.
THE VINTAGE OR INGATHERING OF,
Was a time of great rejoicing. Isa. 16:10.
Sometimes continued to the time of sowing seed. Lev. 26:5.
Failure in, occasioned great grief. Isa. 16:9, 10.
Of red grapes particularly esteemed. Isa. 27:2.
The produce of, was frequently destroyed by enemies. Jer. 48:32.
The whole produce of, often destroyed by insects, &c. Deu. 28:39. Amos 4:9.

In unfavorable seasons produced but little wine. Isa. 5: 10. Hag. 1: 9, 11.
The wicked judicially deprived of the enjoyment of. Amos 5: 11. Zep. 1: 13.
The Rechabites forbidden to plant. Jer. 35: 7—9.
Of the slothful man neglected and laid waste. Pro. 24: 30, 31.
ILLUSTRATIVE
Of the Jewish Church. Isa. 5: 7. Isa. 27: 2. Jer. 12: 10. Mat. 21: 23.
(Failure of,) of severe calamities. Isa. 32: 10.
(Cleaning grapes of,) of the elect. Isa. 24: 13.

Visions.

God often made known His will by. Psa. 89: 19.
God especially made Himself known to prophets by. Num. 12: 6.
OFTEN ACCOMPANIED BY
A representative of the divine person and glory. Isa. 6: 1.
An audible voice from heaven. Gen. 15: 1. 1 Sam. 3: 4, 5.
An appearance of angels. Luke 1: 22, with 11 v. Luke 24: 23. Acts 10: 3.
An appearance of human beings. Acts 9: 12. Acts 16: 9.
Frequently difficult and prelexing to those who received them. Dan. 7: 15. Dan. 8: 15. Acts 10: 17.
OFTEN COMMUNICATED
In the night season. Gen. 46: 2. Dan. 2: 19.
In a trance. Num. 24: 16. Acts 11: 5.
Often recorded for the benefit of the people. Hab. 2: 2.
Often multiplied for the benefit of the people. Hos. 12: 10.
MENTIONED IN SCRIPTURE;
To Abraham. Gen. 15: 1.
To Jacob. Gen. 46: 2.
To Moses. Exo. 3: 2, 3. Acts 7: 30—32.
To Samuel. 1 Sam. 3: 2—15.
To Nathan. 2 Sam. 7: 4, 17.
To Eliphaz. Job 4: 13—16.
To Isaiah. Isa. 6: 1—8.
To Ezekiel. Eze. 1: 4—14. Eze. 8: 2—14. Eze. 10 ch. Eze. 11: 24, 25. Eze. 37: 1—10. Eze. 40 ch. to Eze. 48 ch.
To Nebuchadnezzar. Dan. 2: 28. Dan. 4: 5.
To Daniel. Dan. 2: 19. Dan. 7 ch. Dan. 8 ch. Dan 10 ch.
To Amos. Amos 7: 1—9. Amos 8: 1—6. Amos 9: 1.
To Zechariah. Zec. 1: 8. Zec. 3: 1. Zec. 4: 2. Zec. 5: 2. Zec. 6: 1.
To Paul. Acts 9: 3, 6, 12. Acts 16: 9. Acts 18: 9. Acts 22: 18. Acts 27: 23. 2 Chr. 12: 1—4.
To Ananias. Acts 9: 10, 11.
To Cornelius. Acts 10: 3.
To Peter. Acts 10: 9—17.
To John. Rev. 1: 12, &c. Rev. 4 ch. to Rev. 22 ch.
Sometimes withheld for a long season. 1 Sam. 3: 1.
The withholding of a great calamity. Pro. 29: 18. Lam. 2: 9.
False prophets pretended to have seen. Jer. 14: 14. Jer. 23: 16.
The prophets of God skilled in interpreting. 2 Chr. 26: 5. Dan. 1: 17.

Vows.

Solemn promises to God. Psa. 76: 11.
WERE MADE IN REFERENCE TO
Devoting the person to God. Num. 6: 2.
Dedicating children to God. 1 Sam. 1: 11.
Devoting property to God. Gen. 28: 22.
Offering sacrifices. Lev. 7: 16. Lev. 22: 18, 22. Num. 15: 3.
Afflicting the soul. Num. 30: 13.
To be voluntary. Deu. 23: 21, 22.
To be performed faithfully. Num. 30: 2.
To be performed without delay. Deu. 23: 21, 23.
Danger of inconsiderately making. Pro. 20: 25.
Of children void without consent of parents. Num. 30: 3—5.
Of married women void without consent of husbands. Num. 30: 6—8, 10—13.
Of widows and women divorced from their husbands binding. Num. 30: 9.
Of wives, could only be objected to at the time of making. Num. 30: 14, 15.
Might be redeemed by paying a suitable compensation. Lev. 27: 1—8, 11—23.
Clean beasts the subjects of, not to be redeemed. Lev. 27: 9, 10.
RECORDED IN SCRIPTURE;
Of Jacob. Gen. 28: 20—22. Gen. 31: 13.
Of Israelites. Num. 21: 2.
Of Jephthah. Jud. 11: 30, 31.
Of Hannah. 1 Sam. 1: 11.
Of Elkanah. 1 Sam. 1: 21.
Of David. Psa. 132: 2—5.
Of mariners who cast out Jonah. Jon. 1: 16.
Of Jonah. Jon. 2: 9.
Of Lemuel's mother. Pro. 31: 1, 2.
Of Paul. Acts 18: 18.
Of certain Jews with Paul. Acts 21: 23, 24, 26.
All things dedicated by, to be brought to the tabernacle. Deu. 12: 6, 11, 17, 18, 26.
Of things corrupt or blemished an insult to God. Lev. 22: 23. Mal. 1: 14.

The hire of a prostitute or price of a dog could not be the subject of. Deu. 23: 18.

Waiting upon God.

As the God of providence. Jer. 14: 22.
As the God of salvation. Psa. 25: 5.
As the Giver of all temporal blessings. Psa. 104: 27, 28. Psa. 145: 15, 16.
FOR
- Mercy. Psa. 123: 2.
- Pardon. Psa. 39: 7, 8.
- The consolation of Israel. Luke 2: 25.
- Salvation. Gen. 49: 18. Psa. 62: 1, 2.
- Guidance and teaching. Psa. 25: 5.
- Protection. Psa. 33: 20. Psa. 59: 9, 10.
- The fulfilment of His word. Hab. 2: 3.
- The fulfilment of His promises. Acts 1: 4.
- Hope of righteousness by faith. Gal. 5: 5.
- Coming of Christ. 1 Cor. 1: 7. 1 The. 1: 10.

Is good. Psa. 52: 9.
God calls us to. Zep. 3: 8.
Exhortations and encouragements to. Psa. 27: 14. Psa. 37: 7. Hos. 12: 6.
SHOULD BE
- With the soul. Psa. 62: 1, 5.
- With earnest desire. Psa. 130: 6.
- With patience. Psa. 37: 7. Psa. 40: 1.
- With resignation. Lam. 3: 26.
- With hope in His word. Psa. 130: 5.
- With full confidence. Mic. 7: 7.
- Continually. Hos. 12: 6.
- All the day. Psa. 25: 5.
- Specially in adversity. Psa. 59: 1—9. Isa. 8: 17.
- In the way of His judgments. Isa. 26: 8.

Saints resolve on. Psa. 52: 9. Psa. 59: 9.
Saints have expectation from. Psa. 62: 5.
Saints plead, in prayer. Psa. 25: 21. Isa. 33: 2.
The patience of saints often tried in. Psa. 69: 3.
THEY WHO ENGAGE IN,
- Wait upon Him only. Psa. 62: 5.
- Are heard. Psa. 40: 1.
- Are blessed. Isa. 30: 18. Dan. 12: 12.
- Experience His goodness. Lam. 3: 25.
- Shall not be ashamed. Psa. 25: 3. Isa. 49: 23.
- Shall renew their strength, &c. Isa. 40: 31.
- Shall inherit the earth. Psa. 37: 9.
- Shall be saved. Pro. 20: 22. Isa. 25: 9.
- Shall rejoice in salvation. Isa. 25: 9.
- Shall receive the glorious things prepared by God for them. Isa. 64: 4.

Predicted of the Gentiles. Isa. 42: 4. Isa. 60: 9.
Illustrated. Psa. 123: 2. Luke 12: 36. Jas. 5: 7.
Exemplified. *Jacob*, Gen. 49: 18. *Hannah*, 1 Sam. 1: 2. *David*, Psa. 39: 7. *Isaiah*, Isa. 8: 17. *Micah*, Mic. 7: 7. *Joseph*, Mar. 15: 43.

Walls.

Designed for separation. Eze. 43: 8. Eph. 2: 14.
Designed for defence. 1 Sam. 25: 16.
MENTIONED IN SCRIPTURE;
- Of cities. Num. 13: 28.
- Of temples. 1 Chr. 29: 4. Isa. 56: 5.
- Of houses. 1 Sam. 18: 11.
- Of vineyards. Num. 22: 24. Pro. 24: 31.

Frequently made of stone and wood together. Ezr. 5: 8. Hab. 2: 11.
Were probably often strengthened with plates of iron or brass. Jer. 15: 20. Eze. 4: 3.
OF CITIES
- Often very high. Deu. 1: 28. Deu. 3: 5.
- Strongly fortified. Isa. 2: 15. Isa. 25: 12.
- Had towers built on them. 2 Chr. 26: 9. 2 Chr. 32: 5. Psa. 48: 12. So. of Sol. 8: 10.
- Houses often built on. Jos. 2: 15.
- Were broad and places of public resort. 2 Kin. 6: 26, 30. Psa. 55: 10.
- Were strongly manned in war. 2 Kin. 18: 26.
- Kept by watchmen night and day. So. of Sol. 5: 7. Isa. 62: 6.
- Houses sometimes broken down to repair, and fortify. Isa. 22: 10.
- Danger of approaching too near to, in time of war. 2 Sam. 11: 20, 21.
- Were battered by besieging armies. 2 Sam. 20: 15. Eze. 4: 2, 3.
- Adroitness of soldiers in scaling, alluded to. Joel 2: 7—9.
- Sometimes burned. Jer. 49: 27. Amos 1: 7.
- Frequently laid in ruins. 2 Chr. 25: 23. 2 Chr. 36: 19. Jer. 50: 15.
- Destruction of, a punishment and cause of grief. Deu. 28: 52. Neh. 1: 3. Neh. 2: 12—17.
- The falling of, sometimes occasioned great destruction. 1 Kin. 20: 30.
- The bodies of enemies sometimes fastened on, as a disgrace. 1 Sam. 31: 10.
- Custom of dedicating. Neh. 12: 27.

Idolatrous rites performed on. 2 Kin. 3: 27.
Instances of persons let down from. Jos. 2: 15. Acts 9: 24, 25. 2 Cor. 11: 33.
Small towns and villages were not surrounded by. Lev. 25: 31. Deu. 3: 5.
OF HOUSES
Usually plastered. Eze. 13: 10, with Dan. 5: 5.
Had nails or pegs fastened into them when built. Ecc. 12: 11. Isa. 22: 23.
Liable to leprosy. Lev. 14: 37.
Often infested with serpents. Amos 5: 19.
Could be easily dug through. Gen. 49: 6. Eze. 8: 7, 8. Eze. 12: 5.
The seat next, was the place of distinction. 1 Sam. 20: 25.
Hyssop frequently grew on. 1 Kin. 4: 33.
MIRACLES CONNECTED WITH;
Falling of the walls of Jericho. Jos. 6: 20.
Handwriting on the wall of Belshazzar's palace. Dan. 5: 5, 25—28.
ILLUSTRATIVE
Of salvation. Isa. 26: 1. Isa. 60: 18.
Of the protection of God. Zec. 2: 5.
Of those who afford protection. 1 Sam. 25: 16. Isa. 2: 15.
Of the Church as a protection to the nation. So. of Sol. 8: 9, 10.
Of ordinances as a protection to the Church. So. of Sol. 2: 9. Isa. 5: 5.
Of the wealth of the rich in his own conceit. Pro. 18: 11.
(Brazen,) of prophets in their testimony against the wicked. Jer. 22: 20.
(Bowing or tottering,) of the wicked under judgments. Psa. 62: 3. Isa. 30: 13.
(Of partition,) of separation of Jews and Gentiles. Eph. 2: 14.
(Daubed with untempered mortar,) of the teaching of false prophets. Eze. 13: 10—15.
(Whited,) of hypocrites. Acts 23: 3.

War.

Antiquity of. Gen. 14: 2.
Originates in the lusts of men. Jas. 4: 1.
A time for. Ecc. 3: 8.
GOD
Frequently ordered. Exo. 17: 16. Num. 31: 1, 2. Deu. 7: 1, 2. 1 Sam. 15: 1—3.
Taught His people the art of. 2 Sam. 22: 35.
Strengthens His people for. Lev. 26: 7, 8.
Gives the victory in. Num. 21: 3. Deu. 2: 33. Deu. 3: 3. 2 Sam. 23: 10. Pro. 21: 31. (*marg.*)
Causes, to cease. Psa. 46: 9.
Scatters those who delight in. Psa. 68: 30.
Large armies frequently engaegd in. 2 Chr. 13: 3. 2 Chr. 14: 9.
Weapons used in. Jos. 1: 14. Jud. 18: 11.
PRECEDED BY
Consultation. Luke 14: 31, with Pro. 24: 6.
Great preparation. Joel 3: 9.
Rumors. Jer. 4: 19. Mat. 24: 6.
Frequently long continued. 2 Sam. 3: 1.
Frequently sore and bloody. 1 Sam. 14: 22. 1 Chr. 5: 22. 2 Chr. 14: 13. 2 Chr. 28: 6.
OFTEN ATTENDED BY
Famine. Isa. 51: 19. Jer. 14: 15. Lam. 5: 10.
Pestilence. Jer. 27: 13. Jer. 28: 8.
Cruelty. Jer. 18: 21. Lam. 5: 11—14.
Devastation. Isa. 1: 7.
Records often kept of. Num. 21: 14.
Often sent as a punishment for sin. Jud. 5: 8.
THE JEWS
Were expert in. 1 Chr. 12: 33, 35, 36. So. of Sol. 3: 8.
Frequently engaged in. Jos. 6 ch. to Jos. 11 ch. 1 Kin. 14: 30. 1 Kin. 15: 7, 16.
ILLUSTRATIVE OF
Our contest with death. Ecc. 8: 8.
The contest of saints with the enemies of their salvation. Rom. 7: 23. 2 Cor. 10: 3. Eph. 6: 12. 1 Tim. 1: 18.
The contest between Antichrist and the Church. Rev. 11: 7. Rev. 13: 4, 7.
The malignity of the wicked. Psa. 55: 21.

Warfare of Saints.

Is not after the flesh. 2 Cor. 10: 3.
Is a good warfare. 1 Tim. 1: 18, 19.
Called the good fight of faith. 1 Tim. 6: 12.
IS AGAINST
The devil. Gen. 3: 15. 2 Cor. 2: 11. Eph. 6: 12. Jas. 4: 7. 1 Pet. 5: 8. Rev. 12: 17.
The flesh. Rom. 7: 23. 1 Cor. 9: 25—27. 2 Cor. 12: 7. Gal. 5: 17. 1 Pet. 2: 11.
Enemies. Psa. 38: 19. Psa. 56: 2. Psa. 59: 3.
The world. Jno. 16: 33. 1 Jno. 5: 4, 5.
Death. 1 Cor. 15: 26, with Heb. 2: 14, 15.

Often arises from the opposition of friends or relatives. Mic. 7: 6, with Mat. 10: 35, 36.

TO BE CARRIED ON
- Under Christ, as our captain. Heb. 2: 10.
- Under the Lord's banner. Psa. 60: 4.
- With faith. 1 Tim. 1: 18, 19.
- With a good conscience. 1 Tim. 1: 18, 19.
- With steadfastness in the faith. 1 Cor. 16: 13. 1 Pet. 5: 9, with Heb. 10: 23.
- With earnestness. Jude 3.
- With watchfulness. 1 Cor. 16: 13. 1 Pet. 5: 8.
- With sobriety. 1 The. 5: 6. 1 Pet. 5: 8.
- With endurance of hardness. 2 Tim. 2: 3, 10.
- With self-denial. 1 Cor. 9: 25—27.
- With confidence in God. Psa. 27: 1—3.
- With prayer. Psa. 35: 1—3. Eph. 6: 18.
- Without earthly entanglements. 2 Tim. 2: 4.

Mere professors do not maintain. Jer. 9: 3.

SAINTS
- Are all engaged in. Phi. 1: 30.
- Must stand firm in. Eph. 6: 13, 14.
- Exhorted to diligence in. 1 Tim. 6: 12. Jude 3.
- Encouraged in. Isa. 41: 11, 12. Isa. 51: 12. Mic. 7: 8. 1 Jno. 4: 4.
- Helped by God in. Psa. 118: 13. Isa. 41: 13, 14.
- Protected by God in. Psa. 140: 7.
- Comforted by God in. 2 Cor. 7: 5, 6.
- Strengthened by God in. Psa. 20: 2. Psa. 27: 14. Isa. 41: 10.
- Strengthened by Christ in. 2 Cor. 12: 9. 2 Tim. 4: 17.
- Delivered by Christ in. 2 Tim. 4: 18.
- Thank God for victory in. Rom. 7: 25. 1 Cor. 15: 57.

ARMOR FOR,
- Girdle of truth. Eph. 6: 14.
- Breastplate of righteousness. Eph. 6: 14.
- Preparation of the gospel. Eph. 6: 15.
- Shield of faith. Eph 6: 16.
- Helmet of salvation. Eph. 6: 17. 1 The. 5: 8.
- Sword of the Spirit. Eph. 6: 17.
- Called armor of God. Eph. 6: 11.
- Called armor of righteousness. 2 Cor. 6: 7.
- Called armor of light. Rom. 13: 12.
- Not carnal. 2 Cor. 10: 4.
- Mighty through God. 2 Cor. 10: 4, 5.
- The whole, is required. Eph. 6: 13.
- Must be put on. Rom. 13: 12. Eph. 6: 11.
- To be on right hand and left. 2 Cor. 6: 7.

VICTORY IN, IS
- From God. 1 Cor. 15: 57. 2 Cor. 2: 14.
- Through Christ. Rom. 7: 25. 1 Cor. 15: 27. 2 Cor. 12: 9. Rev. 12: 11.
- By faith. Heb. 11: 33—37. 1 Jno. 5: 4, 5.
- Over the devil. Rom. 16: 20. 1 Jno. 2: 14.
- Over the flesh. Rom. 7: 24, 25. Gal. 5: 24.
- Over the world. 1 Jno. 5: 4, 5.
- Over all that exalts itself. 2 Cor. 10: 5.
- Over death and the grave. Isa. 25: 8. Isa. 26: 19. Hos. 13: 14. 1 Cor. 15: 54, 55.
- Triumphant. Rom. 8: 37. 2 Cor. 10: 5.

THEY WHO OVERCOME IN, SHALL
- Eat of the hidden manna. Rev. 2: 17.
- Eat of the tree of life. Rev. 2: 7.
- Be clothed in white raiment. Rev. 3: 5.
- Be pillars in the temple of God. Rev. 3: 12.
- Sit with Christ in His throne. Rev. 3: 21.
- Have a white stone, and, in it a new name written. Rev. 2: 17.
- Have power over the nations. Rev. 2: 26.
- Have the name of God written upon them by Christ. Rev. 3: 12.
- Have God as their God. Rev. 21: 7.
- Have the morning-star. Rev. 2: 28.
- Inherit all things. Rev. 21: 7.
- Be confessed by Christ before God the Father. Rev. 3: 5.
- Be sons of God. Rev. 21: 7.
- Not be hurt by the second death. Rev. 2: 11.
- Not have their names blotted out of the book of life. Rev. 3: 5.

Illustrated. Isa. 9: 5. Zec. 10: 5.

Watchfulness.

Christ an example of. Mat. 26: 38, 40. Luke 6: 12.

Commanded. Mar. 13: 37. Rev. 3: 2.

Exhortations to. 1 The. 5: 6. 1 Pet. 4: 7.

God especially requires in ministers. Eze. 3: 17, with Isa. 62: 6. Mar. 13: 34.

Ministers exhorted to. Acts 20: 31. 2 Tim. 4: 5.

Faithful ministers exercise. Heb. 13: 17.

Faithful ministers approved by. Mat. 24: 45, 46. Luke 12: 41—44.

SHOULD BE
- With prayer. Luke 21: 36. Eph. 6: 18.
- With thanksgiving. Col. 4: 2.
- With steadfastness in the faith. 1 Cor. 16: 13.

With heedfulness. Mar. 13: 33.
With sobriety. 1 The. 5: 6. 1 Pet. 4: 7.
At all times. Pro. 8: 34.
In all things. 2 Tim. 4: 5.
Saints pray to be kept in a state of. Psa. 141: 3.
MOTIVES TO;
Expected direction from God. Hab. 2: 1.
Uncertain time of the coming of Christ. Mat. 24: 42. Mat. 25: 13. Mar. 13: 35, 36.
Incessant assaults of the devil. 1 Pet. 5: 8.
Liability to temptation. Mat. 26: 41.
Blessedness of. Luke 12: 37. Rev. 16: 15.
Unfaithful ministers devoid of. Isa. 56: 10.
The wicked averse to. 1 The. 5: 7.
Danger of remissness in. Mat. 24: 48—51. Mat. 25: 5, 8, 12. Rev. 3: 3.
Illustrated. Luke 12: 35, 36.
Exemplified. *David*, Psa. 102: 7. *Anna*, Luke 2: 37. *Paul*, 2 Cor. 11: 27.

Watchmen.

Soldiers generally acted as. Mat. 27: 65, 66.
Citizens sometimes acted as. Neh. 7: 3.
WERE STATIONED
On watch towers. 2 Kin. 9: 17. Isa. 21: 5.
On the walls of cities. Isa. 62: 6.
In the streets of cities. Psa. 127: 1.
Around the temple in Jerusalem on special occasions. 2 Kin. 11: 6.
Paraded the streets at night to preserve order. So. of Sol. 3: 3. So. of Sol. 5: 7.
IN TIME OF DANGER
Increased in number. Jer. 51: 12.
Vigilant night and day. Neh. 4: 9. Isa. 21: 8.
Reported the approach of all strangers, &c. 2 Sam. 18: 24—27. 2 Kin. 9: 18—20. Isa. 21: 6, 7, 9.
Sounded an alarm at the approach of enemies. Eze. 33: 2, 3.
Vigilance of, vain without God's protection. Psa. 127: 1.
Were relieved by turns. Neh. 7: 3.
Danger of sleeping on their posts, referred to. Mat. 28: 13, 14.
Neglecting to give warning punished with death. Eze. 33: 6.
Often interrogated by passengers. Isa. 21: 11.
ILLUSTRATIVE
Of ministers. Isa. 52: 8. Isa. 62: 6. Eze. 3: 17. Heb. 13: 17.
(Blind,) of careless ministers. Isa. 56: 10.
(Looking for the morning,) of anxious waiting for God. Psa. 130: 5, 6.

Water.

One of the elements of the world. Gen. 1: 2.
GOD ORIGINALLY
Created the firmament to divide. Gen. 1: 6, 7.
Collected into one place. Gen. 1: 9.
Created fowls and fishes, &c. from. Gen. 1: 20, 21.
Necessary to vegetation. Gen. 2: 5, 6. Job 14: 9. Isa. 1: 30.
Some plants particularly require. Job 8: 11.
Necessary to the comfort and happiness of man. Isa. 41: 17, with Zec. 9: 11.
COLLECTED IN
Springs. Jos. 15: 19.
Pools. 1 Kin. 22: 38. Neh. 2: 14.
Ponds. Exo. 7: 19. Isa. 19: 10.
Fountains. 1 Kin. 18: 5. 2 Chr. 32: 3.
Wells. Gen. 21: 19.
Brooks. 2 Sam. 17: 20. 1 Kin. 18: 5.
Streams. Psa. 78: 16. Isa. 35: 6.
Rivers. Isa. 8: 7. Jer. 2: 18.
The sea. Gen. 1: 9, 10. Isa. 11: 9.
The clouds. Gen. 1: 7. Job 26: 8, 9.
Rises in vapor to the clouds. Ecc. 1: 7, with Psa. 104: 8.
Drops from the clouds in rain. Deu. 11: 11. 2 Sam. 21: 10.
DESCRIBED AS
Fluid. Psa. 78: 16. Pro. 30: 4.
Unstable. Gen. 49: 4.
Penetrating. Psa. 109: 18.
Reflecting images. Pro. 27: 9.
Wearing the hardest substances. Job 14: 19.
Cleansing. Eze. 36: 25. Eph. 5: 26.
Refreshing. Job 22: 7. Pro. 25: 25.
Congealed by cold. Job 38: 29. Psa. 147: 16, 17.
WAS USED BY THE JEWS
As their principal beverage. Gen. 24: 43. 1 Kin. 13: 19, 22. 1 Kin. 18: 4. Hos. 2: 5.
For culinary purposes. Exo. 12: 9.
For washing the person. Gen. 18: 4. Gen. 24: 32.
For legal purification. Exo. 29: 4. Heb. 9: 10, 19.
Kept for purification in large waterpots. Jno. 2: 6.
Carried in vessels. Gen. 21: 14. 1 Sam. 26: 11. Mar. 14: 13.
Artificial mode of conveying, into large cities. 2 Kin. 20: 20.
Frequently brackish and unfit for use. Exo. 15: 23. 2 Kin. 2: 19.
The want of, considered a great calamity. Exo. 17: 1—3. Num. 20: 2. 2 Kin. 3: 9, 10. Isa. 3: 1.

In times of scarcity, sold at an enormous price. Lam. 5:4.

MIRACLES CONNECTED WITH;

- Turned into blood. Exo. 7:17, 20.
- Turned into wine. Jno. 2:7—9.
- Brought from the rock. Exo. 17:6. Num. 20:11.
- Brought from the jaw-bone of an ass. Jud. 15:19.
- Consumed by fire from heaven. 1 Kin. 18:38.
- Divided and made to stand on heap. Exo. 14:21, 22. Jos. 3:16.
- Trenches filled with. 2 Kin. 3:17—22.
- Iron made to swim in. 2 Kin. 6:5, 6.
- Our Lord, &c. walking on. Mat. 14:26—29.
- Healing powers communicated to. 2 Kin. 5:14. Jno. 5:4. Jno. 9:7.

The world and its inhabitants once destroyed by. Gen. 7:20—23, with 2 Pet. 3:6.

The world not to be again destroyed by. Gen. 9:8—15. 2 Pet. 3:7.

ILLUSTRATIVE

- Of the support of God. Isa. 8:6.
- Of the gifts and graces of the Holy Spirit. Isa. 41:17, 18. Isa. 44:3. Eze. 36:25. Jno. 7:38, 39.
- Of persecutors. Psa. 124:4, 5.
- Of persecutions. Psa. 88:17.
- Of hostile armies. Isa. 8:7. Isa. 17:13.
- (Still,) of the ordinances of the gospel. Psa. 23:2.
- (Deep,) of severe affliction. Psa. 66:12. Psa. 69:1. Isa. 30:20. Isa. 43:2.
- (Deep,) of counsel in the heart. Pro. 20:5.
- (Deep,) of the words of the wise. Pro. 18:4.
- (Poured out,) of the wrath of God. Hos. 5:10.
- (Poured out,) of faintness by terror. Psa. 22:14.
- (Pouring, out of buckets,) of a numerous progeny. Num. 24:7.
- (Spilled on the ground,) of death. 2 Sam. 14:14.
- (Its instability,) of a wavering disposition. Gen. 49:4.
- (Its weakness,) of faintness and cowardice. Jos. 7:5. Eze. 7:17.
- (Difficulty of stopping,) of strife and contention. Pro. 17:14.
- (Rapidly flowing away,) of the career of the wicked. Job 24:18. Psa. 58:7.
- (Many,) of different nations and people. Rev. 17:1, 15. Jer. 51:13.
- (Many,) of a variety of afflictions. 2 Sam. 22:17.
- (Noise of many,) of the word of Christ. Rev. 1:15.
- (Covering the sea,) of the general diffusion of the knowledge of God. Isa. 11:9. Hab. 2:14.

Wave-offering.

Placed in the hand of the priest and waved before the Lord. Exo. 29:24. Lev. 8:27.

CONSISTED OF

- The fat, right shoulder, &c. of the priest's consecration-ram. Exo. 29:22, 23. Lev. 8:25, 26.
- The breast of the priest's consecration-ram. Exo. 29:26. Lev. 8:29.
- The breast of all peace-offerings. Lev. 7:30. Lev. 9:18, 21. Num. 6:17, 20.
- Left shoulder, of Nazarite's peace-offering. Num. 6:17, 19.
- The first fruits of barley harvest. Lev. 23:10, 11.
- The first fruits of wheaten bread. Lev. 23:20.
- The jealousy offering. Num. 5:25.
- The leper's trespass offering. Lev. 14:12, 24.

Of the fat, &c. of the consecration-ram burnt on the altar. Exo. 29:25. Lev. 8:28.

Was given to the priest as his due. Exo. 29:26—28. Lev. 7:31, 34. Lev. 8:29. Lev. 10:15. Lev. 23:20. Num. 18:11.

Was to be eaten in a holy place by the priest's family. Lev. 10:14.

Weeks.

A period of time consisting of seven days. Lev. 23:15, 16. Luke 18:12.

A space of seven years sometimes so called. Gen. 29:27, 28. Dan. 9:24, 25, 27.

Origin of computing time by. Gen. 2:2.

The feast of pentecost called the feast of weeks. Exo. 34:22, with Acts 2:1.

Weights.

Generally regulated by the standard of the sanctuary. Exo. 30:24.

Sometimes regulated by the king's standard. 2 Sam. 14:26.

Were frequently used in scales or balances. Job 31:6. Isa. 40:12.

MENTIONED IN SCRIPTURE;

- Gerah. Exo. 30:13. Eze. 45:12.
- Bekah or half-shekel. Gen. 24:22.
- Shekel. Exo. 30:13. Eze. 45:12.
- Dram. Neh. 7:70, 71.
- Maneh or pound. Neh. 7:71. Eze. 45:12.
- Talent. 2 Sam. 12:30. Rev. 16:21.

Value of money estimated according to. Gen. 23:16. Gen. 43:21. Jer. 32:9.

All metals were given by. Exo. 37: 24. 1 Chr. 28: 14.
Provisions were sold by, in times of scarcity. Lev. 26: 26. Eze. 4: 10, 16.
THE JEWS
 Forbidden to have divers. Deu. 25: 13, 14.
 Forbidden to have unjust. Lev. 19: 35, 36.
 Frequently used unjust. Mic. 6: 11.
ILLUSTRATIVE
 Of sins. Heb. 12: 1.
 Of the restraints put on the elements. Job 28: 25.
 (Heavy,) of the exceeding glory reserved for saints. 2 Cor. 4: 17.

Wells.

First mention of. Gen. 16: 14.
FREQUENTLY MADE
 Near encampments. Gen. 21: 30. Gen. 26: 18.
 Outside cities. Gen. 24: 11. Jno. 4: 6, 8.
 In the courts of houses. 2 Sam. 17: 18.
 In the desert. 2 Chr. 26: 10.
Supplied by springs. Pro. 16: 22.
Supplied by the rain. Psa. 84: 6.
Surrounded by trees. Gen. 49: 22. Exo. 15: 27.
Names often given to. Gen. 16: 14. Gen. 21: 31.
Canaan abounded with. Deu. 6: 11.
Many supplied from Lebanon. So. of Sol. 4: 15.
MENTIONED IN SCRIPTURE;
 Beer-lahai-roi. Gen. 16: 14.
 Bethlehem. 2 Sam. 23: 15. 1 Chr. 11: 17, 18.
 Beer (east of Jordan). Num. 21: 16—18.
 Beer-sheba. Gen. 21: 30, 31.
 Elim. Exo. 15: 27.
 Esek. Gen. 26: 20.
 Hagar. Gen. 21: 19.
 Haran. Gen. 29: 3, 4.
 Jacob. Jno. 4: 6.
 Rehoboth. Gen. 26: 22.
 Sitnah. Gen. 26: 21.
Often deep and difficult to draw from. Jno. 4: 11.
Often covered to prevent their being filled with sand. Gen. 29: 2, 3.
Had troughs placed near for watering cattle. Gen. 24: 19, 20. Exo. 2: 16.
FREQUENTED BY
 Women who came to draw water. Gen. 24: 13, 14. Jno. 4: 7.
 Travelers. Gen. 24: 11, 13, 42. Jno. 4: 6.
Strangers not to draw from, without permission. Num. 20: 17.
Water of, frequently sold. Num. 20: 19.
Were a frequent cause of strife. Gen. 21: 25. Gen. 26: 21, 22. Exo. 2: 16, 17.
Were often stopped up by enemies. Gen. 26: 15, 18. 2 Kin. 3: 19, 25.
Often afforded no water. Jer. 14: 3. Zec. 9: 11.
ILLUSTRATIVE
 Of the ordinances of the Church. Isa. 12: 3.
 Of the Holy Spirit in saints. So. of Sol. 4: 15, with Jno. 4: 14.
 Of the mouth of the righteous. Pro. 10: 11.
 Of wisdom and understanding in man. Pro. 16: 22. Pro. 18: 4.
 (A fruitful bough by,) of Joseph's numerous posterity. Gen. 49: 22.
 (Drinking from one's own,) of enjoyment of domestic happiness. Pro. 5: 15.
 (Without water,) of hypocrites. 2 Pet. 2: 17.

Whirlwind.

Generally came from the south. Job 37: 9. Isa. 21: 1. Zec. 9: 14.
Sometimes came from the north. Eze. 1: 4.
Called the whirlwind of the Lord. Jer. 23: 19. Jer. 30: 23.
Arose up from the earth. Jer. 25: 32.
MIRACLES CONNECTED WITH;
 Elijah taken to heaven in. 2 Kin. 2: 1, 11.
 God spake to Job from. Job 38: 1. Job 40: 6.
Frequently continued for a long time. Jer. 30: 23.
Destructive nature of. Pro. 1: 27.
ILLUSTRATIVE OF THE
 Speed with which God executes His purposes. Nah. 1: 3.
 Velocity of Christ's second coming. Isa. 66: 15.
 Velocity of the chariots in hostile armies. Isa. 5: 28. Jer. 4: 13.
 Fury of God's judgments. Jer. 25: 32. Jer. 30: 23.
 Sudden destruction of the wicked. Psa. 58: 9. Pro. 1: 27. Isa. 17: 13. Isa. 40: 24. Isa. 41: 16. Jer. 30: 23.
 Unavoidable fruit of a life of sin and vanity. Hos. 8: 7.

Wicked, The, are compared to.

Abominable branches. Isa. 14: 19.
Ashes under the feet. Mal. 4: 3.
Bad fishes. Mat. 13: 48.
Beasts. Psa. 49: 12. 2 Pet. 2: 12.
Blind, The. Zep. 1: 17. Mat. 15: 14.
Brass and iron, &c. Jer. 6: 28. Eze. 22: 18.
Briars and thorns. Isa. 55: 13. Eze. 2: 6.

Bulls of Bashan. Psa. 22: 12.
Carcasses trodden under feet. Isa. 14: 19.
Chaff. Job 21: 18. Psa. 1: 4. Mat. 3: 12.
Clouds without water. Jude 12.
Corn blasted. 2 Kin. 19: 26.
Corrupt trees. Luke 6: 43.
Deaf adders. Psa. 58: 4.
Dogs. Pro. 26: 11. Mat. 7: 6. 2 Pet. 2: 22.
Dross. Psa. 119: 119. Eze. 22: 18, 19.
Early dew that passeth away. Hos. 13: 3.
Evil figs. Jer. 24: 8.
Fading oaks. Isa. 1: 30.
Fiery oven. Psa. 21: 9. Hos. 7: 4.
Fire of thorns. Psa. 118: 12.
Fools building upon sand. Mat. 7: 26.
Fuel of fire. Isa. 9: 19.
Garden without water. Isa. 1: 30.
Goats. Mat. 25: 32.
Grass. Psa. 37: 2. Psa. 92: 7.
Grass on the housetop. 2 Kin. 19: 26.
Green bay-trees. Psa. 37: 35.
Green herbs. Psa. 37: 2.
Heath in the desert. Jer. 17: 6.
Horses rushing into the battle. Jer. 8: 6.
Idols. Psa. 115: 8.
Lions greedy of prey. Psa. 17: 12.
Melting wax. Psa. 68: 2.
Morning-clouds. Hos. 13: 3.
Moth-eaten garments. Isa. 50: 9. Isa. 51: 8.
Passing whirlwinds. Pro. 10: 25.
Potsherds. Pro. 26: 23.
Raging waves of the sea. Jude 13.
Reprobate silver. Jer. 6: 30.
Scorpions. Eze. 2: 6.
Serpents. Psa. 58: 4. Mat. 23: 33.
Smoke. Hos. 13: 3.
Stony ground. Mat. 13: 5.
Stubble. Job 21: 18. Mal. 4: 1.
Swine. Mat. 7: 6. 2 Pet. 2: 22.
Tares. Mat. 13: 38.
Troubled sea. Isa. 57: 20.
Visions of the night. Job 20: 8.
Wandering stars. Jude 13.
Wayward children. Mat. 11: 16.
Wells without water. 2 Pet. 2: 17.
Wheels. Psa. 83: 13.
Whited sepulchres. Mat. 23: 27.
Wild ass's colts. Job 11: 12.

Widows.

Character of true. Luke 2: 37. 1 Tim. 5: 5, 10.

GOD
- Surely hears the cry of. Exo. 22: 23.
- Judges for. Deu. 10: 18. Psa. 68: 5.
- Relieves. Psa. 146: 9.
- Establishes the border of. Pro. 15: 25.
- Will witness against oppressors of. Mal. 3: 5.

Exhorted to trust in God. Jer. 49: 11.

SHOULD NOT BE
- Afflicted. Exo. 22: 22.
- Oppressed. Jer. 7: 6. Zec. 7: 10.
- Treated with violence. Jer. 22: 3.
- Deprived of raiment in pledge. Deu. 24: 17.

SHOULD BE
- Pleaded for. Isa. 1: 17.
- Honored, if widows indeed. 1 Tim. 5: 3.
- Relieved by their friends. 1 Tim. 5: 4, 16.
- Relieved by the Church. Acts 6: 1. 1 Tim. 5: 9.
- Visited in affliction. Jas. 1: 27.
- Allowed to share in our blessings. Deu. 14: 29. Deu. 16: 11, 14. Deu. 24: 19—21.

Though poor, may be liberal. Mar. 12: 42, 43.
When young, exposed to many temptations. 1 Tim. 5: 11—14.

SAINTS
- Relieve. Acts 9: 39.
- Cause joy to. Job 29: 13.
- Disappoint not. Job 31: 16.

THE WICKED
- Do no good to. Job 24: 21.
- Send, away empty. Job 22: 9.
- Take pledges from. Job 24: 3.
- Reject the cause of. Isa. 1: 23.
- Vex. Eze. 22 7.
- Make a prey of. Isa. 10: 2. Mat. 23: 14.
- Slay. Psa. 94: 6.

Curse for perverting judgment of. Deu. 27: 19.
Woe to those who oppress. Isa. 10: 1, 2.
Blessings on those who relieve. Deu. 14: 29.
A type of Zion in affliction. Lam. 5: 3.
Were released from all obligation to former husbands. Rom. 7: 3.
Were clothed in mourning after the decease of husbands. Gen. 38: 14, 19. 2 Sam. 14: 2, 5.
Reproach connected with. Isa. 54: 4.
Increase of, threatened as a punishment. Exo. 22: 24. Jer. 15: 8. Jer. 18: 21.

LAWS RESPECTING;
- Not to be oppressed. Exo. 22: 22. Deu. 27: 19.
- Raiment of, not to be taken in pledge by creditors. Deu. 24: 17.
- Bound to perform their vows. Num. 30: 9.
- Not to intermarry with priests. Lev. 21: 14.
- To be allowed to glean in fields and vineyards. Deu. 24: 19.
- To have a share of the triennial tithe. Deu. 14: 28, 29. Deu. 26: 12, 13.
- To share in public rejoicings. Deu. 16: 11, 14.

When daughters of priests and childless, to partake of the holy things. Lev. 22:13.
When left without children, to be married by their husband's nearest of kin. Deu. 25:5, 6. Ruth 3:10—13, with Ruth 4:4, 5. Mat. 22:24—26.
Allowed to marry again. Rom. 7:3.
Intermarrying with, of kings considered treason. 1 Kin. 2:21—24.
Not to be deplored by, considered a great calamity. Job 27:15. Psa. 78:64.
Were under the special protection of God. Deu. 10:18. Psa. 68:5.
Were frequently oppressed and persecuted. Job 24:3. Eze. 22:7.
Specially taken care of by the primitive Church. Acts 6:1. 1 Tim. 5:9.
Often devoted themselves entirely to God's service. Luke 2:37. 1 Tim. 5:10.
Instances of great liberality in. 1 Kin. 17:9—15. Mar. 12:42, 43.
ILLUSTRATIVE OF
A desolate condition. Isa. 47:8, 9.
Zion in captivity. Lam. 1:1.

Wind, The.

Variable nature of. Ecc. 1:6.
GOD
Created. Amos 4:13.
Restrains. Job 28:25. Psa. 107:29.
Brings forth, out of His treasuries. Psa. 135:7. Jer. 10:13.
Raises. 107:25. Jon. 4:8.
Changes. Psa. 78:26.
Assuages. Mat. 8:26. Mat. 14:32.
Gathers, in His hand. Pro. 30:4.
Accomplishes the purposes of God. Psa. 148:8.
Theory of, above man's comprehension. Jno. 3:8.
MENTIONED IN SCRIPTURE;
North. Pro. 25:23. So. of Sol. 4:16.
South. Job 37:17. Luke 12:55.
East. Job 27:21. Eze. 17:10. Hos. 13:15.
West. Exo. 10:19.
Euroclydon. Acts 27:14.
The simoon or pestilential wind. 2 Kin. 19:7, with 35 v. Jer. 4:11.
The whirlwind. Job 37:9.
Drying nature of. Gen. 8:1. Isa. 11:15.
Purifying nature of. Job 37:21. Jer. 4:11.
WHEN VIOLENT CALLED
Tempest. Job 9:17. Job 27:20. Jon. 1:4.
Storm. Job 21:18. Psa. 83:15.
Stormy wind. Psa. 148:8. Eze. 13:11, 13.
Windy storm. Psa. 55:8.
Great and strong wind. 1 Kin. 19:11.
Mighty wind. Acts 2:2. Rev. 6:13.
Fierce wind. Jas. 3:4.
Rough wind. Isa. 27:8.
From the north drives away rain. Pro. 25:23.
Frequently brings rain. 1 Kin. 18:44, 45. *See* 2 Kin. 3:17.
Often blighting. Psa. 103:16. Isa. 40:7. (*Hebrew.*)
Movement of the leaves of trees, &c. by, noticed. Isa. 7:2. Mat. 11:7. Rev. 6:13.
TEMPESTUOUS,
Raises the sea in waves. Psa. 107:25. Jno. 6:18.
Drives about the largest ships. Mat. 14:24. Acts 27:18. Jas. 3:4.
Destroys houses. Job 1:19. Mat. 7:27.
MIRACLES CONNECTED WITH;
Locusts brought by. Exo. 10:13.
Locusts removed by. Exo. 10:19.
Red Sea divided by. Exo. 14:21.
Quails brought by. Num. 11:31.
Rocks and mountains rent by. 1 Kin. 19:11.
Raises on account of Jonah. Jon. 1:4.
Calmed by casting out Jonah. Jon. 1:15.
Calmed by Christ. Mat. 8:26. Mat. 14:32.
ILLUSTRATIVE
Of the operations of the Holy Spirit. Eze. 37:9. Jno. 3:8. Acts 2:2.
Of the life of man. Job 7:7.
Of the speeches of the desperate. Job 6:26.
Of terrors which persue the soul. Job 30:15.
Of molten images. Isa. 41:29.
Of iniquity which leads to destruction. Isa. 64:6.
Of false doctrines. Eph. 4:14.
(Chaff or stubble before,) of the wicked. Job 21:18. Psa. 1:4.
(Without rain,) of one who boasts of a false gift. Pro. 25:14.
(When destructive,) of the judgments of God. Isa. 27:8. Isa. 29:6. Isa. 41:16.
(Sowing,) of a course of sin. Hos. 8:7.
(Feeding upon,) of vain hopes. Hos. 12:1.
(Bringing forth,) of disappointed expectations. Isa. 26:18.

Wine.

First mention of. Gen. 9:20, 21.
WAS MADE OF
The juice of the grape. Gen. 49:11.
The juice of the pomegranate. So. of Sol. 8:2.
First mode of making, noticed. Gen. 40:11.

Generally made by treading the grapes in a press. Neh. 13:15. Isa. 63:2, 3.
Refining of, alluded to. Isa. 25:6.
Improved by age. Luke 5:39.
PLACES CELEBRATED FOR;
Canaan in general. Deu. 33:28.
Possessions of Judah. Gen. 49:8, 11, 12.
Lebanon. Hos. 14:17.
Helbon. Eze. 27:18.
Assyria. 2 Kin. 18:32. Isa. 36:17.
Moab. Isa. 16:8—10. Jer. 48:32, 33.
Many kinds of. Neh. 5:18.
Sweet, esteemed for flavor and strength. Isa. 49:26. Amos 9:13. Mic. 6:15.
Red, most esteemed. Pro. 23:31. Isa. 27:2.
Often spiced to increase its strength, &c. Pro. 9:2, 5. Pro. 23:30. So. of Sol. 8:2.
WAS USED
As a beverage from the earliest age. Gen. 9:21. Gen. 27:25.
At all feasts and entertainments. Est. 1:7. Est. 5:6. Isa. 5:12. Dan. 5:1—4. Jno. 2:3.
For drink offerings in the worship of God. Exo. 29:40. Num. 15:4—10.
For drink offerings in idolatrous worship. Deu. 32:37, 38.
As a medicine. Luke 10:34. 1 Tim. 5:23.
First fruits of, to be offered to God. Deu. 18:4. 2 Chr. 31:5.
With corn and oil, denoted all temporal blessings. Gen. 27:28, 37. Psa. 4:7. Hos. 2:8. Joel 2:19.
Given in abundance to the Jews when obedient. Hos. 2:22. Joel 2:19, 24. Zec. 9:17.
The Jews frequently deprived of, as a punishment. Isa. 24:7, 11. Hos. 2:9. Joel 1:10. Hag. 1:11. Hag. 2:16.
The Jews frequently drank, to excess. Isa. 5:11. Joel 3:3. Amos 6:6.
In times of scarcity, was mixed with water. Isa. 1:22.
Sometimes mixed with milk as a beverage. So. of Sol. 5:1.
CHARACTERIZED AS
Cheering God and man. Jud. 9:13. Zec. 9:17.
Gladdening the heart. Psa. 104:15.
Strengthening. 2 Sam. 16:2. So. of Sol. 2:5.
Making mirthful. Est. 1:10. Ecc. 10:19.
Custom of presenting, to travelers. Gen. 14:18. 1 Sam. 25:18.
Custom of giving to persons in pain or suffering, mixed with drugs. Pro. 31:6. Mar. 15:23.
Forbidden to the priests while engaged in the tabernacle. Lev. 10:9.
Forbidden to Nazarites during their separation. Num. 6:3.
The Rechabites never drank. Jer. 35:5, 6.
IN EXCESS
Forbidden. Eph. 5:18.
Infuriates the temper. Pro. 20:1.
Impairs the health. 1 Sam. 25:37. Hos. 4:11.
Impairs the judgment and memory. Pro. 31:4, 5. Isa. 28:7.
Inflames the passions. Isa. 5:11.
Leads to sorrow and contention. Pro. 23:29, 30.
Leads to remorse. Pro. 29:32.
An article of extensive commerce. Eze. 27:18.
Was stored in cellars. 1 Chr. 27:27.
Was kept in bottles. 1 Sam. 25:18. Hab. 2:15.
Consequence of putting (when new), into old bottles. Mar. 2:22.
The love of Christ to be preferred to. So. of Sol. 1:2, 4.
Water miraculously turned into. Jno. 2:9.
ILLUSTRATIVE
Of the blood of Christ. Mat. 26:27—29.
Of the blessings of the gospel. Pro. 9:2, 5. Isa. 25:6. Isa. 55:1.
Of the wrath and judgments of God. Psa. 60:3. Psa. 75:8. Jer. 13:12—14. Jer. 25:15—18.
Of the abominations of the apostacy. Rev. 17:2. Rev. 18:3.
Of violence and rapine. Pro. 4:17

Winter.

God makes. Psa. 74:17.
Yearly return of, secured by covenant. Gen. 8:22.
Coldness and inclemency of, noticed. Pro. 20:4, with (*marg.*) Jno. 10:22.
UNSUITED FOR
Traveling. Mat. 24:20. 2 Tim. 4:21.
Navigation. Acts 27:9.
Ships were laid up in port during. Acts 27:12. Acts 28:11.
The Jews frequently had special houses for. Jer. 36:22. Amos 3:15.
Illustrative of seasons of spiritual adversity. So. of Sol. 2:11.

Wisdom of God, The.

Is one of His attributes. 1 Sam. 2:3. Job 9:4.
DESCRIBED AS
Perfect. Job 36:4. Job 37:16.
Mighty. Job 36:5.
Universal. Job 28:24. Dan. 2:22. Acts 15:18.
Infinite. Psa. 147:5. Rom. 11:33.
Unsearchable. Isa. 40:28. Rom. 11:33.

Wonderful. Psa. 139: 6.
Beyond human comprehension. Psa. 139: 6.
Incomparable. Isa. 44: 7. Jer. 10: 7.
Underived. Job 21: 22. Isa. 40: 44.
The gospel contains treasures of. 1 Cor. 2: 7.
Wisdom of saints is derived from. Ezr. 7: 25.
All human wisdom derived from. Dan. 2: 21.
Saints ascribe to Him. Dan. 2: 20.
EXHIBITED IN
His works. Job 37: 16. Psa. 104: 24. Psa. 136: 5. Pro. 3: 19. Jer. 10: 12.
His counsels. Isa. 28: 29. Jer. 32: 19.
His foreshowing events. Isa. 42: 9. Isa. 46: 10.
Redemption. 1 Cor. 1: 24. Eph. 1: 8. Eph. 3: 10.
Searching the heart. 1 Chr. 28: 9. Rev. 2: 23.
Understanding the thoughts. 1 Chr. 28: 9. Psa. 139: 2.
EXHIBITED IN KNOWING
The heart. Psa. 44: 21. Pro. 15: 11. Luke 16: 15.
The actions. Job 34: 21. Psa. 139: 2, 3.
The words. Psa. 139: 4.
His saints. 2 Sam. 7: 20. 2 Tim. 2: 19.
The way of saints. Job 23: 10. Psa. 1: 6.
The want of saints. Deu. 2: 7. Mat. 6: 8.
The afflictions of saints. Exo. 3: 7. Psa. 142: 3.
The infirmities of saints. Psa. 103: 14.
The minutest matters. Mat. 10: 29, 30.
The most secret things. Mat. 6: 18.
The time of judgment. Mat. 24: 36.
The wicked. Neh. 9: 10. Job 11: 11.
The works, &c. of the wicked. Isa. 66: 18.
Nothing is concealed from. Psa. 139: 12.
The wicked question. Psa. 73: 11. Isa. 47: 10.
Should be magnified. Rom. 16: 27. Jude 25.

Witness of the Holy Ghost.

Is truth. 1 Jno. 5: 6.
To be implicitly received. 1 Jno. 5: 6, 9.
BORNE TO CHRIST
As Messiah. Luke 3: 22, with Jno. 1: 32, 33.
As coming to redeem and sanctify. 1 Jno. 5: 6.
As exalted to be a Prince and Saviour to give repentance, &c. Acts. 5: 31, 32.
As perfecting saints. Heb. 10: 14, 15.
As foretold by Himself. Jno. 15: 26.
In heaven. 1 Jno. 5: 7, 11.
On earth. 1 Jno. 5: 8.
The first preaching of the gospel confirmed by. Acts 14: 3, with Heb. 2: 4.
The faithful preaching of the Apostles accompanied by. 1 Cor. 2: 4. 1 The. 1: 5.
GIVEN TO SAINTS
On believing. Acts 15: 8. 1 Jno. 5: 10.
To testify to them of Christ. Jno. 15: 26.
As an evidence of adoption. Rom. 8: 16.
As an evidence of Christ in them. 1 Jno. 3: 24.
As an evidence of God in them. 1 Jno. 4: 13.
Borne against all unbelievers. Neh. 9: 30. Acts 28: 25—27.

Wives.

Not to be selected from among the ungodly. Gen. 24: 3. Gen. 26: 34, 35. Gen. 28: 1.
DUTIES OF, TO THEIR HUSBANDS
To love them. Tit. 2: 4.
To reverence them. Eph. 5: 33.
To be faithful to them. 1 Cor. 7: 3—5, 10.
To be subject to them. Gen. 3: 16. Eph. 5: 22, 24. 1 Pet. 3: 1.
To obey them. 1 Cor. 14: 34. Tit. 2: 5.
To remain with them for life. Rom. 7: 2, 3.
SHOULD BE ADORNED
Not with ornaments. 1 Tim. 2: 9. 1 Pet. 3: 3.
With modesty and sobriety. 1 Tim. 2: 9.
With a meek and quiet spirit. 1 Pet. 3: 4, 5.
With good works. 1 Tim. 2: 10. 1 Tim. 5: 10.
GOOD,
Are from the Lord. Pro. 19: 14.
Are a token of the favor of God. Pro. 18: 22.
Are a blessing to husbands. Pro. 12: 4. Pro. 31: 10, 12.
Bring honor on husbands. Pro. 31: 23.
Secure confidence of husbands. Pro. 31: 11.
Are praised by husbands. Pro. 31: 28.
Are diligent and prudent. Pro. 31: 13—27.
Are benevolent to the poor. Pro. 31: 20.
Duty of, to unbelieving husbands. 1 Cor. 7: 13, 14, 16. 1 Pet. 3: 1, 2.

Should be silent in the Churches. 1 Cor. 14:34.
Should seek religious instruction from their husbands. 1 Cor. 14:35.
Of ministers should be exemplary. 1 Tim. 3:11.
Good—Exemplified. *Wife of Manoah*, Jud. 13:10. *Orpah and Ruth*, Ruth 1:4, 8. *Abigail*, 1 Sam. 25:3. *Esther*, Est. 2:15—17. *Elizabeth*, Luke 1:6. *Priscilla*, Acts 18:2, 26. *Sarah*, 1 Pet. 3:6.
Bad—Exemplified. *Samson's wife*, Jud. 14:15—17. *Michal*, 2 Sam. 6:16. *Jezebel*, 1 Kin. 21:25. *Zeresh*, Est. 5:14. *Job's wife*, Job 2:9. *Herodias*, Mar. 6:17. *Sapphira*, Acts 5:1, 2.

Wolf, The.

Rapacious nature of. Gen. 49:27.
Particularly fierce in the evening when it seeks its prey. Jer. 5:6. Hab. 1:8.
Destructive to flocks of sheep. Jno. 10:12.
ILLUSTRATIVE
Of the wicked. Mat. 10:16. Luke 10:3.
Of wicked rulers. Eze. 22:27. Zep. 3:3.
Of false teachers. Mat. 7:15. Acts 20:29.
Of the devil. Jno. 10:12.
Of the tribe of Benjamin. Gen. 49:27.
Of fierce enemies. Jer. 5:6. Hab. 1:8.
(Taming of,) of the change effected by conversion. Isa. 11:6. Isa. 65:25.

Woman.

Origin and cause of the name. Gen. 2:23.
ORIGINALLY MADE
By God in His own image. Gen. 1:27.
From one of Adam's ribs. Gen. 2:21, 22.
For man. 1 Cor. 11:9.
To be an helpmeet for man. Gen. 2:18, 20.
Subordinate to man. 1 Cor. 11:3.
To be the glory of man. 1 Cor. 11:7.
Deceived by Satan. Gen. 3:1—6. 2 Cor. 11:3. 1 Tim. 2:14.
Led man to disobey God. Gen. 3:6, 11, 12.
Curse pronounced on. Gen. 3:16.
Salvation promised through the seed of. Gen. 3:15. *See* Isa. 7:14.
Safety in childbirth promised to the faithful and holy. 1 Tim. 2:15.
CHARACTERIZED AS
Weaker than man. 1 Pet. 3:7.
Timid. Isa. 19:16. Jer. 50:37. Jer. 51:30. Nah. 3:13.
Loving and affectionate. 2 Sam. 1:26.
Tender and constant to her offspring. Isa. 49:15. Lam. 4:10.
To wear her hair long as a covering. 1 Cor. 11:15.
Good and virtuous, described. Pro. 31:10—28.
Virtuous, held in high estimation. Ruth 3:11. Pro. 31:10, 30.
FREQUENTLY
Fond of self-indulgence. Isa. 32:9—11.
Subtle and deceitful. Pro. 7:10. Ecc. 7:26.
Silly and easily led into error. 2 Tim. 3:6.
Zealous in promoting superstition and idolatry. Jer. 7:18. Eze. 13:17, 23.
Active in instigating to iniquity. Num. 31:15, 16. 1 Kin. 21:25. Neh. 13:26.
Generally wore a vail in the presence of the other sex. Gen. 24:65.
Generally lived in a separate apartment or tent. Gen. 18:9. Gen. 24:67. Est. 2:9, 11.
Submissive and respectful to husbands. 1 Pet. 3:6, with Gen. 18:12.
OF DISTINCTION
Fair and graceful. Gen. 12:11. Gen. 24:16. So. of Sol. 1:8. Amos 8:13.
Haughty in their deportment. Isa. 3:16.
Fond of dress and ornaments. Isa. 3:17—23.
Wore their hair plaited and adorned with gold and pearls. Isa. 3:24, with 1 Tim. 2:9.
Of the poorer classes swarthy from exposure to the sun. So. of Sol. 1:5, 6.
YOUNG,
Called maids. Exo. 2:8. Luke 8:51, 52.
Called damsels. Gen. 24:55. Mar. 5:39.
Called virgins. Gen. 24:16. Lam. 1:4.
Gay and mirthsome. Jud. 11:34. Jud. 21:21. Jer. 31:13. Zec. 9:17.
Kind and courteous to strangers. Gen. 24:17.
Fond of ornaments. Jer. 2:32.
Required to learn from and imitate their elders. Tit. 2:4.
Inherited parents' property when there was no male heir. Num. 27:8.
Could not marry without consent of parents. Gen. 24:3, 4. Gen. 34:6. Exo. 22:17.
Not to be given in marriage considered a calamity. Jud. 11:37. Psa. 78:63. Isa. 4:1.

Often taken captive. Lam. 1:18. Eze. 30:17, 18.
Punishment for seducing, when betrothed. Deu. 22:23—27.
Punishment for seducing, when not betrothed. Exo. 22:16, 17. Deu. 22:28, 29.
Often treated with great cruelty in war. Deu. 32:25. Lam. 2:21. Lam. 5:11.
Of distinction, dressed in robes of various colors. 2 Sam. 13:18. Psa. 45:14.

Were required to hear and obey the law. Jos. 8:35.
Had a court of the tabernacle assigned to them. Exo. 38:8. 1 Sam. 2:22.
Allowed to join in the temple-music from the time of David. 1 Chr. 25:5, 6. Ezr. 2:65. Neh. 7:67.

OFTEN ENGAGED IN
Domestic employments. Gen. 18:6. Pro. 31:15.
Agriculture. Ruth 2:8. So of Sol. 1:6.
Tending sheep. Gen. 29:9. Exo. 2:16.
Drawing and carrying water. Gen. 24:11, 13, 15, 16. 1 Sam. 9:11. Jno. 4:7.
Grinding corn. Mat. 24:41. Luke 17:35.
Spinning. Pro. 31:13, 14.
Embroidery. Pro. 31:22.
Celebrating the victories of the nation. Exo. 15:20, 21. Jud. 11:34. 1 Sam. 18:6, 7.
Attending funerals as mourners. Jer. 9:17, 20.

Vows of, when married not binding upon the husband. Num. 30:6—8.
Unfaithfulness of, when married found out by the waters of jealousy. Num. 5:14—28.
Punishment for injuring, when with child. Exo. 21:22—25.
To be governed by, considered a calamity by the Jews. Isa. 3:12.
To be slain by, considered a great disgrace. Jud. 9:54.
Considered a valuable booty in war. Deu. 20:14. 1 Sam. 30:2.
Often treated with great cruelty in war. 2 Kin. 8:12. Lam. 5:11. Eze. 9:6. Hos. 13:16.

ILLUSTRATIVE
(Gloriously arrayed,) of the Church of Christ. Psa. 45:13. Gal. 4:26, with Rev. 12:1.
(Delicate,) of backsliding Israel. Jer. 6:2.
(Chaste and holy,) of saints. So. of Sol. 1:3. 2 Cor. 11:2. Rev. 14:4.
(Lewd,) of the Roman apostacy. Rev. 17:4, 18.
(Wise,) of saints. Mat. 25:1, 2, 4.
(Foolish,) of mere professors. Mat. 25:1—3.
(At ease and careless,) of a state of carnal security. Isa. 32:9, 11.
(Forsaken) of the church of Israel in her captivity. Isa. 54:6.

Works, Good.

Christ, an example of. Jno. 10:32. Acts 10:38.

CALLED
Good fruits. Jas. 3:17.
Fruits meet for repentance. Mat. 3:8.
Fruits of righteousness. Phi. 1:11.
Works and labors of love. Heb. 6:10.

Are by Jesus Christ to the glory and praise of God. Phi. 1:11.
They alone, who abide in Christ can perform. Jno. 15:4, 5.
Wrought by God in us. Isa. 26:12. Phi. 2:13.
The Scripture designed to lead us to. 2 Tim. 3:16, 17. Jas. 1:25.
To be performed in Christ's name. Col. 3:17.
Heavenly wisdom is full of. Jas. 3:17.
Justification unattainable by. Rom. 3:20. Gal. 2:16.
Salvation unattainable by. Eph. 2:8, 9. 2 Tim. 1:9. Tit. 3:5.

SAINTS
Created in Christ unto. Eph. 2:10.
Exhorted to put on. Col. 3:12—14.
Are full of. Acts 9:36.
Are zealous of. Tit. 2:14.
Should be furnished unto all. 2 Tim. 3:17.
Should be rich in. 1 Tim. 6:18.
Should be careful to maintain. Tit. 3:8, 14.
Should be established in. 2 The. 2:17.
Should be fruitful in. Col. 1:10.
Should be perfect in. Heb. 13:21.
Should be prepared unto all. 2 Tim. 2:21.
Should abound to all. 2 Cor. 9:8.
Should be ready to all. Tit. 3:1.
Should manifest, with meekness. Jas. 3:13.
Should provoke each other to. Heb. 10:24.
Should avoid ostentation in. Mat. 6:1—18.
Bring to the light their. Jno. 3:21.
Followed into rest by their. Rev. 14:13.

Holy women should manifest. 1 Tim. 2:10. 1 Tim. 5:10.
God remembers. Neh. 13:14, with Heb. 6:9, 10.
Shall be brought into the judgment. Ecc. 12:14, with 2 Cor. 5:10.
In the judgment, will be an evidence of faith. Mat. 25:34—40, with Jas. 2:14—20.

MINISTERS SHOULD
Be patterns of. Tit. 2: 7.
Exhort to. 1 Tim. 6: 17, 18. Tit. 3: 1, 8, 14.
God is glorified by. Jno. 15: 8.
Designed to lead others to glorify God. Mat. 5: 16. 1 Pet. 2: 12.
A blessing attends. Jas. 1: 25.
The wicked reprobate unto. Tit. 1: 16.
Illustrated. Jno. 15: 5.

Years.

The sun and moon appointed to mark out. Gen. 1: 14.
Early computation of time by. Gen. 5: 3.
DIVIDED INTO
Seasons. Gen. 8: 22.
Months. Gen. 7: 11. 1 Chr. 27: 1.
Weeks. Dan. 9: 27. Luke 18: 12.
Days. Gen. 25: 7. Est. 9: 27.
Length of, during the patriarchal age. Gen. 7: 11, and Gen. 8: 13, with Gen. 7: 24, and Gen. 8: 3.
Commencement of, changed after the exodus. Exo. 12: 2.
REMARKABLE;
Sabbatical. Lev. 25: 4.
Jubilee. Lev. 25: 11.
In prophetic computation, days reckoned as. Dan. 12: 11, 12.
ILLUSTRATIVE
(Coming to,) of manhood. Heb. 11: 24.
(Well stricken in,) of old age. Luke 1: 7.
(Being full of,) of old age. Gen. 25: 8.
(Acceptable,) of the dispensation of the gospel. Isa. 61: 2. Luke 4: 19.
(Of the right hand of the Most High,) of prosperity. Psa. 77: 10.
(Of the redeemed,) of redemption by Christ. Isa. 63: 4.
(Of visitation,) of severe judgments. Jer. 11: 23. Jer. 23: 12.
(Of recompenses,) of judgments. Isa. 34: 8.

Zeal.

Christ an example of. Psa. 69: 9. Jno. 2: 17.
Godly sorrow leads to. 2 Cor. 7, 10, 11.
Of saints, ardent. Psa. 119: 139.
Provokes others to do good. 2 Cor. 9: 2.
SHOULD BE EXHIBITED
In spirit. Rom. 12: 11.
In well-doing. Gal. 4: 18. Tit. 2: 14.
In desiring the salvation of others. Acts 26: 29. Rom. 10: 1.
In contending for the faith. Jude 3.
In missionary labors. Rom. 15: 19, 23.
For the glory of God. Num. 25: 11, 13.
For the welfare of saints. Col. 4: 13.
Against idolatry. 2 Kin. 23: 4—14.
Sometimes wrongly directed. 2 Sam. 21: 2. Acts 22: 3, 4. Phi. 3: 6.
Sometimes not according to knowledge. Rom. 10: 2. Gal. 1: 14. Acts 21: 20.
Ungodly men sometimes pretend to. 2 Kin. 10: 16. Mat. 23: 15.
Exhortation to. Rom. 12: 11. Rev. 3: 19.
Holy—Exemplified. *Phinehas*, Num. 25: 11, 13. *Josiah*, 2 Kin. 23: 19—25. *Apollos*, Acts 18: 25. *Corinthians*, 1 Cor. 14: 12. *Epaphras*, Col. 4: 12, 13.

Zebulun, The Tribe of.

Descended from Jacob's tenth son. Gen. 30: 19, 20.
Predictions respecting. Gen. 49: 13. Deu. 33: 18, 19.
PERSONS SELECTED FROM,
To number the people. Num. 1: 9.
To spy out the land. Num. 13: 10.
To divide the land. Num. 34: 25.
Strength of, on leaving Egypt. Num. 1: 30, 31.
Formed the rear of the first division of the army of Israel in its journeys. Num. 10: 14, 16.
Encamped under the standard of Judah, east of the tabernacle. Num. 2: 3, 7.
Offering of, at the dedication. Num. 7: 24—29.
Families of. Num. 26: 26, 27.
Strength of, on entering Canaan. Num. 26: 27.
On Ebal said amen to the curses. Deu. 27: 13.
A naval and commercial people. Gen. 49: 13.
Furnished scribes or writers to Israel. Jud. 5: 14.
Bounds of their inheritance. Jos. 19: 10—16.
Unable to drive out the Canaanites from their cities, but made them tributary. Jud. 1: 30.
Praised for assisting Deborah and Barak in opposing Sisera. Jud. 5: 14, 18, with Jud. 4: 10.
Aided Gideon against the army of the Midianites. Jud. 6: 35.
Furnished a judge to Israel. Jud. 12: 11, 12.
Some of, at David's coronation. 1 Chr. 12: 33.
Officer appointed over by David. 1 Chr. 27: 19.
Only some of, assisted in Hezekiah's reformation. 2 Chr. 30: 10, 11, 18.
Country of, blessed with the presence and instruction of Christ. Isa. 9: 1. Mat. 4: 13—15.

SUMMARY OF THE OUTLINE OF DOCTRINES.

PART I. CONCERNING GOD.

- A. His Being.
  - *I. Attributes.*
  - *II. The Trinity.*
- B. His Works.
  - *I. Creation.*
  - *II. Providence.*
  - *III. Angels.*

PART II. CONCERNING MAN.

- *I. Created.*
- *II. Common origin.*
- *III. Compound being.*
- *IV. Offspring of God.*
- *V. In God's image.*
- *VI. Under law.*

PART III. CONCERNING SIN.

- *I. Its nature.*
- *II. Its extent and penalty.*

PART IV. CONCERNING REDEMPTION.

- A. Introductory and General Statements.
- B. The Person of the Redeemer.
  - *I. Truly God.*
  - *II. Truly man.*
  - *III. Truly God and man.*
- C. The Work of the Redeemer as
  - *I. Prophet.*
  - *II. Priest.*
  - *III. King.*
- D. The Work of the Holy Spirit in Redemption.
- E. The Work of Redemption Viewed in its Relations to the Believer.
  - *I. The union between Christ and the believer.*
  - *II. Related doctrines.*
    1. Repentance.
    2. Faith.
    3. Regeneration.
    4. Justification.
    5. Adoption.
    6. Sanctification.
- F. The Union Between Believers: the Church and its Institutions.
- G. Eschatology.
  - *I. Death, and the state of the soul after death.*
  - *II. The resurrection.*
  - *III. The second advent and the general judgment.*
  - *IV. Heaven and hell.*

OUTLINE OF

THE FUNDAMENTAL DOCTRINES

OF THE BIBLE

BY DAVID ALLEN REED

President of The Bible Normal College, Springfield, Mass.

PART I—Concerning God.

A. His Being.

I. Attributes.

1. Self-existence. Life in Himself; underived; inexhaustible. Gen. 1:1, "In the beginning God." Exo. 3:14, "I AM." Psa. 36:9. Isa. 41:4. Jno. 5:26. Acts 17:24, 25. Rom. 11:35, 36.

2. Spirituality. God is a Spirit. Gen. 1:2. Deu. 4:15—19, (R. V.) Psa. 139:7. Isa. 60:1. Eze. 37:14; 39:29. Joel 2:28, 29. Jno. 4:24. Acts 17:28, with Heb. 12:9. Rom. 8:9, 15, 16. 1 Cor. 2:11. 2 Cor. 3:17.

3. Unity. The *only* God. Exo. 20:3. Deu. 4:35, 39; 6:4. 1 Sam. 2:2. 2 Sam. 7:22. 1 Kin. 8:60. 2 Kin. 19:15. Neh. 9:6. Psa. 86:10. Isa. 44:6—8; 45:22. Jer. 10:10. Joel 2:27, (R. V.) Zec. 14:9. Mar. 12:29. Jno. 17:3. Rom. 1:21—23. 1 Cor. 8:4—6. Gal. 3:20. Eph. 4:6. 1 Tim. 2:5.

4. Eternity. Unlimited by time. Gen. 21:33. Exo. 15:18. Deu. 32:40. 1 Chr. 16:36, (R. V.) Neh. 9:5. Psa. 90:1—4. Isa. 44:6; 48:12; 57:15. Jer. 10:10. Lam. 5:19. Dan. 4:3, 34. Mic. 4:7. Hab. 1:12. Rom. 1:20; 16:26. 1 Tim. 1:17. Heb. 1:10—12. 2 Pet. 3:8. Rev. 4:8—10.

5. Immutability. Unchangeable in nature, or purpose. Exo. 3:15. Num. 23:19. 1 Sam. 15:29. Psa. 33:11. Pro. 19:21. Ecc. 3:14. Isa. 14:24. Eze. 24:14. Mal. 3:6. Rom. 11:29. Heb. 6:17, 18. Jas. 1:17.

6. Omnipresence. Unlimited by space. Gen. 28:15, 16. Deu. 4:39. Jos. 2:11. 1 Kin. 8:27. Psa. 139:7—10. Pro. 15:3, 11. Isa. 66:1. Jer. 23:23, 24. Amos 9:2—4, 6. Acts 7:48, 49; 17:27, 28 (Immanence). Eph. 1:23.

7. Omniscience. Cognizant of all things. Gen. 18:18, 19; 25:23. Exo. 3:19. Deu. 31:21. 1 Sam. 2:3. 1 Kin. 8:39. 2 Kin. 8:10, 13. 1 Chr. 28:9. Psa. 94:9, 11; 139:1—16; 147:4, 5. Pro. 15:3, 11. Isa. 29:15, 16; 40:28. Jer. 1:4, 5; 16:17. Eze. 11:5. Dan. 2:22, 28. Hos. 7:2. Amos 4:13. Nah. 1:7. Zec. 4:10. Mat. 6:4, 6, 8, 18. Luke 16:15. Acts. 15:8, 18. Rom. 8:27, 29. 1 Cor. 3:20. 2 Tim. 2:19. Heb. 4:13. 1 Pet. 1:2. 1 Jno. 3:20.

8. Wisdom. God realizes the best designs by the best possible means. Psa. 104:24. Pro. 3:19. Isa. 28:29, (R. V.) Jer. 10:12. Dan. 2:20, 21. Rom. 11:33. 1 Cor. 1:24, 25, 30; 2:6, 7. Eph. 3:10. Col. 2:2, 3. (See R. V., margin.)

9. Omnipotence. In the truest sense nothing is impossible. Gen. 1:1; 17:1; 18:14. Exo. 15:7. Deu. 3:24; 32:39. 1 Sam. 14:6. 1 Ch. 16:25. 2 Chr. 20:6. Job 40:2, 9; 42:2 (Read together.) Psa. 33:9; 135:6, seq. Isa. 40:12—15. Jer. 32:17. Eze. 10:5. Dan. 3:17; 4:35. Amos 4:13; 5:8. Zec. 12:1. Mat. 19:26. Mar. 10:27. Luke 1:37; 18:27. Rom. 1:20. Eph. 1:19; 3:20. Col. 1:16, 17. Rev. 15:3; 19:6.

10. Holiness. Absolute moral purity. Can neither sin nor tolerate sin. Exo. 15:11. Lev. 11:44, 45; 20:26. Deu. 32:4. Jos. 24:19. 1 Sam. 2:2. 2 Sam. 22:31. Ezr. 9:15. Psa. 5:4; 111:9; 145:17. Isa. 6:3; 43:14, 15. Jer. 23:9. Eze. 39:7. Dan. 9:7, 14. Hab. 1:13. Zec. 8:8. Mal. 2:17. Mat. 5:48. Luke 1:49. Jno. 17:11. Jas. 1:13. 1 Pet. 1:15, 16. 1 Jno. 1:5; 3:3. Rev. 4:8; 15:3, 4.

11. Justice. Demands righteousness of His creatures and deals right-

eously toward them. Gen. 18:23—32. Exo. 20:5, 6. Deu. 7:9, 10; 10:17, 18; 24:16. 2 Chr. 19:7. Neh. 9:33. Psa. 9:8, 16; 89:14. Pro. 24:12. Isa. 9:7; 45:21. Jer. 17:10; 32:19. Lam. 1:18. Eze. 18; 33:18—20. Dan. 9:7, 14. Nah. 1:3. Zep. 3:5. Luke 12:47, 48. Acts 10:34, 35; 17:31. Rom. 11:2, 5—11; 3:26. Gal. 2:6; 6:7, 8. Eph. 6:8, 9. Col. 3:25. Heb. 6:10. 1 Pet. 1:17. 2 Pet. 2:9. 1 Jno. 1:9. Jude 14, 15. Rev. 16:17.

12. Goodness. "Includes benevolence, love, mercy, grace."—*Hodge.* Gen. 19:16. Exo. 34:6, 7. Num. 14:18. Deu. 4:31; 7:7, 8. Jud. 2:18. 1 Kin. 8:23. 2 Kin. 13:23. 1 Chr. 16:34. 2 Chr. 30:9. Neh. 9:17, 31. Psa. 23; 25:8—10; 86:5, 15. Pro. 22:23. Isa. 63:9. Jer. 3:12; 31:3. Lam. 3:22, 23. Eze. 33:11. Dan. 9:9. Hos. 11:1—4, 8, 9. Joel 2:13. Jon. 4:2, 10, 11. Mic. 7:18—20. Nah. 1:7. Zep. 3:17. Zec. 9:17. Mal. 1:2. Mat. 5:45; 19:17. Luke 1:50; 6:36. Jno. 3:16. Acts 14:17. Rom. 2:4; 5:8; 8:38, 39. 2 Cor. 1:3; 13:11. Eph. 2:4, 7. 2 The. 2:16. Tit. 2:11; 3:4, 5. Jas. 5:11. 1 Pet. 1:3. 2 Pet. 3:9. 1 Jno. 3:1; 4:7—10, 16.

13. Faithfulness. Absolutely trustworthy. His words will not fail. Exo. 34:6. Num. 23:19. Deu. 4:31; 31:7:9. Jos. 21:43—45; 23:14. 1 Sam. 15:29. 2 Sam. 7:28. 1 Kin. 8:24, 56. Psa. 105:8; 119:89, 90. Isa. 25:1; 49:7. Jer. 4:28. Lam. 3:23. Eze. 12:25; 16:60, 62. Dan. 9:4. Mic. 7:20. Luke 18:7, 8. Jno. 3:33. Rom. 3:4; 15:8. 1 Cor. 1:9; 10:13. 2 Cor. 1:20. 1 The. 5:24. 2 The. 3:3. 2 Tim. 2:13. Tit. 1:2. Heb. 6:18; 10:23. 1 Pet. 4:19. 2 Pet. 3:9, 13. (Read with verses 3, 4, 8.) 1 Jno. 1:9. Rev. 15:3.

II. The Trinity.

By the Trinity is meant the unity of three persons in one Godhead; Father, Son, Holy Spirit.

Representing God as one, the Scriptures also ascribe divinity to Father, Son, and Holy Spirit.

COURSE OF THE ARGUMENT.

1. God is one. Unity is ascribed to God.
2. The Father is divine: a distinct person.
3. The Son is divine: a distinct person.
4. The Holy Spirit is divine: a distinct person.
5. The Father, Son, and Holy Spirit are classed together, separately from all other beings.

1. God is one. *See passages cited under Attributes, Unity.*

2. The Father is divine and a distinct person. The word "Father" is used in the Scriptures in a two-fold sense in relation to the Godhead: sometimes as equivalant to God, sometimes to the first person in the Trinity.

a. Passages where "Father" is used as equivalent to God, not implying personal distinctions. Deu. 32:6. 2 Sam. 7:14. 1 Chr. 29:10. Psa. 89:26. Isa. 63:16. Jer. 3:19. Mal. 2:10. Mat. 6:9. Mar. 11:25. Luke 12:30. Jno. 4:21, 23, 24. 2 Cor. 6:18. Phi. 4:20. Jas. 1:17. 1 Jno. 2:15, 16.

b. Passages applied to God in contrast with Christ, denoting a special relation to Christ as Son in His office of Redeemer. Psa. 2. Mat. 11:27; 25:34. Mar. 8:38; 14:36. Jno. 5:18—23, 26, 27; 10:15, 30; 17:1. Acts 2:33. Rom. 15:6. 1 Cor. 8:6; 15:24. 2 Cor. 11:31. Gal. 1:1—4. Eph. 1:2, 3; 4:5, 6. Phi. 1:2. 1 The. 3:11, 13. 2 The. 2:16. 1 Tim. 1:2. 2 Tim. 1:2. Tit. 1:4. Phile. 3. 1 Pet. 1:2, 3. 2 Pet. 1:17. 1 Jno. 1:3; 4:14. Jude 1. Rev. 3:21.

3. The Son divine, a distinct person from the Father.

a. Christ pre-existent. Existed as a distinct person before He came into the world. Mic. 5:2. Jno. 8:56—58; 17:5. 1 Cor. 15:47. Phi. 2:6, 7. Col. 1:17. 1 Jno. 1:1. Rev. 22:13, (Read with verse 16).

b. Not merely pre-existent, but pre-eminent, above all things except the Father, co-eternal with the Father. Mat. 11:27; 28:18. Luke 20:41—44. Jno. 3:13, 31. Acts 10:36. Rom. 14:9. Eph. 1:20—22. Phi. 2:9, 10. Col. 1:15, 17, 18. Heb. 1:4—6. 1 Pet. 3:22. Rev. 1:5; 3:14.

c. Creator of the universe. Jno. 1:3. Col. 1:16. Heb. 1:2, 10.

d. Divine attributes ascribed to Him.

(1) Omnipotence. Isa. 9:6. Mat. 28:18. Jno. 10:17, 18; 11:25. 1 Cor. 1:24. Phi. 3:21. Col. 2:10. 2 Tim. 1:10. Heb. 1:3. Rev. 1:8.

(2) Omnipresence. Mat. 18:20; 28:20. Eph. 1:23.

(3) Eternity. Mic. 5:2. Jno. 1:1. Rev. 1:8.

(4) Omniscience. Mat. 11:27. Luke 10:22. Jno. 2:24, 25; 21:17. Acts 1:24. Col. 2:3. Rev. 2:23.

e. The divine name is applied to Him as to no other being except the Father, implying supreme divinity. Psa. 102:24, 25, (See Heb. 1:8—10). Isa. 7:14; 9:6. Mal. 3:1. Mat. 1:23. Jno. 1:1; 20:28. Acts 20:28. Rom. 9:5. Eph. 5:5. Phi. 2:6. Col. 2:9. Tit. 1:3; 2:13, (R. V.). Heb. 1:8—10,

(See Psa. 102: 24, 25). 2 Pet. 1: 1. 1 Jno. 5: 20. Rev. 17: 14; 19: 16.

f. Exhibited in the Scriptures as the object of religious worship. Mat. 2: 11; 14: 33; 15: 25. Luke 24: 52. Jno. 5: 23. Acts 7: 59, 60. 1 Cor. 1: 2. 2 Cor. 12: 8, 9. Gal. 1: 5. Phi. 2: 10. 1 The. 3: 11, 12. 2 Tim. 4: 18. Heb. 1: 6 (Psa. 97: 7). 2 Pet. 3: 18. Rev. 5: 13.

4. The Holy Spirit is divine and a distinct person from the Father and the Son.

a. The Holy Spirit is divine. Called the Spirit of the Father, the Spirit of the Son, the Holy Spirit, the Spirit of truth, the Spirit of life. Gen. 1: 2; 6: 3. Neh. 9: 30. Isa. 63: 10. Eze. 36: 27, 28 (Cf. Acts 2: 16, 17). Joel 2: 28. Mat. 10: 20. Luke 12: 12. Jno. 14: 16, 17; 15: 26. Acts 5: 3, 4; 28: 25. Rom. 8: 14. 1 Cor. 3: 16. Gal. 4: 6. Eph. 1: 13. 1 The. 4: 8. Heb. 2: 4. 1 Pet. 1: 2.

b. Is distinct from Father and Son, and is personal. The personal pronoun *He* applied to Him; personal acts ascribed to Him. Mat. 3: 16, 17; 28: 19. Mar. 1: 10, 11. Luke 3: 21, 22. Jno. 14: 26; 15: 26; 16: 13. Acts 13: 2, 4; 15: 28. Rom. 8: 26, (R. V.). 1 Cor. 12: 11.

c. Converting, regenerating influence ascribed to Him. Neh. 9: 20. Isa. 44: 3. Eze. 36: 26, 27; 37: 14. Joel 2: 28. Mat. 3: 11. Jno. 3: 5, 6; 14: 26. Acts 9: 31. Rom. 8: 9, 11, 14. 1 Cor. 6: 11. 2 Cor. 1: 22; 5: 5. Gal. 4: 6; 5: 22. Eph. 1: 13; 3: 16. 1 The. 1: 6. 2 The. 2: 13. Tit. 3: 5. 1 Pet. 1: 2. 1 Jno. 3: 24. Rev. 22: 17.

5. The Father, Son, and Spirit are classed together, separately from all other beings, as divine. Mat. 28: 19. Rom. 8: 9, 14—17. 2 Cor. 13: 14. 1 Pet. 1: 2. Jude 20, 21.

Result of the Biblical evidence in respect to the divinity of the Father, the Son, and the Holy Spirit.

(1) That the Father, Son, and Holy Spirit are personally distinguished from each other. There is recognized throughout a personal relation of the Father and Son to each other. So of the Holy Spirit to both.

(2) They each have divine names and attributes.

(3) Yet there is only one God.—*H. B. Smith.*

B. His Works.

I. Creation.

1. The Scriptures represent God as the Creator of the universe. Gen. 1: 1. 2 Kin. 19: 15. 1 Chr. 29: 11. Neh. 9: 6. Job 38: 4. Psa. 33: 6; 96: 5; 102; 25; 146: 5, 6. Pro. 3: 19. Isa. 42: 5; 51: 13. Jer. 10: 12; 32: 17. Amos 5: 8; 9: 6. Zec. 12: 1. Jno. 1: 1—3. Acts 4: 24; 17: 25. Rom. 11: 36. Eph. 3: 9. Col. 1: 16, 17. Heb. 3: 4; 11: 3. 2 Pet. 3: 5. Rev. 4: 11.

2. Creation voluntary on God's part. The universe the product of His will. The First Cause is Mind. Gen. 1: 3, 4, 31. Psa. 33: 6, 9. Eph. 1: 11. Heb. 11: 3. Rev. 4: 11.

II. Providence.

"This term, in its widest application, signifies the Divine Presence in the world as sustaining, controlling, and guiding to their destination all things that are made. The will of God determines the end for which His creatures exist; His wisdom and His goodness appoint the means by which that end is attained: in the conservation of the frame of nature, in the care of all creatures that have wants, in the government especially of intelligent and probationary beings; and His power ensures the accomplishment of every design."—*Pope.*

1. The universe as such is the object of conservation. What God has brought into being is continued in existence by His omnipresent agency. Neh. 9: 6. Psa. 36: 6; 66: 9. Isa. 63: 9. Acts 17: 28. Col. 1: 17. Heb. 1: 3.

2. That part of creation which is the subject of wants is the object of ceaseless providential care. Gen. 48: 15. 2 Sam. 22: 2, 3. Psa. 23: 5; 147: 9. Pro. 16: 9. Mat. 5: 45; 6: 26, 30. Luke 12: 6, 7. Acts 14: 17. 1 Pet. 5: 7.

3. That part of creation which consists of intelligent or probationary creatures is the object of providential government. Psa. 37: 23; 64: 12. Pro. 16: 7, 9. Isa. 33: 22. Dan. 4: 17. Mat. 6: 33; 7: 24—27. Mar. 10: 29, 30. Luke 6: 47—49. Acts 5: 38, 39. Rom. 8: 28. Jas. 4: 12.

III. Angels.

1. Existence and nature. Spiritual beings, created before man, high in intelligence and mighty in power.

a. Gen. 18: 19; 32: 1, 2.

b. Gen. 3. Job 38: 7. Rev. 12: 9.

c. Psa. 103: 20. Mat. 13: 41; 24: 36; 25: 31. 1 Cor. 13: 1. 2 The. 1: 7.

2. Orders. There appear to be various orders of angels. Dan. 10: 13; 12: 1. Luke 1: 19. Eph. 1: 21. 1 The. 4: 16. Jude 7. Rev. 12: 7.

3. Number. Exceedingly great. Deu. 33: 2. Psa. 68: 17. Dan. 7: 10. Mat. 26: 53. Luke 2: 13. Heb. 12: 22. Rev. 5: 11.

4. Employment.

a. Adore the presence of God, serve Him, and are happy in His service. Mat. 18:10. 1 Pet. 1:12. Rev. 5:11.

b. Employed in works of providence and in greater work of redemption.

(1) Gen. 28:12. Psa. 34:7; 91:11, 12. Mat. 18:10. Acts 5:19; 12:7; 27: 23. Heb. 1:13, 14.

(2) Acts 7: 53. Gal. 3: 19. Heb. 2:2.

(3) 2 Kin. 19: 35. 1 Chr. 21:16. Acts 12:23.

(4) Luke 2:10, 11. Mar. 1:13. Luke 22:43. Mat. 28: 2—4. Jno. 20:12. Acts 1:10, 11.

(5) Mat. 13:49, 50; 24:31; 25:31. 1 The. 4:16, 17. 2 The. 1:7.

5. Character. As to moral character, divided into two great classes.

a. The good. Psa. 103:20. Luke 9: 26. 1 Tim. 5:21.

b. The bad. Mat. 12:24—27. Eph. 2:2; 6:12. 1 Tim. 4:1.

6. Satan, the chief of the fallen angels.

a. Names applied to him. Satan. 1 Chr. 21:1. The devil. Mat. 4:1, 5, 8. The tempter. Mat. 4:3. Prince of the devils. Mar. 3: 22. Murderer and liar. Jno. 8:44. Prince of this world. Jno. 12:31; 14:30. God of this world. 2 Cor. 4:4. Prince of the power of the air. Eph. 2:2. Adversary. 1 Pet. 5:8. Apollyon. Rev. 9:11. The old serpent, the deceiver. Rev. 12:9. The accuser. Rev. 12:10. The dragon. Rev. 20:2.

b. Personality. Mat. 4:1—11. Jno. 8:44. 2 Cor. 11:3, 14.

c. Other evil angels subordinate to him. Mat. 12:24—28. Luke 10:18. Eph. 2:2; 6:12. Rev. 9:11; 20:2.

d. Power and work of Satan and his angels.

(1) Mat. 4: 1—11. 1 Cor. 5:5. 2 Cor. 4: 4; 11: 14. Eph. 6: 11, 12. 2 The. 2:9, 10. 1 Tim. 3:7. Heb. 2:14. Rev. 12:9.

(2) Prominent examples of temptation. Adam and Eve, David, Christ, Judas, Ananias and Sapphira.

(3) Demoniacs were persons possessed of demons, agents of Satan.

7. Cherubim and Seraphim.

a. Some hold that the cherubim are real, personal creatures; others that they are ideal beings. The term "living creature" is applied to the same beings. May be regarded as symbolical of the highest properties of creature life and typical of redeemed manhood. Gen. 3:24. Exo. 25:22. 1 Sam. 4:4. Eze. 1:5—25; 10. Rev. 4:6—9; 5:6—14; 6:1—7.

b. Seraphim. Mentioned only in Isa. 6. Probably the same as cherubim.

PART II—Concerning Man.

I. Man was Created.

Gen. 1:27. Exo. 20:11. Pro. 20:12. Isa. 45:12. Jer. 27:5. Zec. 12:1. 1 Cor. 11:9, 10.

II. The Race has a Common Origin.

Gen. 1:27; 5:1—3; 7:21—24; 9:18, 19. Isa. 63:16; 64:8. Mal. 2:10. Mat. 6:9. Luke 11:2. Acts 17:26—29. 1 Cor. 8:6. Eph. 4:6.

III. Man a Compound Being, Consisting of Body and Spirit.

Gen. 2:7. Ecc. 12:7. Mat. 10:28; 22:32. Luke 8:55. 1 Cor. 15:45. 2 Cor. 5:6, 8. 1 The. 5:23.

IV. Man is the Offspring of God.

See the texts cited under "Common Origin," also, Luke 3:38. Jno. 20:17.

V. Man was Created in God's Image.

1. This includes knowledge, feeling, and will. Gen. 1:26, 27; 5:1. Cor. 11:7. Jas. 3:9.

2. He was in a state of righteousness and holiness. Ecc. 7:29. 2 Cor. 3:13. Eph. 4:24. Col. 3:10, and the whole teaching of Scripture in regard to the state of the regenerated.

VI. Man Under Moral Law.

Gen. 2:16, 17. Exo. 20. Deu. 6:6—9; 27:26; 32:46. Jos. 1:8. Psa. 1:1—3; 73:5; 119:72, 92. Mat. 5:17, 19; 7:21, 24—27. Jno. 14:21. Rom. 2:13—15; 8:4. Jas. 1:22, 25. 1 Jno. 2:3, 4. Rev. 22:14.

PART III—Concerning Sin.

I. Its Nature.

1. Its origin, as regards the human race. The first man and woman, by their own choice, violated the law of God; they sinned against God. Gen. 3.

2. Words, which describe sin in

some of its forms. Hebrew: "*Chata*," to go out of the way, to miss the mark. "*Pasha*," to transgress. "*Avah*," to twist, to act perversely. Greek "*Hamartia*," a missing of the mark. "*Paraptoma*," a falling away from law, truth, right. "*Parabasis*," a going over or beyond truth and right, transgression. "*Anomia*," lawlessness. "*Asebeia*," irreverence.

3. Definition. "Sin is any want of conformity unto, or transgression of, the law of God."

II. Its Extent and Penalty.

1. By sinning, our first parents incurred the penalty of eternal death, including loss of communion with God, supremacy of worldly affections, and consequent misery, wretchedness, pain. Gen. 2:17. Eze. 18:4. Mat. 25:46. Rom. 5:12; 6:23. 1 Cor. 15: 58. Gal. 6:8. Jas. 1:15. (See also next two sections.)

2. Sin natural to every human being, depravity being hereditary. Psa. 51:5; 58:3. Jer. 17:9. Jno. 3:6. Rom. 5:12—19; 7:14—24; 8:7. 1 Cor. 15:22. Gal. 5:17, 19—21. Eph. 2:1, 3.

3. All men sinners; therefore subject to same penalty incurred by the first sin. Gen. 6:5, 11, 12. 1 Kin. 8: 46. 2 Chr. 6:36. Psa. 53:1—3. Pro. 20: 6, 9. Ecc. 7:20. Jno. 3:19. Rom. 3:9—18, 23; 11:32. Gal. 3:22. 1 Jno. 1: 8, 10.

4. Therefore all need redemption. Jno. 3;5, 6. Rom. 5:18; 7:24, 25. 2 Cor. 5:14, 15, 19. Gal. 3:21, 22. Tit. 2:14. Heb. 2:9. 1 Jno. 2:2

PART IV—Concerning Redemption.

A. Introductory and General Statements.

The sin and ruin of man gave occasion for the gracious interposition of God. In the curse upon the serpent was intimated the purpose of redemption. Gen. 3:15.

I. There is, however, no Self-redemption.

The fall of man wrought a change in both his nature and his condition. To be redeemed he must be placed where he was before, both as to character and as to state. His purity must be restored; his condemnation must be removed. Man cannot redeem himself, because—

1. The legal difficulty is insuperable. The divine law requires a perfect obedience. Mat. 22:37. Gal. 3: 10. Rev. 6:23. *There can be no surplus obedience*, no reparation for sin that is past.

2. The moral difficulty is insuperable. Job 14:14. Jno. 3:6. There is no tendency in that which is sinful to that which is holy. No sinner can regain by self-effort alone the purity which he has lost; but this is indispensable to redemption. Heb. 12:14.

II. No Redemption by other Creatures.

It is equally certain that, while sinful man cannot redeem himself, no other creature can redeem him. The fact of creatureship necessitates dependence and obligation. The highest angel and all the angels are under law to God. That law is perfect, it exacts their whole power of love and service. By no possibility can they love and serve God except for themselves alone. To find a being qualified and able to redeem, we must find one over whom the law has no jurisdiction. In the presence of that being we are in the presence of God.

III. Will God redeem?

1. Nature furnishes presumptive evidence that God will redeem. Nature shows the goodness of God. His gifts are not determined by the moral character of men. Psa. 103:10; 145: 15, 16; 147:8, 9. Mat. 5:45; 6:26.

2. In the world man is subject to many evils as to his body, but all around him are remedies in nature.

3. The universal prevalence of sacrifice is another presumption. It is probable that sacrifice did not originate with man, but in the appointment of God. Gen. 3:21.

4. If nature is uncertain, revelation is clear and conclusive. From the fall of Adam to the birth of Christ the divine purpose was constantly being more fully and clearly revealed. Gen. 3:15; 4:4; 5:24—29; 6: 8; 14:18. Jno. 8:56. Isa. 53:1—12. Dan. 9:24—27. Joel 2:28—32. Zec. 13: 1—7.

5. The presence and work of the Holy Spirit also attested. Gen. 6:3. Exo. 31:2, 3. Jud. 6:34; 11:29. Neh. 9:20. Isa. 44:3, 4; 59:21; 63:11. Hag. 2:5.

IV. The Redeemer, or Messiah, has Already Come.

It is plain from the prophecies and from their historical fulfilment that the Messiah must have long since come. Gen. 49:10. Dan. 9:25. Hag. 2:6—9. Mal. 3:1.

V. Jesus Christ the Messiah, as shown by Fulfilled Prophecies.

1. Was to be from eternity the fellow of God. Isa. 9:6. Mic. 5:2. Zec. 13:7. Mat. 3:17. Jno. 1:1—3. 1 Jno. 5:20.

2. To be born not by ordinary generation, but of a virgin. Isa. 7:14. Mat. 1:18—25. Luke 1:26—33.

3. In Bethlehem of Judea. Mic. 5:2. Luke 2:4, 11. (See also Mat. 2: 4–6. Jno. 7:42.)

4. To come while the scepter still lingered with Judah, near by the close of the weeks predicted Daniel, and while the second temple was yet standing. Gen. 49:10; Mat. 2:1. Dan. 9:25; Luke 2:1. Hag. 2: 6–9; Mat. 24:1, 2.

5. To be of the race of Abraham, of the tribe of Judah, of the family of David. Gen. 22:18. Gen. 49:10. 2 Sam. 7:16. Isa. 11:1—9.

6. To come in humble circumstances. Isa. 53:2; Luke 2:7–24. Isa. 49:7; Mat. 8:20; Mar. 6:3.

7. To make Himself known by works of mercy and of supernatural power. Isa. 35:3—6; Jno. 5:36, 37. Isa. 42:7; 61:1—3; Jno. 10:24, 25.

8. To be despised and rejected of men. Isa. 53:3—7. Jno. 1:10, 11. Luke 23:18—21.

9. To be cut off by a violent death and His body to be pierced. Isa. 53: 8; Dan. 9:26; Luke 23:23, 33. Psa. 22:16; Jno. 20:25. Zec. 12:10; Jno. 19:34.

10. Other prophecies concerning His death. Psa. 22:7, 8; Mat. 27:39—43. Psa. 69:21; Mat. 27:34. Psa. 22: 18; Jno. 19:23, 24. Exo. 12:46; Jno. 19:33, 36. Isa. 53:12; Mar. 15:27. Isa. 53:9; Mat. 27:57—60.

11. To rise from the dead, to ascend on high, leading captivity captive. Psa. 16:9—11; Mat. 28:5—7. Psa. 68:18; Acts 1:9—11.

VI. The Incarnation.

The word incarnation comes from Latin words (*in* and *caro, carnis*, flesh) meaning "in the flesh." To become incarnate is to become a man. Remaining God, Christ became man and as such lived among men. The divine was not changed into the human, or commingled with the human so that it became what it was not before, but *the divine took the human into union with itself and so entered a form or mode of being which was new as well as mysterious.* As by faith we understand that the world was framed by the word of God, so by faith we understand that He who framed the world became incarnate. Heb. 1; 11:3.

While incarnation could not affect the nature and properties of Deity, it did affect their manifestation. The glory which the Son had with the Father was not visible when He was among men. Jno. 17:5. Phi. 2: 7. Jno. 1:14. Luke 1:32.

To the sight of men the human was the more constant and conspicuous. At times, however, there was the clear shining forth of Deity. Mat. 7: 28, 29. Jno. 3:2. Jno. 7:46. Mat. 17:1, 2.

VII. Old Testament Intimations of the Incarnation.

1. In the first promise. In the renewal of the promise to Abraham, Isaac, Jacob, and David He was to be their seed. Gen. 3:15; 22:18; 28:14. 2 Sam. 7:12—29.

2. The theophanies of the old covenant were manifestations of God in the person of His Son. To Abraham. Gen. 18. Jacob. Gen. 32:22—32. Joshua. Jos. 5:13; 6:5. Manoah and his wife. Jud. 13.

3. Isaiah said: "A Virgin shall conceive, and bear a son" (7:14). This would make Him human, at the same time His name was to be Immanuel, *God with us.* (See also Isa. 9:6, and Zec. 13:7; Mat. 26:31.)

VIII. Necessity of the Incarnation.

Its necessity in the fact of sin. God under no obligation to redeem lost men, but, on the supposition of redemption, the Redeemer must become incarnate.

1. God alone could redeem. The law broken must be vindicated, the nature defiled must be renewed. Men and angels are utterly incompetent in such an exigency. The case necessitates a divine Redeemer.

2. God himself in redeeming men must do it righteously. His perfect law cannot be set aside. The Redeemer must come under the law, under its jurisdiction and its power. But to do this He must come out of the sphere of absolute God-head into that of real manhood. (See Heb. 2: 14—16.) It was impossible that He should cease to be God; it was not impossible that He should assume into union with Himself the nature of man.

IX. The Mediator.

The Greek word for mediator is *emites*, meaning *one who goes between,* or *in the middle*. It embraces the additional ideas of *variance* and *reconciliation*.

1. The word *mediator* does not in itself indicate by what means mediation is to be made.

a. In the case of a *misapprehension* the mediator would only need to explain, or be an interpreter.

b. In a case of *deliberate wrong* the mediator would seek the clemency and favor of the offended party, and thus *become an intercessor*.

c. If, further, the case were such that there were grave *liabilities in law and right* resting upon the offending party, it would be requisite for the mediator to obtain for him, or himself become *a sponsor*, or, to use the Scriptural word, a *surety* or *bondsman*.

d. If the obligations resting upon the offending party were *such as he could not in his own person, or by his own resources satisfy*, it would behoove the mediator to take them upon himself, and actually meeting them become his *redemptor*, or *redeemer*.

2. The application of this idea to Christ. The word *mediator* as applied to Jesus Christ has this definite meaning—*He comes between men and God—separated and at variance by reason of sin—to effect their reconciliation, in harmony with eternal truth, right, and holiness*. See Heb. 2:9—18; 4:14—16; 5:1—9.

X. Atonement.

1. The usage of the English word.

a. Its verbal meaning. This is seen by pronouncing it at-one-ment. In this verbal sense the word expresses a *result*, not that by which the result is gained.

b. In theology the word is commonly used to denote *that part of the priestly work of Christ by which He made satisfaction to the law and justice of God for the sins of men, and in view of which men are saved*. In this use it expresses not reconciliation itself, but that which reconciles.

2. Scriptural words in this connection.

a. In the Old Testament the fundamental Hebrew word for atonement means *to cover*. Psa. 32:1. According to it, sin is expiated or atoned for by *covering* it.

b. In the New Testament. (1) *Katallage* (Rom. 5:11), means a change or an exchange; *i. e.*, a change from enmity to love, and so reconciliation. (2) *Apolutrosis* (Rom. 3:24), deliverance by a ransom or by payment of a price. Mat. 20:28. 1 Pet. 1:18, 19. (3) *Hilasmos*, propitiation. Both Jews and Gentiles perfectly understood the meaning of *hilasmos*. When under a sense of sin they would make a propitiation—they approached the altar and laid upon it the sacrificial victim. 1 Jno. 2:2.

3. If now we combine and formulate these ideas, we see that the atonement of Christ is *that satisfaction to the law and justice of God for the sins of men, which, as the one great High Priest, He made by His own obedience unto death, and on the ground of which He carries on His acts of intercession and benediction in heaven.*

XI. Redemption. (In contrast with atonement.)

Atonement is the ground and means of redemption, while *redemption* is the result of atonement. Redemption consists of two parts, the one legal, the other moral. The work of Christ meets the demands of the law and man is justified. The work of the Spirit renews the depraved nature and reforms the sinner in the divine image, and man is sanctified.

B. The Person of the Redeemer.

I. He is truly God.

(See texts on The Trinity.)

II. He is truly Man.

His human nature the same as that of other men, because He is of the stock of Abraham.

1. General references. Mat. 12:8, 13—37; 16:13; 25:31. Jno. 3:14; 8:28; 13:31. Gal. 4:4. 1 Tim. 2:5. Heb. 2:14.

2. References to His human body. Mat. 2:1. Mar. 4:38. Luke 2:52; Jno. 4:6—8; 19:32—34.

3. References to the intellectual and spiritual faculties which He had in common with men. Mat. 4:1—11; 26:38. Mar. 10:14; 11:13. Luke 2:52; 4:16—22. Jno. 2:24; 11:3—5, 33.

III. He is truly God and Man.

These two natures, the divine and the human, combined in Christ as the God-man.

1. In many passages both natures are referred to. Jno. 1:14. Rom. 1:3, 4; 8:3; 9:5. Gal. 4:4. Phi. 2:11. 1 Jno. 4:3.

2. Passages which speak of the human attributes and actions of Christ while the divine title is used. Mat. 1:23. Luke 1:31, 32. Acts 20:28. Rom. 8:32. 1 Cor. 2:8. Col. 1:13—17.

3. Passages which speak of the

divine attributes and actions of Christ while He is designated by the human title. Jno. 3: 13; 6: 62. Rom. 9: 5. Rev. 5: 12, 13.

C. The Work of the Redeemer as Prophet, Priest, and King.

I. As Prophet.

A prophet of God is one who has authority and who has the necessary qualifications to convey God's messages to men. He may also be an interpreter.

1. Christ executed the office of prophet, by His word and by His works. Mat. 5: 24.

2. Also through other agents: through His Spirit, by inspiration, by spiritual illumination, through the officers of the church inspired as apostles, prophets, and teachers. Eph. 4: 11, 12. 1 Jno. 2: 20; 5: 20. He continues to execute the office of prophet through eternity. Rev. 7: 17; 21: 23.

II. As Priest.

A priest is one who is qualified and authorized to "draw near to the Lord for men." Exo. 19: 22. Heb. 5: 1.

1. Must be taken from among men to represent them. Exo. 28: 9, 12, 21, 29. Heb. 5: 12.

2. Must be chosen by God. Exo. 28: 1. Num. 16: 5. Heb. 5: 4.

3. Must be holy—morally pure and consecrated to God. Exo. 39: 30, 31. Lev. 21: 6, 8. Psa. 106: 16.

4. Must have a right to draw near to Jehovah and to offer sacrifices and make intercession. Exo. 19: 22. Lev. 16: 3, 7, 12, 15. Num. 16: 5.

5. The Old Testament declares Christ to be a priest. Psa. 110: 4 (Cf. Heb. 5: 6; 6: 20). Zec. 6: 13.

6. Priestly functions ascribed to Him. Isa. 53: 10. Dan. 9: 24, 25. The temple and its services and all Old Testament sacrifices typical of Christ and His work. He superseded these. Col. 2: 17. Heb. 9: 10—12; 10: 11, 12.

7. New Testament proof. Was taken from among men to stand for them before God. Heb. 2: 16; 4: 15. Was chosen by God. Heb. 5: 5, 6. Was perfectly holy. Luke 1: 35. Heb. 7: 26. Has the right of the nearest access and the greatest influence with the Father. John 11: 42; 16: 28. Heb. 1: 3; 9: 11—24.

a. He "mediated" in the general sense of the term. John 14: 6. 1 Tim. 2: 5. Heb. 8: 6.

b. He offered propitiation. Eph. 5: 25. Heb. 9: 26; 10: 12. 1 Jno. 2: 2.

c. He makes intercession. Rom. 8: 4. Heb. 7: 25. 1 Jno. 2: 1.

8. Christ as priest made atonement for us, was made a substitute for us. A substitute is one appointed or accepted to act or to suffer in the stead of another, and his actions or sufferings are *vicarious.*

a. The Greek preposition *huper*, with the genitive, sometimes signifies *instead of*, and the construction is used to set forth the relation of Christ's work to us. 2 Cor. 5: 14, 15, 20. Gal. 3: 13. Phile. 13. 1 Pet. 3: 18.

b. The preposition *anti* definitely and always expresses substitution. Mat. 2: 22; 5: 38; 20: 28. Mar. 10: 45. 1 Tim. 2: 6.

c. The same is true as to what the Scriptures teach as to our sins being laid upon Christ. Lev. 7: 18. Num. 18: 27. Psa. 106: 31. Isa. 53: 12. Luke 22: 37. Rom. 2: 26; 4: 3—9. 2 Cor. 5: 19—21. Gal. 3: 13.

d. The effects of Christ's action as priest are shown.

(1) As towards God, they are declared to be propitiatory. Rom. 3: 25, 26. Heb. 2: 17. 1 Jno. 2: 2; 4: 10.

(2) As respects the sinner, they are declared to be redemption, deliverance by ransom. Isa. 51: 11; 62: 12. 1 Cor. 7: 23. Gal. 3: 13, 14. 1 Tim. 2: 6. 1 Pet. 1: 18, 19. Rev. 5: 9.

III. As King.

The kingdom of Christ a very prominent subject in Scripture. Dan. 2: 44. Mat. 13; 22: 1—14. Luke 13: 22—30; 17: 20, 21. Rom. 14: 17. Eph. 1: 10, 20—22. 1 Pet. 3: 22.

1. Christ's authority embraces the universe. Mat. 28: 18. Eph. 1: 17—23. Phi. 2: 9—11. It is distinguished as—

a. His kingdom of power, embracing the entire universe in His providential and judicial administration. Jno. 5: 22—27; 9: 39. 1 Cor. 15: 25. Heb. 10: 12, 13.

b. His kingdom of grace, spiritual alike as to its subjects, laws, modes of administration and instrumentalities.

c. His kingdom of glory, the consummation of His gracious administration, will continue forever.

2. The object of Christ's authority is to accomplish the salvation of His church. Eph. 1: 22, 23.

a. To cause all things to work together for the good of His people. Rom. 8: 28.

b. To establish a kingdom for them. Luke 22: 29. Jno. 14: 2.

c. To subjugate all His enemies. 1 Cor. 15: 25.

d. That all should worship Him. Heb. 1:6. Rev. 5:9-13.

3. The following are some of the titles to this kingdom, with the sense in which they are used.

a. The kingdom of God, Luke 4:43, because of divine origin and the authority of God exercised in its administration.

b. The kingdom of Christ, Mat. 16:28; Col. 1:13, because He is in person the immediate sovereign.

c. The kingdom of heaven, Mat. 11:12, because its origin and characteristics are from heaven and its consummation is to be in heaven.

4. Christ's administration of His kingdom presents two aspects:—(1) As militant. Eph. 6:11—17. (2) As glorified, or triumphant. Rev. 3:21. Accordingly Christ is represented as a great Captain (Rev. 19:11, 16), and as a Prince reigning upon His throne. Rev. 21:5, 22, 23.

The throne upon which Christ sits is represented as—A throne of grace. Heb. 4:16. A throne of judgment. Rev. 20:11—15. A throne of glory. Rev. 4:25; 5:6.

5. The sense in which Christ's kingdom is spiritual.

a. The king is a spiritual and not an earthly sovereign. Mat. 20:28. Jno. 18:36.

b. His throne is at the right hand of God. Heb. 1:3.

c. His scepter is spiritual. Psa. 110:2. Isa. 61:1—3; 63:1.

d. The citizens of the kingdom are spiritual men. Jno. 4:24.

e. The mode in which He administers His government is spiritual. Zec. 4:6, 7.

f. His laws are spiritual. Jno. 4:24.

g. The blessings and penalties of His kingdom are spiritual. 1 Cor. 3:4—11. 2 Cor. 10:4. Eph. 1:3—8. 2 Tim. 4:2. Tit. 2:15.

6. Christ as seated at the right hand of the Father. Some of the language may be figurative, but it sets forth the glorification of Christ in heaven. It presents Him as the God-man exalted to supreme and universal glory and power. Psa. 110:1. Dan. 7:13, 14. Mat. 26:64. Mar. 16:19. Jno. 5:22. Rom. 8:34. Eph. 1:20—22. Phi. 2:9—11. Col. 3:1. Heb. 1:3, 4; 2:9; 10:12. 1 Pet. 3:22. Rev. 5:6.

D. The Work of the Holy Spirit in Redemption.

(See Personality and Deity under head of the Trinity.)

I. The Father and the Son work by, and through, the Holy Spirit.

He came upon men and clothed them with the power of God as worker, prophet or leader. Gen. 41:38. Exo. 31:1—3; 35:31. Num. 11:29; 24:2. 1 Sam. 10:10. 2 Chr. 15:1. Isa. 63:11. Eze. 11:23, 24.

II. His special individual work.

1. To convict of sin. Jno. 16:8. Acts 2:37.

2. To regenerate. Jno. 3:3—5; 6:63. Tit. 3:5—7.

3. To witness concerning Jesus. Heb. 10:15. 1 Jno. 5:7.

4. He is the author of assurance to us. Rom. 8:14—16. 1 Jno. 4:13.

5. He is the inspirer of the Scriptures and our personal teacher. Jno. 14:26; 16:13. 1 Cor. 2:9—13; 12:3—8. 1 The. 1:5. 2 Tim 3:16. Heb. 3:7. 2 Pet. 1:21.

6. He dwells in the disciples of Jesus. 1 Cor. 2:9—16; 6:17; 12:13. Gal. 3:5; 4:6; 5:25. Eph. 2:22; 3:16; 5:18. 1 Pet. 1:11. 1 Jno. 3:24.

7. He sheds abroad the love of God in our hearts. Rom. 5:5.

8. He gives hope, joy, peace, liberty. Gal. 5:22. 2 Cor. 3:17.

9. He is the Comforter. Jno. 14:16, 26; 15:26; 16:7. Acts 9:31. Rom. 15:13.

10. He sanctifies. Rom. 8:6—11. 1 Cor. 6:11. Gal. 5:22—26. 2 The. 2:13.

III. The Holy Spirit for Service.

1. The gift. (See texts under I.) Jno. 14:17. 1 Cor. 3:16; 6:19, 20. Luke 4:17—21. Jno. 3:34. Acts 10:38. Isa. 44:3. Acts 1:5, 8; 2:4, 38, 39; 4:31; 6:3; 9:17.

2. How given. Luke 11:13; 24:49. Jno. 20:22. Acts 1:4; 2:38; 5:32; 8:17; 19:6. 1 Jno. 5:14, 15.

3. As to the renewal of the gift. Acts 4:31; 10:44; 11:15; 13:52.

E. The Work of Redemption as Related to the Believer.

I. The Union between Christ and the Believer.

1. As to its nature.

a. Christ as the second Adam (1 Cor. 15:22) assumes in the covenant of grace those broken obligations of the covenant of works which the first Adam failed to discharge, and fulfils them all in behalf of all His "sheep"—those whom the Father has given Him.

b. Its spiritual and vital character.

(1) It is a *spiritual* union. 1 Cor. 6:17; 12:13. 1 Jno. 3:24; 4:13.

(2) It is a *vital* union. Jno. 14:19. Gal 2:20.

(3) It embraces our entire persons. 1 Cor. 6:15, 19.

(4) It is an *indissoluble* union. Jno. 10:28; 14:23; 17:21, 23. 1 The. 4:14, 17.

2. As to its consequences (in general)—

a. Believers have a community with Christ in His covenant standing and rights. Rom. 8:1. Eph. 1:6, 11, 13. Phi. 3:8, 9. Col. 2:10.

His mediatorial office embraces three principal functions:—(1) Prophet. In fellowship with Him the believer is a prophet. Jno. 16:13. 1 Jno. 2:27. (2) Priest. The believer is also a priest in Him. Isa. 61:6. 1 Pet. 2:5. Rev. 20:6. (3) King. In Him the believer is also a king. 1 Pet. 2:9. Rev. 3:21; 5:10.

b. Believers have fellowship with Him in the transforming, assimilating power of His life.

(1) As to their souls. Rom. 8:9. Phi. 2:5. 1 Jno. 3:2.

(2) As to their bodies. Rom. 6:5. 1 Cor. 6:17, 19; 15:47, 49. Phi. 3:21. Thus bearing fruit to Christ, both in their bodies and in their spirits which are His. John 15:5. 2 Cor. 12:9. 1 Jno. 1:6.

c. This leads to fellowship with Christ, in experience, labors, sufferings, temptation, death, and finally, in His glory. Gal. 6:17. Phi. 3:10. Heb, 12:3. 1 Pet. 4:13.

d. Also to Christ's rightful fellowship with them in all *they* possess. Rom. 14:8. 1 Cor. 6:19, 20.

e. Also to the consequence that in the spiritual reception of the sacraments, they do really hold fellowship with Him. They are baptized into Christ. Jno. 6:51, 56. 1 Cor. 10:16; 11:26. Gal. 3:27.

II. Doctrines Connected with the Union of Christ with the Believer.

1. Repentance.

a. Repentance includes a sense of personal guilt, pollution, and helplessness, an apprehension of the mercy of God in Christ, grief and hatred of sin, a resolute turning from it unto God, and a persistent endeavor after a new life of holy obedience.

b. True repentance brings the believer to see and appreciate the holiness of God as revealed alike in the law and in the gospel, and in that light to see and feel the exceeding sinfulness of all sin as well as the sinfulness of his own nature. Job 42:6. Psa. 51:4-9. Rom. 3:20.

c. The awakened conscience echoes God's law, and can be appeased by no less a propitiation than that demanded by divine justice itself.

d. The evidence of genuine repentance.

(1) To be determined by prayerful study of the Scriptures in connection with self-examination.

(2) By the hatred and forsaking of secret as well as of open sins, the choice of God's service as both right and desirable, public confession, and practical consecration.

e. Scripture examples of repentance.

(1) True. 2 Sam. 12:13. Psa. 51:4. 2 Sam. 24:10. Luke 15:18, 21. Luke 18:13.

(2) False. Exo. 9:27, 34; 10:16, 20. 1 Sam. 15:24. Mat. 27:4, 5.

2. Faith.

a. New Testament usage.

(1) That state of mind which is induced by persuasion. Rom. 14:22.

(2) Good faith, fidelity, sincerity. Rom. 3:3. Tit. 2:10.

(3) Assent to the truth. Phi. 1:27. 2 The. 2:13.

(4) Faith toward, on, or in God. Mar. 11:22. 1 The. 1:8. Heb. 6:1. 1 Pet. 1:21. In Christ. Acts. 24:24. Rom. 3:35. Gal. 2:16—20.

(5) The object of faith; viz., the revelation of the gospel. Rom. 1:5; 10:8. 1 Tim. 4:1. Jude 3, 20.

b. *Knowledge* is the apprehension of an object as true, and *faith* is an assent to its truth. In this general sense every exercise of faith includes the knowledge of the object assented to.

c. Religious faith rests, first, upon the faithfulness of God as pledged in His supernatural revelation, (Jno. 3:33); second, upon the evidence of spiritual illumination, personal experience of the power of the truth, and the witness of the Holy Ghost. Thus it rests not in the wisdom of men, but in the power of God. 1 Cor. 2:5—12.

d. The two kinds of evidence by which we know that God has revealed certain truths as objects of faith.

(1) The evidence in the truth itself—moral, spiritual, experimental, rational. Jer. 23:29. Jno. 6:33. Jno. 14:7, 26.

(2) The accrediting evidence of the presence and power of God accompanying the promulgation of the truth, and proving that it is from Him. These are miracles, providential dispensations, and the fulfilment of prophecy. Jno. 5:36. Heb. 2:4.

e. That saving faith includes trust is proved from the uniform and single condition of salvation as presented in the Scriptures, expressed in the words "believe in, or on, Christ." Jno. 7: 38. Acts 9: 42; 16: 31. Gal. 2: 16. To believe in, or on, a person, necessarily implies trust as well as credit. Acts 26: 18. Gal. 3: 26. 2 Tim. 3: 15. Heb. 11: 1.

f. The same proved from expressions used in the Scriptures as equivalent to the phrase "believing in Christ." Such expressions are: Receiving Christ, (Jno. 1: 12). Looking to Christ, (Isa. 45: 22). (Cf. Num. 21: 9. Jno. 3: 14, 15.) Fleeing for refuge, (Heb. 6: 18). Coming to Christ, (Mat. 11: 28. Jno. 6: 35, 37). Committing unto Christ, (2 Tim. 1: 12).

g. The object of faith is the person and work of the Lord Jesus Christ as mediator.

(1) We are justified by that faith of which Christ is the object. Rom. 3: 22, 25. Gal. 2: 16. Phi. 3: 9.

(2) Saved by faith in Christ. Jno. 1: 12; 3: 16, 36; 6: 35. Acts 10: 43; 16: 31.

(3) The rejection of Christ, or refusal to submit to the righteousness of God declared to be the ground of reprobation. Jno. 3: 18, 19; 8: 24.

h. Assurance of salvation attainable through faith.

Directly asserted. Rom. 8: 16. 2 Pet. 1: 10. 1 Jno. 2: 3; 3: 14; 5: 13. Scriptural examples: 2 Tim. 1: 12; 4: 7, 8. Begets unfeigned humility. 1 Cor. 15: 10. Gal. 6: 14. Leads to ever increasing diligence in practical religion. Psa. 51: 12, 13, 19. Also to candid self-examination and a desire to be searched and corrected by God. Psa. 139: 23, 24. Also to constant aspirations after nearer conformity to, and more intimate communion with God. 1 Jno. 3: 2, 3.

i. Living faith leads to good works. Acts 15: 9; 26: 18. Gal. 5: 6. Jas. 2: 14—26. 1 Jno. 5: 4.

3. Regeneration.

a. Scripture terms by which this work of God is designated: Creating. Eph. 4: 24. Begetting. 1 Jno. 4: 7. Quickening. Jno. 5: 21. Eph. 2: 5. Calling out of darkness into marvelous light. 1 Pet. 2: 9.

The subjects of it are said—To be alive from the dead. Rom 6: 13. To be new creatures. 2 Cor. 5: 17. To be born again, or anew. Jno. 3: 3, 7. To be God's workmanship. Eph. 2: 10.

b. Proof that there is such a thing as is commonly called regeneration.

(1) The Scriptures declare that such a change is necessary. 2 Cor. 5: 17. Gal. 6: 15.

(2) The change is described. Eph. 2: 5; 4: 23, 24. Jas. 1: 18. 1 Pet. 1: 23.

(3) It is necessary for the most moral as well as the most profligate. 1 Cor. 15: 10. Gal. 1: 13—16.

(4) That this change is not a mere reformation is proved by its being referred to the Holy Spirit. Tit. 3: 5.

(5) In the comparison of man's state in grace with his state by nature. Rom. 6: 13; 8: 6—10. Eph. 5: 8.

(6) In the experience of all Christians and the testimony of their lives.

c. Proofs that believers are subjects of supernatural, or spiritual illumination.

(1) This is necessary. Jno 16: 3. 1 Cor. 2: 14. 2 Cor. 3: 14; 4: 3.

(2) The Scriptures expressly affirm it. Psa. 19: 7, 8; 43: 3, 4. Jno. 17: 3. 1 Cor. 2: 12, 13. 2 Cor. 4: 6. Eph. 1: 18. Phi. 1: 9. Col. 3: 10. 1 Jno. 4: 7; 5: 20.

The first effect of regeneration is to open the eyes of our understanding to the excellency of divine truth. The second effect is the going forth of the renewed affections toward that excellency perceived.

d. Proof of the absolute necessity of regeneration.

(1) The Scriptures assert it. Jno. 3: 3. Rom. 8: 6, 7. Eph. 2: 10; 4: 21—24.

(2) It is proved from the nature of man as a sinner. Rom. 7: 18; 8: 7—9. 1 Cor. 2: 14. Eph. 2: 1.

(3) Also from the nature of heaven. Isa. 35: 8; 52: 1. Mat. 5: 8; 13: 41. Heb. 12: 14. Rev. 21: 27.

(4) The restoration of holiness is the grand end of the whole plan of salvation. Rom. 8: 28, 29. Eph. 1: 4; 5: 5, 26, 27.

4. Justification.

a. Its fundamental idea is that of perfect conformity to all of the requirements of the moral law.

b. The usage of "to justify."

It means to declare a person to be just.

(1) Because personally conformed to the law as to moral character. Luke 7: 29. Rom. 3: 4.

(2) Because, forensically, the demands of the law as a condition of life have been fully satisfied in regard to Him. Acts 13: 39. Rom. 5: 1, 9; 8: 30, 33. 1 Cor. 6: 11. Gal. 2: 16; 3: 11.

c. (1) The ungodly are said to be justified without the deeds of the law, by the blood of Christ, by faith, freely, and of grace, by means of a satisfaction and of imputed righteousness. Rom. 3: 20—28; 4: 5—7; 5: 1. Gal. 2: 16; 3: 11; 5: 4. 1 Jno. 2: 2.

(2) The contrary of condemnation. Rom. 8: 33, 34.

(3) The same idea conveyed in many equivalent and interchangeable expressions. Jno. 3: 18; 5: 24. Rom. 4: 6, 7. 2 Cor. 5: 19.

d. The terms "righteousness" and "righteousness of God" in the New Testament signify:—

(1) Holiness of character. Mat. 5: 6. Rom. 6: 13. Rom. 10: 3—5. Phi. 3: 9. Tit. 3: 5.

(2) The vicarious obedience and sufferings of Christ our substitute, which become our righteousness, received and appropriated by us through faith. Rom. 3: 22; 4: 6, 11; 10: 4—10. 1 Cor. 1: 30.

The phrase "righteousness of God" means that perfect righteousness or satisfaction to the whole law, precept and penalty alike, which God provides, and which God will accept. Mat. 6: 33. Rom. 1: 17. 2 Cor. 5: 21. Jas. 1: 20.

e. The term "justification," occurs only in Rom. 4: 25; 5: 16, 18. It signifies that relation to the law into which we are brought in consequence of the righteousness of Christ being made legally ours. We are absolved from all liability to the penalty, and the rewards promised to obedience are declared to belong to us.

f. The requirement of the law in order to the justification of a sinner.

The law consists of a rule of duty and a penalty to take effect in case of disobedience. In the case of the sinner, therefore, who has already incurred guilt, the law demands that, besides the rendering of perfect obedience, the penalty also should be suffered. Rom. 10: 5. Gal. 3: 10—13.

g. Proof that works cannot be the ground of a sinner's justification.

(1) Paul repeatedly asserts this. Gal. 2: 16. Phi. 3: 9.

(2) The law demands perfect obedience. No act of obedience at one time can atone for disobedience at another. Gal. 3: 10, 21; 5: 3.

(3) If we are justified by works, then Christ is dead in vain. Gal 2: 21; 5: 4.

(4) If it were of works it would not be of grace. Rom. 11: 6. Eph. 2: 8, 9.

(5) It would afford cause for boasting. Rom. 3: 27; 4: 2.

(6) Paul also quotes the Old Testament to prove that all men are sinners (Rom. 3: 9, 10), and that consequently they cannot be justified by works. Psa. 143: 2. Rom. 3: 20. He quotes Hab. 2: 4 to prove that the just shall live by faith, and cites the example of Abraham. Gal. 3: 6.

h. The ground of justification is the righteousness of Christ. Rom. 10: 4. 1 Cor. 1: 30.

Faith is the essential prerequisite and instrument of receiving that righteousness. Eph. 2: 8.

Justification is a declaration on the part of God that the law is satisfied because of the righteousness of Christ, which is imputed to believers, and the merits of which are received by them through faith.

i. The sense in which Christ's righteousness is imputed.

Imputation is an act of God as sovereign Judge, whereby (1) He makes the guilt and legal responsibilities of our sins really Christ's (Isa. 53: 5, 11. Jno. 1: 29. 2 Cor. 5: 21. Gal. 3: 13); and whereby (2) He makes the righteousness of Christ ours (that is, the legal right to reward, by the gracious covenant conditioned on righteousness), and then treats us as persons legally invested with those rights. Rom. 4: 6; 10: 4. 1 Cor. 1: 30. 2 Cor. 5: 21. Phi. 3: 9.

Imputation is the charging or crediting to one's account as the ground of judicial treatment.

As Christ is not made a sinner by the imputation to Him of our sins, so we are not made holy by the imputation to us of His righteousness. The transfer is only of guilt from us to Him, and of merit from Him to us. Rom. 5: 12—21. Cf. Rom. 4: 6, and 3: 21, with 5: 19.

j. The nature of the peace which flows from justification.

(1) Peace with God, His justice being completely satisfied through the righteousness of Christ. Rom. 5: 1. 2 Cor. 5: 19. Col. 1: 21. Eph. 2: 14. In witness of this His Holy Spirit is given to us. Rom. 8: 15, 16. Heb. 10: 15, 17. His love is shed abroad in our hearts (Rom. 5: 5), and our fellowship with Him is established.

(2) Inward peace of conscience, through the apprehension of the righteousness by which we are justified. Heb. 9: 15; 10: 2, 22.

3. Adoption.

a. Classes of persons to whom the term "sons" or "children of God" is applied in the Scriptures.

(1) In the singular, the term is applied in a supreme sense to the Second Person of the Trinity alone.

(2) In the plural, to angels, because they are God's favored creatures. Job 1: 6; 38: 7.

(3) To human magistrates, be-

cause they possess authority delegated from God. Psa. 82:6.

(4) To good men as the subjects of a divine adoption.

The sonship which this adoption confers is twofold:—

(*a*) General and external. Exo. 4:22. Rom. 9:4.

(*b*) Special, spiritual, and immortal. Gal. 4:5. Eph. 1:4–6.

b. That which is represented in Scripture as involved in being a child of God by adoption.

(1) Derivation of nature from God. Jno. 1:13. Jas. 1:18. 1 Jno. 5:18.

(2) Being born again in the image of God, bearing His likeness. Rom. 8:29. 2 Cor. 3:18. Col. 3:10. 2 Pet. 1:4.

(3) Bearing His name. 1 Jno. 3:1. Rev. 2:17; 3:12.

(4) Being the objects of His peculiar love. Jno. 17:23. Rom. 5:5—8. Tit. 3:4. 1 Jno. 4:7—11.

(5) The indwelling Spirit of His Son (Gal. 4:5, 6), forms in us a spirit becoming the children of God: Obedient (1 Pet. 1:14. 2 Jno. 6); free from sense of guilt, legal bondage, and fear of death (Rom. 8:15. Gal. 5:1. Heb. 2:15); and elevated with a holy boldness and royal dignity. Heb. 10:19, 22. 1 Pet. 2:9; 4:14.

(6) Present protection, consolations, and abundant provisions. Psa. 125:2. Isa. 66:13. Luke 12:27—32. Jno. 14:18. 1 Cor. 3:21—23. 2 Cor. 1:4.

(7) Present fatherly chastisements for our good. Psa. 51:11, 12; Heb. 12:5—11.

(8) The certain inheritance of the riches of our Father's glory, as heirs with God and joint-heirs with Christ (Rom. 8:17. Jas. 2:5. 1 Pet. 1:4; 3:7); including the exaltation of our bodies to the fellowship with Him. Rom. 8:23. Phi. 3:21.

c. Adoption proceeds from the Father, upon the merits of the Son, by the agency of the Holy Spirit. Jno. 1:12, 13. Gal. 4:5, 6. Tit. 3:5, 6. Rom. 8:17, 29. Heb. 2:17; 4:15. All believers being subjects of the same adoption, are brethren. Eph. 3:6. 1 Jno. 3:14; 5:1.

6. Sanctification.

a. (1) To make clean physically or morally. (*a*) Of ceremonial purification. Heb. 9:13. (*b*) To render clean in a moral sense. 1 Cor. 6:11. Heb. 13:12. (*c.*) To set apart from a common to a sacred use, to devote. Mat. 23:17. Jno. 10:36. Mat. 6:9. 1 Pet. 3:15.

b. *Regeneration* is the creative act of the Holy Spirit, implanting a new principle of spiritual life in the soul. *Sanctification* is the sustaining and developing work of the Holy Spirit, bringing all the faculties of the soul more and more perfectly under the purifying and regulating influence of the implanted principle of spiritual life.

c. The sense in which the body is sanctified.

As being the temple of the Holy Ghost. 1 Cor. 6:19.

As being a member of Christ. 1 Cor. 6:15.

It will be made like Christ's glorified body. 1 Cor. 15:44. Phi. 3:21.

d. To whom the work of sanctification is referred.

(1) To the Father. 1 The. 5:23. Heb. 13:21.

(2) To the Son. Eph. 5:25, 26. Tit. 2:14.

(3) To the Holy Spirit. 1 Cor. 6:11. 2 The. 2:13.

f. The agency of the truth in the work of sanctification. Psa. 119:9—11. Jno. 17:19. Jas. 1:18. 1 Pet. 1:22; 2:2. 2 Pet. 1:4.

F. The Union between Believers; the Church and its Institutions.

(Condensed from the Schaff-Herzog Encyclopædia.)

I. The Church.

1. The word *ecclesia* in the New Testament means either the universal church of Christ, or a local congregation.

2. The historical Christian church began on the day of Pentecost; and it was at first composed of the disciples whom Jesus had personally gathered. It was a community inside of Judaism, with peculiar worship and government. It was the *ecclesia;* and by this name Paul calls it in his earliest epistles, whether in Palestine or outside. 1 The. 2:14. Its complete name was the "Church of God," or the "Church of Christ" (Rom. 16:16), whether of a single congregation, or of the whole body of believers. It was made up of the "sanctified in Christ Jesus" (1 Cor. 1:2), the "called saints" (Rom. 1:7), the "holy nation" (1 Pet. 2:9). In the deep conception of Paul every believer was united with Christ, and entered this close union through baptism. 1 Cor. 12:13. Gal. 3:27. The church was Christ's body, of which He was the Head. Col. 1:14; 2:19.

3. For church government, see in

the encyclopædias the articles on the different denominations.

II. The Sacraments.

These are baptism and the Lord's Supper.

For a discussion of the sacraments, consult the leading theological works in your denomination.

G. Eschatology.

Death, and the State of the Soul after Death.

1. The different forms of expression by which death is described in the Scriptures.

Departure out of this world. 2 Tim. 4:6.

Going the way of all the earth Jos. 23:14.

Gathered to one's fathers. Jud. 2:10.

Gathered to one's people. Deu. 32:50.

Dissolving the earthly house of this tabernacle. 2 Cor. 5:1.

Returning to the dust. Ecc. 12:7.

Sleep. Jno. 11:11.

Giving up the ghost. Acts 5:10.

Absent from the body and present with the Lord. 2 Cor. 5:8.

Sleeping in Jesus. 1 The. 4:14. Ecc. 12:7.

2. The relation of death to sin.

The entire penalty of the law, including all the spiritual, physical, and eternal penal consequences of sin, is called death in the Scripture. Gen. 2:17; Rom. 5:12. This included natural death. Rom. 5:13, 14. When Christ bore the penalty of the law, it was necessary for Him to die. Heb. 9:22.

3. Why do the justified die?

It is made necessary from the present constitution of the body, while it is to both body and soul the gateway of heaven. The sting and fear of death are taken away. 1 Cor. 15:55—57. Heb. 2:15. They die "in the Lord" (Rev. 14:13), and shall at last be completely delivered from its power. 1 Cor. 15:26.

4. Immateriality of the soul. Its continual existence after death.

The entire range of human experience fails to make us acquainted with a single instance of the annihilation of matter. Material *bodies*, organized or chemically compounded, constantly come into existence and in turn pass away, yet never through annihilation but simply from the dissolution of that relation which these parts had temporarily sustained to each other. Spirit, however, is essentially simple and single, and therefore incapable of that dissolution of parts to which material bodies are subject. We infer, therefore, that spirits are immortal, since they cannot be subject to that only form of death of which we have any knowledge.

5. Argument derived from its imperfect development in this world.

In every department of organized life every individual creature, in its normal state, tends to grow toward condition of complete development, which is the perfection of its kind. Every human being, however, is conscious that in this life he never attains that completeness which the Creator contemplated in the ideal of His type. He has faculties undeveloped, capacities unfulfilled, natural desires unsatisfied. He knows that he was designed to be much more than he is and to fill a much higher sphere.

6. Argument derived from the distributive justice of God.

It is a judgment of reason, and a fundamental Bible doctrine that moral good is associated with happiness, and moral evil with misery, by the unchangeable nature and purpose of God. But history establishes the fact that this life is not a state of retribution, here wickedness is often associated with prosperity, moral excellence with sorrow. We hence conclude that there is a future state where everything inconsistent with the justice of God shall be adjusted. See Psa. 73.

7. Conscience points to a future state.

Conscience is the voice of God in the soul, witnessing to our sinfulness, God's essential justice. The characteristic testimony of the human conscience has always been in accordance with the word of God, that, "after death comes the judgment."

8. Confirmed by the general consent of mankind.

This has been the universal faith of all men, of all races, and in all ages. Universal consent, like every universal effect, must be referred to an equally universal cause, and this consent, uniform among men differing in every other possible respect, can be referred to no common origin other than the constitution of man's common nature, which is the testimony of his Maker.

9. The Old Testament teaches the same distinction between body and soul that is taught in the New Testament. Gen. 1:26, 27; 2:7. Ecc. 12:7.

10. Our Saviour's argument. Luke 20: 37, 38.

11. Old Testament passages implying a state of blessedness after death. Num. 23: 10. Job 19:26, 27. Psa. 16: 9—11; 17: 15; 49: 14, 15; 73: 24—26. Isa. 25: 8; 26: 19. Dan. 12: 2, 3, 13. Hos. 13: 14.

12. Teaching of the New Testament. Luke 23: 43. 2 Cor. 5: 6—8. Phi. 1: 23, 24. Luke 16: 23, 24. Jude 5—7.

II. The Resurrection.

1. The Greek word is *anastasis*, which signifies " a rising or raising up." It is used in Scripture to designate the future general raising, by the power of God, of the bodies of all men from the sleep of death.

2. Old Testament passages. Job 19: 25—27. Psa. 49: 15. Isa. 26: 19. Dan. 12: 1—3.

3. New Testament passages. Mat. 27; 52, 53. Jno. 5: 28, 29; 6: 39. Acts 2: 25—34; 13: 34. Rom. 8: 11, 22, 23. 1 Cor. 15. Phi. 3: 20, 21. 1 The. 4: 13—17.

4. The body to rise again. Phi. 3: 21. 1 Cor. 15: 53, 54. Jno. 5: 28. 1 The. 4: 13—17. 1 Cor. 6: 15. Jno. 20: 27.

5. The nature of the resurrection body.

a. It is to be spiritual. 1 Cor. 15: 44.

b. Like Christ's body. Phi. 3: 21.

c. Glorious, powerful, and incorruptible, 1 Cor. 15: 54.

d. It shall never die. Rev. 21: 4.

e. Never to be given in marriage. Mat. 22: 30.

7. The resurrection of Christ secures and illustrates that of His people.

a. Because His resurrection seals and consummates His redemptive power, and the redemption of our bodies. Rom. 3: 23.

b. Because of our federal and vital union with Christ. 1 Cor. 15: 21, 22. 1 The. 4: 14.

c. Because of His Spirit who dwells in us (Rom. 8: 11), making our bodies His members. 1 Cor. 6: 15.

d. Because Christ by covenant is Lord both of the living and the dead. Rom. 14: 9.

This same vital union causes the resurrection of the believer to be similar to, as well as consequent upon, that of Christ. 1 Cor. 15: 49. Phi. 3: 21. 1 Jno. 3: 2.

III. The Second Advent and the General Judgment.

1. The meaning of the expression, "the coming" or "the day of the Lord," as used in both the Old and New Testaments.

a. For any special manifestation of God's presence and power. Isa. 13: 6. Jer. 46: 10. Jno. 14: 18, 23.

b. By way of eminence.

(1) In the Old Testament, for the coming of Christ in the flesh, and the abrogation of the Jewish economy. Mal. 3: 2; 4: 5.

(2) In the New Testament, for the second and final coming of Christ.

2. The several terms referring to this last great event are:—

a. His " revelation." 1 Cor. 1: 7. 2 The. 1: 7. 1 Pet. 1: 7, 13; 4: 13.

b. " Presence," " coming." Mat. 24: 3, 27, 37, 39. 1 Cor. 15: 23. 1 The. 2: 19; 3: 13; 4: 15; 5: 23. 2 The. 2: 1—9. Jas. 5: 7, 8. 2 Pet. 1: 16; 3: 4, 12. 1 Jno. 2: 28.

c. "Appearing," "manifestation." 2 The. 2: 8. 1 Tim. 6: 14. 2 Tim. 4: 1, 8. Tit. 2: 13.

d. "The day of the Lord," or a similar expression. Jno. 6: 39—54. Rom. 2: 5. 1 Cor. 1: 8. Phi. 1: 6, 10. 1 The. 5: 2. 2 The. 1: 10. 2 Tim. 1: 12, 18. 2 Pet. 2: 9; 3: 10, 12. Jude 6. Rev. 6: 17.

Christ is called " the coming One " with reference to both advents. Mat. 21: 9. Luke 7: 19, 20; 19: 38. Jno. 3: 31. Rev. 1: 4; 4: 8.

3. Evidence that a literal, personal advent of Christ still future is taught in the Bible.

a. The analogy of the first advent.

b. The coming itself, its manner and purpose, are alike defined. Mat. 16: 27; 24: 30; 25: 31; 26: 64. Mar. 8: 38. Luke 21: 27.

c. The apostles understood these predictions to relate to a literal advent of Christ in person. Acts 1: 11; 3: 19—21. 1 Cor. 4: 5; 11: 26; 15: 23. Heb. 9: 28; 10: 37.

4. The exact time declared to be unknown. Mat. 24: 36. Mar. 13: 32. Luke 12: 40. Acts 1: 6, 7. 1 The. 5: 1—3. 2 Pet. 3: 3, 4, 10. Rev. 16: 15.

5. The Judge of the world.

This will be Jesus Christ, in His official character as mediator, in both natures, as the God-man. This is evident,—

a. Because as judge He is called the "Son of man" (Mat. 25: 31, 32), and " the man ordained by God." Acts 17: 31.

b. Because it pertains to Him as mediator to complete and publicly manifest the salvation of His people and the overthrow of His enemies, together with the glorious righteousness of His work in both respects. 2 The. 1: 7—10. Rev. 1: 7.

6. The subjects of the judgment.

a. The whole race of man. The dead will be raised, and the living changed simultaneously. Mat. 25: 31—46. 1 Cor. 15: 51, 52. 2 Cor. 5: 10. 1 The. 4: 17. 2 The. 1: 6—10. Rev. 20: 11—15.

b. All evil angels. 2 Pet. 2: 4. Jude 6. Good angels appearing as attendants and ministers. Mat. 13: 41, 42.

7. The moral effect of the Scripture teaching as to Christ's second advent.

Christians ought thereby to be comforted when in sorrow, and always stimulated to duty. Phi. 3: 20. Col. 3: 4, 5. Jas. 5: 7. 1 Jno. 3: 2, 3.

Their duty also to love, watch, wait for, and hasten unto, the coming of their Lord. Luke 12: 35—37. 1 Cor. 1: 7, 8. Phi. 3: 20. 1 The. 1: 9, 10. 2 Tim. 4: 8. 2 Pet. 3: 12. Rev. 22: 20.

Unbelievers should be filled with fearful apprehension, and should come to immediate repentance. Mar. 13: 35, 37. 2 Pet. 3: 9, 10. Jude 14, 15.

IV. Heaven and Hell.

1. New Testament usage of the words. "Heaven" used chiefly in three senses:—

(1) The upper air where the birds fly. Mat. 8: 20; 24: 30.

(2) The region in which the stars revolve. Acts 7: 42. Heb. 11: 12.

(3) The abode of Christ's human nature, the scene of the special manifestation of divine glory, and of the eternal blessedness of the saints. Heb. 9: 24. 1 Pet. 3: 22. Sometimes called the "third heaven." 2 Cor. 12: 2. The phrases "new heaven" and "new earth," in contrast with "first heaven" and "first earth," refer to some unexplained change by which God will revolutionize our portion of the physical universe, cleansing it from the stain of sin and qualifying it to be the abode of blessedness.

2. Terms used to designate the future blessedness of the saints.

a. Literal terms:—

Life, eternal life. Mat. 7: 14; 19: 16, 29; 25: 46.

Glory, the glory of God, an eternal weight of glory. Rom. 2: 7, 10; 5: 2. 2 Cor. 4: 17.

Peace. Rom. 2: 10.

Salvation, and eternal salvation. Heb. 5: 7.

b. Figurative terms:—

Paradise, Luke 23: 43. 2 Cor. 12: 4. Rev. 2: 7.

Heavenly Jerusalem. Gal. 4: 26. Rev. 3: 12.

Kingdom of heaven, heavenly kingdom, eternal kingdom, kingdom prepared from the foundation of the world. Mat. 25: 34. 2 Tim. 4: 18. 2 Pet. 1: 11.

Eternal inheritance. 1 Pet. 1: 4. Heb. 9: 15.

The blessed are said to sit down with Abraham, Isaac, and Jacob; to be in Abraham's bosom (Luke 16: 22. Mat. 8: 11); to reign with Christ (2 Tim. 2: 11, 12); to enjoy a Sabbath of rest. Heb. 4: 10, 11.

3. Heaven as a place.

The Scriptures represent heaven as a definite place as well as a state of blessedness. Jno. 17: 24. 2 Cor. 5: 6—10. Rev. 5: 6.

4. Wherein does the blessedness of heaven consist as far as revealed?

a. In perfect deliverance from sin and all its evil consequences, physical, moral, and social. Rev. 7: 16, 17; 21: 4, 27.

b. In the perfection of our nature. 1 Cor. 13: 9—12; 15: 45—49. 1 Jno. 3: 2.

c. In the sight of our Redeemer, communion with His person, and fellowship in all His glory and blessedness, and through Him with saints and angels. Jno. 17: 24. 1 Jno. 1: 3. Rev. 3: 21; 21: 3—5.

d. In that "beatific vision of God" which, consisting in the ever increasingly clear discovery of the divine excellence lovingly apprehended, transforms the soul into the same image, from glory unto glory. Mat. 5: 8. 2 Cor. 3: 18.

5. The principal terms, literal and figurative, which are applied in Scripture to the future condition of the reprobate.

As a *place* it is literally designated by Gehenna (Mat. 5: 22, 29, 30), and by the phrase "place of torment." Luke 16: 28. As a *condition* of suffering, it is literally designated by the phrases "wrath of God" (Rom. 2: 5) and "second death." Rev. 21: 8.

Figurative terms:—

"Everlasting fire, prepared for the devil and his angels." Mat. 25: 41.

"Hell, where their worm dieth not and the fire is not quenched." Mar. 9: 48.

"The lake which burneth with fire and brimstone." Rev. 21: 8.

"The pit of the abyss." Rev. 9: 2.

The dreadful nature of this abode of the wicked is implied in such expressions as "outer darkness," the place where there is "weeping and gnashing of teeth" (Mat. 8: 12); "I am in anguish in this flame" (Luke 16: 24); "unquenchable fire" (Luke 3: 17); "furnace of fire" (Mat. 13: 42); "blackness of darkness" (Jude 13); torment "with fire and brimstone"

(Rev. 14:10); "the smoke of their torment goeth up forever and ever." Rev. 14:11.

6. The teaching of the Scriptures as to the nature of future punishments.

a. These sufferings will consist—

(1) In the loss of all good.

(2) In all the natural consequences of unrestrained sin, judicial abandonment, utter alienation from God, and the society of the lost. 2 The. 1:9.

(3) In the positive infliction of torment, God's wrath abiding upon those who do not believe. Jno. 3:36.

b. The Scriptures also establish the facts that these sufferings must be—

(1) Dreadful in degree.

(2) Endless in duration.

(3) Proportioned to the deserts of the subject. Mat. 10:15. Luke 12:47, 48.

"For God so loved the world, that He gave His only begotten Son, that whosoever believeth in Him should not perish, but have everlasting life." Jno. 3:16.